Taste of Home

Light&Tasty

Annual Recipes 2008

PICTURED ABOVE AND ON THE FRONT COVER: Hot Berries 'n'
Brownie Ice Cream Cake (page 212), Avocado Dip (page 19) and
Marvelous Chicken Enchiladas (page 132).

Taste of Home
Light&Tasty
Annual Recipes 2008

Editor in Chief: Catherine Cassidy
Vice President, Executive Editor/Books: Heidi Reuter Lloyd
Creative Director: Ardyth Cope
Food Director: Diane Werner

Senior Editor/Books: Mark Hagen
Art Director: Gretchen Trautman
Layout Designers: Emma Acevedo, Kathleen Bump
Proofreaders: Linne Bruskewitz, Jean Steiner
Content Production Supervisor: Julie Wagner
Recipe Asset Systems Manager: Coleen Martin
Editorial Assistant: Barb Czysz
Cover Photography: Jim Wieland (photographer);
Jenny Bradley Vent (set stylist); Julie Herzfeldt (food stylist)

Chief Marketing Officer: Lisa Karpinski
Vice President/Book Marketing: Robert Graham Botta
Creative Director/Creative Marketing: James Palmen

Editor: Mary Spencer
Art Director: Nicholas Mork
Food Editor: Peggy Woodward RD
Recipe Editors: Sue A. Jurak (senior), Mary King, Christine Rukavena
Associate Editors: Mary C. Hanson, John McMillan, Elizabeth Russell
Copy Editor: S.K. Enk
Editorial Assistant: Marilyn Iczkowski
Executive Assistant: Marie Brannon
Test Kitchen Manager: Karen Scales
Home Economists: Tina Johnson, Marie Parker, Annie Rose,
Kristen Lingsweiler
Test Kitchen Assistants: Rita Krajcir, Kris Lehman, Sue Megonigle, Megan Taylor
Photographers: Rob Hagen (senior), Dan Roberts, Jim Wieland, Lori Foy
Set Stylists: Jenny Bradley Vent (senior), Stephanie Marchese (senior),
Dee Dee Jacq
Food Stylists: Sarah Thompson (senior), Tamara Kaufman
Assistant Food Stylists: Kaitlyn Besasie, Alynna Malson, Shannon Roum, Leah Rekau
Photo Studio Coordinator: Kathy Swaney

THE READER'S DIGEST ASSOCIATION, INC.
President and Chief Executive Officer: Mary G. Berner
President, RDA Food & Entertaining: Suzanne M. Grimes
President, Consumer Marketing: Dawn Zier

Taste of Home Books
© 2008 Reiman Media Group, Inc.
5400 S. 60th Street, Greendale, WI 53129

International Standard Book Number (10): 0-89821-660-5
International Standard Book Number (13): 978-0-89821-660-8
International Serial Number: 1537-3134

To order additional copies of this book, contact Reiman Media Group at
1-800/344-2560 or visit www.ShopTasteofHome.com.

Contents

Celebrate the Goodness of 534 Family Favorites

MEMORABLE nights around the family supper table...laughter-filled gatherings with friends...spirited holiday celebrations...at the heart of all of these occasions, you're sure to find wonderful food. However, serving those classic standbys doesn't have to mean putting on pounds or straying from healthy-eating commitments.

Now more than ever, family cooks are experimenting in the kitchen, whipping up outstanding edibles guaranteed to strike a chord without breaking the calorie bank. They're finding delicious ways to eat right, and they've shared hundreds of their secrets with *Light & Tasty* magazine over the past year.

We've assembled all of those recipes and more in *2008 Light & Tasty Annual Recipes*. In fact, with this edition at hand, preparing a fantastic meal is easier than ever...no matter what the occasion.

Featuring 534 phenomenal dishes, this edition of *Light & Tasty Annual Recipes* is our largest volume to date. Packed with everything from casual snacks and supper-time lifesavers to eye-appealing appetizers and impressive weekend entrees, the perfect recipe is always at your fingertips.

For nights when time is truly at a premium, turn to page 95 and consider our new chapter, "30-Minutes Entrees." There you'll find dozens of main courses that are table-ready in just half an hour...or less! See "Family-Style Suppers" (p. 247), too. That chapter offers easy menus for hurried nights. In addition, more than 150 entrees can be found between chapters dedicated to beef (p. 109), chicken and turkey (p. 123), pork (p. 147), seafood (p. 159) and meat-free meals (p. 173).

When it's time to "wow" the gang with a sweet treat, simply see the "Dazzling Desserts" chapter (p. 199) where more than 75 luscious surprises await. You might also want to consider the section "Let's Celebrate!" (p. 259), which offers health-smart menus perfect for holidays and special events.

So whether you're whipping up Tuesday's supper or planning Christmas dinner, singing "Happy Birthday" or cheering "Happy New Year," *2008 Light & Tasty Annual Recipes* helps you make delightfully memorable menus while keeping your goals to eat right.

Peggy Woodward, RD

Food Editor, *Light & Tasty*

What's Inside These Recipe-Packed Pages?

WITH the 534 incredible recipes in this volume, *2008 Light & Tasty Annual Recipes* is the largest edition in the series to date; however, that doesn't mean we're taking a rest. We made sure to fill the book with the features you've come to know and trust. Take a look at some of the value-added benefits this title offers:

At-a-Glance Information. If you are on a special diet—or someone you cook for is—finding suitable recipes is a breeze. That's because low-fat, low-sodium, low-carb and meatless dishes are clearly labeled next to the recipe title. (Turn the page for an explanation of these special diet indicators.) As an added bonus, preparation times are provided for *every* recipe in the book.

User-Friendly Chapters. To assist in your menu planning, we've compiled all 534 recipes into 16 chapters, including a new chapter, "30-Minute Entrees" (p. 95). You'll also find your old favorites such as "Trimmed-Down Dishes for Two" (p. 237), "Light Bites & Beverages" (p. 13) and "Dazzling Desserts" (p. 199). For a complete list of chapters, turn back to page 3.

De-Light-Ful Dinner Planner. In addition to the meal chapters mentioned above, we've created 15 menu plans. (See the "De-Light-Ful Dinner Planner" on page 7.) Each meal features recipes found inside the book, as well as suggestions for "appealing partners" (side dishes, desserts or beverages) and meal-preparation pointers.

Mouth-Watering Meals. You'll find 12 complete meals (including pictures!), which are perfect for either weekday family dining (p. 247) or weekend entertaining (page 260).

Easy-to-Use Indexes. Finding all 534 recipes is a snap with our indexes. The general index lists every recipe by food category, major ingredient and/or cooking technique. The alphabetical recipe listing is perfect for anyone looking for a specific family favorite. Both indexes highlight which recipes are table-ready in just 30 minutes or less.

Nutrition Facts Nuggets

Our Nutritional Guidelines

EVERY RECIPE in 2008 *Light & Tasty Annual Recipes* fits the lifestyle of health-conscious cooks. The recipes represent a variety of foods that will fit into any meal plan that is within the standards of the USDA's "My Pyramid Plan" for moderately active adults (see box below). The target nutritional content of recipes, on a per serving basis, is:

- 400 calories (or less)
- 12 grams of fat (or less)
- 1,000 mg sodium (or less)
- 100 mg cholesterol (or less)

How we calculated the Nutrition Facts

- Whenever a choice of ingredients is given in a recipe (such as 1/3 cup of sour cream or plain yogurt), the first ingredient listed is always the one calculated in the Nutrition Facts.
- When a range is given for an ingredient (such as 2 to 3 teaspoons), we calculate the first amount given.
- Only the amount of marinade absorbed during preparation is calculated.
- Garnishes listed in recipes are generally included in our calculations.

Diabetic Exchanges

ALL recipes in this book have been reviewed by a Registered Dietitian. Diabetic Exchanges are assigned to recipes in accordance with guidelines from the American Diabetic and American Dietetic Associations. The majority of recipes in 2008 *Light & Tasty Annual Recipes* are suitable for diabetics.

Special Diet Indicators

TO HELP those on restricted diets easily find dishes to suit their needs, we clearly indicate recipes that are low in carbohydrates, fat or sodium or that contain no meat. You'll find these colored, special diet indicators after the recipe title where appropriate:

FAT One serving contains 3 grams or less of fat

SALT One serving contains 140 milligrams or less of sodium

CARB One serving contains 15 grams or less of carbohydrates

MEAT-LESS Appetizers, salads, savory breads, side dishes and entrees that contain no meat

Your Serving Size Guide

This list is a general guide for healthy eating for most adults.

Grains
1 bread slice, pancake or waffle
Half of an average bagel (the size of a hockey puck)
1 cup dry cereal
1/2 cup cooked cereal, rice or pasta

Vegetables
1 cup raw leafy greens
1/2 cup of any chopped vegetable, raw or cooked
6-ounce glass of vegetable juice
1 small potato

Fruits
1 medium piece of fruit
1/2 cup sliced fruit
6-ounce glass of orange juice or any 100% fruit juice

Dairy
8-ounce container of yogurt
1/2 cup cottage cheese
1-1/2 ounces cheese (size of two dominoes)
8-ounce glass of milk

Meat and Beans
3 ounces cooked lean meat, poultry or fish (size of a deck of cards)
2 tablespoons peanut butter
1/2 cup beans

Daily Nutrition Guide

	Women 30-50	Women over 50	Men 50-65
Calories	2,000	1,800	2,400
Fat	65 g or less	60 g or less	80 g or less
Saturated Fat	22 g or less	20 g or less	27 g or less
Cholesterol	300 mg or less	300 mg or less	300 mg or less
Sodium	2,300 mg or less	2,300 mg or less	2,300 mg or less
Carbohydrates	300 g	270 g	360 g
Fiber	28 g	25 g	34 g
Protein	50 g	45 g	60 g

This chart is only a guide. Calorie requirements vary, depending on age, weight, height and amount of activity. Children's dietary needs vary as they grow.

De-Light-Ful Dinner Planner

Deciding what to make for dinner can be harder than preparing it! The next time you need some culinary inspiration, consider the following menus that use recipes from this book. In addition, "appealing partners" round out the meals and "practical tips" offer various time-saving ideas.

Sweet Maple-Glazed Salmon and Gingered Asparagus, p. 10

Asian Supper Dresses Up Dinners

Skillet Sensation Warms Hearts

Easy Updates on Family Staples

Kick off the week with international flair and delicious **Garlic-Ginger Turkey Tenderloin** (p. 107) from our Test Kitchen. Brown sugar adds a hint of sweetness to the tangy aspect of the warm sauce.

Janice McCloskey shares a colorful and buttery stir-fry of **Pepper Squash Saute** (p. 66) that she relies on to round out many of her meals in Howard, Pennsylvania. It's versatile, flavorful and goes together in just minutes. It's perfect with turkey and chicken, but feel free to add the no-fuss side dish to beefy meals and pork entrees as well.

On chilly nights in Morehead City, North Carolina, Ruth Tamul enjoys serving friends and family her healthy, hearty **Chops 'n' Kraut** (p. 150). Seasoned with garlic, brown sugar and caraway seeds, this mouth-watering meal-in-one is loaded with heart-warming flavor.

For a change-of-pace finale, consider baking the light, luscious **Pound Cake** (p. 190) shared by Rochester, New York's Joyce Grasby. The moist treat is loaded with homemade goodness, and it boasts a delightful hint of lemon flavor.

It just doesn't get much more comforting than this delectable **Beef 'n' Turkey Meat Loaf** (p. 122) from Fern Nead of Florence, Kentucky. With two kinds of meat and shredded potatoes, it's a well-seasoned, old-fashioned entree with a healthy touch.

Pair it with sassy **Spicy Carrot Coins** (p. 67). It's a specialty from Nancy Zimmerman's kitchen in Cape May Court House, New Jersey. "We think that this colorful and easy side dish is a great, low-fat way to boost the beta carotene in everyone's diet," Nancy explains.

APPEALING PARTNERS

- Asian rice noodles
- Mandarin orange segments

PRACTICAL TIPS

- You could also substitute white or brown rice for the Asian rice noodles suggested above.

- For added convenience, mix and match the peppers and squash in the vegetable side dish. It is just as delicious with only red, green or yellow peppers.

- Finish the meal with scoops of fat-free frozen yogurt.

APPEALING PARTNERS

- Italian-Style Green Beans (p. 71)
- Rye bread

PRACTICAL TIPS

- To satisfy even hungrier appetites, try serving the chops and kraut with mashed potatoes.

- Hot apple cider makes a wonderful beverage choice to serve alongside the tender and filling chops, particularly during autumn.

- For an extra-moist dessert, thaw frozen mixed berries and spoon the juices over each slice of pound cake.

APPEALING PARTNERS

- Mashed potatoes
- Mixed greens salad

PRACTICAL TIPS

- For an extra treat, Fern Nead sometimes tops her meat loaf with narrow strips of turkey bacon.

- Line the meat loaf baking pan with foil and spritz it with cooking spray to help make your busy-weeknight cleanup a snap.

- When company is coming, garnish the carrot coins with cinnamon sticks or lemon-peel twists for an eye-appealing presentation.

Wrap Up Weeknights In Savory Style

When every minute matters, you can count on Barbara Blake's effortless **Garden Vegetable Wraps** (p. 104) for a nutritious meal-on-the-go. "They're a cinch to prepare, packed with fresh veggie goodness and a breeze for all ages to handle," explains the West Battleboro, Vermont cook.

Chunks of broccoli and a touch of thyme make creamy **Carrot Broccoli Soup** (p. 31) a first course that folks really enjoy. The filling accompaniment comes from Sandy Smith of London, Ontario.

APPEALING PARTNERS

- Pretzels
- Apple wedges

PRACTICAL TIPS

- For a quick appetizer, wrap the veggie roll-ups in plastic wrap and refrigerate for at least an hour. Then cut into 1-inch slices and serve with party picks.

- Caught without tortillas? Serve the veggie wrap filling in a pita pocket or spread it on slices of wheat bread.

- For added interest and flavor, Sandy Smith tops her soup with a sprinkle of reduced-fat shredded cheddar cheese.

Refreshing Menu's Ready in No Time

You'll put a spring in your step when you serve Anita Dudiwka's **Chicken Veronique** (p. 134). The classic chicken dish from the Akron, Ohio reader features a refreshing sauce that calls for sliced green grapes. It's sure to beat the doldrums and dress up dinners without much work on your part.

Cookies 'n' Cream Berry Desserts (p. 205) will end any meal on a sweet note. A medley of berries, a creamy topping and crumbled meringue cookies make it a special treat for Lillian Julow's friends and family in Gainesville, Florida.

APPEALING PARTNERS

- Long grain and wild rice mix
- Iced tea

PRACTICAL TIPS

- Anita likes to serve the chicken with a side of rice pilaf, but you could boost fiber by serving it with brown rice instead.

- For a little extra flavor in her chicken entree, Anita often adds sauteed green onions to the sauce.

- The berries in the dessert provide nearly 75% of daily needs for vitamin C, so it's a good-for-you treat you can enjoy without any guilt.

Comfy Casserole's Sure to Satisfy

Shake up your supper routine by serving family-friendly **Spaghetti Pizza Casserole** (p. 111). In Mansfield, Ohio, Kim Neer tosses together this simple spaghetti combination with vegetables, lean ground beef, prepared spaghetti sauce and two kinds of cheese in no time.

Folks will never guess that **Creamy Garlic Salad Dressing** (p. 41) is low in fat. The rich dressing from Michele Odstrcilek of Lemont, Illinois has a pleasant garlic flavor that pairs perfectly with the main course.

APPEALING PARTNERS

- Garlic bread
- Peanut Butter Crunch Cookies (p. 28)

PRACTICAL TIPS

- Chop an extra medium onion when preparing the casserole and store it in the refrigerator. The chopped onion will come in handy for preparing meals later in the week.

- Using 1/2 cup of egg substitute saves almost 50 mg of cholesterol per serving in the entree.

- To speed assembly of the dressing, Michele advises using a garlic press to quickly mince the garlic cloves.

Supper Offers Southwestern Taste

Turkey Pecan Enchiladas (p. 129) shared by Cathy Huppe of Georgetown, Massachusetts make the most of lighter ingredients. The creamy main dish has a lean turkey filling with unexpected pecans that offer a surprising crunch. It's sure to be a hit with your gang!

In Amity, Missouri, Kay Dunham assembles her **Avocado Dip** (p. 19) in a matter of minutes. The heart-smart treat is wonderful with tortilla chips or veggies, but it could also be served with light tacos, burritos or other Southwestern fare.

APPEALING PARTNERS

- Steamed broccoli
- Black beans

PRACTICAL TIPS

- Have leftover turkey from another meal? The enchiladas will be the perfect next-day dish.

- The avocados in the dip have monounsaturated fat, which can help boost good cholesterol and decrease bad cholesterol, so you can feel good about serving it in moderation.

- For a fast and refreshing beverage, serve this combination with lemon- or limeade.

Hearty Sandwich Combo Relaxes

A fast-to-fix overnight marinade cuts prep time for **Grilled Pork Tenderloin Sandwiches** (p. 153). These light, handheld greats from Geri Bierschbach of Weidman, Michigan are complemented by a zesty, homemade mustard-horseradish sauce that is loaded with taste.

A side of **Seasoned Yukon Gold Wedges** (p. 60) from Jane Lunch of Scarborough, Ontario rounds out the menu with bold flavor. The rich, buttery potatoes have a slightly spicy flair that makes them an ideal partner to the sandwiches. Try them the next time you're serving up barbecued fare or any casual meal.

APPEALING PARTNERS

- Zucchini sticks with fat-free Ranch dressing
- Fruit medley

PRACTICAL TIPS

- Short on time? Skip the mustard-horseradish sauce and serve the sandwiches with your favorite condiments instead.

- Jane offers the potato wedges with a dollop of fat-free sour cream.

- If you don't have Yukon Gold potatoes on hand, substitute russets.

Salmon Ends Nights On a Tasty Note

Sweet **Maple-Glazed Salmon** (p. 162) turns any night into a special occasion. The recipe from David Krisko of Becker, Minnesota is not only a breeze to prepare, but it offers all of the heart-healthy goodness of salmon in one entree. Best of all, it features weekend flair combined with the work-week ease most family cooks desire.

Light and flavorful **Gingered Asparagus** (p. 59) is sure to fit into most meal plans because it's low in fat and carbs and goes with a variety of main courses. Perfect for any affair, the spring-fresh side dish comes from Nancy Zimmerman of Cape May Court House, New Jersey.

APPEALIN G PARTNERS

- Orzo with herbs
- Lemon Sorbet (p. 243)

PRACTICAL TIPS

- Not only does salmon provide heart-healthy omega-3 fatty acids, but it's also a great source of B vitamins and vitamin D.

- To cut back on sodium, David often uses salt substitute when he prepares the main course.

- For a change of pace, Nancy often makes her side dish with broccoli instead of asparagus.

Stay Cool with Simple Elegance

No need to turn on the oven when you serve **Blackberry-Sauced Pork Chops** (p. 154) for dinner. Cooked on the grill or in a skillet, these unique chops from Priscilla Gilbert of Indian Harbour Beach, Florida are dressed for summer in a sweet homemade berry sauce. What a lovely way to use up a harvest of ripe berries!

Garlic-Herb Orzo Pilaf (p. 79) makes a versatile, good-for-you side dish. It's an easy way to complement many of the meat entrees Mary Relyea serves her family in Canastota, New York. After just one bite, you're sure to think of a host of dishes the pilaf would pair well with.

APPEALING PARTNERS

- Snow peas
- Angel food cake

PRACTICAL TIPS

■ For a change of pace, Priscilla likes to serve the blackberry sauce over grilled chicken.

■ "Any small pasta, such as elbow macaroni, can be used instead of the orzo in the side dish," says Mary.

■ To quickly snip basil for the orzo, Mary recommends using a pair of kitchen scissors.

Tasty Twosome Tempts Appetites

So full of chunky veggies and garden-fresh flavor that you'll never even miss the meat, **Fettuccine with Black Bean Sauce** (p. 183) is a favorite fast and healthy meal for Marianne Neuman's family in East Troy, Wisconsin.

And folks will simply never believe that **Yummy Chocolate Cake** (p. 208) could be so light or so easy to throw together! Special thanks to LaDonna Reed in Ponca City, Oklahoma for sharing the scrumptious dessert recipe. She obviously knows that it's just too good to keep all to herself.

APPEALING PARTNERS

- Tossed green salad
- Sliced French bread

PRACTICAL TIPS

■ Marianne recommends boosting nutrition, flavor and color in her pasta recipe by using spinach fettuccine when available.

■ The entree's beans are a smart choice. They're high in dietary fiber and a good source of protein, so they'll help you feel full longer.

■ For a refreshing treat, LaDonna often prepares the decadent dessert with yellow cake mix and lemon-flavored pudding.

Impressive Meal Leaves Extra Time

You won't believe how easy elegance can be until you try this refreshing entree from Loveland, Colorado's Lindy Bonnell. **Pork with Artichokes and Capers** (p. 148) goes together in mere minutes, but it is moist and special enough to serve weekend guests. And at only 263 calories per serving, you can enjoy it guilt-free!

Pair it with a frosty pitcher of Clara Coulston's **Lemon Quencher** (p. 15). The Washington Court House, Ohio reader uses honey to tame the sweet sipper's natural tartness.

APPEALING PARTNERS

- Steamed baby carrots
- Brown rice

PRACTICAL TIPS

■ Pork tenderloin is the leanest cut of pork. Each serving of the main dish provides well over half the protein you need for the day.

■ Slice up any extra artichoke hearts for tuna casseroles, potato salads or baked pastas. They are a simple way to pump up flavor.

■ For a fancy twist, freeze some mint sprigs and a little lemon peel in ice cubes to serve in tall glasses of the Lemon Quencher.

Hook into Flavor And Fun

Make-Ahead Menu Has Appeal

Citrusy Salad Brightens Meals

Chase away the supper-time blues with Jennifer Maslowski's tangy, fast-to-fix **Broiled Greek Fish Fillets** (p. 170). Seasoned with dill, olives, red onions, feta cheese and a splash of lime, they satisfy friends and family in New York, New York with light, lively Mediterranean flair.

To complement the fish, serve savory **Mushroom Rice** (p. 80), a side-dish specialty of Beth McCaw in Nashville, Tennessee. See how Greek seasoning and crunchy celery and pecans make a quick dish so special.

Looking for something different for your next cookout? Mitzi Sentiff says friends in Alexandria, Virginia can't get enough of juicy **Teriyaki Beef Burgers** (p. 121). As a bonus, you can marinate them overnight for added convenience on busy weekdays.

Pair the Asian-flavored patties with Kathy Rairigh's make-ahead favorite **Veggie Barley Salad** (p. 55). Packed with summer-fresh veggies and herbs, this nutritious side dish always brings compliments to the Milford, Indiana reader.

Pasta, chicken, oranges and avocado make Ann Berger's **Chicken Pasta Salad a l'Orange** (p. 98) a winning blend of textures and tastes. The Howell, Michigan subscriber tosses the meal-in-one with a low-fat dressing she makes herself.

From Columbus, Ohio, Cheryl Hindrichs sends the perfect addition. Our taste-testers simply loved her lighter-than-air **Pesto Muffins** (p. 195) prepared with a hint of whole wheat flour and heart-healthy walnuts. Try them yourself and you'll see how each muffin is filled with terrific basil and garlic flavor.

APPEALING PARTNERS

- Roasted broccoli spears
- Lemonade

PRACTICAL TIPS

- Substitute any other white-fleshed fish, such as sole, flounder or orange roughy, for the tilapia in the entree.

- Tilapia is one of the safest fish for consumption. Not only does it provide heart-healthy omega-3 fatty acids, but it also has one of the lowest reported levels of mercury.

- Buy chopped onion and pre-sliced mushrooms from your grocery store's produce section to speed assembly of the rice.

APPEALING PARTNERS

- Sliced melon
- Fat-free frozen yogurt

PRACTICAL TIPS

- To save time, use store-bought minced garlic for the burgers.

- Besides providing a tasty change of pace from the pasta used in so many summer salads, barley is also a healthy source of cholesterol-lowering fiber and niacin.

- Try the veggie salad with your favorite vegetables. For a sunny look, substitute the tomato with yellow pear tomatoes and the zucchini for yellow summer squash.

APPEALING PARTNERS

- Fresh grapes
- Berry scones

PRACTICAL TIPS

- For 2 cups of cubed cooked chicken, you'll need about 10 ounces of uncooked chicken breast.

- Don't have enough time to bake the muffins? Swing by the grocery store on the way home and pick up some bran muffins instead.

- Always freeze or refrigerate whole wheat flour to keep its natural oils fresh.

Light Bites & Beverages

Load up your appetizer buffet with any of these 45 crowd-pleasers. From elegant and impressive to easy and effortless, each luscious bite is sure to be the life of the party. Best of all, guests can nibble away since all of the recipes fit into heart-smart lifestyles.

Gorgonzola Figs with Balsamic Glaze, p. 19

In a large nonstick skillet coated with cooking spray, cook onion in oil over medium heat for 8 minutes, stirring frequently. Add garlic; cook 3 minutes longer.

Stir in broth and wine or additional broth. Reduce heat to medium-low; cook for 25-30 minutes or until onions are golden brown and liquid is evaporated, stirring occasionally.

Transfer to a bowl. Stir in the sour cream, spinach and salt. Serve with tortilla chips. Refrigerate leftovers.

NUTRITION FACTS: 1/4 cup (calculated without chips) equals 73 calories, 1 g fat (trace saturated fat), 7 mg cholesterol, 250 mg sodium, 11 g carbohydrate, 1 g fiber, 4 g protein. **DIABETIC EXCHANGE:** 1 starch.

Fruity Horseradish Cream Cheese

PREP/TOTAL TIME: 10 Min.   **YIELD:** 1-1/3 Cups

Typically called a "Jezebel Sauce," this sweet, fruity topping has an underlying bite from horseradish. Try it over pork or chicken.
—Rita Reifenstein, Evans City, Pennsylvania

> 1 package (8 ounces) fat-free cream cheese
> 1/3 cup apple jelly, warmed
> 1 tablespoon prepared horseradish
> 1-1/2 teaspoons ground mustard
> 1/3 cup apricot spreadable fruit

Assorted crackers

Place cream cheese on a serving plate. In a small microwave-safe bowl, heat jelly until warmed. Stir in horseradish and mustard until blended. Stir in spreadable fruit; spoon over cream cheese. Serve with crackers. Refrigerate leftovers.

NUTRITION FACTS: 2 tablespoons (calculated without crackers) equals 73 calories, trace fat (trace saturated fat), 2 mg cholesterol, 128 mg sodium, 14 g carbohydrate, trace fiber, 3 g protein. **DIABETIC EXCHANGE:** 1 starch.

Tomato Basil Snackers

(PICTURED ABOVE)

PREP/TOTAL TIME: 15 Min.   **YIELD:** 4 Servings

Fresh basil, summer-ripe tomatoes and melted mozzarella cheese top toasted English muffins in this fabulous nibble from the Light & Tasty Test Kitchen.

> 2 English muffins, split and toasted
> 2 tablespoons fat-free mayonnaise
> 3 plum tomatoes, cut into 1/4-inch slices
> 6 fresh basil leaves, thinly sliced
> 1/8 teaspoon pepper
> 1/2 cup shredded part-skim mozzarella cheese

Place English muffin halves on an ungreased baking sheet; spread with mayonnaise. Top with tomatoes, basil, pepper and cheese. Broil 4 in. from the heat for 3-4 minutes or until cheese is melted.

NUTRITION FACTS: 1 serving equals 118 calories, 3 g fat (2 g saturated fat), 9 mg cholesterol, 261 mg sodium, 17 g carbohydrate, 1 g fiber, 6 g protein. **DIABETIC EXCHANGES:** 1 starch, 1/2 fat.

Apple Oatmeal Bites

PREP: 20 Min.   **BAKE:** 10 Min./Batch   **YIELD:** About 2-1/2 Dozen

Need a snack that's perfect on car trips or hikes? Pack up some of these chewy treats. With lots of oats and apples, you'll find plenty of fruit and fiber in every bite. Best of all, they're much better for you than candy bars or chips. —Sue Violette, Neillsville, Wisconsin

> 2 egg whites
> 1/4 cup fat-free milk
> 2 tablespoons canola oil
> 1/2 teaspoon vanilla extract
> 2 cups quick-cooking oats
> 1/2 cup all-purpose flour
> 1/4 cup sugar
> 1/4 cup packed brown sugar
> 1 teaspoon ground cinnamon
> 1/2 teaspoon baking powder
> 1/2 teaspoon salt
> 1/4 teaspoon ground nutmeg
> 1 cup chopped peeled apple

In a large mixing bowl, beat the egg whites, milk, oil and vanilla. Combine the oats, flour, sugars, cinnamon, baking powder, salt and nutmeg; gradually add to egg white mixture and mix well. Stir in apple.

Drop by tablespoonfuls 2 in. apart onto baking sheets

Caramelized Onion Spinach Dip

PREP: 10 Min.   **COOK:** 40 Min.   **YIELD:** 2-1/2 Cups

I caramelize sweet onions with a hint of wine for a richly delicious appetizer that's guilt-free! It's a decadent update on traditional spinach dip.   —Corrine Rupp, Statesville, North Carolina

> 1 sweet onion, chopped
> 2 teaspoons olive oil
> 3 garlic cloves, minced
> 1/4 cup reduced-sodium chicken broth
> 1/4 cup white wine *or* additional reduced-sodium chicken broth
> 2 cups (16 ounces) fat-free sour cream
> 1 package (10 ounces) frozen chopped spinach, thawed and squeezed dry
> 3/4 teaspoon salt

Tortilla chips

coated with cooking spray. Bake at 350° for 10-12 minutes or until bottoms are lightly browned. Remove to wire racks.

NUTRITION FACTS: 1 cookie equals 51 calories, 1 g fat (trace saturated fat), trace cholesterol, 48 mg sodium, 9 g carbohydrate, 1 g fiber, 1 g protein. **DIABETIC EXCHANGE:** 1/2 starch.

Vegetarian Stuffed Mushrooms

PREP: 15 Min.   **BAKE:** 25 Min.   **YIELD:** 14 Appetizers

Mixed with a blend of parsley, basil, oregano and bread crumbs, soy crumbles make a healthy addition to these stuffed mushrooms.
—Arline Aaron, Brooklyn, New York

       14 large fresh mushrooms
        1 small onion, finely chopped
        4 teaspoons canola oil
      3/4 cup soft bread crumbs
      1/2 cup frozen vegetarian meat crumbles, thawed
        1 teaspoon minced fresh parsley
        1 teaspoon dried basil
      1/2 teaspoon dried oregano
      1/2 teaspoon salt
      1/2 teaspoon pepper

Remove stems from mushrooms and chop; set mushroom caps aside. In a large nonstick skillet coated with cooking spray, saute stems and onion in oil until tender. Stir in the bread crumbs, meat crumbles and seasonings; cook until bread crumbs are lightly browned. Cool slightly.

Stuff into mushroom caps. Place in a 15-in. x 10-in. x 1-in. baking pan coated with cooking spray. Bake at 350° for 25-30 minutes or until heated through and mushrooms are tender. Serve warm.

NUTRITION FACTS: 1 stuffed mushroom equals 34 calories, 2 g fat (trace saturated fat), trace cholesterol, 111 mg sodium, 3 g carbohydrate, 1 g fiber, 2 g protein. **DIABETIC EXCHANGE:** 1/2 fat.

Chive Crab Cakes

PREP: 20 Min. + Chilling   **COOK:** 10 Min./Batch   **YIELD:** 6 Servings

You can either offer these tasty crab cakes as an hors d'oeuvre or alongside a salad for a light meal. Look for panko bread crumbs in the ethnic aisle of your supermarket. —Cindy Worth, Lapwai, Idaho

        4 egg whites
        1 egg
        6 tablespoons minced chives
        3 tablespoons all-purpose flour
        1 to 2 teaspoons hot pepper sauce
        1 teaspoon baking powder
      1/2 teaspoon salt
      1/4 teaspoon pepper
        4 cans (6 ounces *each*) crabmeat, drained, flaked and
          cartilage removed
        2 cups panko (Japanese) bread crumbs
        2 tablespoons canola oil

In a large bowl, lightly beat the egg whites and egg. Add the chives, flour, pepper sauce, baking powder, salt and pepper;

mix well. Fold in crab. Cover and refrigerate for at least 2 hours.

Place bread crumbs in a shallow bowl. Drop crab mixture by 1/4 cupfuls into crumbs. Gently coat and shape into 3/4-in.-thick patties. In a large nonstick skillet, cook crab cakes in oil in batches over medium-high heat for 3-4 minutes on each side or until golden brown.

NUTRITION FACTS: 2 crab cakes equals 242 calories, 7 g fat (1 g saturated fat), 136 mg cholesterol, 731 mg sodium, 12 g carbohydrate, 1 g fiber, 29 g protein. **DIABETIC EXCHANGES:** 4 very lean meat, 1 starch, 1 fat.

Lemon Quencher

(PICTURED BELOW)

PREP: 15 Min. + Chilling   **YIELD:** 8 Servings

Tart and refreshing, this minty summer beverage is sweetened with just a touch of honey.
—Clara Coulston, Washington Court House, Ohio

        5 cups water, *divided*
       10 fresh mint leaves
        1 cup lemon juice
      2/3 cup honey
        2 teaspoons grated lemon peel
Ice cubes
Mint sprigs and lemon peel strips, optional

In a blender, combine 1 cup water and mint leaves; cover and process for 1 minute. Strain mixture into a pitcher, discarding mint. Add the lemon juice, honey, lemon peel and remaining water; stir until blended. Cover and refrigerate for at least 2 hours. Serve over ice. Garnish with mint sprigs and lemon peel if desired.

NUTRITION FACTS: 3/4 cup equals 96 calories, trace fat (trace saturated fat), 0 cholesterol, 2 mg sodium, 27 g carbohydrate, trace fiber, trace protein. **DIABETIC EXCHANGE:** 2 starch.

Quick Stovetop Granola

FAT SALT

PREP/TOTAL TIME: 15 Min.   **YIELD:** 3 Cups

The L&T Test Kitchen staff relied on fiber-rich oats to bulk up this granola and to quell your snack attacks. It makes a hearty alternative to popcorn.

- 2 cups quick-cooking oats
- 2 tablespoons brown sugar
- 2 tablespoons honey
- 1 tablespoon butter
- 1/4 cup slivered almonds
- 2 tablespoons golden raisins
- 2 tablespoons flaked coconut

In a large nonstick skillet, toast oats over medium heat until golden brown. Remove and set aside. In the same skillet, cook and stir the brown sugar, honey and butter over medium-low heat until bubbly, about 1-2 minutes.

Stir in the almonds, raisins, coconut and oats until coated. Cool. Store in an airtight container.

NUTRITION FACTS: 1/4 cup equals 102 calories, 3 g fat (1 g saturated fat), 3 mg cholesterol, 14 mg sodium, 16 g carbohydrate, 2 g fiber, 3 g protein. **DIABETIC EXCHANGES:** 1 starch, 1/2 fat.

Crab-Stuffed Jalapenos

FAT CARB

(PICTURED BELOW)

PREP: 25 Min.   **BAKE:** 40 Min.   **YIELD:** 2 Dozen

Whenever I bring these peppers to a party, guests can't wait to try them. The bites always seem to complement the other food that is served. They come together easily but look like I fussed.
—Susan Dugat, Rockport, Texas

- 24 large jalapeno peppers
- 6 ounces fat-free cream cheese
- 2 teaspoons Worcestershire sauce
- 1/4 teaspoon garlic powder
- 1 package (8 ounces) imitation crabmeat, chopped
- 1/4 cup shredded reduced-fat cheddar cheese
- 12 turkey bacon strips, halved widthwise

Cut stems off jalapenos; remove seeds and membranes. In a small mixing bowl, beat the cream cheese, Worcestershire sauce and garlic powder until blended. Stir in crab and cheddar cheese. Transfer to a resealable plastic bag; cut a small hole in a corner of the bag.

Pipe filling into jalapenos. Wrap each with a piece of bacon; secure with toothpicks. Place on an ungreased baking sheet. Bake at 350° for 40-50 minutes or until the peppers are crisp-tender.

NUTRITION FACTS: 1 stuffed pepper equals 41 calories, 2 g fat (1 g saturated fat), 9 mg cholesterol, 188 mg sodium, 3 g carbohydrate, trace fiber, 3 g protein. **DIABETIC EXCHANGE:** 1/2 lean meat.

Editor's Note: When cutting or seeding hot peppers, use rubber or plastic gloves to protect your hands. Avoid touching your face.

Chickpea Patties with Yogurt Sauce

MEAT-LESS

PREP: 25 Min.   **COOK:** 10 Min./Batch   **YIELD:** 1 Dozen (1 Cup Sauce)

A little dill gives these first-course patties an unexpected flavor boost. Served with a garlic-curry sauce, the plated appetizers please vegetarians and meat lovers alike.
—Jane Hacker, Milwaukee, Wisconsin

- 1 can (15 ounces) chickpeas *or* garbanzo beans, rinsed and drained, *divided*
- 2 green onions, chopped
- 2 tablespoons dry bread crumbs
- 2 tablespoons snipped fresh dill *or* 2 teaspoons dill weed
- 2 tablespoons lemon juice
- 2 tablespoons tahini
- 1/2 teaspoon salt
- 1/2 teaspoon ground cumin
- 1/4 teaspoon pepper
- 4 teaspoons canola oil

SAUCE:
- 1 cup (8 ounces) fat-free plain yogurt
- 2 garlic cloves, minced
- 1/4 teaspoon curry powder

Dash crushed red pepper flakes

Place half of the chickpeas and the onions in a food processor; cover and process until chopped. Transfer to a small bowl. Stir in the bread crumbs, dill and lemon juice; set aside.

Place the tahini, salt, cumin, pepper and remaining chickpeas in food processor; cover and process until blended. Add to chopped chickpea mixture; stir to combine. Shape into 12 patties.

In a large nonstick skillet coated with cooking spray, cook patties in oil over medium heat in batches for 4-5 minutes on each side or until golden brown. Meanwhile, in a small bowl, combine sauce ingredients. Serve with patties.

NUTRITION FACTS: 2 patties with 3 tablespoons sauce equals 159 calories, 8 g fat (1 g saturated fat), 1 mg cholesterol, 332 mg sodium, 18 g carbohydrate, 4 g fiber, 6 g protein. **DIABETIC EXCHANGES:** 1-1/2 fat, 1 starch.

Favorite Recipe Made Lighter

FULL-BODIED Veggie Pizza Squares are packed with good-for-you cauliflower, broccoli, carrots, mushrooms and other vegetables. Under those veggies, however, there's a creamy spread that sits atop a buttery, flaky crust. That's where the problem lays for *L&T* reader Sandra Shafer of Mountain View, California. A big fan of the original recipe, Sandra asked if our Test Kitchen staff could trim down the fat in the dill spread and in the crust.

Our home economists began from the bottom up, with the crescent roll crust. It was an easy transition from full-fat to reduced, because reduced-fat crescent rolls are actually comparable in taste to their counterparts.

The team didn't want to use all fat-free cream cheese in the spread, so the staff opted for half reduced-fat cream cheese and half fat-free. Next, they combined the cream cheese with reduced-fat mayonnaise. To bulk up the milk, they added plain yogurt.

To help matters, the vegetables were perfect as they were, and they carried so much flavor that the fattening ingredients really weren't missed at all. The resulting recipe for Makeover Veggie Pizza Squares is not only delightful, but just as beautiful as the original. Each square contains only 2 grams of saturated fat and boasts an amazing 61% decrease in fat overall.

Makeover Veggie Pizza Squares

(PICTURED ABOVE)

PREP: 30 Min. + Chilling   **YIELD:** 24 Pieces

- 2 tubes (8 ounces *each*) refrigerated reduced-fat crescent rolls
- 1 package (8 ounces) reduced-fat cream cheese
- 1 package (8 ounces) fat-free cream cheese
- 1/2 cup plain yogurt
- 1/3 cup reduced-fat mayonnaise
- 1/4 cup fat-free milk
- 1 tablespoon dill weed
- 1/2 teaspoon garlic salt
- 1 cup shredded carrots
- 1 cup fresh cauliflowerets, chopped
- 1 cup fresh broccoli florets, chopped
- 1 cup julienned green pepper
- 1 cup sliced fresh mushrooms
- 2 cans (2-1/4 ounces *each*) sliced ripe olives, drained
- 1/4 cup finely chopped sweet onion

Unroll both tubes of crescent dough and pat into an ungreased 15-in. x 10-in. x 1-in. baking pan; seal seams and perforations. Bake at 375° for 10-12 minutes or until golden brown. Cool completely on a wire rack.

In a small mixing bowl, beat the cream cheeses, yogurt, mayonnaise, milk, dill and garlic salt until smooth. Spread over crust. Sprinkle with carrots, cauliflower, broccoli, green pepper, mushrooms, olives and onion. Cover and refrigerate for at least 1 hour. Cut into squares before serving. Refrigerate leftovers.

NUTRITION FACTS: 1 piece equals 128 calories, 7 g fat (2 g saturated fat), 9 mg cholesterol, 365 mg sodium, 11 g carbohydrate, 1 g fiber, 4 g protein. **DIABETIC EXCHANGES:** 1 starch, 1 fat.

Veggie Pizza Squares

PREP: 30 Min. + Chilling   **YIELD:** 24 Pieces

- 2 tubes (8 ounces *each*) refrigerated crescent rolls
- 2 packages (8 ounces *each*) cream cheese, softened
- 3/4 cup mayonnaise
- 1/4 cup heavy whipping cream
- 1 tablespoon dill weed
- 1-1/2 teaspoons garlic salt
- 1 cup shredded carrots
- 1 cup fresh cauliflowerets, chopped
- 1 cup fresh broccoli florets, chopped
- 1 cup julienned green pepper
- 1 cup sliced fresh mushrooms
- 2 cans (2-1/4 ounces *each*) sliced ripe olives, drained
- 1/4 cup finely chopped sweet onion

Unroll both tubes of crescent dough and pat into an ungreased 15-in. x 10-in. x 1-in. baking pan; seal seams and perforations. Bake at 375° for 10-12 minutes or until golden brown. Cool completely on a wire rack.

In a small mixing bowl, beat the cream cheese, mayonnaise, cream, dill and garlic salt until smooth. Spread over crust. Sprinkle with carrots, cauliflower, broccoli, green pepper, mushrooms, olives and onion. Cover and refrigerate for at least 1 hour. Cut into squares before serving. Refrigerate leftovers.

NUTRITION FACTS: 1 piece equals 212 calories, 18 g fat (7 g saturated fat), 27 mg cholesterol, 407 mg sodium, 10 g carbohydrate, 1 g fiber, 3 g protein.

2 teaspoons butter
1 cup (4 ounces) crumbled blue cheese
4 tablespoons finely chopped walnuts, toasted, *divided*
1/2 teaspoon salt
1 package (2.1 ounces) frozen miniature phyllo tart shells

In a small nonstick skillet, saute apple and onion in butter until tender. Remove from the heat; stir in the blue cheese, 3 tablespoons walnuts and salt. Spoon a rounded tablespoonful into each tart shell.

Place on an ungreased baking sheet. Bake at 350° for 5 minutes. Sprinkle with remaining walnuts; bake 2-3 minutes longer or until lightly browned.

NUTRITION FACTS: 1 appetizer equals 76 calories, 5 g fat (2 g saturated fat), 7 mg cholesterol, 200 mg sodium, 5 g carbohydrate, trace fiber, 3 g protein. **DIABETIC EXCHANGES:** 1 fat, 1/2 starch.

Southwest Spanakopita Bites

PREP: 40 Min.   BAKE: 10 Min.   YIELD: 2 Dozen (1/2 Cup Sauce)

I'm a big fan of the Southwest-style egg rolls served at restaurants and wanted to re-create them without the fat of deep frying. Using phyllo dough and baking the appetizers in the oven was the solution. Now I can enjoy the bites without the guilt.
—Marianne Shira, Osceola, Wisconsin

2 tablespoons finely chopped sweet red pepper
1 green onion, finely chopped
1 teaspoon canola oil
1 package (10 ounces) frozen chopped spinach, thawed and squeezed dry
3/4 cup shredded reduced-fat Monterey Jack cheese *or* Mexican cheese blend
1/2 cup frozen corn, thawed
1/2 cup canned black beans, rinsed and drained
1 tablespoon chopped seeded jalapeno pepper
1/2 teaspoon ground cumin
1/2 teaspoon chili powder
1/4 teaspoon salt
8 sheets phyllo dough (14 inches x 9 inches)
Butter-flavored cooking spray
SAUCE:
1/3 cup cubed avocado
1/4 cup reduced-fat mayonnaise
1/4 cup reduced-fat sour cream
1-1/2 teaspoons white vinegar

In a small skillet, saute red pepper and onion in oil until tender. Transfer to a small bowl; stir in 1/2 cup spinach (save the rest for another use). Stir in the cheese, corn, beans, jalapeno, cumin, chili powder and salt.

Place one sheet of phyllo dough on a work surface with a short end facing you. (Keep remaining phyllo covered with plastic wrap to prevent it from drying out.) Spray sheet with butter-flavored spray; cut into three 14-in. x 3-in. strips.

Place a scant tablespoon of filling on lower corner of each strip. Fold dough over filling, forming a triangle. Fold triangle up, then over, forming another triangle. Continue folding, like a flag, until you come to the end of the strip. Spritz end of dough with spray and press onto triangle to seal. Turn triangle and spritz top with spray. Repeat with remaining phyllo and filling.

Orange and Jicama Salsa
(PICTURED ABOVE)

PREP/TOTAL TIME: 25 Min.   YIELD: 4 Cups

Tiny cubes of jicama and ripe oranges make for a change-of-pace salsa. Adjust the amount of jalapeno pepper to best fit your taste.
—Cheryl Perry, Elizabeth City, North Carolina

6 medium oranges, peeled, sectioned and chopped
1-1/2 cups cubed peeled jicama
1/4 cup chopped red onion
1/4 cup chopped sweet red pepper
2 green onions, thinly sliced
1/4 cup minced fresh cilantro
1 tablespoon lime juice
2 teaspoons chopped seeded jalapeno pepper
1/2 teaspoon sugar
1/8 teaspoon salt
Baked tortilla chips *or* scoops

In a large bowl, combine the first 10 ingredients. Serve with chips. Refrigerate leftovers.

NUTRITION FACTS: 1/4 cup (calculated without chips) equals 22 calories, trace fat (trace saturated fat), 0 cholesterol, 20 mg sodium, 5 g carbohydrate, 1 g fiber, trace protein. **DIABETIC EXCHANGE:** Free food.

Editor's Note: When cutting or seeding hot peppers, use rubber or plastic gloves to protect your hands. Avoid touching your face.

Apple-Nut Blue Cheese Tartlets

PREP: 25 Min.   BAKE: 10 Min.   YIELD: 15 Appetizers

These appetizers look and taste gourmet, but they're easy to make and have loads of blue cheese flavor. The phyllo shells and filling can even be made in advance. —Trisha Kruse, Eagle, Idaho

1 large apple, peeled and finely chopped
1 medium onion, finely chopped

Place triangles on baking sheets coated with cooking spray. Bake at 375° for 10-12 minutes or until golden brown. Mash avocado with mayonnaise, sour cream and vinegar. Serve with warm appetizers.

NUTRITION FACTS: 1 appetizer with 1 teaspoon sauce equals 50 calories, 3 g fat (1 g saturated fat), 4 mg cholesterol, 103 mg sodium, 5 g carbohydrate, 1 g fiber, 2 g protein. **DIABETIC EXCHANGES:** 1/2 starch, 1/2 fat.

Editor's Note: *When cutting or seeding hot peppers, use rubber or plastic gloves to protect your hands. Avoid touching your face.*

Gorgonzola Figs With Balsamic Glaze

FAT CARB

(PICTURED BELOW)

PREP: 30 Min. **BAKE:** 10 Min. **YIELD:** 16 Appetizers

We received this recipe from another couple and tweaked it slightly to suit our family. Calling for a handful of ingredients, it's an easy appetizer that everyone adores.
—Sarah Vasques, Milford, New Hampshire

　　1 cup balsamic vinegar
　 16 dried figs
　1/2 cup crumbled Gorgonzola cheese
　　8 thin slices prosciutto, halved widthwise
　　2 teaspoons minced fresh rosemary
　1/4 teaspoon pepper

For glaze, in a small saucepan, bring vinegar to a boil over medium heat; cook until reduced to about 1/4 cup.

Cut a lengthwise slit down the center of each fig; fill with 1-1/2 teaspoons cheese. Wrap each with a piece of prosciutto; place on a baking sheet. Sprinkle appetizers with rosemary and pepper.

Bake at 425° for 10-12 minutes or until prosciutto is crisp. Serve warm with glaze.

NUTRITION FACTS: 1 stuffed fig with 3/4 teaspoon glaze equals 90 calories, 2 g fat (1 g saturated fat), 9 mg cholesterol, 190 mg sodium, 15 g carbohydrate, 2 g fiber, 3 g protein. **DIABETIC EXCHANGES:** 1 fruit, 1/2 fat.

Editor's Note: *Amber-colored dried figs (labeled Turkish or Calimyrna) are recommended for this recipe. Mission figs, which are black, are smaller and hold less cheese. If large stems are present, remove them before stuffing the figs.*

Nutty Snack Mix

SALT CARB

PREP: 15 Min. **BAKE:** 20 Min. + Cooling **YIELD:** 7 Cups

This toasty mix from our Test Kitchen offers a little spice and a whole lot of flavor! Make it for a long car ride to Grandma's house or for a party that is sure to last all night.

　　2 cups Bran Chex
　　2 cups Wheat Chex
　　1 cup Cheerios
　　1 cup unblanched almonds
　　1 cup pecan halves
　1/4 cup reduced-fat butter, melted
　1/4 cup Worcestershire sauce
　　2 teaspoons chili powder
　　2 teaspoons paprika
　1/2 teaspoon onion powder
　　4 to 6 drops hot pepper sauce
　1/2 cup dried cranberries

In a large bowl, combine the cereal and nuts. Spread into two ungreased 15-in. x 10-in. x 1-in. baking pans. In a small bowl, combine the butter, Worcestershire sauce, chili powder, paprika, onion powder and pepper sauce; pour over cereal mixture and toss to coat.

Bake at 300° for 20 minutes, stirring once. Stir in cranberries. Cool completely. Store in airtight containers.

NUTRITION FACTS: 1/3 cup equals 128 calories, 9 g fat (1 g saturated fat), 4 mg cholesterol, 121 mg sodium, 12 g carbohydrate, 3 g fiber, 3 g protein.

Editor's Note: *This recipe was tested with Land O'Lakes light stick butter.*

Avocado Dip

CARB MEAT-
LESS

PREP/TOTAL TIME: 15 Min. **YIELD:** 2-1/2 Cups

When I couldn't find a guacamole that I really liked, I came up with this no-stress dip.　　—Kay Dunham, Amity, Missouri

　　2 medium ripe avocados, peeled and pitted
　　1 package (8 ounces) fat-free cream cheese
　1/3 cup plain yogurt
　1/3 cup picante sauce
　　1 tablespoon lime juice
　1/2 teaspoon salt
　1/4 teaspoon garlic powder
Tortilla chips

In a small bowl, mash avocados and cream cheese until smooth. Stir in the yogurt, picante sauce, lime juice, salt and garlic powder. Serve with chips. Refrigerate leftovers.

NUTRITION FACTS: 1/4 cup (calculated without chips) equals 76 calories, 5 g fat (1 g saturated fat), 2 mg cholesterol, 237 mg sodium, 4 g carbohydrate, 1 g fiber, 4 g protein. **DIABETIC EXCHANGE:** 1 fat.

Smoked Salmon Cucumber Canapes

PREP: 25 Min. + Chilling   **YIELD:** 42 Appetizers

This is the one appetizer that I'm always asked to bring to parties. It's simple, comes together quickly and is always a winner.
—Judy Grebetz, Racine, Wisconsin

  2 medium cucumbers, peeled
  4 ounces smoked salmon, flaked
  2 tablespoons lemon juice
  1 tablespoon finely chopped onion
  1 tablespoon capers, drained
  1 tablespoon minced fresh parsley
1/2 teaspoon Dijon mustard
1/8 teaspoon pepper

Cut cucumbers in half lengthwise; remove and discard seeds. In a small bowl, combine the remaining ingredients. Spoon into cucumber halves. Wrap in plastic wrap. Refrigerate for 3-4 hours or until filling is firm. Cut into 1/2-in. slices.

NUTRITION FACTS: 1 canape equals 6 calories, trace fat (trace saturated fat), 1 mg cholesterol, 27 mg sodium, 1 g carbohydrate, trace fiber, 1 g protein. **DIABETIC EXCHANGE:** Free food.

Lemony Hummus

(PICTURED ABOVE)

PREP/TOTAL TIME: 15 Min.   **YIELD:** 1-1/2 Cups

This easy spread makes a welcomed addition to appetizer buffet tables. I love the kick that the tahini gives it.
—Josephine Piro, Easton, Pennsylvania

  2 garlic cloves, peeled
  1 can (15 ounces) chickpeas *or* garbanzo beans, rinsed and drained
1/4 cup lemon juice
  3 tablespoons water
  2 tablespoons tahini
  1 teaspoon ground cumin
1/4 teaspoon salt
1/4 teaspoon pepper
Pita breads, warmed and cut into wedges
Carrot and celery sticks

Process garlic in a food processor until minced. Add the chickpeas, lemon juice, water, tahini, cumin, salt and pepper; cover and process until smooth. Transfer to a small bowl. Serve with pita wedges and vegetables.

NUTRITION FACTS: 1/4 cup (calculated without pita wedges and vegetables) equals 106 calories, 5 g fat (1 g saturated fat), 0 cholesterol, 192 mg sodium, 13 g carbohydrate, 3 g fiber, 4 g protein. **DIABETIC EXCHANGES:** 1 starch, 1/2 fat.

SHOPT SMART

Tahini is a nutty paste that's made from ground sesame seeds. When featuring hulled seeds, tahini is mild in flavor and works well in many recipes. The unhulled version can lend a slightly bitter taste if you're not used to it. A Middle Eastern staple, the spread is available in the ethnic aisle of most grocery stores.

Asparagus Pepperoni Triangles

PREP: 30 Min.   **BAKE:** 10 Min./Batch   **YIELD:** 36 Appetizers

Convenient phyllo dough forms the crispy golden crust for these mouth-watering party starters. Our Test Kitchen staff created the cute triangular bites.

2/3 cup part-skim ricotta cheese
  1 egg yolk
1-1/2 ounces sliced turkey pepperoni, chopped
  6 tablespoons grated Parmesan cheese
1/4 cup minced fresh basil *or* 4 teaspoons dried basil
4-1/2 teaspoons minced chives
4-1/2 teaspoons minced fresh parsley
Dash pepper
  1 cup water
1/2 pound fresh asparagus, trimmed and cut into 1/2-inch pieces
  1 green onion, chopped
  3 garlic cloves, minced
  2 teaspoons plus 3 tablespoons butter, *divided*
 12 sheets phyllo dough (14 inches x 9 inches)
Butter-flavored cooking spray

In a large bowl, combine the first eight ingredients; set aside. In a small saucepan, bring water to a boil. Add asparagus; cover and boil for 3 minutes. Drain and immediately place asparagus in ice water. Drain and pat dry.

In a small nonstick skillet over medium heat, cook onion and garlic in 2 teaspoons butter for 2 minutes or just until tender; add to ricotta mixture. Stir in asparagus. Melt remaining butter; set aside.

Place one sheet of phyllo dough on a work surface with a short end facing you. (Keep remaining phyllo covered with plastic wrap to prevent it from drying out.)

Spray sheet with butter-flavored spray; cut dough into three 14-in. x 3-in. strips. Place a scant tablespoon of asparagus mixture on lower corner of each strip. Fold dough over filling, forming a triangle. Fold triangle up, then fold triangle over, forming another triangle. Continue folding, like a flag, until you come to the end of the strip.

Brush end of dough with butter and press onto triangle to seal. Turn triangle and brush top with melted butter. Repeat with remaining phyllo and filling.

Place triangles on baking sheets coated with cooking spray. Bake at 375° for 10-12 minutes or until triangles are golden brown. Serve warm.

NUTRITION FACTS: 1 appetizer equals 36 calories, 2 g fat (1 g saturated fat), 13 mg cholesterol, 71 mg sodium, 3 g carbohydrate, trace fiber, 2 g protein. DIABETIC EXCHANGE: 1/2 fat.

Mini Pizza Cups

PREP: 25 Min.   BAKE: 15 Min.   YIELD: 32 Appetizers

Served hot or cold, these little pizzas are pure delight. Try them for after-school snacks or kid-friendly party fare.
—Jane Jones, Cedar, Minnesota

    1 tube (11.3 ounces) refrigerated dinner rolls
    1 can (8 ounces) pizza sauce
1/4 cup finely chopped onion
1/3 cup finely chopped green pepper
    2 ounces sliced turkey pepperoni, chopped
    1 cup (4 ounces) shredded part-skim mozzarella cheese

Separate dough into eight rolls; cut each into quarters. Press dough onto the bottom and up the sides of miniature muffin cups coated with cooking spray.

Spoon pizza sauce into each cup. Sprinkle with onion, green pepper, pepperoni and cheese. Bake at 375° for 15-18 minutes or until crusts are browned and cheese is melted.

NUTRITION FACTS: 1 pizza cup equals 44 calories, 1 g fat (1 g saturated fat), 4 mg cholesterol, 134 mg sodium, 6 g carbohydrate, trace fiber, 3 g protein. DIABETIC EXCHANGE: 1/2 starch.

Mango Black Bean Salsa

PREP/TOTAL TIME: 15 Min.   YIELD: 3-1/2 Cups

This colorful salsa takes just minutes to prepare...and that's likely how long it will last at your event!   —Judy Heiser, Uvalde, Texas

    1 can (15 ounces) black beans, rinsed and drained
    1 can (11 ounces) Mexicorn, drained
    1 medium mango, peeled and chopped
1/4 cup finely chopped onion
1/4 cup minced fresh cilantro
    2 tablespoons lime juice
    1 teaspoon garlic salt
1/4 teaspoon ground cumin
Baked tortilla chip scoops

In a large bowl, combine the beans, corn, mango, onion, cilantro, lime juice, garlic salt and cumin. Refrigerate until serving. Serve with chips.

NUTRITION FACTS: 1/4 cup (calculated without chips) equals 53 calories, trace fat (trace saturated fat), 0 cholesterol, 310 mg sodium, 11 g carbohydrate, 2 g fiber, 2 g protein. DIABETIC EXCHANGE: 1 starch.

Cranberry Turkey Crostini

(PICTURED BELOW)

PREP: 30 Min. + Chilling   YIELD: 30 Appetizers

I wasn't quite sure what to expect when I made these, but they're fantastic. The jalapenos balance out the other ingredients perfectly. If you don't have shaved turkey, chicken works just as well.
—Bridgetta Ealy, Pontiac, Michigan

    1 package (12 ounces) fresh *or* frozen cranberries
    1 medium tangerine, peeled and seeded
1/2 cup red wine vinegar
1/4 cup chopped shallots
1/2 cup sugar
1/4 cup chopped seeded jalapeno peppers
1/4 teaspoon pepper
  30 slices French bread (1/4 inch thick)
Cooking spray
    1 package (8 ounces) reduced-fat cream cheese
1/2 pound shaved deli smoked turkey

Place cranberries and tangerine in a food processor; cover and process until coarsely chopped. Set aside.

In a small saucepan, bring vinegar and shallots to a boil. Reduce heat; simmer, uncovered, for 5 minutes or until mixture is reduced to 1/3 cup, stirring occasionally. Stir in the sugar, jalapenos, pepper and reserved cranberry mixture. Cook for 5 minutes over medium heat, stirring frequently. Transfer to a small bowl; refrigerate until chilled.

Place bread on ungreased baking sheets; lightly spray bread on both sides with cooking spray. Broil 3-4 in. from the heat for 1-2 minutes on each side or until lightly browned. Spread each slice with 1-1/2 teaspoons cream cheese; top with turkey and 1 tablespoon cranberry mixture.

NUTRITION FACTS: 1 appetizer equals 79 calories, 3 g fat (1 g saturated fat), 8 mg cholesterol, 131 mg sodium, 11 g carbohydrate, 1 g fiber, 3 g protein. DIABETIC EXCHANGES: 1 starch, 1/2 fat.

Editor's Note: When cutting or seeding hot peppers, use rubber or plastic gloves to protect your hands. Avoid touching your face.

Favorite Recipe Made Lighter

IT'S SURPRISING what a quick substitution or two can do. By switching from full-fat products to reduced- or low-fat ingredients, you can often save fat and calories while keeping the flavor and texture of many recipes.

This is certainly the case with Leigh Thomas' Makeover Mexican Roll-Ups. The Hahira, Georgia reader became an honorary member of our recipe revamp team when she lightened up one of her favorite appetizers. Instead of giving up Mexican Roll-Ups, she revised the recipe with fat-free cream cheese and reduced-fat sour cream.

Doing so cut nearly 70% of the fat and eliminated a whopping 75% of the cholesterol from each appealing bite.

"I've been a health and physical education teacher for the past 19 years," Leigh writes, "so I always try to serve healthier dishes to my guests. The original version of this tasty appetizer is wonderful, but I actually prefer the trimmed-down variation. I can now serve the roll-ups without an ounce of guilt. What a great feeling!"

With their reduced-fat content, fat-free products often require extra care in cooking. Heating them may result in less creamy products. But, since these appetizers don't have to be cooked, they're a perfect fit for fat-free ingredients and Leigh's healthier meals for family and friends.

Mexican Roll-Ups

 SALT CARB MEAT-LESS

PREP: 25 Min. + Chilling   **YIELD:** About 4 Dozen

- 1 package (8 ounces) cream cheese, softened
- 1 cup (8 ounces) sour cream
- 1 cup (4 ounces) shredded cheddar cheese
- 1 can (4 ounces) chopped green chilies, drained
- 4 green onions, chopped
- 1 can (2-1/4 ounces) chopped ripe olives, drained
- 1 teaspoon garlic powder
- 5 flour tortillas (10 inches), room temperature

Salsa, optional

In a small mixing bowl, combine the first seven ingredients. Spread over tortillas. Roll up tightly and wrap in plastic wrap. Refrigerate for 1 hour or until firm.

Unwrap the rolls and cut into scant 1-in. slices. Serve with salsa if desired.

NUTRITION FACTS: 1 piece (calculated without salsa) equals 57 calories, 4 g fat (2 g saturated fat), 11 mg cholesterol, 89 mg sodium, 4 g carbohydrate, 1 g fiber, 2 g protein. **DIABETIC EXCHANGE:** 1 fat.

MAKEOVER TIP

Whether making roll-up appetizers or another south-of-the-border favorite, consider using whole wheat tortillas. As a no-fuss substitution for the flour variety, whole wheat tortillas lend a hint of color to foods and provide a bit of extra fiber as well.

Makeover
Mexican Roll-Ups

 FAT SALT CARB MEAT-LESS

(PICTURED ABOVE)

PREP: 25 Min. + Chilling   **YIELD:** About 4 Dozen

- 1 package (8 ounces) fat-free cream cheese
- 1 cup (8 ounces) fat-free sour cream
- 1 cup (4 ounces) shredded reduced-fat cheddar cheese
- 1 can (4 ounces) chopped green chilies, drained
- 4 green onions, chopped
- 1 can (2-1/4 ounces) chopped ripe olives, drained
- 1 teaspoon garlic powder
- 5 flour tortillas (10 inches), room temperature

Salsa, optional

In a small mixing bowl, combine the first seven ingredients. Spread over tortillas. Roll up tightly and wrap in plastic wrap. Refrigerate for 1 hour or until firm.

Unwrap the rolls and cut into scant 1-in. slices. Serve with salsa if desired.

NUTRITION FACTS: 1 piece (calculated without salsa) equals 40 calories, 1 g fat (trace saturated fat), 3 mg cholesterol, 103 mg sodium, 5 g carbohydrate, 1 g fiber, 2 g protein. **DIABETIC EXCHANGE:** 1/2 starch.

Roasted Red Pepper Hummus

PREP: 30 Min. + Standing   **YIELD:** 3 Cups

My son taught me how to make hummus, which is a great alternative to other calorie-filled dips. Fresh-roasted red bell peppers make this version extra special.

—Nancy Watson-Pistole, Shawnee, Kansas

- 2 large sweet red peppers
- 2 cans (15 ounces *each*) garbanzo beans *or* chickpeas, rinsed and drained
- 1/3 cup lemon juice
- 3 tablespoons tahini
- 1 tablespoon olive oil
- 2 garlic cloves, peeled
- 1-1/4 teaspoons salt
- 1 teaspoon curry powder
- 1/2 teaspoon ground coriander
- 1/2 teaspoon ground cumin
- 1/2 teaspoon pepper
- Pita bread, warmed and cut into wedges, *and* reduced-fat wheat snack crackers
- Additional garbanzo beans or chickpeas, optional

Broil red peppers 4 in. from the heat until skins blister, about 5 minutes. With tongs, rotate peppers a quarter turn. Broil and rotate until all sides are blistered and blackened. Place peppers in a bowl; cover and let stand for 15-20 minutes.

Peel off and discard charred skin. Remove stems and seeds. Place the peppers in a food processor. Add beans, lemon juice, tahini, oil, garlic and seasonings; cover and process until blended. Transfer to a serving bowl. Serve with pita bread and crackers. Garnish with additional beans if desired.

NUTRITION FACTS: 1/4 cup (calculated without pita bread, crackers or additional beans) equals 113 calories, 5 g fat (1 g saturated fat), 0 cholesterol, 339 mg sodium, 14 g carbohydrate, 4 g fiber, 4 g protein. **DIABETIC EXCHANGES:** 1 starch, 1 fat.

Hot Spiced Punch

PREP/TOTAL TIME: 25 Min.   **YIELD:** 12 Servings (2-1/4 Quarts)

Here's a cheery beverage that's guaranteed to warm you up on a chilly winter day. I found that candy red-hots add a touch of cinnamon to the sweet, fruity blend of flavors.

—Bertha Johnson, Indianapolis, Indiana

- 6 cups water
- 2 cups cranberry juice
- 1 cup sugar
- 1/4 cup red-hot candies
- 9 whole cloves
- 1/2 cup unsweetened pineapple juice
- 1/2 cup orange juice
- 1/4 cup lemon juice

In a Dutch oven, combine the water, cranberry juice, sugar, redhots and cloves; bring to a boil. Add the remaining juices; return to a boil. Reduce heat; simmer, uncovered, for 10 minutes to allow flavors to blend. Discard cloves. Serve warm.

NUTRITION FACTS: 3/4 cup equals 113 calories, trace fat (trace saturated fat), 0 cholesterol, 2 mg sodium, 29 g carbohydrate, trace fiber, trace protein.

Deviled Eggs with Dill

CARB

PREP/TOTAL TIME: 20 Min.   **YIELD:** 1 Dozen

Deviled eggs make a great side dish for Easter, but they are also a fantastic snack year-round. My version offers a hint of Worcestershire and a slight tang of mustard.

—Mary Prior, Rush City, Minnesota

- 6 hard-cooked eggs
- 2 tablespoons reduced-fat mayonnaise
- 1-1/2 teaspoons cider vinegar
- 3/4 teaspoon prepared mustard
- 1/4 teaspoon Worcestershire sauce
- 1/4 teaspoon salt
- Dash pepper
- 12 fresh dill sprigs

Cut eggs in half lengthwise. Remove yolks; set aside egg whites and four yolks (discard remaining yolks or save for another use).

In a bowl, mash reserved yolks. Add the mayonnaise, vinegar, mustard, Worcestershire sauce, salt and pepper; mix well. Stuff or pipe into egg whites. Garnish with dill. Refrigerate until serving.

NUTRITION FACTS: 2 egg halves equals 74 calories, 5 g fat (1 g saturated fat), 144 mg cholesterol, 207 mg sodium, 1 g carbohydrate, trace fiber, 5 g protein. **DIABETIC EXCHANGES:** 1 lean meat, 1/2 fat.

Easy Party Bruschetta

PREP/TOTAL TIME: 25 Min.   **YIELD:** 30 Appetizers

This pretty bruschetta packs plenty of fresh flavor and gets a bit of heat from jalapeno pepper. It's perfect for a casual buffet table when tomatoes are at their summer best.

—Del Mason, Martensville, Saskatchewan

- 1-1/2 cups chopped seeded tomatoes
- 2/3 cup finely chopped red onion
- 2 tablespoons minced seeded jalapeno pepper
- 2 garlic cloves, minced
- 1/2 teaspoon dried basil
- 1/4 teaspoon salt
- 1/4 teaspoon coarsely ground pepper
- 2 tablespoons olive oil
- 1 tablespoon cider vinegar
- 1 tablespoon red wine vinegar
- 3 dashes hot pepper sauce
- 1 loaf (8 ounces) French bread, cut into 1/4-inch slices
- 2 tablespoons grated Parmesan cheese

In a small bowl, combine the first seven ingredients. In another bowl, whisk the oil, vinegars and pepper sauce; stir into tomato mixture.

Place bread slices on an ungreased baking sheet. Broil 3-4 in. from the heat for 1-2 minutes or until golden brown. With a slotted spoon, top each slice with tomato mixture. Sprinkle with Parmesan cheese.

NUTRITION FACTS: 1 appetizer equals 34 calories, 1 g fat (trace saturated fat), trace cholesterol, 73 mg sodium, 5 g carbohydrate, trace fiber, 1 g protein. **DIABETIC EXCHANGE:** 1/2 starch.

Editor's Note: *When cutting or seeding hot peppers, use rubber or plastic gloves to protect your hands. Avoid touching your face.*

Fudgy Brownies

(PICTURED AT RIGHT)

SALT ▼

PREP: 20 Min.   **BAKE:** 20 Min. + Cooling   **YIELD:** 1 Dozen

Almond extract enhances these chocolaty treats without adding calories. Each bite is so decadent, no one will realize the brownies are lighter in fat than most.   —Margaret Wilson, Hemet, California

  1/4 cup butter, cubed
    1 square (1 ounce) unsweetened chocolate
 1-1/2 cups sugar
    3 egg whites
    1 egg
  1/4 teaspoon almond extract
    1 cup all-purpose flour
  2/3 cup baking cocoa
  1/2 teaspoon baking powder

In a small saucepan over medium heat, cook and stir the butter and chocolate until melted. Remove from the heat; stir in sugar until blended. Cool for 10 minutes.

Combine the egg whites, egg and extract; stir into chocolate mixture until blended. Combine the flour, cocoa and baking powder; stir into chocolate mixture until blended.

Transfer to a 9-in. square baking pan coated with cooking spray. Bake at 350° for 18-22 minutes or until a toothpick inserted near the center comes out with moist crumbs (do not overbake). Cool on a wire rack. Cut into bars.

NUTRITION FACTS: 1 brownie equals 205 calories, 6 g fat (3 g saturated fat), 28 mg cholesterol, 75 mg sodium, 36 g carbohydrate, 2 g fiber, 4 g protein. **DIABETIC EXCHANGES:** 2 starch, 1 fat.

Vanilla Chip Cranberry Blondies

(PICTURED ABOVE RIGHT)

SALT ▼

PREP: 15 Min.   **BAKE:** 15 Min. + Cooling   **YIELD:** 20 Bars

Our Test Kitchen created these delicious blondies that are sure to satisfy any health-conscious cook. Applesauce, dried cranberries, vanilla chips and heart-smart pecans add flavor to each bite.

    2 eggs
  1/4 cup canola oil
  1/4 cup unsweetened applesauce
 1-1/2 teaspoons vanilla extract
 1-1/3 cups all-purpose flour
  2/3 cup packed brown sugar
    1 teaspoon baking powder
  1/2 teaspoon salt
    1 cup dried cranberries, *divided*
  1/2 cup vanilla *or* white chips
  1/2 cup chopped pecans

In a large mixing bowl, beat the eggs, oil, applesauce and vanilla. Combine the flour, brown sugar, baking powder and salt; stir into egg mixture until blended. Stir in 1/2 cup cranberries (batter will be thick).

Spread into a 13-in. x 9-in. x 2-in. baking pan coated with cooking spray. Top with chips, pecans and remaining cranberries; gently press toppings down.

Bake at 350° for 15-20 minutes or until a toothpick inserted near the center comes out clean. Cool on a wire rack. Cut into bars.

NUTRITION FACTS: 1 bar equals 154 calories, 7 g fat (1 g saturated fat), 22 mg cholesterol, 92 mg sodium, 22 g carbohydrate, 1 g fiber, 2 g protein. **DIABETIC EXCHANGES:** 1-1/2 starch, 1 fat.

Hearty Poppers

FAT ▼ SALT ▼ CARB ▼

PREP: 35 Min.   **BAKE:** 20 Min.   **YIELD:** 24 Appetizers

There are many recipes for jalapeno pepper poppers here in Las Cruces, New Mexico. For our church's potluck, however, my husband and I came up with this lighter version.
        —Janice Vernon, Las Cruces, New Mexico

   12 jalapeno peppers
  1/2 pound lean ground turkey
  1/4 cup finely chopped onion
    4 ounces fat-free cream cheese
 1-1/3 cups shredded part-skim mozzarella cheese, *divided*
    1 tablespoon minced fresh cilantro
    1 teaspoon chili powder
  1/2 teaspoon garlic powder
  1/2 teaspoon ground cumin
  1/8 teaspoon salt
  1/8 teaspoon pepper

Cut jalapenos in half lengthwise, leaving stems intact; discard seeds. Set aside. In a small nonstick skillet over medium heat, cook turkey and onion until meat is no longer pink; drain.

In a small bowl, combine the cream cheese, 1/3 cup mozzarella cheese, cilantro, chili powder, garlic powder, cumin, salt and pepper. Stir in turkey mixture. Spoon generously into pepper halves.

Place in a 15-in. x 10-in. x 1-in. baking pan coated with cooking spray; sprinkle with remaining mozzarella cheese. Bake, uncovered, at 350° for 20 minutes for spicy flavor, 30 minutes for medium and 40 minutes for mild.

NUTRITION FACTS: 1 appetizer equals 38 calories, 2 g fat (1 g saturated fat), 11 mg cholesterol, 78 mg sodium, 1 g carbohydrate, trace fiber, 4 g protein. **DIABETIC EXCHANGE:** 1 lean meat.

Editor's Note: When cutting or seeding hot peppers, use rubber or plastic gloves to protect your hands. Avoid touching your face.

Apple Snack Wedges

FAT SALT

PREP/TOTAL TIME: 10 Min.   **YIELD:** 4 Servings

Kids of all ages will love these easy apples at snack time. With protein from peanut butter and a hint of sweetness and crunch, the quick-to-fix nibbles make nutritious treats.

—Jacquie Berg, St. Cloud, Wisconsin

    2 medium apples
    1 cup Rice Chex, crushed
1-1/2 teaspoons packed brown sugar
    2 tablespoons reduced-fat creamy peanut butter

Core apples; cut each into six wedges. Pat wedges dry with paper towels.

In a small shallow bowl, combine the cereal and brown sugar. Spread cut sides of apples with peanut butter; roll in cereal mixture. Serve immediately.

NUTRITION FACTS: 3 wedges equals 111 calories, 3 g fat (1 g saturated fat), 0 cholesterol, 103 mg sodium, 20 g carbohydrate, 2 g fiber, 3 g protein. **DIABETIC EXCHANGES:** 1 fruit, 1/2 starch, 1/2 fat.

Hot Chicken Swirls

(PICTURED BELOW)

FAT SALT CARB

PREP: 25 Min.   **BAKE:** 10 Min.   **YIELD:** 64 Appetizers

I was trying to use up crescent rolls and leftover chicken breast and came up with this tasty recipe. I lightened it by using reduced-fat dressing and fat-free cream cheese.

—Evelyn McGinnis, Bay City, Michigan

    2 tubes (8 ounces *each*) refrigerated reduced-fat
      crescent rolls
    1 cup shredded cooked chicken breast
    4 ounces fat-free cream cheese
1/4 cup prepared reduced-fat ranch salad dressing
1/4 cup shredded reduced-fat cheddar cheese
1/4 cup finely chopped sweet red pepper
    2 green onions, finely chopped
    2 tablespoons Louisiana-style hot sauce

Separate each tube of crescent dough into four rectangles; gently press perforations to seal. In a small bowl, combine the remaining ingredients; spread evenly over rectangles. Roll up jelly-roll style, starting with a short side; pinch seams to seal.

Cut each into eight slices; place cut side down on ungreased baking sheets. Bake at 375° for 10-12 minutes or until golden brown. Refrigerate leftovers.

NUTRITION FACTS: 1 appetizer equals 34 calories, 2 g fat (trace saturated fat), 2 mg cholesterol, 82 mg sodium, 3 g carbohydrate, trace fiber, 2 g protein. **DIABETIC EXCHANGE:** 1/2 starch.

Taco Dip

FAT CARB MEAT-
LESS

PREP/TOTAL TIME: 10 Min.   **YIELD:** 4 Cups

Serve this at your next party and guests won't have a clue that it's low fat.

—Traci Hoffman, Jamestown, Indiana

    1 can (16 ounces) fat-free refried beans
    2 cups (16 ounces) reduced-fat sour cream
    1 envelope taco seasoning
    1 plum tomato, chopped
1/2 cup shredded reduced-fat Mexican cheese blend
    3 green onions, sliced
1/4 cup sliced ripe olives, drained
Baked tortilla chip scoops

Spread the refried beans into a 9-in. pie plate. Combine sour cream and taco seasoning; spread over beans. Top the dip with the tomato, cheese, onions and olives. Serve with the chips. Refrigerate leftovers.

NUTRITION FACTS: 1/4 cup (calculated without chips) equals 91 calories, 3 g fat (2 g saturated fat), 13 mg cholesterol, 381 mg sodium, 10 g carbohydrate, 2 g fiber, 5 g protein. **DIABETIC EXCHANGES:** 1/2 starch, 1/2 fat.

Banana Chocolate Chip Cookies

FAT SALT CARB

PREP: 20 Min.   **BAKE:** 10 Min./Batch   **YIELD:** 3 Dozen

These soft cookies have a cake-like texture and lots of banana flavor that folks seem to love. —Vicki Raatz, Waterloo, Wisconsin

1/3 cup butter, softened
1/2 cup sugar
    1 egg
1/2 cup mashed ripe banana
1/2 teaspoon vanilla extract
    1 cup all-purpose flour
    1 teaspoon baking powder
1/4 teaspoon salt
1/8 teaspoon baking soda
    1 cup (6 ounces) semisweet chocolate chips

In a small mixing bowl, cream butter and sugar until light and fluffy. Beat in the egg, banana and vanilla. Combine the flour, baking powder, salt and baking soda; gradually add to creamed mixture. Stir in chocolate chips.

Drop by tablespoonfuls 2 in. apart onto baking sheets coated with cooking spray. Bake at 350° for 9-11 minutes or until edges are lightly browned. Remove to wire racks to cool.

NUTRITION FACTS: 1 cookie equals 66 calories, 3 g fat (2 g saturated fat), 10 mg cholesterol, 51 mg sodium, 9 g carbohydrate, trace fiber, 1 g protein. **DIABETIC EXCHANGES:** 1/2 starch, 1/2 fat.

Quince Pear Salsa

PREP: 25 Min.   COOK: 15 Min. + Chilling   YIELD: 3 Cups

When you need a tangy appetizer, our home economists suggest this pretty, peach-colored salsa.

> 2 medium quinces, peeled and chopped
> 1/2 cup orange juice
> 1 tablespoon lime juice
> 2 medium pears, peeled and chopped
> 1/3 cup finely chopped red onion
> 2 tablespoons chopped seeded jalapeno pepper
> 1 tablespoon minced fresh gingerroot
> 1/2 teaspoon honey
> 1/4 teaspoon salt

In a small saucepan, bring quinces and juices to a boil. Reduce heat; cover and simmer for 10 minutes. Stir in pears; cover and simmer 2-3 minutes longer or until quinces are tender. Remove from the heat; cool to room temperature.

Stir in the onion, jalapeno, ginger, honey and salt. Cover and refrigerate for 1 hour before serving.

NUTRITION FACTS: 1/4 cup equals 33 calories, trace fat (trace saturated fat), 0 cholesterol, 50 mg sodium, 8 g carbohydrate, 1 g fiber, trace protein. **DIABETIC EXCHANGE:** 1/2 fruit.

Editor's Note: When cutting or seeding hot peppers, use rubber or plastic gloves to protect your hands. Avoid touching your face.

Coconut Shrimp with Dipping Sauce
(PICTURED BELOW)

PREP: 1-1/4 Hours + Marinating   BAKE: 15 Min.   YIELD: 5 Servings

With crispy coconut-cilantro breading and an apricot sauce, this seafood delight fits any occasion. Our Test Kitchen staff even recommend the shrimp as main course.

> 1 can (14 ounces) light coconut milk, *divided*
> 1 jalapeno pepper, seeded and chopped
> 1/4 cup minced fresh cilantro
> 1-1/4 pounds uncooked medium shrimp
> 3/4 cup all-purpose flour
> 4 egg whites
> 3/4 cup panko (Japanese) bread crumbs
> 3/4 cup flaked coconut, lightly toasted
> 1/3 cup reduced-sugar apricot preserves
> 1 teaspoon spicy brown mustard

Place 2 tablespoons coconut milk in a small bowl; cover and refrigerate. In a large resealable plastic bag, combine the jalapeno, cilantro and remaining coconut milk. Peel and devein shrimp, leaving tails on. Add to bag; seal and turn to coat. Refrigerate for 1 hour.

Place flour in a shallow bowl. In another bowl, lightly beat the egg whites. In a third bowl, combine bread crumbs and coconut. Drain and discard marinade. Dip shrimp in flour and egg whites, then roll in crumb mixture.

Place on a baking sheet coated with cooking spray. Bake at 400° for 7-9 minutes on each side or until lightly browned. Meanwhile, for dipping sauce, add preserves and mustard to the reserved coconut milk. Serve with shrimp.

NUTRITION FACTS: about 10 shrimp with 5 teaspoons sauce equals 324 calories, 11 g fat (8 g saturated fat), 168 mg cholesterol, 316 mg sodium, 30 g carbohydrate, 1 g fiber, 23 g protein. **DIABETIC EXCHANGES:** 3 very lean meat, 2 starch, 2 fat.

Editor's Note: When cutting or seeding hot peppers, use rubber or plastic gloves to protect your hands. Avoid touching your face.

Saucy Asian Meatballs

PREP: 20 Min.   BAKE: 20 Min.   YIELD: 3 Dozen

This meatball recipe originally called for beef and pork and a different combination of seasonings. I used ground turkey and altered the seasonings for a healthy, fresh-flavored sauce.
—Lisa Varner, Greenville, South Carolina

> 2 garlic cloves, minced
> 1/2 teaspoon ground ginger
> 1 teaspoon plus 1/4 cup reduced-sodium soy sauce, *divided*
> 1 pound lean ground turkey
> 1/4 cup rice wine vinegar
> 1/4 cup tomato paste
> 2 tablespoons molasses
> 1 teaspoon hot pepper sauce

In a large bowl, combine the garlic, ginger and 1 teaspoon soy sauce. Crumble turkey over mixture and mix well. Shape into 1-in. balls.

Place in a 13-in. x 9-in. x 2-in. baking dish coated with cooking spray. Bake, uncovered, at 350° for 20-25 minutes or until meat is no longer pink.

In a saucepan, combine the vinegar, tomato paste, molasses, pepper sauce and remaining soy sauce. Cook and stir over medium heat for 3-5 minutes. Add the meatballs; heat through.

NUTRITION FACTS: 1 meatball equals 32 calories, 2 g fat (1 g saturated fat), 9 mg cholesterol, 89 mg sodium, 2 g carbohydrate, trace fiber, 2 g protein. **DIABETIC EXCHANGE:** 1/2 fat.

Favorite Recipe Made Lighter

CHRISTMAS wouldn't be the same for Diana Osborn without creamy Peanut Butter Fudge. A few years ago, however, the Wichita, Kansas cook put herself on a low-fat diet that nearly put an end to her family's Yuletide treat.

In the spirit of the season, however, she rolled up her sleeves and got to work to see if she could lighten the cherished recipe without losing its rich taste. Diana began by replacing the sugar with a sugar blend for baking to reduce calories.

She kept the full-fat butter but used only 2 tablespoons instead of a quarter cup—even though that meant the candy had to be boiled a little bit longer to ensure a fudge that was nice and firm. In addition, Diana greased the foil in her pan with cooking spray instead of butter. Next, reduced-fat peanut butter was substituted for the full-fat variety. Finally, she switched out the evaporated milk for fat-free.

The result? "So far, no one has even been able to tell the difference!" reports a delighted and proud Diana. She was able to pare 15 calories and a third of the fat grams from every piece of Makeover Peanut Butter Fudge. That may not sound like such a drastic cut, but it makes a big difference when you consider that nobody ever stops at just one piece!

Peanut Butter Fudge

FAT SALT CARB

PREP: 30 Min. + Chilling   **YIELD:** 81 Pieces

    1 teaspoon plus 1/4 cup butter, *divided*
1-1/2 cups sugar
    1 can (5 ounces) evaporated milk
1/4 teaspoon salt
1/3 cup butterscotch chips
1/3 cup peanut butter chips
    1 jar (7 ounces) marshmallow creme
    1 cup chunky peanut butter
    1 teaspoon vanilla extract

Line a 9-in. square pan with foil and grease the foil with 1 teaspoon butter; set aside.

Cube remaining butter and place in a large heavy saucepan. Add the sugar, milk and salt; cook and stir over medium heat until sugar is dissolved. Bring to a rapid boil; boil for 5 minutes or until a candy thermometer reads 230°, stirring constantly.

Remove from the heat; stir in chips until melted. Stir in the marshmallow creme, peanut butter and vanilla until blended. Pour into prepared pan; refrigerate for 2 hours or until firm.

Using foil, lift fudge out of pan. Gently peel off foil; cut fudge into 1-in. squares. Store in an airtight container in the refrigerator.

NUTRITION FACTS: 1 piece equals 58 calories, 3 g fat (1 g saturated fat), 2 mg cholesterol, 35 mg sodium, 8 g carbohydrate, trace fiber, 1 g protein.
DIABETIC EXCHANGES: 1/2 starch, 1/2 fat.

Editor's Note: We recommend that you test your candy thermometer before each use by bringing water to a boil; the thermometer should read 212°. Always adjust your recipe temperature up or down based on your test.

Makeover Peanut Butter Fudge

FAT SALT CARB

(PICTURED ABOVE)

PREP: 30 Min. + Chilling   **YIELD:** 81 Pieces

    3/4 cup sugar blend for baking
    2/3 cup fat-free evaporated milk
    2 tablespoons butter
1/4 teaspoon salt
1/3 cup butterscotch chips
1/3 cup peanut butter chips
    1 jar (7 ounces) marshmallow creme
    3/4 cup reduced-fat chunky peanut butter
    1 teaspoon vanilla extract

Line a 9-in. square pan with foil and coat the foil with cooking spray; set aside.

In a large heavy saucepan, combine the sugar blend, milk, butter and salt. Cook and stir over medium heat until sugar blend is dissolved. Bring to a rapid boil; boil for 7 minutes or until a candy thermometer reads 224°, stirring constantly.

Remove from the heat; stir in chips until melted. Stir in the marshmallow creme, peanut butter and vanilla until blended. Pour into prepared pan. Refrigerate for 2 hours or until firm.

Using foil, lift fudge out of pan. Gently peel off foil; cut fudge into 1-in. squares. Store in an airtight container in the refrigerator.

NUTRITION FACTS: 1 piece equals 43 calories, 2 g fat (1 g saturated fat), 1 mg cholesterol, 33 mg sodium, 6 g carbohydrate, trace fiber, 1 g protein.
DIABETIC EXCHANGES: 1/2 starch, 1/2 fat.

Editor's Note: This recipe was tested with Splenda Sugar Blend for Baking. We recommend that you test your candy thermometer before each use by bringing water to a boil; the thermometer should read 212°. Always adjust your recipe temperature up or down based on your test.

Goat Cheese 'n' Veggie Quesadillas

MEAT-LESS

(PICTURED AT RIGHT)

PREP: 55 Min. **BAKE:** 5 Min. **YIELD:** 24 Appetizers

Roasted veggies and goat cheese make this an elegant party food. We love to top them with our favorite salsa for an extra kick.
—Sara Longworth, Philadelphia, Pennsylvania

- 1 small eggplant, peeled, quartered and cut into 1/2-inch slices
- 1 medium zucchini, cut into 1/4-inch slices
- 1 medium sweet red pepper, chopped
- 1 medium onion, chopped
- 1/4 cup chopped ripe olives
- 2 garlic cloves, minced
- 2 tablespoons olive oil
- 1 tablespoon lemon juice
- 1/2 teaspoon chili powder
- 1/2 teaspoon cayenne pepper
- 1 tablespoon minced fresh cilantro
- 1/2 cup semi-soft goat cheese
- 8 whole wheat tortillas (8 inches)

Place the first six ingredients in an ungreased 15-in. x 10-in. x 1-in. baking pan. Combine the oil, lemon juice, chili powder and cayenne; drizzle over vegetables and toss to coat. Bake, uncovered, at 400° for 35-40 minutes or until tender, stirring once. Stir in cilantro.

Spread 1 tablespoon goat cheese over one side of each tortilla. Place two tortillas, plain side down, on an ungreased baking sheet; spread each with 2/3 cup vegetable mixture. Top each with another tortilla. Repeat. Bake at 400° for 5-10 minutes or until golden brown. Cut each quesadilla into six wedges. Serve warm.

NUTRITION FACTS: 2 wedges equals 126 calories, 6 g fat (2 g saturated fat), 7 mg cholesterol, 190 mg sodium, 18 g carbohydrate, 3 g fiber, 5 g protein. **DIABETIC EXCHANGES:** 1 starch, 1 fat.

Mediterranean Polenta Cups

FAT SALT CARB MEAT-LESS

PREP: 40 Min. + Chilling **COOK:** 5 Min. **YIELD:** 24 Appetizers

Need a special appetizer that stands out in a crowd? Our Test Kitchen used garlic, basil and feta cheese to lend flavor to these scrumptious goodies.

- 4 cups water
- 1/2 teaspoon salt
- 1 cup yellow cornmeal
- 1/2 teaspoon minced fresh thyme *or* 1/4 teaspoon dried thyme
- 1/4 teaspoon pepper
- 4 plum tomatoes, finely chopped
- 1/4 cup crumbled feta cheese
- 2 tablespoons chopped fresh basil
- 1 garlic clove, minced

In a large heavy saucepan, bring water and salt to a boil. Reduce heat to a gentle boil; slowly whisk in cornmeal. Cook and stir with a wooden spoon for 15-20 minutes or until polenta is thickened and pulls away cleanly from the sides of the pan. Remove from the heat; stir in thyme and pepper.

Spoon heaping tablespoonfuls into miniature muffin cups

coated with cooking spray. Using the back of a spoon, make an indentation in the center of each. Cover and chill until set. Meanwhile, in a small bowl, combine the tomatoes, feta cheese, basil and garlic.

Unmold polenta cups and place on an ungreased baking sheet. Top each with 1 heaping tablespoon of tomato mixture. Broil cups 4 in. from the heat for 5-7 minutes or until cups are heated through.

NUTRITION FACTS: 1 appetizer equals 26 calories, trace fat (trace saturated fat), 1 mg cholesterol, 62 mg sodium, 5 g carbohydrate, 1 g fiber, 1 g protein. **DIABETIC EXCHANGE:** 1/2 starch.

Peanut Butter Crunch Cookies

FAT SALT CARB

PREP: 15 Min. **BAKE:** 10 Min./Batch **YIELD:** 2-1/2 Dozen

The next time you're craving peanut butter cookies, try this low-fat variation with oats and Grape-Nuts cereal.
—Jack Horst, Westfield, New York

- 1/4 cup butter, softened
- 1/4 cup creamy peanut butter
- 1/4 cup sugar
- 1/4 cup packed brown sugar
- 1 egg
- 1/4 teaspoon vanilla extract
- 1/2 cup all-purpose flour
- 1/4 cup quick-cooking oats
- 1/4 teaspoon baking soda
- 1/8 teaspoon salt
- 1/4 cup Grape-Nuts

In a small mixing bowl, cream the butter, peanut butter and sugars. Beat in egg and vanilla. Combine the flour, oats, baking soda and salt; gradually add to creamed mixture and mix well. Stir in Grape-Nuts.

Drop by rounded teaspoonfuls 3 in. apart onto ungreased baking sheets. Flatten slightly with a fork dipped in flour. Bake at 350° for 9-12 minutes or until lightly browned. Cool for 5 minutes before removing from pans to wire racks.

NUTRITION FACTS: 1 cookie equals 56 calories, 3 g fat (1 g saturated fat), 11 mg cholesterol, 54 mg sodium, 7 g carbohydrate, trace fiber, 1 g protein. **DIABETIC EXCHANGES:** 1/2 starch, 1/2 fat.

Simmer Up A Souper Bowl!

Steaming bowls brimming with pasta…thick, comforting chowders…beefy, five-alarm chili…you can enjoy all of these spirit-warming classics without straying from your healthy-eating commitments. Just turn the page for a hearty array of homemade specialties guaranteed to satisfy.

Meatball Soup, p. 36

Black Bean Chipotle Soup

MEAT-LESS

PREP: 15 Min.   **COOK:** 30 Min.   **YIELD:** 8 Servings (2 Quarts, 1 Cup Sauce)

I am a vegetarian, but the rest of my family isn't. Surprisingly, they prefer this soup to a traditional meaty chili because it's so packed with flavor.   —Janice Schneider, Parkville, Missouri

   1 large onion, chopped
   3 garlic cloves, minced
   1 teaspoon canola oil
   2 cans (15 ounces *each*) black beans, rinsed and drained
   2 cans (14-1/2 ounces *each*) vegetable broth
   1 can (28 ounces) crushed tomatoes
   1 tablespoon chopped chipotle pepper in adobo sauce
   2 bay leaves
   1 tablespoon minced fresh cilantro
   2 teaspoons ground cumin
   1 teaspoon ground coriander
 1/8 teaspoon salt
 1/8 teaspoon pepper

SAUCE:
   1 cup (8 ounces) reduced-fat sour cream
   2 green onion tops, chopped
   1 garlic clove, peeled
 1/8 teaspoon salt
 1/8 teaspoon adobo sauce
   1 tablespoon minced fresh cilantro

In a large saucepan coated with cooking spray, saute onion and garlic in oil until tender. Add the beans, broth, tomatoes, chipotle pepper, bay leaves and seasonings. Bring to a boil. Reduce heat; cover and simmer for 20 minutes.

Meanwhile, in a blender, combine the sour cream, green onion tops, garlic, salt and adobo sauce; cover and process until blended.

Discard bay leaves from soup. Top each serving with sauce and sprinkle with cilantro.

NUTRITION FACTS: 1 cup soup with 2 tablespoons sauce equals 185 calories, 4 g fat (2 g saturated fat), 10 mg cholesterol, 883 mg sodium, 29 g carbohydrate, 7 g fiber, 10 g protein. **DIABETIC EXCHANGES:** 2 vegetable, 1 starch, 1 very lean meat, 1/2 fat.

Editor's Note: When cutting or seeding hot peppers, use rubber or plastic gloves to protect your hands. Avoid touching your face.

Ham 'n' Chickpea Soup

(PICTURED ABOVE)

PREP: 15 Min.   **COOK:** 25 Min.   **YIELD:** 4 Servings

Chock-full of ham, vegetables, chickpeas and orzo, this hearty soup is loaded with good-for-you flair.
   —Linda Arnold, Edmonton, Alberta

 1/2 cup uncooked orzo pasta
   1 small onion, chopped
   2 garlic cloves, minced
   2 teaspoons canola oil
   1 cup cubed fully cooked lean ham
   1 teaspoon dried rosemary, crushed
   1 teaspoon rubbed sage
   2 cups reduced-sodium beef broth
   1 can (14-1/2 ounces) diced tomatoes, undrained
   1 can (15 ounces) chickpeas *or* garbanzo beans, rinsed and drained
   4 tablespoons shredded Parmesan cheese
   1 tablespoon minced fresh parsley

Cook orzo according to package directions. Meanwhile, in a large saucepan, saute onion and garlic in oil for 3 minutes. Add the ham, rosemary and sage; saute 1 minute longer. Stir in broth and tomatoes. Bring to a boil. Reduce heat; simmer, uncovered, for 10 minutes.

Drain orzo; stir into soup. Add chickpeas; heat through. Sprinkle each serving with Parmesan cheese and parsley.

NUTRITION FACTS: 1-1/2 cups equals 312 calories, 8 g fat (2 g saturated fat), 19 mg cholesterol, 1,015 mg sodium, 43 g carbohydrate, 7 g fiber, 18 g protein. **DIABETIC EXCHANGES:** 2-1/2 starch, 2 very lean meat, 1 vegetable, 1/2 fat.

Vegetable Barley Soup

FAT MEAT-LESS

PREP: 25 Min.   **COOK:** 8-1/4 Hours
YIELD: 12 Servings (About 3-1/2 Quarts)

Brimming with veggies and barley, this old-fashioned soup has only 128 calories and 1 gram of fat! Best of all, it simmers in the slow cooker on its own!   —Mary Tallman, Arbor Vitae, Wisconsin

   1 large sweet potato, peeled and cubed
 1-1/2 cups fresh baby carrots, halved
 1-1/2 cups frozen cut green beans
 1-1/2 cups frozen corn
   3 celery ribs, thinly sliced
   1 small onion, chopped
 1/2 cup chopped green pepper
   2 garlic cloves, minced

6 cups water
2 cans (14-1/2 ounces *each*) vegetable broth
1 cup medium pearl barley
1 bay leaf
1-3/4 teaspoons salt
1/2 teaspoon fennel seed, crushed
1/4 teaspoon pepper
1 can (14-1/2 ounces) Italian diced tomatoes, undrained

In a 5-qt. slow cooker, combine the first eight ingredients. Stir in the water, broth, barley, bay leaf and seasonings. Cover and cook on low for 8-9 hours or until barley and vegetables are tender.

Stir in tomatoes; cover and cook on high for 10-20 minutes or until heated through. Discard bay leaf before serving.

NUTRITION FACTS: 1-1/4 cups equals 128 calories, 1 g fat (trace saturated fat), 0 cholesterol, 812 mg sodium, 28 g carbohydrate, 5 g fiber, 4 g protein. **DIABETIC EXCHANGES:** 1-1/2 starch, 1 vegetable.

Hearty Lentil Soup

FAT MEAT-LESS

PREP: 20 Min.   **COOK:** 1-1/2 Hours   **YIELD:** 6 Servings

Chock-full of veggies, this delicious lentil soup is really simple to fix. I like to double the recipe and freeze half of it for busy nights.
—Joy Maynard, St. Ignatius, Montana

3 cups water
3 cups vegetable broth
3 medium carrots, sliced
1 medium onion, chopped
1 cup dried lentils, rinsed
2 celery ribs, sliced
1 small green pepper, chopped
1/4 cup uncooked brown rice
1 teaspoon dried basil
1 garlic clove, minced
1 bay leaf
3/4 cup tomato paste
1/2 cup frozen corn
1/2 cup frozen peas

In a large saucepan, combine the first 11 ingredients. Bring to a boil. Reduce heat; cover and simmer for 1 to 1-1/2 hours or until lentils and rice are tender.

Add the tomato paste, corn and peas; stir until blended. Cook, uncovered, 15-20 minutes or until corn and peas are tender. Discard bay leaf before serving.

NUTRITION FACTS: 1-1/3 cups equals 228 calories, 1 g fat (trace saturated fat), 0 cholesterol, 566 mg sodium, 44 g carbohydrate, 15 g fiber, 14 g protein. **DIABETIC EXCHANGES:** 2 starch, 2 vegetable, 1 very lean meat.

HEALTHY HINT
Hearty Lentil Soup packs 15 g of fiber in every serving. Nearly 10 of the 15 grams come from the cup of lentil beans that the recipe calls for. Lentils are available in several colors, but the most commonly found in supermarkets is the brown variety. Green and red lentils can be found in specialty stores.

Carrot Broccoli Soup

MEAT-LESS

(PICTURED BELOW)

PREP: 15 Min.   **COOK:** 20 Min.   **YIELD:** 4 Servings

This soup is a staple at my house because it is fast, nutritious and so yummy!
—Sandy Smith, London, Ontario

1 medium onion, chopped
2 medium carrots, chopped
2 celery ribs, chopped
1 tablespoon butter
3 cups fresh broccoli florets
3 cups fat-free milk, *divided*
3/4 teaspoon salt
1/2 teaspoon dried thyme
1/8 teaspoon pepper
3 tablespoons all-purpose flour

In a saucepan coated with cooking spray, cook the onion, carrots and celery in butter for 3 minutes. Add broccoli; cook 3 minutes longer. Stir in 2-3/4 cups milk, salt, thyme and pepper.

Bring to a boil. Reduce heat; cover and simmer for 5-10 minutes or until vegetables are tender. Combine the flour and remaining milk until smooth; gradually stir into soup. Bring to a boil; cook 2 minutes longer or until thickened.

NUTRITION FACTS: 1-1/4 cups equals 168 calories, 4 g fat (3 g saturated fat), 14 mg cholesterol, 633 mg sodium, 24 g carbohydrate, 4 g fiber, 10 g protein. **DIABETIC EXCHANGES:** 2 vegetable, 1 fat-free milk, 1/2 fat.

Favorite Recipe Made Lighter

CREAMY SPECIALTIES can be so gratifying, and Doris Davis's Cauliflower Soup is no exception. The Hellertown, Pennsylvania cook writes, "I think that creamy soups satisfy hunger as well as they warm the soul. That's why I was so happy to receive this recipe from a friend. Even though my husband doesn't care for cauliflower, he loves this soup."

What's not to love? Each steaming bowl is full of flavorful vegetables and seasonings…as well as butter, milk and half-and-half cream. In fact, the soup is so fantastic, that when Doris asked *L&T* to lighten it up with a makeover, our home economists gladly obliged.

The first thing they wanted to do was cut back on butter, but the original recipe called for a roux to be made from butter and flour to thicken the soup. They decided to thicken the soup by making a slurry…milk whisked with flour.

To keep the original's flavor, they added a small amount of butter to saute the vegetables. Using fat-free half-and-half and low-fat milk lightened the soup even further.

With these simple changes, Makeover Cauliflower Soup boasts huge savings. It has 75% less fat and saturated fat and 89 fewer calories per serving. Most importantly though, it's just as comforting as the original recipe Doris shared.

Cauliflower Soup

PREP: 30 Min. **COOK:** 30 Min. **YIELD:** 11 Servings (2-3/4 Quarts)

- 6 cups chicken broth
- 2 celery ribs, chopped
- 1 small onion, chopped
- 1 medium carrot, chopped
- 1 large head cauliflower (2 pounds), broken into florets
- 1/2 cup butter
- 3/4 cup all-purpose flour
- 2 cups milk
- 1 cup half-and-half cream
- 1 tablespoon minced fresh parsley
- 1 teaspoon salt
- 1 teaspoon dill weed
- 1/4 teaspoon white pepper

In a Dutch oven, combine the broth, celery, onion and carrot. Bring to a boil. Reduce heat; cover and simmer for 5 minutes. Add cauliflower; cover and simmer 15-20 minutes longer or until vegetables are tender. Cool slightly.

Meanwhile, in a saucepan, melt butter. Stir in flour until smooth; gradually stir in milk. Bring to a boil; cook and stir for 1-2 minutes or until thickened.

In a blender or food processor, process vegetable mixture in batches until smooth; return to pan. Stir in the cream, parsley, salt, dill, pepper and white sauce; heat through.

NUTRITION FACTS: 1 cup equals 195 calories, 12 g fat (8 g saturated fat), 39 mg cholesterol, 874 mg sodium, 16 g carbohydrate, 3 g fiber, 6 g protein.

Makeover Cauliflower Soup

(PICTURED ABOVE)

FAT CARB

PREP: 30 Min. **COOK:** 30 Min. **YIELD:** 11 Servings (2-3/4 Quarts)

- 2 celery ribs, chopped
- 1 small onion, chopped
- 1 medium carrot, chopped
- 2 tablespoons butter
- 1 large head cauliflower (2 pounds), broken into florets
- 6 cups reduced-sodium chicken broth
- 1/2 cup all-purpose flour
- 2 cups 2% milk
- 3/4 cup fat-free half-and-half
- 1 tablespoon minced fresh parsley
- 1 teaspoon salt
- 1 teaspoon dill weed
- 1/4 teaspoon white pepper

In a Dutch oven, saute the celery, onion and carrot in butter for 3-5 minutes or until crisp-tender. Stir in cauliflower and broth; bring to a boil. Reduce heat; cover and simmer for 15-20 minutes or until tender. Cool slightly.

In a blender or food processor, process vegetable mixture in batches until smooth. Return to the pan. Heat over medium heat. In a small bowl, whisk flour and milk until smooth; stir into puree. Bring to a boil; cook and stir for 2 minutes or until thickened. Reduce heat; stir in the half-and-half, parsley, salt, dill and pepper. Heat through.

NUTRITION FACTS: 1 cup equals 106 calories, 3 g fat (2 g saturated fat), 9 mg cholesterol, 641 mg sodium, 14 g carbohydrate, 3 g fiber, 6 g protein. **DIABETIC EXCHANGES:** 1 vegetable, 1/2 starch, 1/2 fat.

Cassoulet for the Gang

PREP: 25 Min.   **COOK:** 40 Min.   **YIELD:** 10 Servings (4 Quarts)

Wine lends a warm touch to this satisfying take on a traditional French stew. Mashed beans thicken the broth and boost nutrition without adding fat. —Lynn Stein, Joseph, Oregon

    1 pork tenderloin (1 pound), cut into 1/2-inch pieces
    1 pound smoked turkey kielbasa, cut into 1/2-inch pieces
    1 tablespoon olive oil
    3 medium carrots, chopped
    1 large onion, cut into wedges
    4 garlic cloves, minced
    2 cans (14-1/2 ounces *each*) no-salt-added stewed tomatoes, cut up
    1 can (14-1/2 ounces) reduced-sodium chicken broth
    3 teaspoons herbes de Provence
1-1/2 teaspoons garlic powder
1-1/2 teaspoons dried basil
    1/2 teaspoon dried oregano
    1/4 teaspoon pepper
    4 cans (15-1/2 ounces *each*) great northern beans, rinsed and drained, *divided*
    3/4 cup white wine *or* additional chicken broth, *divided*

In a Dutch oven coated with cooking spray, saute pork and kielbasa in oil until lightly browned; drain. Add the carrots, onion and garlic; saute 4 minutes longer. Stir in the tomatoes, broth and seasonings. Bring to a boil. Reduce heat; cover and simmer for 10 minutes.

Place one can of beans in a food processor; add 1/4 cup wine or broth. Cover and process until pureed. Stir into meat mixture. Stir in the remaining beans and wine or broth. Bring to a boil. Reduce heat; simmer, uncovered, for 8-10 minutes or until meat and vegetables are tender.

NUTRITION FACTS: 1-1/2 cups equals 316 calories, 5 g fat (1 g saturated fat), 41 mg cholesterol, 959 mg sodium, 40 g carbohydrate, 11 g fiber, 25 g protein.

Editor's Note: Look for herbes de Provence in the spice aisle of your grocery store.

Pumpkin Corn Soup

MEAT-LESS

PREP: 20 Min.   **COOK:** 25 Min.   **YIELD:** 7 Servings

My family loves this recipe. Featuring lots of spices, it's great on chilly nights. Try garnishing it with fresh cilantro. —Melissa Every, Austin, Texas

    1 large onion, chopped
    1 medium sweet red pepper, chopped
    2 tablespoons butter
    2 cups fresh *or* frozen corn, thawed
    1 jalapeno pepper, seeded and chopped
    2 garlic cloves, minced
    2 teaspoons chili powder
    2 cans (14-1/2 ounces *each*) vegetable broth
    1 can (15 ounces) solid-pack pumpkin
    1/2 teaspoon salt
Dash cayenne pepper
    2 tablespoons lime juice

In a large saucepan, saute onion and red pepper in butter until almost tender. Add the corn, jalapeno, garlic and chili powder; saute 2 minutes longer.

Stir in the broth, pumpkin, salt and cayenne until blended. Bring to a boil. Reduce heat; cover and simmer for 10 minutes. Stir in lime juice.

NUTRITION FACTS: 1 cup equals 120 calories, 5 g fat (2 g saturated fat), 9 mg cholesterol, 714 mg sodium, 20 g carbohydrate, 5 g fiber, 4 g protein. **DIABETIC EXCHANGES:** 1 starch, 1/2 fat.

Editor's Note: When cutting or seeding hot peppers, use rubber or plastic gloves to protect your hands. Avoid touching your face.

Cuban Black Bean Soup

FAT   MEAT-LESS

PREP: 15 Min.   **COOK:** 35 Min.   **YIELD:** 9 Servings (2-1/4 Quarts)

I use my blender for this smooth, nutritious heart-warmer. It's just right for cool winter nights. If the soup is too thick, add more vegetable broth to thin it out a bit. —Tracy Lohr, Urbandale, Iowa

    4 celery ribs, sliced
    1 large onion, chopped
    8 garlic cloves, minced
    1 jalapeno pepper, seeded and chopped
    4 teaspoons canola oil
    4 cans (15 ounces *each*) black beans, rinsed and drained
    2 cans (14-1/2 ounces *each*) vegetable broth
    3/4 cup water
    2 teaspoons dried oregano
    2 teaspoons ground cumin
    1 to 2 teaspoons chili powder
    1 to 2 teaspoons pepper
    1/2 teaspoon ground coriander
    1/4 to 1/2 teaspoon crushed red pepper flakes
    1/8 to 1/4 teaspoon hot pepper sauce
GARNISH:
    9 tablespoons chopped tomatoes
    9 teaspoons fat-free sour cream
    9 teaspoons minced fresh cilantro

In a Dutch oven coated with cooking spray, saute the celery, onion, garlic and jalapeno in oil until onion is tender. Stir in the beans, broth, water, seasonings and hot pepper sauce. Bring to a boil. Reduce heat; simmer, uncovered, for 20 minutes. Cool slightly.

In a blender, process soup in batches until smooth. Return to the pan; heat through. Garnish each serving with tomatoes, sour cream and cilantro.

NUTRITION FACTS: 1 cup equals 202 calories, 3 g fat (trace saturated fat), 1 mg cholesterol, 786 mg sodium, 33 g carbohydrate, 9 g fiber, 11 g protein. **DIABETIC EXCHANGES:** 2 starch, 1 very lean meat, 1/2 fat.

Editor's Note: When cutting or seeding hot peppers, use rubber or plastic gloves to protect your hands. Avoid touching your face.

TASTY TIP
With the exception of soups made with cream or potatoes, most soups freeze rather nicely. To retain flavor, don't freeze soup for longer than 3 months.

Chicken Noodle Soup with Rutabaga

FAT

PREP: 20 Min.   **COOK:** 50 Min.   **YIELD:** 6 Servings

Our Test Kitchen simmered a winner with this welcoming delight. Packed with wintry root vegetables, it goes together in a flash.

3 medium carrots, chopped
1 medium onion, chopped
1 celery rib, chopped
2 teaspoons butter
4 cups reduced-sodium chicken broth
1 medium rutabaga (about 1-1/2 pounds), peeled and cut into 1/2-inch cubes
1/2 teaspoon salt
1/4 teaspoon dried thyme
1/8 teaspoon dried marjoram
1/8 teaspoon pepper
2 cups uncooked yolk-free noodles
2 cups cubed cooked chicken breast
1/3 cup minced fresh parsley

In a large saucepan or Dutch oven, saute the carrots, onion and celery in butter until tender. Add the broth, rutabaga, salt, thyme, marjoram and pepper; bring to a boil. Reduce heat; cover and simmer for 15 minutes.

Add noodles; cover and simmer 20 minutes longer or until noodles are tender. Stir in the chicken and parsley; heat through.

NUTRITION FACTS: 1 cup equals 211 calories, 3 g fat (1 g saturated fat), 39 mg cholesterol, 702 mg sodium, 26 g carbohydrate, 5 g fiber, 20 g protein. **DIABETIC EXCHANGES:** 2 very lean meat, 1-1/2 starch, 1 vegetable.

Hearty Meatless Chili

FAT MEAT-LESS

PREP: 20 Min.   **COOK:** 55 Min.   **YIELD:** 8 Servings (2-1/2 Quarts)

Years ago I found a recipe for chili con carne. After trying it, I changed the spices, reduced the oil and added vegetables to make it more attractive. Dozens have enjoyed the results and have asked for my secret.   —Lois Beach, College Station, Texas

1 small onion, chopped
3 garlic cloves, minced
1 tablespoon olive oil
2 medium zucchini, finely chopped
2 medium carrots, finely chopped
3 tablespoons cornmeal
2 tablespoons chili powder
2 tablespoons paprika
1 tablespoon sugar
1/2 teaspoon ground cumin
1/4 to 1/2 teaspoon cayenne pepper
2 cans (one 28 ounces, one 14-1/2 ounces) diced tomatoes, undrained
2 cans (15 ounces *each*) pinto beans, rinsed and drained
1 can (16 ounces) kidney beans, rinsed and drained
GARNISH:
8 tablespoons fat-free sour cream
8 tablespoons thinly sliced green onions
8 teaspoons minced fresh cilantro

In a Dutch oven, saute onion and garlic in oil until tender. Stir in zucchini and carrots. Add the cornmeal, chili powder, pa-

prika, sugar, cumin and cayenne; cook and stir for 1 minute.

Stir in tomatoes and beans. Bring to a boil. Reduce heat; cover and simmer for 45 minutes. Garnish each serving with sour cream, green onions and cilantro.

NUTRITION FACTS: 1-1/4 cups equals 254 calories, 3 g fat (trace saturated fat), 3 mg cholesterol, 466 mg sodium, 47 g carbohydrate, 12 g fiber, 13 g protein.

Hearty Tomato Bisque

MEAT-LESS

(PICTURED BELOW)

PREP: 20 Min.   **COOK:** 20 Min.   **YIELD:** 6 Servings

After just one sip of this comforting bisque, you'll never want canned soup again.   —Lisa Renshaw, Kansas City, Missouri

1 medium onion, chopped
1 tablespoon olive oil
2 cans (15 ounces *each*) crushed tomatoes
1 tablespoon honey
1 teaspoon minced fresh rosemary *or* 1/4 teaspoon dried rosemary, crushed
1/2 teaspoon salt
1/4 teaspoon pepper
8 ounces soft tofu, drained and crumbled (1 cup)
1-1/2 cups soy milk
3/4 cup salad croutons

In a large saucepan, saute onion in oil for 4-6 minutes or until tender. Stir in the tomatoes, honey, rosemary, salt and pepper; bring to a boil. Reduce heat; simmer for 10 minutes, stirring occasionally.

Remove from the heat; stir in tofu and soy milk. Cool slightly. In a blender or food processor, process soup in batches until smooth. Return to the pan and heat through. Garnish each serving with croutons.

NUTRITION FACTS: 1 cup bisque with 2 tablespoons croutons equals 156 calories, 6 g fat (1 g saturated fat), 0 cholesterol, 432 mg sodium, 21 g carbohydrate, 4 g fiber, 8 g protein. **DIABETIC EXCHANGES:** 2 vegetable, 1 lean meat, 1/2 starch, 1/2 fat.

Favorite Recipe Made Lighter

WHEN blustery winds blow into Ypsilanti, Michigan, nothing warms Christine Schenher's family like her Mom's Clam Chowder. "It's fantastic—especially on cold, wintry days," Christine writes. "But because it's so high in fat, I feel guilty preparing it. Can you lighten it up?"

Our team tackled the soup's butter content first, slashing it from 3/4 cup to just 1/4 cup...but that proved to be too little to dissolve the flour. This can be a common problem when lightening cream soups or white sauces that depend on a roux (a mixture of flour and fat).

A simple solution was to combine the flour with milk, stirring the mixture into the cooked soup and bringing it to a boil for thickening at the very end.

They cut the amount of the half-and-half, making up the volume with 2% milk instead of whole. Finally, combining both reduced-sodium chicken broth and bouillon granules instead of regular chicken broth cut sodium from each serving by 22 percent. Makeover Mom's Clam Chowder has less than half the fat, saturated fat and cholesterol...but all of the original's wholesome, down-home flavor. And that should warm any Mom's heart!

Makeover Mom's Clam Chowder CARB
(PICTURED ABOVE)

PREP: 30 Min. COOK: 45 Min. YIELD: 12 Servings (3 Quarts)

   3/4 cup *each* chopped onion, celery and carrots
   1/2 cup chopped green pepper
   1/4 cup butter, cubed
     1 carton (32 ounces) reduced-sodium chicken broth
     1 bottle (8 ounces) clam juice
     2 teaspoons reduced-sodium chicken bouillon granules
     1 bay leaf
   1/2 teaspoon dried parsley flakes
   1/2 teaspoon salt
   1/4 teaspoon curry powder
   1/4 teaspoon pepper
     1 medium potato, peeled and cubed
   2/3 cup all-purpose flour
     2 cups 2% milk, *divided*
     4 cans (6-1/2 ounces *each*) minced clams, undrained
     1 cup half-and-half cream

In a Dutch oven over medium heat, cook the onion, celery, carrots and green pepper in butter until tender. Stir in the broth, clam juice, bouillon and seasonings. Add potato. Bring to a boil. Reduce heat; simmer, uncovered, for 15-20 minutes or until potato is tender.

In a small bowl, combine flour and 1 cup milk until smooth. Gradually stir into soup. Bring to a boil; cook and stir for 1-2 minutes or until thickened.

Stir in the clams, cream and remaining milk; heat through (do not boil). Discard bay leaf before serving.

NUTRITION FACTS: 1 cup equals 155 calories, 7 g fat (4 g saturated fat), 34 mg cholesterol, 726 mg sodium, 15 g carbohydrate, 1 g fiber, 8 g protein. **DIABETIC EXCHANGES:** 1 starch, 1 very lean meat, 1 fat.

Mom's Clam Chowder

PREP: 30 Min. COOK: 45 Min. YIELD: 11 Servings (2-3/4 Quarts)

   1/2 cup *each* chopped onion, celery and carrot
   1/4 cup chopped green pepper
   3/4 cup butter, *divided*
   3/4 cup all-purpose flour
     1 carton (32 ounces) chicken broth
     1 bottle (8 ounces) clam juice
     1 medium potato, peeled and cubed
     1 bay leaf
   1/2 teaspoon salt
   1/2 teaspoon dried parsley flakes
   1/4 teaspoon curry powder
   1/4 teaspoon pepper
     2 cups half-and-half cream
     4 cans (6-1/2 ounces *each*) minced clams, undrained
     1 cup milk

In a Dutch oven over medium heat, cook the onion, celery, carrot and green pepper in 1/4 cup butter until tender. Add the remaining butter; cook until melted. Sprinkle with flour; stir until blended.

Gradually stir in the broth, clam juice, potato and seasonings. Bring to a boil; cook and stir for 2 minutes or until thickened. Reduce heat; simmer, uncovered, for 15-20 minutes or until potato is tender, stirring frequently.

Add the cream, clams and milk; heat through (do not boil). Discard bay leaf before serving.

NUTRITION FACTS: 1 cup equals 266 calories, 18 g fat (11 g saturated fat), 70 mg cholesterol, 927 mg sodium, 16 g carbohydrate, 1 g fiber, 9 g protein.

In a large bowl, combine the turkey, 1-1/2 teaspoons Italian seasoning, paprika, 1/8 teaspoon salt and 1/8 teaspoon pepper. Shape into 36 meatballs.

In a large nonstick skillet coated with cooking spray, brown meatballs in batches in 2 teaspoons oil until no longer pink. Remove and keep warm.

In a large saucepan coated with cooking spray, saute the celery, carrots and onion in remaining oil until tender. Stir in the white kidney beans, tomatoes, broth, cabbage, green beans and remaining Italian seasoning, salt and pepper.

Bring to a boil. Reduce heat; stir in meatballs. Simmer, uncovered, for 15-20 minutes or until green beans are tender. Sprinkle with cheese.

NUTRITION FACTS: 1 cup equals 254 calories, 10 g fat (2 g saturated fat), 62 mg cholesterol, 748 mg sodium, 21 g carbohydrate, 5 g fiber, 19 g protein. **DIABETIC EXCHANGES:** 2 lean meat, 1 starch, 1 vegetable, 1 fat.

Mexican Bean 'n' Barley Chili
FAT MEAT-LESS

(PICTURED ABOVE LEFT)

PREP: 25 Min.   **COOK:** 25 Min.   **YIELD:** 10 Servings (About 3-1/2 Quarts)

Chili powder adds just the right amount of "heat" to this filling, fast and fabulous vegetarian meal. It's an easy, cold-weather recipe the whole family will surely warm up to!
— Lana Day, Bloomington, Indiana

  1 large onion, chopped
  1 garlic clove, minced
  1 tablespoon olive oil
  1 *each* medium green and sweet red pepper, chopped
  2 cups frozen corn, thawed
3/4 cup quick-cooking barley
  2 cups water
  1 can (16 ounces) chili beans in chili sauce, undrained
  1 can (15 ounces) pinto beans, rinsed and drained
  1 can (15 ounces) black beans, rinsed and drained
  1 can (15 ounces) tomato sauce
  1 can (14-1/2 ounces) diced tomatoes, undrained
  1 can (14-1/2 ounces) vegetable broth
  2 cans (4 ounces *each*) chopped green chilies
  2 tablespoons chili powder
1/2 teaspoon pepper

In a Dutch oven coated with cooking spray, saute onion and garlic in oil for 2 minutes. Stir in peppers; cook 3-4 minutes longer or until tender.

Stir in the remaining ingredients; bring to a boil. Reduce heat; cover and simmer for 15-20 minutes or until barley is tender.

NUTRITION FACTS: 1-1/2 cups equals 247 calories, 3 g fat (1 g saturated fat), 0 cholesterol, 836 mg sodium, 46 g carbohydrate, 11 g fiber, 11 g protein. **DIABETIC EXCHANGES:** 2 starch, 2 vegetable, 1 very lean meat, 1/2 fat.

Meatball Soup

(PICTURED ABOVE)

PREP: 30 Min.   **COOK:** 40 Min.   **YIELD:** 6 Servings

My husband and I are both diabetics and like to find tasty recipes such as this one that are in line with our dietary requirements.
— Rebecca Phipps, Rural Hall, North Carolina

    1 pound lean ground turkey
2-1/2 teaspoons Italian seasoning, *divided*
  1/4 teaspoon paprika
  1/4 teaspoon salt, *divided*
  1/4 teaspoon coarsely ground pepper, *divided*
    4 teaspoons olive oil, *divided*
    2 celery ribs, chopped
   15 fresh baby carrots, chopped
    1 small onion, chopped
    1 can (15 ounces) white kidney *or* cannellini beans, rinsed and drained
    1 can (14-1/2 ounces) Italian diced tomatoes, undrained
    1 can (14-1/2 ounces) reduced-sodium chicken broth
  3/4 cup chopped cabbage
  3/4 cup cut fresh green beans
    3 tablespoons shredded part-skim mozzarella cheese

Pea Soup with Quinoa

PREP: 10 Min.   **COOK:** 25 Min.   **YIELD:** 4 Servings

This soup is low in fat, high in fiber, has a fantastically fresh flavor and a wonderful texture. Plus, it's so simple to make!
—Jane Hacker, Milwaukee, Wisconsin

  1 cup water
1/2 cup quinoa, rinsed
  1 medium onion, chopped
  2 teaspoons canola oil
  2 cans (14-1/2 ounces *each*) reduced-sodium chicken broth *or* vegetable broth
  2 packages (10 ounces *each*) frozen peas
1/2 teaspoon salt
1/4 teaspoon pepper
  2 teaspoons reduced-fat plain yogurt

In a small saucepan, bring water and quinoa to a boil. Reduce heat; cover and simmer for 13-15 minutes or until water is absorbed. Meanwhile, in a large saucepan, saute onion in oil until tender. Stir in broth and peas. Bring to a boil. Reduce heat; simmer, uncovered, for 5 minutes or until peas are tender. Cool slightly.

In a blender or food processor, process soup in batches until smooth. Return all to the pan. Stir in the salt, pepper and quinoa; heat through. Garnish each serving with 1/2 teaspoon yogurt.

NUTRITION FACTS: 1-1/2 cups equals 236 calories, 4 g fat (trace saturated fat), trace cholesterol, 858 mg sodium, 38 g carbohydrate, 9 g fiber, 13 g protein. **DIABETIC EXCHANGES:** 2-1/2 starch, 1/2 fat.

Apple Butternut Soup

PREP: 25 Min.   **COOK:** 50 Min.   **YIELD:** 6 Servings

Brighten blustery, gray days with steaming bowlfuls of this colorful soup. It's a rich, velvety creation that's slightly sweet and low in fat.
—Jane Shapton, Tustin, California

  1 small onion, chopped
  1 garlic clove, minced
  1 tablespoon butter
  6 cups cubed peeled butternut squash
  1 can (14-1/2 ounces) reduced-sodium chicken broth *or* vegetable broth
  1 large apple, peeled and chopped
1/2 cup water
1-1/2 teaspoons minced fresh thyme *or* 1/2 teaspoon dried thyme
  1 teaspoon salt
1/2 cup half-and-half cream

In a large saucepan coated with cooking spray, cook and stir the onion and garlic in butter over medium heat until tender. Add the squash, broth, apple, water, thyme and salt. Bring to a boil. Reduce heat; cover and simmer for 20-25 minutes or until squash is tender. Cool slightly.

In a blender, process soup in batches until smooth. Return all to the pan; stir in cream and heat through (do not boil).

NUTRITION FACTS: 1 cup equals 172 calories, 4 g fat (3 g saturated fat), 15 mg cholesterol, 613 mg sodium, 33 g carbohydrate, 9 g fiber, 4 g protein. **DIABETIC EXCHANGES:** 2 starch, 1 fat.

Sausage Lentil Soup

(PICTURED BELOW)

PREP: 25 Min.   **COOK:** 40 Min.   **YIELD:** 6 Servings

I found a recipe in a men's magazine and lightened it up to suit our needs. It's so tasty and loaded with fiber, vitamins and iron.
—Suzanne Dabkowski, Blythewood, South Carolina

  1 medium onion, chopped
  1 celery rib, chopped
1/4 pound reduced-fat smoked sausage, halved and thinly sliced
  1 medium carrot, halved and thinly sliced
  2 garlic cloves, minced
  2 cans (14-1/2 ounces *each*) reduced-sodium chicken broth
1/3 cup water
  1 cup dried lentils, rinsed
1/2 teaspoon dried oregano
1/4 teaspoon ground cumin
1/4 teaspoon pepper
  1 can (14-1/2 ounces) stewed tomatoes, cut up
  1 tablespoon Worcestershire sauce
  1 cup chopped fresh spinach

In a large saucepan coated with cooking spray, cook and stir onion and celery over medium-high heat for 2 minutes. Add the sausage, carrot and garlic; cook 2-3 minutes longer or until onion is tender.

Stir in the broth, water, lentils, oregano, cumin and pepper. Bring to a boil. Reduce heat; cover and simmer for 25-30 minutes or until lentils and vegetables are tender.

Stir in the tomatoes, Worcestershire sauce and spinach; cook until heated through and spinach is wilted.

NUTRITION FACTS: 1 cup equals 180 calories, 1 g fat (trace saturated fat), 7 mg cholesterol, 639 mg sodium, 31 g carbohydrate, 12 g fiber, 14 g protein. **DIABETIC EXCHANGES:** 2 very lean meat, 1 starch, 1 vegetable.

Hearty Sausage-Chicken Chili

PREP: 20 Min. **COOK:** 4 Hours **YIELD:** 11 Servings (2-3/4 Quarts)

We have an annual chili cook-off at work, and this recipe of mine was a winner once. Using boneless chicken thighs made it different from the other varieties. After one bite, it's sure to become a winner in your home, too. —Carolyn Etzler, Thurmont, Maryland

 1 pound Italian turkey sausage links, casings removed
 3/4 pound boneless skinless chicken thighs, cut into 3/4-inch pieces
 1 medium onion, chopped
 2 cans (14-1/2 ounces *each*) diced tomatoes with mild green chilies, undrained
 2 cans (8 ounces *each*) tomato sauce
 1 can (16 ounces) kidney beans, rinsed and drained
 1 can (15 ounces) white kidney *or* cannellini beans, rinsed and drained
 1 can (15 ounces) pinto beans, rinsed and drained
 1 can (15 ounces) black beans, rinsed and drained
 1 teaspoon chili powder
 1/2 teaspoon garlic powder
 1/8 teaspoon pepper

Crumble sausage into a large nonstick skillet coated with cooking spray. Add chicken and onion; cook and stir over medium heat until meat is no longer pink. Drain.

Transfer to a 5-qt. slow cooker. Stir in the remaining ingredients. Cover and cook on low for 4 hours.

NUTRITION FACTS: 1 cup equals 272 calories, 6 g fat (1 g saturated fat), 45 mg cholesterol, 826 mg sodium, 32 g carbohydrate, 8 g fiber, 21 g protein.

Vegetarian Split Pea Soup

FAT MEAT-LESS

PREP: 15 Min. **COOK:** 7 Hours **YIELD:** 8 Servings (2 Quarts)

I adapted this slow-cooker recipe from several I found online. When I was a vegetarian for health reasons, it was a favorite at our house. Even my meat-loving husband asked for seconds! In fact, I still rely on the savory dish regularly. —Corrie Gamache, Palmyra, Virginia

 1 package (16 ounces) dried green split peas, rinsed
 1 medium leek (white portion only), chopped
 3 celery ribs, chopped
 1 medium potato, peeled and chopped
 2 medium carrots, chopped
 1 garlic clove, minced
 1/4 cup minced fresh parsley
 4 cans (14-1/2 ounces *each*) vegetable broth
 1-1/2 teaspoons ground mustard
 1/2 teaspoon pepper
 1/2 teaspoon dried oregano
 1 bay leaf

In a 5-qt. slow cooker, combine all ingredients. Cover and cook on low for 7-8 hours or until peas are tender. Discard bay leaf before serving.

NUTRITION FACTS: 1 cup equals 244 calories, 2 g fat (trace saturated fat), 0 cholesterol, 906 mg sodium, 44 g carbohydrate, 16 g fiber, 17 g protein.

Spill-the-Beans Minestrone

MEAT-LESS

(PICTURED ABOVE)

PREP: 20 Min. **COOK:** 20 Min. **YIELD:** 6 Servings

A meal in itself, here's a hearty soup that's chock-full of good-for-you veggies and vitamins. Serve it with crunchy breadsticks. —Reuben Tsujimura, Walla Walla, Washington

 1 medium onion, chopped
 2 garlic cloves, minced
 1 tablespoon olive oil
 2 cans (14-1/2 ounces *each*) reduced-sodium chicken broth *or* vegetable broth
 1 can (16 ounces) kidney beans, rinsed and drained
 1 can (15 ounces) garbanzo beans *or* chickpeas, rinsed and drained
 1 can (14-1/2 ounces) stewed tomatoes, cut up
 2 cups chopped fresh kale
 1/2 cup water
 1/2 cup uncooked small pasta shells
 1 teaspoon Italian seasoning
 1/4 teaspoon crushed red pepper flakes
 6 teaspoons shredded Parmesan cheese

In a large saucepan, saute onion and garlic in oil until onion is tender. Add the broth, beans, tomatoes, kale, water, pasta, Italian seasoning and pepper flakes. Bring to a boil. Reduce heat; cover and simmer for 10-15 minutes or until pasta is tender. Sprinkle each serving with Parmesan cheese.

NUTRITION FACTS: 1 cup equals 238 calories, 4 g fat (1 g saturated fat), 1 mg cholesterol, 738 mg sodium, 39 g carbohydrate, 8 g fiber, 13 g protein.

HEALTHY HINT
Adding drained, canned beans to soups, stews and other recipes is an easy and delicious way to pump up the fiber and protein in a family-friendly dish.

Step Up to the Salad Bar

When it comes to eating right, one staple constantly rises to the top of heart-smart menus…leafy green salads. But today's health-conscious cooks no longer limit themselves to boring greens. See how they're dressing up salad plates with fruits, cheeses, tangy dressings and more!

Colorful Tomato 'n' Mozzarella Salad, p. 43

Party Tortellini Salad

MEAT-LESS

(PICTURED ABOVE)

PREP/TOTAL TIME: 25 Min.   **YIELD:** 10 Servings

This easy salad with its crowd-pleasing flavors makes a wonderful addition to summer cookouts. It's a winner with folks of all ages.
—Mary Wilt, Ipswich, Massachusetts

- 1 package (19 ounces) frozen cheese tortellini
- 2 cups fresh broccoli florets
- 1 medium sweet red pepper, chopped
- 1/2 cup pimiento-stuffed olives, halved
- 3/4 cup reduced-fat red wine vinaigrette
- 1/2 teaspoon salt

Cook tortellini according to package directions; drain and rinse in cold water.

In a large bowl, combine the tortellini, broccoli, red pepper and olives. Drizzle with dressing and sprinkle with salt; toss to coat. Cover and refrigerate until serving.

NUTRITION FACTS: 3/4 cup equals 156 calories, 7 g fat (2 g saturated fat), 8 mg cholesterol, 596 mg sodium, 19 g carbohydrate, 1 g fiber, 6 g protein. **DIABETIC EXCHANGES:** 1 starch, 1 lean meat, 1/2 fat.

Tangy Cucumber Salad

FAT CARB MEAT-LESS

PREP: 20 Min. + Chilling   **YIELD:** 6 Servings

A splash of lemon juice lends a delightfully tart bite to my zippy, quick-to-fix salad. Cider vinegar adds a tasty, change-of-pace flair to this creamy cucumber dish that everyone seems to love. Best of all, it's so low in calories, you hardly need to count them!
—Sharon Seving, Sidney, Ohio

- 1 cup (8 ounces) fat-free sour cream
- 2 tablespoons cider vinegar
- 2 tablespoons lemon juice
- 3/4 teaspoon salt
- 1/8 teaspoon white pepper
- 3 large cucumbers, peeled and thinly sliced
- 1/2 cup thinly sliced sweet onion

In a large bowl, combine the sour cream, vinegar, lemon juice, salt and pepper. Add cucumbers and onion; toss to coat. Cover and refrigerate for at least 1 hour. Serve with a slotted spoon.

NUTRITION FACTS: 3/4 cup equals 68 calories, trace fat (trace saturated fat), 6 mg cholesterol, 328 mg sodium, 13 g carbohydrate, 1 g fiber, 4 g protein. **DIABETIC EXCHANGES:** 1 vegetable, 1/2 starch.

Fluffy Pineapple-Pear Salad

FAT ↓ SALT ↓ MEAT-LESS

PREP: 25 Min. + Chilling   **YIELD:** 8 Servings

I treat sweet pear and pineapple to a creamy topping that offers a hint of tang. It's a unique salad that's simply perfect for family meals or company dinners alike.

—Bernice Morris, Marshfield, Missouri

- 1 can (20 ounces) unsweetened pineapple tidbits
- 1 can (15 ounces) reduced-sugar pear halves, drained and cubed
- 2 tablespoons sugar
- 2 tablespoons all-purpose flour
- 1/8 teaspoon salt
- 1 egg, beaten
- 1 tablespoon white vinegar
- 1 cup reduced-fat whipped topping

Drain the pineapple, reserving the juice in a 1-cup measuring cup. Add enough water to measure 1 cup; set mixture aside. Combine the pineapple and pears in an 8-in. square dish; cover and refrigerate.

In a small saucepan, combine the sugar, flour and salt. Stir in the pineapple juice mixture until smooth. Cook and stir over medium-high heat until thickened and bubbly. Reduce heat; cook and stir 2 minutes longer.

Remove from the heat. Stir a small amount of hot mixture into egg; return all to the pan, stirring constantly. Bring to a gentle boil; cook and stir for 2 minutes.

Remove from the heat. Gently stir in vinegar. Cool to room temperature without stirring. Fold in whipped topping. Spread over fruit. Cover salad and refrigerate for 1 hour or until chilled.

NUTRITION FACTS: 1/2 cup equals 108 calories, 2 g fat (1 g saturated fat), 27 mg cholesterol, 53 mg sodium, 23 g carbohydrate, 2 g fiber, 1 g protein. **DIABETIC EXCHANGES:** 1 fruit, 1/2 starch.

Mustard Bean Salad

FAT ↓ CARB ↓ MEAT-LESS

PREP/TOTAL TIME: 25 Min.   **YIELD:** 8 Servings

Just a few ingredients are all you'll need for this tasty wax bean specialty. My grandmother and my husband's grandmother, both of whom used to prepare something similar, inspired the recipe that we continue to enjoy regularly.

—Patricia Ritter, Douglassville, Pennsylvania

- **2 pounds fresh wax beans, trimmed and cut into 2-inch pieces**
- 1/4 cup finely chopped onion
- 3 tablespoons Dijon mustard
- 2 tablespoons white vinegar

Dash salt

Place beans in a steamer basket; place in a large saucepan over 1 in. of water. Bring to a boil; cover and steam for 8-10 minutes or until crisp-tender.

Transfer beans to a serving bowl; reserve 2 tablespoons of cooking water. In a small bowl, combine the onion, mustard, vinegar, reserved cooking water and salt. Drizzle over beans; toss to coat. Serve warm or chilled.

NUTRITION FACTS: 3/4 cup equals 44 calories, 1 g fat (trace saturated fat), 0 cholesterol, 167 mg sodium, 9 g carbohydrate, 4 g fiber, 2 g protein. **DIABETIC EXCHANGE:** 2 vegetable.

Creamy Garlic Salad Dressing

FAT ↓ CARB ↓

(PICTURED BELOW)

PREP: 15 Min. + Chilling   **YIELD:** 1-1/2 Cups

Most commercial garlic dressings don't have enough garlic for me, but this homemade version always hits the spot. Try it yourself and you'll see how the thick, creamy dressing jazzes up any salad.

—Michele Odstrcilek, Lemont, Illinois

- 1 cup (8 ounces) reduced-fat sour cream
- 1/2 cup fat-free mayonnaise
- 1/3 cup fat-free milk
- 2 teaspoons sugar
- 2 green onions, finely chopped
- 2 garlic cloves, minced
- 1 teaspoon salt
- 1/8 teaspoon pepper

In a small bowl, whisk the sour cream, mayonnaise, milk and sugar. Stir in the onions, garlic, salt and pepper. Cover and refrigerate for at least 1 hour before serving.

NUTRITION FACTS: 5 teaspoons equals 33 calories, 2 g fat (1 g saturated fat), 6 mg cholesterol, 235 mg sodium, 3 g carbohydrate, trace fiber, 1 g protein. **DIABETIC EXCHANGE:** Free food.

Fiesta Side Salad

(PICTURED BELOW)

PREP: 30 Min. + Chilling   **YIELD:** 8 Servings

Perfect for a buffet, picnic or potluck, this Southwestern salad can be served at room temperature. You'll want to make extra because it tastes even better the second day! —Michelle Chicoine, APO, AE

- 2/3 cup uncooked long grain rice
- 2 cups frozen corn, thawed
- 1 can (15 ounces) black beans, rinsed and drained
- 6 green onions, sliced
- 1/4 cup pickled jalapeno slices, chopped
- 1/4 cup canola oil
- 2 tablespoons cider vinegar
- 1 tablespoon lime juice
- 1 teaspoon chili powder
- 1 teaspoon molasses
- 1/2 teaspoon salt
- 1/2 teaspoon cumin seeds, toasted and ground

Cook rice according to package directions. Meanwhile, in a large bowl, combine the corn, beans, onions and jalapenos. In a jar with a tight-fitting lid, combine the remaining ingredients; shake well.

Stir rice into corn mixture. Add dressing and toss to coat. Cover and refrigerate for at least 2 hours.

NUTRITION FACTS: 2/3 cup equals 206 calories, 8 g fat (1 g saturated fat), 0 cholesterol, 273 mg sodium, 31 g carbohydrate, 4 g fiber, 5 g protein. **DIABETIC EXCHANGES:** 2 starch, 1-1/2 fat.

Festive Slaw

PREP: 25 Min. + Chilling   **YIELD:** 10 Servings

Families will love this crisp, fresh-tasting and tangy slaw from our Test Kitchen. Packed with nutritious ingredients, it's a pretty, sweet-and-sour summer item that's perfect for picnics, covered-dish events or backyard barbecues.

- 5-1/2 cups shredded cabbage
- 3 celery ribs, thinly sliced
- 1 large carrot, shredded
- 1 *each* medium green, sweet red and yellow peppers, julienned
- 1 medium onion, halved and sliced

DRESSING:

- 1/4 cup sugar
- 1/4 cup lime juice
- 2 tablespoons canola oil
- 1 tablespoon white wine vinegar
- 1 tablespoon minced fresh cilantro
- 1 teaspoon salt

In a large bowl, combine the cabbage, celery, carrot, peppers and onion. In a small bowl, whisk the dressing ingredients. Pour over cabbage mixture; toss to coat. Cover and refrigerate for at least 1 hour, stirring occasionally.

NUTRITION FACTS: 3/4 cup equals 76 calories, 3 g fat (trace saturated fat), 0 cholesterol, 257 mg sodium, 13 g carbohydrate, 2 g fiber, 1 g protein. **DIABETIC EXCHANGES:** 1 vegetable, 1/2 starch, 1/2 fat.

Colorful Tomato 'n' Mozzarella Salad
(PICTURED ABOVE)

PREP: 20 Min. + Standing   **YIELD:** 4 Servings

This is my twist on the popular tomato-mozzarella salad. Since the rest of the salad is so light, you can splurge a bit with fresh mozzarella!   —Tari Ambler, Shorewood, Illinois

> 1 cup fresh baby spinach
> 2 medium yellow tomatoes, sliced
> 2 medium red tomatoes, sliced
> 4 ounces fresh mozzarella cheese, sliced
> 2 tablespoons thinly sliced fresh basil leaves
> 1/4 teaspoon salt
> 1/4 teaspoon pepper
> 1 tablespoon balsamic vinegar
> 2 teaspoons olive oil

Arrange spinach on a platter; top with tomato and cheese slices. Sprinkle with basil, salt and pepper. Drizzle with vinegar and oil. Let stand for 15 minutes before serving.

NUTRITION FACTS: 1 serving equals 132 calories, 9 g fat (4 g saturated fat), 22 mg cholesterol, 218 mg sodium, 7 g carbohydrate, 2 g fiber, 7 g protein.

HEALTHY OUTLOOK
At only 30 calories, a medium-size red tomato has nearly as much fiber as a slice of whole wheat bread.

Fruit and Feta Spinach Salad

PREP/TOTAL TIME: 15 Min.   **YIELD:** 6 Servings

This is the salad I served on our 25th wedding anniversary. Everyone commented on the blending of fruits, nuts and spinach, and I continue to serve it today. It's a full-flavored delight that pairs well with mildly seasoned meats.   —Paula Wharton, El Paso, Texas

> 6 cups fresh baby spinach
> 1 medium apple, sliced
> 1/2 cup seedless red grapes, halved
> 1/3 cup dried cranberries
> 3 green onions, thinly sliced
> 1/4 cup chopped walnuts, toasted
> 5 teaspoons olive oil
> 2 teaspoons cider vinegar
> 1 garlic clove, minced
> 1/4 teaspoon salt
> 1/8 teaspoon pepper
> 1/3 cup crumbled feta cheese

In a large salad bowl, combine the spinach, apple, grapes, cranberries, onions and walnuts.

In a small bowl, whisk the oil, vinegar, garlic, salt and pepper. Drizzle over salad and toss to coat. Sprinkle with feta cheese. Serve immediately.

NUTRITION FACTS: 1 cup equals 134 calories, 8 g fat (1 g saturated fat), 3 mg cholesterol, 184 mg sodium, 14 g carbohydrate, 3 g fiber, 4 g protein. **DIABETIC EXCHANGES:** 1-1/2 fat, 1 vegetable, 1/2 fruit.

Watermelon and Tomato Salad

FAT MEAT-LESS

(PICTURED ABOVE)

PREP: 40 Min. **YIELD:** 12 Servings

You cannot beat this light and refreshing salad on hot summer days. The combination of watermelon, cilantro, lime and tasty heirloom tomatoes is just unusual enough to keep folks commenting on the great flavor—and coming back for more!

—Bev Jones, Brunswick, Missouri

3 tablespoons lime juice

2 tablespoons white balsamic vinegar

2 tablespoons olive oil

2 tablespoons honey

1 medium mango, peeled and chopped

1 teaspoon grated lime peel

1 teaspoon kosher salt

1/4 teaspoon white pepper

8 cups cubed seedless watermelon

1-1/2 pounds yellow tomatoes, coarsely chopped (about 5 medium)

1-1/2 pounds red tomatoes, coarsely chopped (about 5 medium)

2 sweet onions, thinly sliced and separated into rings

2/3 cup minced fresh cilantro

For dressing, place the first eight ingredients in a blender; cover and process until pureed. In a large bowl, combine the watermelon, tomatoes, onions and cilantro. Just before serving, add dressing and toss to coat. Serve with a slotted spoon.

NUTRITION FACTS: 1 cup equals 102 calories, 3 g fat (trace saturated fat), 0 cholesterol, 181 mg sodium, 22 g carbohydrate, 3 g fiber, 2 g protein. **DIABETIC EXCHANGES:** 1 vegetable, 1 fruit, 1/2 fat.

Broken Glass Gelatin

SALT CARB ⬇ ⬇

PREP: 40 Min. + Chilling   **YIELD:** 15 Servings

A lightened-up version of an old standby, this eye-appealing treat is pretty enough to double as a light dessert.
— Dorothy Alexander, Martin, Tennessee

  1-1/2 cups reduced-fat graham cracker crumbs (about 8 whole crackers)
     7 tablespoons sugar, *divided*
     5 tablespoons reduced-fat butter, melted
     1 cup unsweetened pineapple juice
     1 envelope unflavored gelatin
     1 package (.3 ounce) sugar-free orange gelatin
  4-1/2 cups boiling water, *divided*
     1 package (.3 ounce) sugar-free lime gelatin
     1 package (.3 ounce) sugar-free strawberry gelatin
     1 carton (8 ounces) frozen reduced-fat whipped topping, thawed

In a large bowl, combine the cracker crumbs, 5 tablespoons sugar and butter; press into an ungreased 13-in. x 9-in. x 2-in. dish. Chill.

In a small saucepan, combine pineapple juice and remaining sugar. Sprinkle unflavored gelatin over juice mixture; let stand for 1 minute. Heat over low heat, stirring until gelatin is completely dissolved. Transfer to a large bowl; cool.

Dissolve orange gelatin in 1-1/2 cups boiling water; pour into an 8-in. x 4-in. x 2-in. loaf pan coated with cooking spray. Refrigerate until firm. Repeat with lime and strawberry gelatins and remaining boiling water, using additional loaf pans.

Gently fold whipped topping into pineapple juice mixture; cover and refrigerate. Cut flavored gelatins into 1-in. cubes; gently fold into whipped topping mixture. Spoon over crust. Refrigerate for several hours or overnight.

NUTRITION FACTS: 1 piece equals 98 calories, 4 g fat (3 g saturated fat), 7 mg cholesterol, 78 mg sodium, 13 g carbohydrate, trace fiber, 2 g protein. **DIABETIC EXCHANGES:** 1 starch, 1/2 fat.

Editor's Note: This recipe was tested with Land O'Lakes light stick butter.

Festive Spinach Salad

PREP: 20 Min. + Chilling   **YIELD:** 8 Servings

Baby spinach leaves get jazzed up with this simple, homemade salad dressing. Walnuts, bacon bits and pomegranate seeds make this attractive salad a regular on my holiday menus.
— JoAnn Scannell, Dubuque, Iowa

  3/4 cup fat-free French salad dressing
     2 tablespoons orange juice
     2 tablespoons honey
  3/4 teaspoon paprika
     6 cups fresh baby spinach
     1 can (11 ounces) mandarin oranges, drained
  3/4 cup pomegranate seeds (about 2 pomegranates) *or* dried cranberries
  1/2 cup sliced fresh mushrooms
  1/2 cup cubed avocado
     3 slices red onion, separated into rings
  1/4 cup crumbled cooked bacon
  1/4 cup chopped walnuts, toasted

In a jar with a tight-fitting lid, combine the salad dressing, orange juice, honey and paprika; shake well. Refrigerate for 1 hour or until chilled.

In a salad bowl, combine the remaining ingredients. Serve with dressing.

NUTRITION FACTS: 1 cup salad with about 2 tablespoons dressing equals 134 calories, 4 g fat (1 g saturated fat), 3 mg cholesterol, 359 mg sodium, 22 g carbohydrate, 3 g fiber, 4 g protein. **DIABETIC EXCHANGES:** 1 starch, 1 vegetable, 1 fat.

Bulgur Wheat Salad

MEAT-LESS

(PICTURED BELOW)

PREP: 35 Min. + Chilling   **YIELD:** 6 Servings

Fresh seasonings jazz up bulgur in my simple side dish. Featuring ripe tomatoes and green onions, it's a scrumptious addition to any meal.
— Millie McDonough, Homeland, California

     1 cup bulgur
     1 cup boiling water
     2 tablespoons lemon juice
     2 tablespoons olive oil
     1 garlic clove, minced
  1/2 teaspoon salt
  1/2 cup minced fresh parsley
     2 medium tomatoes, chopped
     4 green onions, chopped

Place bulgur in a large bowl; stir in water. Cover and let stand for 30 minutes or until liquid is absorbed.

In a small bowl, whisk the lemon juice, oil, garlic and salt. Stir into bulgur. Add parsley.

Cover and refrigerate for at least 1 hour. Just before serving, stir in the tomatoes and onions.

NUTRITION FACTS: 2/3 cup equals 137 calories, 5 g fat (1 g saturated fat), 0 cholesterol, 210 mg sodium, 22 g carbohydrate, 5 g fiber, 4 g protein. **DIABETIC EXCHANGES:** 1-1/2 starch, 1 fat.

Editor's Note: Look for bulgur in the cereal, rice or organic food aisle of your grocery store.

Gobbler Salad

CARB

(PICTURED BELOW)

PREP/TOTAL TIME: 30 Min.   YIELD: 8 Servings

Not only is this surprising salad a good way to use up leftover turkey, it tastes great and it's good for you, too.
—Marcy Kennedy, Wallaceburg, Ontario

 6 cups cubed cooked turkey breast
 3 celery ribs, finely chopped
 1 medium sweet red pepper, chopped
 4 green onions, thinly sliced
 1/2 cup raisins
 1/2 cup frozen peas, thawed
 1/3 cup minced fresh parsley
 4 hard-cooked eggs, chopped

DRESSING:

 3/4 cup plain yogurt
 1/4 cup reduced-fat mayonnaise
 3 tablespoons white vinegar
 1 tablespoon sugar
 1 tablespoon minced fresh dill
 1 tablespoon lemon juice
 1 tablespoon Dijon mustard
 1/2 teaspoon salt
 1/8 teaspoon pepper

In a large bowl, combine the turkey, celery, red pepper, onions, raisins, peas, parsley and eggs. In a small bowl, whisk the dressing ingredients. Pour over salad and toss to coat. Refrigerate until serving.

NUTRITION FACTS: 1-1/4 cups equals 278 calories, 7 g fat (2 g saturated fat), 202 mg cholesterol, 389 mg sodium, 15 g carbohydrate, 2 g fiber, 37 g protein. DIABETIC EXCHANGES: 5 very lean meat, 1 starch, 1 fat.

Strawberry Spinach Salad

SALT CARB

PREP/TOTAL TIME: 25 Min.   YIELD: 6 Servings

Filled with nutritious fruits and laced with a light-purple yogurt dressing, this colorful salad is appreciated by my husband who has diabetes.
—Gladys Nelson, Fort Atkinson, Wisconsin

 4 cups fresh baby spinach
 3 cups sliced fresh strawberries
 1 can (11 ounces) mandarin oranges, drained
 2 tablespoons canola oil
 2 tablespoons cider vinegar
 1/2 cup fat-free sugar-free raspberry yogurt
 1/4 cup slivered almonds, toasted

In a large bowl, combine the spinach, strawberries and mandarin oranges. In a small bowl, whisk together the oil and vinegar. Whisk in yogurt.

Divide spinach mixture among six salad plates. Top each serving with dressing and almonds.

NUTRITION FACTS: 1-1/3 cups spinach mixture with 2 tablespoons dressing and 2 teaspoons almonds equals 127 calories, 7 g fat (1 g saturated fat), trace cholesterol, 31 mg sodium, 14 g carbohydrate, 3 g fiber, 3 g protein. DIABETIC EXCHANGES: 1-1/2 fat, 1 vegetable, 1 fruit.

HEALTHY OUTLOOK

Loaded with spinach, fruits and a sprinkling of almonds, Strawberry Spinach Salad is a heart-smart menu option for anyone trying to eat right. Fruits and veggies are high in vitamins, minerals and fiber but low in calories. Almonds are a good source of monounsaturated fat, protein, fiber and iron.

Fresh Broccoli Salad

(PICTURED ABOVE)

MEAT-
LESS

PREP/TOTAL TIME: 20 Min.   **YIELD:** 8 Servings

This hearty side makes a nice change-of-pace salad on busy week-nights. It's so delicious that no one suspects that it's light.
— Dana Herbert, Goshen, Utah

  6 cups fresh broccoli florets
  1 can (8 ounces) sliced water chestnuts, drained
1/2 cup dried cranberries
1/4 cup chopped red onion
3/4 cup reduced-fat mayonnaise
3/4 cup fat-free plain yogurt
1-1/2 teaspoons sugar
1-1/2 teaspoons cider vinegar
1-1/2 teaspoons Dijon mustard
1/4 teaspoon salt
1/8 teaspoon pepper
1/4 cup slivered almonds, toasted

In a large bowl, combine the broccoli, water chestnuts, cranberries and onion. In a small bowl, whisk the mayonnaise, yogurt, sugar, vinegar, mustard, salt and pepper. Pour over salad; toss to coat. Just before serving, sprinkle with almonds.

NUTRITION FACTS: 3/4 cup equals 144 calories, 8 g fat (1 g saturated fat), 7 mg cholesterol, 272 mg sodium, 16 g carbohydrate, 3 g fiber, 3 g protein. **DIABETIC EXCHANGES:** 1-1/2 fat, 1 vegetable, 1/2 starch.

HEALTHY OUTLOOK

Got broccoli? If not, you should. The healthy vegetable is an excellent source of vitamins A and C. In addition, broccoli is a tasty way to increase the calcium, riboflavin and iron in your diet.

Santa Fe Salad

FAT MEAT-LESS

(PICTURED BELOW)

PREP/TOTAL TIME: 30 Min.   **YIELD:** 10 Servings

People always ask for the recipe when I bring my special salad to a potluck. The zippy dressing and mix of crunchy veggies with beans is a winning combination!   —Gail Park, Newport News, Virginia

 2-1/2 cups cut fresh green beans
     1 cup minced fresh cilantro
   1/4 cup fat-free sour cream
     2 tablespoons lime juice
     2 tablespoons balsamic vinegar
     2 garlic cloves, minced
 1-1/2 teaspoons ground cumin
   1/4 teaspoon salt
Dash cayenne pepper
     2 cups frozen corn, thawed
     1 can (15 ounces) pinto beans, rinsed and drained
     1 can (15 ounces) black beans, rinsed and drained
     1 small sweet red pepper, finely chopped
     1 small red onion, chopped
     1 can (4 ounces) chopped green chilies
     1 can (2-1/4 ounces) sliced ripe olives, drained
   1/2 cup shredded reduced-fat cheddar cheese

Place green beans in a small saucepan and cover with water. Bring to a boil; cover and cook for 3-5 minutes or until crisp-tender. Drain and immediately place beans in ice water. Drain and pat dry.

For dressing, in a small bowl, combine the cilantro, sour cream, lime juice, vinegar, garlic, cumin, salt and cayenne. In a large bowl, combine the green beans, corn, pinto beans, black beans, red pepper, onion, chilies and olives. Add cheese and dressing; toss gently to coat. Cover and refrigerate until serving.

NUTRITION FACTS: 3/4 cup equals 151 calories, 2 g fat (1 g saturated fat), 5 mg cholesterol, 374 mg sodium, 26 g carbohydrate, 6 g fiber, 8 g protein. **DIABETIC EXCHANGES:** 1-1/2 starch, 1/2 fat.

Bean 'n' Rice Picnic Salad

SALT MEAT-LESS

PREP: 30 Min. + Chilling   **YIELD:** 8 Servings

This filling salad is often requested in my home. Orange carrots and green celery also lend colorful crunch to the sweet-and-sour blend of flavors.   —Ruth Andrewson, Leavenworth, Washington

     1 cup uncooked long grain rice
     1 can (16 ounces) kidney beans, rinsed and drained
     1 medium carrot, chopped
     1 celery rib with leaves, chopped
     2 green onions, thinly sliced
   1/4 cup white wine vinegar
     2 tablespoons olive oil
     1 tablespoon sugar
   1/2 teaspoon dill weed
   1/4 teaspoon pepper
     8 lettuce leaves

Prepare rice according to package directions. Transfer to a large bowl; cool to room temperature. Stir in the beans, carrot, celery and onions.

In a jar with a tight-fitting lid, combine the vinegar, oil, sugar, dill and pepper; shake well. Pour over rice mixture; toss to coat. Refrigerate at least 1 hour. Serve on lettuce.

NUTRITION FACTS: 3/4 cup equals 177 calories, 4 g fat (1 g saturated fat), 0 cholesterol, 100 mg sodium, 31 g carbohydrate, 3 g fiber, 5 g protein. **DIABETIC EXCHANGES:** 2 starch, 1/2 fat.

Favorite Recipe Made Lighter

FEW FOODS capture the flavor of fall and winter like cranberries. The ruby red gems add a slightly tart twist and a striking color to many cool-weather dishes.

Combining cranberries with heavy cream, sugar and marshmallows, Alexandra Lypecky created Creamy Cranberry Salad. Her brightly colored delight is a scrumptious way to round out any special meal. However, the Dearborn, Michigan cook's recipe packs 14 g of fat and more than 200 calories per serving, not to mention high levels of cholesterol and saturated fat. Determined to make this treat even more enjoyable, our makeover experts went to work slashing fat and calories.

First went the heavy cream, which was replaced with reduced-fat whipped topping to mimic the original's decadent texture. Next, sugar substitute took the place of 1/2 cup of sugar called for in the recipe, lending sweetness without a large dose of calories.

With just these two simple substitution, Makeover Creamy Cranberry Salad offered a flavor and appearance that was just as terrific as the original...but with 48 percent fewer calories and 86 percent less fat. And the good news doesn't end there! Cholesterol disappeared from the recipe and saturated fat decreased from 8 g to a mere 2 g per serving. Now this is one luscious treat you can enjoy without an ounce of guilt.

Creamy Cranberry Salad

SALT ▼

PREP: 15 Min. + Chilling **YIELD:** 14 Servings

- 3 cups fresh *or* frozen cranberries, thawed and coarsely chopped
- 1 can (20 ounces) unsweetened crushed pineapple, drained
- 2 cups miniature marshmallows
- 1 medium apple, chopped
- 2/3 cup sugar
- 1/8 teaspoon salt
- 2 cups heavy whipping cream
- 1/4 cup chopped walnuts

In a large bowl, combine the cranberries, pineapple, marshmallows, apple, sugar and salt. Cover and refrigerate overnight.

Just before serving, in a large mixing bowl, beat cream until stiff peaks form. Fold the cream and walnuts into the cranberry mixture.

NUTRITION FACTS: 2/3 cup equals 229 calories, 14 g fat (8 g saturated fat), 47 mg cholesterol, 38 mg sodium, 27 g carbohydrate, 1 g fiber, 2 g protein.

> **MAKEOVER TIP**
> Apples, cranberries and pineapple give dishes a sweet-tart flair while offering a good dose of vitamin C. Using them in a recipe beefs up flavor and nutrition.

Makeover Creamy Cranberry Salad

SALT ▼

(PICTURED ABOVE)

PREP: 15 Min. + Chilling **YIELD:** 12 Servings

- 3 cups fresh *or* frozen cranberries, thawed and coarsely chopped
- 1 can (20 ounces) unsweetened crushed pineapple, drained
- 2 cups miniature marshmallows
- 1 medium apple, chopped
- Sugar substitute equivalent to 1/2 cup sugar
- 1/8 teaspoon salt
- 1 carton (8 ounces) frozen reduced-fat whipped topping, thawed
- 1/4 cup chopped walnuts

In a large bowl, combine the cranberries, pineapple, marshmallows, apple, sugar substitute and salt. Cover and refrigerate overnight.

Just before serving, fold in whipped topping and walnuts.

NUTRITION FACTS: 2/3 cup equals 133 calories, 4 g fat (2 g saturated fat), 0 cholesterol, 29 mg sodium, 24 g carbohydrate, 2 g fiber, 1 g protein.
DIABETIC EXCHANGES: 1 starch, 1/2 fruit, 1/2 fat.

Editor's Note: This recipe was tested with Splenda No Calorie Sweetener.

Creamy Succotash

MEAT-
LESS

(PICTURED ABOVE)

PREP: 10 Min.   **COOK:** 20 Min. + Cooling   **YIELD:** 10 Servings

This is a creation my sister invented. When I saw her make it, I didn't think the combination would be very tasty together, but I changed my mind immediately upon trying it.
—Shannon Koene, Blacksburg Virginia

- 4 cups frozen lima beans
- 1 cup water
- 4 cups frozen corn
- 2/3 cup reduced-fat mayonnaise
- 2 teaspoons Dijon mustard
- 1/2 teaspoon onion powder
- 1/2 teaspoon garlic powder
- 1/4 teaspoon salt
- 1/4 teaspoon pepper
- 2 medium tomatoes, finely chopped
- 1 small onion, finely chopped

In a large saucepan, bring lima beans and water to a boil. Reduce heat; cover and simmer for 10 minutes. Add corn; return to a boil. Reduce heat; cover and simmer 5-6 minutes longer or until vegetables are tender. Drain; cool for 10-15 minutes.

Meanwhile, in a large bowl, combine the mayonnaise, mustard, onion powder, garlic powder, salt and pepper. Stir in the bean mixture and chopped tomatoes and onion. Serve immediately or refrigerate.

NUTRITION FACTS: 3/4 cup equals 198 calories, 6 g fat (1 g saturated fat), 6 mg cholesterol, 238 mg sodium, 31 g carbohydrate, 6 g fiber, 7 g protein. **DIABETIC EXCHANGES:** 2 starch, 1 fat.

Dill Vegetable-Pasta Salad

MEAT-
LESS

PREP/TOTAL TIME: 25 Min.   **YIELD:** 10 Servings

We often have this delicious pasta salad for lunch or as a light supper in the summertime—in lieu of a big meal. Chunks of cheese and fresh vegetables eliminate the need for meat, and a light, creamy dill dressing replaces a heavy pasta sauce.
—Darnell Griffin, Estes Park, Colorado

- 3 cups uncooked tricolor spiral pasta
- 1 large cucumber, peeled, seeded and cubed
- 1 cup cherry tomatoes, halved
- 1 cup (4 ounces) shredded reduced-fat cheddar cheese
- 2 tablespoons chopped red onion

1 green onion, chopped
1/3 cup reduced-fat mayonnaise
1/4 cup reduced-fat sour cream
1 tablespoon buttermilk
1 tablespoon snipped fresh dill *or* 1 teaspoon dill weed
1/4 teaspoon salt
1/4 teaspoon pepper
1 cup torn romaine

Cook pasta according to package directions; drain and rinse in cold water.

In a large bowl, combine the cucumber, tomatoes, cheese and onions. In a small bowl, whisk the mayonnaise, sour cream, buttermilk, dill, salt and pepper until smooth.

Add lettuce and pasta to vegetable mixture. Drizzle with mayonnaise mixture; toss to coat. Refrigerate until serving.

NUTRITION FACTS: 3/4 cup equals 174 calories, 6 g fat (2 g saturated fat), 13 mg cholesterol, 229 mg sodium, 22 g carbohydrate, 1 g fiber, 7 g protein. **DIABETIC EXCHANGES:** 1-1/2 starch, 1 fat.

Layered Gelatin Salad

PREP: 25 Min. + Chilling   **YIELD:** 15 Servings

Here's a bright, citrusy salad that combines several of my best-loved recipes. I serve it on Thanksgiving and Christmas.
—Sharen Clark, Sunnyside, Washington

1 package (.3 ounce) sugar-free raspberry gelatin
1 cup boiling water
1 can (16 ounces) jellied cranberry sauce
CREAM LAYER:
1 envelope unflavored gelatin
1/2 cup cold water
2 cups (16 ounces) reduced-fat sour cream
1 teaspoon vanilla extract
1 cup reduced-fat whipped topping
ORANGE LAYER:
2 cans (11 ounces each) mandarin oranges
1 package (.3 ounce) sugar-free orange gelatin
1 cup boiling water

In a small bowl, dissolve raspberry gelatin in boiling water. Whisk in cranberry sauce until blended. Transfer to a 13-in. x 9-in. x 2-in. dish coated with cooking spray. Refrigerate until set but not firm, about 45 minutes.

For the cream layer, in a small saucepan, sprinkle gelatin over cold water. Let stand for 1 minute. Heat over low heat, stirring until gelatin is completely dissolved. Cool to room temperature.

In a small bowl, combine sour cream and vanilla. Fold in gelatin mixture, then whipped topping. Spoon over cranberry layer and gently spread. Refrigerate until set but not firm, about 45 minutes.

Drain oranges, reserving 1 cup syrup; set oranges aside. In a small bowl, dissolve orange gelatin in boiling water. Sir in reserved syrup. Refrigerate until slightly thickened, about 45 minutes. Stir in oranges. Carefully spoon over sour cream layer. Cover and refrigerate for 8 hours or overnight.

NUTRITION FACTS: 1 piece equals 129 calories, 3 g fat (3 g saturated fat), 11 mg cholesterol, 58 mg sodium, 21 g carbohydrate, 1 g fiber, 3 g protein. **DIABETIC EXCHANGES:** 1-1/2 starch, 1 fat.

Holiday Gelatin Mold

(PICTURED BELOW)

PREP: 25 Min. + Chilling   **YIELD:** 12 Servings (3/4 Cup Topping)

Because I care for a teenager with diabetes, I decided to change my annual Thanksgiving salad so she could enjoy this tasty treat.
—Mareen Robinson, Spanish Fork, Utah

1 package (.3 ounce) sugar-free lemon gelatin
1 package (.3 ounce) sugar-free strawberry gelatin
1 package (.3 ounce) sugar-free cherry gelatin
1-3/4 cups boiling water
1 can (20 ounces) unsweetened crushed pineapple
1 can (16 ounces) whole-berry cranberry sauce
1 medium navel orange, peeled and sectioned
3/4 cup reduced-fat whipped topping
1/4 cup fat-free sour cream

In a large bowl, dissolve the gelatins in boiling water. Drain pineapple, reserving juice in a 2-cup measuring cup; add enough cold water to measure 2 cups. Stir into gelatin mixture.

Place the pineapple, cranberry sauce and orange in a food processor; cover and pulse until blended. Stir into gelatin mixture. Transfer to an 8-cup ring mold coated with cooking spray. Refrigerate until firm.

In a small bowl, combine whipped topping and sour cream. Unmold gelatin; serve with topping.

NUTRITION FACTS: 2/3 cup gelatin with 1 tablespoon topping equals 167 calories, 1 g fat (1 g saturated fat), 1 mg cholesterol, 97 mg sodium, 38 g carbohydrate, 2 g fiber, 3 g protein.

Favorite Recipe Made Lighter

LEAFY GREENS can often trick us into thinking a salad is a light option. But tasty toppings and dressings can quickly add fat and calories, making some salads far from healthy. Diann Dinkel of Chandler, Arizona knows this fact well. Her favorite salad, for instance, has over 400 calories per serving and 37 g of fat.

"I received this recipe from my brother-in-law, and it's so delicious," she says. "I frequently prepare it for parties, and people always ask for the recipe. I'm happy to share it, but feel I'm deceiving them with a salad that's really not healthy. Can you help?"

You bet! Our makeover pros lightened Diann's salad dramatically. They started by reducing the amount of Swiss and cheddar cheeses and using reduced-fat or fat-free versions. Next, they swapped the vegetable oil for canola oil and replaced some of the oil with water.

Using four bacon strips instead of eight cut calories and fat, but still gave the salad the robust flavor that Diann and her family so enjoy. Honey-roasted peanuts also gave the salad a flavor boost, but our home economists found that honey-roasted soy nuts worked just as well. Next, our experts used white wine vinegar in place of cider vinegar to jazz up the dressing a bit.

They were thrilled with the makeover results, finding the salad kept its key characteristics and delightful taste. With a few easy alterations, Diann's salad lost 227 calories, 25 g of fat and 36 mg of cholesterol, turning Makeover Silverglade Salad into a dish she can feel good about serving.

Silverglade Salad

PREP/TOTAL TIME: 25 Min.   YIELD: 15 Servings

    6 cups torn green leaf lettuce
    6 cups torn red leaf lettuce
    4 cups seedless red grapes, halved
 3/4 pound Swiss cheese, julienned
 3/4 pound cheddar cheese, julienned
    1 cup vegetable oil
 1/2 cup cider vinegar
    4 teaspoons brown sugar
    4 teaspoons Dijon mustard
    8 bacon strips, cooked and crumbled
    2 green onions, chopped
1-1/2 cups honey-roasted peanuts

In a large bowl, combine the lettuces, grapes and cheeses. In a jar with a tight-fitting lid, combine the oil, vinegar, brown sugar and mustard; shake well.

Add bacon and onions to the dressing; pour over salad and toss to coat. Sprinkle with peanuts. Serve immediately.

NUTRITION FACTS: 1 cup equals 452 calories, 37 g fat (12 g saturated fat), 47 mg cholesterol, 341 mg sodium, 16 g carbohydrate, 2 g fiber, 17 g protein.

Makeover Silverglade Salad

(PICTURED ABOVE)

PREP/TOTAL TIME: 25 Min.   YIELD: 15 Servings

    6 cups torn green leaf lettuce
    6 cups torn red leaf lettuce
    4 cups seedless red grapes, halved
 1/2 pound reduced-fat Swiss cheese, julienned
    2 cups (8 ounces) shredded fat-free cheddar cheese
 1/3 cup water
 1/3 cup white wine vinegar
 1/3 cup canola oil
    5 teaspoons brown sugar
    1 tablespoon Dijon mustard
    2 green onions, chopped
1-1/2 cups honey-roasted soy nuts
    4 bacon strips, cooked and crumbled

In a large bowl, combine the lettuces, grapes and cheeses. In a jar with a tight-fitting lid, combine the water, vinegar, oil, brown sugar and mustard; shake well.

Add onions to the dressing; pour over salad and toss to coat. Sprinkle with soy nuts and bacon. Serve immediately.

NUTRITION FACTS: 1 cup equals 225 calories, 12 g fat (3 g saturated fat), 11 mg cholesterol, 212 mg sodium, 17 g carbohydrate, 3 g fiber, 15 g protein.

MAKEOVER TIP
Using shredded cheddar cheese instead of julienned cheese gives guests the illusion that there's more cheese on the salad.

Tangy Potato Salad

FAT ➤ MEAT-LESS

(PICTURED BELOW)

PREP: 30 Min.   **COOK:** 25 Min.   **YIELD:** 8 Servings

Horseradish adds a special kick to this mouth-watering recipe. No one ever guesses that I lightened it up with low-fat sour cream and fat-free mayo.   —Lesley Pew, Lynn, Massachusetts

        2 pounds red potatoes, cubed
        2 celery ribs, thinly sliced
      1/2 cup fat-free mayonnaise
      1/4 cup reduced-fat sour cream
        2 teaspoons chopped green onion
        2 teaspoons cider vinegar
        2 teaspoons prepared horseradish
        2 teaspoons spicy brown mustard
    1-1/2 teaspoons lemon juice
      1/2 teaspoon salt
      1/8 teaspoon pepper
    Red leaf lettuce

Place potatoes in a large saucepan and cover with water. Bring to a boil. Reduce heat; cover and simmer for 15-20 minutes or until tender. Drain and place in a large bowl; cool to room temperature. Add celery.

In a small bowl, combine the mayonnaise, sour cream, onion, vinegar, horseradish, mustard, lemon juice, salt and pepper. Stir into potato mixture. Serve in a lettuce-lined bowl.

NUTRITION FACTS: 3/4 cup equals 109 calories, 1 g fat (1 g saturated fat), 4 mg cholesterol, 314 mg sodium, 22 g carbohydrate, 3 g fiber, 3 g protein. **DIABETIC EXCHANGE:** 1-1/2 starch.

Jicama Cucumber Salad

CARB ➤ MEAT-LESS

PREP: 25 Min. + Chilling   **YIELD:** 6 Servings

Cool as a cuke and crunchy with jicama, this summery salad dressed with a splash of lime juice is a favorite. It's especially great with Mexican food.   —Debi Williams, Westminster, Colorado

        1 medium jicama, peeled and julienned
        1 small cucumber, seeded and julienned
      1/2 cup thinly sliced red onion
        1 can (4 ounces) chopped green chilies
        2 tablespoons lime juice
        2 tablespoons olive oil
      3/4 teaspoon salt
        1 garlic clove, minced
      1/2 teaspoon grated lime peel
      1/4 teaspoon pepper

In a large bowl, combine the jicama, cucumber, onion and chilies. In a small bowl, whisk the remaining ingredients. Pour over jicama mixture; toss to coat. Cover and refrigerate for at least 1 hour.

NUTRITION FACTS: 3/4 cup equals 96 calories, 5 g fat (1 g saturated fat), 0 cholesterol, 376 mg sodium, 13 g carbohydrate, 6 g fiber, 1 g protein. **DIABETIC EXCHANGES:** 2 vegetable, 1 fat.

TASTY TIP
Add peeled sticks of jicama to your veggie platters. Mild in flavor, crunchy jicama won't discolor.

Romaine Salad with Mint Dressing

 CARB MEAT-LESS

PREP/TOTAL TIME: 15 Min. **YIELD:** 6 Servings

This festive salad features dried cranberries, almonds and a little fresh mint. It's a staple at my home during busy weeknights...particularly when the holidays come around.

—Laurie Balcom, Lynden, Washington

     6 cups torn romaine
  1/4 cup dried cranberries
  1/4 cup slivered almonds, toasted
     2 tablespoons minced fresh mint
     2 tablespoons water
     2 tablespoons red wine vinegar
     2 tablespoons olive oil
     1 garlic clove, minced
  1/2 teaspoon sugar
  1/2 teaspoon salt
  1/4 teaspoon white pepper

In a large salad bowl, combine the romaine, cranberries and almonds. In a small bowl, whisk the remaining ingredients. Drizzle over salad and toss to coat. Serve immediately.

NUTRITION FACTS: 1 cup equals 94 calories, 7 g fat (1 g saturated fat), 0 cholesterol, 202 mg sodium, 8 g carbohydrate, 2 g fiber, 2 g protein. **DIABETIC EXCHANGES:** 1-1/2 fat, 1 vegetable.

Better Than Egg Salad

MEAT-LESS

(PICTURED ABOVE)

PREP/TOTAL TIME: 20 Min. **YIELD:** 4 Servings

Tofu updates a lunchtime classic in this simple sandwich. Try it on whole wheat bread, stuffed into a pita or on an English muffin.

—Lisa Renshaw, Kansas City, Missouri

  1/4 cup chopped celery
     2 green onions, chopped
  1/4 cup reduced-fat mayonnaise
     2 tablespoons sweet pickle relish
     1 tablespoon Dijon mustard
  1/4 teaspoon ground turmeric
  1/4 teaspoon salt
  1/8 teaspoon cayenne pepper
     1 package (12.3 ounces) silken firm tofu, cubed
     8 slices whole wheat bread
     4 lettuce leaves

In a small bowl, combine the first eight ingredients. Gently stir in tofu. Spread over four slices of bread; top with lettuce and remaining bread.

NUTRITION FACTS: 1 sandwich equals 274 calories, 12 g fat (2 g saturated fat), 5 mg cholesterol, 734 mg sodium, 33 g carbohydrate, 5 g fiber, 13 g protein. **DIABETIC EXCHANGES:** 2 starch, 1 lean meat, 1 fat.

Mom's Orange-Spice Gelatin

PREP: 25 Min. + Chilling   **YIELD:** 10 Servings

I remember my mom making this tangy salad frequently when I was growing up. We were always so happy whenever it appeared on the dinner table. It's a refreshing way to complete any meal.

—Karen Grimes, Stephens City, Virginia

- 1 can (15 ounces) sliced peaches in extra-light syrup
- 2 tablespoons cider vinegar
- 3 cinnamon sticks (3 inches)
- 12 whole cloves
- 3 cups boiling water
- 4 packages (.3 ounce *each*) sugar-free orange gelatin
- 2 cups cold water

Sugar substitute equivalent to 1/3 cup sugar

- 1/4 cup finely chopped pecans

Drain peaches, reserving syrup; set peaches aside. In a small saucepan, combine the vinegar, cinnamon sticks, cloves and reserved syrup. Bring to a boil; cook until reduced to about 1/2 cup. Strain, discarding cinnamon and cloves.

Add boiling water to syrup mixture; stir in gelatin until dissolved. Stir in the cold water and sugar substitute. Refrigerate until slightly thickened, about 35 minutes.

Coarsely chop the peaches. Stir peaches and pecans into gelatin mixture. Transfer to a 6-cup ring mold coated with cooking spray (mold will be full). Refrigerate for 3-4 hours or until firm. Unmold onto a serving plate.

NUTRITION FACTS: 2/3 cup equals 62 calories, 2 g fat (trace saturated fat), 0 cholesterol, 91 mg sodium, 8 g carbohydrate, 1 g fiber, 2 g protein. **DIABETIC EXCHANGES:** 1/2 starch, 1/2 fat.

Editor's Note: This recipe was tested with Splenda No Calorie Sweetener.

Veggie Barley Salad

(PICTURED AT RIGHT)

MEAT-LESS

PREP: 30 Min. + Chilling   **YIELD:** 6 Servings

When I took this salad to a family potluck, it was such a hit! I often fix it with basil-flavored vinegar that I make each summer. The longer this chills, the tastier it becomes.

—Kathy Rairigh, Milford, Indiana

- 1-1/4 cups reduced-sodium chicken broth *or* vegetable broth
- 3/4 cup water
- 1 cup quick-cooking barley
- 1 medium tomato, seeded and chopped
- 1 small zucchini, halved and thinly sliced
- 1 small sweet yellow pepper, chopped
- 2 tablespoons minced fresh parsley

DRESSING:

- 3 tablespoons olive oil
- 2 tablespoons white wine vinegar
- 1 tablespoon water
- 1 tablespoon lemon juice
- 1 tablespoon minced fresh basil
- 1/2 teaspoon salt
- 1/4 teaspoon pepper
- 1/4 cup slivered almonds, toasted

In a small saucepan, bring the broth, water and barley to a boil. Reduce heat; cover and simmer for 10-12 minutes or until barley is tender. Remove from the heat; let stand for 5 minutes.

In a large bowl, combine the tomato, zucchini, yellow pepper and parsley. Stir in barley. In a small bowl, whisk the oil, vinegar, water, lemon juice, basil, salt and pepper. Pour over barley mixture; toss to coat. Cover and refrigerate for at least 3 hours. Just before serving, stir in almonds.

NUTRITION FACTS: 3/4 cup equals 211 calories, 10 g fat (1 g saturated fat), 0 cholesterol, 334 mg sodium, 27 g carbohydrate, 7 g fiber, 6 g protein. **DIABETIC EXCHANGES:** 2 fat, 1-1/2 starch.

SHOP SMART

Barley is a flavorful and chewy alternative to white rice. You can find pearl and quick-cooking barley in most grocery stores, with many supermarkets also carrying Scotch barley.

Pearl barley has had its double outer hull and bran layer removed during processing. Quick-cooking barley is pearl barley that was precooked by steaming. Scotch barley has been milled less than pearl barley and retains some of its bran layer.

Company's Coming Salad
(PICTURED ABOVE)

SALT CARB MEAT-
LESS

PREP/TOTAL TIME: 30 Min.   **YIELD:** 8 Servings

Sugared almonds give this special salad an over-the-top kick that will have guests coming back for seconds.
—Dolores Lucken, Ferdinand, Indiana

- 2 tablespoons sugar
- 1/2 cup sliced almonds
- 1 package (5 ounces) spring mix salad greens
- 6 cups torn romaine
- 1 can (11 ounces) mandarin oranges, drained
- 2 celery ribs, thinly sliced
- 1 small red onion, chopped
- 2 green onions, thinly sliced

DRESSING:

- 3 tablespoons canola oil
- 2 tablespoons cider vinegar
- 5 teaspoons sugar
- 1 tablespoon minced fresh parsley
- 1/4 teaspoon salt

In a small heavy skillet, cook and stir the sugar over medium-low heat until melted. Stir in almonds; cook for 1 minute or until lightly browned. Spread onto foil coated with cooking spray; set aside.

In a large salad bowl, combine the mixed greens, romaine, oranges, celery and onions.

In a small bowl, whisk the dressing ingredients. Drizzle over salad; add almonds and toss to coat. Serve immediately.

NUTRITION FACTS: 1-1/4 cups equals 134 calories, 8 g fat (1 g saturated fat), 0 cholesterol, 98 mg sodium, 14 g carbohydrate, 3 g fiber, 3 g protein.
DIABETIC EXCHANGES: 1-1/2 fat, 1 vegetable, 1/2 starch.

TASTY TIP
Company's Coming Salad is ready in half an hour, making it perfect for dinner parties and weeknight suppers alike. You can even prepare the delicious sugared almonds a day or two ahead of time.

Beef up the protein in the recipe and create an entree salad by adding slices of cooked chicken.

Side Dishes & More

With the 53 slimmed-down delights found here, rounding out menus is easier than ever. In addition to hearty potato bakes and colorful vegetable medleys, you'll find savory sauces, stovetop lifesavers and other favorites guaranteed to make any meal a mouth-watering success.

Orzo-Stuffed Tomatoes, p. 65

Italian Veggie Skillet

(PICTURED ABOVE)

CARB MEAT-
LESS

PREP/TOTAL TIME: 20 Min.   **YIELD:** 6 Servings

This colorful blend of sauteed vegetables is as pretty as it is tasty. The recipe was given to me by a dear friend and makes a quick summer side using our garden harvest.
—Sue Spencer, Coarsegold, California

   1 medium onion, halved and sliced
   1 medium sweet red pepper, chopped
   1 tablespoon olive oil
   3 medium zucchini, thinly sliced
   1 garlic clove, minced
1-1/2 cups frozen corn, thawed
   1 large tomato, chopped
   2 teaspoons minced fresh basil
 1/2 teaspoon salt
 1/2 teaspoon Italian seasoning
 1/4 cup shredded Parmesan cheese

In a large nonstick skillet, saute onion and red pepper in oil for 2 minutes. Add zucchini and garlic; saute 4-5 minutes longer or until vegetables are crisp-tender.

Add the corn, tomato, basil, salt and Italian seasoning; cook and stir until heated through. Sprinkle with Parmesan cheese. Serve immediately.

NUTRITION FACTS: 1 cup equals 93 calories, 4 g fat (1 g saturated fat), 3 mg cholesterol, 266 mg sodium, 14 g carbohydrate, 3 g fiber, 4 g protein. **DIABETIC EXCHANGES:** 2 vegetable, 1/2 starch, 1/2 fat.

Orange-Glazed Sweet Potatoes

SALT MEAT-
LESS

PREP/TOTAL TIME: 25 Min.   **YIELD:** 3 Servings

These delicious potatoes from our Test Kitchen bring a little citrus flair to your plate. They make a nice contrast from sticky-sweet, canned candied yams.

   1 pound sweet potatoes, peeled and cut into 1/2-inch slices
 1/2 cup orange juice
   1 tablespoon butter
 1/2 teaspoon grated orange peel
 1/4 teaspoon pumpkin pie spice

Place sweet potatoes in a small saucepan and cover with water. Bring to a boil. Reduce heat; cover and simmer for 4-6 minutes or just until tender.

Meanwhile, in a small skillet, bring the orange juice, butter, orange peel and pumpkin pie spice to a boil. Reduce heat; simmer, uncovered, for 3-4 minutes or until thickened. Drain sweet potatoes; return to pan. Pour glaze over potatoes and stir gently to coat.

NUTRITION FACTS: 2/3 cup equals 147 calories, 4 g fat (2 g saturated fat), 10 mg cholesterol, 48 mg sodium, 27 g carbohydrate, 3 g fiber, 2 g protein. **DIABETIC EXCHANGES:** 1-1/2 starch, 1/2 fat.

Gingered Asparagus

(PICTURED AT RIGHT)

PREP/TOTAL TIME: 15 Min. **YIELD:** 4 Servings

We enjoy asparagus fresh from our garden every spring. This is one of my favorite ways to serve it. It's great for those watching their fat intake and so fast to fix.

—Nancy Zimmerman, Cape May Court House, New Jersey

2 tablespoons sherry *or* reduced-sodium chicken broth

1 tablespoon reduced-sodium soy sauce

2 teaspoons sesame oil

1 teaspoon minced fresh gingerroot

1 teaspoon lemon juice

1 teaspoon rice wine vinegar

1 garlic clove, minced

1-1/4 pounds fresh asparagus, trimmed and cut into 1-inch pieces

In a small bowl, combine the first seven ingredients. Place asparagus in a shallow 1-1/2-qt. microwave-safe dish. Drizzle with half of the sauce; toss to coat.

Cover and microwave on high for 4-6 minutes or until asparagus is crisp-tender, stirring occasionally. Drizzle with remaining sauce. Serve immediately.

NUTRITION FACTS: 3/4 cup equals 61 calories, 3 g fat (trace saturated fat), 0 cholesterol, 155 mg sodium, 7 g carbohydrate, 3 g fiber, 3 g protein. **DIABETIC EXCHANGES:** 1 vegetable, 1/2 fat.

Editor's Note: This recipe was tested in a 1,100-watt microwave.

Slow-Cooked Sausage Dressing

(PICTURED BELOW)

PREP: 20 Min. **COOK:** 3 Hours **YIELD:** 8 Cups

This dressing is so delicious, no one will know it's lower in fat. And best of all, it cooks effortlessly in the slow cooker, so the stove and oven are freed up for other dishes.

—Raquel Haggard, Edmond, Oklahoma

1/2 pound reduced-fat bulk pork sausage

2 celery ribs, chopped

1 large onion, chopped

7 cups seasoned stuffing cubes

1 can (14-1/2 ounces) reduced-sodium chicken broth

1 medium tart apple, chopped

1/3 cup chopped pecans

2 tablespoons reduced-fat butter, melted

1-1/2 teaspoons rubbed sage

1/2 teaspoon pepper

In a large nonstick skillet, cook the sausage, celery and onion over medium heat until meat is no longer pink; drain. Transfer to a large bowl; stir in the remaining ingredients.

Transfer to a 5-qt. slow cooker coated with cooking spray. Cover and cook on low for 3-4 hours or until heated through and apple is tender, stirring once.

NUTRITION FACTS: 2/3 cup equals 201 calories, 8 g fat (2 g saturated fat), 17 mg cholesterol, 640 mg sodium, 26 g carbohydrate, 3 g fiber, 7 g protein.

Editor's Note: This recipe was tested with Land O'Lakes light stick butter.

Baked Parmesan Tomatoes

PREP/TOTAL TIME: 25 Min. **YIELD:** 6 Servings

No matter how many tomatoes I give to neighbors, I always have too many left for my family to eat. So I came up with this yummy recipe that helped us out with my predicament!

—Kay Lunsford, Charlotte, North Carolina

3 medium tomatoes

1/2 teaspoon salt

1/4 teaspoon pepper

1/2 cup grated Parmesan cheese

3 tablespoons seasoned bread crumbs

1 tablespoon minced fresh basil

1 tablespoon minced fresh parsley

2 teaspoons canola oil

Cut tomatoes in half widthwise; place cut side up in an 11-in. x 7-in. x 2-in. baking dish coated with cooking spray. Sprinkle with salt and pepper. Combine the remaining ingredientsl; sprinkle over tomatoes. Bake, uncovered, at 350° for 15-20 minutes or until topping is golden brown.

NUTRITION FACTS: 1 tomato half equals 74 calories, 4 g fat (1 g saturated fat), 5 mg cholesterol, 382 mg sodium, 6 g carbohydrate, 1 g fiber, 4 g protein. **DIABETIC EXCHANGES:** 1 vegetable, 1 fat.

Can't-Be-Beet Roasted Potato Salad

FAT MEAT-LESS

(PICTURED ABOVE)

PREP: 20 Min.   **BAKE:** 35 Min.   **YIELD:** 9 Servings

You'll love the combination of beets and balsamic dressing in this lovely menu addition. I like it during the holidays.
—Jennifer Fisher, Austin, Texas

- 1-1/2 pounds small red potatoes, halved
- 2 medium red onions, cut into wedges
- 1/2 teaspoon salt, *divided*
- 2 tablespoons olive oil
- 1-1/2 pounds fresh beets, peeled and cut into wedges
- 2/3 cup reduced-sodium chicken broth *or* vegetable broth
- 1/3 cup balsamic vinegar
- 2 teaspoons brown sugar
- 2 teaspoons minced fresh thyme *or* 1/2 teaspoon dried thyme
- 1/2 teaspoon pepper
- 2 tablespoons minced fresh parsley

Place potatoes and onions in two 15-in. x 10-in. x 1-in. baking pans coated with cooking spray. Sprinkle with 1/4 teaspoon salt; drizzle with oil and toss to coat.

Place beets in pans (do not stir). Bake, uncovered, at 425° for 35-40 minutes or until vegetables are tender.

For dressing, in a small saucepan, combine the broth, vinegar, brown sugar, thyme, pepper and remaining salt. Bring to a boil. Reduce heat; simmer, uncovered, until reduced to 1/3 cup. Transfer vegetables to a large bowl. Drizzle with dressing and toss to coat. Sprinkle with parsley.

NUTRITION FACTS: 3/4 cup equals 135 calories, 3 g fat (trace saturated fat), 0 cholesterol, 244 mg sodium, 24 g carbohydrate, 3 g fiber, 3 g protein. **DIABETIC EXCHANGES:** 1 starch, 1 vegetable, 1/2 fat.

Broccoli Cauliflower Combo

FAT CARB MEAT-LESS

PREP/TOTAL TIME: 25 Min.   **YIELD:** 6 Servings

Here's a vegetable medley that gets plenty of flavor from shallots and basil. Its vibrant colors really dress up dinner plates.
—Clara Coulston, Washington Court House, Ohio

- 4 cups fresh broccoli florets
- 2 cups fresh cauliflowerets

- 3 shallots, chopped
- 1/2 cup reduced-sodium chicken broth *or* vegetable broth
- 1 teaspoon dried basil
- 1/2 teaspoon seasoned salt
- 1/8 teaspoon pepper

In a large skillet, combine all ingredients. Cover and cook over medium heat for 6-8 minutes or until vegetables are crisp-tender, stirring occasionally.

NUTRITION FACTS: 3/4 cup equals 38 calories, trace fat (trace saturated fat), 0 cholesterol, 204 mg sodium, 8 g carbohydrate, 2 g fiber, 3 g protein. **DIABETIC EXCHANGE:** 2 vegetable.

Seasoned Yukon Gold Wedges

FAT MEAT-LESS

(PICTURED BELOW)

PREP: 10 Min.   **BAKE:** 40 Min.   **YIELD:** 6 Servings

My zesty potatoes are a snap to make. Serve them alongside a roast or pork chops. We even enjoy them as party appetizers.
—Jane Lynch, Scarborough, Ontario

- 1-1/2 pounds Yukon Gold potatoes (about 5 medium), cut into wedges
- 1 tablespoon olive oil
- 1/4 cup dry bread crumbs
- 1-1/2 teaspoons paprika
- 3/4 teaspoon salt
- 1/4 teaspoon dried oregano
- 1/4 teaspoon dried thyme
- 1/4 teaspoon ground cumin
- 1/8 teaspoon pepper
- 1/8 teaspoon cayenne pepper

In a large bowl, toss potatoes with oil. Combine the remaining ingredients; sprinkle over potatoes and toss to coat.

Arrange potatoes in a single layer in a 15-in. x 10-in. x 1-in. baking pan coated with cooking spray. Bake, uncovered, at 425° for 40-45 minutes or until tender, stirring once.

NUTRITION FACTS: 3/4 cup equals 134 calories, 3 g fat (trace saturated fat), 0 cholesterol, 341 mg sodium, 24 g carbohydrate, 2 g fiber, 3 g protein. **DIABETIC EXCHANGES:** 1-1/2 starch, 1/2 fat.

Fettuccine with Green Vegetables

(PICTURED ABOVE)

PREP: 15 Min.   **COOK:** 20 Min.   **YIELD:** 4 Servings

I serve this side dish with all sorts of entrees. It's special even with burgers. —Susan McCartney, Onalaska, Wisconsin

- 4 ounces uncooked fettuccine
- 1/4 pound fresh asparagus, trimmed and cut into 1-inch pieces
- 1 medium zucchini, chopped
- 1 tablespoon canola oil
- 1 green onion, thinly sliced
- 1 garlic clove, minced
- 1/4 cup frozen peas, thawed
- 1/4 teaspoon salt
- 1/8 teaspoon pepper
- 1/4 cup shredded Romano cheese
- 2 tablespoons minced fresh parsley
- 4 teaspoons minced chives

Additional shredded Romano cheese, optional

Cook fettuccine according to package directions. Meanwhile, in a small saucepan, bring 1/2 in. of water to a boil. Add asparagus; cover and boil for 3 minutes. Drain and immediately place asparagus in ice water. Drain and pat dry.

In a large nonstick skillet, saute zucchini in oil for 3 minutes. Add onion and garlic; saute 1 minute longer. Add the peas, salt, pepper and asparagus; saute until vegetables are crisp-tender.

Drain fettuccine; add to vegetable mixture. Stir in the cheese, parsley and chives. Garnish with additional Romano cheese if desired.

NUTRITION FACTS: 3/4 cup (calculated without additional Romano cheese) equals 176 calories, 7 g fat (2 g saturated fat), 8 mg cholesterol, 276 mg sodium, 23 g carbohydrate, 2 g fiber, 8 g protein. **DIABETIC EXCHANGES:** 1-1/2 starch, 1 fat.

HEALTHY OUTLOOK

To boost the nutrition in Fettuccine with Green Vegetables, use whole wheat pasta; for a different look, use spinach pasta.

Not sure what to do with the extra asparagus? Use it as a quiche filler, grill it for a fast side dish or tuck it into an omelet for an elegant addition to breakfast.

Speedy Spanish Rice

(PICTURED ABOVE)

PREP/TOTAL TIME: 25 Min.   **YIELD:** 4 Servings

Mexican food is big with our family; in fact, one of my nephews loves this dish so much that he always requests it on his special birthday menu.   —Angie Rorick, Fort Wayne, Indiana

   1-1/2 cups uncooked instant brown rice
       1 medium onion, chopped
       1 small green pepper, chopped
       1 garlic clove, minced
       1 tablespoon butter
   1-1/2 cups water
       1 tablespoon minced fresh cilantro *or* 1 teaspoon dried
          cilantro flakes
       2 teaspoons ground cumin
   1-1/2 teaspoons chicken bouillon granules
       1/4 teaspoon pepper
       1 cup picante sauce

In a large nonstick skillet, saute the rice, onion, green pepper and garlic in butter until rice is lightly browned and vegetables are crisp-tender. Stir in the water, cilantro, cumin, bouillon and pepper; bring to a boil. Reduce the heat; cover and simmer for 5 minutes.

   Remove from the heat; let stand for 5 minutes. Fluff with a fork. Stir in picante sauce.

NUTRITION FACTS: 3/4 cup equals 201 calories, 4 g fat (2 g saturated fat), 8 mg cholesterol, 615 mg sodium, 35 g carbohydrate, 3 g fiber, 4 g protein. **DIABETIC EXCHANGES:** 2 starch, 1 vegetable, 1 fat.

Tahini Roasted Vegetables

 CARB MEAT-LESS

PREP: 25 Min.   **BAKE:** 25 Min.   **YIELD:** 6 Servings

Hearty vegetables such as eggplant and zucchini are flavored with honey, rice wine vinegar and tahini, then roasted to perfection for this side dish from our Test Kitchen. It's ideal for light and bold main courses alike.

       1 medium eggplant, peeled
       2 medium sweet red peppers
       1 medium zucchini
       1 medium onion
       1 tablespoon olive oil
       1 tablespoon tahini
       2 teaspoons rice wine vinegar
       2 teaspoons honey
     1/2 teaspoon salt
     1/4 teaspoon pepper
       2 tablespoons minced fresh parsley

Cut the eggplant, red peppers, zucchini and onion into 1-in. pieces. Place in a 15-in. x 10-in. x 1-in. baking pan coated with cooking spray. In a small bowl, combine the oil, tahini, vinegar, honey, salt and pepper. Drizzle mixture over vegetables; toss to coat.

   Bake, uncovered, at 450° for 25-30 minutes or until tender, stirring occasionally. Stir in parsley before serving.

NUTRITION FACTS: 2/3 cup equals 91 calories, 4 g fat (1 g saturated fat), 0 cholesterol, 203 mg sodium, 13 g carbohydrate, 4 g fiber, 2 g protein. **DIABETIC EXCHANGES:** 2 vegetable, 1 fat.

Favorite Recipe Made Lighter

WHEN folks think of "Thanksgiving" their thoughts often turn to turkey and dressing, and Kim Kreider of Mount Joy, Pennsylvania is no different. She asked us to lighten up her Best Corn Bread Dressing, and we cut more than 60 percent of the fat.

Best Corn Bread Dressing

PREP: 50 Min. + Simmering   **BAKE:** 45 Min.   **YIELD:** 12 Servings

    4 cups water
Turkey giblets
1-1/4 cups all-purpose flour
    3/4 cup yellow cornmeal
    1/4 cup sugar
      2 teaspoons baking powder
    1/2 teaspoon salt
        1 egg
        1 cup milk
    1/4 cup vegetable oil
        2 celery ribs, finely chopped
        1 large onion, finely chopped
        1 cup chopped pecans
        1 cup butter, cubed
        6 cups cubed soft bread (1/2-inch cubes)
        2 eggs, beaten
1-1/2 teaspoons poultry seasoning
        1 teaspoon salt
    1/2 teaspoon pepper

In a large saucepan, bring water and giblets to a boil. Reduce heat; cover and simmer for 2 hours.

Meanwhile, in a large bowl, combine the flour, cornmeal, sugar, baking powder and salt. Combine the egg, milk and oil; stir into dry ingredients just until moistened. Transfer to a greased 9-in. square baking pan.

Bake at 400° for 18-20 minutes or until a toothpick inserted near the center comes out clean. Cool on a wire rack. Cut corn bread into 1/2-in. cubes; set aside.

Strain broth, discarding giblets. Set broth aside; cool slightly. In a large skillet, saute the celery, onion and pecans in butter until vegetables are tender. Transfer to a large bowl. Stir in the corn bread, cubed bread, eggs, seasonings and enough reserved broth to reach desired moistness (about 1-1/2 cups). Save remaining broth for another use.

Transfer to a greased 13-in. x 9-in. x 2-in. baking dish. Cover and bake at 350° for 35 minutes. Uncover; bake 8-10 minutes longer or until a thermometer reads 160° and top is lightly browned.

NUTRITION FACTS: 3/4 cup equals 434 calories, 30 g fat (12 g saturated fat), 124 mg cholesterol, 651 mg sodium, 34 g carbohydrate, 3 g fiber, 9 g protein.

Editor's Note: This recipe makes enough dressing to stuff a 12-pound turkey. If used to stuff poultry, replace the eggs in the dressing with 1/2 cup egg substitute. Bake until a meat thermometer reads 180° for poultry and 165° for dressing.

Makeover Best Corn Bread Dressing

PREP: 45 Min. + Cooling   **BAKE:** 45 Min.   **YIELD:** 12 Servings

1-1/4 cups all-purpose flour
    3/4 cup yellow cornmeal
    1/4 cup sugar
      2 teaspoons baking powder
    1/2 teaspoon salt
        1 egg
        1 cup fat-free milk
        2 tablespoons canola oil
        2 tablespoons unsweetened applesauce
DRESSING:
        2 celery ribs, finely chopped
        1 large onion, finely chopped
    1/2 cup chopped pecans
    1/2 cup reduced-fat butter
        6 cups cubed day-old bread (1/2-inch cubes)
        2 eggs, beaten
1-1/2 teaspoons poultry seasoning
    3/4 teaspoon salt
    1/2 teaspoon pepper
2-1/4 to 2-3/4 cups reduced-sodium chicken broth

In a large bowl, combine the first five ingredients. Combine the egg, milk, oil and applesauce; stir into dry ingredients just until moistened. Transfer to a 9-in. square baking pan coated with cooking spray.

Bake at 400° for 15-18 minutes or until a toothpick inserted near the center comes out clean. Cool on a wire rack. Place cubed bread on baking sheets; bake for 5-7 minutes or until lightly browned. Cool on a wire rack. Cut corn bread into 1/2-in. cubes; set aside.

In a large skillet, saute the celery, onion and pecans in butter until vegetables are tender. Transfer to a large bowl. Stir in the corn bread, cubed bread, eggs, seasonings and enough broth to reach desired moistness (about 2-1/2 cups).

Transfer to a 13-in. x 9-in. x 2-in. baking dish coated with cooking spray. Cover and bake at 350° for 35 minutes. Uncover; bake 8-10 minutes longer or until a thermometer reads 160° and top is lightly browned.

NUTRITION FACTS: 3/4 cup equals 267 calories, 12 g fat (4 g saturated fat), 67 mg cholesterol, 616 mg sodium, 33 g carbohydrate, 2 g fiber, 8 g protein.

Editor's Note: This recipe was tested with Land O'Lakes light stick butter and makes enough to stuff a 12-pound turkey. If used to stuff poultry, replace the eggs with 1/2 cup egg substitute. Bake until a meat thermometer reads 180° for poultry and 165° for dressing.

MAKEOVER TIP
When preparing Makeover Best Corn Bread Dressing, our home economists found that it's best to use day-old bread cubes. They give the dish just the right consistency. It won't be too moist or too dry.

Green Beans with Dill Cream Sauce

FAT CARB MEAT-LESS

(PICTURED AT RIGHT)

PREP/TOTAL TIME: 20 Min.   YIELD: 5 Servings

A lightly flavored dill sauce dresses up frozen green beans in my quick side dish. —Joan Airey, Rivers, Manitoba

  1 package (16 ounces) frozen cut green beans
  2 tablespoons chopped onion
1-1/2 teaspoons butter
1-1/2 teaspoons all-purpose flour
  1/3 cup reduced-sodium chicken broth *or* vegetable broth
1-1/2 teaspoons white vinegar
  1/4 teaspoon salt
  1/8 teaspoon dill weed
Dash pepper
  1/4 cup reduced-fat sour cream

Cook beans according to package directions. Meanwhile, in a small skillet, saute onion in butter until tender. Stir in flour until blended; gradually add broth.

Stir in the vinegar, salt, dill and pepper. Bring to a boil; cook and stir for 1-2 minutes or until thickened. Reduce heat. Stir in sour cream; heat through (do not boil). Drain beans; serve with sauce.

NUTRITION FACTS: 2/3 cup beans with about 5 teaspoons sauce equals 59 calories, 2 g fat (2 g saturated fat), 7 mg cholesterol, 283 mg sodium, 7 g carbohydrate, 2 g fiber, 2 g protein. **DIABETIC EXCHANGES:** 1 vegetable, 1/2 fat.

Warm Tuscan Bean Salad

MEAT-LESS

(PICTURED BELOW)

PREP/TOTAL TIME: 25 Min.   YIELD: 4 Servings

Coated with a tangy homemade vinaigrette, this white bean salad even makes a quick lunch. —Linda Arnold, Edmonton, Alberta

1 small onion, thinly sliced
1 small green pepper, chopped
1 garlic clove, minced

3 teaspoons olive oil
1 large tomato, coarsely chopped
1 teaspoon dried basil
1 teaspoon dried oregano
1/4 teaspoon salt
1/4 teaspoon pepper
1 can (15 ounces) white kidney *or* cannellini beans, rinsed and drained

In a large nonstick skillet coated with cooking spray, saute the onion, green pepper and garlic in oil until tender. Stir in tomato and seasonings; cook 3-4 minutes longer. Add beans; cook and stir until heated through.

NUTRITION FACTS: 2/3 cup equals 136 calories, 4 g fat (trace saturated fat), 0 cholesterol, 285 mg sodium, 20 g carbohydrate, 6 g fiber, 5 g protein. **DIABETIC EXCHANGES:** 1 starch, 1 vegetable, 1/2 fat.

Roasted Asparagus

SALT CARB MEAT-LESS

PREP/TOTAL TIME: 25 Min.   YIELD: 4 Servings

I rely on a mild lemon dressing to bring out the flavor in roasted asparagus. Try it alongside pork or chicken.
—Kelley Casey, Fairfax, Virginia

1 pound fresh asparagus, trimmed
1 tablespoon olive oil
1 teaspoon lemon juice
1 teaspoon red wine vinegar *or* balsamic vinegar
1 teaspoon Dijon mustard
1 tablespoon shredded Parmesan cheese

Place the asparagus in an 11-in. x 7-in. x 2-in. baking dish coated with cooking spray. In a small bowl, combine the oil, lemon juice, vinegar and mustard. Pour over asparagus. Sprinkle with Parmesan cheese. Bake, uncovered, at 425° for 12-18 minutes or until tender.

NUTRITION FACTS: 1 serving equals 51 calories, 4 g fat (1 g saturated fat), 1 mg cholesterol, 59 mg sodium, 3 g carbohydrate, 1 g fiber, 2 g protein. **DIABETIC EXCHANGES:** 1 vegetable, 1/2 fat.

Orzo-Stuffed Tomatoes

(PICTURED BELOW)

PREP: 35 Min. **BAKE:** 15 Min. **YIELD:** 6 Servings

My neighbor and I used to have a friendly competition for that first ripe tomato! This side dish with orzo is always the one I reach for when I can claim that honor.

—Marian Ridgeway, Desert Hot Springs, California

- 2/3 cup uncooked orzo pasta
- 6 medium tomatoes
- 1 tablespoon butter
- 1/2 cup shredded reduced-fat Swiss cheese
- 1 tablespoon minced fresh basil *or* 1 teaspoon dried basil
- 2 teaspoons minced fresh parsley
- 1 teaspoon salt
- 1/4 teaspoon white pepper

Paprika

Cook orzo according to package directions. Meanwhile, cut a thin slice off the top of each tomato. Scoop out pulp, leaving a 1/2-in. shell. Set aside 6 tablespoons pulp for filling. Invert tomatoes onto paper towels to drain. Drain orzo.

In a small heavy saucepan, cook butter over medium heat for 5-7 minutes or until golden brown. Remove from the heat; stir in the cheese, basil, parsley, salt, pepper, orzo and reserved pulp. Spoon into tomatoes.

Place in an ungreased 2-qt. baking dish; sprinkle with paprika. Bake, uncovered, at 350° for 15-20 minutes or until heated through.

NUTRITION FACTS: 1 stuffed tomato equals 150 calories, 3 g fat (2 g saturated fat), 9 mg cholesterol, 456 mg sodium, 24 g carbohydrate, 2 g fiber, 7 g protein. **DIABETIC EXCHANGES:** 1 starch, 1 vegetable, 1/2 fat.

Brown Rice with Lentils

PREP: 15 Min. **BAKE:** 65 Min. **YIELD:** 6 Servings

In just a few moments, I can have this homey side dish in the oven, leaving me plenty of time to attend to the rest of my meal.

—Michele Doucette, Stephenville, Newfoundland and Labrador

- 1-1/2 cups reduced-sodium chicken broth *or* vegetable broth
- 1/2 cup white wine *or* reduced-sodium chicken broth *or* vegetable broth
- 1 medium onion, chopped
- 1/2 cup dried lentils, rinsed
- 1/2 cup uncooked brown rice
- 1 garlic clove, minced
- 1 bay leaf
- 1/4 teaspoon dried basil
- 1/4 teaspoon dried thyme
- 1/8 teaspoon pepper
- 1 cup Italian stewed tomatoes, cut up
- 1/4 teaspoon salt
- 1/2 cup reduced-fat shredded Swiss cheese

In a 1-1/2-qt. baking dish coated with cooking spray, combine the first 10 ingredients. Cover and bake at 350° for 40 minutes.

Stir in the tomatoes and salt. Cover and bake for 20-30 minutes longer or until rice and lentils are tender. Remove and discard bay leaf. Sprinkle with cheese. Bake, uncovered, for 5-8 minutes or until cheese melts.

NUTRITION FACTS: 3/4 cup equals 169 calories, 1 g fat (trace saturated fat), 4 mg cholesterol, 427 mg sodium, 27 g carbohydrate, 7 g fiber, 10 g protein. **DIABETIC EXCHANGE:** 2 starch.

Pepper Squash Saute

FAT ↓ CARB ↓ MEAT-LESS

(PICTURED ABOVE)

PREP/TOTAL TIME: 25 Min. **YIELD:** 4 Servings

I often double this saute because it's so good reheated later in the week. —Janice McCloskey, Howard, Pennsylvania

- 1 small onion, chopped
- 2 garlic cloves, minced
- 1 tablespoon butter
- 1/3 cup *each* chopped green, sweet red and yellow pepper
- 1 medium zucchini, chopped
- 1 medium yellow summer squash, chopped
- 1 medium carrot, shredded
- 1/2 teaspoon salt
- 1/4 teaspoon pepper

In a large nonstick skillet, saute onion and garlic in butter for 2 minutes. Stir in the peppers; cook for 3 minutes. Stir in the zucchini, summer squash and carrot; saute 3-4 minutes longer or until vegetables are tender. Sprinkle with salt and pepper.

NUTRITION FACTS: 3/4 cup equals 69 calories, 3 g fat (2 g saturated fat), 8 mg cholesterol, 333 mg sodium, 10 g carbohydrate, 3 g fiber, 2 g protein. **DIABETIC EXCHANGES:** 2 vegetable, 1/2 fat.

Tomato Casserole

MEAT-LESS

PREP: 15 Min. **BAKE:** 25 Min. **YIELD:** 6 Servings

Here's a delicious side dish that's simple and fast. It's especially popular when tomatoes are ripe. —Debbie Campbell, Peterborough, Ontario

- 6 medium tomatoes, chopped
- 1 small onion, chopped
- 2 teaspoons sugar
- 1/4 teaspoon salt
- 1/8 teaspoon pepper
- 1/2 cup dry bread crumbs
- 1/2 cup grated Parmesan cheese
- 1 tablespoon butter, melted

In a large bowl, combine the tomatoes, onion, sugar, salt and pepper. Transfer to a 2-qt. baking dish coated with cooking spray. Combine the bread crumbs, Parmesan cheese and butter; sprinkle over tomato mixture. Bake, uncovered, at 350° for 25-30 minutes or until golden brown.

NUTRITION FACTS: 1 serving equals 129 calories, 5 g fat (3 g saturated fat), 10 mg cholesterol, 334 mg sodium, 17 g carbohydrate, 2 g fiber, 6 g protein. **DIABETIC EXCHANGES:** 2 vegetable, 1 fat, 1/2 starch.

Spicy Carrot Coins

(PICTURED AT RIGHT)

FAT MEAT-LESS

PREP/TOTAL TIME: 25 Min.   **YIELD:** 6 Servings

Cumin, coriander and ginger lend unusual zip and flavor to these colorful carrot coins.
    —Nancy Zimmerman, Cape May Court House, New Jersey

     2 pounds carrots, sliced
 1-1/4 cups water
     1 cinnamon stick (3 inches)
     1 teaspoon ground ginger
     1 teaspoon ground cumin
   1/2 teaspoon ground coriander
   1/4 teaspoon salt
   1/8 to 1/4 teaspoon cayenne pepper
   1/4 cup honey
     4 teaspoons lemon juice

In a large nonstick saucepan, combine the first eight ingredients. Bring to a boil. Reduce heat; cover and simmer mixture for 5 minutes.

Discard cinnamon stick. Add honey and lemon juice to carrots. Bring to a boil; cook, uncovered, for 5-8 minutes or until carrots are tender and liquid has evaporated.

NUTRITION FACTS: 2/3 cup equals 112 calories, trace fat (trace saturated fat), 0 cholesterol, 153 mg sodium, 28 g carbohydrate, 5 g fiber, 2 g protein. **DIABETIC EXCHANGES:** 2 vegetable, 1 starch.

Tomatoes Rockefeller

(PICTURED BELOW)

PREP: 20 Min.   **BAKE:** 35 Min.   **YIELD:** 6 Servings

Looking for a unique item to serve with beef? Consider this change-of-pace recipe. The spinach-topped tomatoes look wonderful on the plate.   —Linda Roberson, Collierville, Tennessee

     3 eggs, lightly beaten
     1 cup dry bread crumbs
     3 green onions, chopped
     1 tablespoon butter, melted
     1 teaspoon Italian seasoning

     1 garlic clove, minced
   1/2 teaspoon minced fresh thyme
   1/4 teaspoon salt
   1/4 teaspoon pepper
   1/8 teaspoon Worcestershire sauce
   1/8 teaspoon hot pepper sauce
     1 package (10 ounces) frozen creamed spinach
     2 large tomatoes
   1/4 cup shredded Parmesan cheese

In a large bowl, combine the first 11 ingredients. Cook spinach according to package directions; stir into egg mixture.

Cut each tomato into six slices; arrange in a single layer in a 13-in. x 9-in. x 2-in. baking dish coated with cooking spray. Mound 2 tablespoons of spinach mixture on each slice.

Bake, uncovered, at 350° for 30 minutes. Sprinkle with Parmesan cheese. Bake 5-10 minutes longer or until a thermometer reads 160°.

NUTRITION FACTS: 2 spinach-topped tomato slices equals 190 calories, 8 g fat (3 g saturated fat), 114 mg cholesterol, 595 mg sodium, 21 g carbohydrate, 2 g fiber, 9 g protein. **DIABETIC EXCHANGES:** 1 starch, 1 vegetable, 1 fat.

Vegetable Medley

FAT CARB MEAT-LESS

PREP/TOTAL TIME: 30 Min.   **YIELD:** 5 Servings

My sister-in-law served a healthy vegetable dish to my husband and I. We liked it so much, I just had to share the recipe here.
    —Betty Kleberger, Florissant, Missouri

   1/2 pound sliced fresh mushrooms
     1 medium zucchini, sliced
     1 medium yellow summer squash, sliced
     1 small onion, chopped
     1 can (14-1/2 ounces) Italian diced tomatoes, undrained
   1/2 teaspoon salt
   1/4 teaspoon pepper

In a large saucepan, combine all ingredients. Bring to a boil. Reduce heat; simmer, uncovered, for 15-20 minutes or until vegetables are tender, stirring occasionally. Serve with a slotted spoon.

NUTRITION FACTS: 3/4 cup equals 61 calories, trace fat (trace saturated fat), 0 cholesterol, 557 mg sodium, 13 g carbohydrate, 3 g fiber, 3 g protein. **DIABETIC EXCHANGE:** 2 vegetable.

Favorite Recipe Made Lighter

SOME MENUS just aren't complete without a steaming side of mashed potatoes. And for Kathy Fleming's family in Lisle, Illinois, Patrician Potatoes are a must-have for special occassions.

"I've served this fantastic side dish for years," writes Kathy. "It's a favorite for holidays. I get so many requests for it, and would really like to trim it down a bit."

Our recipe makeover staff took a straightforward approach and replaced the dish's full-fat sour cream and cream cheese with their lower-fat versions. To lighten the dish even more, they decreased the amount of butter and Parmesan cheese. The results were excellent!

Makeover Patrician Potatoes have 70 percent less cholesterol and 73 percent fewer fat grams. Despite the changes, the dish maintains its comforting characteristics, which will ensure that this made-lighter version will be a favorite at the Fleming household for years to come.

Patrician Potatoes
MEAT-LESS

PREP: 45 Min.   **BAKE:** 20 Min.   **YIELD:** 12 Servings

- 5 pounds medium potatoes, peeled and quartered
- 1/4 cup butter, melted
- 1 package (8 ounces) cream cheese, softened
- 1 cup (8 ounces) sour cream
- 2 teaspoons salt
- 2 teaspoons minced chives
- 1/2 cup shredded Parmesan cheese
- 1 teaspoon paprika

Place potatoes in a Dutch oven and cover with water. Bring to a boil. Reduce heat; cover and simmer for 15-20 minutes or until tender.

Drain potatoes and place in a large bowl; mash with butter. In a small mixing bowl, beat the cream cheese, sour cream and salt until light and fluffy; add to potatoes. Stir in chives.

Transfer to a greased 13-in. x 9-in. x 2-in. baking dish. Sprinkle with Parmesan cheese and paprika. Bake, uncovered, at 350° for 20-25 minutes or until heated through.

NUTRITION FACTS: 1 cup equals 292 calories, 15 g fat (9 g saturated fat), 46 mg cholesterol, 560 mg sodium, 34 g carbohydrate, 3 g fiber, 6 g protein.

SHOP SMART
Many supermarkets carry shredded Parmesan in refrigerated cases near the deli area. Look for fresh chives in your grocery store's produce department. If you'd rather not use chives, add a finely chopped green onion instead.

Makeover Patrician Potatoes
MEAT-LESS

(PICTURED ABOVE)

PREP: 45 Min.   **BAKE:** 20 Min.   **YIELD:** 12 Servings

- 5 pounds medium potatoes, peeled and quartered
- 2 tablespoons butter, melted
- 1 package (8 ounces) fat-free cream cheese
- 1 cup (8 ounces) reduced-fat sour cream
- 2 teaspoons salt
- 2 teaspoons minced chives
- 1/4 cup shredded Parmesan cheese
- 1 teaspoon paprika

Place potatoes in a Dutch oven and cover with water. Bring to a boil. Reduce heat; cover and simmer for 15-20 minutes or until tender.

Drain potatoes and place in a large bowl; mash with butter. In a small mixing bowl, beat the cream cheese, sour cream and salt until light and fluffy; add to potatoes. Stir in chives.

Transfer to a 13-in. x 9-in. x 2-in. baking dish coated with cooking spray. Sprinkle with Parmesan cheese and paprika. Bake, uncovered, at 350° for 20-25 minutes or until heated through.

NUTRITION FACTS: 1 cup equals 207 calories, 4 g fat (3 g saturated fat), 14 mg cholesterol, 563 mg sodium, 35 g carbohydrate, 3 g fiber, 8 g protein. **DIABETIC EXCHANGES:** 2 starch, 1 fat.

Cranberry-Walnut Sweet Potatoes

SALT MEAT-
LESS

(PICTURED BELOW)

PREP: 25 Min.   **BAKE:** 1 Hour   **YIELD:** 8 Servings

*For me, the best part of Thanksgiving dinner is the sweet potatoes!
You can make the sauce for these up to a day ahead, just omit the
walnuts until you're ready to serve.*

—Mary Wilhelm, Sparta, Wisconsin

        4 large sweet potatoes
    1/4 cup finely chopped onion
        1 tablespoon butter
        1 cup fresh *or* frozen cranberries
    1/3 cup maple syrup
    1/4 cup water
    1/4 cup cranberry juice
    1/4 teaspoon salt, *divided*
    1/2 cup chopped walnuts, toasted
        1 teaspoon Dijon mustard
    1/4 teaspoon pepper
        2 tablespoons minced chives

Scrub and pierce sweet potatoes. Bake at 400° for 1 hour or
until tender.

In a small saucepan, saute onion in butter until tender.
Add the cranberries, syrup, water, cranberry juice and 1/8
teaspoon salt. Bring to a boil. Reduce heat; cover and simmer
for 10-15 minutes or until berries pop, stirring occasionally.

Stir in walnuts and mustard; heat through.

Cut potatoes in half lengthwise; sprinkle with pepper and
remaining salt. Top each with 2 tablespoons cranberry mixture;
sprinkle with chives.

NUTRITION FACTS: 1/2 potato equals 249 calories, 6 g fat (1 g saturated fat),
4 mg cholesterol, 120 mg sodium, 46 g carbohydrate, 6 g fiber, 5 g protein.

Herb Rice

FAT

PREP/TOTAL TIME: 30 Min.   **YIELD:** 4 Servings

*Here's a delicious side for busy weeknight meals. I even layer the
dry ingredients in a pint mason jar for last-minute hostess gifts.
Turn it into an entree by adding slices of cooked chicken.*

—Sam Prichard, Lexington, South Carolina

        2 cups water
        1 cup uncooked long grain rice
    4-1/4 teaspoons dried parsley flakes
        4 teaspoons butter
        1 teaspoon minced chives
    1/2 teaspoon dried
    1/2 teaspoon dried rosemary, crushed

In a large saucepan, combine all ingredients. Bring to a boil.
Reduce heat; cover and simmer for 16-20 minutes or until rice
is tender.

NUTRITION FACTS: 2/3 cup equals 132 calories, 2 g fat (1 g saturated
fat), 3 mg cholesterol, 222 mg sodium, 26 g carbohydrate, 1 g fiber, 3 g
protein. **DIABETIC EXCHANGES:** 1 starch, 1-1/2 starch, 1/2 fat.

Curried Corn on the Cob

MEAT-LESS

(PICTURED ABOVE)

PREP: 15 Min. + Soaking   **GRILL:** 25 Min.   **YIELD:** 6 Servings

If goat cheese is not to your liking, try queso fresco or any other crumbly cheese such as feta. Parmesan is also good, and even though it won't spread well, you can sprinkle the mixture over the corn.   —Laura Fall-Sutton, Buhl, Idaho

- 6 medium ears sweet corn in husks
- 1/2 cup goat cheese
- 1 tablespoon sugar
- 2 teaspoons salt-free seasoning blend
- 1/2 teaspoon curry powder
- 1/4 teaspoon salt
- 1/4 teaspoon pepper

Carefully peel back cornhusks to within 1 in. of bottoms; remove silk. Rewrap corn in husks and secure with kitchen string. Place in a large kettle; cover with cold water. Soak for 20 minutes; drain.

Grill corn, covered, over medium heat for 25-30 minutes or until tender, turning often. In a small bowl, combine the remaining ingredients; spread over warm corn. Serve the corn immediately.

NUTRITION FACTS: 1 ear of corn with 4 teaspoons cheese mixture equals 203 calories, 7 g fat (4 g saturated fat), 15 mg cholesterol, 214 mg sodium, 33 g carbohydrate, 4 g fiber, 8 g protein. **DIABETIC EXCHANGES:** 2 starch, 1 fat.

Walnut Cranberry Orzo

MEAT-LESS

PREP/TOTAL TIME: 30 Min.   **YIELD:** 6 Servings

After becoming fascinated with tiny orzo pasta, I created this delightful side dish. With red pepper, cranberries, walnuts and Parmesan, it's as colorful as it is flavorful.   —Judith Comstock, Salado, Texas

- 1-1/4 cups uncooked orzo pasta
- 1 medium sweet red pepper, chopped
- 1 small onion, chopped
- 1-1/2 teaspoons olive oil
- 1/2 cup reduced-sodium chicken broth *or* vegetable broth
- 1/2 cup dried cranberries
- 1/4 teaspoon salt
- 1/2 cup chopped walnuts, toasted
- 1/4 cup grated Parmesan cheese

Cook orzo according to package directions. Meanwhile, in a small nonstick skillet coated with cooking spray, saute red pepper and onion in oil until tender. Stir in the broth, cranberries and salt. Bring to a boil. Reduce heat; simmer, uncovered, for 5 minutes.

Drain orzo; toss with vegetable mixture. Sprinkle with walnuts and Parmesan cheese.

NUTRITION FACTS: 2/3 cup equals 283 calories, 9 g fat (1 g saturated fat), 3 mg cholesterol, 216 mg sodium, 43 g carbohydrate, 3 g fiber, 10 g protein.

Italian-Style Green Beans

FAT SALT CARB MEAT-LESS

PREP/TOTAL TIME: 30 Min.   **YIELD:** 8 Servings

Fresh green beans and mushrooms star in this pretty dinner addition. Lightly coated with olive oil, lemon and basil, the no-fuss beans quickly cook to perfection.

—Gloria Warczak, Cedarburg, Wisconsin

- 1-1/2 pounds fresh green beans, trimmed
- 1/2 pound sliced fresh mushrooms
- 1 tablespoon olive oil
- 1 tablespoon minced fresh basil *or* 1 teaspoon dried basil
- 1 teaspoon grated lemon peel
- 1/4 teaspoon sugar
- 1/4 teaspoon salt
- 1/8 teaspoon pepper

Place beans in a large saucepan and cover with water. Bring to a boil. Cook, uncovered, for 8-10 minutes or until crisp-tender; drain.

In a large nonstick skillet, saute mushrooms in oil until crisp-tender; stir in the beans. Sprinkle with basil, lemon peel, sugar, salt and pepper. Cook and stir until combined.

NUTRITION FACTS: 3/4 cup equals 46 calories, 2 g fat (trace saturated fat), 0 cholesterol, 79 mg sodium, 7 g carbohydrate, 3 g fiber, 2 g protein. **DIABETIC EXCHANGES:** 1 vegetable, 1/2 fat.

Multigrain Pilaf

PREP: 20 Min.   **BAKE:** 1 Hour   **YIELD:** 12 Servings

Packed with rice, lentils and barley, this filling side dish has a rich, nutty taste and texture that I hope you'll like. It's as good with beef dishes as it is with chicken or turkey.

—Lillian Zurock, Spirit River, Alberta

- 1 medium onion, chopped
- 1 tablespoon canola oil
- 1/2 cup medium pearl barley
- 1/2 cup uncooked brown rice
- 1/2 cup uncooked wild rice
- 1/2 cup dried lentils, rinsed
- 1/2 cup sliced almonds
- 1 tablespoon chicken bouillon granules
- 4-1/2 cups boiling water
- 1 tablespoon salt-free seasoning blend
- 2 tablespoons sherry *or* additional water

In a large nonstick skillet coated with cooking spray, saute onion in oil for 2 minutes. Add the barley, brown rice, wild rice, lentils and almonds; saute 5-6 minutes longer or until almonds are lightly browned. Transfer to a 3-qt. baking dish coated with cooking spray.

Dissolve bouillon in boiling water; stir in the seasoning blend and sherry or additional water. Carefully pour over grain mixture; stir to combine.

Cover and bake at 350° for 60-70 minutes or until grains are tender.

NUTRITION FACTS: 3/4 cup equals 155 calories, 4 g fat (trace saturated fat), trace cholesterol, 213 mg sodium, 25 g carbohydrate, 5 g fiber, 6 g protein. **DIABETIC EXCHANGES:** 1-1/2 starch, 1/2 fat.

Squash Medley

FAT SALT CARB MEAT-LESS

(PICTURED BELOW)

PREP/TOTAL TIME: 30 Min.   **YIELD:** 6 Servings

I'm trying to cut my risk for cardiac disease by changing the way I eat. Made on the stovetop, this heartwarming dish is packed with nutrition and flavor.

—Marlene Agnelly, Ocean Springs, Mississippi

- 1 yellow summer squash, quartered and sliced
- 1 medium zucchini, quartered and sliced
- 1 medium onion, chopped
- 1 medium sweet red pepper, cut into 1-inch pieces
- 1 tablespoon olive oil
- 2 garlic cloves, minced
- 1/2 teaspoon salt-free spicy seasoning blend
- 1/4 teaspoon salt
- 1/8 teaspoon pepper
- 1 medium tomato, chopped

In a large skillet, saute the yellow squash, zucchini, onion and red pepper in oil for 5 minutes. Add garlic and seasonings; saute 2-3 minutes longer or until vegetables are crisp-tender. Stir in tomato; heat through.

NUTRITION FACTS: 2/3 cup equals 53 calories, 2 g fat (trace saturated fat), 0 cholesterol, 104 mg sodium, 8 g carbohydrate, 2 g fiber, 2 g protein. **DIABETIC EXCHANGES:** 1 vegetable, 1/2 fat.

SHOP SMART

Choose firm summer squash with brightly colored skin that's free from spots and bruises. Generally, the smaller the squash, the more tender it will be. Refrigerate summer squash in a plastic bag for up to 5 days. Before using, wash squash and trim both ends. If sauteing sliced summer squash, blot slices dry first.

Twice-Baked Sweet Potatoes

 FAT SALT MEAT-LESS

(PICTURED ABOVE)

PREP: 70 Min. + Cooling **BAKE:** 20 Min. **YIELD:** 8 Servings

Our Test Kitchen puts a new twist on a classic, using good-for-you sweet potatoes, raisins and almonds. Pineapple juice and cinnamon round out this satisfying recipe.

    4 medium sweet potatoes
    1 can (6 ounces) unsweetened pineapple juice
 1/2 cup golden raisins
    2 tablespoons brown sugar
 1/4 teaspoon ground cinnamon
 1/4 cup sliced almonds

Scrub and pierce sweet potatoes. Bake at 375° for 1 hour or until tender.

When cool enough to handle, cut each potato in half lengthwise. Scoop out pulp, leaving a thin shell. In a small bowl, mash the pulp with pineapple juice. Stir in the raisins, brown sugar and cinnamon. Spoon into potato shells. Sprinkle with almonds.

Place on a baking sheet. Bake for 20 minutes or until heated through.

NUTRITION FACTS: 1/2 potato equals 163 calories, 2 g fat (trace saturated fat), 0 cholesterol, 12 mg sodium, 36 g carbohydrate, 4 g fiber, 3 g protein.

HEALTHY OUTLOOK

Sweet potatoes are a good source of vitamins A and C as well as manganese, which helps the body break down fats, carbohydrates and proteins.

Wholesome Apple-Hazelnut Stuffing

MEAT-LESS

(PICTURED BELOW)

PREP: 20 Min. **BAKE:** 30 Min. **YIELD:** 6 Cups

Try this whole grain, fruit and nut stuffing for a delicious new slant on holiday tradition. Herbs balance the sweetness of the apples and give this dish a wonderful flavor. —Donna Noel, Gray, Maine

    2 celery ribs, chopped
    1 large onion, chopped
    1 tablespoon olive oil
    1 small carrot, shredded
    2 garlic cloves, minced
    3 tablespoons minced fresh parsley *or* 1 tablespoon dried parsley flakes
    1 tablespoon minced fresh rosemary *or* 1 teaspoon dried rosemary, crushed
    4 cups cubed day-old whole wheat bread
 1-1/2 cups shredded peeled tart apples (about 2 medium)
 1/2 cup chopped hazelnuts, toasted
    1 egg, lightly beaten
 3/4 cup apple cider *or* unsweetened apple juice
 1/2 teaspoon coarsely ground pepper
 1/4 teaspoon salt

In a large nonstick skillet, saute celery and onion in oil for 4 minutes. Add the carrot, garlic, parsley and rosemary; saute 2-4 minutes longer or until vegetables are tender.

In a large bowl, combine the vegetable mixture, bread cubes, apples and hazelnuts. In a small bowl, combine the egg, cider, pepper and salt. Add to stuffing mixture and mix well.

Transfer to an 8-in. square baking dish coated with cooking spray. Cover and bake at 350° for 20 minutes. Uncover; bake 10-15 minutes longer or until a thermometer reads 160°.

NUTRITION FACTS: 3/4 cup equals 159 calories, 8 g fat (1 g saturated fat), 27 mg cholesterol, 195 mg sodium, 20 g carbohydrate, 4 g fiber, 4 g protein. **DIABETIC EXCHANGES:** 1-1/2 fat, 1 starch.

Just Delish Veggie Kabobs

(PICTURED AT RIGHT)

FAT ▼ MEAT-LESS

PREP: 30 Min. + Marinating   **GRILL:** 10 Min.   **YIELD:** 4 Servings

Invite your neighbors over for a grilling get-together and serve these scrumptious skewers. —Agnes Ward, Stratford, Ontario

        8 small red potatoes, halved
        3 tablespoons unsweetened apple juice
        3 tablespoons red wine vinegar
        2 tablespoons minced fresh basil
        1 tablespoon Dijon mustard
        1 tablespoon honey
        1 tablespoon reduced-sodium soy sauce
        2 teaspoons olive oil
        2 garlic cloves, minced
    1/4 teaspoon pepper
      12 medium fresh mushrooms
        1 large sweet red pepper, cut into 1-inch pieces
        1 medium zucchini, cut into 1/2-inch slices

Place potatoes in a steamer basket; place in a large saucepan over 1 in. of water. Bring to a boil; cover and steam for 7-9 minutes or just until tender. Cool.

In a large resealable plastic bag, combine the apple juice, vinegar, basil, mustard, honey, soy sauce, oil, garlic and pepper. Add the mushrooms, red pepper, zucchini and cooked potatoes. Seal bag and turn to coat; refrigerate for 2 hours.

Coat grill rack with cooking spray before starting the grill. Drain and reserve marinade; thread vegetables onto four metal or soaked wooden skewers. Grill, covered, over medium heat for 10-15 minutes, turning and basting occasionally with reserved marinade.

NUTRITION FACTS: 1 kabob equals 168 calories, 3 g fat (trace saturated fat), 0 cholesterol, 258 mg sodium, 32 g carbohydrate, 4 g fiber, 5 g protein. **DIABETIC EXCHANGES:** 1-1/2 starch, 1 vegetable, 1/2 fat.

Fiesta Red Potatoes

SALT ▼ MEAT-LESS

PREP: 15 Min.   **COOK:** 30 Min.   **YIELD:** 4 Servings

My son-in-law came up with these fiery potatoes.
—Pat Pennell, El Dorado Springs, Missouri

        4 medium red potatoes, cut into 1/2-inch cubes
        1 medium onion, thinly sliced
        2 jalapeno peppers, seeded and chopped
    1/4 teaspoon salt-free seasoning blend
    1/4 teaspoon pepper
        1 tablespoon canola oil
        2 small tomatoes, chopped

In a large nonstick skillet coated with cooking spray, saute the potatoes, onion, jalapenos, seasoning blend and pepper in oil for 30-35 minutes or until potatoes are tender. Stir in tomatoes; heat through.

NUTRITION FACTS: 1 cup equals 146 calories, 4 g fat (trace saturated fat), 0 cholesterol, 15 mg sodium, 25 g carbohydrate, 4 g fiber, 3 g protein. **DIABETIC EXCHANGES:** 1 starch, 1 vegetable, 1/2 fat.

Editor's Note: When cutting or seeding hot peppers, use rubber or plastic gloves to protect your hands. Avoid touching your face

Spiced Polenta Steak Fries

FAT ▼ MEAT-LESS

(PICTURED ABOVE)

PREP/TOTAL TIME: 30 Min.   **YIELD:** 4 Servings

Adults and kids alike will delight in these healthy stand-ins for steak fries from our home economists.

>   1 tube (1 pound) polenta
>   1 tablespoon olive oil
> 1/4 teaspoon onion powder
> 1/4 teaspoon garlic powder
> 1/4 teaspoon chili powder
> 1/8 teaspoon paprika
> 1/8 teaspoon pepper

Cut polenta in half widthwise; cut each portion in half lengthwise. Cut each section into eight strips. Arrange strips in a single layer in a 15-in. x 10-in. x 1-in. baking pan coated with cooking spray. Combine the oil and seasonings; drizzle over polenta strips and gently toss to coat. Bake at 425° for 7-10 minutes on each side or until golden brown.

NUTRITION FACTS: 8 fries equals 121 calories, 3 g fat (trace saturated fat), 0 cholesterol, 383 mg sodium, 20 g carbohydrate, 1 g fiber, 2 g protein. **DIABETIC EXCHANGES:** 1 starch, 1/2 fat.

> ### SHOP SMART
> Look for packaged polenta (a northern Italian staple) in the produce section or in the pasta and grain aisle at your grocery store.

Vegetable Quinoa

MEAT-LESS

PREP: 20 Min.   **COOK:** 20 Min.   **YIELD:** 4 Servings

This hearty specialty makes a delicious addition to grilled meals. You could even enjoy it as a main course with a salad or an extra vegetable.   —Kate Selner, Lino Lakes, Minnesota

>   1 cup quinoa, rinsed
>   1 can (14-1/2 ounces) reduced-sodium chicken broth
>   *or* vegetable broth
> 1/4 cup water
>   1 small onion, chopped
>   1 tablespoon olive oil
>   1 medium sweet red pepper, chopped
>   1 small carrot, chopped
> 1/2 cup chopped fresh broccoli
>   2 garlic cloves, minced
>   1 teaspoon dried basil
> 1/4 teaspoon pepper

In a small nonstick saucepan coated with cooking spray, toast quinoa over medium heat until lightly browned, stirring occasionally. Add broth and water; bring to a boil. Reduce heat; simmer, uncovered, for 14-18 minutes or until liquid is absorbed.

Meanwhile, in a large nonstick skillet, saute onion in oil for 2 minutes. Add the red pepper, carrot, broccoli and garlic; saute 3 minutes longer. Add basil and pepper; cook and stir just until vegetables are tender. Stir in quinoa; heat through.

NUTRITION FACTS: 1/2 cup equals 221 calories, 6 g fat (1 g saturated fat), 0 cholesterol, 288 mg sodium, 36 g carbohydrate, 4 g fiber, 8 g protein. **DIABETIC EXCHANGES:** 2 starch, 1 vegetable, 1/2 fat.

Lemon Risotto with Peas

(PICTURED BELOW)

PREP: 10 Min.   **COOK:** 30 Min.   **YIELD:** 8 Servings

Lemon adds a refreshing taste to my risotto dish that's perfect for spring. —Sue Dannahower, Denver, Colorado

- 4 to 4-1/2 cups reduced-sodium chicken broth
- 2 shallots, finely chopped
- 1 tablespoon butter
- 1-1/2 cups uncooked arborio rice
- 1/2 teaspoon dried thyme
- 1/4 teaspoon pepper
- 1/3 cup white wine *or* additional reduced-sodium chicken broth
- 3 tablespoons lemon juice
- 1 cup frozen peas, thawed
- 1/2 cup grated Parmesan cheese
- 1-1/2 teaspoons grated lemon peel

In a small saucepan, heat broth and keep warm. In a large non-stick skillet, saute shallots in butter for 2-3 minutes or until tender. Add the rice, thyme and pepper; cook and stir for 2-3 minutes. Stir in wine or additional broth and lemon juice. Cook and stir until all of the liquid is absorbed.

Stir in heated broth, 1/2 cup at a time, stirring constantly. Allow liquid to absorb between additions. Cook just until risotto is creamy and rice is almost tender. Total cooking time is about 20 minutes. Add the peas, Parmesan cheese and lemon peel; cook and stir until heated through. Serve immediately.

NUTRITION FACTS: 1/2 cup equals 207 calories, 3 g fat (2 g saturated fat), 8 mg cholesterol, 440 mg sodium, 35 g carbohydrate, 1 g fiber, 7 g protein. **DIABETIC EXCHANGES:** 2 starch, 1/2 fat.

Southwest Corn and Tomatoes

(PICTURED ABOVE)

REP: 20 Min.   **BAKE:** 20 Min.   **YIELD:** 6 Servings

I came up with this recipe to use an over-abundance of corn from the garden one year. Everyone liked it so much that I substituted frozen corn so I could make it all year-round.
—Trisha Kruse, Eagle, Idaho

- 1 package (16 ounces) frozen corn, thawed
- 5 plum tomatoes, seeded and coarsely chopped
- 1 large onion, chopped
- 2 jalapeno peppers, seeded and finely chopped
- 3 garlic cloves, minced
- 2 tablespoons olive oil
- 1/4 cup minced fresh cilantro
- 1/2 teaspoon salt

In a large bowl, combine the corn, tomatoes, onion, jalapenos and garlic. Drizzle with oil; toss to coat. Transfer to a 15-in. x 10-in. x 1-in. baking pan coated with cooking spray.

Bake at 425° for 20-25 minutes or until onion is tender, stirring twice. Spoon into a bowl. Stir in cilantro and salt. Serve warm.

NUTRITION FACTS: 2/3 cup equals 130 calories, 5 g fat (1 g saturated fat), 0 cholesterol, 205 mg sodium, 21 g carbohydrate, 3 g fiber, 3 g protein. **DIABETIC EXCHANGES:** 1 starch, 1 vegetable, 1 fat.

Editor's Note: When cutting or seeding hot peppers, use rubber or plastic gloves to protect your hands. Avoid touching your face.

Sweet Potatoes and Apples Au Gratin

FAT SALT CARB MEAT-LESS

(PICTURED ABOVE)

PREP: 25 Min. **BAKE:** 45 Min. **YIELD:** 12 Servings

This is a favorite of ours that we make every year, and people on both sides of the family rave about it!
—Erica Vickerman, Hopkins, Minnesota

>   3 cups thinly sliced tart apples (about 3 large)
>   1 teaspoon lemon juice
>   3 pounds sweet potatoes (about 5 medium), peeled and thinly sliced
> 1/4 cup maple syrup
>   1 tablespoon butter, melted
> 1/2 teaspoon salt
> 1/4 teaspoon pepper
>   1 cup soft bread crumbs
>   2 teaspoons olive oil
> 1/4 teaspoon ground cinnamon
> 1/4 teaspoon ground nutmeg
> 1/4 teaspoon cider vinegar

Place apples in a large bowl; sprinkle with lemon juice. Add the sweet potatoes, syrup, butter, salt and pepper; toss to coat.

Transfer to a 3-qt. baking dish coated with cooking spray. Bake, uncovered, at 400° for 35-40 minutes or until apples are tender, stirring once.

In a small bowl, combine the bread crumbs, oil, cinnamon, nutmeg and vinegar; sprinkle over potato mixture. Bake 10-15 minutes longer or until topping is golden brown.

NUTRITION FACTS: 1 serving equals 130 calories, 2 g fat (1 g saturated fat), 3 mg cholesterol, 136 mg sodium, 27 g carbohydrate, 3 g fiber, 2 g protein. **DIABETIC EXCHANGE:** 2 starch.

TASTY TIP
Have extra Sweet Potatoes and Apples Au Gratin? Mash the refrigerated leftovers. Shape the mixture into patties, dipping each in bread crumbs. Fry them in a nonstick pan for unique potato pancakes.

Favorite Recipe Made Lighter

A LIST of traditional side dishes would have to include the consummate classic…green bean casserole. From Kingfisher, Oklahoma, Donna Brockett shares an incredibly rich, cheesy version she's made for ages.

Our makeover team decided they needed to turn Donna's traditional casserole into a healthier product with the same amazing taste.

They began by looking at the sodium. Canned corn and beans were replaced with their frozen counterparts; however, the frozen beans didn't have the right texture, so the testers went back to canned. Using frozen corn alone saved nearly 200 mg of sodium. To lower the numbers further, they opted for a reduced-sodium, reduced-fat creamy soup.

Reduced-fat sour cream is lighter than the original, but it's still a significant source of fat, calories, saturated fat and cholesterol. Yogurt made a good substitution for some of the sour cream. The team tried a reduced-fat cheese, but it didn't melt as well as they would've liked. Instead, they kept the full-fat version, opting for more flavorful sharp cheddar cheese and reducing the amount overall. Finally, they replaced the margarine with a lesser amount of reduced-fat butter in the topping, and slightly reduced the amount of crackers, using their reduced-fat counterpart.

All of the hard work was worth it. The makeover is 44 percent lower in sodium, and a whopping 60 percent lower in fat. While the original is so decadent you might only make it for special occasions, Makeover Corn 'n' Green Bean Bake will be great for any event!

Corn 'n' Green Bean Bake

MEAT-LESS

PREP: 20 Min.   **BAKE:** 40 Min.   **YIELD:** 12 Servings

- 2 cans (15-1/4 ounces *each*) whole kernel corn, drained
- 2 cans (14-1/2 ounces *each*) French-style green beans, drained
- 2 cans (10-3/4 ounces *each*) condensed cream of mushroom soup, undiluted
- 2 cups (16 ounces) sour cream
- 2 cups (8 ounces) shredded cheddar cheese
- 1 large onion, chopped
- 1 celery rib, chopped
- 1 small green pepper, chopped
- 2-3/4 cups crushed butter-flavored crackers (about 70 crackers)
- 1/2 cup margarine, melted

In a large bowl, combine the first eight ingredients. Transfer to a greased 13-in. x 9-in. x 2-in. baking dish.

Toss the cracker crumbss and margarine; sprinkle over vegetable mixture. Bake, uncovered, at 350° for 40-45 minutes or until bubbly.

NUTRITION FACTS: 3/4 cup equals 424 calories, 28 g fat (12 g saturated fat), 49 mg cholesterol, 1,202 mg sodium, 29 g carbohydrate, 4 g fiber, 10 g protein.

Makeover Corn 'n' Green Bean Bake

MEAT-LESS

(PICTURED ABOVE)

PREP: 20 Min.   **BAKE:** 40 Min.   **YIELD:** 12 Servings

- 3-1/2 cups frozen corn, thawed
- 2 cans (14-1/2 ounces *each*) French-style green beans, drained
- 2 cans (10-3/4 ounces *each*) reduced-fat reduced-sodium condensed cream of mushroom soup, undiluted
- 1 cup (8 ounces) reduced-fat sour cream
- 1 cup (8 ounces) plain yogurt
- 1 cup (4 ounces) shredded sharp cheddar cheese
- 1 large onion, chopped
- 1 celery rib, chopped
- 1 small green pepper, chopped
- 2 cups crushed reduced-fat butter-flavored crackers (about 50 crackers)
- 1/3 cup reduced-fat butter, melted

In a large bowl, combine the first nine ingredients. Transfer to a 13-in. x 9-in. x 2-in. baking dish coated with cooking spray.

Toss the cracker crumbs and butter; sprinkle over vegetable mixture. Bake, uncovered, at 350° for 40-45 minutes or until bubbly.

NUTRITION FACTS: 3/4 cup equals 241 calories, 11 g fat (6 g saturated fat), 32 mg cholesterol, 679 mg sodium, 30 g carbohydrate, 3 g fiber, 8 g protein.

Editor's Note: This recipe was tested with Land O'Lakes light stick butter.

Home-Style Gravy

(PICTURED BELOW)

FAT CARB

PREP: 15 Min.   **COOK:** 45 Min.   **YIELD:** 3 Cups

Thinking of skipping the gravy this year because it's "bad" for you? Don't even think of it! Our Test Kitchen created this low-cal, low-fat gravy you won't believe.

   1 large onion, chopped
   1 medium carrot, chopped
   1 celery rib, chopped
   2 teaspoons canola oil
  1/2 cup sherry *or* unsweetened apple juice
2-1/2 cups water
  1/2 cup packed fresh parsley sprigs
   2 bay leaves
  1/4 cup all-purpose flour
   1 can (14-1/2 ounces) reduced-sodium chicken broth
   1 tablespoon turkey drippings
   1 teaspoon rubbed sage
  1/2 teaspoon browning sauce, optional
  1/4 teaspoon salt
  1/4 teaspoon pepper

In a large saucepan, saute the onion, carrot and celery in oil until tender. Add sherry or apple juice; cook and stir 1 minute longer. Add the water, parsley and bay leaves; bring to a boil. Reduce heat; simmer, uncovered, for 30 minutes or until liquid is nearly reduced by half.

   Strain and discard vegetables and herbs; set liquid aside (liquid should measure 1-1/2 cups). In a small saucepan, combine flour and broth until smooth. Stir in the drippings, sage, browning sauce if desired, salt, pepper and reserved liquid. Bring to a boil; cook and stir for 2 minutes or until thickened.

NUTRITION FACTS: 1/4 cup equals 31 calories, 2 g fat (1 g saturated fat), 1 mg cholesterol, 146 mg sodium, 3 g carbohydrate, trace fiber, 1 g protein. **DIABETIC EXCHANGE:** 1/2 fat.

Zucchini Cakes

PREP: 20 Min. + Chilling   **COOK:** 10 Min./Batch   **YIELD:** 4 Servings

I love these "crab cakes" that don't include any crab! Try the crispy zucchini patties when you need a new way to jazz up summer suppers.
          —Mary Wagner, Austin, Pennsylvania

   2 cups shredded zucchini
   1 cup seasoned bread crumbs
  1/2 cup quick-cooking oats
   2 tablespoons finely chopped onion
   1 tablespoon fat-free mayonnaise
1-1/2 teaspoons seafood seasoning
  1/2 teaspoon prepared mustard
   2 eggs, lightly beaten
   4 teaspoons canola oil

In a large bowl, combine the first seven ingredients. Stir in eggs until well blended. Cover and refrigerate for at least 1 hour.

   Shape into eight patties. In a large nonstick skillet coated with cooking spray, cook patties in oil in batches for 3-4 minutes on each side or until golden brown.

NUTRITION FACTS: 2 zucchini cakes equals 241 calories, 10 g fat (1 g saturated fat), 107 mg cholesterol, 750 mg sodium, 30 g carbohydrate, 3 g fiber, 9 g protein. **DIABETIC EXCHANGES:** 2 fat, 1-1/2 starch, 1 vegetable.

Winter Fruit Compote

SALT MEAT-LESS

PREP: 10 Min.   **COOK:** 1-1/4 Hours + Cooling   **YIELD:** 2-1/2 Cups

I like to make this colorful and easy fruit relish a few days early and refrigerate it. It makes a great accompaniment to turkey, chicken or pork throughout the holiday season.
          —Esther Chesney, Carthage, Missouri

   1 package (12 ounces) fresh *or* frozen cranberries, thawed
  2/3 cup packed brown sugar
  1/4 cup orange juice concentrate
   2 tablespoons raspberry vinegar
  1/2 cup chopped dried apricots
  1/2 cup golden raisins
  1/2 cup chopped walnuts, toasted

In a 1-1/2-qt. slow cooker, combine the cranberries, brown sugar, orange juice concentrate and vinegar. Cover and cook on low for 1-1/4 to 1-3/4 hours or until cranberries pop and mixture is thickened.

   Turn off the heat; stir in the apricots, raisins and walnuts. Cool to room temperature. Serve or refrigerate.

NUTRITION FACTS: 1/4 cup equals 161 calories, 4 g fat (trace saturated fat), 0 cholesterol, 12 mg sodium, 32 g carbohydrate, 3 g fiber, 2 g protein.

> **TASTY TIP**
> Feature colorful Winter Fruit Compote on your Thanksgiving or Christmas menu, and you can save yourself a bit of time during the busy holiday season! Simply prepare the dish well in advance and freeze it. It can be frozen for up to 2 months.

Garlic-Herb Orzo Pilaf

(PICTURED ABOVE)

MEAT-LESS

PREP: 10 Min.   **COOK:** 30 Min.   **YIELD:** 4 Servings

Mildly flavored and flecked with garlic and fresh herbs, this creamy side dish is always a welcomed addition to my menus. Best of all, the pilaf is a cinch to put together.

—Mary Relyea, Canastota, New York

    8 garlic cloves, peeled and thinly sliced
    1 tablespoon olive oil
1/2 cup uncooked orzo pasta
1/2 cup uncooked long grain rice
    1 can (14-1/2 ounces) reduced-sodium chicken broth *or* vegetable broth
1/3 cup water
    3 green onions, thinly sliced
1/3 cup thinly sliced fresh basil leaves
1/4 cup minced fresh parsley
1/4 teaspoon salt

In a large nonstick skillet coated with cooking spray, cook garlic in oil over medium-high heat for 2 minutes. Add orzo and rice; cook 4-6 minutes longer or until lightly browned.

Stir in broth and water. Bring to a boil. Reduce heat; cover and simmer for 15-20 minutes or until rice is tender and liquid is absorbed. Stir in the onions, basil, parsley and salt.

NUTRITION FACTS: 3/4 cup equals 227 calories, 4 g fat (1 g saturated fat), 0 cholesterol, 426 mg sodium, 40 g carbohydrate, 1 g fiber, 7 protein. **DIABETIC EXCHANGES:** 2-1/2 starch, 1/2 fat.

Summer Squash Stuffing Bake

PREP: 25 Min.   **BAKE:** 25 Min.   **YIELD:** 8 Servings

A convenient stuffing mix adds effortless flavor to this side dish casserole. I serve it with chicken and pork.

—Ruth Peterson, Jenison, Michigan

3/4 cup water
1/4 teaspoon salt
    4 medium yellow summer squash, cut into 1/4-inch slices
1/4 cup chopped onion
    1 package (8 ounces) stuffing mix
    2 tablespoons butter, melted
    1 can (10-3/4 ounces) reduced-fat reduced-sodium condensed cream of celery soup, undiluted
    1 cup (8 ounces) fat-free sour cream
    2 medium carrots, finely shredded

In a large saucepan, bring water and salt to a boil. Add squash and onion. Reduce heat; cover and simmer for 3-5 minutes or until squash is crisp-tender. In a small bowl, combine stuffing mix and butter; set aside.

In a large bowl, combine the soup, sour cream and carrots. Drain squash mixture; gently stir into soup mixture.

Place half of the stuffing mixture in a 3-qt. baking dish coated with cooking spray. Layer with squash mixture and remaining stuffing mixture. Bake, uncovered, at 350° for 25-30 minutes or until heated through and golden brown.

NUTRITION FACTS: 3/4 cup equals 229 calories, 7 g fat (2 g saturated fat), 14 mg cholesterol, 748 mg sodium, 34 g carbohydrate, 3 g fiber, 7 g protein. **DIABETIC EXCHANGES:** 2 starch, 1 vegetable, 1/2 fat.

Mushroom Rice

(PICTURED ABOVE)

MEAT-
LESS

PREP/TOTAL TIME: 25 Min.   **YIELD:** 8 Servings

Don't count on having any leftovers with this scrumptious dish. A friend gave me the recipe more than a decade ago, and it's been a family favorite ever since! —Beth McCaw, Nashville, Tennessee

    1 small onion, finely chopped
    1 celery rib, chopped
1/2 cup chopped celery leaves
    2 tablespoons butter
    1 pound sliced fresh mushrooms
    3 cups uncooked instant rice
    3 cups water
    4 teaspoons Greek seasoning
1/2 cup chopped pecans, toasted

In a large nonstick skillet coated with cooking spray, saute the onion, celery and celery leaves in butter for 4 minutes. Add mushrooms; cook 4 minutes longer.

Add rice; cook for 4-5 minutes or until lightly browned. Stir in the water and Greek seasoning. Bring to a boil. Remove from the heat; cover and let stand for 5 minutes. Fluff with a fork. Sprinkle with pecans.

NUTRITION FACTS: 1 cup equals 232 calories, 9 g fat (2 g saturated fat), 8 mg cholesterol, 529 mg sodium, 35 g carbohydrate, 2 g fiber, 5 g protein. **DIABETIC EXCHANGES:** 2 starch, 1-1/2 fat, 1 vegetable.

SHOP SMART

It's a snap to speed up the assembly of the moist side dish Mushroom Rice. Simply stop by your grocery store's produce department and pick up a container of chopped onions and a carton of presliced mushrooms. Don't have the pecans on hand? Leave them out or try replacing them with a can of sliced water chestnuts.

Barley Risotto

(PICTURED BELOW)

FAT SALT

PREP: 10 Min.   **COOK:** 30 Min.   **YIELD:** 4 Servings

Low in fat, but high in fiber, this delicious dish from our Test Kitchen puts a twist on typical risotto.

   3 cups water
   3 teaspoons sodium-free chicken bouillon granules
 3/4 cup medium pearl barley
 1/4 cup finely chopped onion
   1 teaspoon olive oil
   1 garlic clove, minced
 1/2 cup white wine *or* additional water
   3 tablespoons minced fresh parsley
   2 teaspoons grated lemon peel
 1/8 teaspoon salt

In a small saucepan, bring water to a boil; add bouillon and stir until dissolved. Reduce heat and keep warm.

In a large nonstick skillet over medium-high heat, cook and stir the barley for 2-4 minutes or until lightly browned. Transfer to a small bowl. In the same skillet, saute onion in oil for 2 minutes. Add garlic; saute 1 minute longer or until onion is tender. Stir in barley and wine or additional water. Cook and stir until all of the liquid is absorbed.

Add heated bouillon, 1/2 cup at a time, stirring constantly and allowing the liquid to absorb between additions. Cook just until barley is almost tender (cooking time is about 20 minutes). Add the parsley, lemon peel and salt; cook and stir until heated through. Serve immediately.

NUTRITION FACTS: 1/2 cup equals 175 calories, 2 g fat (trace saturated fat), 0 cholesterol, 84 mg sodium, 32 g carbohydrate, 6 g fiber, 4 g protein. **DIABETIC EXCHANGES:** 2 starch, 1/2 fat.

Garlic Mashed Cauliflower

(PICTURED ABOVE)

CARB MEAT-LESS

PREP/TOTAL TIME: 20 Min.   **YIELD:** 4 Servings

I've always enjoyed mashed cauliflower at a favorite restaurant, so I came up with this low-carb version I can prepare at home.
          —Jean Keiser, West Chester, Pennsylvania

   5 cups fresh cauliflowerets
   1 garlic clove, minced
   3 tablespoons fat-free milk
   3 tablespoons reduced-fat mayonnaise
 1/2 teaspoon salt
 1/8 teaspoon white pepper

Place 1 in. of water in a large saucepan; add cauliflower and garlic. Bring to a boil. Reduce heat; cover and simmer for 10-15 minutes or until tender.

Drain; transfer to a small mixing bowl. Add the milk, mayonnaise, salt and pepper; beat until blended. If desired, shape into individual molds by packing 1/2 cup mixture at a time into a 2-in. biscuit cutter.

NUTRITION FACTS: 1/2 cup equals 74 calories, 4 g fat (1 g saturated fat), 4 mg cholesterol, 428 mg sodium, 8 g carbohydrate, 3 g fiber, 3 g protein. **DIABETIC EXCHANGES:** 1 vegetable, 1 fat.

Colorful Rice Medley

(PICTURED AT LEFT)

PREP: 10 Min.   **COOK:** 25 Min.   **YIELD:** 6 Servings

I found this recipe while searching for something with peas that was different from what I usually serve guests. It's colorful, tasty and goes well with a variety of entrees.

—Dorothy Pritchett, Wills Point, Texas

   1/4 cup chopped onion
      1 tablespoon butter
   3/4 cup uncooked long grain rice
      1 small sweet red pepper, finely chopped
1-1/2 cups reduced-sodium chicken broth *or* vegetable broth
   1/4 cup white wine *or* additional reduced-sodium chicken broth
   1/2 teaspoon dried thyme
   1/8 teaspoon pepper
      1 cup frozen peas
   1/4 cup plus 1 tablespoon grated Parmesan cheese, *divided*

In a large saucepan coated with cooking spray, saute onion in butter for 1 minute. Add rice and red pepper; cook and stir for 3-4 minutes or until rice is lightly browned.

Stir in the broth, wine or additional broth, thyme and pepper. Bring to a boil. Reduce heat; cover and simmer for 15 minutes.

Stir in peas; cover and simmer 3-5 minutes longer or until rice is tender and peas are heated through. Stir in 1/4 cup Parmesan cheese. Sprinkle remaining Parmesan cheese over the top.

NUTRITION FACTS: 2/3 cup equals 155 calories, 3 g fat (2 g saturated fat), 8 mg cholesterol, 281 mg sodium, 24 g carbohydrate, 2 g fiber, 6 g protein. **DIABETIC EXCHANGES:** 1-1/2 starch, 1 fat.

Tomato Corn Toss

PREP/TOTAL TIME: 15 Min.   **YIELD:** 3 Servings

The microwave makes this medley a snap to prepare. Featuring banana peppers, tomatoes and corn, it's a lovely addition to summer meals. Best of all, it goes with just about any main course.

—Annette Marie Young, West Lafayette, Indiana

1 medium tomato, seeded and diced
1 to 2 banana peppers, seeded and chopped
2 tablespoons water
1 teaspoon salt-free seasoning blend
2 cups frozen corn, thawed
1 tablespoon butter

In a 1-qt. microwave-safe dish, combine the tomato, peppers, water and seasoning blend. Cover and microwave on high for 1 minute; stir. Cook 1 minute longer.

Stir in corn and butter. Cover and microwave for 2-3 minutes or until heated through and butter is melted.

NUTRITION FACTS: 3/4 cup equals 147 calories, 5 g fat (3 g saturated fat), 10 mg cholesterol, 50 mg sodium, 26 g carbohydrate, 4 g fiber, 4 g protein. **DIABETIC EXCHANGES:** 1-1/2 starch, 1/2 fat.

Editor's Note: This recipe was tested in a 1,100-watt microwave. When cutting or seeding hot peppers, use rubber or plastic gloves to protect your hands. Avoid touching your face.

TASTY TIP
Turn the rice medley into a light main course by stirring in a bag of frozen, cooked shrimp. Quickly thaw the shrimp by running cold water over them.

Breakfast & Brunch

Feel your best each and every day with a delicious sunrise delight. Not only are these daybreak specialties tasty, but they make eating right a snap. Whether you're looking for a no-fuss way to start the workday or a contribution to a Sunday brunch, stop here for the perfect eye-opener.

Sweet Berry Bruschetta, p. 90

Pumpkin Seed Cranberry Biscotti

FAT SALT CARB

(PICTURED BELOW)

PREP: 30 Min.   **BAKE:** 35 Min. + Cooling   **YIELD:** 2-1/2 Dozen

A hint of pumpkin seed and almond gives this biscotti a wonderful flavor that's just right for fall!

—Nancy Renner, Sequim, Washington

      3/4 cup sugar
        2 eggs
      1/4 cup canola oil
  1-1/2 teaspoons vanilla extract
      1/2 teaspoon almond extract
  1-3/4 cups all-purpose flour
        1 teaspoon baking powder
      1/2 teaspoon salt
        1 cup pumpkin seeds, toasted
      1/2 cup dried cranberries

In a small mixing bowl, beat the sugar, eggs, oil and extracts. Combine the flour, baking powder and salt; gradually add to sugar mixture and mix well. Stir in pumpkin seeds and cranberries (dough will be sticky).

Divide dough in half; place on a baking sheet coated with cooking spray. With lightly floured hands, shape each portion into a 12-in. x 2-in. rectangle. Bake at 350° for 25-30 minutes or until golden brown.

Carefully remove to wire racks; cool for 10 minutes. Transfer to a cutting board; cut diagonally with a serrated knife into 3/4-in. slices. Place cut side down on ungreased baking sheets.

Bake for 5 minutes or until firm. Turn and bake 5-10 minutes longer or until lightly browned. Remove to wire racks to cool. Store in an airtight container.

NUTRITION FACTS: 1 cookie equals 84 calories, 3 g fat (trace saturated fat), 14 mg cholesterol, 57 mg sodium, 13 g carbohydrate, trace fiber, 2 g protein. **DIABETIC EXCHANGES:** 1 starch, 1/2 fat.

Savory Apple-Chicken Sausage

CARB

(PICTURED ABOVE)

PREP/TOTAL TIME: 25 Min.   **YIELD:** 8 Patties

These easy, healthy sausage patties are very versatile. They can be doubled or tripled for a crowd, and they freeze well.

—Angela Buchanan, Longmont, Colorado

        1 large tart apple, peeled and diced
        2 teaspoons poultry seasoning
        1 teaspoon salt
      1/4 teaspoon pepper
        1 pound ground chicken

In a large bowl, combine the apple, poultry seasoning, salt and pepper. Crumble chicken over mixture and mix well. Shape into eight 3-in. patties.

In a large skillet coated with cooking spray, cook patties over medium heat for 5-6 minutes on each side or until no longer pink. Drain if necessary.

NUTRITION FACTS: 1 patty equals 92 calories, 5 g fat (1 g saturated fat), 38 mg cholesterol, 328 mg sodium, 4 g carbohydrate, 1 g fiber, 9 g protein. **DIABETIC EXCHANGES:** 1 lean meat, 1/2 fruit.

Sun-Kissed Smoothies

FAT SALT

PREP/TOTAL TIME: 10 Min.   **YIELD:** 3 Servings

Grapefruit, banana, pineapple and peaches flavor this refreshing, satisfying summertime smoothie from our Test Kitchen.

      3/4 cup ruby red grapefruit juice
        1 medium ripe banana, cut into chunks and frozen
      1/2 cup cubed fresh pineapple
      1/2 cup frozen unsweetened peach slices
        4 ice cubes
        1 tablespoon sugar

In a blender, combine all ingredients; cover and process for 30-45 seconds or until smooth. Pour into chilled glasses; serve immediately.

NUTRITION FACTS: 3/4 cup equals 100 calories, trace fat (trace saturated fat), 0 cholesterol, 2 mg sodium, 25 g carbohydrate, 2 g fiber, 1 g protein. **DIABETIC EXCHANGES:** 1 fruit, 1/2 starch.

Granola-Topped Pear Crisp

(PICTURED BELOW)

SALT

PREP: 20 Min. **BAKE:** 25 Min. **YIELD:** 8 Servings

Lots of crunchy topping and just the right amount of sweetness make this a delicious dish. With fruit and granola, it's perfect for brunch or breakfast. —Pat Habiger, Spearville, Kansas

  4 medium pears, peeled and thinly sliced
  2 tablespoons cornstarch
  1/2 cup peach preserves, warmed
TOPPING:
  1/3 cup all-purpose flour
  1/3 cup sugar
  3/4 teaspoon ground cinnamon
  1/4 teaspoon salt
  1/8 teaspoon ground nutmeg
  3 tablespoons cold butter
  1 cup granola with fruit and nuts

Place pears in a large bowl; sprinkle with cornstarch and toss to coat. Gently stir in preserves just until combined. Transfer to an 11-in. x 7-in. x 2-in. baking dish coated with cooking spray.

For topping, in a small bowl, combine the flour, sugar, cinnamon, salt and nutmeg. Cut in butter until crumbly; stir in granola. Sprinkle over fruit mixture.

Bake at 375° for 25-30 minutes or until topping is golden brown and fruit is tender. Serve warm.

NUTRITION FACTS: 1 serving equals 244 calories, 7 g fat (3 g saturated fat), 11 mg cholesterol, 132 mg sodium, 46 g carbohydrate, 3 g fiber, 2 g protein.

Triple-Berry Smoothies

FAT SALT

PREP/TOTAL TIME: 15 Min. **YIELD:** 4 Servings

This smoothie is fantastic and is packed with protein and berries. No one knows it calls for tofu until we tell them, but even then, they can't believe it. —Allison Tunaley, Lookout, California

  2 cups vanilla soy milk
  1 teaspoon vanilla extract
  6 ounces silken firm tofu
  1 small banana, sliced and frozen
  1/2 cup *each* frozen unsweetened raspberries, blackberries and strawberries
  1 tablespoon sugar
  4 tablespoons reduced-fat whipped topping

In a blender, combine the soy milk, vanilla, tofu, banana, berries and sugar. Cover and process until smooth. Pour into chilled glasses; garnish with whipped topping and serve immediately.

NUTRITION FACTS: 1 cup equals 146 calories, 3 g fat (1 g saturated fat), 0 cholesterol, 75 mg sodium, 22 g carbohydrate, 2 g fiber, 7 g protein.
DIABETIC EXCHANGES: 1 fruit, 1 reduced-fat milk.

Florence-Inspired Souffle
(PICTURED ABOVE)

PREP: 35 Min.   **BAKE:** 35 Min.   **YIELD:** 4 Servings

This souffle is not only absolutely delicious, but it's light and beautiful as well. Your guests will be impressed every time it graces your brunch buffet.   —Jenny Flake, Gilbert, Arizona

    6 egg whites
  3/4 cup onion and garlic salad croutons
    1 small onion, finely chopped
  1/4 cup finely chopped sweet red pepper
    2 ounces thinly sliced prosciutto, chopped
    1 garlic clove, minced
    2 teaspoons olive oil
    2 cups fresh baby spinach
  1/3 cup all-purpose flour
  1/2 teaspoon salt
  1/4 teaspoon pepper
1-1/4 cups fat-free milk
    1 egg yolk, beaten
  1/4 teaspoon cream of tartar
  1/4 cup shredded Italian cheese blend

Let egg whites stand at room temperature for 30 minutes. Place croutons in a food processor; cover and process until ground. Sprinkle evenly onto the bottom and 1 in. up the sides of a 2-qt. baking dish coated with cooking spray; set aside.

In a large saucepan, saute the onion, red pepper, prosciutto and garlic in oil for 3-5 minutes or until vegetables are crisp-tender. Add spinach; cook just until wilted. Stir in flour, salt and pepper until blended; gradually add milk. Bring to a boil; cook and stir for 2 minutes or until thickened. Transfer to a large bowl.

Stir a small amount of hot mixture into egg yolk; return all to the bowl, stirring constantly. Allow to cool slightly.

In a large mixing bowl, beat egg whites and cream of tartar until stiff peaks form. Fold into vegetable mixture. Transfer to prepared dish; sprinkle with cheese. Bake at 350° for 35-40 minutes or until the top is puffed and center appears set. Serve immediately.

NUTRITION FACTS: 1 serving equals 223 calories, 9 g fat (3 g saturated fat), 73 mg cholesterol, 843 mg sodium, 20 g carbohydrate, 2 g fiber, 16 g protein. **DIABETIC EXCHANGES:** 2 lean meat, 1-1/2 starch.

Quince Orange Marmalade

PREP: 30 Min.   **COOK:** 1-1/2 Hours + Chilling   **YIELD:** 3 Cups

Quince sweetens this unique marmalade from our Test Kitchen. Try it on toasted bagels.

    5 cups chopped peeled quinces (about 4 medium)
1-1/2 cups water
1-1/3 cups sugar
    1 cup orange juice
    1 tablespoon grated orange peel

In a large saucepan, combine all ingredients. Bring to a boil. Reduce heat; simmer, uncovered, for 1-1/2 to 1-3/4 hours or until mixture is reduced to 3 cups, stirring frequently.

Cool slightly; carefully mash. Cool to room temperature. Cover and refrigerate for several hours or overnight before serving. Store in airtight containers in the refrigerator for up to 3 weeks or freeze for longer storage.

NUTRITION FACTS: 2 tablespoons equals 58 calories, trace fat (trace saturated fat), 0 cholesterol, 1 mg sodium, 15 g carbohydrate, trace fiber, trace protein. **DIABETIC EXCHANGE:** 1 starch.

Favorite Recipe Made Lighter

STARTING the day off on a healthy note is easy with a bowl of satisfying granola. "I have a favorite recipe, Toasted Granola, which my family loves," shares Susan Lajeunesse of Colchester, Vermont. "I would like a trimmed-down version we could enjoy anytime."

Susan came to the right place. With some simple changes, our home economists cut half the fat and a third of the calories from each serving.

In addition, the recipe includes a jar of wheat germ. Wheat germ is the "heart" of the wheat kernel. It's a concentrated source of several nutrients including Vitamin E and folate, so it's a healthful addition to the granola. (Look for wheat germ in your grocery store's cereal aisle.)

Even a straightforward recipe can pose some challenges. Initially, the team members wanted to decrease the sugar, while keeping the granola sweet, and decrease the oil, while keeping it crunchy. Substituting naturally sweet bran flakes for some of the oats was the answer.

Unlike oats, which need a light coating of oil to become crunchy, bran flakes are crunchy to begin with. By decreasing water, the resulting Makeover Toasted Granola keeps all of the original's crunch and sweetness.

That's good news for Susan and her family because they can enjoy this lighter treat in all of their favorite ways. "We sprinkle it over yogurt and ice cream; we eat it with milk like cereal; and we love to eat it right from the container," Susan says. Now she and her gang can grab handfuls of the yummy granola and still keep their commitments to eating right!

Toasted Granola

PREP: 20 Min. **BAKE:** 1-3/4 Hours + Cooling **YIELD:** 11-1/2 Cups

2-1/4 cups packed brown sugar
2/3 cup water
6 cups old-fashioned oats
1 jar (12 ounces) toasted wheat germ
1/2 cup all-purpose flour
1 teaspoon salt
1 cup vegetable oil
2 teaspoons vanilla extract

In a large saucepan, bring brown sugar and water to a boil. Cook and stir until sugar is dissolved. Remove from the heat; set aside. In a large bowl, combine the oats, wheat germ, flour and salt. Stir oil and vanilla into sugar mixture; pour over oat mixture and toss to coat.

Transfer to two greased 15-in. x 10-in. x 1-in. baking pans. Bake at 250° for 1-3/4 to 2 hours or until dry and lightly browned, stirring every 15 minutes. Cool completely on wire racks. Store in an airtight container.

NUTRITION FACTS: 1/2 cup equals 307 calories, 12 g fat (2 g saturated fat), 0 cholesterol, 113 mg sodium, 44 g carbohydrate, 4 g fiber, 8 g protein.

Makeover Toasted Granola
(PICTURED ABOVE)

PREP: 20 Min. **BAKE:** 1-1/4 Hours + Cooling **YIELD:** 10-1/2 Cups

1 cup packed brown sugar
1/3 cup water
4 cups old-fashioned oats
2 cups bran flakes
1 jar (12 ounces) toasted wheat germ
2 tablespoons all-purpose flour
3/4 teaspoon salt
1/3 cup canola oil
2 teaspoons vanilla extract

In a large saucepan, bring brown sugar and water to a boil. Cook and stir until sugar is dissolved. Remove from the heat; set aside. In a large bowl, combine the oats, bran flakes, wheat germ, flour and salt. Stir oil and vanilla into sugar mixture; pour over oat mixture and toss to coat.

Transfer to two 15-in. x 10-in. x 1-in. baking pans coated with cooking spray. Bake at 250° for 1-1/4 to 1-1/2 hours or until dry and lightly browned, stirring every 15 minutes. Cool completely on wire racks. Store in an airtight container.

NUTRITION FACTS: 1/2 cup equals 202 calories, 6 g fat (1 g saturated fat), 0 cholesterol, 118 mg sodium, 32 g carbohydrate, 4 g fiber, 8 g protein. **DIABETIC EXCHANGES:** 2 starch, 1 fat.

> **MAKEOVER TIP**
> Canola oil is a healthy substitution for vegetable oil in recipes. Replace the oil in equal amounts and you should find little to no difference in taste.

Spinach Omelet Brunch Roll

CARB

(PICTURED BELOW)

PREP: 20 Min.   **BAKE:** 15 Min.   **YIELD:** 8 Servings

This recipe uses the combination of veggies from one of my favorite recipes and the rolling technique of another. The result is this stunning presentation, which tastes as good as it looks.

—Laine Beal, Topeka, Kansas

      2 cups egg substitute
      4 eggs
  1/2 teaspoon salt
  1/8 teaspoon hot pepper sauce
      1 package (10 ounces) frozen chopped spinach, thawed
         and squeezed dry
  1/4 cup chopped red onion
      1 teaspoon Italian seasoning
      5 turkey bacon strips, diced and cooked, *divided*
      1 pound sliced fresh mushrooms
      2 teaspoons canola oil
      1 cup (4 ounces) shredded part-skim mozzarella cheese,
         divided

Line a 15-in. x 10-in. x 1-in. baking pan with parchment paper; coat paper with cooking spray and set aside. In a large bowl, whisk the egg substitute, eggs, salt and pepper sauce. Stir in the spinach, onion, Italian seasoning and 1/4 cup bacon.

Pour into prepared pan. Bake at 375° for 15-20 minutes or until set. Meanwhile, in a large nonstick skillet, saute mushrooms in oil for 6-8 minutes or until tender. Drain on paper towels; blot to remove excess moisture. Keep warm.

Turn omelet onto a work surface; peel off parchment paper. Sprinkle omelet with mushrooms and 3/4 cup cheese; roll up jelly-roll style, starting with a short side. Place on a serving platter. Sprinkle with remaining cheese and bacon.

NUTRITION FACTS: 1 slice equals 160 calories, 8 g fat (3 g saturated fat), 122 mg cholesterol, 505 mg sodium, 6 g carbohydrate, 2 g fiber, 17 g protein. **DIABETIC EXCHANGES:** 2 lean meat, 1 vegetable, 1/2 fat.

Coffee Angel Food Cake

FAT

PREP: 20 Min.   **BAKE:** 35 Min. + Cooling   **YIELD:** 12 Servings

This special cake tastes great with minimal calories. It's a tender treat with a subtle coffee flavor that's sure to be a hit. You'll find that it's wonderful for nearly any occasion.

—Patricia Bristow, St. Louis, Missouri

       12 egg whites
        2 tablespoons instant coffee granules
        2 tablespoons boiling water
  1-1/4 cups cake flour
     3/4 cup sugar
        1 teaspoon cream of tartar
  1-1/2 teaspoons vanilla extract
     1/2 teaspoon almond extract
     1/2 teaspoon salt
     3/4 cup packed brown sugar

Place egg whites in a large mixing bowl; let stand at room temperature for 30 minutes. In a small bowl, dissolve coffee granules in boiling water; set aside. Sift flour and sugar together twice; set aside.

Add the cream of tartar, extracts, salt and coffee mixture to egg whites; beat on medium speed until soft peaks form. Gradually add brown sugar, about 2 tablespoons at a time, beating on high until stiff glossy peaks form and sugar is dissolved. Gradually fold in flour mixture, about 1/2 cup at a time.

Gently spoon into an ungreased 10-in. tube pan. Cut through batter with a knife to remove air pockets. Bake on the lowest oven rack at 350° for 35-40 minutes or until lightly browned and entire top appears dry. Immediately invert pan; cool completely, about 1 hour.

Run a knife around side and center tube of pan. Remove cake to a serving plate.

NUTRITION FACTS: 1 slice equals 172 calories, trace fat (trace saturated fat), 0 cholesterol, 159 mg sodium, 38 g carbohydrate, trace fiber, 5 g protein.

So-Healthy Smoothies

FAT SALT

PREP/TOTAL TIME: 15 Min.   **YIELD:** 4 Servings

This tastes like a milk shake, but it doesn't have all the guilt or fat. My husband and I look forward to it every day for breakfast. It keeps you energized for hours.

—Jessica Gerschitz, Jericho, New York

      1 cup fat-free milk
  1/4 cup orange juice
      2 tablespoons vanilla yogurt
      1 tablespoon honey
      1 small banana, sliced and frozen
  2/3 cup frozen blueberries
  1/2 cup chopped peeled mango, frozen
  1/4 cup frozen unsweetened peach slices

In a blender, combine all ingredients; cover and process until smooth. Pour into chilled glasses; serve immediately.

NUTRITION FACTS: 3/4 cup equals 107 calories, 1 g fat (trace saturated fat), 2 mg cholesterol, 38 mg sodium, 24 g carbohydrate, 2 g fiber, 3 g protein. **DIABETIC EXCHANGES:** 1 fruit, 1/2 starch.

Christmas Morning Wreaths

(PICTURED ABOVE)

PREP: 40 Min. + Rising   **BAKE:** 20 Min. + Cooling
YIELD: 3 Wreaths (15 Slices Each)

We like to keep one of these three wreaths and deliver the others to family and friends on Christmas Eve.
—Virginia Kreamer-Lutz, Fort Wayne, Indiana

  2 packages (1/4 ounce *each*) active dry yeast
1/2 cup warm water (110° to 115°)
2-1/2 cups whole wheat flour
2-1/2 cups all-purpose flour
1/4 cup sugar
  1 teaspoon salt
  1 cup cold reduced-fat butter, cubed
  1 egg white, lightly beaten
  1 cup warm fat-free milk (110° to 115°)

FILLING:
1-1/2 cups chopped dates
  1 cup chopped pecans
  1 cup packed brown sugar
3/4 cup golden raisins
3/4 cup raisins
  3 teaspoons ground cinnamon
  3 tablespoons reduced-fat butter, melted

ICING:
  2 cups confectioners' sugar
  2 to 3 tablespoons fat-free evaporated milk

In a small bowl, dissolve yeast in warm water. In a large mixing bowl, combine the whole wheat flour, 1 cup all-purpose flour, sugar and salt. Cut in butter until crumbly. Combine egg white and milk; add to flour mixture. Add yeast mixture; beat until smooth. Stir in enough remaining all-purpose flour to form a firm dough.

Turn onto a lightly floured surface; knead until smooth and elastic, about 6-8 minutes. Place in a bowl coated with cooking spray, turning once to coat the top. Cover and refrigerate overnight.

Punch dough down. Turn onto a lightly floured surface; divide into three equal portions. Roll each portion into an 18-in. x 12-in. rectangle. In a large bowl, combine the dates, pecans, brown sugar, raisins and cinnamon. Brush dough with butter; sprinkle with filling to within 1/2 in. of edges. Roll up tightly jelly-roll style, starting with a long side; pinch seam to seal.

Place seam side down on baking sheets coated with cooking spray; pinch ends together to form a ring. With scissors, cut from outside edge two-thirds of the way toward center of ring at 1-in. intervals. Separate strips slightly; twist so filling shows. Cover and let rise until doubled, about 40 minutes.

Bake at 350° for 18-23 minutes or until golden brown. Cool on wire racks. Combine icing ingredients; drizzle over wreaths.

NUTRITION FACTS: 1 slice equals 166 calories, 5 g fat (2 g saturated fat), 9 mg cholesterol, 90 mg sodium, 30 g carbohydrate, 2 g fiber, 3 g protein. **DIABETIC EXCHANGES:** 2 starch, 1/2 fat.

Editor's Note: This recipe was tested with Land O'Lakes light stick butter.

TASTY TIP
The wreaths are much easier to create than they appear. Knead the dough on the first day, and on the second day, shape and bake the three loaves.

Sweet Berry Bruschetta

FAT CARB

(PICTURED ABOVE)

PREP/TOTAL TIME: 20 Min.   **YIELD:** 10 Pieces

I've made this recipe by toasting the bread on a grill at cookouts, but any way I serve it, I never have any leftovers.
—Patricia Nieh, Portola Valley, California

      10 slices French bread (1/2 inch thick)
       5 teaspoons sugar, *divided*
       6 ounces fat-free cream cheese
      1/2 teaspoon almond extract
      3/4 cup fresh blackberries
      3/4 cup fresh raspberries
      1/4 cup slivered almonds, toasted
       2 teaspoons confectioners' sugar

Place bread on an ungreased baking sheet; lightly coat with cooking spray. Sprinkle with 2 teaspoons sugar. Broil 3-4 in. from the heat for 1-2 minutes or until lightly browned.

   In a small bowl, combine the cream cheese, almond extract and remaining sugar. Spread over toasted bread. Top with berries and almonds; dust with confectioners' sugar.

NUTRITION FACTS: 1 piece equals 92 calories, 2 g fat (trace saturated fat), 1 mg cholesterol, 179 mg sodium, 14 g carbohydrate, 2 g fiber, 4 g protein. **DIABETIC EXCHANGES:** 1 starch, 1/2 fat.

Oat 'n' Nut Griddle Cakes

MEAT-LESS

PREP: 15 Min.   **COOK:** 10 Min./Batch   **YIELD:** 12 Griddle Cakes

I created this recipe to satisfy my craving for something sweet.
—Sharon Schenker, Walkertown, North Carolina

   1-1/4 cups all-purpose flour
       2 teaspoons baking powder
      1/2 teaspoon salt
      1/2 teaspoon ground cinnamon
       1 egg, beaten
       1 cup fat-free milk
       1 tablespoon canola oil
       1 tablespoon honey
      1/2 cup quick-cooking oats
      1/2 cup chopped pecans

In a small bowl, combine the flour, baking powder, salt and cinnamon. Combine the egg, milk, oil and honey; stir into dry ingredients just until moistened. Fold in oats and pecans.

   Pour batter by scant 1/4 cupfuls onto a hot griddle coated with cooking spray. Turn when bubbles form on top; cook until the second side is golden brown.

NUTRITION FACTS: 2 griddle cakes equals 248 calories, 11 g fat (1 g saturated fat), 36 mg cholesterol, 363 mg sodium, 31 g carbohydrate, 2 g fiber, 7 g protein. **DIABETIC EXCHANGES:** 2 starch, 2 fat.

Berry Best Smoothies

(PICTURED BELOW)

FAT SALT

PREP/TOTAL TIME: 10 Min.   **YIELD:** 3 Servings

This fun recipe is a wonderful way to use up over-ripened bananas and to help my family get more servings of fruit. It's so quick, easy and filling—and my kids absolutely love it!
—Pamela Klim, Bettendorf, Iowa

- 3 tablespoons orange juice concentrate
- 3 tablespoons fat-free half-and-half
- 12 ice cubes
- 1 cup fresh strawberries, hulled
- 1 medium ripe banana, cut into chunks
- 1/2 cup fresh *or* frozen blueberries
- 1/2 cup fresh *or* frozen raspberries

In a blender, combine all ingredients; cover and process for 30-45 seconds or until smooth. Pour into chilled glasses; serve immediately.

NUTRITION FACTS: 1 cup equals 108 calories, 1 g fat (trace saturated fat), 0 cholesterol, 14 mg sodium, 26 g carbohydrate, 4 g fiber, 2 g protein. **DIABETIC EXCHANGE:** 1-1/2 fruit.

Mini Ham 'n' Cheese Frittatas

(PICTURED ABOVE)

CARB

PREP: 15 Min.   **BAKE:** 25 Min.   **YIELD:** 8 Frittatas

I found this recipe a few years ago and tried to make it with a few changes. I'm diabetic, and this fits into my low-carb and low-fat diet. Every time I serve a brunch, the frittatas are the first thing to disappear, and nobody knows they are low in fat!
—Susan Watt, Basking Ridge, New Jersey

- 1/4 pound cubed fully cooked lean ham
- 1 cup (4 ounces) shredded fat-free cheddar cheese
- 6 eggs
- 4 egg whites
- 3 tablespoons minced chives
- 2 tablespoons fat-free milk
- 1/4 teaspoon salt
- 1/4 teaspoon pepper

Divide ham evenly among eight muffin cups coated with cooking spray; top with cheese. In a large bowl, beat eggs and whites. Beat in the chives, milk, salt and pepper. Pour over cheese, filling each muffin cup three-fourths full.

Bake at 375° for 22-25 minutes or until a knife inserted near the center comes out clean. Carefully run a knife around edges to loosen; remove from pan. Serve warm.

NUTRITION FACTS: 1 frittata equals 106 calories, 4 g fat (1 g saturated fat), 167 mg cholesterol, 428 mg sodium, 2 g carbohydrate, trace fiber, 14 g protein. **DIABETIC EXCHANGE:** 2 lean meat.

Favorite Recipe Made Lighter

YOU CAN'T BEAT a good coffee cake. And Janice Kuhlmann's Sour Cream Coffee Cake is exactly that. With a tender interior and a slightly crunchy crust, it has lovely lemon, almond and walnut flavors. It's an ideal addition to a Sunday brunch buffet, a wonderful hostess gift or a heartwarming snack cake to enjoy with a cup of steaming hot coffee or tea.

The Stafford Springs, Connecticut reader thought the original sweet was high in fat and calories, so she decided to give our makeover process a try. And, wow, did she succeed! As she writes, "I'd like to share with everyone a makeover recipe that I created myself."

With some smart substitutions and decisions, Janice earned an honorary spot on our makeover team. She began by halving the original recipe's butter and swapped egg whites for some of the whole eggs. To make up for the loss in tenderness and richness, she added extra reduced-fat sour cream. And, to cut back on fat and calories, she decreased the walnuts, opting to toast a smaller amount in order to maintain the nutty taste.

Janice's Makeover Sour Cream Coffee Cake is a delectable success! She cut over half of the fat, saturated fat and cholesterol and saved more than 100 calories per serving without losing any of the scrumptious taste that really makes this treat take the cake!

Sour Cream Coffee Cake

PREP: 30 Min. BAKE: 50 Min. + Cooling YIELD: 16 Servings

 1 cup butter, softened
 2 cups sugar
 6 eggs
 2 teaspoons lemon juice
 1 teaspoon grated lemon peel
1/2 teaspoon almond extract
 3 cups all-purpose flour
 1 teaspoon baking soda
3/4 teaspoon salt
 1 cup (8 ounces) sour cream
 1 cup chopped walnuts
 2 teaspoons confectioners' sugar

In a large mixing bowl, cream butter and sugar. Add eggs, one at a time, beating well after each addition. Stir in the lemon juice, lemon peel and extract. Combine the flour, baking soda and salt; add to creamed mixture alternately with sour cream. Fold in walnuts.

Transfer to a greased and floured 10-in. fluted tube pan. Bake at 350° for 50-60 minutes or until a toothpick comes out clean. Cool for 10 minutes before removing from pan to a wire rack to cool completely. Dust with confectioners' sugar.

NUTRITION FACTS: 1 slice equals 390 calories, 20 g fat (10 g saturated fat), 120 mg cholesterol, 337 mg sodium, 45 g carbohydrate, 1 g fiber, 7 g protein.

Makeover Sour Cream Coffee Cake
(PICTURED ABOVE)

PREP: 30 Min. BAKE: 50 Min. + Cooling YIELD: 16 Servings

 1/2 cup butter, softened
 2 cups sugar
 1 egg
 4 egg whites
 2 teaspoons lemon juice
 1 teaspoon grated lemon peel
1/2 teaspoon almond extract
 3 cups all-purpose flour
 1 teaspoon baking soda
3/4 teaspoon salt
1-1/2 cups (12 ounces) reduced-fat sour cream
 1/4 cup chopped walnuts, toasted
 2 teaspoons confectioners' sugar

In a large mixing bowl, beat butter and sugar until crumbly, about 2 minutes. Add egg, then egg whites, beating well after each addition. Stir in the lemon juice, lemon peel and extract. Combine the flour, baking soda and salt; add to butter mixture alternately with sour cream. Fold in walnuts.

Coat a 10-in. fluted tube pan with cooking spray and dust with flour; add batter. Bake at 350° for 50-60 minutes or until a toothpick comes out clean. Cool for 10 minutes before removing from pan to a wire rack to cool completely. Dust with confectioners' sugar.

NUTRITION FACTS: 1 slice equals 285 calories, 9 g fat (5 g saturated fat), 36 mg cholesterol, 280 mg sodium, 45 g carbohydrate, 1 g fiber, 6 g protein.

Gingerbread Cinnamon Rolls

PREP: 25 Min. + Rising **BAKE:** 20 Min. **YIELD:** 1 Dozen

Molasses and ginger make these cinnamon rolls an exceptional choice for holiday breakfasts. —Marilyn Stroud, Larsen, Wisconsin

 1 cup water (70° to 80°)
 1/2 cup molasses
 1 egg, beaten
 2 tablespoons canola oil
 2 tablespoons toasted wheat germ
 1 teaspoon ground ginger
 3/4 teaspoon salt
 1/2 teaspoon ground cinnamon
 1/4 teaspoon ground nutmeg
 1/4 teaspoon ground cloves
 3-3/4 cups all-purpose flour
 1 package (1/4 ounce) active dry yeast
FILLING:
 2 tablespoons butter, softened
 1/3 cup packed brown sugar
 1/4 cup raisins
 1 teaspoon ground cinnamon
 Confectioners' sugar, optional

In bread machine pan, place the first 12 ingredients in order suggested by manufacturer. Select dough setting (check dough after 5 minutes of mixing; add 1 to 2 tablespoons of water or flour if needed). When cycle is completed, turn dough onto a well-floured surface.

Roll into a 12-in. x 8-in. rectangle; spread with butter. Combine the brown sugar, raisins and cinnamon; sprinkle over dough to within 1/2 in. of edges. Roll up jelly-roll style, starting with a long side; pinch seam to seal. Cut into 12 slices.

Place cut side down in an 11-in. x 7-in. x 2-in. baking dish coated with cooking spray. Cover and let rise until nearly doubled, about 40 minutes. Bake at 375° for 20-25 minutes or until golden brown. Dust with confectioners' sugar if desired.

NUTRITION FACTS: 1 roll equals 261 calories, 5 g fat (2 g saturated fat), 23 mg cholesterol, 181 mg sodium, 49 g carbohydrate, 2 g fiber, 5 g protein.

Fruit Skewers with Ginger Dip

SALT MEAT-
↓ LESS

PREP: 20 Min. + Chilling **YIELD:** 8 Skewers (1-1/2 Cups Dip)

A friend shared this refreshing recipe with us, and my husband and I thought it was simply delicious. Laced with lime, ginger and honey, the creamy dip is great all year-round.
—Cindy Winter-Hartley, Apex, North Carolina

 2/3 cup reduced-fat spreadable strawberry cream cheese
 2/3 cup reduced-fat sour cream
 1/4 cup lime juice
 3 tablespoons honey
 1/2 teaspoon ground ginger
 2 cups green grapes
 2 cups fresh *or* canned unsweetened pineapple chunks
 2 large red apples, cut into 1-inch pieces

For dip, in a small mixing bowl, beat cream cheese and sour cream until smooth. Add the lime juice, honey and ginger; mix well. Cover and refrigerate for at least 1 hour.

On eight 12-in. skewers, alternately thread the grapes, pineapple and apples. Serve immediately with dip.

NUTRITION FACTS: 1 skewer with 3 tablespoons dip equals 180 calories, 5 g fat (1 g saturated fat), 18 mg cholesterol, 104 mg sodium, 28 g carbohydrate, 2 g fiber, 4 g protein. **DIABETIC EXCHANGES:** 1 starch, 1 fruit, 1 fat.

Coffee Lover's Coffee Cake
(PICTURED BELOW)

PREP: 25 Min. **BAKE:** 25 Min. **YIELD:** 9 Servings

I had this cake at a friend's brunch, and she graciously shared the recipe. Now people always request it from me because it's so delightful. —Gale Lalmond, Deering, New Hampshire

 1/3 cup sugar
 4-1/2 teaspoons instant coffee granules
 1-1/2 teaspoons ground cinnamon
BATTER:
 3 tablespoons butter, softened
 1/2 cup sugar
 1 egg
 1 teaspoon vanilla extract
 1-1/2 cups all-purpose flour
 1 teaspoon baking powder
 1/2 teaspoon baking soda
 1/8 teaspoon salt
 1 cup (8 ounces) plain yogurt
 2 tablespoons chopped walnuts *or* pecans

In a small bowl, combine the sugar, coffee granules and cinnamon; set aside. In a large mixing bowl, beat butter and sugar until crumbly, about 2 minutes. Add egg and vanilla; mix well. Combine the flour, baking powder, baking soda and salt; add to butter mixture alternately with yogurt, beating just until combined.

Spread half of the batter evenly into a 9-in. square baking pan coated with cooking spray; sprinkle with half of the reserved sugar mixture. Repeat layers; cut through batter with a knife to swirl. Sprinkle with nuts.

Bake at 350° for 25-30 minutes or until a toothpick inserted near the center comes out clean. Cool for 5 minutes on a wire rack. Serve warm.

NUTRITION FACTS: 1 piece equals 219 calories, 6 g fat (3 g saturated fat), 37 mg cholesterol, 206 mg sodium, 36 g carbohydrate, 1 g fiber, 4 g protein. **DIABETIC EXCHANGES:** 2 starch, 1 fat.

Waffles with Peach-Berry Compote

MEAT-LESS

(PICTURED ABOVE)

PREP: 25 Min.　**COOK:** 5 Min./Batch
YIELD: 12 Waffles (1-1/2 Cups Compote)

When I was looking for a more healthful alternative to butter and maple syrup to top my waffles, this recipe was born!
　　　　　　　　　　　　—Brandi Waters, Fayetteville, Arkansas

　　1 cup fresh *or* frozen peeled peach slices, chopped
　1/2 cup orange juice
　　2 tablespoons brown sugar
　1/4 teaspoon ground cinnamon
　　1 cup fresh *or* frozen blueberries
　1/2 cup sliced fresh *or* frozen strawberries
BATTER:
　1-1/4 cups all-purpose flour
　1/2 cup whole wheat flour
　　2 tablespoons flaxseed
　　1 teaspoon baking powder
　　1 teaspoon baking soda
　1/2 teaspoon ground cinnamon
　　1 cup buttermilk
　3/4 cup orange juice
　　1 tablespoon canola oil
　　1 teaspoon vanilla extract

In a small saucepan, combine the peaches, orange juice, brown sugar and cinnamon; bring to a boil over medium heat. Add berries; cook and stir for 8-10 minutes or until thickened.

In a large bowl, combine the flours, flaxseed, baking powder, baking soda and cinnamon. Combine the buttermilk, orange juice, oil and vanilla; stir into dry ingredients just until moistened.

Bake in a preheated waffle iron according to manufacturer's directions until golden brown. Serve with compote.

NUTRITION FACTS: 2 waffles with 1/4 cup compote equals 251 calories, 4 g fat (1 g saturated fat), 2 mg cholesterol, 324 mg sodium, 47 g carbohydrate, 4 g fiber, 7 g protein. **DIABETIC EXCHANGES:** 2-1/2 starch, 1/2 fruit, 1/2 fat.

Mexican Breakfast Casserole

PREP: 15 Min. + Chilling　**BAKE:** 40 Min.　**YIELD:** 4 Servings

I make this recipe whenever I'm having overnight guests.
　　　　　　　　　　—Leona Hansen, Kennedy Meadows, California

　　4 cups cubed day-old French bread
　　1 cup cubed fully cooked lean ham
　　1 can (4 ounces) chopped green chilies
　1/4 cup chopped sweet red pepper
　1-1/4 cups egg substitute
　　1 cup fat-free milk
　1/4 teaspoon onion powder
　1/4 teaspoon ground cumin
　1/4 teaspoon ground mustard
　1/8 to 1/4 teaspoon cayenne pepper
　1/4 teaspoon paprika
　1-1/4 cups shredded reduced-fat cheddar cheese
Salsa, optional

In an 8-in. square baking dish coated with cooking spray, combine the bread cubes, ham, chilies and red pepper.

In a small bowl, whisk the egg substitute, milk, onion powder, cumin, mustard and cayenne. Pour over bread mixture; sprinkle with paprika. Cover and refrigerate overnight.

Remove from the refrigerator 30 minutes before baking. Bake at 350° for 30 minutes. Uncover; sprinkle with cheese. Bake 10-15 minutes longer or until a knife inserted near the center comes out clean. Let stand for 5 minutes before cutting. Serve with salsa if desired.

NUTRITION FACTS: 1 serving (calculated without salsa) equals 305 calories, 11 g fat (6 g saturated fat), 40 mg cholesterol, 1,154 mg sodium, 25 g carbohydrate, 2 g fiber, 28 g protein.

Brunch Risotto

PREP: 10 Min.　**COOK:** 30 Min.　**YIELD:** 8 Servings

This light risotto makes a surprising addition to brunch.
　　　　　　　　　　—Jennifer Dines, Brighton, Massachusetts

　5-1/4 to 5-3/4 cups reduced-sodium chicken broth
　3/4 pound Italian turkey sausage links, casings removed
　　2 cups uncooked arborio rice
　　1 garlic clove, minced
　1/4 teaspoon pepper
　　1 tablespoon olive oil
　　1 medium tomato, chopped

In a large saucepan, heat broth and keep warm. In a large nonstick skillet, cook sausage until no longer pink; drain and set aside. In the same skillet, saute rice, garlic and pepper in oil for 2-3 minutes. Return sausage to skillet. Carefully stir in 1 cup heated broth. Cook and stir until all of the liquid is absorbed.

Add remaining broth, 1/2 cup at a time, stirring constantly. Allow liquid to absorb between additions. Cook just until risotto is creamy and rice is almost tender. Total cooking time is about 20 minutes. Add tomato; cook and stir until heated through. Serve immediately.

NUTRITION FACTS: 2/3 cup equals 279 calories, 6 g fat (2 g saturated fat), 23 mg cholesterol, 653 mg sodium, 42 g carbohydrate, 1 g fiber, 12 g protein. **DIABETIC EXCHANGES:** 2-1/2 starch, 1 lean meat, 1/2 fat.

30-Minute Entrees

Cooking light doesn't mean spending hours in the kitchen. The next time you're in a rush, don't neglect healthy eating habits—turn to this new chapter instead. Every dish comes together in just half an hour…or less!

Mediterranean-Style Red Snapper, p. 100

Chicken with Creamy Jalapeno Sauce
(PICTURED ABOVE)

PREP/TOTAL TIME: 25 Min.   YIELD: 4 Servings (2 Cups Sauce)

My sister came up with this recipe that does a great job of making boring old chicken breasts a lot more exciting. My husband and I just love the wonderful sauce.

—Molly Cappone, Lewis Center, Ohio

4 boneless skinless chicken breast halves (4 ounces *each*)
1/4 teaspoon salt
1 tablespoon canola oil
2 medium onions, chopped
1/2 cup reduced-sodium chicken broth
2 jalapeno peppers, seeded and minced
2 teaspoons ground cumin
3 ounces reduced-fat cream cheese, cubed
1/4 cup reduced-fat sour cream
3 plum tomatoes, seeded and chopped
2 cups hot cooked rice

Sprinkle chicken with salt. In a large nonstick skillet over medium-high heat, brown chicken in oil on both sides.

Add the onions, broth, jalapenos and cumin. Bring to a boil. Reduce heat; cover and simmer for 5-7 minutes or until a meat thermometer reads 170°. Remove chicken and keep warm.

Stir cream cheese and sour cream into onion mixture until blended. Stir in tomatoes; heat through. Serve with chicken and rice.

NUTRITION FACTS: 1 chicken breast half with 1/2 cup sauce and 1/2 cup rice equals 376 calories, 13 g fat (5 g saturated fat), 83 mg cholesterol, 389 mg sodium, 34 g carbohydrate, 3 g fiber, 30 g protein. **DIABETIC EXCHANGES:** 3 very lean meat, 2 vegetable, 2 fat, 1-1/2 starch.

Editor's Note: *When cutting or seeding hot peppers, use rubber or plastic gloves to protect your hands. Avoid touching your face.*

Hawaiian Ham Salad Pockets

PREP/TOTAL TIME: 15 Min.   YIELD: 4 Servings

Pineapple and mustard are traditional flavors with baked ham, and they work well in these sandwiches. Not only do they come together in minutes, but they use up leftover ham deliciously.

—Mitzi Sentiff, Alexandria, Virginia

1-1/4 cups cubed fully cooked lean ham
3/4 cup unsweetened pineapple tidbits
1 large carrot, chopped
1/4 cup fat-free mayonnaise
1 tablespoon honey mustard
2 pita breads (6 inches), halved
4 lettuce leaves

In a small bowl, combine the ham, pineapple and carrot. Stir in the mayonnaise and mustard until blended. Line each pita half with a lettuce leaf; fill with ham salad.

NUTRITION FACTS: 1 filled pita half equals 194 calories, 3 g fat (1 g saturated fat), 21 mg cholesterol, 945 mg sodium, 29 g carbohydrate, 2 g fiber, 13 g protein. **DIABETIC EXCHANGES:** 2 starch, 1 lean meat.

Pasta Fagioli Soup

PREP/TOTAL TIME: 30 Min. **YIELD:** 5 Servings

My husband enjoys my version of this soup so much, he doesn't order it at restaurants anymore. With fresh spinach, pasta and seasoned sausage, it's a fast-to-fix soup that eats like a meal.
—Brenda Thomas, Springfield, Missouri

    1/2 pound Italian turkey sausage links, casings removed, crumbled
      1 small onion, chopped
  1-1/2 teaspoons canola oil
      1 garlic clove, minced
      2 cups water
      1 can (15-1/2 ounces) great northern beans, rinsed and drained
      1 can (14-1/2 ounces) diced tomatoes, undrained
      1 can (14-1/2 ounces) reduced-sodium chicken broth
    3/4 cup uncooked elbow macaroni
    1/4 teaspoon pepper
      1 cup fresh spinach leaves, cut into strips
      5 teaspoons shredded Parmesan cheese

In a large saucepan, cook sausage over medium heat until no longer pink; drain and set aside. In the same pan, saute onion in oil until tender. Add garlic; saute 1 minute longer.

Add the water, beans, tomatoes, broth, macaroni and pepper; bring to a boil. Cook, uncovered, for 8-10 minutes or until macaroni is tender.

Reduce heat to low; stir in sausage and spinach. Cook for 2-3 minutes or until spinach is wilted. Garnish with Parmesan cheese.

NUTRITION FACTS: 1-1/3 cups equals 228 calories, 7 g fat (1 g saturated fat), 29 mg cholesterol, 841 mg sodium, 27 g carbohydrate, 6 g fiber, 16 g protein. **DIABETIC EXCHANGES:** 1-1/2 starch, 1 lean meat, 1 vegetable, 1/2 fat.

Gnocchi with Hearty Meat Sauce

PREP/TOTAL TIME: 30 Min. **YIELD:** 6 Servings

When time's at a premium, turn to this hearty, full-flavored meat sauce, mellowed with a hint of wine from our home economists.

      1 package (16 ounces) potato gnocchi
      1 package (20 ounces) Italian turkey sausage links, casings removed
      1 large green pepper, cut into 1-inch pieces
      1 large sweet red pepper, cut into 1-inch pieces
    1/4 cup dry red wine *or* reduced-sodium chicken broth
      1 can (14-1/2 ounces) diced tomatoes, undrained
      1 can (8 ounces) no-salt-added tomato sauce
      2 tablespoons tomato paste
      2 teaspoons brown sugar

Cook gnocchi according to package directions. Meanwhile, crumble the sausage into a large nonstick skillet; add peppers. Cook over medium heat until meat is no longer pink and peppers are tender; drain.

Add wine or broth; cook and stir for 2 minutes. Stir in the tomatoes, tomato sauce, tomato paste and brown sugar; heat through. Drain gnocchi; serve with meat sauce.

NUTRITION FACTS: 1-1/3 cups equals 371 calories, 10 g fat (3 g saturated fat), 56 mg cholesterol, 1,022 mg sodium, 45 g carbohydrate, 4 g fiber, 22 g protein. **DIABETIC EXCHANGES:** 3 lean meat, 2 starch, 2 vegetable.

Editor's Note: Look for potato gnocchi in the pasta, ethnic or frozen section of your grocery store.

Teriyaki Turkey Tossed Salad

(PICTURED BELOW)

PREP/TOTAL TIME: 20 Min. **YIELD:** 4 Servings

Here's a fast and colorful salad perfect for lunches. With a whole wheat roll and frozen yogurt for dessert, you have the perfect meal!
—Mary Wilhelm, Sparta, Wisconsin

      2 cups fresh snow peas
      6 cups spring mix salad greens
    3/4 pound thinly sliced deli turkey, julienned
      1 medium sweet red pepper, chopped
    1/2 cup sliced almonds, toasted
      3 green onions, thinly sliced
      2 tablespoons orange juice
      2 tablespoons reduced-sodium teriyaki sauce
      2 tablespoons honey
    1/2 teaspoon crushed red pepper flakes

In a small saucepan, bring 1 in. of water to a boil. Add peas. Reduce heat; cover and simmer for 2-3 minutes or until crisp-tender. Drain and immediately place peas in ice water. Drain and pat dry.

In a large salad bowl, combine the greens, turkey, red pepper, almonds, onions and peas. In a small bowl, whisk the orange juice, teriyaki sauce, honey and pepper flakes. Drizzle over salad and toss to coat.

NUTRITION FACTS: 1-1/2 cups equals 240 calories, 7 g fat (1 g saturated fat), 38 mg cholesterol, 1,073 mg sodium, 25 g carbohydrate, 5 g fiber, 23 g protein. **DIABETIC EXCHANGES:** 2 very lean meat, 2 vegetable, 1-1/2 fat, 1/2 starch.

Family-Pleasing Spaghetti

PREP/TOTAL TIME: 30 Min.   YIELD: 6 Servings

I'm a big fan of pasta, smoked sausage and cheese, and I love spicy food. This dish has it all! Paired with a salad and bread, it makes a complete meal in no time.
—Lisa Varner, Greenville, South Carolina

 12 ounces uncooked spaghetti
  1 small onion, chopped
  2 garlic cloves, minced
  2 teaspoons canola oil
  1 pound reduced-fat smoked sausage, casings removed and cut into 1/2-inch slices
  1 small green pepper, chopped
  1 can (14-1/2 ounces) diced tomatoes, undrained
 3/4 cup salsa
  1 teaspoon chili powder
 1/2 teaspoon dried oregano
 1/2 cup shredded reduced-fat cheddar cheese

Cook spaghetti according to package directions. Meanwhile, in a large nonstick skillet coated with cooking spray, cook onion and garlic in oil over medium heat for 2 minutes. Add sausage and green pepper; cook 4-6 minutes longer or until sausage is lightly browned and vegetables are tender.

Stir in the tomatoes, salsa, chili powder and oregano. Bring to a boil. Reduce heat; simmer, uncovered, for 5 minutes. Drain spaghetti; toss with sauce. Sprinkle with cheese.

NUTRITION FACTS: 1-1/3 cups equals 379 calories, 7 g fat (2 g saturated fat), 33 mg cholesterol, 936 mg sodium, 57 g carbohydrate, 3 g fiber, 20 g protein.

Greek Turkey Burgers

PREP/TOTAL TIME: 25 Min.   YIELD: 4 Servings

These burgers are absolutely mouth-watering! Greek dressing is the secret ingredient that gives each bite extra kick.
—Sheri McCafferty, Richmond, Virginia

 1/2 cup crumbled feta cheese
  2 tablespoons Greek vinaigrette
  2 garlic cloves, minced
 1/8 teaspoon salt
 1/8 teaspoon dried oregano
 1/8 teaspoon pepper
  1 pound extra-lean ground turkey
  4 hamburger buns, split
  4 lettuce leaves
  4 slices tomato

In a large bowl, combine the first six ingredients. Crumble turkey over mixture and mix well. Shape into four patties.

If using the grill, coat grill rack with cooking spray before starting. Grill patties, covered, over medium-hot heat or broil 4 in. from the heat for 5-7 minutes on each side or until a meat thermometer reads 165° and juices run clear. Serve on buns with lettuce and tomato.

NUTRITION FACTS: 1 burger equals 324 calories, 10 g fat (3 g saturated fat), 53 mg cholesterol, 593 mg sodium, 25 g carbohydrate, 2 g fiber, 35 g protein. **DIABETIC EXCHANGES:** 4 very lean meat, 1-1/2 starch, 1 fat.

Chicken Pasta Salad a l'Orange
(PICTURED BELOW)

PREP/TOTAL TIME: 30 Min.   YIELD: 6 Servings

I found this recipe in an old cookbook just after I was married 25 years ago. All of my six kids like it—even those who don't usually eat salad!
—Ann Berger, Howell, Michigan

 2-1/2 cups uncooked bow tie pasta
  2 cups cubed cooked chicken breast
  2 celery ribs, thinly sliced
  1 can (11 ounces) mandarin oranges, drained
  1 can (2-1/4 ounces) sliced ripe olives, drained
 1/3 cup fat-free plain yogurt
 1/3 cup reduced-fat mayonnaise
 1/4 cup orange juice concentrate
  1 tablespoon white vinegar
  2 teaspoons sugar
 1/4 teaspoon salt
 1/4 teaspoon ground mustard
  6 cups torn mixed salad greens
 1/2 cup cubed avocado

Cook pasta according to package directions; drain and rinse in cold water. In a large bowl, combine the pasta, chicken, celery, oranges and olives.

For dressing, in a small bowl, combine the yogurt, mayonnaise, orange juice concentrate, vinegar, sugar, salt and mustard. Pour over pasta mixture and toss to coat.

For each serving, spoon 1-1/3 cups pasta mixture over 1 cup of greens; top with about 1 tablespon avocado.

NUTRITION FACTS: 1 serving equals 269 calories, 9 g fat (2 g saturated fat), 41 mg cholesterol, 368 mg sodium, 29 g carbohydrate, 3 g fiber, 18 g protein. **DIABETIC EXCHANGES:** 2 very lean meat, 1-1/2 fat, 1 starch, 1 vegetable, 1/2 fruit.

Sweet 'n' Tangy Shrimp
(PICTURED ABOVE)

PREP/TOTAL TIME: 30 Min. **YIELD:** 4 Servings

My husband and I adapted this recipe from one in a magazine, and we just love it. With its delightfully sweet-tangy flavor, it's an easy entree I turn to often. —Kathleen Davis, North Bend, Washington

- 1/2 cup ketchup
- 2 tablespoons sugar
- 2 tablespoons cider vinegar
- 2 tablespoons reduced-sodium soy sauce
- 1 teaspoon sesame oil
- 1/4 teaspoon crushed red pepper flakes
- 1-1/2 pounds uncooked medium shrimp, peeled and deveined
- 1 tablespoon minced fresh gingerroot
- 3 garlic cloves, minced
- 1 tablespoon canola oil
- 2 green onions, sliced
- 1 teaspoon sesame seeds, toasted

Hot cooked rice, optional

In a small bowl, combine the first six ingredients; set aside. In a large nonstick skillet or wok, stir-fry the shrimp, ginger and garlic in oil until shrimp turn pink.

Add the ketchup mixture; cook and stir for 2-3 minutes or until heated through. Sprinkle with onions and sesame seeds. Serve with rice if desired.

NUTRITION FACTS: 3/4 cup (calculated without rice) equals 241 calories, 7 g fat (1 g saturated fat), 252 mg cholesterol, 954 mg sodium, 17 g carbohydrate, 1 g fiber, 28 g protein. **DIABETIC EXCHANGES:** 4 very lean meat, 1 starch, 1/2 fat.

Garlic-Mushroom Turkey Slices

PREP/TOTAL TIME: 30 Min. **YIELD:** 4 Servings

Even my 17-year-old likes this dish! It's super for weeknight dining.
—Rick Fleishman, Beverly Hills, California

- 1/2 cup all-purpose flour
- 1/2 teaspoon dried oregano
- 1/2 teaspoon paprika
- 3/4 teaspoon salt, *divided*
- 1/4 teaspoon pepper, *divided*
- 1 package (17.6 ounces) turkey breast slices
- 1 tablespoon olive oil
- 3/4 cup reduced-sodium chicken broth
- 1/4 cup white wine *or* additional reduced-sodium chicken broth
- 1/2 pound sliced fresh mushrooms
- 2 garlic cloves, minced

In a large resealable plastic bag, combine the flour, oregano, paprika, 1/2 teaspoon salt and 1/8 teaspoon pepper. Add turkey, a few pieces at a time, and shake to coat.

In a large nonstick skillet coated with cooking spray, cook turkey in oil in batches over medium heat for 1-2 minutes on each side or until no longer pink. Remove and keep warm.

Add broth and wine or additional broth to the skillet; stir in the mushrooms, garlic and remaining salt and pepper. Cook and stir for 4-6 minutes or until mushrooms are tender. Return turkey to the pan; heat through.

NUTRITION FACTS: 4 ounces cooked turkey with 1/3 cup mushroom mixture equals 218 calories, 4 g fat (1 g saturated fat), 77 mg cholesterol, 440 mg sodium, 8 g carbohydrate, 1 g fiber, 34 g protein. **DIABETIC EXCHANGES:** 4 very lean meat, 1/2 starch, 1/2 fat.

Mediterranean-Style Red Snapper

(PICTURED ABOVE)

CARB

PREP/TOTAL TIME: 30 Min.   **YIELD:** 4 Servings

This entree is both time-saving and nutritious. Seasoned with spices and served with a zesty sauce, it's a favorite at our house.
—Josephine Piro, Easton, Pennsylvania

　　1 teaspoon lemon-pepper seasoning
　1/2 teaspoon garlic powder
　1/2 teaspoon dried thyme
　1/8 teaspoon cayenne pepper
　　4 red snapper fillets (6 ounces *each*)
　　2 teaspoons olive oil, *divided*
　1/2 medium sweet red pepper, julienned
　　3 green onions, chopped
　　1 garlic clove, minced
　　1 can (14-1/2 ounces) diced tomatoes, undrained
　1/2 cup chopped pimiento-stuffed olives
　1/4 cup chopped ripe olives
　1/4 cup minced fresh chives

Combine the lemon-pepper, garlic powder, thyme and cayenne; rub over fillets. In a large nonstick skillet coated with cooking spray, cook fillets in 1 teaspoon oil over medium heat for 4-5 minutes on each side or until fish flakes easily with a fork. Remove and keep warm.

　In the same pan, saute the red pepper, onions and garlic in remaining oil until crisp-tender. Stir in tomatoes. Bring to a boil. Reduce heat; simmer, uncovered, for 3 minutes or until liquid has evaporated. Serve over snapper. Sprinkle with the olives and chives.

NUTRITION FACTS: 1 fillet with 1/3 cup tomato mixture and 3 tablespoons olives equals 258 calories, 9 g fat (1 g saturated fat), 60 mg cholesterol, 754 mg sodium, 10 g carbohydrate, 3 g fiber, 35 g protein. **DIABETIC EXCHANGES:** 5 very lean meat, 1-1/2 fat, 1 vegetable.

Orange Chicken Spinach Salad

PREP/TOTAL TIME: 20 Min.   **YIELD:** 4 Servings

In less than half an hour, you can enjoy this refreshing and satisfying entree salad. It's always well received by friends and family.
—Jean Murawski, Grosse Pointe Park, Michigan

　　3 cups cubed cooked chicken breast
　　1 can (15 ounces) mandarin oranges, drained
　　1 package (6 ounces) fresh baby spinach
　　1 medium sweet red pepper, diced
　　1 small red onion, chopped
　　2 tablespoons orange juice
　　2 tablespoons cider vinegar
　　1 tablespoon olive oil
　1/2 teaspoon Italian seasoning
　　1 garlic clove, minced
　1/8 teaspoon salt
　　2 tablespoons crumbled goat cheese

In a large bowl, combine the chicken, oranges, spinach, red pepper and onion. In a small bowl, whisk the orange juice, vinegar, oil, Italian seasoning, garlic and salt. Pour over salad and toss to coat. Top with goat cheese.

NUTRITION FACTS: 2-1/2 cups equals 293 calories, 9 g fat (3 g saturated fat), 86 mg cholesterol, 211 mg sodium, 18 g carbohydrate, 2 g fiber, 34 g protein. **DIABETIC EXCHANGES:** 4 very lean meat, 1 vegetable, 1 fruit, 1 fat.

Bean 'n' Pepper Burritos

MEAT-LESS

PREP/TOTAL TIME: 25 Min.   **YIELD:** 8 Servings

My family loves this dish's flavor, but I love its microwave ease!
—Alicia Luttrell, Mobile, Alabama

      1 medium onion, chopped
      1 medium green pepper, chopped
      1 medium sweet red pepper, chopped
      1 medium tomato, chopped
      1 can (16 ounces) fat-free refried beans
      8 flour tortillas (8 inches), warmed
      1 cup (4 ounces) shredded reduced-fat cheddar cheese
      1 cup (4 ounces) shredded part-skim mozzarella cheese
      1 cup salsa
   1/2 cup fat-free sour cream

In a small microwave-safe dish, combine onion and peppers. Cover and microwave on high for 3-5 minutes or until tender. Drain; stir in tomato.

Spread refried beans down the center of each tortilla. Top with pepper mixture and cheeses. Fold sides and ends over filling and roll up.

Place four burritos in a shallow microwave-safe dish; cover and microwave at 70% power for 4-6 minutes or until heated through. Repeat with remaining burritos. Serve with salsa and sour cream.

NUTRITION FACTS: 1 burrito with 2 tablespoons salsa and 1 tablespoon sour cream equals 328 calories, 8 g fat (4 g saturated fat), 21 mg cholesterol, 782 mg sodium, 46 g carbohydrate, 5 g fiber, 17 g protein.

Editor's Note: This recipe was tested in a 1,100-watt microwave.

New Mexico-Style Pizza

PREP/TOTAL TIME: 25 Min.   **YIELD:** 6 Slices

This outrageously delicious pizza really was created from leftovers.
—Lisa Renshaw, Kansas City, Missouri

      1 prebaked thin Italian bread shell crust (10 ounces)
   1-1/2 cups salsa verde
      1 tablespoon lime juice
      1 teaspoon ground cumin
   1/2 teaspoon salt
   1/4 teaspoon dried oregano
      2 cups shredded cooked chicken breast
   1/2 cup frozen corn, thawed
      3 green onions, thinly sliced
   1/2 cup shredded reduced-fat cheddar cheese
      2 tablespoons minced fresh cilantro
      6 tablespoons fat-free sour cream

Place crust on a pizza pan or baking sheet. In a small bowl, combine the salsa verde, lime juice, cumin, salt and oregano; spread over crust. Top with chicken, corn, onions and cheese.

Bake at 450° for 8-10 minutes or until heated through and cheese is melted. Sprinkle with cilantro. Serve with sour cream.

NUTRITION FACTS: 1 slice with 1 tablespoon sour cream equals 285 calories, 7 g fat (2 g saturated fat), 45 mg cholesterol, 923 mg sodium, 32 g carbohydrate, 2 g fiber, 23 g protein. **DIABETIC EXCHANGES:** 2 starch, 2 very lean meat, 1 fat.

Grilled Feta Quesadillas

FAT CARB MEAT-LESS

(PICTURED BELOW)

PREP/TOTAL TIME: 20 Min.   **YIELD:** 12 Wedges

Here's a perfect dish when you have to eat and run...and still watch your diet. It's lower in fat than other quesadillas, but very big on taste.
—Jacqui Correa, Landing, New Jersey

      3 ounces fat-free cream cheese
   1/2 cup shredded reduced-fat Mexican cheese blend
   1/3 cup crumbled feta cheese
   1/2 teaspoon dried oregano
      4 flour tortillas (6 inches)
   1/4 cup chopped pitted ripe olives
      2 tablespoons diced pimientos
      1 green onion, chopped

In a small mixing bowl, beat cheeses with oregano until blended. Spread 3 tablespoons of cheese mixture over half of each tortilla; top with olives, pimientos and onion. Fold tortillas over.

Coat grill rack with cooking spray before starting the grill. Grill quesadillas, uncovered, over medium heat for 1-2 minutes on each side or until golden brown. Cut each quesadilla into three wedges. Serve warm.

NUTRITION FACTS: 1 wedge equals 62 calories, 3 g fat (1 g saturated fat), 6 mg cholesterol, 198 mg sodium, 5 g carbohydrate, trace fiber, 4 g protein. **DIABETIC EXCHANGES:** 1/2 starch, 1/2 fat.

Curried Pineapple Turkey Salad

PREP/TOTAL TIME: 30 Min. **YIELD:** 6 Servings

I serve this refreshing salad with date-nut bread on the side.
—Teri Lindquist, Gurnee, Illinois

 1 can (8 ounces) unsweetened pineapple chunks
 5 cups cubed cooked turkey breast
 1 celery rib, thinly sliced
 1/3 cup raisins
 1 green onion, chopped
 1/2 cup reduced-fat mayonnaise
 1 tablespoon Dijon mustard
 1 teaspoon curry powder
 1/4 teaspoon salt
 1/8 teaspoon pepper
 6 lettuce leaves
 1 cup seedless red grapes, halved
 1/3 cup slivered almonds, toasted

Drain pineapple, reserving 2 tablespoons juice. In a large bowl, combine the pineapple, turkey, celery, raisins and onion. In a small bowl, combine the mayonnaise, mustard, curry, salt, pepper and reserved pineapple juice. Stir into turkey mixture.

Cover and refrigerate until serving. Spoon onto lettuce-lined plates; top with grapes and almonds.

NUTRITION FACTS: 1 cup equals 335 calories, 12 g fat (2 g saturated fat), 107 mg cholesterol, 398 mg sodium, 20 g carbohydrate, 2 g fiber, 38 g protein. **DIABETIC EXCHANGES:** 5 very lean meat, 2 fat, 1 fruit.

Country Chicken with Gravy

(PICTURED AT RIGHT)

PREP/TOTAL TIME: 30 Min. **YIELD:** 4 Servings

This lightened-up dinner entree is so hearty, quick and simple!
—Ruth Helmuth, Abbeville, South Carolina

 3/4 cup crushed cornflakes
 1/2 teaspoon poultry seasoning
 1/2 teaspoon paprika
 1/4 teaspoon dried thyme
 1/4 teaspoon salt
 1/4 teaspoon pepper
 2 tablespoons fat-free evaporated milk
 4 boneless skinless chicken breast halves (4 ounces *each*)
 2 teaspoons canola oil
GRAVY:
 1 tablespoon butter
 1 tablespoon all-purpose flour
 1/4 teaspoon pepper
 1/8 teaspoon salt
 1/2 cup fat-free evaporated milk
 1/4 cup condensed chicken broth, undiluted
 1 teaspoon sherry *or* additional condensed chicken broth
 2 tablespoons snipped chives

In a shallow bowl, combine the first six ingredients. Place milk in another shallow bowl. Dip chicken in milk, then roll in cornflake mixture.

In a large nonstick skillet coated with cooking spray, cook chicken in oil over medium heat for 6-8 minutes on each side or until juices run clear.

Meanwhile, in a small saucepan, melt butter. Stir in the flour, pepper and salt until smooth. Gradually stir in the milk, broth and sherry or additional broth. Bring to a boil; cook and stir for 1-2 minutes or until thickened. Stir in chives. Serve with chicken.

NUTRITION FACTS: 1 chicken breast half with 2 tablespoons gravy equals 274 calories, 8 g fat (3 g saturated fat), 72 mg cholesterol, 569 mg sodium, 20 g carbohydrate, trace fiber, 28 g protein. **DIABETIC EXCHANGES:** 3 very lean meat, 1 starch, 1 fat.

Cucumber Chicken Salad Sandwiches

PREP/TOTAL TIME: 10 Min. **YIELD:** 2 Servings

I like to dress up chicken salad with crunchy cucumber and dill for a summery sandwich that's ready in just 10 minutes.
—Eva Wright, Grant, Alabama

 1 cup cubed cooked chicken breast
 1/3 cup chopped seeded peeled cucumber
 1/4 cup fat-free mayonnaise
 1/4 teaspoon salt
 1/8 teaspoon dill weed
 2 lettuce leaves
 4 slices tomato
 2 sandwich buns, split

In a small bowl, combine the first five ingredients. Place lettuce and tomato on bun bottoms; top with chicken salad. Replace bun tops.

NUTRITION FACTS: 1 sandwich equals 350 calories, 8 g fat (3 g saturated fat), 57 mg cholesterol, 930 mg sodium, 42 g carbohydrate, 3 g fiber, 28 g protein. **DIABETIC EXCHANGES:** 3 very lean meat, 2-1/2 starch, 2 vegetable.

Sweet Onion 'n' Sausage Spaghetti
(PICTURED ABOVE)

PREP/TOTAL TIME: 30 Min.   **YIELD:** 5 Servings

I toss sweet onion and turkey sausage with light cream, basil and tomatoes for a quick, springy meal in minutes.
                                    —Mary Relyea, Canastota, New York

   6 ounces uncooked whole wheat spaghetti
   3/4 pound Italian turkey sausage links, casings removed
   2 teaspoons olive oil
   1 sweet onion, thinly sliced
   1 pint cherry tomatoes, halved
   1/2 cup loosely packed fresh basil leaves, thinly sliced
   1/2 cup half-and-half cream
Shaved Parmesan cheese, optional

Cook spaghetti according to package directions. Meanwhile, in a large nonstick skillet over medium heat, cook sausage in oil for 5 minutes. Add onion; cook 8-10 minutes longer or until meat is no longer pink and onion is tender.

Stir in tomatoes and basil; heat through. Add cream; bring to a boil. Drain spaghetti; toss with sausage mixture. Garnish with Parmesan cheese if desired.

NUTRITION FACTS: 1-1/4 cups (calculated without Parmesan cheese) equals 305 calories, 11 g fat (4 g saturated fat), 48 mg cholesterol, 442 mg sodium, 33 g carbohydrate, 6 g fiber, 18 g protein. **DIABETIC EXCHANGES:** 2 lean meat, 1-1/2 starch, 1 vegetable, 1 fat.

White Beans and Veggies with Couscous   MEAT-LESS

PREP/TOTAL TIME: 30 Min.   **YIELD:** 4 Servings

With its variety in taste and texture, this meatless dish is a favorite with my gang.   —Heather Savage, Corydon, Indiana

   1 medium zucchini, quartered lengthwise and thinly sliced
   1 medium onion, finely chopped
   4 garlic cloves, minced
   1 tablespoon olive oil
   1 can (15 ounces) white kidney *or* cannellini beans, rinsed and drained
   1 can (14-1/2 ounces) diced tomatoes, undrained
   1/2 teaspoon dried basil
   1/4 teaspoon dried rosemary, crushed
   1/4 teaspoon pepper
   1/8 teaspoon salt
COUSCOUS:
   1-1/2 cups water
   1 tablespoon butter
   1/4 teaspoon salt
   1 cup uncooked couscous

In a large skillet, saute the zucchini, onion and garlic in oil until tender. Stir in the beans, tomatoes and seasonings. Cook, stirring occasionally, for 5 minutes.

Meanwhile, in a small saucepan, bring the water, butter and salt to a boil. Stir in couscous. Cover and remove from the heat; let stand for 5 minutes or until water is absorbed. Fluff with a fork. Serve with bean mixture.

NUTRITION FACTS: 1 cup bean mixture with 3/4 cup couscous equals 350 calories, 8 g fat (2 g saturated fat), 8 mg cholesterol, 521 mg sodium, 60 g carbohydrate, 9 g fiber, 13 g protein.

TASTY TIP
Make couscous a staple. It's a healthy item that comes together in no time, making it perfect for weeknights.

Shrimp and Asparagus Penne

(PICTURED BELOW)

PREP/TOTAL TIME: 30 Min.   YIELD: 4 Servings

This pretty pasta dish has only a few ingredients, so it's a breeze to whip up. We used to prepare it with heavy cream, but I substituted half-and-half to cut fat, and it's just as good.

—Diane Shipley, Concord, Ohio

    3 cups uncooked penne pasta
    1 pound fresh asparagus, trimmed and cut into 1-inch pieces
    1 tablespoon butter
    1 pound uncooked medium shrimp, peeled and deveined
    2 teaspoons all-purpose flour
1/4 teaspoon salt
1/2 cup half-and-half
1/2 cup grated Parmesan cheese, *divided*

Cook pasta according to package directions. Meanwhile, in a large nonstick skillet, saute asparagus in butter for 4 minutes. Add shrimp; cook and stir for 3-4 minutes or until shrimp turn pink. Remove and keep warm.

In a small bowl, combine the flour, salt and half-and-half until smooth; add to the skillet. Bring mixture to a boil; cook and stir for 1-2 minutes or until thickened. Stir in 1/4 cup Parmesan cheese.

Remove from the heat. Drain pasta; toss with shrimp mixture and sauce. Sprinkle with remaining Parmesan cheese.

NUTRITION FACTS: 2 cups equals 417 calories, 11 g fat (6 g saturated fat), 199 mg cholesterol, 580 mg sodium, 46 g carbohydrate, 3 g fiber, 32 g protein. DIABETIC EXCHANGES: 3 very lean meat, 2-1/2 starch, 2 fat, 1 vegetable.

Orange Chicken Stir-Fry

PREP/TOTAL TIME: 25 Min.   YIELD: 6 Servings

A burst of citrus easily brightens up the dinner table in this stress-free chicken staple. With it's thick and glossy orange sauce, the healthy stir-fry tastes great over rice.

—Janice Mitchell, Aurora, Colorado

    1 tablespoon cornstarch
  2/3 cup orange juice
1-1/4 teaspoons salt
  1/4 teaspoon ground ginger
  1/4 teaspoon pepper
1-1/2 pounds boneless skinless chicken breasts, cut into strips
    3 large carrots, julienned
    1 medium onion, thinly sliced and separated into rings
    3 teaspoons canola oil, *divided*
  1/3 cup reduced-sugar orange marmalade
    3 tablespoons brown sugar
    1 tablespoon lemon juice
Hot cooked rice, optional

In a small bowl, combine cornstarch and orange juice until smooth; set aside. Combine the salt, ginger and pepper; sprinkle over chicken. Set aside.

In a large nonstick skillet or wok, stir-fry carrots and onion in 1 teaspoon oil until crisp-tender. Remove and keep warm.

In the same pan, stir-fry chicken in remaining oil until no longer pink. Stir in the marmalade, brown sugar and lemon juice until marmalade is dissolved.

Return carrot mixture to the pan. Stir orange juice mixture; add to pan. Bring to a boil; cook and stir for 2 minutes or until thickened. Serve with rice if desired.

NUTRITION FACTS: 1 cup (calculated without rice) equals 229 calories, 5 g fat (1 g saturated fat), 63 mg cholesterol, 562 mg sodium, 21 g carbohydrate, 1 g fiber, 24 g protein. DIABETIC EXCHANGES: 3 very lean meat, 1 starch, 1 vegetable, 1/2 fat.

Garden Vegetable Wraps

PREP/TOTAL TIME: 25 Min.   YIELD: 4 Servings

My husband and I love these no-fuss wraps on hectic nights. I found the recipe years ago, and it was an instant keeper. It's a fun take on a BLT, but feel free to add strips of cooked chicken or beef if you have any on hand.

—Barbara Blake, West Brattleboro, Vermont

  1/2 cup reduced-fat garlic-herb cheese spread
    4 flour tortillas (10 inches)
1-1/4 cups chopped seeded tomatoes
1-1/4 cups julienned fresh spinach
  3/4 cup chopped sweet red pepper
    2 bacon strips, cooked and crumbled
  1/4 teaspoon coarsely ground pepper

Spread 2 tablespoons cheese spread over each tortilla. Sprinkle with tomatoes, spinach, red pepper, bacon and pepper. Roll up tightly.

NUTRITION FACTS: 1 wrap equals 314 calories, 10 g fat (5 g saturated fat), 21 mg cholesterol, 614 mg sodium, 37 g carbohydrate, 8 g fiber, 12 g protein. DIABETIC EXCHANGES: 2-1/2 starch, 2 fat, 1 vegetable.

Zesty Turkey Burgers
(PICTURED ABOVE)

PREP/TOTAL TIME: 25 Min. YIELD: 4 Servings

My husband and I were watching our weight last summer and we found that this recipe was really quick to prepare, and it's delicious!
—Louise Gilbert, Quesnel, British Columbia

    1/2 cup ketchup
      1 tablespoon cider vinegar
      1 tablespoon Worcestershire sauce
      2 garlic cloves, minced
    1/4 teaspoon pepper
    1/4 teaspoon crushed red pepper flakes
    1/4 teaspoon hot pepper sauce
    1/3 cup quick-cooking oats
      1 pound lean ground turkey
      4 lettuce leaves
      4 hamburger buns, split

In a small bowl, combine the first seven ingredients. Transfer half of the mixture to a large bowl; stir in oats. Set remaining ketchup mixture aside for basting. Crumble turkey over oat mixture and mix well. Shape into four patties.

Coat grill rack with cooking spray before starting the grill. Grill patties, covered, over medium heat for 5-7 minutes on each side or until a meat thermometer reads 165°, basting occasionally with ketchup mixture. Serve on lettuce-lined buns.

NUTRITION FACTS: 1 burger equals 355 calories, 12 g fat (3 g saturated fat), 90 mg cholesterol, 746 mg sodium, 36 g carbohydrate, 2 g fiber, 25 g protein. DIABETIC EXCHANGES: 3 lean meat, 2 starch.

Chicken Creole

PREP/TOTAL TIME: 30 Min. YIELD: 4 Servings

I've relied on this easy skillet dish for years. Every time I serve it to guests, they ask for the recipe.
—Leeanne Grether, Woodbury, Minnesota

      1 pound boneless skinless chicken breasts, cut into
        3/4-inch pieces

      4 teaspoons canola oil, *divided*
      1 medium onion, chopped
      1 small green pepper, chopped
      1 celery rib, chopped
      1 can (14-1/2 ounces) diced tomatoes, undrained
      1 cup reduced-sodium chicken broth
    1/3 cup tomato paste
    1/2 teaspoon pepper
    1/2 teaspoon *each* dried basil, oregano, thyme and
        marjoram
      2 cups hot cooked rice

In a large nonstick skillet, saute chicken in 2 teaspoons oil until no longer pink. Remove and keep warm. In the same skillet, saute the onion, green pepper and celery in remaining oil until tender.

Stir in the tomatoes, broth, tomato paste and seasonings. Bring to a boil. Reduce heat; cover and simmer for 8 minutes. Return chicken to the pan; heat through. Serve with rice.

NUTRITION FACTS: 1-1/4 cups chicken mixture with 1/2 cup rice equals 334 calories, 8 g fat (1 g saturated fat), 63 mg cholesterol, 368 mg sodium, 38 g carbohydrate, 5 g fiber, 28 g protein. DIABETIC EXCHANGES: 3 very lean meat, 2-1/2 starch, 1 fat.

Saucy Peach Chicken

PREP/TOTAL TIME: 30 Min. YIELD: 4 Servings

I quickly pair basil and peaches with tender chicken breast to create this tangy main course. —Ellen Schroeder, Reedsburg, Wisconsin

      4 boneless skinless chicken breast halves (4 ounces *each*)
    1/2 teaspoon salt
    1/8 teaspoon pepper
      1 teaspoon canola oil
SAUCE:
      2 tablespoons brown sugar
      1 tablespoon cornstarch
    1/2 teaspoon dried basil
      1 can (15 ounces) sliced peaches in extra-light syrup
      1 tablespoon cider vinegar
      1 tablespoon reduced-sodium soy sauce
      2 cups hot cooked rice

Sprinkle chicken with salt and pepper. In a large nonstick skillet coated with cooking spray, cook chicken in oil over medium heat for 5-6 minutes on each side or until the juices run clear.

Meanwhile, in a small bowl, combine the brown sugar, cornstarch and basil. Drain peaches, reserving syrup in a measuring cup; add enough water to measure 1 cup. Set peaches aside. Stir the syrup mixture, vinegar and soy sauce into the brown sugar mixture until smooth.

Remove chicken and keep warm. Stir syrup mixture and add to the pan. Bring to a boil; cook and stir for 2 minutes or until thickened. Return chicken to the pan. Add peaches; heat through. Serve with rice.

NUTRITION FACTS: 1 chicken breast half with 1/3 cup sauce and 1/2 cup rice equals 329 calories, 4 g fat (1 g saturated fat), 63 mg cholesterol, 510 mg sodium, 47 g carbohydrate, 2 g fiber, 26 g protein. DIABETIC EXCHANGES: 3 very lean meat, 2 starch, 1 fruit, 1/2 fat.

Turkey Cutlets with Cool Pepper Sauce

CARB

(PICTURED ABOVE)

PREP/TOTAL TIME: 25 Min.   **YIELD:** 4 Servings (1/2 Cup Sauce)

Crisp breading surrounds tender turkey cutlets in this easy recipe.
—Jeannie Klugh, Lancaster, Pennsylvania

   3 tablespoons reduced-fat sour cream
   2 tablespoons reduced-fat mayonnaise
   2 tablespoons minced seeded jalapeno pepper
   2 teaspoons lemon juice
1/4 teaspoon grated lemon peel
1/8 teaspoon plus 1/4 teaspoon pepper, *divided*
1/2 cup seasoned bread crumbs
   2 tablespoons grated Parmesan cheese
   1 tablespoon minced fresh parsley
   1 garlic clove, minced
   1 package (17.6 ounces) turkey breast slices
   1 tablespoon olive oil
Lemon wedges and sliced jalapeno peppers, optional

For sauce, in a small bowl, combine the sour cream, mayonnaise, jalapeno, lemon juice and peel and 1/8 teaspoon pepper; set aside.

In a large resealable plastic bag, combine the bread crumbs, Parmesan cheese, parsley, garlic and remaining pepper. Add turkey, a few pieces at a time, and shake to coat.

In a large nonstick skillet, cook turkey in oil in batches over medium heat for 1-2 minutes on each side or until no longer pink. Serve with sauce. Garnish with lemon wedges and jalapenos if desired.

NUTRITION FACTS: 3 ounces cooked turkey with 2 tablespoons sauce equals 242 calories, 9 g fat (2 g saturated fat), 78 mg cholesterol, 296 mg sodium, 9 g carbohydrate, 1 g fiber, 31 g protein. **DIABETIC EXCHANGES:** 4 very lean meat, 1-1/2 fat, 1/2 starch.

Editor's Note: *When cutting or seeding hot peppers, use rubber or plastic gloves to protect your hands. Avoid touching your face.*

Chicken with Cranberry-Hoisin Sauce

PREP/TOTAL TIME: 30 Min.   **YIELD:** 6 Servings (1 Cup Sauce)

My husband and I have high cholesterol, so I've been trying to lighten recipes to meet our needs. This main course is so good, even my two small grandsons come back for more.
—Mary Lou Foley, London, Ontario

1/4 cup all-purpose flour
1/2 teaspoon salt
1/4 teaspoon pepper
   6 boneless skinless chicken breast halves (4 ounces *each*)
   1 teaspoon canola oil
SAUCE:
   1 can (20 ounces) unsweetened pineapple tidbits
   3 tablespoons hoisin sauce
   2 tablespoons reduced-sodium soy sauce
   1 tablespoon honey
   2 teaspoons rice wine vinegar
   1 garlic clove, minced
1/2 teaspoon hot pepper sauce
1/4 cup dried cranberries

In a large resealable plastic bag, combine the flour, salt and pepper. Add chicken, one piece at a time, and shake to coat.

In a large nonstick skillet coated with cooking spray, cook chicken in oil over medium heat for 5-6 minutes on each side or until juices run clear. Remove and keep warm.

Reserve 1/3 cup pineapple and 1/3 cup pineapple juice (save remainder for another use). In the skillet, combine the hoisin sauce, soy sauce, honey, vinegar, garlic, pepper sauce and reserved pineapple juice.

Stir in the cranberries and reserved pineapple. Cook and stir until mixture comes to a boil. Reduce heat; simmer, uncovered, for 2 minutes. Serve with chicken.

NUTRITION FACTS: 1 chicken breast half with about 3 tablespoons sauce equals 209 calories, 4 g fat (1 g saturated fat), 63 mg cholesterol, 585 mg sodium, 19 g carbohydrate, 1 g fiber, 24 g protein. **DIABETIC EXCHANGES:** 3 very lean meat, 1 starch, 1/2 fruit.

Garlic-Ginger Turkey Tenderloins

PREP/TOTAL TIME: 30 Min.   **YIELD:** 4 Servings

This good-for-you Asian entree can be on your family's plates quicker than Chinese takeout…and for a lot less money! Shared by our Test Kitchen, it has a ginger-brown sugar sauce that spices up the turkey tenderloins as they bake.

   1 package (20 ounces) turkey breast tenderloins
   3 tablespoons brown sugar, *divided*
   8 teaspoons reduced-sodium soy sauce, *divided*
   2 tablespoons minced fresh gingerroot
   6 garlic cloves, minced
1/2 teaspoon pepper
   1 tablespoon cornstarch
   1 cup reduced-sodium chicken broth

Place turkey in a shallow 3-qt. baking dish coated with cooking spray. In a small bowl, combine 2 tablespoons brown sugar, 6 teaspoons soy sauce, ginger, garlic and pepper. Set half aside; sprinkle remaining mixture over turkey.

Bake, uncovered, at 375° for 25-30 minutes or until a meat thermometer reads 170°. Let turkey stand for 5 minutes before slicing.

Meanwhile, in a small saucepan, combine the cornstarch and broth until smooth. Stir in reserved soy sauce mixture and remaining brown sugar and soy sauce. Bring to a boil; cook and stir for 2 minutes or until thickened. Serve with the turkey.

NUTRITION FACTS: 5 ounces cooked turkey with about 2 tablespoons sauce equals 212 calories, 2 g fat (1 g saturated fat), 69 mg cholesterol, 639 mg sodium, 14 g carbohydrate, trace fiber, 35 g protein. **DIABETIC EXCHANGES:** 5 very lean meat, 1 starch.

SHOP SMART
Save time by picking up a jar of minced garlic from your grocer's produce department. You can also mince several cloves of garlic at once, covering the garlic in oil, wine or vinegar and storing it in the refrigerator in a jar with a tight-fitting lid. Unbroken heads of garlic can be stored for about 8 weeks.

Shrimp Pizza
(PICTURED BELOW)

PREP/TOTAL TIME: 30 Min.   **YIELD:** 6 Slices

Here's a lightened-up version of one of my staples. Topped with fresh shrimp and melted cheese, this seafood pizza makes a timely supper with a special touch.   —Susan LeBrun, Sulphur, Louisiana

   1 tablespoon butter
4-1/2 teaspoons all-purpose flour
1/4 to 1/2 teaspoon ground mustard
1/8 to 1/4 teaspoon cayenne pepper
1/8 teaspoon salt
   1 cup 2% milk
   1 small onion, chopped
   1 pound uncooked medium shrimp, peeled and deveined
   1 prebaked Italian bread shell crust (14 ounces)
3/4 cup shredded part-skim mozzarella cheese

For white sauce, in a small nonstick saucepan, melt butter. Stir in the flour, mustard, cayenne and salt until smooth; gradually add milk. Bring to a boil; cook and stir for 2 minutes or until thickened. Remove from the heat; set aside.

In a large nonstick skillet coated with cooking spray, cook onion over medium heat for 2 minutes. Add shrimp; cook and stir 2-3 minutes longer. Drain.

Place crust on a pizza pan or baking sheet; spread with white sauce. Top with shrimp mixture and cheese. Bake at 425° for 8-12 minutes or until the shrimp turn pink and the cheese is melted.

NUTRITION FACTS: 1 slice equals 317 calories, 9 g fat (3 g saturated fat), 128 mg cholesterol, 633 mg sodium, 34 g carbohydrate, trace fiber, 24 g protein. **DIABETIC EXCHANGES:** 2 starch, 2 lean meat, 1 fat.

Chicken Caesar Pasta Toss

PREP/TOTAL TIME: 30 Min.   YIELD: 6 Servings

When looking for a no-hassle dinner to feed my hungry family, I came up with this recipe. Flavored with Caesar salad dressing, the combination of pasta, chicken and asparagus was a hit.
— Joy Bilbey, Holt, Michigan

   3 quarts water
2-1/2 cups uncooked tricolor spiral pasta
1-1/2 cups cut fresh asparagus (1-inch pieces)
1-1/2 pounds boneless skinless chicken breasts, cut into 1-inch pieces
   2 teaspoons olive oil
   2 large tomatoes, chopped
  2/3 cup reduced-fat Caesar salad dressing
   3 green onions, chopped
   3 tablespoons grated Parmesan cheese

In a Dutch oven, bring water to a boil. Add pasta. Return to a boil; cook for 4 minutes. Add asparagus; cook 6-8 minutes longer or until pasta and asparagus are tender.

Meanwhile, in a large nonstick skillet, saute chicken in oil until no longer pink. Remove from the heat.

Drain pasta mixture; return to the pan. Add the chicken, tomatoes and salad dressing. Cook over low heat until heated through. Sprinkle with onions and Parmesan cheese.

NUTRITION FACTS: 1-1/3 cups equals 363 calories, 10 g fat (2 g saturated fat), 67 mg cholesterol, 609 mg sodium, 35 g carbohydrate, 2 g fiber, 31 g protein. DIABETIC EXCHANGES: 3 very lean meat, 2 starch, 1 vegetable, 1 fat.

Chicken with Black Bean Salsa

FAT ▼

(PICTURED ABOVE)

PREP/TOTAL TIME: 25 Min.   YIELD: 4 Servings

There's nothing timid about the flavors in this Southwestern-style staple. Prepared on the grill or broiled, it's a fast, fun meal for a busy weeknight or a weekend get-together with friends.
— Trisha Kruse, Eagle, Idaho

   1 can (15 ounces) black beans, rinsed and drained
   1 can (8 ounces) unsweetened crushed pineapple, drained
   1 small red onion, chopped
   1 plum tomato, chopped
   1 garlic clove, minced
   2 tablespoons lime juice
 1/4 teaspoon salt
 1/4 teaspoon coarsely ground pepper
RUB:
   1 tablespoon brown sugar
   1 teaspoon hot pepper sauce
 1/2 teaspoon garlic powder
 1/2 teaspoon salt
 1/2 teaspoon coarsely ground pepper
   4 boneless skinless chicken breast halves (4 ounces *each*)

For salsa, in a large bowl, combine the first eight ingredients; refrigerate until serving. Combine the brown sugar, pepper sauce, garlic powder, salt and pepper; rub over both sides of the chicken.

If grilling the chicken, coat grill rack with cooking spray before starting the grill. Grill chicken, covered, over medium heat or broil 4 in. from the heat for 4-7 minutes on each side or until juices run clear. Serve with salsa.

NUTRITION FACTS: 1 chicken breast half with 3/4 cup salsa equals 269 calories, 3 g fat (1 g saturated fat), 63 mg cholesterol, 710 mg sodium, 31 g carbohydrate, 5 g fiber, 29 g protein. DIABETIC EXCHANGES: 3 very lean meat, 1-1/2 starch, 1/2 fruit.

Broiled Cod with Herb Sauce

 CARB ▼

PREP/TOTAL TIME: 25 Min.   YIELD: 4 Servings

A flavorful white sauce dresses up cod fillets in my high-protein entree. Pine nuts lend a little crunch for a special finishing touch.
— Rachel Niemeyer, Tacoma, Washington

   4 cod fillets (6 ounces *each*)
 1/2 teaspoon salt, *divided*
 1/4 teaspoon pepper, *divided*
   2 tablespoons butter
   2 tablespoons all-purpose flour
 1/2 teaspoon *each* dried oregano, tarragon and rosemary, crushed
   1 cup fat-free milk
 1/4 cup pine nuts, toasted

Sprinkle fillets with 1/4 teaspoon salt and 1/8 teaspoon pepper. Place on a broiler pan coated with cooking spray. Broil 3-4 in. from the heat for 8-12 minutes or until fish flakes easily with a fork.

Meanwhile, in a small saucepan, melt butter. Stir in the flour, herbs and remaining salt and pepper until blended. Gradually stir in milk. Bring to a boil; cook and stir for 2 minutes or until thickened. Spoon over cod; sprinkle with pine nuts.

NUTRITION FACTS: 1 fillet with 3 tablespoons sauce and 1 tablespoon pine nuts equals 259 calories, 11 g fat (4 g saturated fat), 81 mg cholesterol, 477 mg sodium, 8 g carbohydrate, 1 g fiber, 31 g protein. DIABETIC EXCHANGES: 5 very lean meat, 2 fat.

Beefed-Up Main Courses

Even your most serious meat-and-potato lover will happily sink his teeth into these hearty favorites. Loaded with all of the juicy flavor…and less fat…than you'd expect, the meaty entrees are sure to become staples at your table.

Hot 'n' Spicy Flank Steak, p. 116

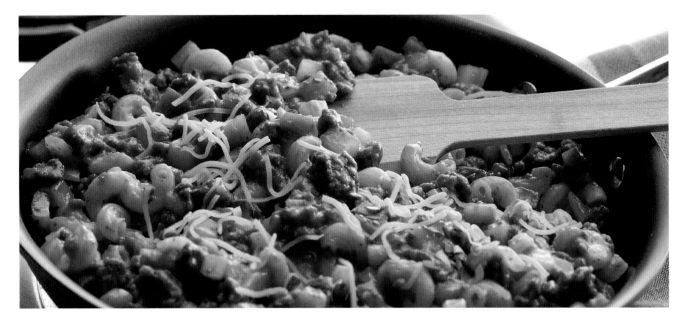

Macaroni Scramble

(PICTURED ABOVE)

PREP/TOTAL TIME: 25 Min.   **YIELD:** 3 Servings

This quick-and-easy dinner immediately became a family-pleasing classic in my home.   —Patricia Kile, Nokomis, Florida

- 1 cup uncooked cellentani (corkscrew pasta) *or* elbow macaroni
- 1/2 pound lean ground beef
- 1 small onion, chopped
- 1 celery rib, chopped
- 1 small green pepper, chopped
- 1 garlic clove, minced
- 1 can (10-3/4 ounces) reduced-sodium condensed tomato soup, undiluted
- 1 tablespoon minced fresh parsley *or* 1 teaspoon dried parsley flakes
- 1 teaspoon dried oregano
- 1/4 teaspoon salt
- 1/4 teaspoon pepper
- 1/2 cup shredded reduced-fat cheddar cheese

Cook pasta according to package directions. Meanwhile, in a large skillet, cook the beef, onion, celery, green pepper and garlic over medium heat until meat is no longer pink and vegetables are tender; drain. Drain pasta; add to the beef mixture. Stir in the soup, parsley, oregano, salt and pepper. Bring to a boil. Reduce heat; simmer, uncovered, for 4-5 minutes or until heated through. Sprinkle with cheese.

NUTRITION FACTS: 1-1/3 cups equals 351 calories, 11 g fat (5 g saturated fat), 50 mg cholesterol, 758 mg sodium, 38 g carbohydrate, 3 g fiber, 24 g protein. **DIABETIC EXCHANGES:** 3 lean meat, 2 starch, 1 vegetable.

TASTY TIP
Feel free to get creative with Macaroni Scramble. Add your favorite herbs and spices or jazz it up with a little cayenne pepper, chili powder or red pepper flakes.

Savory Beef Stew

PREP: 25 Min.   **COOK:** 1-1/4 Hours   **YIELD:** 4 Servings

Wine lends a warm accent to this satisfying take on a traditional French stew. I like to use low-fat mashed beans to thicken the broth and boost the nutrition.
—Margaret McCully, St. John, New Brunswick

- 1/4 cup all-purpose flour
- 1 pound lean beef stew meat, cut into 1-inch cubes
- 1 small onion, chopped
- 1 tablespoon canola oil
- 1-1/2 cups water
- 1 can (10-1/2 ounces) condensed beef consomme, undiluted
- 1/2 cup sherry *or* reduced-sodium beef broth
- 1 teaspoon Worcestershire sauce
- 1 teaspoon dried parsley flakes
- 1/4 teaspoon salt
- 1/4 teaspoon garlic powder
- 1/8 teaspoon pepper
- 2 medium carrots, chopped
- 2 medium parsnips, peeled and chopped
- 1 large potato, peeled and chopped
- 1 medium turnip, peeled and chopped

Place flour in a large resealable plastic bag; add beef, a few pieces at a time, and shake to coat.

In a large saucepan coated with cooking spray, cook beef and onion in oil over medium-high heat until beef is browned on all sides. Stir in the water, consomme, sherry or broth, Worcestershire sauce and seasonings. Bring to a boil. Reduce heat; cover and simmer for 1 hour.

Stir in the carrots, parsnips, potato and turnip. Bring to a boil. Reduce heat; cover and simmer for 30-45 minutes or until meat and vegetables are tender.

NUTRITION FACTS: 1-1/4 cups equals 349 calories, 12 g fat (3 g saturated fat), 73 mg cholesterol, 742 mg sodium, 29 g carbohydrate, 5 g fiber, 27 g protein. **DIABETIC EXCHANGES:** 3 lean meat, 2 vegetable, 1 starch, 1/2 fat.

Italian Beef on Rolls

(PICTURED BELOW)

PREP: 15 Min.   COOK: 8 Hours   YIELD: 8 Servings

Here's one of my all-time favorite slow cooker recipes. With 28 grams of protein per serving, it's a great way to meet your daily protein needs. —Jami Hilker, Fair Grove, Missouri

      1 boneless beef sirloin tip roast (2 pounds)
      1 can (14-1/2 ounces) diced tomatoes, undrained
      1 medium green pepper, chopped
  1/2 cup water
      1 tablespoon sesame seeds
1-1/2 teaspoons garlic powder
      1 teaspoon fennel seed, crushed
  1/2 teaspoon salt
  1/2 teaspoon pepper
      8 hard rolls, split

Place the roast in a 3-qt. slow cooker. In a small bowl, combine the tomatoes, green pepper, water and seasonings; pour over roast. Cover and cook on low for 8-9 hours or until meat is very tender.

Remove roast; cool slightly. Skim fat from cooking juices; shred beef and return to the slow cooker. Serve on rolls.

NUTRITION FACTS: 2/3 cup beef mixture on 1 roll equals 326 calories, 8 g fat (2 g saturated fat), 60 mg cholesterol, 572 mg sodium, 34 g carbohydrate, 3 g fiber, 28 g protein. DIABETIC EXCHANGES: 3 lean meat, 2 starch.

Spaghetti Pizza Casserole

(PICTURED ABOVE)

PREP: 25 Min.   BAKE: 25 Min.   YIELD: 9 Servings

I first tried this great-tasting dish at an office Christmas party. A wonderful alternative to ordinary spaghetti, it quickly became everyone's most-requested supper. —Kim Neer, Mansfield, Ohio

      1 package (7 ounces) spaghetti
  1/2 cup egg substitute
  1/4 cup grated Parmesan cheese
      1 pound lean ground beef
      1 medium onion, chopped
  1/2 cup chopped green pepper
  1/2 cup chopped sweet yellow pepper
      2 garlic cloves, minced
      1 jar (26 ounces) meatless spaghetti sauce
      1 teaspoon Italian seasoning
      1 teaspoon dried basil
  1/2 teaspoon salt
  1/4 teaspoon pepper
  1/2 pound sliced fresh mushrooms
1-1/2 cups (6 ounces) shredded part-skim mozzarella cheese

Cook spaghetti according to package directions. Rinse with cold water and drain. In a large bowl, toss spaghetti with egg substitute and Parmesan cheese. Spread spaghetti evenly into a 15-in. x 10-in. x 1-in. baking pan coated with cooking spray; set aside.

In a large nonstick skillet, cook the beef, onion and peppers over medium heat until meat is no longer pink; drain. Add garlic; cook 1 minute longer. Stir in spaghetti sauce and seasonings; heat through.

Spoon over spaghetti. Top with mushrooms and cheese. Bake, uncovered, at 350° for 25-30 minutes or until lightly browned. Let stand for 5 minutes before serving.

NUTRITION FACTS: 1 piece equals 274 calories, 8 g fat (4 g saturated fat), 37 mg cholesterol, 685 mg sodium, 29 g carbohydrate, 3 g fiber, 22 g protein. DIABETIC EXCHANGES: 2 lean meat, 1-1/2 starch, 1 vegetable.

Three-Pepper Beef Wraps
(PICTURED AT RIGHT)

PREP: 25 Min.   **COOK:** 20 Min.   **YIELD:** 6 Servings

This recipe is as versatile as the cook preparing it. Quick, simple-to-fix and good for you, it's a meal all ages seem to love.
—Doreen Muench, Chandler, Arizona

  1 *each* large green, sweet red and yellow peppers, julienned
  1 medium onion, halved and sliced
  2 tablespoons olive oil, *divided*
3/4 pound lean ground beef
  1 can (16 ounces) kidney beans, rinsed and drained
3/4 cup salsa
1/4 teaspoon steak seasoning
1/4 teaspoon pepper
  6 flour tortillas (8 inches), warmed
1/2 cup shredded reduced-fat cheddar cheese

In a large nonstick skillet, saute peppers and onion in 1 tablespoon oil until crisp-tender. Remove and keep warm.

In the same skillet, cook beef over medium heat until no longer pink; drain. Place the kidney beans, salsa and remaining oil in a food processor; cover and process until chopped. Add to beef. Sprinkle with steak seasoning and pepper; cook and stir until heated through.

Spoon about 1/3 cup beef mixture down the center of each tortilla; top each with 1/2 cup pepper mixture. Sprinkle with cheese. Fold sides and ends over filling and roll up.

NUTRITION FACTS: 1 wrap equals 390 calories, 14 g fat (4 g saturated fat), 34 mg cholesterol, 637 mg sodium, 43 g carbohydrate, 6 g fiber, 23 g protein. **DIABETIC EXCHANGES:** 2-1/2 starch, 2 lean meat, 2 vegetable, 1-1/2 fat.

Editor's Note: This recipe was tested with McCormick's Montreal Steak Seasoning. Look for it in the spice aisle of your grocery store.

Herbed Beef with Noodles

PREP: 25 Min.   **COOK:** 5 Hours   **YIELD:** 8 Servings

Just a handful of ingredients and a sprinkling of spices go into this slow-cooked dish. But although it's very simple, it's just wonderful and full of subtle flavors. Try it tonight.
—Roslyn Hurst, Belmont, California

  2 pounds boneless beef top round steak
1/2 teaspoon salt
1/2 teaspoon pepper, *divided*
  2 teaspoons canola oil
  1 can (10-3/4 ounces) reduced-fat reduced-sodium condensed cream of celery soup, undiluted
  1 medium onion, chopped
  1 tablespoon fat-free milk
  1 teaspoon dried oregano
1/2 teaspoon dried thyme
  6 cups cooked wide egg noodles
Chopped celery leaves, optional

Cut steak into serving-size pieces; sprinkle with salt and 1/4 teaspoon pepper.

In a large nonstick skillet coated with cooking spray,

brown the meat in oil on both sides. Transfer to a 3-qt. slow cooker.

In a small bowl, combine the soup, onion, milk, oregano, thyme and remaining pepper. Pour over meat. Cover and cook on low for 5-6 hours or until meat is tender. Serve over noodles. Sprinkle with celery leaves if desired.

NUTRITION FACTS: 3 ounces cooked beef with 3/4 cup noodles equals 290 calories, 7 g fat (2 g saturated fat), 92 mg cholesterol, 334 mg sodium, 26 g carbohydrate, 2 g fiber, 30 g protein. **DIABETIC EXCHANGES:** 3 lean meat, 1-1/2 starch.

time for a checkup?

To be considered safe, a slow cooker must be able to cook slow enough so that it can be left unattended, yet fast enough to keep the food at a healthy temperature. Here's how to check your device:

• Fill the slow cooker with 2 quarts of lukewarm water (or one-half to two-thirds full).

• Heat on low for 8 hours with the lid on.

• Use a food thermometer to check the water's temperature. Move quickly since the temperature drops fast once the lid is removed.

• The temperature should read 185 degrees. If it's higher, food cooked for 8 hours would likely be overdone. If the temperature is lower, the cooker may not heat food to a temperature adequate to deter bacteria growth and should be replaced.

Paprika Beef Stroganoff
(PICTURED BELOW)

PREP: 15 Min.   **COOK:** 55 Min.   **YIELD:** 8 Servings

Everyone looks forward to this wonderful meal. I can let it simmer on the stovetop while I do other things and it fills my home with a delightful aroma. —Lara Taylor, Virginia Beach, Virginia

- 2 pounds boneless beef top round steak, cut into thin strips
- 1 tablespoon plus 2 teaspoons canola oil, *divided*
- 1 large onion, sliced
- 1 large green pepper, cut into strips
- 1/2 pound sliced fresh mushrooms
- 1-1/4 cups reduced-sodium beef broth, *divided*
- 1 can (8 ounces) tomato sauce
- 3/4 cup sherry or additional reduced-sodium beef broth
- 2 tablespoons Worcestershire sauce
- 2 tablespoons prepared mustard
- 2 teaspoons paprika
- 1 bay leaf
- 1/2 teaspoon dried thyme
- 1/4 teaspoon pepper
- 1 package (12 ounces) yolk-free noodles
- 3 tablespoons all-purpose flour
- 1 cup (8 ounces) reduced-fat sour cream

In a large nonstick skillet coated with cooking spray, cook beef in 1 tablespoon oil until no longer pink; drain and set aside.

In the same skillet, saute onion and green pepper in remaining oil for 1 minute. Stir in mushrooms; cook for 3-4 minutes or until tender. Stir in 1 cup broth, tomato sauce, sherry or additional broth, Worcestershire sauce, mustard, paprika, bay leaf, thyme and pepper. Return beef to the pan; bring to a boil. Reduce heat; cover and simmer for 40-50 minutes or until meat is tender.

Cook noodles according to package directions. Meanwhile, combine flour and remaining broth until smooth; gradually stir into beef mixture. Bring to a boil; cook and stir for 2 minutes or until thickened. Discard bay leaf. Remove from the heat; stir in sour cream until blended. Drain noodles; serve with stroganoff.

NUTRITION FACTS: 3/4 cup stroganoff with 1 cup noodles equals 414 calories, 10 g fat (3 g saturated fat), 74 mg cholesterol, 360 mg sodium, 42 g carbohydrate, 4 g fiber, 36 g protein. **DIABETIC EXCHANGES:** 3 lean meat, 2-1/2 starch, 1 vegetable, 1 fat.

Sirloin Strips over Rice

(PICTURED BELOW)

PREP: 15 Min.   **COOK:** 30 Min.   **YIELD:** 6 Servings

I found this recipe in a movie magazine some 20 years ago. Its great flavor and the fact that leftovers just get better have made it a staple in my home. —Karen Dunn, Kansas City, Missouri

- 1-1/2 pounds boneless beef sirloin steak, cut into thin strips
- 1 teaspoon salt
- 1/4 teaspoon pepper
- 2 teaspoons olive oil, *divided*
- 2 medium onions, thinly sliced
- 1 garlic clove, minced
- 1 can (14-1/2 ounces) diced tomatoes, undrained
- 1/2 cup reduced-sodium beef broth
- 1/3 cup dry red wine *or* additional reduced-sodium beef broth
- 1 bay leaf
- 1/2 teaspoon dried basil
- 1/2 teaspoon dried thyme
- 3 cups hot cooked rice

Sprinkle beef strips with salt and pepper. In a large nonstick skillet coated with cooking spray, brown beef in 1 teaspoon oil. Remove and keep warm.

In the same skillet, saute onions and garlic in remaining oil until tender. Stir in the tomatoes, broth, wine or additional broth, bay leaf, basil and thyme. Bring to a boil. Reduce heat; simmer, uncovered, for 10 minutes.

Return beef to the pan; cook for 2-4 minutes or until tender and mixture is heated through. Discard bay leaf. Serve beef over rice.

NUTRITION FACTS: 2/3 cup beef mixture with 1/2 cup rice equals 299 calories, 7 g fat (2 g saturated fat), 63 mg cholesterol, 567 mg sodium, 31 g carbohydrate, 3 g fiber, 25 g protein. **DIABETIC EXCHANGES:** 3 lean meat, 1-1/2 starch, 1 vegetable, 1 fat.

Tex-Mex Lasagna

(PICTURED ABOVE)

PREP: 20 Min.   **BAKE:** 45 Min. + Standing   **YIELD:** 12 Servings

This recipe combines my love of lasagna with my love of Mexican food. I tried to make the lasagna healthier by using extra-lean ground beef and I increased the fiber by adding beans. —Athena Russell, Florence, South Carolina

- 1 pound lean ground beef
- 1 can (16 ounces) refried black beans
- 1 can (15 ounces) black beans, rinsed and drained
- 1/2 cup frozen corn, thawed
- 1 jalapeno pepper, seeded and chopped
- 1 envelope taco seasoning
- 1 can (15 ounces) tomato sauce, *divided*
- 2-1/2 cups salsa
- 12 no-cook lasagna noodles
- 1-1/2 cups (6 ounces) shredded reduced-fat Monterey Jack cheese *or* Mexican cheese blend
- 1-1/2 cups (6 ounces) shredded reduced-fat cheddar cheese
- 1 cup (8 ounces) fat-free sour cream
- 1 medium ripe avocado, peeled and cubed
- 4 green onions, thinly sliced

In a large nonstick skillet, cook beef over medium heat until no longer pink; drain. Stir in the beans, corn, jalapeno, taco seasoning and 3/4 cup tomato sauce.

Combine salsa and remaining tomato sauce. Spread 1/4 cup into a 13-in. x 9-in. x 2-in. baking dish coated with cooking spray. Layer with four noodles (noodles will overlap slightly), half of the meat sauce, 1 cup salsa mixture, 1/2 cup Monterey Jack cheese and 1/2 cup cheddar cheese. Repeat layers. Top with the remaining noodles, salsa mixture and cheeses.

Cover and bake at 350° for 45-50 minutes or until edges are bubbly and cheese is melted. Let stand for 10 minutes before cutting. Serve with sour cream, avocado and onions.

NUTRITION FACTS: 1 piece equals 381 calories, 13 g fat (7 g saturated fat), 47 mg cholesterol, 1,170 mg sodium, 39 g carbohydrate, 5 g fiber, 25 g protein.

Editor's Note: *When cutting or seeding hot peppers, use rubber or plastic gloves to protect your hands. Avoid touching your face.*

Pizza Spaghetti

PREP: 20 Min. **COOK:** 30 Min. **YIELD:** 6 Servings

I had the idea for this dinner when I saw someone dip a slice of pizza into a pasta dish. My wife and kids love it!
—Robert Smith, Las Vegas, Nevada

- 1/2 **pound lean ground beef**
- 1/2 **pound Italian turkey sausage links, casings removed, crumbled**
- 1/2 **cup chopped sweet onion**
- 4 **cans (8 ounces *each*) no-salt-added tomato sauce**
- 3 **ounces sliced turkey pepperoni**
- 1 **tablespoon sugar**
- 2 **teaspoons minced fresh parsley *or* 1/2 teaspoon dried parsley flakes**
- 2 **teaspoons minced fresh basil *or* 1/2 teaspoon dried basil**
- 9 **ounces uncooked whole wheat spaghetti**
- 3 **tablespoons grated Parmesan cheese**

In a large nonstick skillet, cook beef, sausage and onion over medium heat until meat is no longer pink; drain.

Stir in the tomato sauce, pepperoni, sugar, parsley and basil. Bring to a boil. Reduce heat; simmer, uncovered, for 20-25 minutes or until thickened. Meanwhile, cook spaghetti according to package directions.

Drain the spaghetti; toss with the sauce. Sprinkle with the Parmesan cheese.

NUTRITION FACTS: 1-1/3 cups equals 369 calories, 9 g fat (3 g saturated fat), 60 mg cholesterol, 614 mg sodium, 46 g carbohydrate, 7 g fiber, 25 g protein.

Beef on a Stick

PREP: 15 Min. + Marinating **GRILL:** 10 Min. **YIELD:** 6 Kabobs

My daughter's friend gave her this simply great-tasting marinade recipe. We made it healthier just by using a reduced-sodium soy sauce. —Lois Weigel, Mountain Home, Arkansas

- 1/3 **cup reduced-sodium soy sauce**
- 3 **tablespoons honey**
- 2 **tablespoons canola oil**
- 2 **tablespoons cider vinegar**
- 2 **tablespoons hoisin sauce**
- 1 **tablespoon brown sugar**
- 1-1/2 **teaspoons Worcestershire sauce**
- 2 **garlic cloves, minced**
- 1 **boneless beef top sirloin steak (1-1/2 pounds), cut into 1-inch cubes**

In a large resealable plastic bag, combine the first eight ingredients; add beef. Seal bag and turn to coat; refrigerate for 8 hours or overnight.

Coat grill rack with cooking spray before starting the grill. Drain and discard marinade. Thread beef onto six metal or soaked wooden skewers. Grill, covered, over medium heat for 8-10 minutes or until meat reaches desired doneness, turning kabobs occasionally.

NUTRITION FACTS: 1 kabob equals 161 calories, 6 g fat (2 g saturated fat), 64 mg cholesterol, 174 mg sodium, 3 g carbohydrate, trace fiber, 22 g protein. **DIABETIC EXCHANGE:** 3 lean meat.

Citrus Steaks

(PICTURED BELOW)

PREP/TOTAL TIME: 25 Min. **YIELD:** 2 Servings

Brighten up those cold winter nights with a burst of citrus. Clementines and beef make a delicious pairing in this special dinner for two from our Test Kitchen staff.

- 2 **boneless beef sirloin steaks (5 ounces *each*)**
- 1/4 **teaspoon salt**
- 1/4 **teaspoon pepper**
- 2 **teaspoons canola oil**
- 2 **clementines, peeled and sectioned**
- 1 **green onion, chopped**
- 1 **tablespoon finely chopped walnuts, toasted**
- 1/3 **cup dry red wine *or* reduced-sodium beef broth**

Hot cooked rice, optional

Sprinkle steaks with salt and pepper. In a large nonstick skillet coated with cooking spray, cook steaks in oil over medium heat for 5-6 minutes on each side or until meat reaches desired doneness (for medium-rare, a meat thermometer should read 145°; medium, 160°; well-done, 170°).

Meanwhile, combine the clementines, onion and walnuts; set aside. Remove steaks and keep warm.

Add wine or broth to the skillet, stirring to loosen browned bits. Bring to a boil. Reduce heat; simmer, uncovered, for 1-2 minutes or until liquid is reduced to 2 tablespoons. Spoon over steaks. Serve with clementine mixture and rice if desired.

NUTRITION FACTS: 1 steak with about 1/3 cup clementine mixture (calculated without the rice) equals 311 calories, 14 g fat (3 g saturated fat), 79 mg cholesterol, 357 mg sodium, 13 g carbohydrate, 3 g fiber, 29 g protein.

Japanese Steak Salad

(PICTURED BELOW)

PREP: 25 Min. + Marinating   **COOK:** 20 Min.   **YIELD:** 4 Servings

We enjoy all kinds of ethnic foods, and this beef recipe is a snap to toss together. With its sweet soy marinade and fresh veggies, there's lots to love about the main-dish salad.

—Diane Halferty, Corpus Christi, Texas

3 tablespoons sherry *or* reduced-sodium chicken broth
3 tablespoons rice wine vinegar
3 tablespoons reduced-sodium soy sauce
2 tablespoons hoisin sauce
1/2 teaspoon minced fresh gingerroot
1 boneless beef sirloin steak (1 inch thick and 1-1/4 pounds)
2 green onions, chopped
1 tablespoon sugar
1 tablespoon sesame oil
1/3 cup fresh snow peas
3 cups sliced Chinese *or* napa cabbage
3 cups torn romaine
1/3 cup uncooked instant rice
1/2 cup julienned carrot
1/2 cup thinly sliced cucumber
1/2 cup sliced radishes

In a small bowl, combine the first five ingredients. Pour 1/3 cup into a large resealable plastic bag; add beef. Seal bag and turn to coat; refrigerate for at least 2 hours. For dressing, add the onions, sugar and sesame oil to the remaining marinade. Cover and refrigerate until serving.

In a small saucepan, bring 1 in. of water to a boil. Add peas. Reduce heat; cover and simmer for 2-3 minutes or until crisp-tender. Drain and immediately place peas in ice water. Drain and pat dry. Combine the cabbage, romaine and peas; place on a serving platter.

Drain and discard marinade. Broil beef 4-6 in. from the heat for 8-10 minutes on each side or until meat reaches desired doneness (for medium-rare, a meat thermometer should read 145°; medium, 160°; well-done, 170°). Let stand for 5 minutes before slicing.

Meanwhile, cook rice according to package directions. Arrange the carrot, cucumber and radishes on cabbage mixture. Top with rice and beef; drizzle with dressing.

NUTRITION FACTS: 1 serving equals 298 calories, 10 g fat (3 g saturated fat), 80 mg cholesterol, 438 mg sodium, 19 g carbohydrate, 3 g fiber, 30 g protein. **DIABETIC EXCHANGES:** 4 lean meat, 1 vegetable, 1/2 starch, 1/2 fat.

Barbecue Beef Sandwiches

PREP/TOTAL TIME: 30 Min.   **YIELD:** 6 Servings

A quick, tangy sauce gives these family-pleasing sandwiches lots of zip. I've had this recipe for years, and I've given it out many, many times.

—Sharon Zagar, Gardner, Illinois

1-1/2 pounds lean ground beef
2 celery ribs, finely chopped
1 large onion, finely chopped
1 can (8 ounces) tomato sauce
1/4 cup ketchup
2 tablespoons brown sugar
2 tablespoons barbecue sauce
1 tablespoon prepared mustard
1 tablespoon Worcestershire sauce
6 hamburger buns, split

In a large nonstick skillet, cook the beef, celery and onion over medium heat until meat is no longer pink; drain.

Stir in the tomato sauce, ketchup, brown sugar, barbecue sauce, mustard and Worcestershire sauce. Bring to a boil. Reduce heat; simmer, uncovered, for 10-15 minutes to allow flavors to blend. Spoon 3/4 cup onto each bun.

NUTRITION FACTS: 1 sandwich equals 348 calories, 11 g fat (4 g saturated fat), 56 mg cholesterol, 719 mg sodium, 35 g carbohydrate, 2 g fiber, 27 g protein. **DIABETIC EXCHANGES:** 3 lean meat, 2 starch.

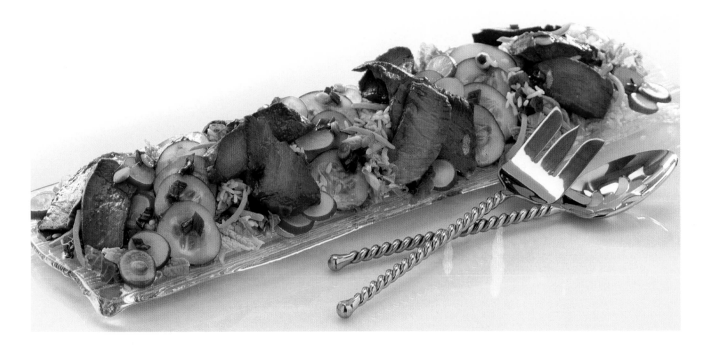

Mexi-Mac Skillet

(PICTURED ABOVE)

PREP/TOTAL TIME: 30 Min.   **YIELD:** 5 Servings

This dish really saves time because it eliminates the need to precook the pasta and makes a family-pleasing supper in minutes! It's the tastiest and quickest recipe I have.
— Maurane Ramsey, Fort Wayne, Indiana

  1 pound lean ground beef
  1 large onion, chopped
  1 can (14-1/2 ounces) diced tomatoes, undrained
  1 can (8 ounces) tomato sauce
  1 cup fresh *or* frozen corn
  1/2 cup water
1-1/4 teaspoons chili powder
  1 teaspoon dried oregano
  1/2 teaspoon salt
  2/3 cup uncooked elbow macaroni
  2/3 cup shredded reduced-fat cheddar cheese

In a large nonstick skillet over medium-high heat, cook beef and onion until meat is no longer pink; drain. Stir in the tomatoes, tomato sauce, corn, water, chili powder, oregano and salt.

Bring to a boil; stir in macaroni. Reduce heat; cover and simmer for 18-22 minutes or until macaroni is tender. Sprinkle with cheese.

NUTRITION FACTS: 1 cup equals 283 calories, 11 g fat (5 g saturated fat), 55 mg cholesterol, 716 mg sodium, 23 g carbohydrate, 4 g fiber, 25 g protein. **DIABETIC EXCHANGES:** 3 lean meat, 1 starch, 1 vegetable.

TASTY TIP

For a meal in a jiffy, Maurane Ramsey likes to serve her Mexi-Mac Skillet with a simple side salad and a fresh fruit medley for dessert. You could also add a loaf of bread or rolls from the local bakery.

Hot 'n' Spicy Flank Steak

CARB

(PICTURED BELOW)

PREP: 15 Min. + Marinating   **GRILL:** 15 Min.   **YIELD:** 6 Servings

With its flavorful marinade, this flank steak makes a succulent meal. I received the recipe from a friend, and it's been a regular on my table ever since. — Julee Wallberg, Reno, Nevada

  3 tablespoons brown sugar
  3 tablespoons red wine vinegar
  3 tablespoons sherry *or* reduced-sodium chicken broth
  3 tablespoons reduced-sodium soy sauce
  1 tablespoon canola oil
1-1/2 teaspoons crushed red pepper flakes
1-1/2 teaspoons paprika
1-1/2 teaspoons chili powder
1-1/2 teaspoons Worcestershire sauce
  3/4 teaspoon seasoned salt
  3/4 teaspoon garlic powder
  3/4 teaspoon dried parsley flakes
  1 beef flank steak (1-1/2 pounds)

In a small bowl, combine the first 12 ingredients. Pour 1/3 cup marinade into a large resealable plastic bag; add the steak. Seal bag and turn to coat; refrigerate for 1-3 hours. Cover and refrigerate remaining marinade for basting.

Coat grill rack with cooking spray before starting the grill. Drain and discard marinade. Grill steak, uncovered, over medium heat for 6-8 minutes on each side or until meat reaches desired doneness (for medium-rare, a meat thermometer should read 145°; medium, 160°; well-done, 170°), basting frequently with remaining marinade. Thinly slice steak across the grain.

NUTRITION FACTS: 3 ounces cooked beef equals 201 calories, 9 g fat (4 g saturated fat), 54 mg cholesterol, 326 mg sodium, 5 g carbohydrate, trace fiber, 22 g protein. **DIABETIC EXCHANGE:** 3 lean meat.

Taco Stuffed Peppers

PREP: 30 Min.   **BAKE:** 15 Min.   **YIELD:** 4 Servings

Sometimes I use rice instead of orzo pasta in this zesty take on stuffed bell peppers.   —Shannon Talmage, Alexandria, Indiana

    4 medium green peppers
1/3 cup uncooked orzo pasta
3/4 pound lean ground beef
1/4 pound reduced-fat bulk pork sausage
    3 tablespoons chopped onion
    2 plum tomatoes, seeded and chopped
    2 tablespoons taco seasoning
    1 garlic clove, minced
3/4 cup shredded reduced-fat cheddar cheese, *divided*

Cut tops off peppers and remove seeds. In a large kettle, cook peppers in boiling water for 3-5 minutes. Drain and rinse in cold water; set aside.

Cook orzo according to package directions. Meanwhile, in a large nonstick skillet, cook the beef, sausage and onion over medium heat until meat is no longer pink; drain. Reduce heat to low. Add the tomatoes, taco seasoning and garlic. Cook, uncovered, for 10 minutes, stirring occasionally.

Drain orzo; stir into meat mixture. Add 1/2 cup cheese. Spoon into peppers. Place in an 11-in. x 7-in. x 2-in. baking dish coated with cooking spray.

Cover and bake at 350° for 10 minutes. Uncover; sprinkle with remaining cheese. Bake 5 minutes longer or until cheese is melted.

NUTRITION FACTS: 1 pepper equals 379 calories, 17 g fat (8 g saturated fat), 87 mg cholesterol, 772 mg sodium, 28 g carbohydrate, 3 g fiber, 30 g protein. **DIABETIC EXCHANGES:** 3 lean meat, 2 vegetable, 1-1/2 fat, 1 starch.

Hamburger Noodle Casserole
(PICTURED ABOVE)

PREP: 30 Min.   **BAKE:** 35 Min.   **YIELD:** 10 Servings

People have a hard time believing this homey and hearty casserole uses light ingredients. The taste is so rich and creamy...a great weeknight family entree.   —Martha Henson, Winnsboro, Texas

    5 cups uncooked egg noodles
1-1/2 pounds lean ground beef
    2 garlic cloves, minced
    3 cans (8 ounces *each*) tomato sauce
1/2 teaspoon sugar
1/2 teaspoon salt
1/8 teaspoon pepper
    1 package (8 ounces) reduced-fat cream cheese
    1 cup reduced-fat ricotta cheese
1/4 cup reduced-fat sour cream
    3 green onions, thinly sliced, *divided*
2/3 cup shredded reduced-fat cheddar cheese

Cook noodles according to package directions. Meanwhile, in a large nonstick skillet over medium heat, cook beef and garlic until meat is no longer pink; drain. Stir in the tomato sauce, sugar, salt and pepper; heat through. Drain noodles; stir into beef mixture.

In a small mixing bowl, beat the cream cheese, ricotta cheese and sour cream until blended. Stir in half of the onions.

Spoon half of the noodle mixture into a 13-in. x 9-in. x 2-in. baking dish coated with cooking spray. Top with cheese mixture and remaining noodle mixture.

Cover casserole and bake at 350° for 30 minutes. Uncover; sprinkle with cheddar cheese. Bake 5-10 minutes longer or until heated through and cheese is melted. Sprinkle with the remaining onions.

NUTRITION FACTS: 1 cup equals 319 calories, 14 g fat (8 g saturated fat), 92 mg cholesterol, 635 mg sodium, 23 g carbohydrate, 1 g fiber, 24 g protein. **DIABETIC EXCHANGES:** 3 lean meat, 1-1/2 starch, 1 fat.

All-American Rub

FAT SALT CARB

PREP/TOTAL TIME: 5 Min.   **YIELD:** 3/4 cup

This wonderful salt-free rub is great on steaks, as well as pork and chicken.   —Heather Bonser, Laurel, Montana

1/2 cup packed brown sugar
    2 tablespoons dried minced onion
    1 tablespoon garlic powder
    1 tablespoon ground mustard
1/2 teaspoon cayenne pepper
1/8 teaspoon ground nutmeg

In a small bowl, combine all ingredients; store in an airtight container.

Rub over beef; cover and refrigerate for up to 4 hours before grilling or broiling.

NUTRITION FACTS: 1 tablespoon equals 43 calories, trace fat (trace saturated fat), 0 cholesterol, 4 mg sodium, 10 g carbohydrate, trace fiber, trace protein. **DIABETIC EXCHANGE:** 1/2 starch.

> **TASTY TIP**
> If you have friends who are watching their sodium intake, keep All-American Rub in mind. Small bottles of the low-salt rub make great gifts.

Flank Steak with Wine Sauce

(PICTURED BELOW)

CARB

PREP: 40 Min. + Cooling   **COOK:** 30 Min.   **YIELD:** 6 Servings (3/4 Cup Sauce)

For best results, I always serve this lean flank steak medium rare. Deglaze the pan with wine, making sure to scrape up all the savory browned bits with a wooden spoon.
—Warner Beatty, Niagara Falls, Ontario

- 1 whole garlic bulb
- 1-1/2 teaspoons olive oil, *divided*
- 1 beef flank steak (1-1/2 pounds)
- 1 teaspoon coarsely ground pepper
- 3/4 teaspoon salt
- 2 tablespoons butter, *divided*
- 1/2 cup reduced-sodium beef broth
- 1 cup dry red wine *or* 1/4 cup grape juice and 3/4 cup additional reduced-sodium beef broth
- 1/4 cup thinly sliced green onions

Remove papery outer skin from garlic bulb (do not peel or separate cloves). Cut top off of garlic bulb; brush with 1/2 teaspoon oil. Wrap bulb in heavy-duty foil. Bake at 425° for 30-35 minutes or until softened. Cool for 10-15 minutes. Squeeze softened garlic into a small bowl; mash and set aside.

Sprinkle steak with pepper and salt. In a large non-stick skillet coated with cooking spray, cook steak over medium-high heat in remaining oil for 3-4 minutes on each side or until the steak is browned.

Reduce heat to medium; add 1 tablespoon butter. Cook for 4-8 minutes on each side or until meat reaches desired doneness (for medium-rare, a meat thermometer should read 145°; medium, 160°; well-done, 170°). Remove steak and keep warm.

Gradually add broth and wine or grape juice and additional broth to pan, stirring to loosen browned bits. Bring to a boil. Stir in mashed garlic. Reduce heat; simmer, uncovered, until liquid is reduced by half.

Strain sauce and return to pan; stir in remaining butter until melted. Thinly slice steak across the grain. Sprinkle with onions; serve with sauce.

NUTRITION FACTS: 3 ounces cooked beef with 2 tablespoons sauce equals 227 calories, 13 g fat (6 g saturated fat), 65 mg cholesterol, 439 mg sodium, 1 g carbohydrate, trace fiber, 22 g protein. **DIABETIC EXCHANGES:** 3 lean meat, 1 fat.

storage savvy

Keep the following in mind when storing beef:

- Uncooked ground beef and stew meat as well as beef broth keep in the refrigerator 1 to 2 days.
- Cooked meats and meaty casseroles and meat pizzas can stay in the refrigerator for 3 to 4 days.
- Fresh steaks and roasts will keep in the refigerator for 3 to 5 days.

Favorite Recipe Made Lighter

HOMECOMINGS are all the sweeter when the aroma of your favorite comfort food awaits your return. And for Mandy Anderson's husband, that food is the hearty, meat-cheese-and-stuffing casserole, Zucchini Supper.

"Chris works on the road and eats truck-stop food all the time, so I like making this dinner when he's home," she writes from East Moline, Illinois. "I know it can't be good for him, so I'd like to make it more nutritional."

Our team first eliminated the boxed stuffing mix, which is high in sodium but low on nutrition. Instead, they created a savory homemade stuffing with whole-wheat bread cubes, onion, carrot and celery, adding flavor, color, minerals and vitamins in the process. Next, they "beefed up" Mandy's recipe by decreasing the pork sausage. They made up the difference with additional lean ground beef.

They also used egg substitute for eggs, replaced full-fat with reduced-fat process cheese and eliminated the cheese soup altogether.

Mandy's revised one-dish wonder boasts nearly 60% less saturated fat, 199 fewer calories and 46% less sodium per serving! But it's more colorful and nutritious than the original. And it still has the cheesy, melt-in-your-mouth flavor her husband loves.

Makeover Zucchini Supper
(PICTURED ABOVE)

PREP: 30 Min.   BAKE: 50 Min.   YIELD: 8 Servings

- 1-1/2 pounds lean ground beef
- 1/2 pound reduced-fat bulk pork sausage
- 1 large onion, chopped
- 1 medium carrot, chopped
- 1 celery rib, chopped
- 2 cups cubed day-old whole wheat bread
- 1/2 cup fat-free milk
- 1 tablespoon all-purpose flour
- 4 cups chopped zucchini
- 3/4 pound reduced-fat process cheese (Velveeta), cubed
- 1 can (10-3/4 ounces) reduced-fat reduced-sodium condensed cream of mushroom soup, undiluted
- 3/4 cup egg substitute
- 1 teaspoon garlic powder
- 1/2 teaspoon onion powder
- 1/2 teaspoon rubbed sage
- 1/2 teaspoon dried thyme
- 1/2 teaspoon pepper

In a Dutch oven, cook the beef, sausage, onion, carrot and celery over medium heat until meat is no longer pink and vegetables are crisp-tender. Meanwhile, in a small bowl, combine bread cubes and milk; set aside.

Remove meat mixture from the heat; drain. Stir in flour until blended. Stir in bread mixture and remaining ingredients.

Transfer to a 13-in. x 9-in. x 2-in. baking dish coated with cooking spray. Cover and bake at 350° for 40-45 minutes or until a meat thermometer reads 160°. Uncover and stir. Bake 8-12 minutes longer or until golden brown.

NUTRITION FACTS: 1-1/3 cups equals 373 calories, 17 g fat (7 g saturated fat), 80 mg cholesterol, 1,119 mg sodium, 21 g carbohydrate, 2 g fiber, 34 g protein.

Zucchini Supper

PREP: 25 Min.   BAKE: 35 Min.   YIELD: 8 Servings

- 1 pound ground beef
- 1 pound bulk pork sausage
- 4 cups chopped zucchini
- 1 pound process cheese (Velveeta), cubed
- 1 can (10-3/4 ounces) condensed cream of mushroom soup, undiluted
- 1 can (10-3/4 ounces) condensed cheddar cheese soup, undiluted
- 1 package (6 ounces) stuffing mix
- 3 eggs, lightly beaten
- 1 small onion, chopped
- 1/2 teaspoon salt
- 1/2 teaspoon garlic powder
- 1/4 teaspoon pepper

In a Dutch oven, cook beef and sausage over medium heat until no longer pink; drain. Stir in the remaining ingredients. Cook, stirring occasionally, until heated through.

Transfer to a greased 13-in. x 9-in. x 2-in. baking dish. Cover and bake at 350° for 30-35 minutes or until a meat thermometer reads 160°. Uncover and stir. Bake 4-6 minutes longer or until golden brown.

NUTRITION FACTS: 1-1/4 cups equals 572 calories, 37 g fat (17 g saturated fat), 170 mg cholesterol, 2,064 mg sodium, 29 g carbohydrate, 2 g fiber, 33 g protein.

Sweet-and-Sour Beef

PREP/TOTAL TIME: 30 Min.   **YIELD:** 4 Servings

This healthful stir-fry can't be beat when you're short on time. I've used a variety of meats and apples and sometimes replace the green onion with yellow onion. It always tastes great!
—Brittany McCloud, Kenyon, Minnesota

   1 pound boneless beef sirloin steak, cut into 1/2-inch cubes
   1 teaspoon salt
1/2 teaspoon pepper
   3 teaspoons canola oil, *divided*
   1 large green pepper, cut into 1/2-inch pieces
   1 large sweet red pepper, cut into 1/2-inch pieces
   2 medium tart apples, chopped
1/2 cup plus 2 tablespoons thinly sliced green onions, *divided*
2/3 cup packed brown sugar
1/2 cup cider vinegar
   1 tablespoon cornstarch
   2 tablespoons cold water
Hot cooked rice, optional

Sprinkle beef with salt and pepper. In a large nonstick skillet or wok coated with cooking spray, stir-fry beef in 2 teaspoons oil until no longer pink. Remove and keep warm.

In the same pan, stir-fry peppers and apples in remaining oil for 3 minutes. Add 1/2 cup green onions. Stir-fry 2-3 minutes longer or until peppers are crisp-tender. Remove and keep warm.

Add brown sugar and vinegar to pan; bring to a boil. Combine cornstarch and water until smooth; stir into brown sugar mixture. Return to a boil; cook and stir for 2 minutes or until thickened and bubbly.

Return beef and vegetable mixture to pan; heat through. Garnish with remaining onions. Serve with rice if desired.

NUTRITION FACTS: 1-1/2 cups (calculated without rice) equals 390 calories, 10 g fat (3 g saturated fat), 63 mg cholesterol, 656 mg sodium, 56 g carbohydrate, 4 g fiber, 23 g protein.

Teriyaki Beef Burgers

PREP: 15 Min. + Marinating   **GRILL:** 10 Min.   **YIELD:** 6 Servings

Everyone who tastes them agrees that these are not your ordinary burgers! A flavorful Asian-inspired marinade and crunchy water chestnuts make them a surefire crowd-pleaser.
—Mitzi Sentiff, Alexandria, Virginia

1-1/2 pounds lean ground beef
   1 can (8 ounces) water chestnuts, drained and chopped
1/2 cup reduced-sodium soy sauce
1/3 cup sherry *or* reduced-sodium beef broth
   2 green onions, chopped
   1 tablespoon brown sugar
   2 garlic cloves, minced
1/2 teaspoon ground ginger
   6 lettuce leaves
   6 hamburger buns, split

In a large bowl, combine the beef and water chestnuts. Shape into six patties. Place in a 13-in. x 9-in. x 2-in. dish.

In a small bowl, combine the soy sauce, sherry or broth, onions, brown sugar, garlic and ginger. Pour 1/2 cup over patties; cover and refrigerate for 2-3 hours or overnight. Cover and refrigerate remaining marinade for basting.

Coat grill rack with cooking spray before starting the grill. Drain and discard marinade. Grill patties, covered, over medium heat for 5-7 minutes on each side or until meat is no longer pink, basting occasionally with reserved marinade. Serve on lettuce-lined buns.

NUTRITION FACTS: 1 burger equals 335 calories, 10 g fat (4 g saturated fat), 56 mg cholesterol, 924 mg sodium, 29 g carbohydrate, 2 g fiber, 27 g protein. **DIABETIC EXCHANGES:** 3 lean meat, 2 starch, 1 vegetable.

Taco Pasta Shells
(PICTURED BELOW)

PREP: 25 Min.   **BAKE:** 25 Min.   **YIELD:** 6 Servings

Here's a kid-friendly dish so flavorful and fun, nobody is likely to guess that it's also lower in fat. It's a healthy supper perfect for busy weeknights.
—Anne Thomsen, Westchester, Ohio

  18 uncooked jumbo pasta shells
1-1/2 pounds lean ground beef
   1 bottle (16 ounces) taco sauce, *divided*
   3 ounces fat-free cream cheese, cubed
   2 teaspoons chili powder
3/4 cup shredded reduced-fat Mexican cheese blend, *divided*
  20 baked tortilla chip scoops, coarsely crushed

Cook pasta according to package directions. Meanwhile, in a large nonstick skillet over medium heat, cook beef until no longer pink; drain. Add 1/2 cup taco sauce, cream cheese and chili powder; cook and stir until blended. Stir in 1/4 cup cheese blend.

Drain pasta and rinse in cold water; stuff each shell with about 2 tablespoons beef mixture. Arrange in an 11-in. x 7-in. x 2-in. baking dish coated with cooking spray. Spoon remaining taco sauce over the top.

Cover and bake at 350° for 20 minutes. Uncover; sprinkle with remaining cheese blend. Bake 5-10 minutes longer or until heated through and cheese is melted. Sprinkle with chips.

NUTRITION FACTS: 3 stuffed shells equals 384 calories, 13 g fat (5 g saturated fat), 67 mg cholesterol, 665 mg sodium, 33 g carbohydrate, 3 g fiber, 33 g protein.

Layered Italian Casserole
(PICTURED ABOVE)

PREP: 30 Min.   **BAKE:** 50 Min.   **YIELD:** 10 Servings

Here's a wonderful dish that tastes just like lasagna but with less preparation time. —Joyce Benninger, Owen Sound, Ontario

   12 ounces uncooked spaghetti
1-1/2 pounds lean ground beef
    1 large onion, chopped
    2 garlic cloves, minced
    2 cans (15 ounces *each*) Italian tomato sauce
    3 tablespoons minced fresh parsley
    1 tablespoon dried oregano
    4 cups (32 ounces) 1% cottage cheese
2-1/2 cups (10 ounces) shredded part-skim mozzarella cheese, *divided*
   1/2 cup grated Parmesan cheese, *divided*

Cook spaghetti according to package directions. Meanwhile, in a large nonstick skillet over medium heat, cook the beef, onion and garlic until meat is no longer pink; drain. Add the tomato sauce, parsley and oregano; heat through.

In a large bowl, combine the cottage cheese, 2 cups mozzarella cheese and 1/4 cup Parmesan cheese. Drain the spaghetti.

Spread 1 cup meat sauce into a 13-in. x 9-in. x 2-in. baking dish coated with cooking spray. Layer with half of the spaghetti, cheese mixture and remaining meat sauce. Repeat layers (dish will be full).

Cover and bake at 350° for 45 minutes. Uncover; sprinkle with remaining mozzarella and Parmesan cheeses. Bake 5-10 minutes longer or until heated through and cheese is melted.

NUTRITION FACTS: 1-1/4 cups equals 413 calories, 12 g fat (6 g saturated fat), 56 mg cholesterol, 1,067 mg sodium, 36 g carbohydrate, 3 g fiber, 39 g protein.

Beef Taco Salad

PREP/TOTAL TIME: 30 Min.   **YIELD:** 2 Servings

This entree salad is a flavorful, colorful way to impress that special someone. —Jan Koellen, Baton Rouge, Louisiana

   1/3 pound lean ground beef
   1/3 cup water
    3 teaspoons reduced-sodium taco seasoning
Dash hot pepper sauce
    3 cups torn romaine
   1/2 cup canned black beans, rinsed and drained
   1/3 cup crumbled baked tortilla chip scoops (about 10 scoops)
   1/4 cup shredded reduced-fat Mexican cheese blend
   1/2 cup canned diced tomatoes with mild green chilies, drained
   1/2 medium ripe avocado, peeled and cubed
   1/3 cup *each* chopped green, sweet red and yellow pepper
   1/4 cup chopped red onion

In a small nonstick skillet, cook beef over medium heat until no longer pink; drain. Stir in the water, taco seasoning and pepper sauce. Bring to a boil; cook and stir for 2 minutes or until thickened. Remove from the heat.

Divide beef mixture between two plates. Layer with romaine, beans, tortilla chips, cheese, tomatoes, avocado, peppers and onion.

NUTRITION FACTS: 1 serving equals 377 calories, 16 g fat (5 g saturated fat), 47 mg cholesterol, 809 mg sodium, 35 g carbohydrate, 10 g fiber, 25 g protein. **DIABETIC EXCHANGES:** 2 lean meat, 2 vegetable, 1-1/2 starch, 1-1/2 fat.

Beef 'n' Turkey Meat Loaf

PREP: 15 Min.   **BAKE:** 50 Min. + Standing   **YIELD:** 6 Servings

Shredded potatoes bulk up my hefty meat loaf recipe. It's seasoned with garlic and thyme. Due to the combination of meats, no one thinks that it is light. —Fern Nead, Florence, Kentucky

    2 egg whites
   2/3 cup ketchup, *divided*
    1 medium potato, peeled and finely shredded
    1 medium green pepper, finely chopped
    1 small onion, grated
    3 garlic cloves, minced
    1 teaspoon salt
    1 teaspoon dried thyme
   1/2 teaspoon pepper
   3/4 pound lean ground beef
   3/4 pound lean ground turkey

In a large bowl, combine egg whites and 1/3 cup ketchup. Stir in the potato, green pepper, onion, garlic, salt, thyme and pepper. Crumble beef and turkey over mixture and mix well. Shape into a 10-in. x 4-in. loaf.

Line a 15-in. x 10-in. x 1-in. baking pan with heavy-duty foil and coat the foil with cooking spray. Place loaf in pan. Bake, uncovered, at 375° for 45 minutes; drain.

Brush with remaining ketchup. Bake 5-10 minutes longer or until a meat thermometer reads 165°. Let stand for 10 minutes before slicing.

NUTRITION FACTS: 1 slice equals 240 calories, 9 g fat (3 g saturated fat), 79 mg cholesterol, 808 mg sodium, 16 g carbohydrate, 2 g fiber, 23 g protein. **DIABETIC EXCHANGES:** 3 lean meat, 1 starch.

Chicken & Turkey Entrees

Whether you need a no-fuss meal during the week or an elegant main course for Saturday dinner guests, you simply can't wrong with chicken and turkey. Versatile, flavorful and low in fat, the following poultry dishes are certain to grace your table time and again.

Chicken Tostadas with Mango Sauce, p. 135

Cranberry Chicken and Wild Rice

(PICTURED BELOW)

PREP: 10 Min.   **BAKE:** 40 Min.   **YIELD:** 6 Servings

This chicken is delicious, and it's so easy to prepare. I love that I can do other things while it bakes.

—Evelyn Lewis, Independence, Missouri

 6 boneless skinless chicken breast halves (4 ounces *each*)
 1-1/2 cups hot water
 1 package (6.2 ounces) fast-cooking long grain and wild rice mix
 1 can (16 ounces) whole-berry cranberry sauce
 1 tablespoon lemon juice
 1 tablespoon reduced-sodium soy sauce
 1 tablespoon Worcestershire sauce

Place the chicken in a 13-in. x 9-in. x 2-in. baking dish coated with cooking spray. In a small bowl, combine the water and rice mix with contents of the seasoning packet. Pour around the chicken.

In a small bowl, combine the cranberry sauce, lemon juice, soy sauce and Worcestershire sauce; pour over chicken. Cover and bake at 350° for 40-50 minutes or until chicken juices run clear and rice is tender.

NUTRITION FACTS: 1 chicken breast half with 1/2 cup rice mixture and 1/4 cup sauce equals 332 calories, 3 g fat (1 g saturated fat), 63 mg cholesterol, 592 mg sodium, 50 g carbohydrate, 2 g fiber, 26 g protein.

TASTY TIP
For a simple supper, toss together a spinach salad as the chicken nears the end of its baking time. For a no-fuss dessert consider scoops of lemon frozen yogurt.

Cajun Chicken Penne

PREP: 20 Min.   **COOK:** 20 Min.   **YIELD:** 4 Servings

I tasted a wonderful Cajun pasta dish on a kayaking trip and attempted to re-create the delicious flavors from memory. With whole wheat pasta, this is as tasty as the original.

—Mary Spikowski, Columbus, Ohio

 1-1/2 cups uncooked whole wheat penne pasta
 1 pound boneless skinless chicken breasts, cut into 3/4-inch pieces
 3 teaspoons Cajun seasoning, *divided*
 3 teaspoons olive oil, *divided*
 1 medium green pepper, julienned
 1 medium sweet red pepper, julienned
 1 medium onion, halved and sliced
 3 garlic cloves, minced
 2 medium tomatoes, chopped
 1 cup fat-free evaporated milk, *divided*
 3 tablespoons all-purpose flour

Cook pasta according to package directions. Meanwhile, toss chicken with 2 teaspoons Cajun seasoning. In a large non-stick skillet coated with cooking spray, cook chicken in 2 teaspoons oil until no longer pink; drain. Remove and keep warm.

In the same skillet, saute peppers and onion in remaining oil for 1 minute. Add garlic; saute 1 minute longer. Add tomatoes; saute 2 minutes longer. Stir in 3/4 cup milk.

Bring to a boil. Combine flour with remaining Cajun seasoning and milk until smooth; gradually stir into skillet. Cook for 1-2 minutes or until thickened. Return chicken to the pan; heat through. Drain pasta; toss with chicken mixture.

NUTRITION FACTS: 1-3/4 cups equals 432 calories, 8 g fat (1 g saturated fat), 65 mg cholesterol, 635 mg sodium, 55 g carbohydrate, 5 g fiber, 35 g protein.

Turkey Thyme Risotto

PREP: 20 Min.   **COOK:** 25 Min.   **YIELD:** 4 Servings

Thanks to a little Romano cheese, this entree is a delicious way to use up extra turkey. —Sunny McDaniel, Cary, North Carolina

2-3/4 to 3-1/4 cups reduced-sodium chicken broth
   2 cups sliced fresh mushrooms
   1 small onion, chopped
   1 garlic clove, minced
   1 tablespoon olive oil
   1 cup uncooked arborio rice
   1 teaspoon minced fresh thyme *or* 1/4 teaspoon dried thyme
 1/2 cup white wine *or* additional reduced-sodium chicken broth
1-1/2 cups cubed cooked turkey breast
   2 tablespoons grated Romano cheese
 1/4 teaspoon salt
 1/4 teaspoon pepper

In a small saucepan, heat broth and keep warm. In a large non-stick skillet, saute the mushrooms, onion and garlic in oil until tender, about 3 minutes. Add rice and thyme; cook and stir for 2-3 minutes. Stir in wine or additional broth. Cook and stir until all of the liquid is absorbed.

Add heated broth, 1/2 cup at a time, stirring constantly. Allow liquid to absorb between additions. Cook just until risotto is creamy and rice is almost tender. Total cooking time is about 20 minutes. Add the turkey, Romano cheese, salt and pepper; cook and stir until heated through. Serve immediately.

NUTRITION FACTS: 1 cup equals 334 calories, 6 g fat (1 g saturated fat), 49 mg cholesterol, 698 mg sodium, 44 g carbohydrate, 1 g fiber, 24 g protein. **DIABETIC EXCHANGES:** 3 starch, 2 very lean meat, 1/2 fat.

Peanut-Crusted Chicken   CARB

PREP: 20 Min. + Marinating   **BAKE:** 25 Min.   **YIELD:** 4 Servings

With the flavors of ginger, honey and garlic, this aromatic chicken from our Test Kitchen is sure to please.

 1/4 cup reduced-sodium soy sauce
   2 tablespoons rice wine vinegar
   3 garlic cloves, minced
   1 green onion, thinly sliced
   1 tablespoon honey
   1 teaspoon minced fresh gingerroot
   4 boneless skinless chicken breast halves (4 ounces *each*)
 1/2 cup panko (Japanese) bread crumbs
 1/4 cup chopped unsalted peanuts
 1/4 teaspoon paprika
 1/4 teaspoon pepper

In a large resealable plastic bag, combine the first six ingredients; add chicken. Seal bag and turn to coat; refrigerate for up to 4 hours.

In another large resealable plastic bag, combine the bread crumbs, peanuts, paprika and pepper. Drain and discard marinade. Add chicken to crumb mixture, one piece at a time, and shake to coat.

Place in a 13-in. x 9-in. x 2-in. baking pan coated with cooking spray. Bake, uncovered, at 350° for 25-30 minutes or until juices run clear.

NUTRITION FACTS: 1 chicken breast half equals 197 calories, 6 g fat (1 g saturated fat), 63 mg cholesterol, 267 mg sodium, 8 g carbohydrate, 1 g fiber, 26 g protein. **DIABETIC EXCHANGES:** 3 very lean meat, 1 fat, 1/2 starch.

Grilled Basil Chicken and Tomatoes   CARB
(PICTURED ABOVE)

PREP: 15 Min. + Marinating   **GRILL:** 10 Min.   **YIELD:** 4 Servings

Here's the perfect recipe for midweek summer barbecues! Relax after work with a cold drink while your savory chicken marinates, then toss it on the grill. —Laura Lunardi, Exton, Pennsylvania

   8 plum tomatoes, *divided*
 3/4 cup balsamic vinegar
 1/4 cup tightly packed fresh basil leaves
   2 tablespoons olive oil
   1 garlic clove, minced
 1/2 teaspoon salt
   4 boneless skinless chicken breast halves (4 ounces *each*)

Cut four tomatoes into quarters and place in a food processor. Add the vinegar, basil, oil, garlic and salt; cover and process until blended.

Pour 1/2 cup dressing into a small bowl; cover and refrigerate until serving. Pour remaining dressing into a large resealable plastic bag; add chicken. Seal bag and turn to coat; refrigerate for up to 1 hour.

Coat grill rack with cooking spray before starting the grill. Drain and discard marinade. Grill chicken, covered, over medium heat for 4-6 minutes on each side or until juices run clear. Cut remaining tomatoes in half; grill for 2-3 minutes on each side or until tender. Serve with the chicken and the reserved dressing.

NUTRITION FACTS: 1 chicken breast half with 1 tomato and 2 tablespoons dressing equals 174 calories, 5 g fat (1 g saturated fat), 63 mg cholesterol, 179 mg sodium, 7 g carbohydrate, 1 g fiber, 24 g protein. **DIABETIC EXCHANGES:** 3 very lean meat, 1 vegetable, 1/2 fat.

Favorite Recipe Made Lighter

PURE DELIGHT is what you'll find when you dive into homemade enchiladas...especially if they taste anything like Diane Witmer's Cheesy Chicken Enchiladas. However, the high nutritional numbers caused concern for Diane. From Spencer, Wisconsin, she explains, "I'd love to cut calories from this dish. Could you look at it?"

The recipe offers a cup of cheese and nearly 1,000 calories per serving, so it was obvious that Diane was on the right track in asking for help.

The first thing our makeover team tackled was the cheese. By choosing a reduced-fat substitute, they were able to maintain the savory goodness while keeping a whopping two cups of cheese in the recipe.

When baking, it's important to remember that fat-free ingredients sometimes don't perform well. So when the team went after the sour cream and soup, they relied on reduced-fat varieties to maintain the original dish's rich characteristics. They then chose fat-free tortillas, which hold up well when baked, and a lean choice of chicken.

The results are impressive. Half the calories were cut, and an amazing 45 grams of fat removed. But with all the cheesy flavor, it definitely doesn't taste light. Now the Witmer family can dig into Makeover Chicken Cheese Enchiladas for dinner knowing that they're eating good food that doesn't break the calorie bank!

Chicken Cheese Enchiladas

PREP: 25 Min.   **BAKE:** 50 Min.   **YIELD:** 6 Servings

- 2 cups (16 ounces) sour cream
- 1 can (10-3/4 ounces) condensed cream of chicken soup, undiluted
- 1 can (4 ounces) chopped green chilies
- 1 can (2-1/4 ounces) sliced ripe olives, drained
- 4 cups cubed cooked chicken
- 3 cups (12 ounces) shredded Monterey Jack cheese, *divided*
- 3 cups (12 ounces) shredded cheddar cheese, *divided*
- 12 flour tortillas (6 inches), warmed
- 4 green onions, thinly sliced

In a large bowl, combine the sour cream, soup, chilies and olives. Set aside 1-1/2 cups for topping. Add the chicken, 2 cups Monterey Jack cheese and 2 cups cheddar cheese to remaining soup mixture.

Spoon about 1/2 cup chicken mixture down the center of each tortilla; roll up tightly. Place seam side down in a greased 13-in. x 9-in. x 2-in. baking dish. Top with reserved soup mixture.

Bake, uncovered, at 350° for 40 minutes. Sprinkle with remaining cheeses; top with onions. Bake 10-15 minutes longer or until cheese is melted.

NUTRITION FACTS: 2 enchiladas equals 992 calories, 63 g fat (35 g saturated fat), 251 mg cholesterol, 1,765 mg sodium, 36 g carbohydrate, 1 g fiber, 63 g protein.

Makeover Chicken Cheese Enchiladas
(PICTURED ABOVE)

PREP: 25 Min.   **BAKE:** 45 Min.   **YIELD:** 6 Servings

- 1-1/2 cups (12 ounces) reduced-fat sour cream
- 1 can (10-3/4 ounces) reduced-fat reduced-sodium condensed cream of chicken soup, undiluted
- 1 can (4 ounces) chopped green chilies
- 1 can (2-1/4 ounces) sliced ripe olives, drained
- 4 cups cubed cooked chicken breast
- 1 cup (4 ounces) shredded reduced-fat Monterey Jack *or* Mexican cheese blend, *divided*
- 1 cup (4 ounces) shredded reduced-fat cheddar cheese, *divided*
- 12 fat-free flour tortillas (6 inches), warmed
- 4 green onions, thinly sliced

In a large bowl, combine the sour cream, soup, chilies and olives. Set aside 1-1/2 cups for topping. Add the chicken, 1/2 cup Monterey Jack cheese and 1/2 cup cheddar cheese to remaining soup mixture.

Spoon about 1/3 cup chicken mixture down the center of each tortilla; roll up tightly. Place seam side down in a 13-in. x 9-in. x 2-in. baking dish coated with cooking spray. Top with reserved soup mixture.

Bake, uncovered, at 350° for 35 minutes. Sprinkle with remaining cheeses; top with onions. Bake 10-15 minutes longer or until cheese is melted.

NUTRITION FACTS: 2 enchiladas equals 508 calories, 18 g fat (11 g saturated fat), 123 mg cholesterol, 1,164 mg sodium, 40 g carbohydrate, 2 g fiber, 46 g protein.

Smothered Chicken Italiano

CARB

(PICTURED BELOW)

PREP: 15 Min. **BAKE:** 20 Min. **YIELD:** 4 Servings

Here's one of my husband's most-requested dinners. It's become an "old reliable" to serve dinner guests as well because it's impressive but easy. —Mary Kretschmer, Miami, Florida

> 1/2 teaspoon dried oregano
> 1/4 teaspoon garlic powder
> 1/4 teaspoon salt, *divided*
> 1/4 teaspoon pepper, *divided*
> 4 boneless skinless chicken breast halves (4 ounces *each*)
> 2 teaspoons canola oil
> 1 cup part-skim ricotta cheese
> 1 cup crushed tomatoes
> 4 slices part-skim mozzarella cheese

In a small bowl, combine the oregano, garlic powder, 1/8 teaspoon salt and 1/8 teaspoon pepper; rub over chicken. In a large nonstick skillet coated with cooking spray, brown chicken in oil for 3-4 minutes on each side.

Transfer to an 11-in. x 7-in. x 2-in. baking dish coated with cooking spray. Combine ricotta cheese and remaining salt and pepper; spoon over chicken. Top with tomatoes.

Bake, uncovered, at 350° for 15 minutes. Top with cheese. Bake 5-10 minutes longer or until cheese is melted and chicken juices run clear.

NUTRITION FACTS: 1 serving equals 252 calories, 11 g fat (5 g saturated fat), 85 mg cholesterol, 341 mg sodium, 6 g carbohydrate, 1 g fiber, 32 g protein. **DIABETIC EXCHANGES:** 4 very lean meat, 1-1/2 fat.

Mini Turkey Meat Loaves

CARB

PREP: 25 Min. **BAKE:** 25 Min. **YIELD:** 6 Servings

These convenient turkey loaves are moist, hearty and loaded with flavor. Bake them ahead and top them off with cheese before serving. —Janice Christofferson, Eagle River, Wisconsin

> 1 egg, lightly beaten
> 1 large onion, finely chopped
> 1 small sweet red pepper, finely chopped
> 3/4 cup shredded part-skim mozzarella cheese, *divided*
> 1/2 cup plus 6 tablespoons spaghetti sauce, *divided*
> 3 tablespoons grated Parmesan cheese, *divided*
> 3 tablespoons quick-cooking oats
> 1 teaspoon Italian seasoning
> 1/4 teaspoon salt
> 1/4 teaspoon pepper
> 1 pound lean ground turkey

In a large bowl, combine the egg, onion, red pepper, 1/2 cup mozzarella cheese, 1/2 cup spaghetti sauce, 2 tablespoons Parmesan cheese, oats and seasonings. Crumble turkey over mixture and mix well.

Coat six jumbo muffin cups with cooking spray; fill with turkey mixture. Bake at 350° for 20 minutes; drain.

Top each loaf with 1 tablespoon spaghetti sauce, 2 teaspoons mozzarella cheese and 1/2 teaspoon Parmesan cheese. Bake 5-10 minutes longer or until a meat thermometer reads 165° and cheese is melted. Let stand for 5 minutes before removing from pan.

NUTRITION FACTS: 1 loaf equals 210 calories, 10 g fat (4 g saturated fat), 105 mg cholesterol, 447 mg sodium, 9 g carbohydrate, 2 g fiber, 20 g protein. **DIABETIC EXCHANGES:** 3 lean meat, 1/2 starch.

Porcini Turkey Meatballs

(PICTURED BELOW)

PREP: 45 Min.   **COOK:** 35 Min.   **YIELD:** 6 Servings

My husband loves meatballs, but I don't like all the fat they typically have. One day, I fooled him by making this recipe with ground turkey, and he loved it!   —Alison Hyde, St. Louis, Missouri

- 1 egg, lightly beaten
- 1 egg white, lightly beaten
- 3/4 cup finely chopped sweet onion
- 3/4 cup seasoned bread crumbs
- 1/3 cup shredded part-skim mozzarella cheese
- 1/3 cup grated Parmesan cheese
- 1/3 cup minced fresh parsley
- 2 tablespoons ketchup
- 2 tablespoons Worcestershire sauce
- 1 garlic clove, minced
- 1/4 teaspoon salt
- 1/4 teaspoon pepper
- 1 package (1 ounce) dried porcini mushrooms, *divided*
- 1 pound extra-lean ground turkey
- 1 cup water
- 2 tablespoons balsamic vinegar

TOMATO MARSALA SAUCE:

- 1 cup chopped sweet onion
- 2 garlic cloves, minced
- 1 tablespoon olive oil
- 3/4 cup marsala wine *or* 1/2 cup reduced-sodium chicken broth plus 1/4 cup white grape juice
- 2 tablespoons balsamic vinegar
- 1 teaspoon dried basil
- 1 can (14-1/2 ounces) diced tomatoes, undrained
- 9 ounces uncooked spaghetti, cooked and drained

In a large bowl, combine the first 12 ingredients. Place half of the mushrooms in a food processor; cover and process to a fine powder. Add to bowl. Crumble turkey over mixture and mix well. Shape into 18 balls.

Place on a rack coated with cooking spray in a shallow baking pan. Cover and bake at 350° for 20 minutes. Meanwhile, in a small saucepan, bring water and remaining mushrooms to a boil. Remove from the heat; let stand for 15-20 minutes. Drain, reserving liquid. Chop mushrooms; set aside.

Turn meatballs; drizzle with vinegar. Bake, uncovered, for 15 minutes or until no pink remains and a meat thermometer reads 165°.

In the same small saucepan, saute onion and garlic in oil until tender. Stir in wine or broth plus juice, vinegar, basil and mushrooms with liquid. Bring to a boil. Reduce heat; simmer, uncovered, for 20-25 minutes or until reduced to 1-1/3 cups. Add tomatoes; heat through. Serve the sauce over the meatballs and spaghetti.

NUTRITION FACTS: 3 meatballs with 1/2 cup sauce and 2/3 cup spaghetti equals 451 calories, 8 g fat (2 g saturated fat), 73 mg cholesterol, 700 mg sodium, 58 g carbohydrate, 5 g fiber, 34 g protein.

Crumb-Coated Baked Chicken

CARB

PREP: 15 Min.   **BAKE:** 30 Min.   **YIELD:** 6 Servings

This light, oven-fried chicken has a pretty golden coating and a slightly crunchy texture. My family really loves it, and I like that it has less fat than traditional fried chicken.
—Suzanne Zick, Lincolnton, North Carolina

- 1/3 cup buttermilk
- 2 teaspoons hot pepper sauce
- 3/4 cup seasoned bread crumbs
- 3/4 cup yellow cornmeal
- 3/4 teaspoon salt
- 3/4 teaspoon dried cilantro flakes
- 3/4 teaspoon chili powder
- 3/4 teaspoon cayenne pepper
- 1/4 teaspoon ground cumin
- 6 bone-in chicken breast halves (6 ounces *each*), skin removed

Line a 15-in. x 10-in. x 1-in. baking pan with foil and coat the foil with cooking spray; set aside.

In a shallow bowl, combine buttermilk and hot pepper sauce. In another shallow bowl, combine the bread crumbs, cornmeal and seasonings. Dip chicken in buttermilk mixture, then roll in crumb mixture. Place bone side down in prepared pan.

Spritz chicken with cooking spray. Bake at 425° for 15-20 minutes. Remove from oven; spritz again with cooking spray. Bake 15-20 minutes longer or until a meat thermometer reads 170°.

NUTRITION FACTS: 1 chicken breast half equals 197 calories, 4 g fat (1 g saturated fat), 68 mg cholesterol, 340 mg sodium, 13 g carbohydrate, 1 g fiber, 27 g protein. **DIABETIC EXCHANGES:** 4 very lean meat, 1 starch.

Broccoli Chicken Casserole

PREP: 15 Min. **BAKE:** 35 Min. **YIELD:** 5 Servings

I came across this hot bake when I was in high school, and it's been a staple ever since. Basil gives this casserole wonderful flavor. No one will know it's good for them. They'll be too busy asking for seconds.
—Sharie Blevins, Chisholm, Minnesota

2-1/2 cups uncooked yolk-free noodles

2-1/2 cups cubed cooked chicken breast

  1 package (10 ounces) frozen broccoli florets, thawed

  1 small onion, chopped

  1 can (10-3/4 ounces) reduced-fat reduced-sodium condensed cream of chicken soup, undiluted

1/2 cup fat-free milk

1/2 cup shredded part-skim mozzarella cheese

  1 teaspoon dried basil

1/4 teaspoon salt

1/8 teaspoon pepper

Paprika, optional

Cook noodles according to package directions; drain and place in a large bowl. Add the chicken, broccoli and onion. In a small bowl, combine the soup, milk, cheese, basil, salt and pepper. Pour over chicken mixture and stir until combined.

Transfer to a 2-qt. baking dish coated with cooking spray. Cover and bake at 350° for 35-40 minutes or until bubbly. Sprinkle with paprika if desired.

NUTRITION FACTS: 1-1/2 cups equals 284 calories, 5 g fat (2 g saturated fat), 66 mg cholesterol, 489 mg sodium, 27 g carbohydrate, 3 g fiber, 29 g protein. **DIABETIC EXCHANGES:** 3 very lean meat, 1-1/2 starch, 1 vegetable, 1 fat.

Cranberry-Glazed Turkey Breast

PREP: 20 Min. **BAKE:** 1-1/2 Hours + Standing **YIELD:** 12 Servings

A tasty, golden brown turkey breast is just four ingredients away! And with low sodium, fat and cholesterol levels, you can feel good about preparing this recipe.
—Audrey Petterson, Maidstone, Saskatchewan

1-1/4 cups jellied cranberry sauce

  2/3 cup unsweetened apple juice concentrate

    2 tablespoons butter

    1 bone-in turkey breast (5 to 6 pounds)

In a small saucepan, bring the cranberry sauce, apple juice concentrate and butter to a boil. Remove from the heat; cool.

Carefully loosen skin of turkey breast. Set aside 1/2 cup sauce for basting and 3/4 cup for serving. Spoon remaining sauce onto the turkey, rubbing mixture under and over the skin.

Place turkey on a rack in a shallow roasting pan. Bake, uncovered, at 325° for 1-1/2 to 2 hours or until a meat thermometer reads 170°, basting occasionally with reserved sauce. Cover and let stand for 10 minutes before carving. Warm reserved 3/4 cup sauce; serve with turkey.

NUTRITION FACTS: 5 ounces cooked turkey (without skin) and 1 tablespoon sauce equals 244 calories, 3 g fat (1 g saturated fat), 103 mg cholesterol, 91 mg sodium, 17 g carbohydrate, trace fiber, 36 g protein. **DIABETIC EXCHANGES:** 5 very lean meat, 1 starch.

Turkey Pecan Enchiladas

(PICTURED ABOVE)

PREP: 25 Min. **BAKE:** 45 Min. **YIELD:** 12 Servings

I got this recipe from a friend, and I've often served it at church potlucks. There are never leftovers!
—Cathy Huppe, Georgetown, Massachusetts

  1 medium onion, chopped

  4 ounces reduced-fat cream cheese

  1 tablespoon water

  1 teaspoon ground cumin

1/4 teaspoon pepper

1/8 teaspoon salt

  4 cups cubed cooked turkey breast

1/4 cup chopped pecans, toasted

 12 flour tortillas (6 inches), warmed

  1 can (10-3/4 ounces) reduced-fat reduced-sodium condensed cream of chicken soup, undiluted

  1 cup (8 ounces) reduced-fat sour cream

  1 cup fat-free milk

  2 tablespoons canned chopped green chilies

1/2 cup shredded reduced-fat cheddar cheese

  2 tablespoons minced fresh cilantro

In a small nonstick skillet coated with cooking spray, cook and stir onion over medium heat until tender. Set aside. In a large mixing bowl, beat the cream cheese, water, cumin, pepper and salt until smooth. Stir in the onion, turkey and pecans.

Spoon 1/3 cup turkey mixture down the center of each tortilla. Roll up and place seam side down in a 13-in. x 9-in. x 2-in. baking dish coated with cooking spray. Combine the soup, sour cream, milk and chilies; pour over enchiladas.

Cover and bake at 350° for 40 minutes. Uncover; sprinkle with cheese. Bake 5 minutes longer or until heated through and cheese is melted. Sprinkle with cilantro.

NUTRITION FACTS: 1 enchilada equals 263 calories, 10 g fat (4 g saturated fat), 59 mg cholesterol, 472 mg sodium, 20 g carbohydrate, 1 g fiber, 22 g protein. **DIABETIC EXCHANGES:** 2 lean meat, 1-1/2 starch, 1/2 fat.

Saucy Tarragon Chicken
(PICTURED BELOW)

PREP: 10 Min.   **COOK:** 25 Min.   **YIELD:** 4 Servings

This delightful chicken recipe boasts plenty of mushroom gravy and a mild, satisfying taste with just a hint of lemon and tarragon.
— Mary Steiner, West Bend, Wisconsin

    3 cups uncooked egg noodles
    4 boneless skinless chicken breast halves (4 ounces *each*)
    3/4 teaspoon dried tarragon
    3/4 teaspoon lemon-pepper seasoning
    1 tablespoon butter
    2 cups sliced fresh mushrooms
    4 garlic cloves, minced
    1 can (14-1/2 ounces) reduced-sodium chicken broth, *divided*
    3 tablespoons sherry *or* additional reduced-sodium chicken broth
    3 tablespoons all-purpose flour
    1/4 cup reduced-fat sour cream

Cook noodles according to package directions. Meanwhile, sprinkle chicken with tarragon and lemon-pepper. In a large nonstick skillet over medium-high heat, brown chicken in butter on both sides. Remove and keep warm.

In the same skillet, saute mushrooms and garlic until tender. Add 1 cup broth and sherry or additional broth, stirring to loosen browned bits from pan. Return chicken to the pan; bring to a boil. Reduce heat; simmer, uncovered, for 7-10 minutes or until chicken juices run clear. Remove chicken and keep warm.

Combine flour and remaining broth until smooth; stir into pan juices. Bring to a boil; cook and stir for 1-2 minutes or until thickened. Remove from the heat; stir in sour cream. Drain noodles; serve with chicken and sauce.

NUTRITION FACTS: 1 chicken breast half with 1/4 cup sauce and 3/4 cup noodles equals 379 calories, 9 g fat (4 g saturated fat), 116 mg cholesterol, 454 mg sodium, 39 g carbohydrate, 2 g fiber, 33 g protein. **DIABETIC EXCHANGES:** 3 lean meat, 2-1/2 starch.

TASTY TIP
Saucy Tarragon Chicken is a great way to use up noodles you may have left in the refrigerator. If you have extra cooked rice or orzo on hand, use that instead.

Favorite Recipe Made Lighter

SUPER-CHEESY casseroles are usually taboo for the health conscious, but with a little bit of tweaking, they can often be lightened a bit. That's exactly what Jessica Salts was counting on when she sent us Cheddar Tot Casserole.

"I used to love making this recipe for functions and as a family treat," she writes from Corpus Christi, Texas. "I found it in one of the *Taste of Home* brand magazines a few years ago. However, I've since switched to the *Light & Tasty* way of cooking and no longer make the casserole because of the high level of fat."

We can see why it became a staple. The delicious dish is truly comfort food at its finest. Sour cream, butter and cream of chicken soup combine with Tater Tots to create a creamy filling. Topped with crushed potato chips and cheddar cheese, it makes a truly decadent dish.

But, as good as it tastes, it's a nutritional nightmare. So Jessica decided to do something about it; she sent us the recipe with a request. "Can you help me cut some of the fat out of this recipe without losing the flavor or fun?"

Sure thing, Jessica! Our makeover staff got down to business by replacing the ingredients they could with low-fat or fat-free substitutions. Because some fat-free ingredients don't perform well while baking, they chose mostly low-fat variations instead. They also cut the butter in half to reduce the fat and switched to sour cream and onion chips to enhance the taste.

With just a few changes, the team was able to lose 13 grams of fat and halve the amount of saturated fat, all without sacrificing flavor. So go ahead, Jessica, bring your family's favorite back to the table! We're sure you'll find Makeover Cheddar Tot Casserole a resounding success.

Makeover Cheddar Tot Casserole

(PICTURED ABOVE)

PREP: 15 Min.   BAKE: 30 Min.   YIELD: 10 Servings

- 1 can (12 ounces) fat-free evaporated milk
- 1 can (10-3/4 ounces) reduced-fat reduced-sodium condensed cream of chicken soup, undiluted
- 1 cup (8 ounces) reduced-fat sour cream
- 1/4 cup butter, melted
- 1 teaspoon onion powder
- 1 teaspoon garlic powder
- 1 package (32 ounces) frozen Tater Tots
- 1 cup (4 ounces) shredded reduced-fat cheddar cheese
- 1 cup crushed baked sour cream and onion potato chips

In a large bowl, combine the first six ingredients. Gently stir in Tater Tots. Transfer to a 13-in. x 9-in. x 2-in. baking dish coated with cooking spray. Sprinkle with cheese and potato chips.

Bake, uncovered, at 350° for 30-35 minutes or until bubbly and heated through.

NUTRITION FACTS: 3/4 cup equals 326 calories, 19 g fat (8 g saturated fat), 32 mg cholesterol, 690 mg sodium, 35 g carbohydrate, 2 g fiber, 10 g protein.

Cheddar Tot Casserole

PREP: 15 Min.   BAKE: 30 Min.   YIELD: 10 Servings

- 1 can (12 ounces) evaporated milk
- 1 can (10-3/4 ounces) condensed cream of chicken soup, undiluted
- 1 cup (8 ounces) sour cream
- 1/2 cup butter, melted
- 1 teaspoon onion powder
- 1 teaspoon garlic powder
- 1 package (32 ounces) frozen Tater Tots
- 1-1/2 cups (6 ounces) shredded cheddar cheese
- 1 cup crushed potato chips

In a large bowl, combine the first six ingredients. Gently stir in Tater Tots. Transfer to a greased 13-in. x 9-in. x 2-in. baking dish. Sprinkle with cheese and potato chips.

Bake, uncovered, at 350° for 30-35 minutes or until bubbly and heated through.

NUTRITION FACTS: 3/4 cup equals 446 calories, 32 g fat (16 g saturated fat), 72 mg cholesterol, 871 mg sodium, 33 g carbohydrate, 3 g fiber, 10 g protein.

MAKEOVER TIP
The jump from full-fat to fat-free can sometimes leave makeovers short on flavor. Try a combination of reduced-fat and fat-free ingredients for a happy medium.

cocoa; stir until blended.

Gradually stir in milk. Bring to a boil; cook and stir for 2 minutes or until thickened. Add the corn, onions, chilies and salt; cook and stir 2 minutes longer or until heated through. Remove from the heat. Stir in 1/4 cup cilantro.

Spread 2/3 cup filling down the center of each tortilla. Roll up and place seam side down in a 13-in. x 9-in. x 2-in. baking dish coated with cooking spray.

In a small bowl, combine the salsa, tomato sauce and remaining cilantro; pour over enchiladas. Sprinkle with cheese. Cover and bake at 375° for 25 minutes or until heated through.

NUTRITION FACTS: 1 enchilada equals 270 calories, 7 g fat (2 g saturated fat), 49 mg cholesterol, 768 mg sodium, 35 g carbohydrate, 4 g fiber, 24 g protein. **DIABETIC EXCHANGES:** 2 starch, 2 very lean meat, 1 fat.

Chipotle-Onion Turkey Cutlets

PREP: 25 Min.   **COOK:** 20 Min.   **YIELD:** 4 Servings

Adobo sauce gives this turkey dish its smoky kick. The cutlets make for a special dinner any night of the week.
—Jim Davis, Montgomery Village, Maryland

- 1/4 cup egg substitute
- 1 teaspoon water
- 2 teaspoons adobo sauce plus 1 teaspoon minced chipotle pepper in adobo sauce, *divided*
- 1 cup panko (Japanese) bread crumbs
- 1 teaspoon pepper
- 3/4 teaspoon salt
- 1 package (17.6 ounces) turkey breast slices
- 2 tablespoons olive oil, *divided*
- 1 medium onion, halved and sliced
- 1 garlic clove, minced
- 2 teaspoons all-purpose flour
- 3/4 cup reduced-sodium chicken broth

In a shallow bowl, combine the egg substitute, water and 1 teaspoon adobo sauce. In another shallow bowl, combine the bread crumbs, pepper and salt. Dip turkey in egg mixture, then coat with crumbs.

In a large nonstick skillet coated with cooking spray, cook turkey in batches over medium heat in 1 tablespoon oil for 2-3 minutes on each side or until no longer pink. Remove and keep warm.

In the same skillet, saute onion in remaining oil until tender; stir in garlic and chipotle pepper. Sprinkle with flour; stir until blended. Gradually add broth. Bring to a boil; cook and stir for 2 minutes or until thickened. Stir in remaining adobo sauce. Serve with turkey.

NUTRITION FACTS: 2 turkey slices with 3 tablespoons sauce equals 291 calories, 8 g fat (1 g saturated fat), 77 mg cholesterol, 717 mg sodium, 16 g carbohydrate, 1 g fiber, 36 g protein. **DIABETIC EXCHANGES:** 4 very lean meat, 1-1/2 fat, 1 starch.

Marvelous Chicken Enchiladas

(PICTURED ABOVE)

PREP: 30 Min.   **BAKE:** 25 Min.   **YIELD:** 6 Enchiladas

I love Mexican food, and this is one of my specialties. Try using Monterey Jack cheese in place of the cheddar for a slightly milder flavor.
—Rebekah Sabo, Rochester, New York

- 1 pound boneless skinless chicken breasts, cut into thin strips
- 4 teaspoons chili powder
- 2 teaspoons olive oil
- 2 tablespoons all-purpose flour
- 1-1/2 teaspoons ground coriander
- 1 teaspoon baking cocoa
- 1 cup fat-free milk
- 1 cup frozen corn, thawed
- 4 green onions, chopped
- 1 can (4 ounces) chopped green chilies, drained
- 1/2 teaspoon salt
- 1/2 cup minced fresh cilantro, *divided*
- 6 whole wheat tortillas (8 inches)
- 1/2 cup salsa
- 1/2 cup tomato sauce
- 1/2 cup shredded reduced-fat cheddar cheese

Sprinkle chicken with chili powder. In a large nonstick skillet coated with cooking spray, cook chicken in oil over medium heat until juices run clear. Sprinkle with flour, coriander and

Burgers Cacciatore

(PICTURED BELOW)

PREP: 20 Min. **COOK:** 20 Min. **YIELD:** 4 Servings

Broiled portobello mushrooms take center stage in this change-of-pace main course. —Kendra Doss, Smithville, Missouri

　　5 large portobello mushrooms (4 to 4-1/2 inches)
　3/4 teaspoon salt, *divided*
　　1 small onion, finely chopped
　1/2 cup chopped sweet red pepper
　1/3 cup shredded part-skim mozzarella cheese
　　3 tablespoons tomato paste
　　3 tablespoons minced fresh parsley
　　1 tablespoon Worcestershire sauce
　　2 garlic cloves, minced
　1/4 teaspoon pepper
　　1 pound lean ground turkey
　　2 cups chopped fresh arugula *or* baby spinach
　　4 slices part-skim mozzarella cheese
　　2 plum tomatoes, sliced
　　2 slices red onion, separated into rings

Remove stems from mushrooms and set aside. Place four mushroom caps on a broiler pan coated with cooking spray; sprinkle with 1/4 teaspoon salt. Broil 4 in. from the heat for 4-6 minutes on each side or until tender; keep warm.

Finely chop mushroom stems and remaining mushroom cap; place in a large bowl. Add the chopped onion, red pepper, shredded cheese, tomato paste, parsley, Worcestershire sauce, garlic, pepper and remaining salt. Crumble turkey over mixture; mix well.

Shape into four patties. Broil 4 in. from the heat for 5-7 minutes on each side or until a meat thermometer reads 165°.

Place 1/2 cup arugula on each mushroom cap; top with a turkey patty and a cheese slice. Broil for 1 minute or until cheese is melted. Top with tomato and onion slices.

NUTRITION FACTS: 1 burger equals 347 calories, 16 g fat (7 g saturated fat), 110 mg cholesterol, 809 mg sodium, 16 g carbohydrate, 4 g fiber, 34 g protein.

Lemon Chicken with Pasta

(PICTURED ABOVE)

PREP: 20 Min. **COOK:** 20 Min. **YIELD:** 4 Servings

I combine chicken with a few pantry staples for a healthy, comforting entree in minutes. Even my "pasta-hating husband" asks for seconds! —Karen Hall, South Hamilton, Massachusetts

1-1/2 cups uncooked medium pasta shells
　1/4 cup dry bread crumbs
　　1 teaspoon garlic powder
　1/2 teaspoon salt
　1/2 teaspoon pepper
　　1 pound boneless skinless chicken breasts, cubed
　　6 teaspoons canola oil, *divided*
　　1 medium onion, chopped
　　2 tablespoons all-purpose flour
　　1 cup reduced-sodium chicken broth
　1/4 cup lemon juice
　1/4 cup shredded Parmesan cheese

Cook pasta according to package directions. Meanwhile, in a large resealable plastic bag, combine the bread crumbs, garlic powder, salt and pepper. Add chicken, a few pieces at a time, and shake to coat.

In a large nonstick skillet coated with cooking spray, saute chicken in 4 teaspoons oil until juices run clear. Remove and keep warm.

In the same skillet, cook onion in remaining oil over medium heat until tender. Sprinkle with flour; stir until blended. Gradually stir in broth and lemon juice. Bring to a boil; cook and stir for 2 minutes or until thickened.

Drain pasta; toss with lemon sauce. Serve with chicken; sprinkle with Parmesan cheese.

NUTRITION FACTS: 1 serving equals 428 calories, 12 g fat (2 g saturated fat), 66 mg cholesterol, 652 mg sodium, 46 g carbohydrate, 2 g fiber, 33 g protein. **DIABETIC EXCHANGES:** 3 starch, 3 very lean meat, 2 fat.

Chicken Veronique

(PICTURED BELOW)

PREP: 15 Min. **COOK:** 20 Min. **YIELD:** 6 Servings

I found this recipe in a gardening book. My family just loves it, and it's super easy! We think it's excellent served with rice pilaf on the side. —Anita Dudiwka, Akron, Ohio

> 6 boneless skinless chicken breast halves (4 ounces *each*)
> 1/4 teaspoon salt
> 1/8 teaspoon ground nutmeg
> 4 teaspoons butter
> 2/3 cup white wine *or* reduced-sodium chicken broth
> 2 tablespoons orange marmalade spreadable fruit
> 3/4 teaspoon dried tarragon
> 2 teaspoons all-purpose flour
> 1/2 cup half-and-half cream
> 1-1/2 cups green grapes, halved

Sprinkle chicken with salt and nutmeg. In a large nonstick skillet coated with cooking spray, cook chicken in butter over medium heat for 3-5 minutes on each side or until chicken is lightly browned.

In a small bowl, combine the wine, marmalade and tarragon. Add to skillet; bring to a boil. Reduce heat; cover and simmer for 7-11 minutes or until chicken juices run clear. Remove chicken and keep warm.

Combine flour and cream until smooth. Gradually stir into skillet. Bring to a boil; cook 2 minutes longer or until thickened. Stir in grapes; heat through. Serve over chicken.

NUTRITION FACTS: 1 chicken breast half with 1/3 cup sauce equals 226 calories, 7 g fat (4 g saturated fat), 79 mg cholesterol, 191 mg sodium, 13 g carbohydrate, 1 g fiber, 24 g protein. **DIABETIC EXCHANGES:** 3 very lean meat, 1 fat, 1/2 starch, 1/2 fruit.

Company Casserole

PREP: 35 Min. **BAKE:** 40 Min. **YIELD:** 6 Servings

Full of chicken, ham and rice, this hot bake will chase away winter's chill. —Ruth Andrewson, Leavenworth, Washington

> 1 package (6 ounces) long grain and wild rice mix
> 1 package (10 ounces) frozen broccoli florets, thawed and drained
> 1-1/2 cups cubed cooked chicken breast
> 1 cup cubed fully cooked lean ham
> 1/2 cup shredded reduced-fat cheddar cheese
> 1 cup sliced fresh mushrooms
> 1 can (10-3/4 ounces) reduced-fat reduced-sodium condensed cream of mushroom soup, undiluted
> 2/3 cup reduced-fat plain yogurt
> 1/3 cup reduced-fat mayonnaise
> 1 teaspoon prepared mustard
> 1/4 teaspoon curry powder
> 2 tablespoons grated Parmesan cheese

Prepare rice according to package directions, omitting the butter. In a 13-in. x 9-in. x 2-in. baking dish coated with cooking spray, layer the rice, broccoli, chicken, ham, cheddar cheese and mushrooms.

In a small bowl, combine the soup, yogurt, mayonnaise, mustard and curry powder. Spread evenly over top of casserole; sprinkle with Parmesan cheese. Bake, uncovered, at 350° for 40-45 minutes or until heated through.

NUTRITION FACTS: 1-1/3 cups equals 318 calories, 11 g fat (4 g saturated fat), 54 mg cholesterol, 1,129 mg sodium, 31 g carbohydrate, 2 g fiber, 24 g protein. **DIABETIC EXCHANGES:** 2 starch, 2 lean meat, 1 fat.

Barbecued Turkey on Buns

PREP: 10 Min. **COOK:** 35 Min. **YIELD:** 6 Servings

Not only do I feel good about serving these heart-smart sandwiches, but they taste great. —Christa Norwalk, La Valle, Wisconsin

> 1 pound lean ground turkey
> 1/2 cup chopped onion
> 1/2 cup chopped green pepper
> 1 can (6 ounces) tomato paste
> 1 can (6 ounces) unsweetened pineapple juice
> 1/4 cup water
> 2 teaspoons Dijon mustard
> 1/2 teaspoon garlic powder
> 1/2 teaspoon salt
> 1/8 teaspoon pepper
> 6 whole wheat hamburger buns, split and toasted

In a large saucepan coated with cooking spray, cook the turkey, onion and green pepper over medium heat until meat is no longer pink; drain.

Stir in the tomato paste, pineapple juice, water, mustard, garlic powder, salt and pepper. Bring to a boil. Reduce heat; simmer, uncovered, for 20-30 minutes or until sauce is thickened. Spoon 1/3 cup onto each bun.

NUTRITION FACTS: 1 sandwich equals 280 calories, 8 g fat (2 g saturated fat), 60 mg cholesterol, 538 mg sodium, 34 g carbohydrate, 6 g fiber, 18 g protein. **DIABETIC EXCHANGES:** 2 starch, 2 lean meat, 1 vegetable.

Chicken Tostadas with Mango Salsa

(PICTURED ABOVE)

PREP: 30 Min. + Marinating   **COOK:** 20 Min.   **YIELD:** 6 Servings

Ginger adds a pleasant zing to this twist on a traditional tostada. It's so easy to eat healthful foods when good fresh salsa is around.
—Erin Renouf Mylroie, St. George, Utah

- 1/3 cup orange juice
- 5 tablespoons lime juice, *divided*
- 1 teaspoon garlic powder
- 1 teaspoon ground cumin
- 1 pound boneless skinless chicken breast halves
- 2 medium mangoes, peeled and diced
- 1 small red onion, chopped
- 1/2 cup minced fresh cilantro
- 1 serrano pepper, seeded and minced
- 2 tablespoons finely chopped candied ginger
- 1 tablespoon brown sugar
- 1/4 teaspoon salt
- 6 corn tortillas (6 inches)
- 3 cups coleslaw mix
- 6 tablespoons fat-free sour cream

In a large resealable plastic bag, combine the orange juice, 3 tablespoons lime juice, garlic powder and cumin; add chicken. Seal bag and turn to coat; refrigerate for at least 20 minutes.

For salsa, in a small bowl, combine the mangoes, onion, cilantro, serrano pepper, ginger, brown sugar, salt and remaining lime juice. Cover and chill until serving.

Drain and discard marinade. Place chicken on a broiler pan coated with cooking spray. Broil 4-6 in. from the heat for 5-7 minutes on each side or until juices run clear. Cut into thin strips.

In a nonstick skillet, cook tortillas over medium heat for 1-2 minutes on each side or until lightly browned. Top each with coleslaw mix, chicken, mango salsa and sour cream.

NUTRITION FACTS: 1 serving equals 238 calories, 3 g fat (1 g saturated fat), 44 mg cholesterol, 203 mg sodium, 35 g carbohydrate, 3 g fiber, 19 g protein. **DIABETIC EXCHANGES:** 2 very lean meat, 1-1/2 starch, 1 fat.

Editor's Note: When cutting or seeding hot peppers, use rubber or plastic gloves to protect your hands. Avoid touching your face.

Dicing a Mango

■ Wash the fruit. Lay it on the counter, then turn it so the top and bottom are now the sides. Using a sharp knife, make a lengthwise cut as close to the long, flat seed as possible to remove each side of the fruit. Trim fruit away from the seed.

■ Score each side of the fruit lengthwise and widthwise, without cutting through the skin.

■ Using your hand, push the skin up, turning the fruit out. Cut fruit off at the skin with a knife.

Skillet Arroz con Pollo
(PICTURED ABOVE)

PREP: 15 Min.   **COOK:** 25 Min.   **YIELD:** 4 Servings

This chicken-and-rice dish is great for both family and special occasion dinners. It's a tasty meal that comes together in one skillet…and it smells so good while it cooks!
— Cheryl Battaglia, Dalton, Pennsylvania

- 1 medium onion, chopped
- 1 medium sweet red pepper, cut into 1/2-inch pieces
- 1 garlic clove, minced
- 2 teaspoons olive oil
- 1 cup uncooked long grain rice
- 1 can (14-1/2 ounces) reduced-sodium chicken broth
- 1/4 cup sherry *or* water
- 1/2 teaspoon grated lemon peel
- 1/4 teaspoon salt
- 1/4 teaspoon cayenne pepper
- 2 cups cubed cooked chicken breast
- 1 cup frozen peas, thawed
- 1/4 cup sliced ripe olives, drained
- 2 tablespoons minced fresh cilantro

In a large nonstick skillet coated with cooking spray, saute the onion, red pepper and garlic in oil for 1 minute. Add rice; cook and stir for 4-5 minutes or until lightly browned.

Stir in the broth, sherry or water, lemon peel, salt and cayenne. Bring to a boil. Reduce heat; cover and simmer for 15 minutes.

Stir in the chicken, peas and olives. Cover and simmer 3-6 minutes longer or until rice is tender and chicken is heated through. Sprinkle with cilantro.

NUTRITION FACTS: 1-1/2 cups equals 373 calories, 6 g fat (1 g saturated fat), 54 mg cholesterol, 582 mg sodium, 49 g carbohydrate, 4 g fiber, 28 g protein. **DIABETIC EXCHANGES:** 3 starch, 3 very lean meat, 1 vegetable, 1/2 fat.

HEALTHY OUTLOOK
Always trim all visible fat from chicken breasts before cooking, and try to consider low-fat cooking methods such as grilling or broiling.

When preparing chicken on the stovetop, use a nonstick skillet coated with cooking spray instead of cooking the poultry in oil.

Chicken 'n' Summer Squash Packets

PREP: 20 Min. **BAKE:** 25 Min. **YIELD:** 4 Servings

Tender chicken and delightfully seasoned veggies are tucked inside each of these packs. —Sharon Salvador, Lakeport, California

  4 boneless skinless chicken breast halves (4 ounces *each*)
1/4 teaspoon salt, *divided*
1/4 teaspoon pepper, *divided*
  1 medium onion, sliced
  2 tablespoons Dijon mustard
  1 small zucchini, cut into 1/4-inch slices
  1 small yellow summer squash, cut into 1/4-inch slices
  2 cups sliced fresh mushrooms
3/4 teaspoon dried basil
1/8 teaspoon garlic powder
1/8 teaspoon paprika
  1 tablespoon butter
  1 tablespoon grated Parmesan cheese

Flatten chicken to 1/4-in. thickness; sprinkle with 1/8 teaspoon each salt and pepper. Cut eight 15-in. x 12-in. rectangles of heavy-duty foil; place one rectangle on top of another to make four. Divide onion slices among the four rectangles; top with chicken, mustard, zucchini, yellow squash and mushrooms.

Combine the basil, garlic powder, paprika and remaining salt and pepper; sprinkle over vegetables. Dot with butter. Fold foil around vegetable mixture and seal tightly. Place packets on a baking sheet.

Bake at 425° for 25-30 minutes or until chicken juices run clear. Open foil carefully to allow steam to escape. Sprinkle with Parmesan cheese.

NUTRITION FACTS: 1 packet equals 206 calories, 7 g fat (3 g saturated fat), 71 mg cholesterol, 449 mg sodium, 10 g carbohydrate, 3 g fiber, 27 g protein. **DIABETIC EXCHANGES:** 3 very lean meat, 2 vegetable, 1 fat.

Mushroom Turkey Tetrazzini

(PICTURED AT RIGHT)

PREP: 35 Min. **BAKE:** 25 Min. **YIELD:** 8 Servings

This creamy, comforting casserole makes a fantastic way to use up leftover turkey. And it's a real family pleaser, too!
—Linda Howe, Lisle, Illinois

 12 ounces uncooked spaghetti, broken into 2-inch pieces
  2 teaspoons chicken bouillon granules
1/2 pound sliced fresh mushrooms
  2 tablespoons butter
  2 tablespoons all-purpose flour
1/4 cup sherry *or* reduced-sodium chicken broth
3/4 teaspoon salt-free lemon-pepper seasoning
1/2 teaspoon salt
1/8 teaspoon ground nutmeg
  1 cup fat-free evaporated milk
2/3 cup grated Parmesan cheese, *divided*
  4 cups cubed cooked turkey breast
1/4 teaspoon paprika

Cook spaghetti according to package directions. Drain, reserving 2-1/2 cups cooking liquid. Stir bouillon into cooking liquid and set aside. Place spaghetti in a 13-in. x 9-in. x 2-in. baking dish coated with cooking spray; set aside.

In a large nonstick skillet, saute mushrooms in butter until tender. Stir in flour until blended. Gradually stir in sherry or broth and reserved cooking liquid. Add the lemon-pepper, salt and nutmeg. Bring to a boil; cook and stir for 2 minutes or until thickened.

Reduce heat to low; stir in milk and 1/3 cup Parmesan cheese until blended. Add turkey; cook and stir mixture until heated through.

Pour turkey mixture over spaghetti and toss to combine. Sprinkle with paprika and remaining Parmesan cheese. Cover and bake at 375° for 25-30 minutes or until bubbly.

NUTRITION FACTS: 1 cup equals 362 calories, 7 g fat (3 g saturated fat), 75 mg cholesterol, 592 mg sodium, 40 g carbohydrate, 2 g fiber, 33 g protein. **DIABETIC EXCHANGES:** 3 starch, 3 very lean meat, 1/2 fat.

> **TASTY TIP**
> Not only is Mushroom Turkey Tetrazzini a time-saver (it relies on turkey that's already been cooked), but it's low in calories and fat, too.
> The heartwarming main dish calls for fat-free evaporated milk...which has none of the fat and half the calories of the regular variety.

Turkey Enchilada Casserole

(PICTURED BELOW)

PREP: 30 Min.   **BAKE:** 25 Min.   **YIELD:** 10 Servings

Every time I make this turkey hot bake for guests, I end up sharing the recipe. —Debra Martin, Belleville, Michigan

- 1 pound lean ground turkey
- 1 medium green pepper, chopped
- 1 medium onion, chopped
- 3 garlic cloves, minced
- 2 cans (15 ounces *each*) black beans, rinsed and drained
- 1 jar (16 ounces) salsa
- 1 can (15 ounces) tomato sauce
- 1 can (14-1/2 ounces) Mexican stewed tomatoes
- 1 teaspoon *each* onion powder, garlic powder and ground cumin
- 12 corn tortillas (6 inches)
- 2 cups (8 ounces) shredded reduced-fat cheddar cheese, *divided*

In a large nonstick saucepan coated with cooking spray, cook the turkey, green pepper, onion and garlic over medium heat until meat is no longer pink. Stir in the beans, salsa, tomato sauce, tomatoes, onion powder, garlic powder and cumin. Bring to a boil. Reduce heat; simmer mixture, uncovered, for 10 minutes.

Spread 1 cup meat sauce into a 13-in. x 9-in. x 2-in. baking dish coated with cooking spray. Top with six tortillas. Spread with half of the remaining meat sauce; sprinkle with 1 cup cheese. Layer with remaining tortillas and meat sauce.

Cover and bake at 350° for 20 minutes. Uncover; sprinkle with remaining cheese. Bake 5-10 minutes longer or until bubbly and cheese is melted.

NUTRITION FACTS: 1 piece equals 318 calories, 9 g fat (4 g saturated fat), 52 mg cholesterol, 936 mg sodium, 37 g carbohydrate, 7 g fiber, 21 g protein. **DIABETIC EXCHANGES:** 3 lean meat, 2 starch, 2 vegetable.

Chicken 'n' Rice Hot Dish

PREP: 15 Min.   **BAKE:** 30 Min.   **YIELD:** 4 Servings

Try this simple dish when you need a fast meal. It's a surefire crowd-pleaser. —Faye Labatt, Minneapolis, Minnesota

- 1/2 cup uncooked instant brown rice
- 1/4 cup boiling water
- 1 package (10 ounces) frozen chopped spinach, thawed and squeezed dry
- 1 tablespoon butter
- 3 tablespoons all-purpose flour
- 1/2 teaspoon curry powder
- 1/4 teaspoon salt
- Dash pepper
- Dash garlic powder
- 3/4 cup reduced-sodium chicken broth
- 3/4 cup fat-free milk
- 1/4 cup reduced-fat mayonnaise
- 3 cups cubed cooked chicken breast
- 1/3 cup shredded Parmesan cheese

Combine rice and water; transfer to an 11-in. x 7-in. x 2-in. baking dish coated with cooking spray. Top with spinach.

In a nonstick saucepan coated with cooking spray, melt butter. Stir in the flour, curry, salt, pepper and garlic powder until blended. Gradually whisk in broth and milk until smooth. Bring to a boil; cook and stir for 2 minutes or until thickened.

Remove from the heat; whisk in mayonnaise until blended. Pour half of the sauce over spinach. Top with chicken and remaining sauce.

Cover and bake at 350° for 25 minutes. Uncover; sprinkle with Parmesan cheese. Bake 5-10 minutes longer or until heated through and rice is tender.

NUTRITION FACTS: 1 serving equals 325 calories, 13 g fat (5 g saturated fat), 81 mg cholesterol, 659 mg sodium, 20 g carbohydrate, 3 g fiber, 31 g protein. **DIABETIC EXCHANGES:** 3 very lean meat, 2 fat, 1 starch, 1 vegetable.

HEALTHY OUTLOOK

When checking chicken breasts for doneness, use an instant-read thermometer to make sure it's cooked thoroughly. Chicken breasts should register 170° and dark meat 180°. If using boneless chicken in a bone-in recipe, test the chicken 20 minutes before the time stated in the recipe.

Weeknight Chicken Potpie

(PICTURED ABOVE)

PREP: 25 Min.   **BAKE:** 25 Min.   **YIELD:** 8 Servings

I have long days at work, so I really appreciate quick recipes like this casserole.   —Lisa Sjursen-Darling, Scottsville, New York

  1 small onion, chopped
  1 teaspoon canola oil
1-1/2 cups fat-free milk, *divided*
  1/2 cup reduced-sodium chicken broth
  3/4 teaspoon rubbed sage
  1/8 teaspoon pepper
  1/4 cup all-purpose flour
  4 cups cubed cooked chicken breast
  1 package (10 ounces) frozen chopped broccoli, thawed and drained
1-1/2 cups (6 ounces) shredded reduced-fat cheddar cheese
  1 tube (11.3 ounces) refrigerated dinner rolls

In a large nonstick saucepan, saute onion in oil until tender. Stir in 3/4 cup milk, broth, sage and pepper. In a small bowl, combine flour and remaining milk until smooth; gradually stir into onion mixture. Bring to a boil; cook and stir for 1-2 minutes or until thickened. Stir in the chicken, broccoli and cheese; heat through.

Transfer to a 2-qt. baking dish coated with cooking spray. Separate rolls; arrange over chicken mixture. Bake, uncovered, at 350° for 25-30 minutes or until filling is bubbly and rolls are golden brown.

NUTRITION FACTS: 3/4 cup chicken mixture with 1 roll equals 326 calories, 9 g fat (4 g saturated fat), 70 mg cholesterol, 511 mg sodium, 28 g carbohydrate, 2 g fiber, 33 g protein. **DIABETIC EXCHANGES:** 4 very lean meat, 2 starch, 1 fat.

Spinach-Feta Chicken Rolls

CARB

PREP: 25 Min.   **BAKE:** 45 Min.   **YIELD:** 6 Servings

This dish was inspired from a favorite Greek appetizer. It may take a bit of extra work, but it's worth it!
—Linda Gregg, Spartanburg, South Carolina

  1/2 cup sun-dried tomatoes (not packed in oil)
  1 cup boiling water
  1 package (10 ounces) frozen chopped spinach, thawed and squeezed dry
  1 cup (4 ounces) crumbled feta cheese
  4 green onions, thinly sliced
  1/4 cup Greek olives, chopped
  1 garlic clove, minced
  6 boneless skinless chicken breast halves (6 ounces *each*)
  1/4 teaspoon salt
  1/4 teaspoon pepper

Place tomatoes in a small bowl; add boiling water. Let stand for 5 minutes. In another bowl, combine the spinach, feta cheese, onions, olives and garlic. Drain and chop tomatoes; add to spinach mixture.

Flatten chicken to 1/4-in. thickness; sprinkle with salt and pepper. Spread spinach mixture over chicken. Roll up and secure with toothpicks. Place in a 13-in. x 9-in. x 2-in. baking dish coated with cooking spray.

Cover and bake at 350° for 30 minutes. Uncover; bake 15-20 minutes longer or until a meat thermometer reads 170°. Discard toothpicks.

NUTRITION FACTS: 1 stuffed chicken breast half equals 272 calories, 9 g fat (3 g saturated fat), 104 mg cholesterol, 583 mg sodium, 7 g carbohydrate, 3 g fiber, 40 g protein. **DIABETIC EXCHANGES:** 5 very lean meat, 1 vegetable, 1 fat.

Favorite Recipe Made Lighter

BEAUTIFUL braided breads really dress up events…just consider Chicken 'n' Broccoli Braid. It's full of chicken and veggies, and it's surrounded by a buttery crust; however, it's also full of fat and calories, which is an issue for Dana Rabe of West Richland, Washington.

"I love to make this simple, tasty dish for my family, but it doesn't fit in with our lifestyle anymore," Dana explains. "It's one of our favorite meals. Can it be lightened without losing the fabulous flavor?"

The *L&T* home economists were up for the challenge. Taking a long, hard look at the original, they decided there were three main ingredients to focus on: cheese, crescent roll dough and mayonnaise. The first two were easy to fix by simply using reduced-fat varieties of the products. However, the reduced-fat mayo they used is a bit higher in fat and calories than they'd like to see. To keep the flavor and creaminess, they replaced some of it with reduced-fat plain yogurt.

Our tasting panel found Makeover Chicken 'n' Broccoli Braid a delightful improvement. It has all of the original's taste and creamy comfort without the guilt. By taking out a quarter of the calories and nearly half the fat, the resulting makeover is both nutritious and delicious.

Makeover Chicken 'n' Broccoli Braid
(PICTURED ABOVE)

PREP: 25 Min.   BAKE: 15 Min.   YIELD: 8 Servings

- 2 cups cubed cooked chicken breast
- 1 cup chopped fresh broccoli
- 1 cup (4 ounces) shredded reduced-fat cheddar cheese
- 1/2 cup chopped sweet red pepper
- 2 teaspoons dill weed
- 2 garlic cloves, minced
- 1/4 teaspoon salt
- 1/4 cup reduced-fat mayonnaise
- 1/4 cup reduced-fat plain yogurt
- 2 tubes (8 ounces *each*) refrigerated reduced-fat crescent rolls
- 1 egg white, lightly beaten
- 1 tablespoon slivered almonds

In a large bowl, combine the first seven ingredients. Stir in mayonnaise and yogurt. Unroll both tubes of crescent dough onto an ungreased baking sheet; press together, forming a 15-in. x 12-in. rectangle. Seal seams and perforations. Spoon filling lengthwise down the center third of dough.

On each long side, cut dough 3 in. toward the center at 1-1/2-in. intervals, forming strips. Bring one strip from each side over filling; pinch ends to seal. Repeat. Pinch ends of the loaf to seal.

Brush with egg white; sprinkle with almonds. Bake at 375° for 15-20 minutes or until crust is golden brown and filling is heated through.

NUTRITION FACTS: 1 slice equals 338 calories, 16 g fat (5 g saturated fat), 40 mg cholesterol, 723 mg sodium, 28 g carbohydrate, 1 g fiber, 19 g protein.

Chicken 'n' Broccoli Braid

PREP: 25 Min.   BAKE: 15 Min.   YIELD: 8 Servings

- 2 cups cubed cooked chicken
- 1 cup chopped fresh broccoli
- 1 cup (4 ounces) shredded sharp cheddar cheese
- 1/2 cup chopped sweet red pepper
- 2 teaspoons dill weed
- 1 garlic clove, minced
- 1/4 teaspoon salt
- 1/2 cup mayonnaise
- 2 tubes (8 ounces *each*) refrigerated crescent rolls
- 1 egg white, lightly beaten
- 2 tablespoons slivered almonds

In a large bowl, combine the first seven ingredients. Stir in mayonnaise. Unroll both tubes of crescent dough onto an ungreased baking sheet; press together, forming a 15-in. x 12-in. rectangle. Seal seams and perforations. Spoon filling lengthwise down the center third of dough.

On each long side, cut dough 3 in. toward the center at 1-1/2-in. intervals, forming strips. Bring one strip from each side over filling; pinch ends to seal. Repeat. Pinch ends of the loaf to seal.

Brush with egg white; sprinkle with almonds. Bake at 375° for 15-20 minutes or until crust is golden brown and filling is heated through.

NUTRITION FACTS: 1 slice equals 457 calories, 31 g fat (8 g saturated fat), 51 mg cholesterol, 719 mg sodium, 24 g carbohydrate, 1 g fiber, 18 g protein.

Grilled Thai Chicken Salad

(PICTURED BELOW)

PREP: 20 Min. + Marinating   **GRILL:** 10 Min.   **YIELD:** 4 Servings

My husband and I love to eat Thai and Indian food, but notice that most of these cuisines do not offer fresh salads on their menus. We developed this recipe to capture those ethnic flavors when we wanted to eat light.   —Grace Kunert, Salt Lake City, Utah

  1/2 cup hot water
    2 tablespoons lime juice
  3/4 cup flaked coconut
    2 teaspoons curry powder
    2 teaspoons minced fresh gingerroot
    1 teaspoon salt
    4 boneless skinless chicken breast halves (4 ounces *each*)
    4 cups torn mixed salad greens
  1/2 medium sweet red pepper, julienned
  1/2 cup canned bean sprouts, rinsed and drained
  1/2 cup fresh sugar snap peas
DRESSING:
  1/4 cup reduced-sodium soy sauce
    2 tablespoons lime juice
    2 tablespoons coconut milk
    2 tablespoons reduced-fat creamy peanut butter
    4 teaspoons sugar

In a blender or food processor, combine the first six ingredients; cover and process until blended. Pour into a large resealable plastic bag; add chicken. Seal bag and turn to coat; refrigerate for at least 1 hour.

If grilling the chicken, coat grill rack with cooking spray before starting the grill. Drain and discard marinade. Grill chicken, covered, over medium heat or broil 4 in. from the heat for 4-7 minutes on each side or until juices run clear.

In a large salad bowl, combine the greens, red pepper, bean sprouts and peas. In a small bowl, whisk the dressing ingredients until smooth. Pour over salad and toss to coat. Cut chicken into strips; arrange over salad.

NUTRITION FACTS: 1 serving equals 261 calories, 9 g fat (4 g saturated fat), 63 mg cholesterol, 936 mg sodium, 17 g carbohydrate, 4 g fiber, 29 g protein. **DIABETIC EXCHANGES:** 3 very lean meat, 1 starch, 1 vegetable, 1 fat.

Chicken Stuffing Casserole

PREP: 15 Min.   **BAKE:** 35 Min.   **YIELD:** 8 Servings

I was frequently asked to make this casserole for the monthly potluck dinners in our retirement complex and never had any leftovers. It's so moist and comforting.
          —Carmelia Saxon, Chapel Hill, North Carolina

    2 eggs, lightly beaten
    1 package (16 ounces) crushed corn bread stuffing
    4 cups cubed cooked chicken breast
    3 cups reduced-sodium chicken broth, warmed
    1 can (10-1/2 ounces) reduced-fat reduced-sodium condensed cream of chicken soup, undiluted
    1 small onion, chopped
  1/4 cup chopped celery
    1 teaspoon rubbed sage

In a large bowl, combine all ingredients. Transfer to a 13-in. x 9-in. x 2-in. baking dish coated with cooking spray.

Cover and bake at 375° for 25 minutes. Uncover; bake 10-15 minutes longer or until a knife inserted near the center comes out clean.

NUTRITION FACTS: 1 cup equals 382 calories, 7 g fat (1 g saturated fat), 110 mg cholesterol, 1,073 mg sodium, 49 g carbohydrate, 3 g fiber, 29 g protein.

Roasted Pepper Chicken Sandwiches

(PICTURED BELOW)

PREP: 30 Min. + Marinating   **GRILL:** 10 Min.   **YIELD:** 4 Servings

This is such a wonderful, flavorful sandwich. It's perfect for a casual dinner or special lunch. The grilled chicken is so juicy, you'll prepare it time and time again.   —Laura Merkle, Dover, Delaware

- 1 tablespoon lemon juice
- 1 tablespoon Dijon mustard
- 2 teaspoons olive oil
- 1 garlic clove, minced
- 1/4 teaspoon dried thyme
- 1/4 teaspoon dried marjoram
- 4 boneless skinless chicken breast halves (4 ounces each)

PEPPER MIXTURE:

- 1 large onion, thinly sliced
- 4 garlic cloves, minced
- 1 teaspoon sugar
- 3/4 teaspoon fennel seed, crushed
- 1/4 teaspoon crushed red pepper flakes
- 1/8 teaspoon salt
- 1/8 teaspoon pepper
- 1 jar (7 ounces) roasted sweet red peppers, drained and sliced
- 1 tablespoon red wine vinegar

SANDWICHES:

- 1 loaf (8 ounces) focaccia bread
- 4 teaspoons fat-free mayonnaise
- 4 slices reduced-fat Swiss cheese

In a large resealable plastic bag, combine the first six ingredients; add chicken. Seal bag and turn to coat; refrigerate for 1 hour.

In a large nonstick skillet coated with cooking spray, cook and stir the onion, garlic, sugar and seasonings over medium heat until tender. Stir in roasted peppers and vinegar; cook 2 minutes longer. Remove from the heat; keep warm.

Coat grill rack with cooking spray before starting the grill. Drain chicken if necessary, discarding any excess marinade. Grill chicken, covered, over medium heat for 4-7 minutes on each side or until juices run clear. Cut into 1/2-in. strips.

Cut focaccia bread in half lengthwise; spread mayonnaise over cut side of bread bottom. Layer with cheese, chicken strips and pepper mixture. Replace bread top; lightly press down. Grill, covered, for 2-3 minutes or until cheese is melted. Cut into four sandwiches.

NUTRITION FACTS: 1 sandwich equals 404 calories, 11 g fat (3 g saturated fat), 73 mg cholesterol, 795 mg sodium, 41 g carbohydrate, 2 g fiber, 35 g protein. **DIABETIC EXCHANGES:** 4 lean meat, 2 starch, 1 vegetable.

Favorite Recipe Made Lighter

THE FIRST TIME Todd Richards tasted creamy Chicken Artichoke Bake at a friend's get-together, he noted how much everyone loved it. "All of the party guests went for seconds...and thirds," he shares from his home in West Allis, Wisconsin.

Always on the lookout for fantastic party fare, Todd called his friend for the recipe the next day. "I couldn't believe how easy it was," he says. "It comes together in no time flat, and it's perfect on a buffet."

The moist and delicious casserole was so high in fat and sodium, Todd felt a little guilty serving it. "If someone could just figure out a way to lighten up this casserole without losing the comforting flavor," he writes, "I'd really like to hear about it."

Our makeover experts began by replacing some of the heavier ingredients, such as the soup and mayonnaise, with smaller amounts of reduced-fat or lower-sodium counterparts.

Because lighter products don't always lend a creamy texture, the team used a thickened milk mixture and yogurt to make up the difference. Next, cubed chicken breast took the place of white and dark chicken meat for a lighter dish our home economists could approve.

The result? Makeover Chicken Artichoke Bake has a third fewer calories and about a fourth of the original's fat grams per serving. Now that's one guilt-free entree we can all celebrate!

Chicken Artichoke Bake

PREP: 15 Min.   BAKE: 55 Min.   YIELD: 6 Servings

- 2 cans (10-3/4 ounces *each*) condensed cream of celery soup, undiluted
- 1 cup mayonnaise
- 3 cups cubed cooked chicken
- 1 can (14 ounces) water-packed artichoke hearts, rinsed, drained and chopped
- 1 can (8 ounces) sliced water chestnuts, drained
- 1 package (6 ounces) long grain and wild rice mix
- 1 cup sliced fresh mushrooms
- 1 medium onion, finely chopped
- 1 jar (2 ounces) diced pimientos, drained
- 1/4 teaspoon pepper
- 1 cup seasoned stuffing cubes

In a large bowl, combine soup and mayonnaise. Stir in the chicken, artichokes, water chestnuts, rice mix with the contents of the seasoning packet, mushrooms, onion, pimientos and the pepper.

Spoon into a greased 2-1/2-qt. baking dish. Sprinkle with stuffing cubes. Bake, uncovered, at 350° for 55-65 minutes or until edges are bubbly and rice is tender.

NUTRITION FACTS: 1-1/3 cups equals 659 calories, 39 g fat (7 g saturated fat), 80 mg cholesterol, 1,666 mg sodium, 47 g carbohydrate, 4 g fiber, 29 g protein.

Makeover Chicken Artichoke Bake

(PICTURED ABOVE)

PREP: 25 Min.   BAKE: 45 Min.   YIELD: 6 Servings

- 3 tablespoons all-purpose flour
- 1 teaspoon sodium-free chicken bouillon granules
- 1-1/3 cups fat-free milk
- 1 can (10-3/4 ounces) reduced-fat reduced-sodium condensed cream of celery soup, undiluted
- 1 cup (8 ounces) plain yogurt
- 1/3 cup reduced-fat mayonnaise
- 3 cups cubed cooked chicken breast
- 1 can (14 ounces) water-packed artichoke hearts, rinsed, drained and chopped
- 1 can (8 ounces) sliced water chestnuts, drained
- 1 package (6 ounces) long grain and wild rice mix
- 1 cup sliced fresh mushrooms
- 1 medium onion, finely chopped
- 1 celery rib, finely chopped
- 1 jar (2 ounces) diced pimientos, drained
- 1/4 teaspoon pepper
- 1 cup seasoned stuffing cubes

In a small saucepan, combine the flour, bouillon and milk until smooth. Bring to a boil over medium heat, stirring constantly; cook and stir 1-2 minutes longer or until thickened. Transfer to a large bowl.

Stir in the soup, yogurt and mayonnaise until blended. Stir in the chicken, artichokes, water chestnuts, rice mix with contents of seasoning packet, mushrooms, onion, celery, pimientos and pepper.

Transfer to a 2-1/2-qt. baking dish coated with cooking spray. Sprinkle with the stuffing cubes. Bake, uncovered, at 350° for 45-55 minutes or until edges are bubbly and the rice is tender.

NUTRITION FACTS: 1-1/3 cups equals 431 calories, 11 g fat (3 g saturated fat), 67 mg cholesterol, 1,240 mg sodium, 52 g carbohydrate, 3 g fiber, 31 g protein.

In a large saucepan, combine the first 10 ingredients. Bring to a boil. Reduce heat; cover and simmer for 15-20 minutes or until potatoes are tender.

In a small bowl, whisk flour and evaporated milk until smooth; stir into broth mixture. Bring to a boil; cook and stir for 2 minutes or until thickened. Stir in vegetables and turkey; heat through. Transfer to an ungreased 8-in. square baking dish.

For crust, combine the flours, baking powder and salt in a small bowl. Stir in 3 tablespoons milk and oil just until combined. Roll out and cut into strips; make a lattice crust over filling. Trim and seal edges. Brush lattice top with remaining milk; sprinkle with paprika.

Bake, uncovered, at 400° for 20-25 minutes or until filling is bubbly. Let stand for 10 minutes before serving.

NUTRITION FACTS: 1 serving equals 272 calories, 3 g fat (trace saturated fat), 42 mg cholesterol, 661 mg sodium, 38 g carbohydrate, 7 g fiber, 23 g protein. **DIABETIC EXCHANGES:** 2 starch, 2 very lean meat, 1 vegetable, 1/2 fat.

Lattice-Topped Turkey Casserole

FAT

(PICTURED ABOVE)

PREP: 45 Min.   **BAKE:** 20 Min. + Standing   **YIELD:** 6 Servings

My friends tell me this is the best potpie they've tasted. Hearty and full-flavored, it's a meal-in-one that never lets on that it's low fat.
—Agnes Ward, Stratford, Ontario

 1 can (14-1/2 ounces) reduced-sodium chicken broth
 2 cups diced red potatoes
 2 celery ribs, chopped
 1 large onion, finely chopped
 1/2 cup water
 2 teaspoons chicken bouillon granules
 1/2 teaspoon dried rosemary, crushed
 1/4 teaspoon garlic powder
 1/4 teaspoon dried thyme
 1/8 teaspoon pepper
 3 tablespoons all-purpose flour
 2/3 cup fat-free evaporated milk
 3 cups frozen mixed vegetables, thawed and drained
 2 cups cubed cooked turkey breast
CRUST:
 1/4 cup all-purpose flour
 1/4 cup whole wheat flour
 1/2 teaspoon baking powder
 1/8 teaspoon salt
 4 tablespoons fat-free milk, *divided*
 1 tablespoon canola oil
Paprika

Sausage-Topped Polenta Wedges

PREP: 25 Min.   **COOK:** 30 Min.   **YIELD:** 6 Servings

I combine crushed tomatoes, Italian turkey sausage and green beans for a nutritious sauce that my whole family savors.
—Nanci Huyser, Kilgore, Texas

 4 cups water
 1/4 teaspoon salt
 1 cup yellow cornmeal
 3/4 cup shredded Parmesan cheese, *divided*
 1 tablespoon butter
 1/4 teaspoon pepper, *divided*
 1 pound Italian turkey sausage links, casings removed, crumbled
 1 large onion, chopped
 1 can (28 ounces) crushed tomatoes
 1 package (9 ounces) frozen cut green beans, thawed

In a large heavy saucepan, bring water and salt to a boil. Reduce heat to a gentle boil; slowly whisk in cornmeal. Cook and stir with a wooden spoon for 15-20 minutes or until polenta is thickened and pulls away cleanly from the sides of the pan.

Remove from the heat; stir in 1/2 cup Parmesan cheese, butter and 1/8 teaspoon pepper. Transfer to a 9-in. round pan coated with cooking spray; cool (polenta will thicken as it stands).

Meanwhile, in a large nonstick skillet coated with cooking spray, cook sausage and onion over medium heat until meat is no longer pink; drain. Stir in tomatoes and beans. Bring to a boil. Reduce heat; simmer, uncovered, for 9-12 minutes or until thickened.

Unmold polenta; cut into six wedges. Place on a baking sheet coated with cooking spray. Broil 4-6 in. from the heat for 4-5 minutes or until lightly toasted. Sprinkle with remaining pepper. Top each wedge with sausage mixture, about 1 cup on each; sprinkle with remaining Parmesan cheese. Serve immediately.

NUTRITION FACTS: 1 serving equals 330 calories, 13 g fat (5 g saturated fat), 53 mg cholesterol, 967 mg sodium, 34 g carbohydrate, 5 g fiber, 21 g protein. **DIABETIC EXCHANGES:** 2 lean meat, 2 vegetable, 1-1/2 starch, 1 fat.

Busy Mom's Chicken Fajitas

PREP: 15 Min.   **COOK:** 5 Hours   **YIELD:** 6 Servings

Staying at home with a 9-month-old makes preparing dinner a challenge, but a slow cooker provides an easy way to serve a low-fat meal. The tender meat in these fajitas is a hit, and the veggies and beans provide a dose of fiber.
—Sarah Newman, Brooklyn Center, Minnesota

- 1 pound boneless skinless chicken breast halves
- 1 can (16 ounces) kidney beans, rinsed and drained
- 1 can (14-1/2 ounces) diced tomatoes with mild green chilies, drained
- 1 *each* medium green, sweet red and yellow peppers, julienned
- 1 medium onion, halved and sliced
- 2 teaspoons ground cumin
- 2 teaspoons chili powder
- 1 garlic clove, minced
- 1/4 teaspoon salt
- 6 flour tortillas (8 inches), warmed

Shredded lettuce and chopped tomatoes, optional

In a 3-qt. slow cooker, combine the chicken, beans, tomatoes, peppers, onion and seasonings. Cover and cook on low for 5-6 hours or until chicken is tender.

Remove chicken; cool slightly. Shred chicken and return to the slow cooker; stir to combine. Spoon about 3/4 cup chicken mixture down the center of each tortilla. Top with lettuce and tomatoes if desired.

NUTRITION FACTS: 1 fajita (calculated without optional toppings) equals 347 calories, 5 g fat (1 g saturated fat), 42 mg cholesterol, 778 mg sodium, 49 g carbohydrate, 7 g fiber, 26 g protein.

Pepper 'n' Chicken Fettuccine

SALT

PREP: 20 Min.   **COOK:** 15 Min.   **YIELD:** 5 Servings

My husband discovered this healthful recipe, and it's become a favorite main dish. He's apt to sneak a hot pepper into the skillet since he believes that hotter is always better.
—Nancy High, Raleigh, North Carolina

- 6 ounces uncooked fettuccine
- 1 pound boneless skinless chicken breasts, cut into strips
- 2 tablespoons olive oil, *divided*
- 2-1/2 teaspoons salt-free herb seasoning blend, *divided*
- 1 large sweet red pepper, julienned
- 1 large sweet yellow pepper, julienned
- 1 small green pepper, julienned
- 1 small onion, halved and sliced
- 1 cup sliced fresh mushrooms
- 1/2 cup reduced-sodium chicken broth
- 1 tablespoon shredded Parmesan cheese

Cook fettuccine according to package directions. Meanwhile, in a large nonstick skillet, saute chicken in 1 tablespoon oil until no longer pink. Sprinkle with 1 teaspoon seasoning blend; cook 30 seconds longer. Remove and keep warm.

In the same skillet, saute the peppers and onion in remaining oil for 3 minutes. Add mushrooms; cook 2 minutes longer or until vegetables are crisp-tender. Stir in broth and remaining seasoning blend.

Return chicken to pan; heat through. Drain fettuccine; toss with chicken mixture. Sprinkle with Parmesan cheese.

NUTRITION FACTS: 1-1/4 cups equals 300 calories, 9 g fat (2 g saturated fat), 51 mg cholesterol, 136 mg sodium, 31 g carbohydrate, 3 g fiber, 25 g protein. **DIABETIC EXCHANGES:** 3 very lean meat, 1-1/2 starch, 1 vegetable, 1 fat.

Chicken with Rosemary-Onion Sauce

CARB

(PICTURED BELOW)

PREP: 15 Min.   **BAKE:** 20 Min.   **YIELD:** 4 Servings

Here's a wonderful dish for company because it tastes like you fussed. To me, there's nothing more aromatic or flavorful than chicken with rosemary.
—Donna Roberts, Shumway, Illinois

- 4 boneless skinless chicken breast halves (6 ounces *each*)
- 1/2 teaspoon salt
- 1/4 teaspoon pepper
- 3 teaspoons butter, *divided*
- 1 medium onion, chopped
- 1 garlic clove, minced
- 4 teaspoons all-purpose flour
- 1/2 cup reduced-sodium chicken broth
- 1/2 cup fat-free milk
- 1 teaspoon dried rosemary, crushed

Sprinkle chicken with salt and pepper. In a large nonstick skillet, brown chicken in 1 teaspoon butter. Transfer to an 11-in. x 7-in. x 2-in. baking dish coated with cooking spray.

In the same skillet, saute onion and garlic in remaining butter until tender. Stir in flour until blended. Gradually stir in broth and milk. Add rosemary. Bring to a boil; cook and stir for 2 minutes or until thickened.

Pour sauce over chicken. Cover and bake at 350° for 20-25 minutes or until chicken juices run clear.

NUTRITION FACTS: 1 chicken breast half with 1/4 cup sauce equals 247 calories, 7 g fat (3 g saturated fat), 102 mg cholesterol, 501 mg sodium, 8 g carbohydrate, 1 g fiber, 37 g protein. **DIABETIC EXCHANGES:** 5 very lean meat, 1/2 starch, 1/2 fat.

pepper. Drain chicken, discarding marinade; stuff with apple mixture. Secure with soaked toothpicks.

Coat grill rack with cooking spray before starting the grill. Grill chicken, covered, over medium heat for 5-8 minutes on each side or until a meat thermometer reads 170°. Discard toothpicks before serving.

NUTRITION FACTS: 1 stuffed chicken breast half equals 247 calories, 11 g fat (3 g saturated fat), 72 mg cholesterol, 274 mg sodium, 11 g carbohydrate, 1 g fiber, 25 g protein.

Black Bean Chicken Casserole

PREP: 25 Min.   BAKE: 35 Min.   YIELD: 10 Servings

This casserole never fails to receive compliments. The ingredients come together so nicely to give it a wonderful flavor.
—Tracy Kimzey, Blacksburg, Virginia

> 1 large onion, chopped
> 1 small green pepper, chopped
> 2 garlic cloves, minced
> 1 tablespoon canola oil
> 1 can (14-1/2 ounces) diced tomatoes, undrained
> 1/2 cup salsa
> 1 teaspoon ground cumin
> 1/2 teaspoon salt
> 1/2 teaspoon dried oregano
> 1/4 teaspoon pepper
> 2 cans (15 ounces *each*) black beans, rinsed and drained
> 3 cups cubed cooked chicken breast
> 8 corn tortillas (6 inches)
> 1-1/2 cups (6 ounces) shredded reduced-fat Monterey Jack *or* Mexican cheese blend, *divided*
> Fat-free sour cream, chopped green onions and sliced ripe olives, optional

In a large saucepan, saute the onion, green pepper and garlic in oil until tender. Stir in the tomatoes, salsa, cumin, salt, oregano and pepper. Add beans and chicken; heat through.

Spread a third of the mixture into a 13-in. x 9-in. x 2-in. baking dish coated with cooking spray. Layer with four tortillas, a third of the chicken mixture and 1 cup cheese. Repeat with remaining tortillas and chicken mixture.

Cover and bake at 350° for 25-30 minutes or until heated through. Uncover; sprinkle with remaining cheese. Bake 8-10 minutes longer or until cheese is melted. Serve with sour cream, green onions and olives if desired.

NUTRITION FACTS: 1 serving (calculated without optional toppings) equals 283 calories, 9 g fat (4 g saturated fat), 50 mg cholesterol, 664 mg sodium, 27 g carbohydrate, 6 g fiber, 24 g protein. **DIABETIC EXCHANGES:** 3 very lean meat, 2 starch, 1/2 fat.

Fontina-Fruit Chicken Breasts

CARB

(PICTURED ABOVE)

PREP: 30 Min. + Marinating   GRILL: 10 Min.   YIELD: 8 Servings

This is one of my favorite chicken dishes, festive enough for a special occasion but not loaded with fat and sugar.
—Lillian Julow, Gainesville, Florida

> 1/3 cup olive oil
> 3 tablespoons cider vinegar
> 2 tablespoons red wine vinegar
> 2 teaspoons honey
> 1 teaspoon Dijon mustard
> 1/2 teaspoon ground mustard
> 8 boneless skinless chicken breast halves (4 ounces *each*)
> 1 large tart apple, peeled and chopped
> 1 teaspoon butter
> 1/2 cup shredded fontina cheese
> 1/2 cup dried cherries, coarsely chopped
> 1/2 teaspoon salt
> 1/2 teaspoon pepper

In a large resealable plastic bag, combine the first six ingredients. Carefully cut a pocket in each chicken breast half; place in bag. Seal and turn to coat; refrigerate for 1 hour.

In a small nonstick skillet, saute apple in butter until tender. Transfer to a small bowl. Stir in the cheese, cherries, salt and

Pork Favorites

Today's health-minded cooks are turning to succulent cuts of pork when it comes to preparing a memorable meal. Savory pork medallions, barbecued chops and tender roasts are only a few of the mouth-watering options you'll find in this chapter.

Pepper-Stuffed Pork Chops, p. 149

Maple-Orange Pork Tenderloin

CARB ⬇

PREP: 10 Min. + Marinating   **BAKE:** 30 Min. + Standing   **YIELD:** 6 Servings

A marinade with maple syrup, curry and orange peel gives this lean entree a wonderful glaze and a tangy, citrusy sauce.
— Penny Fraser, Calgary, Alberta

  1/2 cup maple syrup
    2 tablespoons reduced-sodium soy sauce
    2 tablespoons ketchup
    1 tablespoon Dijon mustard
 1-1/2 teaspoons curry powder
 1-1/2 teaspoons ground coriander
    1 teaspoon Worcestershire sauce
    1 teaspoon grated orange peel
    2 garlic cloves, minced
    2 pork tenderloins (1 pound *each*)

In a bowl, combine the first nine ingredients. Pour 2/3 cup into a large resealable plastic bag; add pork. Seal bag and turn to coat; refrigerate for 1 hour. Set aside remaining maple mixture until serving.

Drain and discard marinade. Place pork in a roasting pan lined with heavy-duty foil. Bake, uncovered, at 375° for 30-40 minutes or until a meat thermometer reads 160°. Let stand for 10 minutes before slicing. Drizzle with reserved maple mixture.

NUTRITION FACTS: 4 ounces cooked pork equals 219 calories, 5 g fat (2 g saturated fat), 84 mg cholesterol, 228 mg sodium, 11 g carbohydrate, trace fiber, 30 g protein. **DIABETIC EXCHANGES:** 4 lean meat, 1/2 starch.

Pork with Artichokes and Capers

CARB ⬇

(PICTURED ABOVE)

PREP: 20 Min.   **COOK:** 20 Min.   **YIELD:** 4 Servings

After dating my husband for a month, I wanted to impress him with my cooking. This dish convinced him that I was "the one."
— Lindy Bonnell, Loveland, Colorado

    2 pork tenderloins (3/4 pound *each*)
    1 tablespoon butter
    1 green onion, finely chopped
    1 can (14 ounces) water-packed artichoke hearts, rinsed, drained and chopped
  1/4 cup reduced-sodium chicken broth
    1 tablespoon capers, drained
    1 teaspoon Dijon mustard
    1 tablespoon minced fresh parsley
Lemon slices

Cut pork into 1-in. slices; flatten to 1/4-in. thickness. In a large nonstick skillet over medium heat, cook pork in butter in batches until juices run clear. Transfer to a serving platter and keep warm.

In the same skillet, cook and stir onion until tender. Stir in the artichokes, broth, capers and mustard; heat through. Serve over pork; sprinkle with parsley. Garnish with lemon.

NUTRITION FACTS: 5 ounces cooked pork with 1/4 cup artichoke mixture equals 263 calories, 9 g fat (4 g saturated fat), 102 mg cholesterol, 479 mg sodium, 7 g carbohydrate, trace fiber, 37 g protein. **DIABETIC EXCHANGES:** 5 lean meat, 1 vegetable.

SHOP SMART
Look for capers near the pickles at your supermarket. If you don't like their saltiness, rinse them before using or replace them with chopped green olives.

Baked Barbecue Pork Chops

CARB ⬇

PREP: 20 Min.   **BAKE:** 15 Min.   **YIELD:** 4 Servings

Here's a recipe that my mom used to prepare when I was growing up. Our whole family adored it, and now I enjoy preparing it for my gang.
— Bonnie Schiltz, Menlo, Kansas

    4 boneless pork loin chops (3/4 inch thick and 4 ounces *each*)
  1/2 teaspoon salt, *divided*
  1/4 teaspoon pepper
    2 teaspoons canola oil
  1/3 cup water
  1/4 cup ketchup
    2 tablespoons cider vinegar
  1/4 teaspoon celery seed
  1/8 teaspoon ground nutmeg
    1 bay leaf

Sprinkle pork chops with 1/4 teaspoon salt and pepper. In a large nonstick skillet coated with cooking spray, cook chops in oil for 3-4 minutes on each side or until browned.

Transfer to an 8-in. square baking dish coated with cooking spray. In a small saucepan, combine the water, ketchup, vinegar, celery seed, nutmeg, bay leaf and remaining salt; bring to a boil. Pour over pork.

Cover and bake at 350° for 15-20 minutes or until a meat thermometer reads 160°. Discard bay leaf.

NUTRITION FACTS: 1 pork chop equals 190 calories, 9 g fat (3 g saturated fat), 55 mg cholesterol, 505 mg sodium, 5 g carbohydrate, trace fiber, 22 g protein. **DIABETIC EXCHANGES:** 3 lean meat, 1/2 fat.

Honey-Herb Pork Tenderloin

PREP: 10 Min.   **BAKE:** 30 Min.   **YIELD:** 6 Servings

Just two bites of this mouth-watering entree, and I asked for the recipe! Low enough in fat to fit my husband's heart-smart diet, it's also tasty enough to serve company.

—Nancy Kopp, Manhattan, Kansas

1/2 teaspoon *each* dried marjoram, oregano and thyme

1/2 teaspoon *each* garlic powder, seasoned salt, paprika and pepper

2 pork tenderloins (3/4 pound *each*)

SAUCE:

1 small onion, chopped

1 teaspoon canola oil

1/2 cup tomato puree

1/2 cup honey

1/4 cup cider vinegar

1 teaspoon dried oregano

3/4 teaspoon garlic powder

In a small bowl, combine the marjoram, oregano, thyme, garlic powder, seasoned salt, paprika and pepper. Rub over pork. Line a roasting pan with heavy-duty foil; place tenderloins on a rack in prepared pan. Bake at 350° for 10 minutes.

Meanwhile, in a small nonstick saucepan, saute onion in oil until tender. Stir in the remaining sauce ingredients; bring to a boil. Remove from the heat. Set aside 1 cup; keep warm.

Spoon half of the remaining sauce over pork. Bake 20-30 minutes longer or until a meat thermometer reads 160°, brushing once more with sauce. Let stand for 5 minutes before slicing. Serve with reserved sauce.

NUTRITION FACTS: 3 ounces cooked pork with about 3 tablespoons sauce equals 243 calories, 5 g fat (1 g saturated fat), 63 mg cholesterol, 181 mg sodium, 28 g carbohydrate, 1 g fiber, 23 g protein. **DIABETIC EXCHANGES:** 3 lean meat, 2 starch.

Pepper-Stuffed Pork Chops

(PICTURED BELOW)

PREP: 25 Min.   **COOK:** 15 Min.   **YIELD:** 4 Servings

I love how these succulent pork chops overflow with delicious stuffing. They are a great change of pace.

—Hope MacFarlane, Lincoln, Nebraska

1 medium sweet red pepper, chopped

1/4 cup finely chopped onion

1 garlic clove, minced

2 teaspoons olive oil, *divided*

1 cup cubed bread

1 can (4 ounces) chopped green chilies, drained

1/2 cup frozen corn, thawed

1/2 cup shredded part-skim mozzarella cheese

4 bone-in pork rib chops (3/4 inch thick and 7 ounces *each*)

1/4 teaspoon salt

1/4 teaspoon pepper

In a large nonstick skillet coated with cooking spray, saute the red pepper, onion and garlic in 1 teaspoon oil until tender. Stir in the bread cubes, chilies and corn; cook 2 minutes longer. Transfer to a bowl; stir in cheese.

Cut a pocket in each pork chop by slicing almost to the bone; fill with stuffing. Secure with toothpicks if necessary. Sprinkle chops with salt and pepper.

Coat the same skillet with cooking spray; add remaining oil. Cook chops over medium heat for 5-7 minutes on each side or until browned. Reduce heat; cover and cook 5-8 minutes longer or until a meat thermometer reads 160°. Discard toothpicks before serving.

NUTRITION FACTS: 1 pork chop equals 307 calories, 14 g fat (5 g saturated fat), 72 mg cholesterol, 425 mg sodium, 15 g carbohydrate, 2 g fiber, 31 g protein. **DIABETIC EXCHANGES:** 4 lean meat, 1 starch.

Chops 'n' Kraut
(PICTURED BELOW)

PREP: 25 Min.   **BAKE:** 20 Min.   **YIELD:** 6 Servings

Diced tomatoes lend color to this satisfying dinner-in-one. A little brown sugar sweetens the sauerkraut nicely.
—Ruth Tamul, Morehead City, North Carolina

> 6 bone-in pork loin chops (3/4 inch thick and 7 ounces *each*)
> 1/4 teaspoon salt
> 1/4 teaspoon pepper
> 3 teaspoons canola oil, *divided*
> 1 medium onion, thinly sliced
> 2 garlic cloves, minced
> 1 can (14-1/2 ounces) petite diced tomatoes, undrained
> 1 can (14 ounces) sauerkraut, rinsed and well drained
> 1/3 cup packed brown sugar
> 1-1/2 teaspoons caraway seeds

Sprinkle both sides of pork chops with salt and pepper. In a large nonstick skillet coated with cooking spray, cook three chops in 1 teaspoon oil for 2-3 minutes on each side or until browned; drain. Repeat with remaining chops and 1 teaspoon oil.

Place pork chops in a 13-in. x 9-in. x 2-in. baking dish coated with cooking spray; set aside. In the same skillet, cook onion and garlic in remaining oil until tender. Stir in the tomatoes, sauerkraut, brown sugar and caraway seeds. Cook and stir until mixture comes to a boil.

Carefully pour over chops. Cover and bake at 350° for 20-25 minutes or until meat is tender.

NUTRITION FACTS: 1 pork chop with 2/3 cup sauerkraut mixture equals 311 calories, 11 g fat (3 g saturated fat), 86 mg cholesterol, 691 mg sodium, 21 g carbohydrate, 3 g fiber, 32 g protein. **DIABETIC EXCHANGES:** 4 lean meat, 1 vegetable, 1/2 starch, 1/2 fat.

Dijon-Honey Pork Chops

PREP/TOTAL TIME: 20 Min.   **YIELD:** 4 Servings

Treated to a flavorful honey-orange-Dijon sauce, these tender pork chops come together in less than a half hour!
—Shirley Goehring, Lodi, California

> 4 boneless pork loin chops (5 ounces *each*)
> 1 teaspoon salt-free lemon-pepper seasoning
> 2 teaspoons canola oil
> 1/2 cup orange juice
> 1 tablespoon Dijon mustard
> 1 tablespoon honey

Sprinkle pork chops with lemon-pepper. In a large nonstick skillet coated with cooking spray, cook chops in oil over medium heat for 2-3 minutes on each side or until lightly browned.

In a small bowl, combine the orange juice, mustard and honey; pour over pork. Bring to a boil. Reduce heat; cover and simmer for 5-8 minutes or until a meat thermometer reads 160°. Remove chops and keep warm.

Cook sauce, uncovered, for 2-3 minutes or until reduced to 1/4 cup. Spoon over chops.

NUTRITION FACTS: 1 pork chop with 1 tablespoon sauce equals 244 calories, 11 g fat (3 g saturated fat), 68 mg cholesterol, 134 mg sodium, 9 g carbohydrate, trace fiber, 28 g protein. **DIABETIC EXCHANGES:** 4 lean meat, 1/2 starch.

Lemon-Caper Pork Medallions

PREP/TOTAL TIME: 30 Min.   **YIELD:** 4 Servings

Looking for an elegant but easy supper? These lightly breaded medallions from the Light & Tasty Test Kitchen are truly special. Serve them with rice pilaf on the side.

> 1 pork tenderloin (1 pound), cut into 12 slices
> 1/2 cup all-purpose flour
> 1/2 teaspoon salt
> 1/4 teaspoon pepper
> 1 tablespoon butter
> 1 tablespoon olive oil
> 1 cup reduced-sodium chicken broth
> 1/4 cup white wine *or* additional reduced-sodium chicken broth
> 1 garlic clove, minced
> 1 tablespoon capers, drained
> 1 tablespoon lemon juice
> 1/2 teaspoon dried rosemary, crushed

Flatten pork slices to 1/4-in. thickness. In a large resealable plastic bag, combine the flour, salt and pepper. Add pork, a few pieces at a time, and shake to coat.

In a large nonstick skillet over medium heat, cook pork in butter and oil in batches until juices run clear. Remove and keep warm.

Add the broth, wine or additional broth and garlic to the pan, stirring to loosen browned bits. Bring to a boil; cook until liquid is reduced by half. Stir in the capers, lemon juice and rosemary; heat through. Serve with pork.

NUTRITION FACTS: 3 slices pork with 1 tablespoon sauce equals 232 calories, 10 g fat (4 g saturated fat), 71 mg cholesterol, 589 mg sodium, 7 g carbohydrate, trace fiber, 24 g protein. **DIABETIC EXCHANGES:** 3 lean meat, 1 fat, 1/2 starch.

Chinese Pork Chops

PREP: 15 Min.　**COOK:** 3 Hours　**YIELD:** 6 Servings

Saucy and tender, these slow-cooked chops get their flavor from simple ingredients such as ketchup, brown sugar and soy sauce.
　　　　　　　　　　—Sharon Crider, Junction City, Kansas

　6 boneless pork loin chops (4 ounces *each*)
　1 small onion, finely chopped
1/3 cup ketchup
　3 tablespoons brown sugar
　3 tablespoons water
　3 tablespoons reduced-sodium soy sauce
　1 garlic clove, minced
　1 teaspoon ground ginger
　3 cups hot cooked rice

Place the pork chops in a 3-qt. slow cooker coated with cooking spray.

In a small bowl, combine the onion, ketchup, brown sugar, water, soy sauce, garlic and ginger. Pour over chops. Cover and cook on low for 3-4 hours or until meat is tender. Serve with rice and cooking juices.

NUTRITION FACTS: 1 pork chop with 1/2 cup rice and 3 tablespoons juices equals 305 calories, 7 g fat (2 g saturated fat), 55 mg cholesterol, 496 mg sodium, 34 g carbohydrate, 1 g fiber, 25 g protein. **DIABETIC EXCHANGES:** 3 lean meat, 2 starch.

Pork Chops with Cranberry Sauce

SALT ⬇

PREP/TOTAL TIME: 30 Min.　**YIELD:** 6 Servings

Moist and tender pork is treated to a sweet, light cranberry glaze in this weeknight-friendly dinner. Served over rice, the chops looked like you fussed over them.
　　　　　　　　—Stephanie Homme, Baton Rouge, Louisiana

　6 boneless pork loin chops (4 ounces *each*)
1/4 teaspoon coarsely ground pepper
1/8 teaspoon salt
　2 teaspoons cornstarch
　1 cup cranberry-apple juice
　2 teaspoons honey
3/4 cup dried cranberries
　1 tablespoon minced fresh tarragon
　1 tablespoon minced fresh parsley
　3 cups hot cooked brown rice

Sprinkle pork chops with pepper and salt. In a large nonstick skillet coated with cooking spray, cook chops over medium heat for 3-4 minutes on each side or until lightly browned. Remove and keep warm.

In a small bowl, combine the cornstarch, juice and honey until smooth. Add to pan, stirring to loosen browned bits. Stir in the cranberries, tarragon and parsley. Bring to a boil; cook 2 minutes longer or until thickened and bubbly.

Return pork to the pan. Reduce heat; cover and simmer for 4-6 minutes or until a meat thermometer reads 160°. Serve with rice.

NUTRITION FACTS: 1 pork chop with 3 tablespoons sauce and 1/2 cup rice equals 336 calories, 7 g fat (3 g saturated fat), 55 mg cholesterol, 92 mg sodium, 43 g carbohydrate, 3 g fiber, 24 g protein. **DIABETIC EXCHANGES:** 3 lean meat, 2 starch, 1/2 fruit.

Slow-Cooked Pork Tacos

(PICTURED ABOVE)

PREP: 20 Min.　**COOK:** 4 Hours　**YIELD:** 10 Tacos

Sometimes I'll substitute Bibb lettuce leaves for the tortillas in these unique tacos. Leftovers are perfect for burritos later in the week.
　　　　　　　　—Kathleen Wolf, Naperville, Illinois

　1 boneless pork sirloin roast (2 pounds), cut into 1-inch pieces
1-1/2 cups salsa verde
　1 medium sweet red pepper, chopped
　1 medium onion, chopped
1/4 cup chopped dried apricots
　2 tablespoons lime juice
　2 garlic cloves, minced
　1 teaspoon ground cumin
1/2 teaspoon salt
1/4 teaspoon white pepper
Dash hot pepper sauce
　10 flour tortillas (8 inches), warmed
Reduced-fat sour cream, thinly sliced green onions, cubed avocado, shredded reduced-fat cheddar cheese and chopped tomato, optional

In a 3-qt. slow cooker, combine the first 11 ingredients. Cover and cook on high for 4-5 hours or until meat is very tender.

Shred pork with two forks. Place about 1/2 cup pork mixture down the center of each tortilla. Serve with assorted toppings if desired.

NUTRITION FACTS: 1 taco (calculated without optional toppings) equals 301 calories, 8 g fat (2 g saturated fat), 54 mg cholesterol, 616 mg sodium, 32 g carbohydrate, 1 g fiber, 24 g protein. **DIABETIC EXCHANGES:** 3 lean meat, 2 starch.

6 minutes on each side or until a meat thermometer reads 160°, basting frequently with reserved marinade.

NUTRITION FACTS: 1 pork chop equals 212 calories, 12 g fat (3 g saturated fat), 55 mg cholesterol, 550 mg sodium, 3 g carbohydrate, 1 g fiber, 22 g protein. **DIABETIC EXCHANGES:** 3 lean meat, 1 fat.

Pork Parmigiana

PREP/TOTAL TIME: 30 Min.   **YIELD:** 4 Servings

Bring home the flavors of Italy with my tantalizing Parmigiana. Baked in mere minutes, it's an easy dinner that's sure to please.
—Julee Wallberg, Reno, Nevada

> 1-1/3 cups uncooked spiral pasta
> 2 cups meatless spaghetti sauce
> 1 pork tenderloin (1 pound)
> 1/4 cup egg substitute
> 1/3 cup seasoned bread crumbs
> 3 tablespoons grated Parmesan cheese, *divided*
> 1/4 cup shredded part-skim mozzarella cheese

Cook pasta according to package directions. Place spaghetti sauce in a small saucepan; cook over low heat until heated through, stirring occasionally.

Meanwhile, cut tenderloin into eight slices; flatten to 1/4-in. thickness. Place egg substitute in a shallow bowl. In another shallow bowl, combine bread crumbs and 1 tablespoon Parmesan cheese. Dip pork slices in egg substitute, then roll in crumb mixture.

Place on a baking sheet coated with cooking spray. Bake at 425° for 5-6 minutes on each side or until juices run clear. Drain pasta; serve with pork and spaghetti sauce. Sprinkle with mozzarella cheese and remaining Parmesan cheese.

NUTRITION FACTS: 2 slices of pork with 1/2 cup pasta and 1/2 cup sauce equals 365 calories, 7 g fat (3 g saturated fat), 70 mg cholesterol, 878 mg sodium, 39 g carbohydrate, 3 g fiber, 34 g protein. **DIABETIC EXCHANGES:** 4 lean meat, 2 starch, 2 vegetable.

Grilled Marinated Pork Chops

CARB

(PICTURED ABOVE)

PREP: 15 Min. + Marinating   **GRILL:** 10 Min.   **YIELD:** 4 Servings

I created this recipe several years ago. Since then, I always prepare pork chops this way. Onion, basil, garlic and rosemary pack flavor in every bite. —Jill McDeavitt, Greybull, Wyoming

> 1/4 cup tomato juice
> 1/4 cup chopped onion
> 1/4 cup minced fresh parsley
> 2 tablespoons white wine vinegar
> 2 tablespoons lemon juice
> 2 tablespoons canola oil
> 1 tablespoon Worcestershire sauce
> 2 garlic cloves, minced
> 1 teaspoon salt
> 1 teaspoon dried basil
> 1 teaspoon dried marjoram
> 1 teaspoon dried thyme
> 1/2 teaspoon dried rosemary, crushed
> 1/2 teaspoon pepper
> 1/4 teaspoon hot pepper sauce
> 4 boneless pork loin chops (3/4 inch thick and 4 ounces each)

In a small bowl, combine the first 15 ingredients. Pour 1/2 cup marinade into a large resealable plastic bag; add pork. Seal bag and turn to coat; refrigerate for 8 hours or overnight. Cover and refrigerate remaining marinade for basting.

If grilling the pork, coat grill rack with cooking spray before starting the grill. Drain and discard marinade. Grill pork, covered, over medium heat or broil 4 in. from the heat for 4-

Calypso Pork Chops

CARB

PREP: 30 Min. + Marinating   **GRILL:** 10 Min.
YIELD: 6 Servings (3 Cups Salsa)

Perfect for guests, these fun chops receive rave reviews. They're absolutely mouth-watering! —Jessie Heying, Mitchell, South Dakota

> 2/3 cup reduced-sodium soy sauce
> 1/3 cup packed brown sugar
> 1/3 cup water
> 1/4 cup rice wine vinegar
> 2 tablespoons minced fresh gingerroot
> 2 garlic cloves, minced
> 6 boneless pork loin chops (4 ounces *each*)

SALSA:

> 2 cups cubed fresh pineapple
> 1 cup chopped peeled papaya
> 1 small sweet red pepper, chopped
> 1 small onion, chopped
> 1 serrano pepper, seeded and minced
> 1 garlic clove, minced

In a small saucepan, combine the first six ingredients. Bring to a boil, stirring frequently until sugar is dissolved. Remove from the heat; cool to room temperature.

Pour 1 cup marinade into a large resealable plastic bag; add pork chops. Seal bag and turn to coat; refrigerate overnight. Pour remaining marinade into a small bowl for basting; cover and refrigerate.

In a large bowl, combine salsa ingredients. Let stand at room temperature for 1 hour.

Coat grill rack with cooking spray before starting the grill. Drain and discard marinade. Grill pork, covered, over medium heat for 4-5 minutes on each side or until a meat thermometer reads 160°, basting frequently with reserved marinade. Serve with salsa.

NUTRITION FACTS: 1 pork chop with 1/2 cup salsa equals 214 calories, 7 g fat (2 g saturated fat), 55 mg cholesterol, 297 mg sodium, 15 g carbohydrate, 2 g fiber, 23 g protein. **DIABETIC EXCHANGES:** 3 lean meat, 1/2 fruit.

Editor's Note: When cutting or seeding hot peppers, use rubber or plastic gloves to protect your hands. Avoid touching your face.

Grilled Pork Tenderloin Sandwiches
(PICTURED BELOW)

PREP: 15 Min. + Marinating **GRILL:** 25 Min. **YIELD:** 6 Servings

I received the recipe for these quick-fixing pork sandwiches from a friend at work years ago. I'm always asked for my secrets when I serve the sandwiches to someone new.

—Geri Bierschbach, Weidman, Michigan

    2 tablespoons canola oil
    2 tablespoons reduced-sodium soy sauce
    2 tablespoons steak sauce
    2 garlic cloves, minced
1-1/2 teaspoons brown sugar

    1/2 teaspoon ground mustard
    1/2 teaspoon minced fresh gingerroot
      2 pork tenderloins (1 pound *each*)
MUSTARD HORSERADISH SAUCE:
    1/4 cup fat-free mayonnaise
    1/4 cup reduced-fat sour cream
1-1/2 teaspoons lemon juice
      1 teaspoon sugar
    1/2 teaspoon ground mustard
    1/2 teaspoon Dijon mustard
    1/2 teaspoon prepared horseradish
      6 kaiser rolls, split
      6 lettuce leaves

In a large resealable plastic bag, combine the first seven ingredients; add pork. Seal bag and turn to coat; refrigerate for 8 hours or overnight.

Coat grill rack with cooking spray before starting the grill. Prepare grill for indirect heat. Drain and discard marinade. Grill pork, covered, over indirect medium-hot heat for 25-40 minutes or until a meat thermometer reads 160°. Let stand for 5 minutes before slicing.

In a small bowl, combine the mayonnaise, sour cream, lemon juice, sugar, ground mustard, Dijon mustard and horseradish. Serve pork on rolls with lettuce and mustard horseradish sauce.

NUTRITION FACTS: 1 sandwich equals 382 calories, 10 g fat (3 g saturated fat), 89 mg cholesterol, 528 mg sodium, 34 g carbohydrate, 2 g fiber, 37 g protein. **DIABETIC EXCHANGES:** 4 lean meat, 2 starch.

Glazed Pork Chops and Apples
PREP/TOTAL TIME: 30 Min. **YIELD:** 4 Servings

This hearty dish was always a dinner staple when I was growing up. Mom called the tender chops "fried monkey ears." Now it's a favorite meal with my own family.

—Kathy Barry, Lake Forest, California

      4 boneless pork loin chops (4 ounces *each*)
    3/4 teaspoon rubbed sage
    1/2 teaspoon salt
      1 tablespoon canola oil
      1 tablespoon all-purpose flour
    1/2 cup reduced-sodium chicken broth
      1 tablespoon cider vinegar
      2 medium tart apples, thinly sliced
      4 teaspoons brown sugar

Sprinkle pork chops with sage and salt. In a large skillet, brown chops in oil on both sides. Transfer to an 11-in. x 7-in. x 2-in. baking dish coated with cooking spray.

Stir flour into the pan drippings until blended. Gradually stir in broth and vinegar. Bring to a boil; cook and stir for 1-2 minutes or until thickened. Remove from the heat.

Arrange apples over chops; sprinkle with brown sugar. Drizzle with broth mixture. Bake, uncovered, at 350° for 20-25 minutes or until a meat thermometer reads 160°.

NUTRITION FACTS: 1 pork chop with 1/2 cup apples equals 250 calories, 10 g fat (3 g saturated fat), 55 mg cholesterol, 406 mg sodium, 17 g carbohydrate, 2 g fiber, 22 g protein. **DIABETIC EXCHANGES:** 3 lean meat, 1 fruit, 1/2 fat.

Blackberry-Sauced Pork Chops
(PICTURED ABOVE)

PREP/TOTAL TIME: 30 Min.   **YIELD:** 4 Servings

These yummy chops are always a hit. As tasty in a skillet as they are grilled, you can enjoy them all year long. The sauce is just a incredible with chicken.
> —Priscilla Gilbert, Indian Harbour Beach, Florida

> 1/2 cup seedless blackberry spreadable fruit
>   1 tablespoon lemon juice
>   1 tablespoon reduced-sodium soy sauce
> Dash ground cinnamon
>   4 boneless pork loin chops (5 ounces *each*)
>   2 teaspoons steak seasoning
>   2 teaspoons olive oil
>   1 cup fresh blackberries

In a small saucepan, combine the spreadable fruit, lemon juice, soy sauce and cinnamon. Cook and stir over low heat until spreadable fruit is melted. Remove from the heat; set aside.

Sprinkle both sides of pork chops with steak seasoning. In a large nonstick skillet coated with cooking spray, cook chops in oil over medium-high heat for 5-7 minutes on each side or until a meat thermometer reads 160°. Serve with the sauce and blackberries.

NUTRITION FACTS: 1 pork chop with 2 tablespoons sauce and 1/4 cup berries equals 311 calories, 10 g fat (3 g saturated fat), 68 mg cholesterol, 531 mg sodium, 25 g carbohydrate, 2 g fiber, 28 g protein. **DIABETIC EX-CHANGES:** 4 lean meat, 1-1/2 fruit, 1/2 fat.

Editor's Note: This recipe was tested with McCormick's Montreal Steak Seasoning. Look for it in the spice aisle of your grocery store.

TASTY TIP
If preparing Blackberry-Sauced Pork Chops, feel free to use different flavors of spreadable fruit and whichever fresh berries you enjoy most.

Roast Pork with Currant Sauce   SALT

PREP: 10 Min. + Marinating   **BAKE:** 1 Hour + Standing   **YIELD:** 6 Servings

Our Test Kitchen perked up a pork roast by marinating it in fruit juices and a handful of spices.

> 1-1/2 cups orange juice
>   1/4 cup lemon juice
>   2 teaspoons minced fresh gingerroot
>   2 teaspoons minced garlic, *divided*
>   1 teaspoon dried oregano
>   1 teaspoon ground cinnamon
>   1/2 teaspoon ground coriander
>   1 boneless pork loin roast (2 pounds)
>   1 small onion, sliced
>   1 shallot, chopped
>   1 tablespoon butter
>   1 tablespoon all-purpose flour
>   1/2 cup reduced-sodium chicken broth
>   1/2 cup red currant jelly

In a bowl, combine the orange juice, lemon juice, ginger, 1 teaspoon garlic, oregano, cinnamon and coriander. Cover and refrigerate 1 cup for sauce. Pour remaining marinade into a large resealable plastic bag; add pork and onion. Seal bag and turn to coat; refrigerate for 4 hours, turning occasionally.

Drain and discard marinade; place the roast on a rack in a shallow roasting pan coated with cooking spray. Bake at 350° for 1 hour or until a meat thermometer reads 160°. Let stand for 10 minutes before slicing.

In a small nonstick saucepan, saute shallot and remaining garlic in butter for 1 minute. Sprinkle with flour; cook and stir until blended. Gradually stir in the broth, jelly and reserved juice mixture. Bring to a boil; cook and stir for 2 minutes or until thickened. Serve with pork.

NUTRITION FACTS: 4 ounces cooked pork with 3 tablespoons sauce equals 307 calories, 9 g fat (4 g saturated fat), 80 mg cholesterol, 115 mg sodium, 26 g carbohydrate, trace fiber, 30 g protein. **DIABETIC EX-CHANGES:** 4 lean meat, 1-1/2 starch, 1/2 fat.

Spiced Pork Tenderloin   CARB

PREP: 10 Min.   **BAKE:** 30 Min.   **YIELD:** 3 Servings

Ginger and pepper are the stars in this super-easy tenderloin. There's so much flavor in each bite, but if you really love ginger, increase the amount. —Tammy Bishop, Smyrna, New York

> 1-1/4 teaspoons ground ginger
>   1/2 teaspoon salt
>   1/2 teaspoon pepper
>   1/4 teaspoon ground mustard
>   1/8 teaspoon ground nutmeg
>   1 pork tenderloin (1 pound)

In a small bowl, combine the ginger, salt, pepper, mustard and nutmeg; sprinkle over pork. Place on a rack in a shallow roasting pan.

Bake at 375° for 30-35 minutes or until a meat thermometer reads 160°. Let stand for 5 minutes before slicing.

NUTRITION FACTS: 4 ounces cooked pork equals 182 calories, 5 g fat (2 g saturated fat), 84 mg cholesterol, 454 mg sodium, 1 g carbohydrate, trace fiber, 30 g protein. **DIABETIC EXCHANGE:** 4 lean meat.

Sweet-and-Sour Pork

(PICTURED BELOW)

PREP/TOTAL TIME: 30 Min. **YIELD:** 4 Servings

You'll find that red currant jelly gives this traditional Chinese dish a tangy kick. —Joanne Albers, Garden Grove, California

    4 teaspoons cornstarch
1/2 teaspoon salt
1/2 teaspoon ground ginger
1/8 teaspoon pepper
    1 can (8 ounces) unsweetened pineapple chunks
1/4 cup cider vinegar
    1 pork tenderloin (1 pound), cut into 1-inch cubes
    5 teaspoons canola oil, *divided*
    1 medium green pepper, cut into 1-inch pieces
    1 medium sweet red pepper, cut into 1-inch pieces
    1 small onion, cut into 1-inch pieces
1/3 cup red currant jelly
Hot cooked rice, optional

In a small bowl, combine the cornstarch, salt, ginger and pepper. Drain pineapple, reserving juice; set pineapple aside. Stir juice and vinegar into cornstarch mixture until smooth; set aside.

In a large nonstick skillet or wok, stir-fry pork in 3 teaspoons oil until no longer pink. Remove and keep warm. In the same pan, stir-fry peppers and onion in remaining oil until crisp-tender. Stir in the pork, pineapple and jelly.

Stir cornstarch mixture and add to the pan. Bring to a boil; cook and stir for 2 minutes or until thickened. Serve with rice if desired.

NUTRITION FACTS: 1-1/4 cups (calculated without rice) equals 311 calories, 10 g fat (2 g saturated fat), 63 mg cholesterol, 347 mg sodium, 33 g carbohydrate, 2 g fiber, 23 g protein. **DIABETIC EXCHANGES:** 3 lean meat, 1 starch, 1 vegetable, 1 fat, 1/2 fruit.

Slow-Cooked Pork Loin

CARB

PREP: 20 Min. **COOK:** 5 Hours **YIELD:** 12 Servings

Sweet apple undertones lend special flair to my low-calorie main course. —Kathleen Hendrick, Alexandria, Kentucky

    1 boneless whole pork loin roast (3-1/2 to 4 pounds)
    1 tablespoon canola oil
    1 medium onion, chopped
    1 celery rib, cut into 1-inch pieces
    1 envelope brown gravy mix
    1 cup water
    1 cup unsweetened apple juice
1/2 cup unsweetened applesauce
    2 teaspoons Worcestershire sauce
1/2 teaspoon seasoned salt
1/2 teaspoon pepper

Cut roast in half. In a large skillet, brown roast in oil on all sides. Transfer to a 5-qt. slow cooker. In the same skillet, saute onion and celery until tender; add to slow cooker.

In a small bowl, combine gravy mix and water. Stir in the remaining ingredients; pour over pork. Cover and cook on low for 5-6 hours or until a meat thermometer reads 160° and meat is tender. Skim fat from cooking juices; serve with roast.

NUTRITION FACTS: 3 ounces cooked pork with 1/3 cup juices equals 204 calories, 8 g fat (2 g saturated fat), 66 mg cholesterol, 294 mg sodium, 6 g carbohydrate, trace fiber, 26 g protein. **DIABETIC EXCHANGES:** 3 lean meat, 1/2 starch.

Pork and Sweet Potatoes

PREP/TOTAL TIME: 30 Min.   **YIELD:** 4 Servings

Sweet potatoes and sliced apple blend perfectly in this simple meal.
—Mary Relyea, Canastota, New York

   1 pork tenderloin (1 pound), cut into 12 slices
1/2 cup all-purpose flour
1/2 teaspoon salt
1/4 teaspoon pepper
   1 tablespoon canola oil
   1 can (14-1/2 ounces) reduced-sodium chicken broth
   2 medium sweet potatoes, peeled and cubed
1/2 cup dried cranberries
   1 tablespoon Dijon mustard
   1 medium red apple, sliced
   4 green onions, chopped

Flatten pork to 1/4-in. thickness. In a large resealable plastic bag, combine the flour, salt and pepper; add pork, a few pieces at a time, and shake to coat.

In a large nonstick skillet coated with cooking spray, brown pork in oil in batches. Remove and keep warm. Add the broth, sweet potatoes and cranberries to the skillet. Bring to a boil. Reduce heat; cover and simmer for 4-6 minutes or until potatoes are almost tender. Stir in mustard.

Return pork to the pan; add apple and onions. Cover and simmer for 4-6 minutes or until meat juices run clear.

NUTRITION FACTS: 3 slices pork with 1 cup potato mixture equals 352 calories, 8 g fat (2 g saturated fat), 63 mg cholesterol, 496 mg sodium, 45 g carbohydrate, 5 g fiber, 27 g protein. **DIABETIC EXCHANGES:** 3 starch, 3 lean meat, 1/2 fat.

Porcini-Crusted Pork with Polenta

(PICTURED ABOVE)

PREP: 20 Min.   **BAKE:** 20 Min.   **YIELD:** 4 Servings

Porcini mushrooms surround these luscious chops with earthy undertones and a delectable flavor. Hints of rosemary and Parmesan cheese make polenta a sophisticated accompaniment.
—Casandra Rittenhouse, North Hollywood, California

   1 package (1 ounce) dried porcini mushrooms
1/4 teaspoon salt
1/4 teaspoon pepper
   4 bone-in pork loin chops (7 ounces *each*)
   2 teaspoons olive oil
   1 tube (1 pound) polenta
1/2 cup grated Parmesan cheese
1/4 teaspoon dried rosemary, crushed

Process the mushrooms in a food processor until coarsely chopped. Transfer to a shallow bowl; stir in salt and pepper. Press one side of each pork chop into mushroom mixture.

In a large ovenproof skillet coated with cooking spray, heat oil over medium-high heat. Place chops, mushroom side down, in skillet; cook for 2 minutes. Turn over; cook 2 minutes longer. Bake, uncovered, at 375° for 20-25 minutes or until a meat thermometer reads 160°.

Prepare polenta according to package directions for soft polenta. Stir in the Parmesan cheese and rosemary. Serve with the pork chops.

NUTRITION FACTS: 1 pork chop with 2/3 cup polenta equals 397 calories, 14 g fat (5 g saturated fat), 94 mg cholesterol, 825 mg sodium, 26 g carbohydrate, 3 g fiber, 38 g protein. **DIABETIC EXCHANGES:** 5 lean meat, 1-1/2 starch.

Honey-Mustard Pork Chops

PREP: 10 Min. + Marinating   **GRILL:** 10 Min.   **YIELD:** 6 Servings

Looking for a change from the usual barbecue sauce? These pork chops fit the bill!
—Linda Shupe, Berthoud, Colorado

1/3 cup Dijon mustard
1/4 cup cider vinegar
1/4 cup honey
   2 tablespoons reduced-sodium soy sauce
   1 tablespoon sherry *or* reduced-sodium chicken broth
   1 tablespoon minced fresh parsley
   2 garlic cloves, minced
   1 teaspoon ground ginger
   6 boneless pork loin chops (3/4 inch thick and 6 ounces *each*)

In a small bowl, combine the first eight ingredients. Pour half of the marinade into a large resealable bag; add pork chops. Seal bag and turn to coat; refrigerate for 6-8 hours or overnight. Cover and refrigerate remaining marinade for basting.

Coat grill rack with cooking spray before starting the grill. Drain and discard marinade. Grill pork, covered, over medium heat for 4-5 minutes on each side or until a meat thermometer reads 160°, basting frequently with reserved marinade.

NUTRITION FACTS: 1 pork chop equals 254 calories, 10 g fat (4 g saturated fat), 82 mg cholesterol, 256 mg sodium, 6 g carbohydrate, trace fiber, 33 g protein. **DIABETIC EXCHANGE:** 5 lean meat.

Peachy Ginger Pork

(PICTURED BELOW)

PREP/TOTAL TIME: 25 Min. **YIELD:** 4 Servings

Sliced peaches and red pepper strips add vibrant color to these quick-to-fix pork slices. A hint of Dijon mustard and gingerroot perks up the slightly sweet sauce.

—Terri Glauser, Appleton, Wisconsin

    1 pork tenderloin (1 pound), cut into 1/2-inch slices
1/2 teaspoon salt
1/8 teaspoon pepper
    1 teaspoon olive oil
    1 medium sweet red pepper, julienned
    1 cup canned sliced peaches in extra-light syrup
1/2 cup reduced-sodium chicken broth
1/3 cup peach spreadable fruit
    1 tablespoon Dijon mustard
    2 teaspoons minced fresh gingerroot

Flatten pork to 1/4-in. thickness; sprinkle with salt and pepper. In a large nonstick skillet coated with cooking spray, saute pork in oil in batches until juices run clear. Remove and keep warm.

In the same skillet, saute red pepper and peaches until red pepper is tender. Add the broth, spreadable fruit, mustard and ginger. Cook and stir over medium heat for 4 minutes. Return pork to the pan. Reduce heat; cover and simmer until mixture is heated through.

NUTRITION FACTS: 1 serving equals 236 calories, 5 g fat (2 g saturated fat), 63 mg cholesterol, 517 mg sodium, 23 g carbohydrate, 1 g fiber, 23 g protein. **DIABETIC EXCHANGES:** 3 lean meat, 1 fruit.

> ### TASTY TIP
> For a slightly heartier dish, serve Peachy Ginger Pork over a bed of rice.

Grilled Stuffed Pork Tenderloin

PREP: 20 Min. + Marinating **GRILL:** 25 Min. **YIELD:** 6 Servings

We serve this stuffed tenderloin with a salad and a glass of wine. It's so good, you won't believe how easy it is.

—Bobbie Carr, Lake Oswego, Oregon

     2 pork tenderloins (3/4 pound *each*)
3/4 cup dry red wine *or* reduced-sodium beef broth
1/3 cup packed brown sugar
1/4 cup ketchup
     2 tablespoons reduced-sodium soy sauce
     2 garlic cloves, minced
     1 teaspoon curry powder
1/2 teaspoon minced fresh gingerroot
1/4 teaspoon pepper
1-1/4 cups water
     2 tablespoons butter
     1 package (6 ounces) stuffing mix

Cut a lengthwise slit down the center of each tenderloin to within 1/2 in. of bottom. In a large resealable plastic bag, combine the wine or broth, brown sugar, ketchup, soy sauce, garlic, curry, ginger and pepper; add pork. Seal bag and turn to coat; refrigerate for 2-3 hours.

In a small saucepan, bring water and butter to a boil. Stir in stuffing mix. Remove from the heat; cover and let stand for 5 minutes. Cool.

Drain and discard marinade. Open tenderloins so they lie flat; spread stuffing down the center of each. Close tenderloins; tie at 1-1/2-in. intervals with kitchen string.

Coat grill rack with cooking spray before starting the grill. Prepare grill for indirect heat. Grill pork, covered, over indirect medium-hot heat for 25-40 minutes or until a meat thermometer reads 160°. Let stand for 5 minutes before slicing.

NUTRITION FACTS: 1 serving equals 296 calories, 9 g fat (4 g saturated fat), 73 mg cholesterol, 678 mg sodium, 24 g carbohydrate, 1 g fiber, 27 g protein.

Dijon-Rubbed Pork with Rhubarb Sauce

(PICTURED BELOW)

PREP: 15 Min.   **BAKE:** 1 Hour + Standing
YIELD: 12 Servings (1-1/2 Cups Sauce)

Served with a creamy rhubarb sauce, this pork specialty is one you'll turn to time and again. It's great for company, but it makes an extra special weeknight meal, too.

—Marilyn Rodriguez, Fairbanks, Alaska

- 1 boneless pork loin roast (3 pounds)
- 1/4 cup Dijon mustard
- 6 garlic cloves, minced
- 1 tablespoon minced fresh rosemary *or* 1 teaspoon dried rosemary, crushed
- 3/4 teaspoon salt
- 1/2 teaspoon pepper

SAUCE:
- 3 cups sliced fresh *or* frozen rhubarb
- 1/3 cup orange juice
- 1/3 cup sugar
- 1 tablespoon cider vinegar

Score the surface of the pork, making diamond shapes 1/4 in. deep. In a small bowl, combine the mustard, garlic, rosemary, salt and pepper; rub over pork.

Coat a roasting pan and rack with cooking spray; place pork on rack in pan. Bake, uncovered, at 350° for 1 to 1-1/4 to hours or until a meat thermometer reads 160°. Let stand for 10 minutes before slicing.

In a small saucepan, bring the sauce ingredients to a boil. Reduce heat; cover and simmer for 8-12 minutes or until rhubarb is tender. Serve warm with pork.

NUTRITION FACTS: 3 ounces cooked pork with 2 tablespoons sauce equals 181 calories, 6 g fat (2 g saturated fat), 56 mg cholesterol, 308 mg sodium, 9 g carbohydrate, 1 g fiber, 23 g protein. **DIABETIC EXCHANGES:** 3 lean meat, 1/2 starch.

Editor's Note: If using frozen rhubarb, measure rhubarb while still frozen, then thaw completely. Drain in a colander, but do not press liquid out.

Saucy Southwestern Pork Chops

PREP: 15 Min.   **COOK:** 25 Min.   **YIELD:** 4 Servings

The pairing of green chilies and enchilada sauce gives this dinner a Southwestern kick.   —Jeannette Mitchell, Frederic, Wisconsin

- 4 bone-in pork loin chops (3/4 inch thick and 7 ounces each)
- 1/4 teaspoon pepper
- 2 teaspoons olive oil, *divided*
- 1 large onion, halved and sliced
- 1 can (14-1/2 ounces) stewed tomatoes, cut up
- 1 can (4 ounces) chopped green chilies
- 1/3 cup water
- 2 tablespoons enchilada sauce mix
- 4 tablespoons sliced ripe olives, *divided*
- 1 small green pepper, sliced into eight rings
- 1/2 cup reduced-fat sour cream
- 2 cups hot cooked rice

Sprinkle pork chops with pepper. In a large nonstick skillet coated with cooking spray, cook chops in 1 teaspoon oil over medium heat for 2-3 minutes on each side or until browned. Remove and keep warm.

In the same skillet, saute onion in remaining oil until tender. Stir in the tomatoes, chilies, water, sauce mix and 2 tablespoons olives. Bring to a boil.

Reduce heat; simmer, uncovered, for 3 minutes. Return chops to the pan; top with green pepper rings. Cover and simmer for 9-12 minutes or until meat is tender. Remove chops and pepper rings; keep warm. Stir sour cream into sauce until blended. Serve with pork and rice. Garnish with remaining olives.

NUTRITION FACTS: 1 pork chop with 3/4 cup sauce and 1/2 cup rice equals 439 calories, 14 g fat (6 g saturated fat), 96 mg cholesterol, 861 mg sodium, 40 g carbohydrate, 4 g fiber, 36 g protein. **DIABETIC EXCHANGES:** 4 lean meat, 2 starch, 2 vegetable, 1/2 fat.

Honey-Soy Pork Chops

SALT CARB

PREP: 10 Min. + Marinating   **GRILL:** 10 Min.   **YIELD:** 4 Servings

Summer is always a special time for relaxed and casual meals...and these grilled chops make a great main course.

—Edie DeSpain, Logan, Utah

- 1/4 cup lemon juice
- 1/4 cup honey
- 2 tablespoons reduced-sodium soy sauce
- 1 tablespoon sherry *or* unsweetened apple juice
- 2 garlic cloves, minced
- 4 boneless pork loin chops (4 ounces *each*)

In a small bowl, combine the first five ingredients. Pour 1/2 cup into a large resealable plastic bag; add pork chops. Seal bag and turn to coat; refrigerate for 2-3 hours. Cover and refrigerate remaining marinade for basting.

Coat grill rack with cooking spray before starting the grill. Drain and discard marinade. Grill pork, covered, over medium heat for 4-5 minutes on each side or until a meat thermometer reads 160°, basting frequently with remaining marinade.

NUTRITION FACTS: 1 pork chop equals 176 calories, 6 g fat (2 g saturated fat), 55 mg cholesterol, 132 mg sodium, 6 g carbohydrate, trace fiber, 22 g protein. **DIABETIC EXCHANGE:** 3 lean meat.

Fish & Seafood Fare

Jazz up your meal plan with a from-the-sea delight that's a true taste sensation. Turn the page for an incredible variety of shrimp dishes, salmon dinners, tuna delights and so many more. You'll find dozens of fresh favorites to choose from.

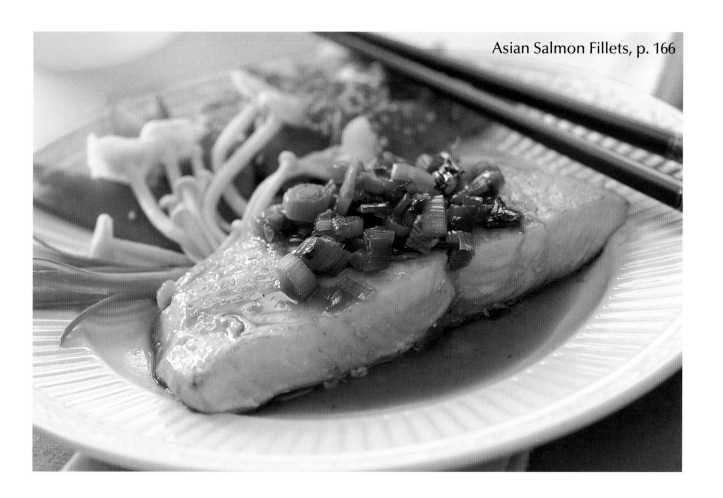

Asian Salmon Fillets, p. 166

Dilled Shrimp with Angel Hair

PREP: 25 Min.   **COOK:** 15 Min.   **YIELD:** 4 Servings

When I first prepared this pasta dish, my husband was surprised that it was actually on the lighter side. It's a great meal that comes together quickly, particularly when I serve a simple green salad or a loaf of crusty garlic bread on the side.
—Linda O'Brien, Girard, Pennsylvania

   6 ounces uncooked angel hair pasta
   6 green onions, thinly sliced
   2 garlic cloves, minced
   1 tablespoon butter
   1 pound uncooked medium shrimp, peeled and deveined
   3 tablespoons lemon juice
   4 ounces reduced-fat cream cheese, cubed
 1/2 cup fat-free half-and-half
   2 tablespoons snipped fresh dill
 1/2 teaspoon salt

Cook pasta according to package directions. Meanwhile, in a large nonstick skillet, saute the onions and garlic in butter for 1 minute.

Stir in shrimp and lemon juice; cook 4-5 minutes longer or until shrimp turn pink. Remove and keep warm.

In the same skillet, cook and stir cream cheese and half-and-half until blended. Stir in dill and salt. Return shrimp mixture to the pan; heat through. Drain pasta; toss with shrimp mixture.

NUTRITION FACTS: 1 serving equals 369 calories, 9 g fat (6 g saturated fat), 191 mg cholesterol, 698 mg sodium, 40 g carbohydrate, 2 g fiber, 28 g protein. **DIABETIC EXCHANGES:** 4 very lean meat, 2-1/2 starch, 1-1/2 fat.

Tomato Walnut Tilapia

CARB

(PICTURED ABOVE)

PREP/TOTAL TIME: 20 Min.   **YIELD:** 4 Servings

Tomato, bread crumbs and crunchy walnuts dress up fish fillets in my tilapia recipe. I usually serve it with cooked julienne carrots and green beans. —Phyl Broich-Wessling, Garner, Iowa

   4 tilapia fillets (4 ounces *each*)
 1/4 teaspoon salt
 1/4 teaspoon pepper
   1 tablespoon butter
   1 medium tomato, thinly sliced
TOPPING:
 1/2 cup soft bread crumbs
 1/4 cup chopped walnuts
   2 tablespoons lemon juice
1-1/2 teaspoons butter, melted

Sprinkle fillets with salt and pepper. In a large ovenproof skillet coated with cooking spray, cook fillets in butter over medium-high heat for 2-3 minutes on each side or until lightly browned.

Place tomato slices over fish. Combine the topping ingredients; spoon over tomato. Broil 3-4 in. from the heat for 2-3 minutes or until topping is lightly browned and fish flakes easily with a fork.

NUTRITION FACTS: 1 fillet equals 205 calories, 10 g fat (3 g saturated fat), 67 mg cholesterol, 265 mg sodium, 7 g carbohydrate, 1 g fiber, 24 g protein. **DIABETIC EXCHANGES:** 3 very lean meat, 2 fat, 1/2 starch.

HEALTHY OUTLOOK
If you prefer to brown the tomato-topped tilapia fillets in cooking spray instead of butter, you'll save another 25 calories and 3 grams of fat per serving.

Lobster 'n' Artichoke Quesadillas

PREP/TOTAL TIME: 30 Min.   **YIELD:** 6 Servings

Lobster, artichokes and cheese turn plain quesadillas into fantastic fare. Try them alongside avocado slices that have been seasoned with fresh lemon juice and lemon-pepper.
—Allene Bary-Cooper, Ramona, Oklahoma

 1/2 cup grated Parmesan cheese
 1/2 cup fat-free mayonnaise
   1 can (14 ounces) water-packed artichoke hearts, rinsed, drained and chopped
4-1/2 teaspoons chopped roasted sweet red pepper
   1 garlic clove, minced
   6 flour tortillas (10 inches)
   1 cup cooked lobster meat *or* canned flaked lobster meat
 1/2 cup shredded part-skim mozzarella cheese

In a small bowl, combine the Parmesan cheese, mayonnaise, artichokes, red pepper and garlic. Spread over three tortillas. Top with lobster, mozzarella cheese and remaining tortillas; press down lightly.

On a griddle coated with cooking spray, cook quesadillas over medium heat for 2 minutes on each side or until cheese is melted. Cut each into six wedges.

NUTRITION FACTS: 3 wedges equals 333 calories, 8 g fat (3 g saturated fat), 30 mg cholesterol, 991 mg sodium, 39 g carbohydrate, 6 g fiber, 18 g protein. **DIABETIC EXCHANGES:** 2 starch, 1 lean meat, 1 vegetable, 1 fat.

Sauteed Spiced Salmon
(PICTURED ABOVE)

SALT CARB

PREP/TOTAL TIME: 15 Min.   **YIELD:** 4 Servings

My friends love this crusty salmon dish. Not only is it positively delectable, but it's rich in heart-healthy omega-3 fatty acids.
—Kathy Garrison, Fort Worth, Texas

- 2 teaspoons dill weed
- 2 teaspoons chili powder
- 1 teaspoon salt-free lemon-pepper seasoning
- 1/2 teaspoon ground cumin
- 4 salmon fillets (4 ounces *each*), skin removed
- 1 tablespoon canola oil

Lemon wedges, optional

Combine the dill, chili powder, lemon-pepper and cumin; rub over fillets.

In a large nonstick skillet coated with cooking spray, cook salmon in oil over medium-high heat for 5-6 minutes on each side or until fish flakes easily with a fork. Serve with lemon wedges if desired.

NUTRITION FACTS: 1 fillet equals 246 calories, 16 g fat (3 g saturated fat), 67 mg cholesterol, 82 mg sodium, 2 g carbohydrate, 1 g fiber, 23 g protein. **DIABETIC EXCHANGES:** 3 lean meat, 1-1/2 fat.

Shrimp Tostadas with Avocado Salsa
(PICTURED AT RIGHT)

PREP/TOTAL TIME: 30 Min.   **YIELD:** 6 Servings

Try this quick and easy recipe for a fun Southwest meal that you likely haven't tried before. A splash of lime in the black beans balances the shrimp and rich avocado salsa.
—Karen Gulkin, Greeley, Colorado

- 1 medium ripe avocado, peeled and chopped, *divided*
- 1 tablespoon water
- 3 teaspoons lime juice, *divided*
- 2 teaspoons blackened seasoning, *divided*
- 1 teaspoon ground cumin
- 1 can (15 ounces) black beans, rinsed and drained, *divided*
- 1 small navel orange, peeled and chopped
- 1/4 cup chopped red onion
- 1 jalapeno pepper, seeded and chopped
- 1 tablespoon minced fresh cilantro
- 6 tostada shells
- 1 cup (4 ounces) shredded reduced-fat Mexican cheese blend
- 1 pound uncooked large shrimp, peeled and deveined

In a small bowl, combine 2 tablespoons avocado, water, 1 teaspoon lime juice, 1 teaspoon blackened seasoning and cumin. Set aside 1/4 cup beans; add remaining beans to avocado mixture and mash with a fork. Stir in reserved beans. Set aside.

For salsa, in a small bowl, combine the orange, onion, jalapeno, cilantro and remaining avocado and lime juice. Cover and refrigerate until serving.

Place tostada shells on ungreased baking sheets; spread with bean mixture. Sprinkle with cheese. Bake at 350° for 4-6 minutes or until cheese is melted.

Meanwhile, in a large nonstick skillet coated with cooking spray, cook shrimp and remaining blackened seasoning over medium-high heat for 4-6 minutes or until shrimp turn pink. Arrange over tostada shells; serve with salsa.

NUTRITION FACTS: 1 tostada with 2 tablespoons salsa equals 285 calories, 12 g fat (3 g saturated fat), 125 mg cholesterol, 517 mg sodium, 23 g carbohydrate, 6 g fiber, 22 g protein. **DIABETIC EXCHANGES:** 3 very lean meat, 2 fat, 1-1/2 starch.

Editor's Note: *When cutting or seeding hot peppers, use rubber or plastic gloves to protect your hands. Avoid touching your face.*

Maple-Glazed Salmon

(PICTURED BELOW)

PREP/TOTAL TIME: 20 Min.   **YIELD:** 4 Servings

I have a few good recipes for heart-healthy salmon, but this one is always preferred. I prepare the fish this way at least once a week and sometimes more! —David Krisko, Becker, Minnesota

- 1/4 cup ruby red grapefruit juice
- 2 tablespoons balsamic vinegar
- 2 tablespoons maple syrup
- 2 garlic cloves, minced
- 2 teaspoons olive oil
- 4 salmon fillets (4 ounces *each*)
- 1/4 teaspoon salt
- 1/4 teaspoon pepper

In a small saucepan, bring the grapefruit juice, vinegar, syrup and garlic to a boil. Reduce heat; simmer, uncovered, for 5 minutes. Transfer 2 tablespoons to a small bowl; add oil. Set remaining glaze aside.

If grilling the salmon, coat grill rack with cooking spray before starting the grill. Sprinkle salmon with salt and pepper; place skin side down on grill rack. Grill, covered, over medium heat or broil 4-6 in. from the heat for 10-12 minutes or until fish flakes easily with a fork, basting occasionally with maple-oil mixture. Drizzle with reserved glaze.

NUTRITION FACTS: 1 fillet equals 266 calories, 15 g fat (3 g saturated fat), 67 mg cholesterol, 218 mg sodium, 10 g carbohydrate, trace fiber, 23 g protein. **DIABETIC EXCHANGES:** 3 meat, 1/2 fruit.

Flounder with Cucumber Sauce

PREP/TOTAL TIME: 20 Min.   **YIELD:** 4 Servings

We live on Chesapeake Bay, and my husband goes fishing every chance he gets. Whenever he comes home with flounder, you can bet this microwave supper is on the menu.
—Carole Dishman, Toano, Virginia

- 4 flounder fillets (6 ounces *each*)
- 1 tablespoon butter, melted
- 1/8 teaspoon salt
- 1/8 teaspoon lemon-pepper seasoning

CUCUMBER SAUCE:

- 1/3 cup chopped seeded peeled cucumber
- 3 tablespoons reduced-fat mayonnaise
- 3 tablespoons reduced-fat sour cream
- 3/4 teaspoon minced chives
- 1/4 teaspoon salt
- 1/4 teaspoon onion powder

Place the flounder in a 2-qt. microwave-safe dish coated with cooking spray. Drizzle with butter; sprinkle with salt and lemon-pepper. Cover and microwave on high for 5-6 minutes or until fish flakes easily with a fork.

Meanwhile, in a small bowl, combine the sauce ingredients. Serve with flounder.

NUTRITION FACTS: 1 fillet with 2 tablespoons sauce equals 217 calories, 9 g fat (4 g saturated fat), 95 mg cholesterol, 485 mg sodium, 2 g carbohydrate, trace fiber, 29 g protein. **DIABETIC EXCHANGES:** 5 very lean meat, 1 fat.

Editor's Note: This recipe was tested in a 1,100-watt microwave.

Tangy Parmesan Tilapia

PREP/TOTAL TIME: 15 Min.   **YIELD:** 4 Servings

I was looking for a fish coating that didn't have bread crumbs or flour when I came across this full-flavored solution.
—Deborah Purdue, Westland, Michigan

- 1/4 cup grated Parmesan cheese
- 2 tablespoons reduced-fat mayonnaise
- 1 tablespoon reduced-fat butter, softened
- 1 tablespoon lime juice
- 1/8 teaspoon garlic powder
- 1/8 teaspoon dried basil
- 1/8 teaspoon pepper
- Dash onion powder
- 4 tilapia fillets (5 ounces *each*)
- 1/4 teaspoon salt

In a small bowl, combine the first eight ingredients; set aside. Line a broiler pan with foil and coat the foil with cooking spray. Place fillets in prepared pan; sprinkle with salt.

Broil 3-4 in. from the heat for 2-3 minutes on each side. Spread 1 tablespoon cheese mixture over the top of each fillet; broil 1-2 minutes longer or until topping is golden and fish flakes easily with a fork.

NUTRITION FACTS: 1 fillet equals 179 calories, 7 g fat (3 g saturated fat), 81 mg cholesterol, 368 mg sodium, 1 g carbohydrate, trace fiber, 29 g protein. **DIABETIC EXCHANGES:** 4 very lean meat, 1 fat.

Editor's Note: This recipe was tested with Land O'Lakes light stick butter.

Creamy Scallop Crepes
(PICTURED ABOVE)

PREP: 45 Min. + Chilling   **BAKE:** 15 Min.   **YIELD:** 6 Servings

This Swiss cheese-and-scallop-filled crepe recipe is a remarkable change of pace from dinner standbys. For extra flavor, I sometimes add 1/4 teaspoon fresh dill weed to the crepe batter before I refrigerate it.   —Doreen Kelly, Hatboro, Pennsylvania

    2 egg whites
    1 egg
1-1/2 cups fat-free milk
    1 cup all-purpose flour
    1/2 teaspoon salt
FILLING:
    1 pound bay scallops
    1/2 cup white wine *or* reduced-sodium chicken broth
    1/8 teaspoon white pepper
    1 pound sliced fresh mushrooms
    4 green onions, sliced
    2 tablespoons butter

> **TASTY TIP**
> When preparing her Creamy Scallop Crepes, Doreen Kelly sometimes replaces the scallops with chicken and adds bread crumbs for a somewhat heartier entree.

    1/4 cup all-purpose flour
    2/3 cup fat-free evaporated milk
    1/2 cup shredded reduced-fat Swiss cheese

In a small mixing bowl, beat the egg whites, egg and milk. Combine flour and salt; add to milk mixture and mix well. Cover and refrigerate for 1 hour.

Coat an 8-in. nonstick skillet with cooking spray; heat. Stir crepe batter; pour 2 tablespoons into center of skillet. Lift and tilt pan to coat bottom evenly. Cook until top appears dry; turn and cook 15-20 seconds longer. Remove to a wire rack. Repeat with remaining batter, coating skillet with cooking spray as needed. When cool, stack crepes with waxed paper or paper towels in between.

In a large nonstick skillet, bring the scallops, wine or broth and pepper to a boil. Reduce heat; simmer for 3-4 minutes or until scallops are firm and opaque. Drain, reserving cooking liquid; set liquid and scallops aside.

In the same skillet, saute mushrooms and onions in butter until almost tender. Sprinkle with flour; stir until blended. Gradually stir in evaporated milk and reserved cooking liquid. Bring to a boil; cook and stir for 2 minutes or until thickened. Remove from the heat. Stir in cheese and scallops.

Spread 1/3 cup filling down the center of each crepe; roll up and place in a 13-in. x 9-in. x 2-in. baking dish coated with cooking spray. Cover and bake at 350° for 12-15 minutes.

NUTRITION FACTS: 2 filled crepes equals 319 calories, 8 g fat (4 g saturated fat), 79 mg cholesterol, 463 mg sodium, 32 g carbohydrate, 2 g fiber, 27 g protein. **DIABETIC EXCHANGES:** 3 very lean meat, 2 starch, 1 fat.

Couscous Paella

(PICTURED ABOVE)

PREP: 25 Min.   **COOK:** 20 Min.   **YIELD:** 8 Servings

Featuring fabulous seasoning and herbs—including coriander, turmeric and garlic—this shrimp paella makes eating healthy completely enjoyable. —Marcella Stevenson, Westminster, California

- 1 medium sweet red pepper, chopped
- 4 garlic cloves, minced
- 1 tablespoon canola oil
- 6 green onions, thinly sliced
- 2 cans (14-1/2 ounces *each*) vegetable broth
- 2 teaspoons ground coriander
- 1 teaspoon ground turmeric
- 1/2 teaspoon salt
- 1/4 teaspoon pepper
- 1/8 teaspoon cayenne pepper
- 2 pounds uncooked medium shrimp, peeled and deveined
- 2 cups uncooked couscous
- 2 cups frozen peas, thawed
- 1 tablespoon butter
- 2 tablespoons chopped almonds, toasted
- 2 tablespoons minced fresh parsley

Lemon wedges

In a large nonstick skillet coated with cooking spray, saute red pepper and garlic in oil for 2 minutes. Add onions; cook 2 minutes longer or until red pepper is tender.

Stir in broth and seasonings; bring to a boil. Add shrimp; cook for 2-3 minutes or just until shrimp turn pink. Return to a boil. Stir in the couscous, peas and butter.

Remove from the heat; cover and let stand for 5 minutes.

Fluff with a fork. Sprinkle with almonds and parsley. Serve with lemon wedges.

NUTRITION FACTS: 1-1/4 cups equals 343 calories, 7 g fat (2 g saturated fat), 172 mg cholesterol, 841 mg sodium, 45 g carbohydrate, 5 g fiber, 28 g protein. **DIABETIC EXCHANGES:** 3 starch, 3 very lean meat, 1 fat.

Veggie-Topped Tilapia

CARB

PREP: 15 Min.   **BAKE:** 20 Min.   **YIELD:** 4 Servings

I invented this fast weeknight dish using frozen tilapia fillets. My entire family loved it, particularly with crusty rolls and rice on the side. —Christine Bissonette, Scotia, New York

- 4 tilapia fillets (5 ounces *each*)
- 1/3 cup white wine *or* reduced-sodium chicken broth
- 1/2 teaspoon seafood seasoning
- 1 medium onion, finely chopped
- 1 medium green pepper, finely chopped
- 1 small tomato, chopped
- 3 tablespoons lemon juice
- 1 teaspoon olive oil
- 1/4 teaspoon garlic powder
- 1/4 cup shredded Parmesan cheese

Place fillets in a 13-in. x 9-in. x 2-in. baking dish coated with cooking spray. Drizzle with wine or broth; sprinkle with seafood seasoning. Combine the onion, green pepper, tomato, lemon juice, oil and garlic powder; spoon over fillets.

Cover and bake at 425° for 15 minutes. Uncover; sprinkle with Parmesan cheese. Bake 5-10 minutes longer or until vegetables are tender and fish flakes easily with a fork.

NUTRITION FACTS: 1 fillet equals 192 calories, 4 g fat (2 g saturated fat), 73 mg cholesterol, 223 mg sodium, 8 g carbohydrate, 2 g fiber, 29 g protein. **DIABETIC EXCHANGES:** 4 very lean meat, 1 vegetable, 1/2 fat.

Grilled Salmon with Dill Sauce

PREP/TOTAL TIME: 20 Min. **YIELD:** 6 Servings (3/4 Cup Sauce)

With its fresh flavors, this rich dinner staple is perfect for elegant meals or casual family dinners. I'll even heat up my grill in the middle of winter just to prepare it.
—Chris Otis, New Canaan, Connecticut

  1 tablespoon minced fresh gingerroot
  1 tablespoon minced fresh cilantro
  3/4 teaspoon salt
  3/4 teaspoon pepper
  1/8 teaspoon cayenne pepper
  6 salmon fillets (4 ounces *each*)
SAUCE:
  1/4 cup reduced-fat sour cream
  1/4 cup fat-free plain yogurt
  1/4 cup fat-free mayonnaise
  1 green onion, chopped
  1-1/2 teaspoons minced fresh parsley
  1-1/2 teaspoons snipped fresh dill *or* 1/2 teaspoon dill weed

In a small bowl, combine the ginger, cilantro, salt, pepper and cayenne; rub over fillets. Coat grill rack with cooking spray before starting the grill. Place salmon skin side down on rack. Grill, covered, over high heat for 5-10 minutes or until fish flakes easily with a fork.

In a small bowl, combine the sauce ingredients. Serve with salmon.

NUTRITION FACTS: 1 fillet with 2 tablespoons sauce equals 235 calories, 13 g fat (3 g saturated fat), 72 mg cholesterol, 455 mg sodium, 3 g carbohydrate, trace fiber, 24 g protein. **DIABETIC EXCHANGES:** 3 lean meat, 1 fat.

Shrimp 'n' Spinach Risotto

PREP: 20 Min. **COOK:** 35 Min. **YIELD:** 4 Servings

I enjoy concocting new, healthy recipes. Spinach is one of the few vegetables that my husband will eat, so this creamy risotto was bound to appear on my dinner table sooner or later.
—Jennifer Neilsen, Winterville, North Carolina

3-1/4 to 3-3/4 cups reduced-sodium chicken broth
1-1/2 cups chopped fresh mushrooms
  1 small onion, chopped
  3 garlic cloves, minced
  1 tablespoon butter
  1 cup uncooked arborio rice
  1 package (6 ounces) fresh baby spinach, coarsely chopped
  1 pound cooked medium shrimp, peeled and deveined
  1/2 cup shredded Parmesan cheese
  1/4 teaspoon pepper

In a small saucepan, heat broth and keep warm. In a large nonstick skillet, saute the mushrooms, onion and garlic in butter until tender, about 3 minutes. Add rice; cook and stir for 2-3 minutes. Carefully stir in 1 cup heated broth. Cook and stir until all of the liquid is absorbed.

Add remaining broth, 1/2 cup at a time, stirring constantly. Allow liquid to absorb between additions. Cook just until risotto is creamy and rice is almost tender. Total cooking time is about 20 minutes. Add the spinach, shrimp, cheese and pepper; cook and stir until spinach is wilted and shrimp are heated through. Serve immediately.

NUTRITION FACTS: 1-1/4 cups equals 405 calories, 8 g fat (4 g saturated fat), 187 mg cholesterol, 906 mg sodium, 47 g carbohydrate, 2 g fiber, 35 g protein. **DIABETIC EXCHANGES:** 4 very lean meat, 2-1/2 starch, 1 vegetable, 1 fat.

Catfish with Savory Strawberry Sauce
(PICTURED BELOW)

PREP/TOTAL TIME: 25 Min. **YIELD:** 4 Servings

Friends and family love the delicate balance between spicy and sweet in my catfish specialty. Serve it with red beans and rice to round out the Cajun menu. —Heather Sapp, Arlington, Virginia

  4 catfish fillets (6 ounces *each*)
  1/4 teaspoon salt
  1/4 teaspoon pepper
  1 teaspoon hot pepper sauce
  1/4 cup strawberry spreadable fruit
  2 tablespoons red wine vinegar
  1 tablespoon seafood cocktail sauce
  3/4 teaspoon reduced-sodium soy sauce
  1/2 teaspoon grated horseradish
  1 garlic clove, minced
  1/3 cup all-purpose flour
  1/3 cup cornmeal
  1 tablespoon olive oil

Sprinkle catfish with salt, pepper and hot pepper sauce; set aside. In a small saucepan, combine the spreadable fruit, vinegar, seafood sauce, soy sauce, horseradish and garlic. Cook over low heat until heated through, stirring occasionally.

Meanwhile, in a large resealable plastic bag, combine flour and cornmeal. Add catfish, one fillet at a time, and shake to coat. In a large nonstick skillet, cook fillets in oil over medium-high heat for 2-3 minutes on each side or until fish flakes easily with a fork. Drain on paper towels. Serve with strawberry sauce.

NUTRITION FACTS: 1 fillet with 2 tablespoons sauce equals 350 calories, 17 g fat (4 g saturated fat), 80 mg cholesterol, 309 mg sodium, 21 g carbohydrate, 1 g fiber, 28 g protein.

Asian Salmon Fillets

(PICTURED BELOW)

CARB

PREP/TOTAL TIME: 25 Min.   YIELD: 4 Servings

This is a recipe I concocted after a visit to Hawaii. It's perfect for hurried work nights and weekend dinner parties alike.
                                    —Susan Coryell, Huddleston, Virginia

    4 green onions, thinly sliced
    1 garlic clove, minced
    1 teaspoon olive oil
    1 teaspoon minced fresh gingerroot
    4 salmon fillets (5 ounces *each*)
1/4 cup white wine *or* reduced-sodium chicken broth
    2 tablespoons reduced-sodium soy sauce
    2 tablespoons oyster sauce

In a large nonstick skillet over medium heat, cook onions and garlic in oil for 1 minute. Add ginger; cook 1 minute longer. Transfer to a small bowl; set aside.

Spritz fillets with cooking spray; add to skillet. Cook for 4-6 minutes on each side or until lightly browned.

Combine the wine or broth, soy sauce, oyster sauce and reserved onion mixture; pour over salmon. Cook for 2-3 minutes or until fish flakes easily with a fork. Remove fillets. Cook sauce 1-2 minutes longer or until thickened; serve over salmon.

NUTRITION FACTS: 1 fillet with 1 tablespoon sauce equals 300 calories, 17 g fat (3 g saturated fat), 84 mg cholesterol, 725 mg sodium, 3 g carbohydrate, trace fiber, 30 g protein. DIABETIC EXCHANGES: 4 lean meat, 1 fat.

Grilled Tuna with Pineapple Salsa

CARB

PREP/TOTAL TIME: 30 Min.   YIELD: 4 Servings (1 Cup Salsa)

Easy-to-mix salsa adds tropical flair to sweet and spicy glazed tuna steaks. Best of all, it requires just an ounce of prep work.
                                    —Bonnie Hogan, Rochester, New Hampshire

    1 cup cubed fresh pineapple
    1 tablespoon finely chopped red onion
    1 tablespoon minced fresh cilantro
    3 teaspoons cider vinegar, *divided*
    1 teaspoon minced jalapeno pepper, optional
    2 tablespoons hoisin sauce
    1 tablespoon ketchup

    4 tuna steaks (1 inch thick and 6 ounces *each*)
    1 tablespoon olive oil
1/4 teaspoon salt
1/4 teaspoon pepper

In a small bowl, combine the pineapple, red onion, cilantro, 1-1/2 teaspoons vinegar and jalapeno if desired. Cover and refrigerate until serving. In a small bowl, combine the hoisin sauce, ketchup and remaining vinegar; set aside.

Coat grill rack with cooking spray before starting the grill. Rub both sides of fish with oil; sprinkle with salt and pepper. Grill, covered, over medium heat for 3-6 minutes on each side or until fish flakes easily with a fork, basting frequently with reserved hoisin sauce mixture and turning once. Serve with pineapple salsa.

NUTRITION FACTS: 1 tuna steak with 1/4 cup salsa equals 256 calories, 5 g fat (1 g saturated fat), 77 mg cholesterol, 385 mg sodium, 10 g carbohydrate, 1 g fiber, 40 g protein. DIABETIC EXCHANGES: 5 very lean meat, 1 fat, 1/2 fruit.

Editor's Note: When cutting or seeding hot peppers, use rubber or plastic gloves to protect your hands. Avoid touching your face.

Shrimp and Plum Salad

PREP: 15 Min.   COOK: 35 Min. + Cooling   YIELD: 4 Servings

Fruit pairs beautifully with seafood in this charming main course salad from the L&T home economists. Served with a sweet-spicy Asian dressing, it's ideal for a luncheon or light summer supper.

2/3 cup uncooked brown rice
1-1/3 cups water
    1 pound cooked medium shrimp, peeled and deveined
    2 large fresh plums, sliced
1/2 cup chopped peeled cucumber
    2 tablespoons minced fresh cilantro
    1 green onion, chopped
    1 jalapeno pepper, seeded and chopped
DRESSING:
    3 tablespoons rice wine vinegar
    3 tablespoons canola oil
    2 teaspoons honey
1/2 teaspoon ground mustard
1/2 teaspoon minced fresh gingerroot
1/2 teaspoon Thai chili sauce
    1 garlic clove, minced
    4 cups spring mix salad greens

In a small saucepan, bring rice and water to a boil. Reduce heat; cover and simmer for 30-35 minutes or until liquid is absorbed and rice is tender. Transfer to a large bowl; cool completely.

Stir in the shrimp, plums, cucumber, cilantro, onion and jalapeno. In a jar with a tight-fitting lid, combine the vinegar, oil, honey, mustard, ginger, chili sauce and garlic; shake well. Pour over shrimp mixture and toss to coat. Serve over salad greens.

NUTRITION FACTS: 1 cup shrimp mixture with 1 cup salad greens equals 377 calories, 14 g fat (1 g saturated fat), 172 mg cholesterol, 197 mg sodium, 36 g carbohydrate, 4 g fiber, 27 g protein. DIABETIC EXCHANGES: 3 very lean meat, 2 fat, 1-1/2 starch, 1 vegetable, 1/2 fruit.

Editor's Note: When cutting or seeding hot peppers, use rubber or plastic gloves to protect your hands. Avoid touching your face.

Favorite Recipe Made Lighter

OVEN-FRESH CASSEROLES are the stuff families dream of when the dinner bell rings. After all, those piping hot creations just can't be beat. Creamy and hearty, Spinach Tuna Casserole from Karla Hamrick of Wapakoneta, Ohio is one of those classics.

With spinach and tuna, the gooey dish is a hit with Karla's family. "I adapted the recipe from one I found in another magazine. I stopped making it when I decided to lose weight," writes Karla. "I've lost 80 pounds, but I miss this entree a lot."

Our home economists set out to re-create Karla's yummy recipe but in a lighter form. First, they decreased the noodles and increased the amount of tuna to balance the starch and protein. Cutting back on mayonnaise and sour cream and using their fat-free and reduced-fat counterparts slashed even more fat.

To make up for the lost mayo and sour cream, they added a white sauce of flour, butter and fat-free milk to help hold the ingredients together and boost the creamy texture. In addition, they added a little bit more Parmesan cheese to give the remade dish a flavorful boost reminiscent of Karla's original submission.

Makeover Spinach Tuna Casserole is a huge success. A whopping 80% of the fat has been removed as well as 327 calories—nearly half of the total number of calories! Best of all, it offers all the nutrition Karla had hoped for in a family-pleasing meal.

Makeover Spinach Tuna Casserole
(PICTURED ABOVE)

PREP: 25 Min. **BAKE:** 40 Min. **YIELD:** 8 Servings

- 5 cups uncooked egg noodles
- 1 cup (8 ounces) reduced-fat sour cream
- 1/2 cup fat-free mayonnaise
- 2 to 3 teaspoons lemon juice
- 2 tablespoons butter
- 1/4 cup all-purpose flour
- 2 cups fat-free milk
- 1/3 cup plus 2 tablespoons shredded Parmesan cheese, *divided*
- 1 package (10 ounces) frozen chopped spinach, thawed and squeezed dry
- 1 package (6 ounces) reduced-sodium chicken stuffing mix
- 1/3 cup seasoned bread crumbs
- 2 cans (6 ounces *each*) light water-packed tuna, drained and flaked

Cook noodles according to package directions. Meanwhile, in a small bowl, combine the sour cream, mayonnaise and lemon juice; set aside.

In a large saucepan or Dutch oven, melt butter. Stir in flour until blended. Gradually stir in milk. Bring to a boil; cook and stir for 2 minutes or until thickened. Reduce heat; stir in 1/3 cup Parmesan cheese until melted. Remove from the heat; stir in the sour cream mixture. Add the spinach, stuffing mix, bread crumbs and tuna; mix well.

Drain noodles and place in a 13-in. x 9-in. x 2-in. baking dish coated with cooking spray. Top with tuna mixture; sprinkle with remaining Parmesan cheese.

Cover and bake at 350° for 35 minutes. Uncover; bake 5-10 minutes longer or until lightly browned and heated through.

NUTRITION FACTS: 1 serving equals 346 calories, 9 g fat (5 g saturated fat), 50 mg cholesterol, 734 mg sodium, 41 g carbohydrate, 2 g fiber, 24 g protein. **DIABETIC EXCHANGES:** 2-1/2 starch, 2 very lean meat, 1-1/2 fat.

Spinach Tuna Casserole

PREP: 25 Min. **BAKE:** 50 Min. **YIELD:** 8 Servings

- 5 cups uncooked egg noodles
- 2 cups (16 ounces) sour cream
- 1-1/2 cups mayonnaise
- 2 to 3 teaspoons lemon juice
- 2 to 3 teaspoons milk
- 1/4 teaspoon salt
- 1 package (10 ounces) frozen chopped spinach, thawed and squeezed dry
- 1 package (6 ounces) chicken stuffing mix
- 1/3 cup seasoned bread crumbs
- 1 can (6 ounces) tuna, drained and flaked
- 3 tablespoons grated Parmesan cheese

Cook noodles according to package directions. Meanwhile, in a large bowl, combine the sour cream, mayonnaise, lemon juice, milk and salt. Add the spinach, stuffing mix, bread crumbs and tuna; mix well.

Drain noodles and place in a greased 13-in. x 9-in. x 2-in. baking dish. Top with tuna mixture; sprinkle with cheese. Cover and bake at 350° for 45 minutes. Uncover; bake 5-10 minutes longer or until lightly browned and heated through.

NUTRITION FACTS: 1 serving equals 673 calories, 46 g fat (12 g saturated fat), 90 mg cholesterol, 927 mg sodium, 42 g carbohydrate, 2 g fiber, 17 g protein

Scampi Adobo

(PICTURED ABOVE)

PREP/TOTAL TIME: 30 Min.   **YIELD:** 4 Servings

Being a homegrown Texan, I love this Southwestern take on shrimp scampi.   —Laurie LaClair, North Richland Hills, Texas

- 2 plum tomatoes, seeded and chopped
- 1 poblano pepper, seeded and chopped
- 1 tablespoon minced chipotle pepper in adobo sauce
- 3 garlic cloves, minced
- 1 tablespoon olive oil
- 1 pound uncooked medium shrimp, peeled and deveined
- 1/2 cup white wine *or* reduced-sodium chicken broth
- 1/3 cup minced fresh cilantro
- 3 tablespoons lime juice
- 2 tablespoons reduced-fat butter
- 1/2 teaspoon salt
- 1/4 cup shredded part-skim mozzarella cheese

Lime slices, optional

In a large nonstick skillet, saute the tomatoes, peppers and garlic in oil for 2 minutes. Reduce heat to medium; stir in the shrimp, wine or broth, cilantro, lime juice, butter and salt. Cook and stir for 3-4 minutes or until shrimp turn pink.

Remove from the heat; sprinkle with mozzarella cheese. Garnish with lime slices if desired.

NUTRITION FACTS: 3/4 cup equals 196 calories, 9 g fat (3 g saturated fat), 182 mg cholesterol, 562 mg sodium, 5 g carbohydrate, 1 g fiber, 21 g protein. **DIABETIC EXCHANGES:** 3 very lean meat, 1-1/2 fat.

Editor's Note: This recipe was tested with Land O'Lakes light stick butter.

De-Lightful Tuna Casserole

PREP: 15 Min.   **BAKE:** 25 Min.   **YIELD:** 5 Servings

Looking to satisfy your family's craving for comfort food without all the fat? Give this homemade tuna casserole a try! Loaded with tuna and elbow macaroni, it gets its creamy goodness from a can of cream soup and cheddar cheese.

—Colleen Willey, Hamburg, New York

- 1 package (7 ounces) elbow macaroni
- 1 can (10-3/4 ounces) reduced-fat reduced-sodium condensed cream of mushroom soup, undiluted
- 1 cup sliced fresh mushrooms
- 1 cup (4 ounces) shredded reduced-fat cheddar cheese
- 1 cup fat-free milk
- 1 can (6 ounces) light water-packed tuna, drained and flaked
- 2 tablespoons diced pimientos
- 3 teaspoons dried minced onion
- 1 teaspoon ground mustard
- 1/4 teaspoon salt
- 1/3 cup crushed cornflakes

Cook macaroni according to package directions. Meanwhile, in a large bowl, combine the soup, mushrooms, cheese, milk, tuna, pimientos, onion, mustard and salt. Drain macaroni; add to tuna mixture and mix well.

Transfer to a 2-qt. baking dish coated with cooking spray. Sprinkle with cornflakes. Bake, uncovered, at 350° for 25-30 minutes or until bubbly.

NUTRITION FACTS: 1-1/4 cups equals 329 calories, 8 g fat (4 g saturated fat), 32 mg cholesterol, 684 mg sodium, 43 g carbohydrate, 2 g fiber, 23 g protein. **DIABETIC EXCHANGES:** 3 starch, 2 lean meat.

Poached Salmon with Chimichurri

SALT CARB

PREP: 40 Min.   **COOK:** 10 Min.   **YIELD:** 4 Servings

Tender, flaky salmon is treated to a scrumptious wine sauce in this elegant dish from our Test Kitchen. Though it takes a little extra prep time, the impressive entree is a must-try.

    4 cups water
    1/2 cup white wine *or reduced-sodium chicken broth*
    1/2 cup white wine vinegar
    1 medium carrot, coarsely chopped
    1 celery rib with leaves, coarsely chopped
    1 medium onion, coarsely chopped
    4 sprigs fresh parsley
    4 whole peppercorns
    1 bay leaf
    4 salmon fillets (4 ounces *each*)
CHIMICHURRI:
    2 tablespoons lemon juice
    1 tablespoon white wine vinegar
    1 tablespoon olive oil
    3 tablespoons finely chopped onion
    3 tablespoons minced fresh parsley
    1 garlic clove, minced
    1/8 teaspoon pepper
    1/8 teaspoon cayenne pepper

In a large saucepan or Dutch oven, bring the first nine ingredients to a boil. Reduce heat; simmer, uncovered, for 15 minutes. Strain, reserving liquid (discard vegetables and spices).

Return liquid to the pan and bring to a boil. Reduce heat; add salmon. Poach, uncovered, for 8-10 minutes or until fish flakes easily with a fork.

Meanwhile, in a small bowl, whisk the lemon juice, vinegar and oil. Stir in the onion, parsley, garlic, pepper and cayenne. Serve with salmon.

NUTRITION FACTS: 1 fillet with 1 tablespoon chimichurri equals 246 calories, 16 g fat (3 g saturated fat), 67 mg cholesterol, 69 mg sodium, 2 g carbohydrate, trace fiber, 23 g protein.

Dilled Fish and Vegetable Packet

FAT CARB

PREP: 15 Min.   **BAKE:** 20 Min.   **YIELD:** 4 Servings

Ideal for anyone counting calories, this convenient, foil-packet meal is a simple solution that couldn't be much easier. I recommend serving it with baked potatoes. —Shirley Gever, Toms River, New Jersey

    4 tilapia fillets (4 ounces *each*)
Refrigerated butter-flavored spray
    1/2 teaspoon salt, *divided*
    1/4 teaspoon pepper, *divided*
    2 cups fresh snow peas
    2 cups fresh baby carrots, halved lengthwise
    1 green onion, thinly sliced
    2 tablespoons minced fresh dill
    2 garlic cloves, minced
    1/2 cup white wine *or reduced-sodium chicken broth*

Place an 18-in. x 12-in. piece of heavy-duty foil on a large baking sheet. Arrange fillets in a single layer on foil; spritz with but-ter-flavored spray. Sprinkle with 1/4 teaspoon salt and 1/8 teaspoon pepper.

Combine the peas, carrots, onion, dill, garlic and remaining salt and pepper; spoon over fish. Drizzle with wine or broth. Top with a second large piece of foil. Bring edges of foil pieces together; crimp to seal, forming a large packet.

Bake at 400° for 20-25 minutes or until fish flakes easily with a fork and vegetables are crisp-tender. Open foil carefully to allow steam to escape.

NUTRITION FACTS: 1 fillet with 3/4 cup vegetables equals 178 calories, 2 g fat (1 g saturated fat), 55 mg cholesterol, 396 mg sodium, 13 g carbohydrate, 4 g fiber, 24 g protein. **DIABETIC EXCHANGES:** 3 very lean meat, 2 vegetable.

Editor's Note: This recipe was tested with I Can't Believe It's Not Butter Spray.

Baked Horseradish Salmon

SALT CARB

(PICTURED BELOW)

PREP/TOTAL TIME: 30 Min.   **YIELD:** 4 Servings

When I created this heart-smart dish, I knew I had a winner on my hands. Now, all we have to do is mention to friends that we're having salmon for dinner and happy guests show up at our door.
    —James Ockerman, Floral City, Florida

    1 salmon fillet (1 pound)
    1 tablespoon butter, melted
    1 tablespoon prepared horseradish, drained
    2 teaspoons lemon juice
    1/4 teaspoon garlic powder
    1/8 teaspoon pepper

Place salmon skin side down in an 11-in. x 7-in. x 2-in. baking dish coated with cooking spray. In a small bowl, combine the butter, horseradish, lemon juice, garlic powder and pepper; spread over salmon.

Bake, uncovered, at 375° for 20-25 minutes or until fish flakes easily with a fork.

NUTRITION FACTS: 3 ounces cooked salmon equals 236 calories, 15 g fat (4 g saturated fat), 75 mg cholesterol, 108 mg sodium, 1 g carbohydrate, trace fiber, 23 g protein. **DIABETIC EXCHANGES:** 3 lean meat, 1-1/2 fat.

Broiled Greek Fish Fillets

CARB

(PICTURED BELOW)

PREP/TOTAL TIME: 25 Min.   **YIELD:** 8 Servings

Olives, onion, dill and feta cheese combine in this tangy, Greek-inspired topping to boost the flavor of tilapia or your favorite whitefish. I usually serve it with a side of rice.
— Jennifer Maslowski, New York, New York

   8 tilapia fillets (4 ounces *each*)
 1/4 teaspoon salt
 1/4 teaspoon pepper
 1/4 cup plain yogurt
   2 tablespoons butter, softened
   1 tablespoon lime juice
   1 small red onion, finely chopped
 1/2 cup pitted Greek olives
   1 teaspoon dill weed
 1/2 teaspoon paprika
 1/4 teaspoon garlic powder
 1/2 cup crumbled feta cheese

Sprinkle tilapia with salt and pepper. Place on a broiler pan coated with cooking spray.

In a small bowl, combine the yogurt, butter and lime juice. Stir in the onion, olives and seasonings. Spread down the middle of each fillet; sprinkle with feta cheese. Broil 3-4 in. from the heat for 6-9 minutes or until fish flakes easily with a fork.

NUTRITION FACTS: 1 fillet equals 169 calories, 7 g fat (3 g saturated fat), 68 mg cholesterol, 353 mg sodium, 3 g carbohydrate, 1 g fiber, 23 g protein. **DIABETIC EXCHANGES:** 3 very lean meat, 1-1/2 fat.

Baked Dill Halibut

CARB

(PICTURED ABOVE)

PREP: 15 Min.   **BAKE:** 25 Min.   **YIELD:** 4 Servings

This healthy dish goes together in no time. I make it regularly and there is never much to clean.   — Sharon Semph, Salem, Oregon

 1/3 cup all-purpose flour
 1/2 teaspoon salt
 1/8 teaspoon pepper
   4 halibut steaks (6 ounces *each*)
 1/4 cup reduced-fat sour cream
 1/4 cup reduced-fat mayonnaise
   1 tablespoon chopped dill pickle
   1 tablespoon chopped green onion
 1/2 teaspoon dill weed
 1/2 teaspoon lemon juice
 1/8 teaspoon seasoned salt
   3 tablespoons grated Parmesan cheese

In a large resealable plastic bag, combine the flour, salt and pepper. Add halibut, one piece at a time, and shake to coat. Place in a 13-in. x 9-in. x 2-in. baking dish coated with cooking spray.

In a small bowl, combine the sour cream, mayonnaise, pickle, onion, dill, lemon juice and seasoned salt; spread evenly over the halibut. Sprinkle with Parmesan cheese. Bake, uncovered, at 350° for 25-30 minutes or until fish flakes easily with a fork.

NUTRITION FACTS: 1 halibut steak equals 314 calories, 11 g fat (3 g saturated fat), 68 mg cholesterol, 663 mg sodium, 11 g carbohydrate, trace fiber, 39 g protein. **DIABETIC EXCHANGES:** 6 very lean meat, 1-1/2 fat, 1/2 starch.

Asparagus Fish Bundles
(PICTURED ABOVE)

PREP: 25 Min.   **BAKE:** 30 Min.   **YIELD:** 4 Servings

Low-fat food can look just as appealing as heavy entrees. Wrapped around asparagus bundles, these mouth-watering fish fillets are an ideal example. The basil-thyme sauce is an exceptional touch to the lovely dinner.   —Jane Shapton, Tustin, California

    4 orange roughy fillets (6 ounces *each*)
   20 fresh asparagus spears, trimmed
  1/2 teaspoon salt
  1/4 teaspoon pepper
    2 green onions, chopped
SAUCE:
  2/3 cup white wine *or* reduced-sodium chicken broth
    2 tablespoons lemon juice
    2 teaspoons cornstarch
    1 teaspoon minced fresh basil *or* 1/4 teaspoon dried basil
    1 teaspoon minced fresh thyme *or* 1/4 teaspoon dried thyme
  1/8 teaspoon pepper

Wrap each fillet around five asparagus spears; secure with toothpicks. Place in a 13-in. x 9-in. x 2-in. baking dish coated with cooking spray. Sprinkle with salt and pepper.

Cover and bake at 350° for 15 minutes. Uncover; sprinkle with onions. Bake, uncovered, 12-15 minutes longer or until fish flakes easily with a fork and asparagus is crisp-tender.

Meanwhile, in a small saucepan, combine the sauce ingredients until blended. Bring to a boil; cook and stir for 1-2 minutes or until thickened. Discard toothpicks from bundles; serve with sauce.

NUTRITION FACTS: 1 bundle with 2 tablespoons sauce equals 172 calories, 1 g fat (trace saturated fat), 34 mg cholesterol, 414 mg sodium, 6 g carbohydrate, 2 g fiber, 27 g protein. **DIABETIC EXCHANGES:** 5 very lean meat, 1 vegetable.

Oven-Fried Fish Nuggets

PREP/TOTAL TIME: 25 Min.   **YIELD:** 4 Servings

My husband and I love fresh fried fish, but we're both trying to cut back on fats. I made up this recipe, and we've enjoyed it regularly since. He tells me that he likes it as much as deep-fried fish, and that's saying a lot!   —LaDonna Reed, Ponca City, Oklahoma

  1/3 cup seasoned bread crumbs
  1/3 cup crushed cornflakes
    3 tablespoons grated Parmesan cheese
  1/2 teaspoon salt
  1/4 teaspoon pepper
1-1/2 pounds cod fillets, cut into 1-inch cubes
Butter-flavored cooking spray

In a shallow bowl, combine the bread crumbs, cornflakes, Parmesan cheese, salt and pepper. Coat fish with butter-flavored spray, then roll in crumb mixture.

Place on a baking sheet coated with cooking spray. Bake at 375° for 15-20 minutes or until fish flakes easily with a fork.

NUTRITION FACTS: 1 serving equals 171 calories, 2 g fat (1 g saturated fat), 66 mg cholesterol, 415 mg sodium, 7 g carbohydrate, trace fiber, 29 g protein. **DIABETIC EXCHANGES:** 5 very lean meat, 1/2 starch.

In a small saucepan coated with cooking spray, cook garlic over medium heat for 1 minute. Add spreadable fruit, soy sauce and ginger. Bring to a boil. Combine cornstarch and lemon juice until smooth; stir into pan. Return to a boil; cook and stir for 1-2 minutes or until thickened. Serve with shrimp.

NUTRITION FACTS: about 9 shrimp with 2 tablespoons sauce equals 327 calories, 9 g fat (4 g saturated fat), 237 mg cholesterol, 892 mg sodium, 37 g carbohydrate, 1 g fiber, 23 g protein. **DIABETIC EXCHANGES:** 3 very lean meat, 2 starch, 1 fat.

Herbed Tuna Sandwiches
(PICTURED BELOW)

PREP/TOTAL TIME: 20 Min.   **YIELD:** 4 Servings

A delightful combination of herbs and reduced-fat cheese make this simple tuna sandwich a memorable lunch or light supper.
— Marie Connor, Virginia Beach, Virginia

    2 cans (6 ounces *each*) light water-packed tuna, drained and flaked
    2 hard-cooked eggs, chopped
  1/3 cup fat-free mayonnaise
  1/4 cup minced fresh chives
    2 teaspoons minced fresh parsley
  1/2 teaspoon dried basil
  1/4 teaspoon onion powder
    8 slices whole wheat bread, toasted
  1/2 cup shredded reduced-fat cheddar cheese

In a small bowl, combine the first seven ingredients. Place four slices of toast on an ungreased baking sheet; top with tuna mixture and sprinkle with cheese.

Broil 3-4 in. from the heat for 1-2 minutes or until cheese is melted. Top with remaining toast.

NUTRITION FACTS: 1 sandwich equals 332 calories, 9 g fat (4 g saturated fat), 144 mg cholesterol, 864 mg sodium, 30 g carbohydrate, 4 g fiber, 34 g protein. **DIABETIC EXCHANGES:** 4 very lean meat, 2 starch, 1 fat.

Breaded Curry Shrimp
(PICTURED ABOVE)

PREP/TOTAL TIME: 30 Min.   **YIELD:** 4 Servings (1/2 Cup Sauce)

A fruity dipping sauce adds to the fun of this simply wonderful, fast-fixing entree.   — Ann Nace, Perkasie, Pennsylvania

    1 egg
    2 tablespoons water
  3/4 cup dry bread crumbs
1-1/2 teaspoons curry powder
  1/4 teaspoon salt
Dash pepper
    1 pound uncooked medium shrimp, peeled and deveined
    2 tablespoons butter, melted
MARMALADE DIPPING SAUCE:
    2 garlic cloves, minced
  1/2 cup orange marmalade spreadable fruit
    2 tablespoons reduced-sodium soy sauce
  1/8 teaspoon ground ginger
    1 teaspoon cornstarch
    2 tablespoons lemon juice

In a shallow bowl, beat egg and water. In another bowl, combine the bread crumbs, curry, salt and pepper. Dip shrimp in egg mixture, then roll in crumb mixture.

Place in a 15-in. x 10-in. x 1-in. baking pan coated with cooking spray. Drizzle with butter. Bake at 400° for 7-9 minutes on each side or until golden brown.

Meatless Main Dishes

Everyone at the table will give the dishes in this chapter thumbs-up approval. In fact, each entree is so sensational, your family members won't even realize they're enjoying a meat-free meal. Try any of these delightful favorites and you'll be surprised how delicious meatless fare can be.

Spinach-Tomato Phyllo Bake, p. 184

Italian Cheese-Stuffed Shells

(PICTURED ABOVE)

MEAT-LESS

PREP: 1 Hour   **BAKE:** 50 Min.   **YIELD:** 7 Servings

I found this recipe in a church cookbook and thought it was a great twist on traditional lasagna. I omitted the meat, and it's just as yummy.   —Patty Tappendorf, Galesville, Wisconsin

    1 medium onion, chopped
  1/2 cup chopped green pepper
  1/2 cup chopped sweet red pepper
    2 garlic cloves, minced
  1/2 pound sliced fresh mushrooms
1-1/2 cups water
    1 can (14-1/2 ounces) Italian stewed tomatoes
    1 can (6 ounces) tomato paste
1-1/2 teaspoons Italian seasoning
    2 eggs, lightly beaten
    1 carton (15 ounces) reduced-fat ricotta cheese
    2 cups (8 ounces) shredded part-skim mozzarella cheese, *divided*
  1/2 cup grated Parmesan cheese
   21 jumbo pasta shells, cooked and drained

In a large nonstick skillet coated with cooking spray, cook the onion, peppers and garlic over medium heat for 2 minutes. Add mushrooms; cook 4-5 minutes longer or until tender. Stir in the water, tomatoes, tomato paste and Italian seasoning. Bring to a boil. Reduce heat; cover and simmer for 30 minutes.

Meanwhile, in a small bowl, combine the eggs, ricotta, 1/2 cup mozzarella and Parmesan cheese. Stuff into shells. Spread 1 cup vegetable sauce into a 13-in. x 9-in. x 2-in. baking dish coated with cooking spray. Arrange shells over sauce; top with remaining sauce.

Cover and bake at 350° for 45 minutes. Uncover; sprinkle with remaining mozzarella. Bake 5-10 minutes longer or until bubbly and cheese is melted. Let stand for 5 minutes before serving.

NUTRITION FACTS: 3 stuffed shells with 3/4 cup sauce equals 351 calories, 11 g fat (6 g saturated fat), 99 mg cholesterol, 457 mg sodium, 39 g carbohydrate, 4 g fiber, 23 g protein. **DIABETIC EXCHANGES:** 2 lean meat, 2 vegetable, 1-1/2 starch, 1 fat.

Black Bean Burritos

MEAT-LESS

PREP: 20 Min.   **BAKE:** 25 Min.   **YIELD:** 8 Servings

My husband and I love this flavorful recipe that's perfect on a chili day or any time at all.   —Beth Cooper, Columbus, Ohio

    1 can (16 ounces) refried beans
    1 can (15 ounces) black beans, rinsed and drained
1-1/2 cups salsa, *divided*
    1 cup fresh broccoli florets, chopped
    1 cup (4 ounces) shredded reduced-fat cheddar cheese, *divided*
    1 small onion, finely chopped
    2 teaspoons ground cumin
    8 flour tortillas (8 inches), warmed

In a large bowl, combine the refried beans, black beans, 1 cup salsa, broccoli, 3/4 cup cheese, onion and cumin. Spoon down the center of each tortilla; roll up. Place seam side down in a 13-in. x 9-in. x 2-in. baking dish coated with cooking spray.

Cover and bake at 350° for 20 minutes or until heated through. Uncover; top with remaining salsa and cheese. Bake 5 minutes longer or until cheese is melted.

NUTRITION FACTS: 1 burrito equals 305 calories, 7 g fat (3 g saturated fat), 15 mg cholesterol, 823 mg sodium, 45 g carbohydrate, 6 g fiber, 14 g protein. **DIABETIC EXCHANGES:** 3 starch, 1 very lean meat, 1 vegetable, 1/2 fat.

Sweet Onion Pie

PREP: 35 Min.　**BAKE:** 20 Min.　**YIELD:** 8 Servings

Here's a creamy, quiche-like dish that makes a scrumptious addition to brunch buffets. It's a nice change of pace and goes well with just about anything.　—Barbara Reese, Catawissa, Pennsylvania

　　2 sweet onions, halved and sliced
　　1 tablespoon butter
　　1 unbaked pastry shell (9 inches)
　　1 cup egg substitute
　　1 cup fat-free evaporated milk
　　1 teaspoon salt
　1/4 teaspoon pepper

In a large nonstick skillet, cook onions in butter over medium-low heat for 30 minutes or until very tender. Meanwhile, line unpricked pastry shell with a double thickness of heavy-duty foil.

　　Bake at 450° for 6 minutes. Remove foil; cool on a wire rack. Reduce heat to 425°.

　　Spoon onions into pastry shell. In a small bowl, whisk the egg substitute, milk, salt and pepper; pour over onions. Bake for 20-25 minutes or until a knife inserted near the center comes out clean. Let stand for 5-10 minutes before cutting.

NUTRITION FACTS: 1 piece equals 187 calories, 9 g fat (4 g saturated fat), 10 mg cholesterol, 510 mg sodium, 20 g carbohydrate, 1 g fiber, 7 g protein. **DIABETIC EXCHANGES:** 1-1/2 fat, 1 starch, 1 very lean meat.

Marjoram Lentils

PREP: 30 Min.　**COOK:** 45 Min.　**YIELD:** 6 Servings

You can enjoy this homey dish with a side of corn bread or rice. Or, seve it as a hearty side with a light meat entree.　—Mildred Sherrer, Fort Worth, Texas

　　4 medium carrots, chopped
　　2 medium onions, chopped
　　6 garlic cloves, minced
　　1 tablespoon olive oil
　　1 can (14-1/2 ounces) vegetable broth
　　1 cup dried lentils, rinsed
　　3 tablespoons minced fresh marjoram *or* 1 tablespoon
　　　　dried marjoram
　1-1/2 teaspoons rubbed sage
　　1 can (14-1/2 ounces) diced tomatoes, undrained
　1/4 cup sherry *or* additional vegetable broth
　1/4 cup minced fresh parsley
　　3 tablespoons shredded Swiss cheese

In a large nonstick saucepan, saute the carrots, onions and garlic in oil until tender. Stir in the broth, lentils, marjoram and sage. Bring to a boil. Reduce heat; cover and simmer for 30-45 minutes or until lentils are tender.

　　Stir in the tomatoes, sherry or additional broth and parsley; heat through. Sprinkle with cheese.

NUTRITION FACTS: 3/4 cup equals 212 calories, 4 g fat (1 g saturated fat), 3 mg cholesterol, 399 mg sodium, 33 g carbohydrate, 13 g fiber, 13 g protein. **DIABETIC EXCHANGES:** 2 vegetable, 1-1/2 starch, 1 very lean meat, 1/2 fat.

Grilled Bean Burgers

(PICTURED BELOW)

PREP: 25 Min.　**GRILL:** 10 Min.　**YIELD:** 8 Servings

I first sampled these salsa-topped burgers at an "Eating Right" session at our local library. They can hold their own against any veggie burger you'd buy at the supermarket.　—Marguerite Shaeffer, Sewell, New Jersey

　　1 large onion, finely chopped
　　4 garlic cloves, minced
　　1 tablespoon olive oil
　　1 medium carrot, shredded
　　1 to 2 teaspoons chili powder
　　1 teaspoon ground cumin
　　1 can (15 ounces) pinto beans, rinsed and drained
　　1 can (15 ounces) black beans, rinsed and drained
　1-1/2 cups quick-cooking oats
　　2 tablespoons Dijon mustard
　　2 tablespoons reduced-sodium soy sauce
　　1 tablespoon ketchup
　1/4 teaspoon pepper
　　8 whole wheat hamburger buns, split
　　8 lettuce leaves
　　8 tablespoons salsa

In a large nonstick skillet coated with cooking spray, saute onion and garlic in oil for 2 minutes. Stir in the carrot, chili powder and cumin; cook 2 minutes longer or until carrot is tender. Remove from the heat; set aside.

　　In a large bowl, mash the pinto beans and black beans. Stir in the oats. Add the mustard, soy sauce, ketchup, pepper and carrot mixture; mix well. Shape into eight 3-1/2-in. patties.

　　Coat grill rack with cooking spray before starting the grill. Grill patties, covered, over medium heat for 4-5 minutes on each side or until heated through. Serve on buns with lettuce and salsa.

NUTRITION FACTS: 1 burger equals 307 calories, 5 g fat (1 g saturated fat), 0 cholesterol, 723 mg sodium, 53 g carbohydrate, 10 g fiber, 12 g protein. **DIABETIC EXCHANGES:** 3-1/2 starch, 1 very lean meat.

Veggie Cheese Ravioli
(PICTURED ABOVE)

MEAT-
LESS

PREP/TOTAL TIME: 20 Min.   **YIELD:** 3 Servings

You can have the best of both worlds with this easy weeknight dish. Not only is it hearty and filling, but it's light as well.
—Gertrudis Miller, Evansville, Indiana

    1 package (9 ounces) refrigerated cheese ravioli
    2 small zucchini, julienned
    1 medium onion, chopped
    1 can (14-1/2 ounces) diced tomatoes, undrained
    2 tablespoons chopped ripe olives
  3/4 teaspoon Italian seasoning
    3 tablespoons shredded Parmesan cheese

Cook ravioli according to package directions. Meanwhile, in a large nonstick skillet coated with cooking spray, cook and stir the zucchini and onion until tender. Stir in the tomatoes, olives and Italian seasoning. Bring to a boil. Reduce heat; simmer, uncovered, for 5 minutes.

Drain ravioli and add to the pan; stir gently to combine. Sprinkle with Parmesan cheese.

NUTRITION FACTS: 1-1/2 cups equals 322 calories, 8 g fat (4 g saturated fat), 37 mg cholesterol, 649 mg sodium, 48 g carbohydrate, 6 g fiber, 17 g protein.

Triple-Mushroom Stroganoff

MEAT-
LESS

PREP: 20 Min.   **COOK:** 30 Min.   **YIELD:** 6 Servings

Three types of mushrooms lend flavor and texture to the creamy sauce of my rustic entree. —Cheri Neustifter, Sturtevant, Wisconsin

5-1/2 cups uncooked egg noodles
  1/2 pound fresh button mushrooms, halved
2-2/3 cups sliced baby portobello mushrooms
    1 package (3-1/2 ounces) sliced fresh shiitake mushrooms
    3 shallots, chopped
    3 garlic cloves, minced
    2 tablespoons butter

1-1/2 cups vegetable broth, *divided*
    2 teaspoons Dijon mustard
  1/2 teaspoon salt
  1/4 teaspoon pepper
    2 tablespoons all-purpose flour
    1 cup (8 ounces) fat-free sour cream
    1 tablespoon minced fresh parsley

Cook noodles according to package directions. Meanwhile, in a large nonstick skillet over medium heat, cook the mushrooms, shallots and garlic in butter for 6-8 minutes or until tender.

Stir in 1-1/4 cups broth, mustard, salt and pepper. Bring to a boil. Reduce heat; simmer, uncovered, for 10 minutes, stirring occasionally.

Combine flour with remaining broth until smooth; gradually stir into mushroom mixture. Bring to a boil; cook and stir for 2 minutes or until thickened and bubbly. Reduce heat to low; gradually stir in sour cream (do not boil). Drain noodles; serve with mushroom sauce. Sprinkle with parsley.

NUTRITION FACTS: 2/3 cup mushroom sauce with 1 cup noodles equals 296 calories, 6 g fat (3 g saturated fat), 57 mg cholesterol, 575 mg sodium, 49 g carbohydrate, 2 g fiber, 12 g protein.

Meatless Stuffed Cabbage

FAT MEAT-
     LESS

PREP: 45 Min.   **BAKE:** 40 Min.   **YIELD:** 6 Servings

These stuffed cabbage bundles make a delicious alternative for the real thing, especially during meatless holidays.
—Linda Evancoe-Coble, Leola, Pennsylvania

  1/2 cup uncooked brown rice
    1 cup water
    1 medium head cabbage
    1 package (12 ounces) frozen vegetarian meat crumbles, thawed
    1 large onion, chopped
  1/2 teaspoon pepper
    1 can (10-3/4 ounces) reduced-sodium condensed tomato soup, undiluted
    1 can (8 ounces) Italian tomato sauce, *divided*
    1 can (14-1/2 ounces) Italian diced tomatoes, undrained

In a small saucepan, bring rice and water to a boil. Reduce heat; cover and simmer for 25-30 minutes or until tender. Meanwhile, cook cabbage in boiling water just until leaves fall off head. Set aside 12 large leaves for rolls (refrigerate remaining cabbage for another use).

In a large bowl, combine the meat crumbles, onion, pepper, cooked rice and half of the soup. Cut out the thick vein from the bottom of each reserved leaf, making a V-shaped cut. Place 1/3 cup rice mixture on each cabbage leaf; overlap cut ends. Fold in sides, beginning from the cut end. Roll up completely to enclose filling.

Spread half of the tomato sauce into a 13-in. x 9-in. x 2-in. baking dish coated with cooking spray. Place rolls seam side down in dish.

In a small bowl, combine the tomatoes with the remaining soup and tomato sauce. Pour over rolls. Cover and bake at 350° for 40-45 minutes or until bubbly and cabbage is tender.

NUTRITION FACTS: 2 cabbage rolls equals 232 calories, 3 g fat (trace saturated fat), trace cholesterol, 1,000 mg sodium, 37 g carbohydrate, 7 g fiber, 15 g protein. **DIABETIC EXCHANGES:** 2 starch, 1 lean meat, 1 vegetable.

Tomato Gnocchi with Pesto

(PICTURED BELOW)

MEAT-LESS

PREP: 70 Min. **COOK:** 5 Min. **YIELD:** 4 Servings

Our taste panel simply loved the blend of pesto sauce and pine nuts in this delectable and impressive dish from our Test Kitchen.

    1 pound russet potatoes, peeled and quartered
    3 quarts water
  2/3 cup all-purpose flour
    1 egg
    3 tablespoons tomato paste
  3/4 teaspoon salt, *divided*
PESTO:
    2 tablespoons olive oil
    1 tablespoon water
    1 cup loosely packed fresh basil
    1 garlic clove, peeled
    3 tablespoons grated Parmesan cheese
    3 tablespoons pine nuts, toasted

Place potatoes in a saucepan and cover with water. Bring to a boil. Reduce heat; cover and simmer for 15-20 minutes or until tender. Drain.

Over warm burner or very low heat, stir potatoes for 1-2 minutes or until steam is evaporated. Press through a potato ricer or strainer into a small bowl; cool slightly. In a Dutch oven, bring water to a boil.

Using a fork, make a well in the potatoes. Sprinkle flour over potatoes and into well. Whisk the egg, tomato paste and 1/2 teaspoon salt; pour into well. Stir until blended. Knead 10-12 times, forming a soft dough.

Divide dough into four portions. On a floured surface, roll portions into 1/2-in.-thick ropes; cut into 3/4-in. pieces. Press and roll each piece with a lightly floured fork. Cook gnocchi in boiling water in batches for 30-60 seconds or until they float. Remove with a strainer and keep warm.

For pesto, place the oil, water, basil, garlic and remaining salt in a food processor; cover and process until blended. Stir in Parmesan cheese. Spoon over gnocchi; toss gently to coat. Sprinkle with pine nuts.

NUTRITION FACTS: 1 cup equals 312 calories, 13 g fat (3 g saturated fat), 56 mg cholesterol, 545 mg sodium, 41 g carbohydrate, 4 g fiber, 10 g protein. **DIABETIC EXCHANGES:** 2-1/2 starch, 2-1/2 fat.

Black Bean Cakes

MEAT-LESS

PREP/TOTAL TIME: 25 Min. **YIELD:** 4 Servings

Topped with a corn salsa, these vegetarian patties are absolutely delicious.   —Barbara Nowakowski, Mesa, Arizona

    2 cans (15 ounces *each*) black beans, rinsed and drained
    1 egg white, lightly beaten
    2 green onions, finely chopped
  1/4 cup plus 2 tablespoons minced fresh cilantro, *divided*
    1 teaspoon chili powder
  1/4 teaspoon dried oregano
  1/4 teaspoon ground cumin
    4 teaspoons canola oil
  1/2 cup frozen corn, thawed
  1/2 cup chunky salsa
  1/4 cup fat-free sour cream

In a large bowl, mash beans with a fork. Stir in the egg white, onions, 1/4 cup cilantro, chili powder, oregano and cumin. Shape into eight 2-1/2-in. patties.

In a small nonstick skillet coated with cooking spray, cook patties in batches in oil for 2-4 minutes on each side or until golden brown.

In a small bowl, combine the corn, salsa and remaining cilantro; spoon over cakes. Garnish with sour cream.

NUTRITION FACTS: 2 cakes with 1/4 cup salsa mixture and 1 tablespoon sour cream equals 264 calories, 5 g fat (trace saturated fat), 3 mg cholesterol, 577 mg sodium, 40 g carbohydrate, 9 g fiber, 13 g protein. **DIABETIC EXCHANGES:** 2-1/2 starch, 2 very lean meat, 1 fat.

Zucchini-Tomato Pasta Sauce

CARB **MEAT-LESS**

PREP: 20 Min. **COOK:** 1 Hour **YIELD:** 5 Cups

I came up with this recipe after planting too many zucchini plants in our vegetable garden one year. My husband loves it.
          —Joy Turner, Amherst, Ohio

    2 medium onions, chopped
    2 tablespoons butter
    2 tablespoons canola oil
    8 large tomatoes, chopped
    2 medium zucchini, cut into 1/2-inch cubes
    4 garlic cloves, minced
    2 teaspoons dried oregano
    1 teaspoon salt
  1/2 teaspoon pepper
Hot cooked pasta

In a large saucepan, saute onions in butter and oil until tender. Stir in the tomatoes, zucchini, garlic, oregano, salt and pepper; bring to a boil. Reduce heat; simmer, uncovered, for 50-60 minutes or until zucchini is tender. Serve with pasta.

NUTRITION FACTS: 1/2 cup sauce (calculated without pasta) equals 96 calories, 6 g fat (2 g saturated fat), 6 mg cholesterol, 275 mg sodium, 11 g carbohydrate, 3 g fiber, 2 g protein. **DIABETIC EXCHANGES:** 2 vegetable, 1 fat.

Favorite Recipe Made Lighter

"SLOW-COOKED Mac 'n' Cheese." The words alone are enough to make mouths water. A longtime staple in homes from coast to coast, macaroni and cheese is as American as apple pie and hot dogs. Whether enjoyed as a side dish, a cozy lunch or beefed up a bit for a fast weeknight entree, big and little appetites alike clamor for the classic comfort food.

All too often, however, folks give up this heartwarming dish when they want to pare down the fat and cholesterol in their diets. Such is the case of Shelby Molina from Whitewater, Wisconsin.

Her easy-to-fix Slow-Cooked Mac 'n' Cheese is loaded with creamy goodness, but it also offers an excess of fat. "It has so much fat and cholesterol that I simply can't bring myself to feed it to my family," Shelby notes. "Is there any way to lighten this recipe and still prepare it in the slow cooker?"

No problem, Shelby! The makeover teammates rolled up their sleeves and began by cutting down the butter and choosing fat-free milk to trim fat. They replaced the original's mild cheddar cheese with reduced-fat processed cheese and scaled back on sharp cheddar cheese in order to maintain the original's distinct flavor.

As a result, Makeover Slow-Cooked Mac 'n' Cheese has 15 less grams of fat, and the cholesterol is slashed by more than half. Best of all, it's a hit with Shelby's family.

"My husband and teenage son really like the new version," she notes. "Now that this recipe is lighter, I'll be able to serve it more often. That's something we are all very excited about!"

Slow-Cooked Mac 'n' Cheese   MEAT-LESS

PREP: 25 Min.   COOK: 2-3/4 Hours   YIELD: 9 Servings

    2 cups uncooked elbow macaroni
    1 can (12 ounces) evaporated milk
1-1/2 cups milk
   1/2 cup egg substitute
   1/4 cup butter, melted
    1 teaspoon salt
2-1/2 cups (10 ounces) shredded cheddar cheese
2-1/2 cups (10 ounces) shredded sharp cheddar cheese, *divided*

Cook macaroni according to package directions; drain and rinse in cold water. In a large bowl, combine the evaporated milk, milk, egg substitute, butter and salt. Stir in the cheddar cheese, 2 cups sharp cheddar cheese and macaroni.

Transfer to a greased 3-qt. slow cooker. Cover and cook on low for 2-3/4 to 3 hours or until center is set, stirring once. Sprinkle with remaining sharp cheddar cheese.

NUTRITION FACTS: 3/4 cup equals 437 calories, 27 g fat (19 g saturated fat), 98 mg cholesterol, 776 mg sodium, 26 g carbohydrate, 1 g fiber, 22 g protein.

Makeover Slow-Cooked Mac 'n' Cheese   MEAT-LESS
(PICTURED ABOVE)

PREP: 25 Min.   COOK: 2-3/4 Hours   YIELD: 9 Servings

    2 cups uncooked elbow macaroni
    1 can (12 ounces) reduced-fat evaporated milk
1-1/2 cups fat-free milk
   1/3 cup egg substitute
    1 tablespoon butter, melted
    8 ounces reduced-fat process cheese (Velveeta), cubed
    2 cups (8 ounces) shredded sharp cheddar cheese, *divided*

Cook macaroni according to package directions; drain and rinse in cold water. In a large bowl, combine the evaporated milk, milk, egg substitute and butter. Stir in the process cheese, 1-1/2 cups sharp cheddar cheese and macaroni.

Transfer to a 3-qt. slow cooker coated with cooking spray. Cover and cook on low for 2-3/4 to 3 hours or until center is set, stirring once. Sprinkle with remaining sharp cheddar cheese.

NUTRITION FACTS: 3/4 cup equals 300 calories, 12 g fat (9 g saturated fat), 45 mg cholesterol, 647 mg sodium, 29 g carbohydrate, 1 g fiber, 19 g protein. DIABETIC EXCHANGES: 2 starch, 2 lean meat, 1 fat.

MAKEOVER TIP
When cutting fat from a favorite casserole, it's important to maintain the creamy texture the original recipe offers. To keep a light casserole creamy, try substituting some of the cheese with reduced-fat processed American cheese.

Asparagus Tofu Stir-Fry

MEAT-LESS

(PICTURED ABOVE)

PREP: 15 Min.   **COOK:** 20 Min.   **YIELD:** 4 Servings

With its flavorful ginger sauce and fresh vegetables, this tasty meal-in-one is always popular at my house.
— Phyllis Smith, Chimacum, Washington

    1 tablespoon cornstarch
  1/2 teaspoon sugar
1-1/4 cups vegetable broth
    4 teaspoons reduced-sodium soy sauce
    2 teaspoons minced fresh gingerroot, *divided*
    3 teaspoons canola oil, *divided*
    1 pound fresh asparagus, trimmed and cut into 1-inch
      pieces
    1 medium yellow summer squash, halved and sliced
    2 green onions, thinly sliced
    1 package (14 ounces) extra-firm tofu, drained and cut
      into 1/2-inch cubes
  1/4 teaspoon salt
  1/4 teaspoon pepper
    2 cups hot cooked brown rice
    2 tablespoons sliced almonds, toasted

In a small bowl, combine the cornstarch, sugar, broth and soy sauce until smooth; set aside.

In a large nonstick skillet or wok, stir-fry 1 teaspoon ginger in 1 teaspoon oil for 1 minute. Add asparagus; stir-fry for 2 minutes. Add squash; stir-fry 2 minutes longer. Add onions; stir-fry 1 minute longer or until vegetables are crisp-tender. Remove and keep warm.

In the same pan, stir-fry tofu, salt, pepper and remaining ginger in remaining oil for 7-9 minutes or until lightly browned. Remove and keep warm.

Stir cornstarch mixture and add to the pan. Bring to a boil; cook and stir for 2 minutes or until thickened. Add asparagus and tofu; heat through. Serve with rice; sprinkle with almonds.

NUTRITION FACTS: 1 cup stir-fry with 1/2 cup rice equals 278 calories, 11 g fat (1 g saturated fat), 0 cholesterol, 682 mg sodium, 34 g carbohydrate, 4 g fiber, 14 g protein. **DIABETIC EXCHANGES:** 2 starch, 1 lean meat, 1 vegetable, 1 fat.

Portobello Spinach Frittata

CARB MEAT-LESS

PREP: 10 Min.   **BAKE:** 30 Min. + Standing   **YIELD:** 6 Servings

This delicious quiche is perfect for breakfast, brunch or even a meatless lunch.
— Irene Turner, Alma, Wisconsin

    2 eggs
  1/2 cup egg substitute
    1 cup fat-free ricotta cheese
  3/4 cup grated Parmesan cheese
    1 package (10 ounces) frozen chopped spinach, thawed
      and squeezed dry
  1/2 teaspoon salt
  1/4 teaspoon pepper
  3/4 cup sliced baby portobello mushrooms
    4 green onions, chopped

In a large bowl, combine the eggs, egg substitute, ricotta cheese, Parmesan cheese, spinach, salt and pepper. Stir in mushrooms and onions.

Transfer to a 9-in. pie plate coated with cooking spray. Bake at 350° for 30-35 minutes or until a knife inserted near the center comes out clean. Let stand for 10 minutes before cutting.

NUTRITION FACTS: 1 piece equals 130 calories, 5 g fat (2 g saturated fat), 85 mg cholesterol, 526 mg sodium, 7 g carbohydrate, 2 g fiber, 13 g protein. **DIABETIC EXCHANGE:** 2 lean meat.

Broccoli Pasta Bake

PREP: 30 Min. **BAKE:** 45 Min. **YIELD:** 8 Servings

I came up with this recipe in the middle of broccoli season, using ingredients I had on hand. It's a pleasing casserole that's light, too.
—Evelyn Peterson, Corvallis, Montana

- 12 ounces uncooked spaghetti
- 8 cups chopped fresh broccoli
- 2 cans (10-3/4 ounces *each*) reduced-fat reduced-sodium condensed cream of mushroom soup, undiluted
- 1/4 cup fat-free milk
- 2 cups sliced fresh mushrooms
- 1 medium onion, finely chopped
- 1 can (8 ounces) whole water chestnuts, drained, halved and thinly sliced
- 1 can (3.8 ounces) sliced ripe olives, drained
- 1 teaspoon salt
- 1/2 teaspoon pepper
- 2 cups (8 ounces) shredded reduced-fat cheddar cheese, *divided*
- 1/4 cup sunflower kernels

Boil spaghetti according to package directions for 7 minutes. Add broccoli; return to a boil. Cook 2 minutes longer or until spaghetti is tender; drain.

In a large bowl, combine soup and milk. Stir in the mushrooms, onion, water chestnuts, olives, salt, pepper and 1 cup cheese. Add spaghetti and broccoli; mix well.

Transfer to a 13-in. x 9-in. x 2-in. baking dish coated with cooking spray (dish will be full). Cover and bake at 350° for 40 minutes. Uncover; sprinkle with sunflower kernels and remaining cheese. Bake 5-10 minutes longer or until heated through and cheese is melted.

NUTRITION FACTS: 1-1/2 cups equals 369 calories, 12 g fat (5 g saturated fat), 26 mg cholesterol, 942 mg sodium, 50 g carbohydrate, 5 g fiber, 17 g protein.

Vegetarian Tortilla Stack
(PICTURED ABOVE)

PREP: 25 Min. **BAKE:** 35 Min. **YIELD:** 6 Servings

Nearly all the meals I make are meatless, and this hot bake is a regular in my house.
—Wendy Fenstermacher, Allentown, Pennsylvania

- 1 medium green pepper, chopped
- 1 medium sweet red pepper, chopped
- 1 small onion, chopped
- 2 teaspoons olive oil
- 1 package (12 ounces) frozen vegetarian meat crumbles, thawed
- 2 tablespoons minced fresh cilantro
- 1 teaspoon ground cumin
- 1-1/2 cups salsa
- 5 flour tortillas (8 inches)
- 1-1/4 cups shredded reduced-fat Mexican cheese blend, *divided*
- 1/3 cup pickled jalapeno slices
- 5 tablespoons sliced ripe olives

In a large nonstick skillet coated with cooking spray, saute the peppers and onion in oil until tender. Stir in the meat crumbles, cilantro and cumin; heat through.

Spread 1/4 cup salsa into a 9-in. deep-dish pie plate coated with cooking spray. Layer with one tortilla, a fourth of the meat crumble mixture, 1/4 cup salsa, 1/4 cup cheese, 2 or 3 jalapeno slices and 1 tablespoon olives. Repeat the layers three times. Top with the remaining tortilla, salsa, olives and jalapeno slices.

Cover and bake at 350° for 30 minutes. Uncover; sprinkle with remaining cheese. Bake 5-10 minutes longer or until heated through and cheese is melted.

NUTRITION FACTS: 1 piece equals 335 calories, 12 g fat (3 g saturated fat), 17 mg cholesterol, 1,111 mg sodium, 38 g carbohydrate, 8 g fiber, 26 g protein. **DIABETIC EXCHANGES:** 2 starch, 2 lean meat, 1 vegetable, 1 fat.

Eggplant-Mushroom Pasta Toss

PREP: 15 Min. **COOK:** 20 Min. **YIELD:** 6 Servings

Mushrooms make an ideal substitute for meat in this Italian pasta dinner. I serve crisp rolls or garlic bread and a green salad on the side.
—Priscilla Gilbert, Indian Harbour Beach, Florida

- 2-1/2 cups uncooked penne pasta
- 4-1/2 cups cubed peeled eggplant (about 1 pound)
- 1 tablespoon olive oil
- 2 packages (3-1/2 ounces *each*) sliced fresh shiitake mushrooms
- 4 garlic cloves, minced
- 1 can (14-1/2 ounces) Italian diced tomatoes, undrained
- 1/2 cup water
- 1/4 cup tomato paste
- 1 teaspoon dried oregano
- 1/2 teaspoon salt
- 1/4 teaspoon pepper
- 1/3 cup sliced ripe olives
- 2/3 cup crumbled feta cheese
- 1/4 cup minced fresh parsley

Cook pasta according to package directions. Meanwhile, in a large nonstick skillet coated with cooking spray, cook eggplant in oil over medium heat for 3 minutes. Add mushrooms and garlic; cook 3-4 minutes longer or until vegetables are tender.

Stir in the tomatoes, water, tomato paste, oregano, salt and pepper. Bring to a boil. Reduce heat; simmer, uncovered, for 5 minutes. Stir in olives; heat through.

Drain pasta; toss with eggplant mixture. Sprinkle with feta cheese and parsley.

NUTRITION FACTS: 1-1/4 cups equals 231 calories, 6 g fat (2 g saturated fat), 7 mg cholesterol, 659 mg sodium, 37 g carbohydrate, 5 g fiber, 9 g protein. **DIABETIC EXCHANGES:** 3 vegetable, 1-1/2 starch, 1 fat.

Tomato Garden Pasta
MEAT-LESS

(PICTURED BELOW)

PREP/TOTAL TIME: 30 Min. **YIELD:** 8 Servings

I have served this supper many times, using fresh tomatoes from my garden. It's a wonderful treat.
—Aileen Sheehan, Stafford, Virginia

   5 cups uncooked bow tie pasta
 1/2 pound fresh green beans, trimmed and cut into 1-inch pieces
   2 tablespoons olive oil
   2 tablespoons balsamic vinegar
   1 teaspoon salt
 1/4 teaspoon pepper
1-1/2 pounds tomatoes, seeded and chopped
   2 garlic cloves, minced
   2 tablespoons minced chives
4-1/2 teaspoons minced fresh basil
 1/2 cup crumbled feta cheese

Cook pasta according to package directions, adding beans during the last 5-6 minutes.

Meanwhile, in a large bowl, whisk the oil, vinegar, salt and pepper. Stir in the tomatoes, garlic, chives and basil. Drain pasta mixture and add to tomato mixture; toss to coat. Serve warm or at room temperature. Sprinkle with cheese just before serving.

NUTRITION FACTS: 1 cup equals 230 calories, 6 g fat (1 g saturated fat), 4 mg cholesterol, 376 mg sodium, 38 g carbohydrate, 4 g fiber, 8 g protein. **DIABETIC EXCHANGES:** 2 starch, 1 vegetable, 1 fat.

Two-Cheese Ziti
MEAT-LESS

(PICTURED ABOVE)

PREP: 25 Min. **BAKE:** 25 Min. **YIELD:** 5 Servings

Cheddar and Parmesan cheeses combine in this comforting casserole. Kids and adults both reach for second helpings.
—Flo Burtnett, Gage, Oklahoma

   3 cups uncooked ziti *or* small tube pasta
   1 tablespoon butter
   2 tablespoons all-purpose flour
 1/2 teaspoon salt
 1/4 teaspoon pepper
1-3/4 cups fat-free milk
 3/4 cup shredded reduced-fat cheddar cheese
   2 tablespoons grated Parmesan cheese
TOPPING:
   3 tablespoons dry bread crumbs
1-1/2 teaspoons butter, melted
 1/4 cup shredded reduced-fat cheddar cheese
   3 tablespoons grated Parmesan cheese

Cook ziti according to package directions. Meanwhile, in a large nonstick skillet, melt butter. Stir in the flour, salt and pepper until smooth; gradually add milk. Bring to a boil; cook and stir for 2 minutes or until thickened. Remove from the heat; stir in cheeses until melted.

Drain ziti; add to sauce and stir to coat. Transfer to a shallow 1-1/2-qt. baking dish coated with cooking spray. Cover and bake at 350° for 20 minutes.

In a small bowl, combine bread crumbs and butter; stir in cheeses. Sprinkle over ziti. Bake, uncovered, for 5-10 minutes or until heated through and topping is lightly browned.

NUTRITION FACTS: 3/4 cup equals 340 calories, 11 g fat (7 g saturated fat), 31 mg cholesterol, 590 mg sodium, 44 g carbohydrate, 2 g fiber, 18 g protein. **DIABETIC EXCHANGES:** 3 starch, 1 lean meat, 1 fat.

Rustic Phyllo Vegetable Pie

(PICTURED ABOVE)

MEAT-LESS

PREP: 30 Min.   **BAKE:** 50 Min. + Standing   **YIELD:** 6 Servings

Phyllo dough creates a delicately crisp crust for this veggie pie.
—Peggy Gwillim, Strasbourg, Saskatchewan

- 1 egg, lightly beaten
- 2 cups cooked long grain rice
- 1 cup (8 ounces) 1% cottage cheese
- 1 cup (4 ounces) shredded part-skim mozzarella cheese, *divided*
- 1 tablespoon lemon juice
- 1 teaspoon grated lemon peel
- 1 medium onion, chopped
- 4 garlic cloves, minced
- 1 tablespoon olive oil
- 2 packages (10 ounces *each*) fresh spinach, torn
- 1/2 cup golden raisins
- 1/4 teaspoon ground cinnamon
- 1/8 teaspoon salt
- 12 sheets phyllo dough (14 inches x 9 inches)

Butter-flavored cooking spray

- 1-1/2 cups meatless spaghetti sauce

In a large bowl, combine the egg, rice, cottage cheese, 1/2 cup mozzarella, lemon juice and peel; set aside. In a Dutch oven, saute onion and garlic in oil until tender. Add spinach, raisins, cinnamon and salt. Cook and stir until spinach is wilted, about 3 minutes. Remove from the heat; stir in remaining mozzarella.

Spritz one sheet of phyllo dough with butter-flavored spray. Place in a 9-in. deep-dish pie plate coated with cooking spray, allowing short sides of dough to hang over edges. (Keep remaining phyllo covered with plastic wrap and a damp towel to prevent it from drying out.)

Place remaining phyllo sheets in pie plate in a crisscross fashion resembling the spokes of a wheel, spritzing between layers with butter-flavored spray. Spread half of rice mixture into crust; layer with half of spinach mixture and half of spaghetti sauce. Repeat layers.

Gently fold edges of dough over filling, leaving center of pie uncovered. Spritz with butter-flavored spray. Cover loosely with foil; bake at 350° for 45 minutes. Uncover; bake 5-10 minutes longer or until filling reaches 160°. Let stand for 10 minutes before cutting.

NUTRITION FACTS: 1 piece equals 341 calories, 8 g fat (3 g saturated fat), 48 mg cholesterol, 745 mg sodium, 51 g carbohydrate, 5 g fiber, 18 g protein. **DIABETIC EXCHANGES:** 3 starch, 1 lean meat, 1 vegetable, 1/2 fat.

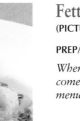

Tortellini Primavera

(PICTURED ABOVE)

PREP/TOTAL TIME: 30 Min.   **YIELD:** 5 Servings

This decadent tortellini with spinach, mushrooms and tomatoes always brings compliments. Dressed up with fresh Parmesan cheese, no one even notices it's meatless.

—Susie Pietrowski, Belton, Texas

   1 package (19 ounces) frozen cheese tortellini
1/2 pound sliced fresh mushrooms
   1 small onion, chopped
   2 garlic cloves, minced
   2 teaspoons butter
2/3 cup fat-free milk
   1 package (8 ounces) fat-free cream cheese, cubed
   1 package (10 ounces) frozen chopped spinach, thawed and squeezed dry
   1 teaspoon Italian seasoning
   1 large tomato, chopped
1/4 cup shredded Parmesan cheese

Cook tortellini according to package directions. Meanwhile, in a large nonstick skillet coated with cooking spray, saute the mushrooms, onion and garlic in butter until tender. Stir in milk; heat through. Stir in cream cheese until blended. Add spinach and Italian seasoning; heat through.

Drain tortellini; toss with sauce and tomato. Sprinkle with Parmesan cheese.

NUTRITION FACTS: 1-1/4 cups equals 341 calories, 10 g fat (5 g saturated fat), 28 mg cholesterol, 671 mg sodium, 41 g carbohydrate, 4 g fiber, 23 g protein. **DIABETIC EXCHANGES:** 2-1/2 starch, 2 lean meat, 1 vegetable.

HEALTHY OUTLOOK

If you're looking to trim a little of the red meat from your dinner plans, you can do so without neglecting your favorite recipes.

• When making chili, tacos or spaghetti sauces, try replacing the meat with soy crumbles found in the freezer section of your supermarket.

• Big brown portobello mushrooms offer a meaty flavor and texture that works well in sandwiches, or even recipes for beef patties.

• Replace some of a recipe's ground beef with beans.

Fettuccine with Black Bean Sauce

(PICTURED BELOW)

PREP/TOTAL TIME: 30 Min.   **YIELD:** 5 Servings

When my husband needed to go on a heart-smart diet, I had to come up with new ways to get more vegetables into our daily menus. This meatless spaghetti sauce was a winner!

—Marianne Neuman, East Troy, Wisconsin

   6 ounces uncooked fettuccine
   1 small green pepper, chopped
   1 small onion, chopped
   1 tablespoon olive oil
   2 cups garden-style pasta sauce
   1 can (15 ounces) black beans, rinsed and drained
   2 tablespoons minced fresh basil *or* 2 teaspoons dried basil
   1 teaspoon dried oregano
1/2 teaspoon fennel seed
1/4 teaspoon garlic salt
   1 cup (4 ounces) shredded part-skim mozzarella cheese

Cook fettuccine according to package directions. Meanwhile, in a large saucepan, saute green pepper and onion in oil until tender. Stir in the pasta sauce, black beans and seasonings. Bring to a boil. Reduce heat; simmer, uncovered, for 5 minutes.

Drain fettuccine. Top with sauce and sprinkle with mozzarella cheese.

NUTRITION FACTS: 3/4 cup pasta with about 3/4 cup sauce and 3 tablespoons cheese equals 350 calories, 10 g fat (3 g saturated fat), 17 mg cholesterol, 761 mg sodium, 51 g carbohydrate, 8 g fiber, 16 g protein. **DIABETIC EXCHANGES:** 2-1/2 starch, 2 vegetable, 1 lean meat, 1 fat.

Editor's Note: This recipe was tested with Ragu Super Vegetable Primavera pasta sauce.

Gnocchi in Sage Butter

(PICTURED BELOW)

MEAT-LESS

PREP: 70 Min.   **COOK:** 5 Min.   **YIELD:** 4 Servings

A buttery garlic-sage sauce adds melt-in-your-mouth flavor to these feather-light potato puffs from the L&T home economists.

- 1 pound russet potatoes, peeled and quartered
- 3 quarts water
- 2/3 cup all-purpose flour
- 1 egg
- 1/2 teaspoon salt
- Dash ground nutmeg
- 2 tablespoons butter
- 2 garlic cloves, thinly sliced
- 4 fresh sage leaves, thinly sliced

Place potatoes in a saucepan and cover with water. Bring to a boil. Reduce heat; cover and simmer for 15-20 minutes or until tender. Drain.

Over warm burner or very low heat, stir potatoes for 1-2 minutes or until steam is evaporated. Press through a potato ricer or strainer into a small bowl; cool slightly. In a Dutch oven, bring water to a boil.

Using a fork, make a well in the potatoes. Sprinkle flour over potatoes and into well. Whisk the egg, salt and nutmeg; pour into well. Stir until blended. Knead 10-12 times, forming a soft dough.

Divide dough into four portions. On a floured surface, roll portions into 1/2-in.-thick ropes; cut into 3/4-in. pieces. Press and roll each piece with a lightly floured fork. Cook gnocchi in boiling water in batches for 30-60 seconds or until they float. Remove with a strainer and keep warm.

In a large heavy saucepan, cook butter over medium heat for 3 minutes. Add garlic and sage; cook for 2-4 minutes or until butter and garlic are golden brown. Add gnocchi; stir gently to coat. Serve immediately.

NUTRITION FACTS: 2/3 cup equals 232 calories, 7 g fat (4 g saturated fat), 68 mg cholesterol, 373 mg sodium, 36 g carbohydrate, 2 g fiber, 6 g protein. **DIABETIC EXCHANGES:** 2 starch, 1-1/2 fat.

Spinach-Tomato Phyllo Bake

(PICTURED ABOVE)

MEAT-LESS

PREP: 25 Min.   **BAKE:** 55 Min. + Standing   **YIELD:** 6 Servings

For a special meal, consider this flaky, phyllo specialty. Low in fat, it features tomatoes, feta and spinach with a pleasant amount of dill and nutmeg.   —Shirley Kacmarik, Glasgow, Scotland

- 4 eggs, lightly beaten
- 2 packages (10 ounces *each*) frozen chopped spinach, thawed and squeezed dry
- 1 cup (4 ounces) crumbled feta cheese
- 1/2 cup 1% cottage cheese
- 3 green onions, sliced
- 1 teaspoon dill weed
- 1/2 teaspoon salt
- 1/4 teaspoon pepper
- 1/4 teaspoon ground nutmeg
- 10 sheets phyllo dough (14 inches x 9 inches)
- Butter-flavored cooking spray
- 3 large tomatoes, sliced

In a large bowl, combine the first nine ingredients; set aside.

Spritz one sheet of phyllo dough with butter-flavored cooking spray. Place in an 8-in. square baking dish coated with cooking spray, allowing one end of dough to hang over edge of dish. Repeat with four more phyllo sheets, staggering the overhanging phyllo around edges of dish. (Keep remaining phyllo covered with plastic wrap and a damp towel to prevent it from drying out.)

Spoon a third of the spinach mixture into crust. Layer with half of the tomatoes, another third of the spinach mixture, remaining tomatoes and remaining spinach mixture. Spritz and layer remaining phyllo dough as before.

Gently fold ends of dough over filling and toward center of baking dish; spritz with butter-flavored spray. Cover edges with foil. Bake at 350° for 55-60 minutes or until a meat thermometer reads 160°. Let stand for 15 minutes before cutting.

NUTRITION FACTS: 1 piece equals 216 calories, 9 g fat (3 g saturated fat), 153 mg cholesterol, 652 mg sodium, 21 g carbohydrate, 5 g fiber, 15 g protein. **DIABETIC EXCHANGES:** 2 vegetable, 1 starch, 1 lean meat, 1 fat.

Colorful Pepper Frittata

CARB → MEATLESS

PREP: 35 Min.   **BAKE:** 20 Min.   **YIELD:** 6 Servings

This basic brunch dish is so filling and tasty, even the biggest meat-lovers will enjoy it.   —Jessie Apfel, Berkeley, California

- 1 large onion, chopped
- 3 garlic cloves, minced
- 2 teaspoons canola oil
- 2 cups chopped sweet red peppers
- 1 cup chopped sweet yellow pepper
- 1 cup chopped sweet orange pepper
- 4 eggs
- 8 egg whites
- 1/4 cup minced fresh basil
- 1 teaspoon salt
- 1/2 teaspoon pepper
- 1 cup (4 ounces) shredded part-skim mozzarella cheese
- 2 tablespoons shredded Parmesan cheese

In a 10-in. ovenproof skillet coated with cooking spray, cook onion and garlic in oil over medium heat for 2 minutes. Stir in peppers; cook for 3-4 minutes or until crisp-tender.

In a small bowl, combine the eggs, egg whites, basil, salt and pepper. Stir in mozzarella cheese; pour over pepper mixture. Sprinkle with Parmesan cheese.

Bake, uncovered, at 350° for 20-25 minutes or until a knife inserted near the center comes out clean. Let stand for 5 minutes before cutting.

NUTRITION FACTS: 1 piece equals 187 calories, 9 g fat (4 g saturated fat), 155 mg cholesterol, 639 mg sodium, 11 g carbohydrate, 2 g fiber, 16 g protein. **DIABETIC EXCHANGES:** 2 lean meat, 2 vegetable, 1/2 fat.

Pasta Primavera with Soy Cream Sauce

FAT → MEATLESS

PREP/TOTAL TIME: 30 Min.   **YIELD:** 6 Servings

I invented this recipe so I could enjoy a creamy sauce without the guilt.   —Amber Rife, Columbus, Ohio

- 6 ounces uncooked angel hair pasta
- 1/2 pound fresh asparagus, trimmed and cut into 1-inch pieces
- 3/4 cup fresh baby carrots, halved lengthwise
- 1 small zucchini, quartered and sliced
- 1 yellow summer squash, quartered and sliced
- 4 teaspoons cornstarch
- 1-1/2 cups soy milk
- 1/2 teaspoon salt
- 1/2 teaspoon dried basil
- 1/2 teaspoon dried oregano

Cook pasta according to package directions. Meanwhile, place asparagus and carrots in a steamer basket; place in a small saucepan over 1 in. of water. Bring to a boil; cover and steam for 2 minutes. Add zucchini and squash; cover and steam 2-3 minutes longer or until vegetables are crisp-tender. Keep warm.

In a small saucepan, combine cornstarch and soy milk until smooth. Stir in the salt, basil and oregano. Bring to a boil; cook and stir for 1-2 minutes or until thickened. Drain pasta; toss with vegetables and sauce.

NUTRITION FACTS: 1 cup equals 158 calories, 2 g fat (trace saturated fat), 0 cholesterol, 235 mg sodium, 29 g carbohydrate, 2 g fiber, 7 g protein. **DIABETIC EXCHANGES:** 1-1/2 starch, 1 vegetable.

Tofu Spinach Lasagna

MEATLESS

(PICTURED BELOW)

PREP: 45 Min.   **BAKE:** 30 Min. + Standing   **YIELD:** 12 Servings

No one guesses that tofu is buried in the layers of my delicious lasagna!   —Christine Laba, Arlington, Virginia

- 9 lasagna noodles
- 1 medium onion, chopped
- 3 garlic cloves, minced
- 1 tablespoon olive oil
- 2 cups sliced fresh mushrooms
- 1 package (14 ounces) firm tofu
- 1 carton (15 ounces) part-skim ricotta cheese
- 1/2 cup minced fresh parsley
- 1 teaspoon salt, *divided*
- 2 packages (10 ounces *each*) frozen chopped spinach, thawed and squeezed dry
- 1-3/4 cups marinara *or* meatless spaghetti sauce
- 1 cup (4 ounces) shredded part-skim mozzarella cheese
- 1/3 cup shredded Parmesan cheese

Cook noodles according to package directions. Meanwhile, in a large nonstick skillet, saute onion and garlic in oil for 1 minute. Add mushrooms; saute until tender. Set aside.

Drain tofu, reserving 2 tablespoons liquid. Place tofu and reserved liquid in a food processor; cover and process until blended. Add ricotta cheese; cover and process for 1-2 minutes or until smooth. Transfer to a large bowl; stir in the parsley, 1/2 teaspoon salt and mushroom mixture. Combine spinach and remaining salt; set aside.

Drain noodles. Spread half of the marinara sauce into a 13-in. x 9-in. x 2-in. baking dish coated with cooking spray. Layer with three noodles, half of the tofu mixture and half of the spinach mixture. Repeat layers of noodles, tofu and spinach. Top with remaining noodles and marinara sauce. Sprinkle with cheeses.

Bake, uncovered, at 350° for 30-35 minutes or until heated through and cheese is melted. Let stand for 10 minutes before cutting.

NUTRITION FACTS: 1 piece equals 227 calories, 8 g fat (4 g saturated fat), 18 mg cholesterol, 429 mg sodium, 25 g carbohydrate, 3 g fiber, 15 g protein. **DIABETIC EXCHANGES:** 1-1/2 starch, 1 lean meat, 1 vegetable, 1/2 fat.

Spread with pizza sauce. Top with green pepper, mushrooms, onion, tomato and cheese. Bake at 400° for 25-30 minutes or until cheese is melted and edges are lightly browned.

NUTRITION FACTS: 1 slice equals 240 calories, 4 g fat (2 g saturated fat), 11 mg cholesterol, 370 mg sodium, 40 g carbohydrate, 4 g fiber, 11 g protein. **DIABETIC EXCHANGES:** 2 starch, 1 lean meat, 1 vegetable.

Veggie Pizza with Herbed Tomato Crust

MEAT-LESS

(PICTURED ABOVE)

PREP: 30 Min. + Rising   **BAKE:** 25 Min.   **YIELD:** 6 Slices

I love this recipe because the crust is so flavorful—tomato juice replaces most of the oil. It's one of my kids' favorite suppers.
—Karen Shipp, San Antonio, Texas

- 1/2 cup whole wheat flour
- 1-1/2 teaspoons minced fresh parsley *or* 1/2 teaspoon dried parsley flakes
- 1-1/2 teaspoons minced fresh rosemary *or* 1/2 teaspoon dried rosemary, crushed
- 1 teaspoon active dry yeast
- 1/2 teaspoon sugar
- 1/4 teaspoon salt
- 1/4 teaspoon pepper
- 1/2 cup water
- 1/2 cup tomato juice
- 1 teaspoon olive oil
- 1-1/2 to 1-3/4 cups all-purpose flour

TOPPINGS:
- 1 can (8 ounces) pizza sauce
- 1 medium green pepper, chopped
- 1 cup sliced fresh mushrooms
- 1 small red onion, chopped
- 1 medium tomato, chopped
- 1 cup (4 ounces) shredded part-skim mozzarella cheese

In a large mixing bowl, combine the first seven ingredients. In a small saucepan, heat the water, tomato juice and oil to 120°-130°. Add to dry ingredients; beat until smooth. Stir in enough all-purpose flour to form a soft dough.

Turn onto a lightly floured surface; knead until smooth and elastic, about 5 minutes. Place in a bowl coated with cooking spray, turning once to coat top. Cover and let rise until doubled, about 45 minutes.

Punch dough down; roll into a 12-in. circle. Transfer to a 14-in. pizza pan coated with cooking spray; build up the edges slightly.

Spinach Gnocchi in Portobello Sauce

MEAT-LESS

PREP: 1-1/4 Hours   **COOK:** 10 Min.   **YIELD:** 6 Servings

Mushrooms and white wine add rich flavor to a creamy sauce for our Test Kitchen's potato dumplings.

- 2 pounds russet potatoes, peeled and quartered
- 4 quarts water
- 1-1/3 cups all-purpose flour
- 1 egg
- 3/4 teaspoon salt
- 5 ounces frozen chopped spinach, thawed and squeezed dry

SAUCE:
- 1/2 pound sliced baby portobello mushrooms
- 1 small onion, finely chopped
- 1 tablespoon butter
- 1/2 cup white wine *or* vegetable broth
- 1/4 cup all-purpose flour
- 1 cup vegetable broth
- 1 cup 2% milk
- 4 tablespoons grated Parmigiano-Reggiano cheese, *divided*
- 1/2 teaspoon Italian seasoning
- 1/4 teaspoon salt
- 1/4 teaspoon pepper

Place potatoes in a saucepan and cover with water. Bring to a boil. Reduce heat; cover and simmer for 15-20 minutes or until tender. Drain.

Over warm burner or very low heat, stir potatoes for 1-2 minutes or until steam is evaporated. Press through a potato ricer or strainer into a small bowl; cool slightly. In a Dutch oven, bring water to a boil.

Using a fork, make a well in the potatoes. Sprinkle flour over potatoes and into well. Combine the egg, salt and spinach; pour into well. Stir until blended. Knead 10-12 times, forming a soft dough.

Divide dough into four portions. On a floured surface, roll portions into 1/2-in.-thick ropes; cut into 3/4-in. pieces. Press and roll each piece with a lightly floured fork. Cook gnocchi in boiling water in batches for 30-60 seconds or until they float. Remove with a strainer and keep warm.

In a large nonstick saucepan, saute mushrooms and onion in butter until tender. Add wine or broth; cook and stir for 1 minute. Combine flour and broth until smooth; stir into pan. Stir in milk. Bring to a boil; cook and stir for 2 minutes or until thickened. Stir in 2 tablespoons cheese and seasonings. Spoon sauce over gnocchi. Sprinkle with remaining cheese.

NUTRITION FACTS: 1 cup gnocchi with 1/2 cup sauce equals 331 calories, 5 g fat (3 g saturated fat), 46 mg cholesterol, 691 mg sodium, 57 g carbohydrate, 4 g fiber, 12 g protein.

From the
Bread Basket

Has low-carb eating got you down? Are you getting enough grains? You can take advantage of the health benefits of whole wheat, oats and more while satisfying your cravings for freshly baked breads and steaming hot dinner rolls. Turn the page to learn how!

Cran-Orange Streusel Muffins, p. 193

Apple Cranberry Muffins
(PICTURED ABOVE)

PREP: 20 Min. **BAKE:** 20 Min. **YIELD:** 1-1/2 Dozen

I like to bake several varieties of bread to give as gifts to family and friends on special occasions. These fruity, crumb-topped muffins are a favorite. —Maureen Collop, Bothell, Washington

    2 **cups all-purpose flour**
   3/4 **cup sugar**
2-1/2 **teaspoons baking powder**
    1 **teaspoon ground cinnamon**
  1/2 **teaspoon salt**
  1/2 **teaspoon ground nutmeg**
  1/4 **teaspoon baking soda**
  1/8 **teaspoon ground allspice**
  1/8 **teaspoon ground cloves**
    2 **eggs**
1-1/2 **cups (12 ounces) reduced-fat sour cream**
  1/4 **cup butter, melted**
    1 **teaspoon vanilla extract**
    1 **cup chopped peeled tart apple**
    1 **cup dried cranberries**
TOPPING:
  1/4 **cup packed brown sugar**
    3 **tablespoons all-purpose flour**
    2 **tablespoons cold butter**

In a large bowl, combine the first nine ingredients. In another bowl, whisk the eggs, sour cream, butter and vanilla. Stir into dry ingredients just until moistened. Fold in the apple and the cranberries.

Coat muffin cups with cooking spray or use paper liners; fill two-thirds full with batter. For topping, combine brown sugar and flour. Cut in butter until mixture resembles coarse crumbs. Sprinkle over batter.

Bake at 375° for 20-25 minutes or until a toothpick comes out clean. Cool for 5 minutes before removing from pans to wire racks.

NUTRITION FACTS: 1 muffin equals 192 calories, 6 g fat (4 g saturated fat), 40 mg cholesterol, 199 mg sodium, 31 g carbohydrate, 1 g fiber, 4 g protein. **DIABETIC EXCHANGES:** 2 starch, 1 fat.

Banana Oat Muffins

(PICTURED AT LEFT)

PREP/TOTAL TIME: 30 Min.   **YIELD:** 1 Dozen

These muffins are low in cholesterol, but you'd never know it. Chopped pecans add pleasant crunch to these hearty treats with rich banana flavor.   —Marjorie Mott, Galatia, Illinois

    3/4 cup all-purpose flour
    3/4 cup quick-cooking oats
      1 teaspoon baking powder
      1 teaspoon ground cinnamon
    1/2 teaspoon baking soda
    1/4 teaspoon ground nutmeg
      2 egg whites
      1 cup mashed ripe bananas (about 2 medium)
    1/2 cup packed brown sugar
    1/4 cup fat-free milk
    1/4 cup canola oil
    1/2 cup chopped pecans

In a large bowl, combine the first six ingredients. In a small mixing bowl, beat the egg whites, bananas, brown sugar, milk and oil. Stir into dry ingredients just until moistened. Stir in pecans.

Coat muffin cups with cooking spray; fill two-thirds full with batter. Bake at 400° for 15-20 minutes or until a toothpick comes out clean. Cool for 5 minutes before removing from pan to a wire rack.

NUTRITION FACTS: 1 muffin equals 180 calories, 9 g fat (1 g saturated fat), trace cholesterol, 102 mg sodium, 24 g carbohydrate, 2 g fiber, 3 g protein. **DIABETIC EXCHANGES:** 1-1/2 fat, 1 starch, 1/2 fruit.

Buttermilk Bran Muffins

(PICTURED AT LEFT)

PREP: 20 Min.   **BAKE:** 15 Min.   **YIELD:** 22 Muffins

Over the years, I've altered the recipe of these sweet muffins to reduce sugar and fat. Even after the changes, they're still a hit!   —Anita Kay Brown, Greenbush, Michigan

      1 cup All-Bran
      2 cups buttermilk, *divided*
  1-1/2 cups raisin bran
  2-3/4 cups all-purpose flour
    3/4 cup sugar
    1/2 cup sugar blend for baking
    1/4 cup packed brown sugar
      1 teaspoon baking powder
    1/2 teaspoon baking soda
    1/2 teaspoon salt
      1 egg
      2 egg whites
    1/2 cup unsweetened applesauce
    1/4 cup canola oil

In a small bowl, combine All-Bran and 1 cup buttermilk; let stand for 5 minutes. Stir in raisin bran; let stand 5 minutes longer.

Meanwhile, in a large bowl, combine the flour, sugar, sugar blend, brown sugar, baking powder, baking soda and salt.

In another bowl, whisk the egg, egg whites, applesauce, oil and remaining buttermilk. Stir into dry ingredients just until moistened. Stir in bran mixture.

Coat muffin cups with cooking spray; fill three-fourths full with batter. Bake at 375° for 15-20 minutes or until a toothpick comes out clean. Cool for 5 minutes before removing from pans to wire racks.

NUTRITION FACTS: 1 muffin equals 169 calories, 3 g fat (trace saturated fat), 11 mg cholesterol, 165 mg sodium, 33 g carbohydrate, 2 g fiber, 4 g protein. **DIABETIC EXCHANGES:** 2 starch, 1/2 fat.

Editor's Note: This recipe was tested with Splenda Sugar Blend for Baking.

Orange Yogurt Muffins

(PICTURED AT FAR LEFT)

PREP/TOTAL TIME: 30 Min.   **YIELD:** 1-1/2 Dozen

Bold orange flavor and a sweet glaze make these light bites extra special. You can add them to just about any menu.
   —Anne Prince, Courtland, Virginia

    1/2 cup sugar, *divided*
      2 tablespoons grated orange peel
      2 tablespoons water
      5 tablespoons butter, cubed
      2 cups all-purpose flour
      1 teaspoon baking powder
      1 teaspoon baking soda
    1/2 teaspoon salt
      2 eggs
    3/4 cup plain yogurt
    3/4 cup 2% milk
  GLAZE:
      1 cup confectioners' sugar
      2 tablespoons orange juice
      1 teaspoon grated orange peel

In a small saucepan, combine 1/4 cup sugar, orange peel and water. Cook and stir over low heat for 3-5 minutes or until sugar is dissolved. Add butter; stir until melted. Remove from the heat; set aside.

In a large bowl, combine the flour, baking powder, baking soda, salt and remaining sugar. In another bowl, whisk the eggs, yogurt, milk and reserved butter mixture. Stir into dry ingredients just until moistened.

Coat muffin cups with cooking spray; fill each with a scant 1/4 cup of batter. Bake at 375° for 13-18 minutes or until a toothpick comes out clean. Combine glaze ingredients; spoon about 1-1/2 teaspoons over each warm muffin. Remove from pans to wire racks.

NUTRITION FACTS: 1 muffin equals 147 calories, 4 g fat (2 g saturated fat), 34 mg cholesterol, 207 mg sodium, 24 g carbohydrate, trace fiber, 3 g protein. **DIABETIC EXCHANGES:** 1-1/2 starch, 1/2 fat.

TASTY TIP

Batters for muffins and quick breads are often lumpy, so don't overmix them. Stirring a batter too much can make the final product tough and rubbery.

after each addition. Stir in the applesauce, vanilla and lemon peel. Combine the flour, baking powder and salt; add to creamed mixture just until blended.

Transfer to an 8-in. x 4-in. x 2-in. loaf pan coated with cooking spray. Bake at 350° for 45-55 minutes or until golden brown and a toothpick inserted near the center comes out clean. Cool for 10 minutes before removing loaf from pan to a wire rack to cool completely.

NUTRITION FACTS: 1 slice equals 185 calories, 9 g fat (5 g saturated fat), 74 mg cholesterol, 159 mg sodium, 23 g carbohydrate, trace fiber, 3 g protein. **DIABETIC EXCHANGES:** 1-1/2 starch, 1-1/2 fat.

Poppy Seed-Banana Mini Loaves

PREP: 20 Min.   **BAKE:** 30 Min.   **YIELD:** 3 Loaves (6 Slices Each)

A surprising hint of orange adds a unique touch to these lovely loaves of banana bread. They're perfect for holiday gift giving.
—Katherine Stallwood, Kennewick, Washington

  1/3 cup butter, softened
  3/4 cup sugar
    1 egg
    2 medium ripe bananas, mashed
    2 cups all-purpose flour
    2 teaspoons baking powder
  1/2 teaspoon salt
 4-1/2 teaspoons poppy seeds
    2 teaspoons grated orange peel
TOPPING:
    2 tablespoons cold butter
  1/4 cup packed brown sugar
    2 tablespoons chopped walnuts

In a small mixing bowl, beat butter and sugar for 2 minutes or until crumbly. Beat in egg and bananas. Combine the flour, baking powder and salt; beat into banana mixture just until blended. Stir in poppy seeds and orange peel.

Transfer to three 5-3/4-in. x 3-in. x 2-in. loaf pans coated with cooking spray. For topping, cut butter into brown sugar until crumbly. Stir in walnuts. Sprinkle over batter.

Bake at 350° for 30-40 minutes or until a toothpick comes out clean. Cool for 10 minutes before removing from pans to a wire rack.

NUTRITION FACTS: 1 slice equals 160 calories, 6 g fat (3 g saturated fat), 24 mg cholesterol, 162 mg sodium, 25 g carbohydrate, 1 g fiber, 2 g protein. **DIABETIC EXCHANGES:** 1-1/2 starch, 1 fat.

Pound Cake
(PICTURED ABOVE)

PREP: 15 Min.   **BAKE:** 45 Min. + Cooling   **YIELD:** 12 Servings

After preparing this low-fat treat, I often cube the cake for a wonderfully light blueberry trifle. You can dress things up a bit by spooning fresh or frozen fruit or berries over each slice.
—F. Joyce Grasby, Rochester, New York

  1/2 cup butter, softened
  3/4 cup sugar
    3 eggs
  1/4 cup unsweetened applesauce
 1-1/4 teaspoons vanilla extract
  1/2 teaspoon grated lemon peel
 1-1/4 cups all-purpose flour
  1/2 teaspoon baking powder
  1/4 teaspoon salt

In a small mixing bowl, cream butter and sugar until light and fluffy, about 5 minutes. Add eggs, one at a time, beating well

Cheddar Dill Biscuits
(PICTURED ABOVE RIGHT)

PREP/TOTAL TIME: 30 Min.   **YIELD:** 1 Dozen

We try to eat in a healthful way, decreasing fat and calories when possible. Thanks to these homemade biscuits, we still enjoy hearty weekend breakfasts.   —Carol Braly, South Fork, Colorado

    2 cups all-purpose flour
    2 teaspoons sugar
    1 teaspoon dill weed
  1/2 teaspoon baking soda
  1/2 teaspoon cream of tartar

Eggnog Bread
(PICTURED BELOW)

PREP: 20 Min. **BAKE:** 40 Min. + Cooling **YIELD:** 2 Loaves (12 Slices Each)

I always try to prepare this loaf the day before I intend to serve it. Doing so seems to gives the flavors just the right amount of time to blend. —Judi Malhotra, Toledo, Ohio

> 3 cups all-purpose flour
> 1/2 cup sugar
> 4 teaspoons baking powder
> 1 teaspoon salt
> 1/2 teaspoon ground nutmeg
> 1 egg
> 1-3/4 cups reduced-fat eggnog
> 1/4 cup unsweetened applesauce
> 1/4 cup canola oil
> 1 cup golden raisins
> 1/2 cup chopped pecans

In a large bowl, combine the flour, sugar, baking powder, salt and nutmeg. In a small bowl, whisk the egg, eggnog, applesauce and oil. Stir into dry ingredients just until moistened. Fold in raisins and pecans.

Transfer to two 8-in. x 4-in. x 2-in. loaf pans coated with cooking spray. Bake at 350° for 40-45 minutes or until a toothpick inserted near the center comes out clean. Cool for 10 minutes before removing from pans to wire racks.

NUTRITION FACTS: 1 slice equals 147 calories, 5 g fat (1 g saturated fat), 23 mg cholesterol, 180 mg sodium, 23 g carbohydrate, 1 g fiber, 3 g protein. **DIABETIC EXCHANGES:** 1-1/2 starch, 1 fat.

Editor's Note: This recipe was tested with commercially prepared eggnog.

> 1/2 teaspoon salt
> 1/4 cup cold butter
> 2/3 cup buttermilk
> 1/4 cup egg substitute
> 1/2 cup shredded reduced-fat cheddar cheese

In a large bowl, combine the first six ingredients. Cut in butter until mixture resembles coarse crumbs. Combine buttermilk and egg substitute; stir into flour mixture just until moistened. Stir in cheese.

Turn onto a lightly floured surface; knead 8-10 times. Pat to 3/4-in. thickness; cut with a floured 2-1/2-in. biscuit cutter.

Place 1 in. apart on an ungreased baking sheet. Bake at 400° for 12-16 minutes or until golden brown. Serve warm.

NUTRITION FACTS: 1 biscuit equals 134 calories, 5 g fat (3 g saturated fat), 14 mg cholesterol, 245 mg sodium, 18 g carbohydrate, 1 g fiber, 4 g protein. **DIABETIC EXCHANGES:** 1 starch, 1 fat.

TASTY TIP
Keep the following in mind when preparing savory Cheddar Dill Biscuits:
- Using reduced-fat cheese cuts the total fat to just about half that of using full-fat cheddar.
- When adding the wet ingredients to the crumb mixture, stir by hand only until moistened. Don't overmix.
- Leftover biscuits make a great breakfast the next day. Split a biscuit and set a lean slice of ham inside. Reheat in the microwave, and you're good to go!

Favorite Recipe Made Lighter

WARM on the inside with a slightly crunchy crust, Pineapple Zucchini Bread from Nancy Skramsted is a satisfying addition to any plate. But as good as the bread tastes, it comes up a bit short in the "health" department. So the reader from Billings, Montana asked for our help.

Our makeover pros realized that canola oil was a healthier choice than vegetable oil because it consists of a significantly larger percentage of healthy monounsaturated fat than vegetable oil. But our team didn't replace all of the vegetable oil with canola oil; they replaced the majority of it with unsweetened applesauce. Doing so maintained much of the bread's moistness, while adding sweetness...which allowed the team to decrease sugar.

Next, they removed one of the eggs and replaced another with 2 egg whites to reduce cholesterol. With a slight decrease in the nuts, the amount of fat was lowered without taking much flavor away from the finished bread.

Makeover Pineapple Zucchini Bread is a wonderful success. The crunchy crust stayed intact as did the loaf's moist center. The made-over bread tastes just as delightful as the original, minus more than half the fat and over a third of the calories.

Makeover Pineapple Zucchini Bread
(PICTURED ABOVE)

PREP: 20 Min.   BAKE: 50 Min. + Cooling   YIELD: 2 Loaves (12 Slices Each)

  1-1/2 cups sugar
    2/3 cup unsweetened applesauce
    1/3 cup canola oil
      2 egg whites
      1 egg
      2 teaspoons vanilla extract
      3 cups all-purpose flour
      2 teaspoons ground cinnamon
  1-1/2 teaspoons baking powder
      1 teaspoon salt
    3/4 teaspoon ground nutmeg
    1/2 teaspoon baking soda
      2 cups shredded zucchini
      1 can (8 ounces) unsweetened crushed pineapple, drained
    1/3 cup chopped walnuts

In a large mixing bowl, beat the sugar, applesauce, oil, egg whites, egg and vanilla until well blended. Combine the flour, cinnamon, baking powder, salt, nutmeg and baking soda; gradually beat into sugar mixture until blended. Stir in the zucchini, pineapple and walnuts.

Transfer to two 8-in. x 4-in. x 2-in. loaf pans coated with cooking spray. Bake at 350° for 50-60 minutes or until a toothpick inserted near the center comes out clean. Cool loaves for 10 minutes before removing loaves from pans to wire racks to cool completely.

NUTRITION FACTS: 1 slice equals 159 calories, 5 g fat (trace saturated fat), 9 mg cholesterol, 158 mg sodium, 27 g carbohydrate, 1 g fiber, 3 g protein. DIABETIC EXCHANGES: 2 starch, 1 fat.

Pineapple Zucchini Bread

PREP: 20 Min.   BAKE: 50 Min. + Cooling   YIELD: 2 Loaves (12 Slices Each)

      2 cups sugar
      1 cup vegetable oil
      3 eggs
      2 teaspoons vanilla extract
      3 cups all-purpose flour
      2 teaspoons ground cinnamon
  1-1/2 teaspoons baking powder
      1 teaspoon salt
    3/4 teaspoon ground nutmeg
    1/2 teaspoon baking soda
      2 cups shredded zucchini
      1 can (8 ounces) unsweetened crushed pineapple, drained
    3/4 cup chopped walnuts

In a large mixing bowl, beat the sugar, oil, eggs and vanilla until well blended. Combine the flour, cinnamon, baking powder, salt, nutmeg and baking soda; gradually beat into sugar mixture until blended. Stir in the zucchini, pineapple and walnuts.

Transfer to two greased 8-in. x 4-in. x 2-in. loaf pans. Bake at 350° for 50-60 minutes or until a toothpick inserted near the center comes out clean. Cool the loaves for 10 minutes before removing from pans to wire racks to cool completely.

NUTRITION FACTS: 1 slice equals 243 calories, 12 g fat (2 g saturated fat), 27 mg cholesterol, 158 mg sodium, 31 g carbohydrate, 1 g fiber, 4 g protein.

Cran-Orange Streusel Muffins

(PICTURED BELOW)

PREP: 20 Min.   **BAKE:** 20 Min.   **YIELD:** 1 Dozen

In less than 45 minutes, you can have a dozen hot muffins on the table. In addition, the recipe is a snap to double, so preparing an extra batch for company isn't a problem.

—Hannah Barringer, Loudon, Tennessee

- 1/4 cup butter, softened
- 1/2 cup sugar
- 1 egg
- 1 cup fat-free milk
- 1/4 cup unsweetened applesauce
- 1/2 teaspoon vanilla extract
- 2 cups all-purpose flour
- 2 teaspoons baking powder
- 1/2 teaspoon salt
- 1 cup fresh *or* frozen cranberries, coarsely chopped
- 2-1/2 teaspoons grated orange peel

STREUSEL TOPPING:

- 2 tablespoons all-purpose flour
- 2 tablespoons brown sugar
- 1/4 teaspoon ground cinnamon
- 2 tablespoons cold butter

In a large mixing bowl, beat butter and sugar until crumbly, about 2 minutes. Add egg; mix well. Beat in the milk, applesauce and vanilla. Combine the flour, baking powder and salt; stir into butter mixture just until moistened. Fold in cranberries and orange peel.

Coat muffin cups with cooking spray; fill three-fourths full with batter. For topping, combine the flour, brown sugar and cinnamon in a small bowl. Cut in butter until crumbly. Sprinkle over batter.

Bake at 400° for 18-22 minutes or until a toothpick comes out clean. Cool for 5 minutes before removing from pan to a wire rack.

NUTRITION FACTS: 1 muffin equals 192 calories, 6 g fat (4 g saturated fat), 33 mg cholesterol, 240 mg sodium, 30 g carbohydrate, 1 g fiber, 4 g protein. **DIABETIC EXCHANGES:** 2 starch, 1 fat.

Good-for-You Grain Bread

FAT ▼ MEAT-LESS

PREP: 20 Min. + Rising   **BAKE:** 25 Min. + Cooling   **YIELD:** 1 Loaf (16 Slices)

I developed this recipe for my sister when I learned she's diabetic. Filled with whole grains, the moist loaf is wonderful for morning toast or afternoon sandwiches.   —Kandi Lilley, Wilton, Maine

- 1 package (1/4 ounce) active dry yeast
- 1-1/3 cups warm water (110° to 115°)
- 1 cup whole wheat flour
- 3/4 cup quick-cooking oats
- 1/3 cup nonfat dry milk powder
- 2 tablespoons ground flaxseed
- 2 tablespoons toasted wheat germ
- 4 teaspoons canola oil
- 4 teaspoons brown sugar
- 1-1/2 teaspoons salt
- 2 to 2-1/2 cups all-purpose flour

In a large mixing bowl, dissolve yeast in warm water. Add the whole wheat flour, oats, milk powder, flaxseed, wheat germ, oil, brown sugar and salt. Beat until smooth. Stir in enough all-purpose flour to form a stiff dough.

Turn onto a lightly floured surface; knead until smooth and elastic, about 6-8 minutes. Place in a bowl coated with cooking spray, turning once to coat the top. Cover and let rise in a warm place until doubled, about 1 hour.

Punch dough down; shape into a loaf. Place in a 9-in. x 5-in. x 3-in. loaf pan coated with cooking spray. Cover and let rise until doubled, about 45 minutes.

Bake at 400° for 25-30 minutes or until golden brown. Remove from pan to a wire rack to cool.

NUTRITION FACTS: 1 slice equals 125 calories, 2 g fat (trace saturated fat), trace cholesterol, 236 mg sodium, 23 g carbohydrate, 2 g fiber, 5 g protein. **DIABETIC EXCHANGE:** 1-1/2 starch.

HEALTHY OUTLOOK

Found in the baking aisle, flaxseed offers calcium, iron and vitamin E and is a source of omega-3 fatty acids.

Cranberry Pumpkin Bread

(PICTURED ABOVE)

PREP: 30 Min.   **BAKE:** 40 Min. + Cooling   **YIELD:** 2 Loaves (12 Slices Each)

I wanted to add extra flavor to one of my favorite pumpkin bread recipes. I started experimenting, and this sweet bread was the result.
—Betty Jackson, White Pine, Tennessee

- 1/2 cup golden raisins
- 1/4 cup dried cranberries
- 3 tablespoons orange juice
- 3 cups self-rising flour
- 1/2 cup packed brown sugar
- 1 teaspoon ground cinnamon
- 1/4 teaspoon ground nutmeg
- 3/4 cup canned pumpkin
- 3/4 cup whole-berry cranberry sauce
- 1/2 cup molasses
- 2 eggs
- 1/4 cup canola oil
- 1 teaspoon vanilla extract
- 1/2 cup chopped pecans
- 1 tablespoon grated orange peel

In a small saucepan, combine the raisins, cranberries and orange juice. Bring to a boil. Remove from the heat; cover and let stand for 5 minutes.

Meanwhile, in a large bowl, combine the flour, brown sugar, cinnamon and nutmeg. In a small mixing bowl, combine the pumpkin, cranberry sauce and molasses. Beat in the eggs, oil and vanilla until blended. Stir into dry ingredients just until moistened. Fold in the pecans, orange peel and raisin mixture.

Transfer to two 8-in. x 4-in. x 2-in. loaf pans coated with cooking spray. Bake at 350° for 40-45 minutes or until a toothpick inserted near the center comes out clean. Cool for 10 minutes before removing from pans to wire racks.

NUTRITION FACTS: 1 slice equals 159 calories, 5 g fat (trace saturated fat), 18 mg cholesterol, 192 mg sodium, 28 g carbohydrate, 1 g fiber, 2 g protein. **DIABETIC EXCHANGES:** 2 starch, 1/2 fat.

Editor's Note: *As a substitute for each cup of self-rising flour, place 1-1/2 teaspoons baking powder and 1/2 teaspoon salt in a measuring cup. Add all-purpose flour to measure 1 cup.*

Scrumptious Blueberry-Lemon Bread

PREP: 20 Min.   **BAKE:** 1 Hour + Cooling   **YIELD:** 1 Loaf (12 Slices)

We enjoy slices of this moist, berry loaf for breakfast or as an afternoon snack. My family doesn't even know they're eating light.
—Karen Strzelecki, Arlington, Texas

- 1-1/3 cups all-purpose flour
- 2/3 cup whole wheat flour
- 2/3 cup sugar
- 2 teaspoons baking powder
- 1/2 teaspoon salt
- 1 egg
- 1 egg white
- 1/2 cup unsweetened applesauce
- 1/2 cup fat-free milk
- 3 tablespoons butter, melted
- 1 cup fresh *or* frozen blueberries
- 2 teaspoons grated lemon peel

GLAZE:
- 1/3 cup confectioners' sugar
- 2 tablespoons lemon juice

In a large bowl, combine the flours, sugar, baking powder and salt. In a small bowl, beat the egg, egg white, applesauce, milk and butter. Stir into dry ingredients just until moistened. Fold in blueberries and lemon peel.

Transfer to an 8-in. x 4-in. x 2-in. loaf pan coated with cooking spray. Bake at 350° for 60-65 minutes or until a toothpick inserted near the center comes out clean.

Combine the glaze ingredients; pour over warm loaf. Cool for 10 minutes before removing loaf from pan to a wire rack to cool completely.

NUTRITION FACTS: 1 slice equals 180 calories, 4 g fat (2 g saturated fat), 27 mg cholesterol, 210 mg sodium, 34 g carbohydrate, 2 g fiber, 4 g protein. **DIABETIC EXCHANGES:** 2 starch, 1/2 fat.

Editor's Note: If using frozen blueberries, do not thaw before adding to batter.

Oniony Wheat Biscuits

PREP: 30 Min.   **BAKE:** 10 Min.   **YIELD:** 10 Biscuits

This recipe has graced my files for more than 10 years. I bake the sweet-savory biscuits often because they complement all kinds of meals. —Bernice Janowski, Stevens Point, Wisconsin

    1 tablespoon butter
    2 teaspoons brown sugar
    1 sweet onion, halved and thinly sliced
DOUGH:
    1 cup all-purpose flour
  3/4 cup whole wheat flour
    2 tablespoons brown sugar
    1 teaspoon baking powder
  3/4 teaspoon rubbed sage
  1/2 teaspoon salt
  1/2 teaspoon baking soda
    3 tablespoons cold butter
    1 egg
    1 cup (8 ounces) plain yogurt

In a large nonstick skillet coated with cooking spray, melt butter. Stir in brown sugar until blended; add onion. Cook over medium heat for 15-20 minutes or until onion is golden brown, stirring frequently. Set aside.

In a large bowl, combine the flours, brown sugar, baking powder, sage, salt and baking soda. Cut in butter until mixture resembles coarse crumbs. Combine egg and yogurt; stir into crumb mixture just until combined (dough will be sticky). Stir in a third of the onion mixture.

Drop by 1/4 cupfuls 2 in. apart onto a baking sheet coated with cooking spray. Gently press remaining onion mixture onto dough. Bake at 425° for 10-15 minutes or until golden brown. Serve warm.

NUTRITION FACTS: 1 biscuit equals 158 calories, 6 g fat (4 g saturated fat), 37 mg cholesterol, 287 mg sodium, 22 g carbohydrate, 2 g fiber, 4 g protein. **DIABETIC EXCHANGES:** 1-1/2 starch, 1 fat.

TASTY TIP
Avoid opening the oven when baking biscuits. Doing so causes a heat loss that may affect the final product.

Pesto Muffins

MEAT-LESS

(PICTURED BELOW)

PREP/TOTAL TIME: 30 Min.   **YIELD:** 1 Dozen

Looking for a change-of-pace addition to a party buffet? Give these basil-flavored bites a try. I also like them alongside a bowl of steaming soup. —Cheryl Hindrichs, Columbus, Ohio

1-1/2 cups all-purpose flour
  1/2 cup whole wheat flour
  1/2 teaspoon baking powder
  1/2 teaspoon baking soda
  1/4 teaspoon salt
    1 egg
    1 cup buttermilk
  3/4 cup vegetable broth
    3 tablespoons canola oil
  1/2 cup grated Parmesan cheese, *divided*
  1/2 cup loosely packed basil leaves, chopped
  1/4 cup chopped walnuts
    2 garlic cloves, minced

In a large bowl, combine the first five ingredients. In another bowl, whisk the egg, buttermilk, broth and oil. Stir into dry ingredients just until moistened.

Set aside 1 tablespoon Parmesan cheese. Fold the basil, walnuts, garlic and remaining Parmesan cheese into batter. Fill paper-lined muffin cups two-thirds full; sprinkle with reserved Parmesan cheese.

Bake at 400° for 15-20 minutes or until a toothpick comes out clean. Cool for 5 minutes before removing from pan to a wire rack.

NUTRITION FACTS: 1 muffin equals 153 calories, 7 g fat (1 g saturated fat), 21 mg cholesterol, 270 mg sodium, 17 g carbohydrate, 1 g fiber, 6 g protein. **DIABETIC EXCHANGES:** 1-1/2 fat, 1 starch.

Multigrain Raisin Bread

(PICTURED BELOW)

FAT MEAT-
LESS

PREP: 40 Min. + Rising **BAKE:** 40 Min. + Cooling
YIELD: 2 Loaves (16 Slices Each)

After years of searching for the perfect recipe for whole-grain raisin bread, I finally whipped up my own version. It's fantastic when making French toast. —Debra Van Den Heuvel, Gilman, Wisconsin

    2 cups raisins
1-1/2 cups water
  1/2 cup old-fashioned oats
    1 tablespoon active dry yeast
1-1/4 cups warm water (110° to 115°)
  1/4 cup honey
    2 eggs
  3/4 cup nonfat dry milk powder
    2 teaspoons salt
1-1/2 teaspoons ground cinnamon
    2 cups whole wheat flour
    3 to 3-1/2 cups all-purpose flour

In a small saucepan, bring raisins and water to a boil. Reduce heat; cover and simmer for 5 minutes. Drain, reserving 1/2 cup liquid. Stir oats into reserved liquid; set raisins and oat mixture aside.

In a large mixing bowl, dissolve yeast in warm water. Stir in honey; let stand for 5 minutes. Add the eggs, milk powder, salt, cinnamon, whole wheat flour, 1 cup all-purpose flour and oat mixture; beat on medium speed until blended. Stir in enough remaining all-purpose flour to form a firm dough. Stir in raisins (dough will be sticky).

Turn onto a lightly floured surface; knead until smooth and elastic, about 6-8 minutes. Place in a bowl coated with cooking spray, turning once to coat the top. Cover and let rise in a warm place until doubled, about 1 hour.

Punch dough down. Turn onto a lightly floured surface; shape into two loaves. Place in two 9-in. x 5-in. x 3-in. loaf pans coated with cooking spray. Cover and let rise until doubled, about 40 minutes.

Bake at 350° for 40-45 minutes or until golden brown. Cover loosely with foil if tops brown too quickly. Remove from pans to wire racks to cool.

NUTRITION FACTS: 1 slice equals 124 calories, 1 g fat (trace saturated fat), 14 mg cholesterol, 169 mg sodium, 26 g carbohydrate, 2 g fiber, 4 g protein. **DIABETIC EXCHANGES:** 1 starch, 1/2 fruit.

Favorite Recipe Made Lighter

FINDING a great recipe makes it hard to adjust or change anything about it. So when Jean Irving of Thousand Oaks, California decided to make over her favorite bread, she turned to us for help.

"I love Fiesta Corn Bread—it's my most requested recipe and has won blue ribbons at county fairs in three different states," she writes. "But it's loaded with butter, sugar, cheese and calories. I'm afraid to try to make it lighter myself. Do you think you could give it a try?"

We'd love to! Our home economists went after the butter first, which weighed in at 3/4 of a pound. Unsweetened applesauce and a little extra cream-style corn filled in beautifully, letting our makeover team reduce the butter to 1/4 cup without losing the bread's moist texture. The applesauce and corn also provided enough sweetness to cut back on the amount of sugar.

Next, the team used two whole eggs and four egg whites instead of four whole eggs, which reduced cholesterol, fat and calories. Finally, they decreased the amount of cheese, replacing it with a smaller amount of reduced-fat Mexican cheese blend.

The results couldn't be any more fantastic. Every tender piece of Makeover Fiesta Corn Bread is filled with the original's contest-winning flavor. It's so delicious, we think our Test Kitchen pros deserve their own blue ribbon!

Makeover Fiesta Corn Bread

MEAT-LESS

(PICTURED ABOVE)

PREP: 20 Min.   **BAKE:** 30 Min.   **YIELD:** 15 Servings

- 1/4 cup butter, softened
- 1/2 cup sugar
- 2 eggs
- 2 cans (8-3/4 ounces *each*) cream-style corn
- 4 egg whites
- 1/4 cup unsweetened applesauce
- 1 cup all-purpose flour
- 1 cup cornmeal
- 3 teaspoons baking powder
- 1/4 teaspoon salt
- 1-1/2 cups (6 ounces) shredded reduced-fat Mexican cheese blend
- 1 can (4 ounces) chopped green chilies
- 1 jar (4 ounces) diced pimientos, drained

In a large mixing bowl, beat butter and sugar until crumbly, about 2 minutes. Add eggs, one at a time, beating well after each addition. Beat in the corn, egg whites and applesauce (mixture will appear curdled).

Combine the flour, cornmeal, baking powder and salt; add to egg mixture just until moistened. Fold in the cheese, chilies and pimientos.

Transfer to a 13-in. x 9-in. x 2-in. baking pan coated with cooking spray. Bake at 350° for 30-35 minutes or until a toothpick inserted near the center comes out clean. Serve warm. Refrigerate leftovers.

NUTRITION FACTS: 1 piece equals 192 calories, 7 g fat (3 g saturated fat), 45 mg cholesterol, 379 mg sodium, 28 g carbohydrate, 2 g fiber, 7 g protein. **DIABETIC EXCHANGES:** 2 starch, 1 fat.

Fiesta Corn Bread

MEAT-LESS

PREP: 20 Min.   **BAKE:** 35 Min.   **YIELD:** 15 Servings

- 3/4 cup butter, softened
- 3/4 cup sugar
- 4 eggs
- 1 can (14-3/4 ounces) cream-style corn
- 1 cup all-purpose flour
- 1 cup cornmeal
- 3 teaspoons baking powder
- 1/4 teaspoon salt
- 1 cup (4 ounces) shredded Monterey Jack cheese
- 1 cup (4 ounces) shredded cheddar cheese
- 1 can (4 ounces) chopped green chilies
- 1 jar (4 ounces) diced pimientos, drained

In a large mixing bowl, cream butter and sugar. Add eggs, one at a time, beating well after each addition. Beat in corn (mixture will appear curdled). Combine the flour, cornmeal, baking powder and salt; add to creamed mixture just until moistened. Fold in the cheeses, chilies and pimientos.

Transfer to a greased 13-in. x 9-in. x 2-in. baking pan. Bake at 350° for 35-40 minutes or until a toothpick inserted near the center comes out clean. Serve warm. Refrigerate any leftovers.

NUTRITION FACTS: 1 piece equals 281 calories, 15 g fat (9 g saturated fat), 96 mg cholesterol, 425 mg sodium, 30 g carbohydrate, 2 g fiber, 7 g protein.

Festive Fruit Ladder

(PICTURED AT RIGHT)

FAT SALT

PREP: 45 Min. + Rising   **BAKE:** 25 Min. + Cooling   **YIELD:** 1 Loaf (24 Slices)

"Festive" is the perfect word to describe this impressive Christmas specialty.   —Cathrine Emerson, Arlington, Washington

1 package (1/4 ounce) active dry yeast
1 cup warm fat-free milk (110° to 115°)
1/2 cup sugar
2 tablespoons butter, softened
1 egg
1/2 teaspoon salt
3-1/2 to 4 cups all-purpose flour

FILLING:
1/2 cup sugar
2 tablespoons plus 2 teaspoons cornstarch
3/4 teaspoon ground cinnamon
2/3 cup apple cider *or* unsweetened apple juice
4 cups thinly sliced peeled tart apples
2/3 cup dried cranberries
1 egg
1 tablespoon water

ICING:
1 cup confectioners' sugar
4 teaspoons water
1/2 teaspoon almond extract
1/4 cup dried cranberries
2 tablespoons sliced almonds, toasted

In a large mixing bowl, dissolve yeast in warm milk. Add sugar, butter, egg, salt and 3 cups flour. Beat on medium speed for 2 minutes. Stir in enough remaining flour to form a soft dough.

Turn onto a lightly floured surface; knead until smooth and elastic, about 6-8 minutes. Place in a bowl coated with cooking spray, turning once to coat the top. Cover and let rise in a warm place until doubled, about 45 minutes.

In a large saucepan, combine the sugar, cornstarch, cinnamon and cider. Bring to a boil; cook and stir for 1 minute or until thickened. Stir in apples; cook 5-10 minutes longer or until crisp-tender. Remove from the heat; stir in cranberries. Cool to room temperature.

Punch dough down; roll into a 15-in. x 12-in. rectangle. Place on a baking sheet coated with cooking spray. Spread filling lengthwise down center of dough. On each long side, cut 1-in.-wide strips 3 in. into center. Fold strips at an angle across filling; seal ends. Cover and let rise until doubled.

Beat egg and water; brush over dough. Bake at 350° for 25-30 minutes or until golden brown. Cool on a wire rack. Combine confectioners' sugar, water and extract; drizzle over loaf. Sprinkle with cranberries and almonds.

NUTRITION FACTS: 1 slice equals 172 calories, 2 g fat (1 g saturated fat), 20 mg cholesterol, 71 mg sodium, 36 g carbohydrate, 1 g fiber, 3 g protein. **DIABETIC EXCHANGE:** 2 starch.

TASTY TIP
Catherine Emerson suggests trying apricots and cinnamon in her Festive Fruit Ladder.

PREP: 25 Min.   **BAKE:** 20 Min.   **YIELD:** 1 Dozen

Pears are a great source of vitamin C, and these tender treats feature plenty of them. Seasonal spices such as cinnamon, allspice and grated orange peel round out the muffins' holiday flair.
—Kay Tanberg, Duluth, Minnesota

1-1/2 cups all-purpose flour
1/2 cup oat bran
1/2 cup packed brown sugar
2 teaspoons baking powder
1/4 teaspoon salt
1/4 teaspoon ground cinnamon
1/8 teaspoon ground allspice
2 egg whites
1/2 cup fat-free milk
1/4 cup canola oil
1 egg
4 teaspoons grated orange peel
1/2 teaspoon vanilla extract
2 medium pears, peeled and chopped

In a large bowl, combine the first seven ingredients. In a small mixing bowl, beat egg whites on high speed until stiff peaks form. In another bowl, whisk the milk, oil, egg, orange peel and vanilla; stir into dry ingredients just until moistened. Fold in pears, then egg whites.

Coat muffin cups with cooking spray; fill three-fourths full. Bake at 350° for 20-25 minutes or until a toothpick comes out clean. Cool for 5 minutes before removing from pan to a wire rack.

NUTRITION FACTS: 1 muffin equals 172 calories, 6 g fat (1 g saturated fat), 18 mg cholesterol, 140 mg sodium, 28 g carbohydrate, 2 g fiber, 4 g protein. **DIABETIC EXCHANGES:** 2 starch, 1 fat.

Spiced Pear Muffins

SALT

Dazzling Desserts

There's always room for dessert, and *Light & Tasty's* trimmed-down favorites turn decadent delights into guilt-free goodies. Thanks to the 78 recipes found here, eating right never tasted so sweet.

Chocolate Peanut Butter Bombes, p. 208

2 packages (.3 ounce *each*) sugar-free lemon gelatin
2 cups boiling water
2 cups diet lemon-lime soda
1/4 cup lemon juice
1 carton (8 ounces) frozen reduced-fat whipped topping, thawed
1/4 teaspoon yellow food coloring, optional
3/4 cup fresh blueberries
3/4 cup sliced fresh strawberries
2 medium kiwifruit, peeled and sliced

In a large mixing bowl, dissolve gelatin in boiling water. Stir in soda and lemon juice. Cover and refrigerate for 2 hours or until set.

Add whipped topping; beat on high speed for 4-5 minutes or until smooth. Stir in food coloring if desired. Place 3/4 cup mixture in each of eight dessert dishes. Refrigerate until set. Just before serving, top with berries and kiwi.

NUTRITION FACTS: 1 serving equals 97 calories, 3 g fat (3 g saturated fat), 0 cholesterol, 58 mg sodium, 13 g carbohydrate, 1 g fiber, 2 g protein. **DIABETIC EXCHANGES:** 1/2 starch, 1/2 fruit, 1/2 fat.

Peach Cheese Pie

(PICTURED ABOVE)

PREP: 15 Min. + Chilling   **YIELD:** 8 Servings

I whip up this cool, creamy dessert in the morning, so my family can enjoy it after dinner on warm summer evenings. With only six ingredients, it couldn't be easier!

—Janine Wich, Farmingdale, New York

1 can (15 ounces) sliced peaches in extra-light syrup
1/4 cup cold water
1 envelope unflavored gelatin
1 package (8 ounces) reduced-fat cream cheese, cubed
1/4 cup sugar
1 graham cracker crust (9 inches)

Drain peaches, reserving syrup; set peaches aside. In a small saucepan, combine water and reserved syrup; sprinkle with gelatin. Let stand for 1 minute. Heat over low heat, stirring until gelatin is completely dissolved, about 2 minutes. Cool mixture slightly.

Transfer to a food processor. Add the peaches, cream cheese and sugar; cover and process until smooth. Pour into crust. Cover pie and refrigerate until set, about 1 hour. Refrigerate leftovers.

NUTRITION FACTS: 1 piece equals 231 calories, 11 g fat (5 g saturated fat), 20 mg cholesterol, 246 mg sodium, 29 g carbohydrate, 1 g fiber, 5 g protein. **DIABETIC EXCHANGES:** 2 starch, 2 fat.

Lemon Cloud Desserts

PREP: 20 Min. + Chilling   **YIELD:** 8 Servings

Family and friends love the bright colors and refreshing lemon-lime taste of this fruity no-bake treat.

—Barbara Robbins, Chandler, Arizona

Bread Pudding

PREP: 10 Min.   **BAKE:** 25 Min.   **YIELD:** 6 Servings

"Sugar and spice and everything nice" go into this moist and mouth-watering bread pudding from our Test Kitchen. A traditional, homey treat, this one is light, economical, so easy—and a soothing antidote for wintry chills.

2 eggs
2 cups fat-free milk
Sugar substitute equivalent to 1/4 cup sugar
1/4 cup sugar
1 tablespoon butter, melted
1 teaspoon ground cinnamon
1/2 teaspoon vanilla extract
1/4 teaspoon salt
1/4 teaspoon ground nutmeg
1/8 teaspoon ground cloves
5 cups cubed day-old French bread

In a large bowl, combine the first 10 ingredients. Add bread cubes; stir gently to coat. Pour into an 8-in. square baking dish coated with cooking spray.

Bake at 350° for 25-30 minutes or until a knife inserted near the center comes out clean. Serve warm.

NUTRITION FACTS: 2/3 cup equals 187 calories, 5 g fat (2 g saturated fat), 78 mg cholesterol, 338 mg sodium, 28 g carbohydrate, 1 g fiber, 7 g protein. **DIABETIC EXCHANGES:** 2 starch, 1/2 fat.

Editor's Note: This recipe was tested with Splenda No Calorie Sweetener.

TASTY TIP
Have cooked oatmeal left from breakfast? Grab your favorite bread pudding recipe and substitute the extra oatmeal for the bread. The texture may be slightly different, but in the end you'll have a healthy take on an old standby.

Holiday Cheesecake

(PICTURED BELOW)

PREP: 35 Min. **BAKE:** 55 Min. + Chilling **YIELD:** 16 Servings

Nothing rounds out holiday meals like this impressive cheesecake. It's lovely sitting on a dessert buffet or when brought out after the big meal. —Meredith Dodson, St. Joseph, Michigan

- 1 cup reduced-fat cinnamon graham cracker crumbs (about 5 whole crackers)
- 2 tablespoons reduced-fat butter, melted
- 1 package (12 ounces) fresh *or* frozen cranberries
- 3/4 cup sugar
- 1/4 cup water

FILLING:

- 2 packages (8 ounces *each*) reduced-fat cream cheese
- 2 packages (8 ounces *each*) fat-free cream cheese
- 1 cup (8 ounces) reduced-fat sour cream
- 1/2 cup sugar
- Sugar substitute equivalent to 1/2 cup sugar
- 1 tablespoon cornstarch
- 1 teaspoon grated orange peel
- 2 eggs, lightly beaten
- 2 egg whites, lightly beaten

In a small bowl, combine cracker crumbs and butter. Press onto the bottom of a 9-in. springform pan coated with cooking spray. Place on a baking sheet. Bake at 325° for 8-10 minutes or until set. Cool on a wire rack.

In a small saucepan, combine the cranberries, sugar and water. Cook over medium heat until berries pop, about 10 minutes; cool.

In a large mixing bowl, combine the first seven filling ingredients; beat until blended. Add eggs and egg whites; beat on low speed just until combined. Pour over crust.

Place pan on a double thickness of heavy-duty foil (about 18 in. square). Securely wrap foil around pan. Place in a large baking pan; add 1 in. of hot water to larger pan.

Bake at 325° for 55-60 minutes or until center is just set and top appears dull. Remove pan from water bath. Cool on a wire rack for 10 minutes. Carefully run a knife around edge of pan to loosen; cool 1 hour longer.

Gently spoon cranberry mixture over cheesecake. Refrigerate overnight. Remove the sides of the pan before cutting.

NUTRITION FACTS: 1 slice equals 230 calories, 9 g fat (6 g saturated fat), 56 mg cholesterol, 335 mg sodium, 27 g carbohydrate, 1 g fiber, 10 g protein. **DIABETIC EXCHANGES:** 2 starch, 2 fat.

Editor's Note: This recipe was tested with Land O'Lakes light stick butter and Splenda No Calorie Sweetener.

Favorite Recipe Made Lighter

A CRISP TOPPING, an oh-so-chocolaty crust and a soft cream cheese filling make these delectable bars over-the-top indulgent. Maybe too indulgent.

Writes Janet Coops of Duarte, California, "I was given this recipe at a Christmas party. It comes together in no time and everyone likes it, but it's really rich. Is there any way to make it lighter?"

After just one bite of the heavenly treat, our makeover team knew this would be a tough job. The home economists wanted to keep the creamy smoothness found in the filling; however, they also wanted to cut calories and fat—especially the saturated fat, which was high at 12 grams per serving.

First, they focused on the topping and crust and cut the amount of butter in half, which drastically reduced the amount of saturated fat. To make up for the butter lost, the team had to review and readjust the amounts of several other ingredients to make sure there wasn't a loss of crispness or chocolate flavor.

Next, they tackled the filling. They easily substituted reduced-fat cream cheese and fat-free sweetened condensed milk for their heavier counterparts, but there was a surprising drawback. When they put the topping on the uncooked filling, the bars sank. To remedy this problem, they baked the filling and the crust just until set, then added the topping.

The resulting Makeover Cream Cheese Streusel Bars are magnificent. With all the original's creamy indulgence but half the fat and over a third less calories, this is one divine dessert.

Cream Cheese Streusel Bars

PREP: 20 Min. **BAKE:** 30 Min. + Cooling **YIELD:** 15 Servings

1-3/4 cups all-purpose flour
1-1/2 cups confectioners' sugar
1/2 cup baking cocoa
1/2 teaspoon salt
1 cup cold butter
1 package (8 ounces) cream cheese, softened
1 can (14 ounces) sweetened condensed milk
1 egg, lightly beaten
2 teaspoons vanilla extract

In a large bowl, combine the flour, confectioners' sugar, cocoa and salt; cut in butter until crumbly. Set aside 1 cup for topping; press remaining crumb mixture into a greased 11-in. x 7-in. x 2-in. baking pan. Bake at 325° for 8-12 minutes or until set.

In a small mixing bowl, beat the cream cheese, milk, egg and vanilla until blended. Pour over crust; top with reserved crumb mixture. Bake for 20-25 minutes or until filling is set. Cool on a wire rack. Store in the refrigerator.

NUTRITION FACTS: 1 bar equals 359 calories, 20 g fat (12 g saturated fat), 72 mg cholesterol, 285 mg sodium, 40 g carbohydrate, 1 g fiber, 6 g protein.

Makeover Cream Cheese Streusel Bars

(PICTURED ABOVE)

PREP: 20 Min. **BAKE:** 30 Min. + Cooling **YIELD:** 15 Servings

1-1/4 cups confectioners' sugar
1 cup all-purpose flour
1/3 cup baking cocoa
1/4 teaspoon salt
1/2 cup cold butter
1 package (8 ounces) reduced-fat cream cheese
1 can (14 ounces) fat-free sweetened condensed milk
1 egg, lightly beaten
2 teaspoons vanilla extract

In a large bowl, combine the confectioners' sugar, flour, cocoa and salt; cut in butter until crumbly. Set aside 1/2 cup for topping; press remaining crumb mixture into an 11-in. x 7-in. x 2-in. baking pan coated with cooking spray. Bake at 325° for 8-12 minutes or until set.

In a small mixing bowl, beat the cream cheese, milk, egg and vanilla until blended. Pour over crust. Bake for 15 minutes. Top with the reserved crumb mixture; bake 5-10 minutes longer or until the filling is set. Cool on a wire rack. Store in the refrigerator.

NUTRITION FACTS: 1 bar equals 245 calories, 10 g fat (6 g saturated fat), 43 mg cholesterol, 197 mg sodium, 34 g carbohydrate, 1 g fiber, 6 g protein. **DIABETIC EXCHANGES:** 2 starch, 2 fat.

Bake, uncovered, at 400° for 28-32 minutes or until bubbly and topping is golden brown. Let stand for 15 minutes. Serve warm.

NUTRITION FACTS: 1 serving equals 216 calories, 4 g fat (1 g saturated fat), 2 mg cholesterol, 78 mg sodium, 46 g carbohydrate, 3 g fiber, 3 g protein.

Dark Chocolate Fondue
(PICTURED BELOW)

SALT

PREP/TOTAL TIME: 20 Min.   **YIELD:** 2 Cups

Savor all the decadence without a lick of guilt! Our Test Kitchen kept all the velvety, melt-in-your-mouth texture of fudgy fondue in this lusciously light version.

> 2 tablespoons all-purpose flour
> 1-1/2 cups 2% milk
> 2 dark chocolate candy bars (1.55 ounces *each*), chopped
> 3 squares (1 ounce *each*) milk chocolate, chopped
> 2 tablespoons light corn syrup
> Cubed angel food cake and assorted fresh fruit

In a small saucepan, combine flour and milk until smooth. Bring to a boil over medium-high heat; cook and stir for 1 minute or until thickened. Reduce heat to low. Stir in chocolate and corn syrup. Cook and stir until melted.

Transfer to a small fondue pot and keep warm. Serve with cake cubes and fruit.

NUTRITION FACTS: 1/4 cup (calculated without cake and fruit) equals 154 calories, 7 g fat (5 g saturated fat), 6 mg cholesterol, 29 mg sodium, 21 g carbohydrate, 1 g fiber, 2 g protein. **DIABETIC EXCHANGES:** 1-1/2 fat, 1 starch.

Plum Good Crisp
(PICTURED ABOVE)

SALT

PREP: 20 Min.   **BAKE:** 30 Min. + Standing   **YIELD:** 9 Servings

Here is a great crisp that goes well with any meal, but you can also serve it as a breakfast treat or snack. It combines interesting flavors. When it's warm, it can't be beat!
—Peter Halferty, Corpus Christi, Texas

> 4 cups sliced fresh plums (about 1-1/2 pounds)
> 3 medium nectarines, sliced
> 1-1/2 cups fresh blueberries
> 3 tablespoons brown sugar
> 2 tablespoons cornstarch
> 1/4 cup maple syrup
> 2 tablespoons lemon juice
> 1/4 teaspoon ground ginger
> 1/8 teaspoon ground nutmeg
> TOPPING:
> 1/2 cup all-purpose flour
> 1/2 cup old-fashioned oats
> 1/4 cup packed brown sugar
> 1/4 teaspoon salt
> 4 teaspoons unsweetened apple juice
> 4 teaspoons canola oil
> 1-1/2 teaspoons butter, melted

In a large bowl, combine the plums, nectarines and blueberries. Combine the brown sugar, cornstarch, syrup, lemon juice, ginger and nutmeg until smooth; drizzle over plum mixture and toss to coat. Transfer to an 11-in. x 7-in. x 2-in. baking dish coated with cooking spray.

For topping, in a small bowl, combine the flour, oats, brown sugar and salt. Stir in the apple juice, oil and butter until crumbly. Sprinkle over fruit mixture.

Creamy Banana-Berry Pie

(PICTURED ABOVE)

PREP: 30 Min. + Chilling   **YIELD:** 8 Servings

Cool, creamy and topped with bananas and blueberries, this pretty pie from our Test Kitchen is sure to melt all resistance to dessert!

> 1 sheet refrigerated pie pastry
> 1/4 cup chopped pecans
> 1-1/4 cups cold fat-free milk
> 1/2 cup reduced-fat sour cream

Sugar substitute equivalent to 1/4 cup sugar

> 1 package (.9 ounce) sugar-free instant banana pudding mix
> 2 cups reduced-fat whipped topping
> 1 tablespoon lemon juice
> 2 medium bananas
> 1/3 cup fresh blueberries

Unroll pastry on a lightly floured surface. Sprinkle with pecans; lightly roll pecans into pastry. Transfer to a 9-in. pie plate. Line unpricked pastry shell with a double thickness of heavy-duty foil. Bake at 450° for 8 minutes. Remove foil; bake 5 minutes longer. Cool on a wire rack.

In a small mixing bowl, combine the milk, sour cream and sugar substitute. Gradually whisk in pudding mix. Fold in whipped topping.

Place lemon juice in a bowl. Slice bananas into juice and stir gently to coat. Set aside 1/3 cup; spoon remaining banana slices into crust. Top with pudding mixture, blueberries and reserved bananas. Cover and refrigerate for 30 minutes.

NUTRITION FACTS: 1 piece equals 263 calories, 13 g fat (6 g saturated fat), 11 mg cholesterol, 266 mg sodium, 31 g carbohydrate, 1 g fiber, 4 g protein. **DIABETIC EXCHANGES:** 2 starch, 2 fat, 1/2 fruit.

Editor's Note: This recipe was tested with Splenda No Calorie Sweetener.

Black Forest Frozen Dessert

SALT

PREP: 40 Min. + Freezing   **YIELD:** 12 Servings

I think that the chocolate and cherries make a sweet taste combo in my layered icebox dessert.   —Ruth Lee, Troy, Ontario

> 1 cup crushed reduced-fat cream-filled chocolate sandwich cookies (about 10 cookies)
> 2 tablespoons butter, melted
> 1 can (15 ounces) pitted dark sweet cherries
> 2 cups black cherry-vanilla swirl frozen yogurt blend
> 3 cups reduced-fat chocolate ice cream, softened
> 1 tablespoon cornstarch
> 2 tablespoons lemon juice
> 3/4 cup reduced-fat whipped topping
> 12 mint sprigs

In a small bowl, combine cookies and butter. Press onto the bottom of a 9-in. springform pan coated with cooking spray. Place pan on a baking sheet. Bake at 350° for 8-10 minutes or until set. Cool on a wire rack.

Drain cherries, reserving syrup. Cover and refrigerate syrup. Chop half of the cherries; refrigerate whole cherries. Spread frozen yogurt evenly over crust; sprinkle with chopped cherries. Cover and freeze for 30 minutes. Spread ice cream over cherries; cover and freeze for 2 hours or until firm.

For sauce, in a small saucepan, combine cornstarch and reserved cherry syrup until smooth. Bring to a boil; cook and stir for 2 minutes or until thickened. Remove from the heat; stir in lemon juice and whole cherries.

Remove sides of springform pan; cut dessert into slices. Serve with sauce. Garnish with whipped topping and mint.

NUTRITION FACTS: 1 slice with 1 tablespoon sauce and 1 tablespoon whipped topping equals 193 calories, 7 g fat (4 g saturated fat), 23 mg cholesterol, 112 mg sodium, 31 g carbohydrate, 1 g fiber, 3 g protein. **DIABETIC EXCHANGES:** 2 starch, 1/2 fat.

Banana Brown Betty

PREP: 20 Min. **BAKE:** 15 Min. **YIELD:** 6 Servings

My three children used to go bananas over this delicious, down-home dessert flavored with a sunny splash of orange juice, brown sugar, bananas and cinnamon. —Kathleen Starcevich, Bremen, Indiana

  1 cup orange juice, *divided*
  3 tablespoons sugar
  1 tablespoon butter
  6 small firm bananas, cut into chunks
  6 tablespoons dry bread crumbs
TOPPING:
  1/3 cup quick-cooking oats
  3 tablespoons brown sugar
  1 teaspoon grated orange peel
  1/2 teaspoon ground cinnamon
  1/8 teaspoon salt
  3 tablespoons cold butter

In a large skillet, combine 1/4 cup orange juice, sugar and butter. Cook and stir over medium heat until light caramel in color, about 3 minutes. Remove from the heat. Add bananas and stir gently to combine.

Spoon half of banana mixture into six 6-oz. ramekins or custard cups coated with cooking spray. Sprinkle each with 1 tablespoon bread crumbs. Top with remaining banana mixture. Spoon 2 tablespoons remaining orange juice over each.

In a bowl, combine the oats, brown sugar, orange peel, cinnamon and salt; cut in butter until mixture resembles coarse crumbs. Sprinkle over bananas.

Place ramekins in a 15-in. x 10-in. x 1-in. baking pan. Bake at 400° for 15-20 minutes or until golden brown. Serve warm.

NUTRITION FACTS: 1 serving equals 272 calories, 9 g fat (5 g saturated fat), 20 mg cholesterol, 188 mg sodium, 49 g carbohydrate, 3 g fiber, 3 g protein.

TASTY TIP
When preparing her Banana Brown Betty, Kathleen Starcevich likes to juice fresh oranges for the juice that the recipe calls for. Not only does the home-squeezed juice lend an extra burst of citrus flavor, but Kathleen doesn't have to purchase orange juice or open a whole container for 1 cup.

Cookies 'n' Cream Berry Desserts

(PICTURED BELOW)

PREP: 10 Min. + Standing **YIELD:** 6 Servings

This sweet berry delight makes an especially pretty final course in the spring. With berries, a creamy topping and a sprinkle of meringue cookies, it always earns praise.
—Lillian Julow, Gainesville, Florida

  2 cups quartered fresh strawberries
1-1/4 cups fresh raspberries
1-1/4 cups fresh blackberries
  2/3 cup fresh blueberries
  4 tablespoons sugar, *divided*
  2 teaspoons lemon juice
  4 ounces reduced-fat cream cheese
1-1/2 cups fat-free whipped topping
Dash ground cinnamon
  12 miniature meringue cookies, quartered

In a large bowl, combine the berries, 2 tablespoons sugar and lemon juice; let stand at room temperature for 30 minutes.

In a small mixing bowl, beat cream cheese until smooth. Beat in the whipped topping, cinnamon and remaining sugar until combined. Just before serving, divide the berry mixture among six dessert dishes. Dollop with topping and sprinkle with cookies.

NUTRITION FACTS: 2/3 cup berries with 3 tablespoons topping and 2 cookies equals 179 calories, 4 g fat (3 g saturated fat), 13 mg cholesterol, 94 mg sodium, 32 g carbohydrate, 5 g fiber, 3 g protein. **DIABETIC EXCHANGES:** 1 starch, 1 fruit, 1 fat.

Watermelon Granita

(PICTURED BELOW)

PREP: 15 Min. + Freezing   **YIELD:** 8 Servings

Say a sweet "ciao" to summer with this four-ingredient Italian specialty from our Test Kitchen.

1-1/4 cups sugar
1-1/4 cups water
6 cups cubed watermelon
Small watermelon wedges, optional

In a small saucepan, bring sugar and water to a boil. Cook and stir until sugar is dissolved; set aside. In a blender, process watermelon in batches until smooth. Strain; discard pulp and seeds. Transfer to an 8-in. square dish; stir in sugar mixture. Cover and freeze overnight.

Remove from the freezer just before serving. Using a fork, scrape granita into serving glasses. Garnish with melon wedges if desired.

NUTRITION FACTS: 2/3 cup equals 151 calories, 0 fat (0 saturated fat), 0 cholesterol, 4 mg sodium, 41 g carbohydrate, 1 g fiber, trace protein.

Panna Cotta with Mixed Berries

SALT

PREP: 30 Min. + Chilling   **YIELD:** 6 Servings

Looking for something new to end meals? Panna cotta, Italian for "cooked cream," is a silky dessert. I serve mine with a sweet berry-wine sauce you won't soon forget! Once you have the basic recipe, however, you can come up with whatever topping you like best.
—Mary Bergfeld, Eugene, Oregon

1 envelope unflavored gelatin
3 cups whole milk
1/3 cup sugar
1/2 teaspoon almond extract
1 cup water
Sugar substitute equivalent to 1/2 cup sugar
2 cups frozen unsweetened mixed berries
1/2 cup port wine *or* grape juice

1/2 cup fresh raspberries
1/2 cup fresh blueberries

In a small saucepan, sprinkle gelatin over milk; let stand for 1 minute. Heat over low heat, stirring until gelatin is completely dissolved. Stir in sugar until dissolved. Stir in extract.

Pour into six 6-oz. ramekins or custard cups coated with cooking spray. Cover and refrigerate until set.

Meanwhile, in a small saucepan, bring water and sugar substitute to a boil. Add the frozen berries and wine or juice; return to a boil. Reduce heat; simmer, uncovered, for 5 minutes. Mash and strain berries, reserving juice. Discard seeds.

Return juice to the pan; bring to a boil. Reduce heat; simmer, uncovered, for 5-10 minutes or until sauce is reduced to 3/4 cup. Transfer to a bowl; cover and refrigerate until chilled.

Unmold panna cotta onto dessert plates. Serve with sauce and fresh berries.

NUTRITION FACTS: 1 serving equals 174 calories, 4 g fat (3 g saturated fat), 17 mg cholesterol, 64 mg sodium, 27 g carbohydrate, 2 g fiber, 6 g protein. **DIABETIC EXCHANGES:** 1 starch, 1/2 fruit, 1/2 milk.

Editor's Note: This recipe was tested with Splenda No Calorie Sweetener.

Spiced Apple Dessert

PREP: 20 Min.   **BAKE:** 25 Min.   **YIELD:** 9 Servings

Drizzled with warm caramel sauce, this classic and comforting, old-fashioned dessert is an heirloom recipe that was passed down from my great aunt. It's so good in wintertime.
—Anne Livingston, Evanston, Illinois

1 cup all-purpose flour
1 cup sugar
1 teaspoon baking soda
1 teaspoon ground cinnamon
1/4 teaspoon salt
1 egg, lightly beaten
2 cups shredded peeled tart apples (about 2 large)
1/4 cup chopped walnuts
CARAMEL SAUCE:
1/2 cup packed light brown sugar
2 tablespoons all-purpose flour
1/8 teaspoon salt
1 cup water
1 tablespoon butter
1/4 teaspoon vanilla extract

In a large bowl, combine the flour, sugar, baking soda, cinnamon and salt. Combine egg and apples; add to flour mixture and mix well. Stir in walnuts.

Transfer to an 8-in. square baking dish coated with cooking spray. Bake at 350° for 25-30 minutes or until a toothpick inserted near the center comes out clean.

For sauce, in a small nonstick saucepan, combine the brown sugar, flour and salt. Gradually add water; stir until smooth. Cook and stir over medium heat until mixture comes to a boil. Cook and stir 1-2 minutes longer or until thickened. Remove from the heat; stir in butter and vanilla. Serve with warm apple dessert.

NUTRITION FACTS: 1 piece with 2 tablespoons sauce equals 251 calories, 4 g fat (1 g saturated fat), 27 mg cholesterol, 264 mg sodium, 52 g carbohydrate, 2 g fiber, 3 g protein.

Favorite Recipe Made Lighter

THANKSGIVING isn't the same at Shirley Dellenger's Elwood, Indiana home until she serves her Pumpkin Cake. "I know how much everyone loves it, but I also know how much fat is in it."

The *Light & Tasty* home economists set out to cut not only fat but also calories and cholesterol from the devine dessert. They reduced the sugar and used only half the eggs, making up the difference with egg substitute.

Vegetable oil was replaced with half as much healthier canola oil and unsweetened applesauce. And a splash of buttermilk helped replace the moistness and tender texture lost with some of the oil.

Reduced-fat cream cheese was an easy and obvious substitution in the frosting. And using only half as much butter and a little less confectioners' sugar kept the creamy texture and taste intact.

The finished Makeover Pumpkin Cake is a winner! Packed with warm pumpkin flavor and spices, it's taller than the original cake but weighs in with just about half the fat, saturated fat and cholesterol and 187 fewer calories per piece. And if you ask us, that's sweet success no matter how you slice it!

Makeover Pumpkin Cake
(PICTURED ABOVE)

PREP: 25 Min. BAKE: 35 Min. + Cooling YIELD: 18 Servings

       1 can (15 ounces) solid-pack pumpkin
  1-2/3 cups sugar
       2 eggs
    1/2 cup egg substitute
    1/2 cup buttermilk
    1/2 cup canola oil
    1/4 cup unsweetened applesauce
       1 teaspoon vanilla extract
       2 cups all-purpose flour
       3 teaspoons ground cinnamon
       2 teaspoons baking soda
       1 teaspoon salt
    1/4 cup chopped pecans
FROSTING:
       1 package (8 ounces) reduced-fat cream cheese
    1/4 cup butter, softened
       3 cups confectioners' sugar
       2 teaspoons vanilla extract

In a large mixing bowl, combine the first eight ingredients; beat until well blended. Combine the flour, cinnamon, baking soda and salt; gradually beat into pumpkin mixture until blended. Stir in pecans.

Transfer to a 13-in. x 9-in. x 2-in. baking pan coated with cooking spray. Bake at 350° for 35-45 minutes or until a toothpick inserted near the center comes out clean. Cool cake on a wire rack.

For frosting, in a small mixing bowl, beat cream cheese and butter until fluffy. Add confectioners' sugar and vanilla; beat until smooth. Frost cake. Store in the refrigerator.

NUTRITION FACTS: 1 piece equals 345 calories, 13 g fat (4 g saturated fat), 40 mg cholesterol, 380 mg sodium, 53 g carbohydrate, 2 g fiber, 5 g protein.

Pumpkin Cake

PREP: 20 Min. BAKE: 40 Min. + Cooling YIELD: 18 Servings

       1 can (15 ounces) solid-pack pumpkin
       2 cups sugar
  1-1/2 cups vegetable oil
       4 eggs
       2 cups all-purpose flour
       3 teaspoons ground cinnamon
       2 teaspoons baking soda
       1 teaspoon salt
    1/2 cup chopped pecans
FROSTING:
       1 package (8 ounces) cream cheese, softened
    1/2 cup butter, softened
  3-3/4 cups confectioners' sugar
       2 teaspoons vanilla extract

In a large mixing bowl, beat the pumpkin, sugar, oil and eggs until well blended. Combine the flour, cinnamon, baking soda and salt; gradually beat into pumpkin mixture until blended. Stir in pecans.

Transfer to a greased 13-in. x 9-in. x 2-in. baking pan. Bake at 350° for 40-50 minutes or until a toothpick inserted near the center comes out clean. Cool on a wire rack.

For frosting, in a small mixing bowl, beat cream cheese and butter until fluffy. Add confectioners' sugar and vanilla; beat until smooth. Frost cake. Store in the refrigerator.

NUTRITION FACTS: 1 piece equals 532 calories, 31 g fat (9 g saturated fat), 75 mg cholesterol, 376 mg sodium, 61 g carbohydrate, 2 g fiber, 5 g protein.

Yummy Chocolate Cake

(PICTURED ABOVE)

PREP: 20 Min.   **BAKE:** 15 Min. + Cooling   **YIELD:** 16 Servings

*My husband and I are trying to eat lighter but still crave sweets.
This moist chocolate cake really helps with that. With the rich
frosting, it makes a decadent close to meals.*

—LaDonna Reed, Ponca City, Oklahoma

>   1 package (18-1/4 ounces) chocolate cake mix
>   1 package (2.1 ounces) sugar-free instant chocolate
>   pudding mix
> 1-3/4 cups water
>   3 egg whites

FROSTING:

> 1-1/4 cups cold fat-free milk
>   1/4 teaspoon almond extract
>   1 package (1.4 ounces) sugar-free instant chocolate
>   pudding mix
>   1 carton (8 ounces) frozen reduced-fat whipped topping,
>   thawed

Chocolate curls, optional

In a large mixing bowl, combine the cake mix, pudding mix,
water and egg whites. Beat on low speed for 1 minute; beat
on medium for 2 minutes.

Pour into a 15-in. x 10-in. x 1-in. baking pan coated with
cooking spray. Bake at 350° for 12-18 minutes or until a toothpick inserted near the center comes out clean. Cool on a wire
rack.

For frosting, place milk and extract in a large bowl. Sprinkle with a third of the pudding mix; let stand for 1 minute.
Whisk pudding into milk. Repeat twice with remaining pudding mix. Whisk pudding 2 minutes longer. Let stand for 15
minutes. Fold in whipped topping. Frost cake. Garnish with
chocolate curls if desired.

NUTRITION FACTS: 1 piece (calculated without chocolate curls) equals
197 calories, 5 g fat (3 g saturated fat), trace cholesterol, 409 mg sodium,
35 g carbohydrate, 1 g fiber, 3 g protein. **DIABETIC EXCHANGES:** 2
starch, 1/2 fat.

Chocolate Peanut Butter Bombes

(PICTURED BELOW)

PREP: 25 Min. + Freezing   **YIELD:** 8 Servings

*Kids of all ages will love these creamy frozen bombes with the
peanut butter "surprise" inside! The creative combo comes from
our Test Kitchen staff.*

>   1 package (8 ounces) fat-free cream cheese
>   3 tablespoons chocolate syrup
> 1/2 cup confectioners' sugar
>   1 carton (12 ounces) frozen reduced-fat whipped
>   topping, thawed
>   8 miniature peanut butter cups
> 1/2 cup fat-free hot fudge ice cream topping, warmed
>   2 tablespoons chopped salted peanuts

Line eight 6-oz. ramekins or custard cups with plastic wrap; set
aside. In a large mixing bowl, beat cream cheese and chocolate syrup until smooth. Beat in confectioners' sugar; fold in
whipped topping.

Spoon into prepared cups; insert a peanut butter cup into
the center of each. Cover and freeze for 4-5 hours or until firm.

Invert bombes into dessert dishes; remove cups and plastic wrap. Drizzle with hot fudge topping and sprinkle with
peanuts.

NUTRITION FACTS: 1 bombe equals 270 calories, 8 g fat (6 g saturated fat),
3 mg cholesterol, 224 mg sodium, 40 g carbohydrate, 1 g fiber, 7 g protein. **DIABETIC EXCHANGES:** 3 starch, 1 fat.

TASTY TIP
You can replace the peanut butter cups called for in
the bombes with another bite-size candy bar. Swap out
the hot fudge with low-fat caramel ice cream topping.

Apple Quince Pie
(PICTURED ABOVE)

PREP: 40 Min.   BAKE: 50 Min. + Cooling   YIELD: 8 Servings

Quince adds a sweet harvest flavor to this luscious, old-fashioned apple pie from our Test Kitchen. It's topped with a crumbly mix of oats, brown sugar, butter and cinnamon.

> 3 cups thinly sliced peeled quinces (about 2 medium)
> 1 can (5-1/2 ounces) unsweetened apple juice
> 1 teaspoon whole cloves

Pastry for single-crust pie (9 inches)

> 5 cups thinly sliced peeled tart apples (about 5 medium)
> 1/2 cup sugar
> 3 tablespoons all-purpose flour
> 1/2 teaspoon ground cinnamon
> 1/4 teaspoon salt
> 1/4 teaspoon ground nutmeg

TOPPING:

> 1/3 cup quick-cooking oats
> 2 tablespoons all-purpose flour
> 2 tablespoons brown sugar
> 1/4 teaspoon ground cinnamon
> 1 tablespoon cold butter

In a large saucepan, combine the quinces and apple juice. Place cloves on a double thickness of cheesecloth; bring up corners of cloth and tie with string to form a bag. Add to pan. Bring to a boil. Reduce heat; cover and simmer for 12-15 minutes or until quinces are crisp-tender.

Uncover; simmer 8-12 minutes longer or until liquid is reduced to 2 tablespoons. Discard spice bag. Cool for 5 minutes.

Line a 9-in. pie plate with pastry. Trim to 1/2 in. beyond edge of plate; flute edges. In a large bowl, combine the apples, sugar, flour, cinnamon, salt and nutmeg. Gently stir in quince mixture. Spoon into crust.

For topping, in a small bowl, combine the oats, flour, brown sugar and cinnamon; cut in butter until crumbly. Sprinkle over filling.

Bake at 375° for 50-60 minutes or until apples are tender and crust is golden brown. Cool on a wire rack.

NUTRITION FACTS: 1 piece equals 287 calories, 9 g fat (4 g saturated fat), 9 mg cholesterol, 191 mg sodium, 51 g carbohydrate, 2 g fiber, 2 g protein.

Lime 'n' Spice Peach Cobbler

(PICTURED BELOW)

PREP: 25 Min. **BAKE:** 35 Min. **YIELD:** 8 Servings

This was my grandmother's favorite recipe to make when peaches were in season. Now I bake it regularly for my family and friends.
—Mary Ann Dell, Phoenixville, Pennsylvania

8 medium peaches, peeled and sliced
3 tablespoons sugar
3 tablespoons brown sugar
2 tablespoons minced candied ginger
4-1/2 teaspoons cornstarch
1 tablespoon lime juice
2 teaspoons ground cinnamon
1/2 teaspoon grated lime peel
TOPPING:
1/4 cup packed brown sugar
2 tablespoons sugar
3 tablespoons butter, softened
1 cup cake flour
1/2 teaspoon baking powder
1/4 teaspoon salt
2 tablespoons cold water
1/4 cup chopped pecans
2 tablespoons buttermilk
1 egg yolk

In a large bowl, combine the first eight ingredients. Transfer to an 8-in. square baking dish coated with cooking spray.

For topping, in a small mixing bowl, beat sugars and butter until crumbly, about 2 minutes. Combine the flour, baking powder and salt; gradually add to butter mixture. Beat in water just until moistened (mixture will be crumbly). Stir in pecans. Crumble over fruit mixture.

Combine buttermilk and egg yolk; drizzle over topping. Bake at 375° for 35-40 minutes or until filling is bubbly and topping is golden brown. Serve warm.

NUTRITION FACTS: 1 serving equals 275 calories, 8 g fat (3 g saturated fat), 38 mg cholesterol, 155 mg sodium, 51 g carbohydrate, 3 g fiber, 3 g protein.

Chocolate Cream Delight

(PICTURED ABOVE)

PREP: 30 Min. + Chilling **YIELD:** 9 Servings

It's wonderful to have so many sugar-free and reduced-fat products to work with today. This after-dinner specialty satisfies our chocolate cravings and is easy to double for guests.
—Wanda Benda, Jackson, Minnesota

1 cup chocolate wafer crumbs
1 tablespoon sugar
2 tablespoons butter, melted
2 packages (1.3 ounces each) sugar-free cook-and-serve chocolate pudding mix
3-1/2 cups fat-free milk
3 ounces reduced-fat cream cheese, cubed
2 cups reduced-fat whipped topping
2 tablespoons chopped pecans

In a small bowl, combine the wafer crumbs, sugar and butter; press onto the bottom of an 8-in. square dish coated with cooking spray. Cover and refrigerate.

In a large saucepan, combine the pudding mixes and milk until smooth. Bring to a boil, stirring constantly. Remove from the heat; cool slightly.

Spread half of the pudding over crust. Stir cream cheese into remaining pudding until smooth; gently spread over pudding layer. Cover and refrigerate for at least 2 hours or until set.

Spread whipped topping over dessert. Sprinkle with pecans. Cut into squares.

NUTRITION FACTS: 1 piece equals 211 calories, 10 g fat (6 g saturated fat), 16 mg cholesterol, 276 mg sodium, 25 g carbohydrate, 1 g fiber, 6 g protein. **DIABETIC EXCHANGES:** 2 fat, 1-1/2 starch.

Favorite Recipe Made Lighter

AFTER A BITE of Geri Frahm's Moist Carrot Cake, you'll be on cloud nine. The only one problem is that one slice of cake has 32 grams of fat. "Can you make it over for a healthier recipe?" she asked from Gretna, Nebraska.

Much of the cake's moisture was from oil, so our staff replaced some of it with applesauce. The most difficult part of the makeover, however, involved the frosting.

The team tried several versions and finally succeeded with a combination of reduced-fat and full-fat cream cheeses.

These steps resulted in the oh-so-decadent Makeover Moist Carrot Cake. An amazing 215 calories and 17 grams of fat have been removed from each slice. But don't worry, each slice is so wonderful, you won't feel like you're missing a thing!

Moist Carrot Cake

PREP: 35 Min.   **BAKE:** 1 Hour + Cooling   **YIELD:** 16 Servings

- 1-1/2 cups sugar
- 1/2 cup packed brown sugar
- 1-1/2 cups vegetable oil
- 3 eggs
- 2 teaspoons vanilla extract
- 2-1/2 cups all-purpose flour
- 2 teaspoons baking powder
- 2 teaspoons ground cinnamon
- 1/2 teaspoon salt
- 1/2 teaspoon baking soda
- 2 cups shredded carrots
- 1 can (8 ounces) unsweetened crushed pineapple, drained
- 1 cup golden raisins
- 1 cup chopped walnuts

FROSTING:
- 1 package (8 ounces) cream cheese, softened
- 1 tablespoon margarine, softened
- 1 teaspoon vanilla extract
- 3-3/4 cups confectioners' sugar

In a large mixing bowl, beat the sugars, oil, eggs and vanilla until well blended. Combine the flour, baking powder, cinnamon, salt and baking soda; gradually beat into sugar mixture until blended. Stir in the carrots, pineapple, raisins and walnuts.

Transfer to a greased 10-in. fluted tube pan. Bake at 350° for 60-70 minutes or until a toothpick inserted near the center comes out clean. Cool for 10 minutes before removing from pan to wire rack to cool completely.

For frosting, in a large mixing bowl, beat cream cheese, margarine and vanilla until fluffy. Beat in confectioners' sugar until smooth. Frost cake. Store in the refrigerator.

NUTRITION FACTS: 1 slice equals 621 calories, 32 g fat (6 g saturated fat), 55 mg cholesterol, 235 mg sodium, 81 g carbohydrate, 2 g fiber, 7 g protein.

Makeover Moist Carrot Cake

(PICTURED ABOVE)

PREP: 35 Min.   **BAKE:** 45 Min. + Cooling   **YIELD:** 16 Servings

- 1-1/3 cups sugar
- 1/2 cup packed brown sugar
- 1 cup unsweetened applesauce
- 1/2 cup canola oil
- 2 eggs
- 2 egg whites
- 2 teaspoons vanilla extract
- 2-1/2 cups all-purpose flour
- 2 teaspoons baking powder
- 2 teaspoons ground cinnamon
- 1/2 teaspoon salt
- 1/2 teaspoon baking soda
- 2 cups shredded carrots
- 1 can (8 ounces) unsweetened crushed pineapple, drained
- 1/2 cup golden raisins
- 1/2 cup finely chopped walnuts

FROSTING:
- 5 ounces reduced-fat cream cheese
- 1 package (3 ounces) cream cheese, softened
- 1 teaspoon vanilla extract
- 2 cups confectioners' sugar
- 1/4 cup finely chopped walnuts, toasted

In a large mixing bowl, beat the sugars, applesauce, oil, eggs, egg whites and vanilla until well blended. Combine the flour, baking powder, cinnamon, salt and baking soda; gradually beat into sugar mixture until blended. Stir in the carrots, pineapple, raisins and walnuts.

Transfer to a 10-in. fluted tube pan coated with cooking spray. Bake at 350° for 45-55 minutes or until a toothpick inserted near the center comes out clean. Cool for 10 minutes before removing from pan to wire rack to cool completely.

For frosting, in a large mixing bowl, beat cream cheeses and vanilla until fluffy. Beat in confectioners' sugar until smooth. Frost cake. Sprinkle with walnuts. Store in the refrigerator.

NUTRITION FACTS: 1 slice equals 406 calories, 15 g fat (3 g saturated fat), 39 mg cholesterol, 240 mg sodium, 64 g carbohydrate, 2 g fiber, 6 g protein.

Hot Berries 'n' Brownie Ice Cream Cake

(PICTURED ABOVE)

PREP: 20 Min.   **BAKE:** 30 Min. + Freezing   **YIELD:** 24 Servings

This decadent dessert is a taste of heaven. The hot mixed berry topping seeps through the brownie layer into the cool vanilla ice cream for an incredible icebox cake.

—Allene Bary-Cooper, Ramona, Oklahoma

   1 package fudge brownie mix (13-inch x 9-inch pan size)

1/4 cup water

1/4 cup unsweetened applesauce

1/4 cup canola oil

   2 eggs

   1 carton (1-3/4 quarts) reduced-fat no-sugar-added vanilla ice cream, softened

BERRY SAUCE:

   2 tablespoons butter

1/3 cup sugar

1/4 cup honey

   2 tablespoons lime juice

   1 tablespoon balsamic vinegar

   1 teaspoon ground cinnamon

1/4 to 1/2 teaspoon cayenne pepper

   1 quart fresh strawberries, hulled and sliced

   2 cups fresh blueberries

   2 cups fresh raspberries

Prepare brownie mix using water, applesauce, oil and eggs. Bake according to package directions; cool completely on a wire rack.

Crumble brownies into 1-in. pieces; sprinkle half into a 13-in. x 9-in. x 2-in. dish coated with cooking spray. Spread evenly with ice cream. Press remaining brownie pieces into ice cream. Cover and freeze for 1 hour or until firm.

Remove from the freezer 5 minutes before serving. For sauce, in a large skillet, melt butter over medium heat. Stir in the sugar, honey, lime juice, vinegar, cinnamon and cayenne. Add berries; cook for 3-5 minutes or until heated through, stirring occasionally. Cut cake into squares; top with hot berry sauce.

NUTRITION FACTS: 1 piece with 3 tablespoons berry sauce equals 233 calories, 9 g fat (3 g saturated fat), 27 mg cholesterol, 140 mg sodium, 36 g carbohydrate, 2 g fiber, 4 g protein. **DIABETIC EXCHANGES:** 2 starch, 1-1/2 fat, 1/2 fruit.

Clementine Tapioca

PREP: 25 Min. + Chilling   **YIELD:** 4 Servings

Because tapioca doesn't have a lot of flavor on its own, the L&T Test Kitchen used nutmeg, vanilla extract and clementines to jazz up the dessert.

   2 cups fat-free milk

1/4 cup quick-cooking tapioca

3 tablespoons sugar

1/2 teaspoon vanilla extract

1/8 teaspoon ground nutmeg

1/2 cup clementine juice (about 5 clementines)

1/2 cup reduced-fat whipped topping

2 clementines, peeled and sectioned

In a small saucepan, combine the milk, tapioca and sugar; let stand for 5 minutes. Cook and stir over medium heat until mixture comes to a full boil. Transfer to a small bowl; stir in vanilla and nutmeg. Cool for 20 minutes. Stir in clementine juice; cover and refrigerate until chilled.

Fold in whipped topping. Spoon into four dessert dishes, 2/3 cup in each. Top with clementine segments.

NUTRITION FACTS: 1 serving equals 176 calories, 1 g fat (1 g saturated fat), 2 mg cholesterol, 64 mg sodium, 36 g carbohydrate, 1 g fiber, 5 g protein.

Cranberry Pecan Bars
(PICTURED BELOW RIGHT)

PREP: 30 Min.　**BAKE:** 30 Min. + Cooling　**YIELD:** 1 Dozen

I have relied on these bars for almost 40 years. The yummy treats are great with vanilla ice cream. Try them for bake sales, potluck dinners or after-school snacks. You can even add the bars to holiday cookie trays. They are just wonderful with a hot cup of coffee or tea.　　　—Sandra Bunte, Covina, California

3/4 cup all-purpose flour

3/4 cup quick-cooking oats

1/3 cup packed brown sugar

1/3 cup butter, melted

FILLING:

1 package (12 ounces) fresh *or* frozen cranberries

1/2 cup cranberry juice, *divided*

1/2 cup golden raisins

1/3 cup honey

Sugar substitute equivalent to 3 tablespoons sugar

1/2 teaspoon ground cinnamon

1/4 teaspoon ground cloves

1/2 teaspoon cornstarch

1/4 cup chopped pecans

In a small bowl, combine the flour, oats and brown sugar. Stir in butter until blended. Set aside 2/3 cup. Pat remaining mixture onto the bottom of a 9-in. square baking pan coated with cooking spray; set aside.

In a small saucepan, combine the cranberries, 7 tablespoons cranberry juice, raisins, honey, sugar substitute, cinnamon and cloves. Cook and stir over medium heat for 10-12 minutes or until berries pop. Combine the cornstarch and remaining cranberry juice until smooth; stir into berry mixture. Bring to a boil; cook and stir for 1-2 minutes or until thickened.

Pour filling over crust. Sprinkle with pecans and reserved oat mixture. Bake at 350° for 30-35 minutes or until lightly browned. Cool on a wire rack. Cut into squares. Store in the refrigerator.

NUTRITION FACTS: 1 bar equals 199 calories, 7 g fat (3 g saturated fat), 14 mg cholesterol, 56 mg sodium, 33 g carbohydrate, 2 g fiber, 2 g protein.
DIABETIC EXCHANGES: 1 starch, 1 fruit, 1 fat.

Editor's Note: This recipe was tested with Splenda No Calorie Sweetener.

Frosty Chocolate Treat

PREP: 10 Min. + Freezing　**YIELD:** About 3-1/2 Quarts

This recipe has been in our family for many years. The thing we like most about it is that if you have any left over, which we rarely do, you can place it in the freezer and it will stay slightly soft.
　　　—Juanita Michael, Florence, Alabama

1/2 gallon 2% chocolate milk

1 can (14 ounces) fat-free sweetened condensed milk

1 teaspoon vanilla extract

1 carton (16 ounces) frozen reduced-fat whipped topping, thawed

In a large bowl, whisk the chocolate milk, condensed milk and vanilla. Whisk in whipped topping until combined. Fill cylinder of ice cream freezer two-thirds full; freeze according to manufacturer's directions.

Refrigerate remaining mixture until ready to freeze. Transfer to freezer containers; freeze for 2-4 hours before serving.

NUTRITION FACTS: 3/4 cup equals 198 calories, 5 g fat (4 g saturated fat), 9 mg cholesterol, 90 mg sodium, 30 g carbohydrate, 1 g fiber, 6 g protein.

Favorite Recipe Made Lighter

AT GATHERINGS certain desserts are often expected. But as those at the table grow older, some cooks worry that their luscious traditions might not fit into everyone's special dietary needs.

Cindy Evanoff of Louisville, Ohio was as determined to please her family as she was to end her heavy holiday meals on a lighter note. So she wrote our Test Kitchen for help in slimming down her family's favorite dessert—French Silk Pie.

We began by using similar ingredients...just lighter versions and fewer of them. The flavor wasn't bad, but the texture needed work. We soon realized this recipe would call for a completely reformulated approach. As such, we tried and tried again.

Some 10 attempts later, we finally hit the jackpot! How? We decreased the butter and sugar, used only egg yolks but fewer of them, and added fat-free milk, whipped topping, gelatin and cornstarch.

We ended up with a chocolaty, smooth and creamy dream of a makeover that mimics Cindy's original recipe in everything but calories, fat and cholesterol. Even our taste-testing panel had a hard time believing this fantastic makeover, with nearly 200 fewer calories and half the fat and saturated fat, wasn't the original recipe!

Bite into a piece of our Makeover French Silk Pie and we think you'll agree: This is one delectable dessert. Perfect for holidays and special menus, it's a dessert that all of your family members can celebrate!

French Silk Pie

PREP: 50 Min. + Chilling   YIELD: 8 Servings

Pastry for single-crust pie (9 inches)
- 4 eggs, beaten
- 1-1/2 cups sugar
- 2 teaspoons vanilla extract
- 1 cup butter, softened
- 1/4 cup baking cocoa

Line a 9-in. pie plate with pastry; trim and flute edges. Line pastry shell with a double thickness of heavy-duty foil. Bake at 450° for 8 minutes. Remove foil; bake 5 minutes longer. Cool on a wire rack.

In a small saucepan, combine eggs and sugar until blended. Cook over low heat, stirring constantly, until mixture reaches 160° and coats the back of a metal spoon. Remove from the heat; stir in vanilla. Cool to lukewarm (about 90°), stirring occasionally.

In a large mixing bowl, beat butter until light and fluffy. Beat in cocoa until blended. Add the cooled sugar mixture; beat on high speed for 5 minutes. Spread evenly into crust. Refrigerate for 4-6 hours before serving. Refrigerate leftovers.

NUTRITION FACTS: 1 piece equals 513 calories, 32 g fat (18 g saturated fat), 173 mg cholesterol, 363 mg sodium, 52 g carbohydrate, 1 g fiber, 5 g protein.

Makeover French Silk Pie

(PICTURED ABOVE)

PREP: 50 Min. + Chilling   YIELD: 8 Servings

Pastry for single-crust pie (9 inches)
- 1-1/2 teaspoons unflavored gelatin
- 1-1/4 cups cold fat-free milk, *divided*
- 2/3 cup sugar
- 1/4 cup cornstarch
- 1/4 cup baking cocoa
- 3 egg yolks
- 3 tablespoons butter
- 2 teaspoons vanilla extract
- 1-1/2 cups whipped topping
Chocolate curls, optional

Line a 9-in. pie plate with pastry; trim and flute edges. Line pastry shell with a double thickness of heavy-duty foil. Bake at 450° for 8 minutes. Remove foil; bake 5 minutes longer. Cool on a wire rack.

In a small heavy saucepan, sprinkle gelatin over 1 cup milk; let stand for 1 minute. Cook over medium-low heat until bubbles form around sides of pan. Meanwhile, sift the sugar, cornstarch and cocoa into a small bowl. Combine egg yolks and remaining milk; whisk into sugar mixture until blended.

Add a small amount of hot milk mixture to sugar mixture; return all to the pan, whisking constantly. Whisk vigorously over medium heat as mixture begins to thicken (mixture will become very thick). Bring to a boil; whisk 2 minutes longer. Remove from the heat; whisk in butter and vanilla.

Transfer to a large metal mixing bowl. Lightly coat waxed paper with cooking spray; press onto surface of cocoa mixture. Refrigerate for 45-60 minutes or until mixture reaches 80°.

Beat the cocoa mixture on high speed for 3-4 minutes or until smooth and glossy, scraping sides of bowl occasionally. Fold in whipped topping. Spread evenly into crust. Refrigerate for 2 hours. Garnish with chocolate curls if desired. Cover leftovers tightly with foil; store in the refrigerator.

NUTRITION FACTS: 1 piece (calculated without chocolate curls) equals 322 calories, 16 g fat (9 g saturated fat), 97 mg cholesterol, 167 mg sodium, 40 g carbohydrate, 1 g fiber, 4 g protein.

Citrus Berry Sherbet

(PICTURED BELOW RIGHT)

FAT SALT

PREP: 25 Min. + Freezing   **YIELD:** 1 Quart

When you serve this fruity sherbet, no one will guess it's light. It certainly doesn't taste like any "diet" food I've ever eaten! With a burst of strawberry and citrus flavors, it's a great way to top off a summer meal. —Wilma Jones, Mobile, Alabama

    3 teaspoons unflavored gelatin
1-1/2 cups cold orange juice
   1/3 cup sugar
    3 tablespoons lemon juice
    1 tablespoon grated lemon peel
1-1/2 pounds fresh *or* frozen strawberries
   3/4 cup unsweetened applesauce

In a small saucepan, sprinkle gelatin over orange juice; let stand for 1 minute. Stir in the sugar, lemon juice and peel. Cook over low heat, stirring until gelatin and sugar are completely dissolved. Remove from the heat; cool for 10 minutes.

Place the strawberries and applesauce in a blender. Add gelatin mixture; cover and process until smooth. Pour into a shallow freezer container. Cover and freeze for 1 to 1-1/2 hours or until partially set.

Transfer to a large mixing bowl; beat on medium speed for 2 minutes. Return to the freezer container; freeze 2-3 hours longer or until firm. Remove from the freezer 10 minutes before serving.

NUTRITION FACTS: 3/4 cup equals 130 calories, trace fat (trace saturated fat), 0 cholesterol, 6 mg sodium, 32 g carbohydrate, 3 g fiber, 2 g protein. **DIABETIC EXCHANGES:** 1 starch, 1 fruit.

Rich Peach Ice Cream

(PICTURED AT FAR RIGHT)

FAT SALT

PREP: 15 Min. + Freezing   **YIELD:** 4 Quarts

Our family loves ice cream, and this homemade version is a favorite. I created the recipe to use up homegrown fruit.
—Catherine MacRae Lyerly, Winston-Salem, North Carolina

2 cups cold fat-free milk
1 package (3.4 ounces) instant vanilla pudding mix
4 medium peaches, peeled and chopped
2 cans (12 ounces *each*) fat-free evaporated milk
1 can (14 ounces) sweetened condensed milk
1/2 cup sugar
1/4 cup lemon juice
1 teaspoon vanilla extract
1/2 teaspoon almond extract
1/8 teaspoon salt
1 carton (8 ounces) fat-free frozen whipped topping, thawed

In a large mixing bowl, beat milk and pudding mix on low speed for 2 minutes. Beat in the peaches, evaporated milk, condensed milk, sugar, lemon juice, extracts and salt. Beat in whipped topping just until combined.

Fill cylinder of ice cream freezer two-thirds full; freeze according to manufacturer's directions. Refrigerate remaining mixture until ready to freeze. Transfer to freezer containers; freeze for 2-4 hours before serving.

NUTRITION FACTS: 2/3 cup equals 140 calories, 2 g fat (1 g saturated fat), 7 mg cholesterol, 139 mg sodium, 27 g carbohydrate, trace fiber, 4 g protein. **DIABETIC EXCHANGES:** 1-1/2 starch, 1/2 fat.

Sour Cherry Sorbet

(PICTURED BELOW)

FAT

PREP: 10 Min. + Freezing   **YIELD:** 6 Servings

My mother-in-law has a sour cherry tree in her yard that yields many quarts of cherries each June, and this is a great way to take advantage of them. —Carol Gaus, Itasca, Illinois

3 cups frozen pitted tart cherries
1 cup sugar
1/3 cup white wine *or* grape juice
1/2 teaspoon almond extract
1/2 teaspoon salt

Place cherries in a food processor; cover and process until smooth. Add remaining ingredients; cover and pulse until blended. Pour into a freezer container. Cover and freeze until firm.

NUTRITION FACTS: 1/3 cup equals 175 calories, trace fat (trace saturated fat), 0 cholesterol, 198 mg sodium, 42 g carbohydrate, 1 g fiber, 1 g protein.

Pumpkin Cheesecake Bars

(PICTURED AT LEFT)

PREP: 15 Min. **BAKE:** 35 Min. + Chilling **YIELD:** 20 Bars

These bars are absolutely delightful and easy to make. They are a fun alternative to pumpkin pie.
—Sharon Kurtz, Emmaus, Pennsylvania

  2 cups graham cracker crumbs
1/4 cup sugar
1/4 cup reduced-fat butter, melted
FILLING:
  2 packages (8 ounces *each*) reduced-fat cream cheese
  1 package (8 ounces) fat-free cream cheese
3/4 cup sugar
  1 can (15 ounces) solid-pack pumpkin
  2 tablespoons all-purpose flour
3/4 teaspoon pumpkin pie spice
3/4 teaspoon vanilla extract
  2 eggs, lightly beaten
20 walnut halves

In a small bowl, combine cracker crumbs and sugar; stir in butter. Press onto the bottom of a 13-in. x 9-in. x 2-in. baking dish coated with cooking spray. Cover and refrigerate for at least 15 minutes.

In a large mixing bowl, beat cream cheese and sugar until smooth. Beat in the pumpkin, flour, pie spice and vanilla. Add eggs; beat on low speed just until combined. Pour over crust.

Bake at 325° for 35-45 minutes or until center is almost set. Cool on a wire rack for 1 hour. Cover and refrigerate for 8 hours or overnight.

Cut cheesecake into 20 bars; top each with a walnut half.

NUTRITION FACTS: 1 bar equals 186 calories, 9 g fat (5 g saturated fat), 42 mg cholesterol, 230 mg sodium, 21 g carbohydrate, 1 g fiber, 6 g protein. **DIABETIC EXCHANGES:** 1-1/2 starch, 1-1/2 fat.

Editor's Note: This recipe was tested with Land O'Lakes light stick butter.

Cranberry Rhubarb Upside-Down Cake

PREP: 20 Min. + Standing **BAKE:** 40 Min. **YIELD:** 12 Servings

With a few alterations over the years, this has become one of my families' most-requested desserts. I'm asked for the recipe every time I make it for guests. —Toni Fohey, Waukesha, Wisconsin

1/2 cup quick-cooking oats
2/3 cup boiling water
  2 tablespoons butter, melted
1/3 cup plus 1/2 cup packed brown sugar, *divided*
  1 cup fresh *or* frozen cranberries, coarsely chopped
  1 cup chopped fresh *or* frozen rhubarb
  1 egg
1/2 cup sugar
1/4 cup canola oil
  1 cup all-purpose flour
  1 teaspoon baking powder
1/2 teaspoon ground cinnamon
1/4 teaspoon salt
1/4 cup chopped walnuts, toasted

Place oats in a small bowl; add boiling water. Cover and let stand for 20 minutes. Meanwhile, pour butter into an 8-in. square baking dish coated with cooking spray; sprinkle with 1/3 cup brown sugar. Add cranberries and rhubarb.

In a large mixing bowl, beat the egg, sugar, oil and remaining brown sugar. Stir in oat mixture. Combine the flour, baking powder, cinnamon and salt; gradually beat into egg mixture until blended. Fold in walnuts. Spoon over fruit.

Bake at 350° for 40-45 minutes or until a toothpick inserted near the center comes out clean. Immediately invert onto a serving plate. Serve warm.

NUTRITION FACTS: 1 piece equals 227 calories, 9 g fat (2 g saturated fat), 23 mg cholesterol, 114 mg sodium, 35 g carbohydrate, 1 g fiber, 3 g protein. **DIABETIC EXCHANGES:** 2 starch, 2 fat.

Applesauce Bars

SALT ▼

PREP: 15 Min. **BAKE:** 20 Min. + Cooling **YIELD:** 20 Bars

This low-cholesterol treat couldn't be easier to make or better to eat! Applesauce creates a moist texture without the fat of oil, and sweet golden raisins complement the cinnamon-spice flavor.
—Stephanie Bosma, Madison, Indiana

    1 cup sugar
    1 cup unsweetened applesauce
  1/4 cup canola oil
    2 cups all-purpose flour
1-1/4 teaspoons baking powder
    1 teaspoon ground cinnamon
  1/2 teaspoon salt
  1/4 teaspoon baking soda
  1/4 teaspoon ground nutmeg
  1/4 teaspoon ground cloves
    1 cup golden raisins
GLAZE:
    1 cup confectioners' sugar
    1 tablespoon butter, melted
  1/2 teaspoon vanilla extract
    2 to 3 tablespoons fat-free milk

In a large mixing bowl, beat the sugar, applesauce and oil until well blended. In a small bowl, combine the flour, baking powder, cinnamon, salt, baking soda, nutmeg and cloves; gradually beat into sugar mixture until blended. Stir in raisins.

Transfer to a 13-in. x 9-in. x 2-in. baking pan coated with cooking spray. Bake at 350° for 20-25 minutes or until a toothpick inserted near the center comes out clean.

In a small mixing bowl, beat the confectioners' sugar, butter, vanilla and enough milk to achieve a glaze consistency. Spread over warm bars. Cool on a wire rack. Cut into bars.

NUTRITION FACTS: 1 bar equals 166 calories, 4 g fat (1 g saturated fat), 2 mg cholesterol, 108 mg sodium, 33 g carbohydrate, 1 g fiber, 2 g protein. **DIABETIC EXCHANGES:** 2 starch, 1/2 fat.

TASTY TIP
Dress up the Applesauce Bars by garnishing individual servings with thin slices of apples. Use green, yellow and red apples, leaving the skin on for a bit of color.

Crunchy Peach-Blueberry Crisp
(PICTURED BELOW)

PREP: 20 Min. **BAKE:** 20 Min. **YIELD:** 4 Servings

A friend of mine gave me this recipe. To make it healthier, I cut down a bit on the butter in the topping and substituted fat-free vanilla frozen yogurt.
—Lillian Charves, New Bern, North Carolina

    3 medium peaches, peeled and sliced
    1 cup fresh blueberries
    1 tablespoon cornstarch
    2 tablespoons orange juice
    2 teaspoons lemon juice
TOPPING:
  1/4 cup Grape-Nuts
  1/4 cup quick-cooking oats
    3 tablespoons brown sugar
    1 tablespoon butter, melted
  1/8 teaspoon salt
  1/8 teaspoon ground cinnamon
    1 cup fat-free vanilla frozen yogurt

In a small bowl, combine the peaches, blueberries and cornstarch. Transfer to an ungreased 1-qt. baking dish. Combine juices; drizzle over fruit.

For the topping, in a small bowl, combine the Grape-Nuts, oats, brown sugar, butter, salt and cinnamon. Sprinkle over the fruit mixture.

Bake at 375° for 20-25 minutes or until topping is golden brown and fruit is tender. Serve warm with frozen yogurt.

NUTRITION FACTS: 1 serving with 1/4 cup frozen yogurt equals 226 calories, 4 g fat (2 g saturated fat), 8 mg cholesterol, 184 mg sodium, 46 g carbohydrate, 4 g fiber, 5 g protein.

Cranberry Pear Crisp

(PICTURED ABOVE)

PREP: 20 Min. **BAKE:** 30 Min. **YIELD:** 8 Servings

A dollop of frozen yogurt tames the tart cranberries in this treasured crisp. I don't recall just where I found it, but it's been a family favorite for at least 20 years. —Ruth Fox, Elmhurst, Illinois

- 1 package (12 ounces) fresh *or* frozen cranberries, thawed
- 2 large pears, peeled and sliced

Sugar substitute equivalent to 1/2 cup sugar

- 1/4 cup sugar
- 6 teaspoons all-purpose flour, *divided*
- 3/4 teaspoon ground cinnamon
- 1/3 cup old-fashioned oats
- 2 tablespoons brown sugar
- 2 tablespoons cold butter
- 1/4 cup chopped walnuts
- 1 cup fat-free frozen vanilla yogurt

In a large bowl, combine cranberries and pears. Combine the sugar substitute, sugar, 1 teaspoon flour and cinnamon; sprinkle over cranberry mixture and toss to coat. Transfer to an 8-in. square baking dish coated with cooking spray.

In a small bowl, combine the oats, brown sugar and remaining flour. Cut in butter until crumbly; stir in walnuts. Sprinkle over cranberry mixture.

Bake, uncovered, at 375° for 30-35 minutes or until topping is golden brown and pears are tender. Serve warm with frozen yogurt.

SALT ▼

NUTRITION FACTS: 1 serving equals 187 calories, 6 g fat (2 g saturated fat), 8 mg cholesterol, 47 mg sodium, 33 g carbohydrate, 4 g fiber, 3 g protein. **DIABETIC EXCHANGES:** 1 starch, 1 fruit, 1 fat.

Editor's Note: This recipe was tested with Splenda No Calorie Sweetener.

Little Orange Dream Cups

PREP: 30 Min. + Chilling **YIELD:** 1 Dozen

Our Test Kitchen used a combination of fat-free and reduced-fat dairy products for these creamy orange-flavored cups.

- 1 envelope unflavored gelatin
- 3/4 cup fat-free milk
- 1 package (8 ounces) fat-free cream cheese
- 1 cup (8 ounces) reduced-fat sour cream

Sugar substitute equivalent to 1/4 cup sugar

- 3/4 teaspoon grated orange peel
- 1/2 teaspoon vanilla extract
- 1 carton (8 ounces) frozen reduced-fat whipped topping, thawed, *divided*
- 12 chocolate wafers

In a small saucepan, sprinkle gelatin over milk; let stand for 1 minute. Heat over low heat, stirring until gelatin is completely dissolved. Remove from the heat; cool slightly.

In a mixing bowl, beat the cream cheese, sour cream, sugar substitute, orange peel and vanilla until smooth. Gradually beat in the gelatin mixture. Fold in 2 cups whipped topping.

Place chocolate wafers in foil-lined muffin cups. Top each

with 1/2 cup cream cheese mixture. Refrigerate for 2 hours or until set. Gently remove foil just before serving; garnish with remaining whipped topping.

NUTRITION FACTS: 1 dessert with about 1 tablespoon whipped topping equals 123 calories, 5 g fat (4 g saturated fat), 9 mg cholesterol, 160 mg sodium, 12 g carbohydrate, trace fiber, 5 g protein. **DIABETIC EXCHANGES:** 1 starch, 1 fat.

Editor's Note: This recipe was tested with Splenda No Calorie Sweetener.

Chocolate Banana Cheesecake

PREP: 30 Min. **BAKE:** 30 Min. + Chilling **YIELD:** 16 Servings

I came up with this special treat for my son, who loves cheesecake and anything with bananas. The lightened recipe quickly became a family favorite! —Eileen Sears, Eagle, Wisconsin

   1 cup chocolate graham cracker crumbs (about 5 whole crackers)
   1 tablespoon sugar
   3 tablespoons butter, melted
FILLING:
   3 packages (8 ounces *each*) reduced-fat cream cheese
  2/3 cup sugar
   1 egg, lightly beaten
   3 egg whites, lightly beaten
  1/2 cup mashed ripe banana
  1/2 cup miniature semisweet chocolate chips
   1 teaspoon vanilla extract
   3 tablespoons baking cocoa
   1 tablespoon canola oil

In a small bowl, combine cracker crumbs and sugar; stir in butter. Set aside 1/4 cup for topping. Press remaining crumb mixture onto the bottom of a 9-in. springform pan coated with cooking spray. Place on a baking sheet. Bake at 350° for 7-9 minutes or until set. Cool on a wire rack.

In a large mixing bowl, beat cream cheese and sugar until smooth. Add egg and egg whites; beat on low speed just until combined. Gently stir in the banana, chocolate chips and vanilla. Pour half of the batter over crust.

Combine cocoa and oil until blended; stir into remaining batter. Drop by tablespoonfuls over batter in pan; gently spread into an even layer. Sprinkle with reserved crumb mixture.

Place pan on a double thickness of heavy-duty foil (about 18 in. square). Securely wrap foil around pan. Place in a large baking pan; add 1 in. of hot water to larger pan.

Bake at 350° for 30-35 minutes or just until center is set. Remove pan from water bath. Cool on a wire rack for 10 minutes. Carefully run a knife around edge of pan to loosen; cool 1 hour longer. Refrigerate overnight. Remove sides of pan before cutting.

NUTRITION FACTS: 1 slice equals 231 calories, 15 g fat (9 g saturated fat), 49 mg cholesterol, 246 mg sodium, 20 g carbohydrate, 1 g fiber, 6 g protein.

Mixed Berry Cake
(PICTURED RIGHT)

PREP: 15 Min. **BAKE:** 35 Min. + Cooling **YIELD:** 8 Servings

Even in the dead of winter I serve up the fabulous flavor of summer-fresh fruit with this yummy cake. Use sliced strawberries or any mix of berries you like.
—Nancy Zimmerman, Cape May Court House, New Jersey

1-3/4 cups all-purpose flour, *divided*
1-1/2 teaspoons baking powder
  1/2 teaspoon salt
  1/4 teaspoon baking soda
   2 egg whites
   1 egg
  2/3 cup unsweetened applesauce
  1/4 cup plain yogurt
   2 tablespoons sugar
   1 teaspoon grated lemon peel
   1 package (12 ounces) frozen unsweetened mixed berries
  1/4 cup packed brown sugar
   2 tablespoons cold butter
   8 tablespoons reduced-fat whipped topping

In a small bowl, combine 1-1/2 cups flour, baking powder, salt and baking soda. In another bowl, whisk the egg whites, egg, applesauce, yogurt, sugar and lemon peel; add to flour mixture, stirring gently until blended.

Spread into a 9-in. round baking pan coated with cooking spray; sprinkle with berries. In a small bowl, combine brown sugar and remaining flour; cut in butter until mixture resembles fine crumbs. Sprinkle over berries.

Bake at 350° for 35-40 minutes or until a toothpick inserted near the center comes out clean. Cool on a wire rack for 15 minutes. Serve with whipped topping.

NUTRITION FACTS: 1 slice equals 218 calories, 4 g fat (3 g saturated fat), 35 mg cholesterol, 320 mg sodium, 39 g carbohydrate, 2 g fiber, 5 g protein. **DIABETIC EXCHANGES:** 2 starch, 1 fat, 1/2 fruit.

Old-Fashioned Molasses Cake

(PICTURED ABOVE)

PREP: 15 Min. **BAKE:** 25 Min. + Cooling **YIELD:** 9 Servings

Serve this old-time spice cake warm for breakfast on a frosty morning or have a square with hot cider on a snowy afternoon.
—Deanne Bagley, Bath, New York

    2 tablespoons reduced-fat butter, softened
    1/4 cup sugar
    1 egg
    1/2 cup molasses
    1 cup all-purpose flour
    1 teaspoon baking soda
    1/4 teaspoon ground ginger
    1/4 teaspoon ground cinnamon
    1/8 teaspoon salt
    1/2 cup hot water
    9 tablespoons fat-free whipped topping

In a small mixing bowl, beat butter and sugar until crumbly, about 2 minutes. Add egg, then molasses, beating well after each addition. Combine the flour, baking soda, ginger, cinnamon and salt; add to butter mixture alternately with water.

Transfer to a 9-in. square baking pan coated with cooking spray. Bake at 350° for 25-30 minutes or until a toothpick inserted near the center comes out clean. Cool on a wire rack. Cut into squares; garnish with whipped topping.

NUTRITION FACTS: 1 piece with 1 tablespoon whipped topping equals 148 calories, 2 g fat (1 g saturated fat), 28 mg cholesterol, 205 mg sodium, 30 g carbohydrate, trace fiber, 2 g protein. **DIABETIC EXCHANGES:** 2 starch, 1/2 fat.

Editor's Note: This recipe was tested with Land O'Lakes light stick butter.

TASTY TIP
Adding dry and wet ingredients alternately to cake batter helps avoid a tough texture to the final product. Begin by adding a third of the flour mixture and mixing until the batter is smooth. Then add half of the liquid, gently mixing until combined. Continue adding ingredients alternately, mixing just until combined.

Clementine Cupcakes

(PICTURED BELOW)

PREP: 25 Min. **BAKE:** 15 Min. + Cooling **YIELD:** 2 Dozen

You can have your cupcake and eat it, too! The Light & Tasty home economists relied on clementines to give the cupcakes a fancy feel that is sure to please.

    1 package (18-1/4 ounces) white cake mix
    3/4 cup water
    4 egg whites
    1/2 cup clementine juice (about 5 clementines)
    1/4 cup canola oil
    1 teaspoon grated clementine peel
    4 clementines, peeled, sectioned and membrane
      removed

FROSTING:

    1/3 cup butter, softened
    3 cups confectioners' sugar
    1/2 teaspoon grated clementine peel
    5 to 6 teaspoons clementine juice

GARNISH:

    3/4 cup semisweet chocolate chips
    24 clementine sections with membrane (about 2-1/2
       clementines)

In a large mixing bowl, combine the first six ingredients. Beat on low speed for 2 minutes. Fill paper-lined muffin cups half full. Place one clementine section in the center of each; gently press down into batter. Chop remaining sections; sprinkle over batter.

Bake at 350° for 15-20 minutes or until a toothpick comes out clean. Cool for 10 minutes before removing from pans to wire racks to cool completely.

For frosting, in a small mixing bowl, beat butter until light and fluffy. Beat in the confectioners' sugar, clementine peel and enough juice to achieve spreading consistency. Frost cupcakes.

In a small microwave-safe bowl, melt chocolate chips; stir until smooth. Dip clementine sections halfway into chocolate; allow excess to drip off. Place on a waxed paper-lined baking sheet; refrigerate until set. Place one on each cupcake.

NUTRITION FACTS: 1 cupcake equals 238 calories, 9 g fat (3 g saturated fat), 7 mg cholesterol, 176 mg sodium, 40 g carbohydrate, 1 g fiber, 2 g protein.

Favorite Recipe Made Lighter

THE SYRUPY-SWEET sauce makes Mom's Apple Dumplings from Gina Hill of Ottawa, Kansas a true delight. But it comes with too much guilt for Gina. "My mother and I would like to find a healthy way to fix these," she says.

Our makeover team tackled the sauce by reducing the sugar to 1/2 cup and adding 1/3 cup of sugar substitute. The staff also decreased the amount of pastry without altering the final product. They eliminated the dumplings' shortening to cut trans fats, and they created a combination of butter and better-for-you canola oil to keep the dumpling's buttery flavory. In addition, they switched from heavy cream to half-and-half for the dessert's lip-smacking topping.

As a result, Makeover Mom's Apple Dumplings are decadent with about half the calories of the original. As a bonus, the recipe has 60% less fat, saturated fat and cholesterol, and it's much lower in sodium, too.

Mom's Apple Dumplings

PREP: 45 Min.   BAKE: 35 Min.   YIELD: 6 Servings

- 1-1/2 cups water
- 1-1/2 cups sugar
- 1/4 teaspoon ground cinnamon
- 1/4 teaspoon ground nutmeg
- 3 tablespoons butter
- 3 to 6 drops red food coloring, optional

DUMPLINGS:
- 2 cups all-purpose flour
- 2 teaspoons baking powder
- 1 teaspoon salt
- 2/3 cup shortening
- 1/3 cup milk
- 6 small tart apples, peeled and cored
- 4 teaspoons sugar, *divided*
- 1/2 teaspoon ground cinnamon
- 1/4 teaspoon ground nutmeg
- 6 teaspoons butter, softened
- 3/4 cup heavy whipping cream

For syrup, in a small saucepan, bring the water, sugar, cinnamon and nutmeg to a boil, stirring occasionally. Remove from the heat; add butter and food coloring if desired. Stir until butter is melted; set aside.

For dumplings, in a small bowl, combine the flour, baking powder and salt; cut in shortening until crumbly. Gradually add milk, tossing with a fork until dough forms a ball. On a lightly floured surface, roll dough into an 18-in. x 12-in. rectangle. Cut into six squares. Place an apple in the center of each square.

Combine 2 teaspoons sugar, cinnamon and nutmeg; sprinkle over the apples. Dot with butter. Bring up the corners of the pastry to center; pinch edges to seal. Place dumplings in a greased 11-in. x 7-in. x 2-in. baking dish.

Pour syrup over dumplings; sprinkle with remaining sugar. Bake at 375° for 35 minutes or until pastry is golden brown and apples are tender. Serve warm with cream.

NUTRITION FACTS: 1 dumpling with 1/4 cup syrup and 2 tablespoons cream equals 810 calories, 43 g fat (19 g saturated fat), 68 mg cholesterol, 642 mg sodium, 102 g carbohydrate, 4 g fiber, 6 g protein.

Makeover Mom's Apple Dumplings

PREP: 50 Min. + Chilling   BAKE: 35 Min.   YIELD: 6 Servings

- 1-1/4 cups water
- 1/2 cup sugar
- Sugar substitute equivalent to 1/3 cup sugar
- 1/4 teaspoon ground cinnamon
- 1/4 teaspoon ground nutmeg
- 1 tablespoon butter
- 2 to 4 drops red food coloring, optional

DUMPLINGS:
- 1-3/4 cups all-purpose flour
- 1-1/4 teaspoons baking powder
- 1/2 teaspoon salt
- 1/4 cup cold butter
- 2 tablespoons canola oil
- 1/3 cup 2% milk
- 2 teaspoons sugar, *divided*
- 1/2 teaspoon ground cinnamon
- 1/4 teaspoon ground nutmeg
- 6 small tart apples, peeled and cored
- 3/4 cup fat-free half-and-half

For syrup, in a small saucepan, bring the water, sugar, sugar substitute, cinnamon and nutmeg to a boil, stirring occasionally. Remove from the heat; add butter and food coloring if desired. Stir until butter is melted. Pour into an 11-in. x 7-in. x 2-in. baking dish coated with cooking spray; set aside.

For dumplings, in a small bowl, combine the flour, baking powder and salt; cut in butter until crumbly. Gently stir in oil. Gradually add milk, tossing with a fork until dough forms a ball. Shape into a log. Cover and refrigerate for 30 minutes. Combine 1 teaspoon sugar, cinnamon and nutmeg; set aside.

Divide dough into six portions (return five portions to the refrigerator until ready to use). On a lightly floured surface, roll one portion into a 6-in. square. Place an apple in the center; sprinkle with about 1/4 teaspoon reserved spice mixture. Bring up corners of pastry to center and pinch edges to seal.

Place dumpling in syrup in baking dish. Repeat with remaining pastry, apples and spice mixture. Sprinkle with remaining sugar. Bake at 375° for 35 minutes or until pastry is golden brown and apples are tender. Serve warm with half-and-half.

NUTRITION FACTS: 1 dumpling with 1/4 cup syrup and 2 tablespoons fat-free half-and-half equals 424 calories, 15 g fat (7 g saturated fat), 27 mg cholesterol, 409 mg sodium, 67 g carbohydrate, 4 g fiber, 6 g protein.

Editor's Note: This recipe was tested with Splenda No Calorie Sweetener.

Cherry Chocolate Parfaits

(PICTURED BELOW)

PREP: 15 Min. + Chilling   **YIELD:** 4 Servings

This refreshing layered dessert from Light & Tasty's Test Kitchen really looks and tastes special. Families will go for this yummy blend of chocolate cookies, cherry gelatin and creamy topping.

- 1 package (.3 ounce) sugar-free cherry gelatin
- 1 cup boiling water
- 1/2 cup reduced-fat sour cream
- 1/4 teaspoon almond extract
- 1/2 cup diet lemon-lime soda
- 8 reduced-fat cream-filled chocolate sandwich cookies, crushed
- 1/4 cup reduced-fat whipped topping

In a small bowl, dissolve gelatin in boiling water. Transfer 1/2 cup to another bowl; stir in sour cream and extract. Divide among four parfait glasses or dessert dishes.

Refrigerate until firm, about 35 minutes. Stir soda into the remaining gelatin; cover and refrigerate until partially set.

To assemble, sprinkle half of the cookies over cherry layer. Top with soda mixture and remaining cookies. Refrigerate until firm.

Just before serving, dollop with whipped topping.

NUTRITION FACTS: 1 parfait equals 146 calories, 5 g fat (3 g saturated fat), 10 mg cholesterol, 207 mg sodium, 20 g carbohydrate, 1 g fiber, 4 g protein. **DIABETIC EXCHANGES:** 1 starch, 1 fat.

Caramel Apple-Pear Crisp

 SALT

PREP: 20 Min.   **BAKE:** 40 Min. + Standing   **YIELD:** 6 Servings

This crisp is packed with a combination of healthy pears and apples, and just the right amount of tasty walnuts in the topping. You'll love it! —Amanda Pettit, Logan, Ohio

- 3 medium pears, peeled and sliced
- 2 medium tart apples, peeled and sliced
- 2 tablespoons sugar
- 1/4 teaspoon ground allspice
- 1/3 cup sugar-free caramel topping

TOPPING:

- 1/4 cup quick-cooking oats
- 1/4 cup packed brown sugar
- 2 tablespoons all-purpose flour
- 3 tablespoons cold reduced-fat butter
- 1/4 cup chopped walnuts
- 3/4 cup reduced-fat whipped topping

In a large bowl, combine the pears, apples, sugar and allspice. Transfer to an 8-in. square baking dish coated with cooking spray. Drizzle with caramel topping.

For topping, in a small bowl, combine the oats, brown sugar and flour. Cut in butter until crumbly; stir in walnuts. Sprinkle over fruit mixture.

Bake at 375° for 40-45 minutes or until topping is golden brown and fruit is tender. Let stand for 15 minutes.

Spoon cooking juices over each serving; garnish with whipped topping.

NUTRITION FACTS: 1 serving with 2 tablespoons whipped topping equals 260 calories, 8 g fat (3 g saturated fat), 10 mg cholesterol, 65 mg sodium, 49 g carbohydrate, 3 g fiber, 3 g protein.

Editor's Note: This recipe was tested with Land O'Lakes light stick butter.

TASTY TIP

When making a gelatin-based parfait, feel free to use gelatin flavors you think your family will enjoy most.

If you are preparing the Cherry Chocolate Parfaits for instance, you can swap out the cherry gelatin and use sugar-free raspberry instead. You could also consider using vanilla cream-filled sandwich cookies instead of the chocolate cookies for a totally different look and flavor. Or, you could try using vanilla extract instead of the almond.

Raspberry Lemon Pavlova
(PICTURED ABOVE)

 SALT

PREP: 40 Min. **BAKE:** 55 Min. + Standing **YIELD:** 10 Servings

Featuring a hard-baked meringue shell topped with lemon curd, this lovely treat includes whipped topping and fresh berries.
—Denise Nyland, Panama City, Florida

    4 egg whites
    1 teaspoon cornstarch
    1 teaspoon white vinegar
    1 teaspoon vanilla extract
    1 cup sugar
TOPPING:
    3/4 cup lemon curd
    1 carton (8 ounces) frozen reduced-fat whipped topping, thawed
1-1/2 cups fresh raspberries

Place egg whites in a large mixing bowl; let stand at room temperature for 30 minutes. Line a large pizza pan with parchment paper; set aside.

Add cornstarch, vinegar and vanilla to egg whites; beat on medium speed until soft peaks form. Gradually beat in sugar, 1 tablespoon at a time, on high until stiff peaks form.

Spread into a 12-in. circle on prepared pan, forming a shallow well in the center. Bake at 225° for 55-65 minutes or until set and lightly browned. Turn oven off; leave meringue in oven for 1 to 1-1/4 hours.

Just before serving, spread lemon curd into meringue shell. Top with whipped topping and raspberries.

NUTRITION FACTS: 1 slice equals 229 calories, 4 g fat (3 g saturated fat), 18 mg cholesterol, 40 mg sodium, 44 g carbohydrate, 1 g fiber, 2 g protein. **DIABETIC EXCHANGE:** 3 starch.

Berry Sponge Cakes
FAT SALT

PREP: 25 Min. + Chilling **YIELD:** 8 Servings

This is such a wonderful departure from ho-hum strawberry shortcake. And with two types of berries, the cakes deliver twice the antioxidants! —Lisa Renshaw, Kansas City, Missouri

    1 package (12 ounces) fresh *or* frozen cranberries
    1 cup fresh *or* frozen blackberries
    1 cup orange juice
    1/2 cup sugar
    1 teaspoon ground cinnamon
1-1/2 cups fat-free whipped topping
    1/4 teaspoon Chinese five-spice powder
    8 individual round sponge cakes

In a large saucepan, combine the berries, orange juice, sugar and cinnamon. Bring to a boil. Reduce heat; simmer, uncovered, for 8-10 minutes or until cranberries pop. Transfer to a small bowl; refrigerate until chilled.

Combine whipped topping and five-spice powder. Place sponge cakes on dessert plates; top with berry mixture and whipped topping.

NUTRITION FACTS: 1 sponge cake with 1/3 cup berry mixture and 3 tablespoons whipped topping equals 229 calories, 1 g fat (trace saturated fat), 39 mg cholesterol, 102 mg sodium, 52 g carbohydrate, 3 g fiber, 2 g protein.

Favorite Recipe Made Lighter

THERE IS something wonderful about Joanie Ward's White Texas Sheet Cake. The reader from Brownsburg, Indiana sent in her recipe in 1993 and the *Taste of Home* group quickly published it. The recipe caught the eye of many readers, including Springfield, Massachusetts' Kaye Buckley, who asked if we could make it lighter.

The makeover staff tackled the cake's batter, replacing half the butter with unsweetened applesauce. To do this, they also had to reduce the amount of water to keep the same proportions of water to butter. Then, they reduced the sugar by 1/2 cup.

Full-fat butter was changed to reduced-fat, and they trimmed back on the nuts and toasted them for additional flavor.

Makeover White Texas Sheet Cake is a mouth-watering success. Without a noticeable difference in flavor, our team cut over 50% of the fat and more than a third of the calories.

White Texas Sheet Cake

PREP: 15 Min.   **BAKE:** 20 Min. + Cooling   **YIELD:** 20 Servings

    1 cup butter, cubed
    1 cup water
    2 cups all-purpose flour
    2 cups sugar
    2 eggs, beaten
  1/2 cup sour cream
    1 teaspoon salt
    1 teaspoon baking powder
    1 teaspoon almond extract
  1/4 teaspoon baking soda

FROSTING:

  1/2 cup butter, cubed
  1/4 cup milk
4-1/2 cups confectioners' sugar
  1/2 teaspoon almond extract
    1 cup chopped walnuts

In a large saucepan, bring butter and water just to a boil. Immediately remove from the heat; stir in the flour, sugar, eggs, sour cream, salt, baking powder, extract and baking soda until smooth.

Pour into a greased 15-in. x 10-in. x 1-in. baking pan. Bake at 375° for 18-22 minutes or until golden brown and a toothpick inserted near the center comes out clean. Cool on a wire rack for 20 minutes.

For frosting, in a large saucepan, bring butter and milk just to a boil. Immediately remove from the heat; stir in confectioners' sugar and extract. Stir in walnuts; spread over warm cake. Cool completely.

NUTRITION FACTS: 1 piece equals 409 calories, 19 g fat (10 g saturated fat), 62 mg cholesterol, 304 mg sodium, 58 g carbohydrate, 1 g fiber, 4 g protein.

Makeover White Texas Sheet Cake
(PICTURED ABOVE)

PREP: 15 Min.   **BAKE:** 15 Min. + Cooling   **YIELD:** 20 Servings

  1/2 cup butter, cubed
  1/2 cup water
    2 cups all-purpose flour
1-1/2 cups sugar
    2 eggs, beaten
  1/2 cup reduced-fat sour cream
  1/2 cup unsweetened applesauce
    1 teaspoon salt
    1 teaspoon baking powder
    1 teaspoon almond extract
  1/4 teaspoon baking soda

FROSTING:

  1/3 cup reduced-fat butter
  1/2 teaspoon almond extract
    3 cups confectioners' sugar
    2 tablespoons fat-free milk
  1/2 cup finely chopped walnuts, toasted

In a large saucepan, bring butter and water just to a boil. Immediately remove from the heat; stir in the flour, sugar, eggs, sour cream, applesauce, salt, baking powder, extract and baking soda until smooth.

Pour into a 15-in. x 10-in. x 1-in. baking pan coated with cooking spray. Bake at 375° for 15-20 minutes or until golden brown and a toothpick inserted near the center comes out clean. Cool on a wire rack for 20 minutes.

For frosting, in a small mixing bowl, beat butter and extract until smooth. Gradually beat in confectioners' sugar. Add milk; beat until smooth. Spread over warm cake; sprinkle with walnuts. Cool completely.

NUTRITION FACTS: 1 piece equals 266 calories, 9 g fat (5 g saturated fat), 41 mg cholesterol, 230 mg sodium, 44 g carbohydrate, 1 g fiber, 3 g protein.

Editor's Note: This recipe was tested with Land O'Lakes light stick butter.

Peach Blackberry Cobbler

(PICTURED BELOW)

PREP: 40 Min. **BAKE:** 40 Min. **YIELD:** 12 Servings

This cobbler is great for a large family group or church dinner during peach season. The rest of the year canned peaches are fine, but, of course, fresh is best. —Marguerite Shaeffer, Sewell, New Jersey

    12 medium peaches, peeled and sliced
   1/3 cup all-purpose flour
   1/4 cup honey
     3 tablespoons lemon juice
   1/4 teaspoon salt
     3 cups fresh blackberries
TOPPING:
     2 cups all-purpose flour
   1/2 cup sugar
     1 teaspoon baking powder
   1/2 teaspoon salt
   1/4 teaspoon baking soda
   1/3 cup cold butter
 1-1/4 cups buttermilk
     1 tablespoon coarse sugar

In a large bowl, combine the peaches, flour, honey, lemon juice and salt; let stand for 15 minutes. Fold in blackberries. Transfer to a 13-in. x 9-in. x 2-in. baking dish coated with cooking spray.

For topping, in a large bowl, combine the flour, sugar, baking powder, salt and baking soda. Cut in butter until crumbly. Make a well in the center; pour in buttermilk. Stir just until a soft dough forms. Drop by tablespoonfuls over fruit mixture; sprinkle with coarse sugar.

Bake at 400° for 40-45 minutes or until filling is bubbly and a toothpick inserted in topping comes out clean. Serve warm.

NUTRITION FACTS: 1 serving equals 263 calories, 6 g fat (3 g saturated fat), 15 mg cholesterol, 286 mg sodium, 51 g carbohydrate, 5 g fiber, 4 g protein.

Chocolate Angel Food Cake

(PICTURED BELOW)

PREP: 20 Min.   **BAKE:** 40 Min. + Cooling   **YIELD:** 12 Servings

Light as air and loaded with the sort of chocolate flavor that everyone craves, here's a cake that offers all of the flavor and none of the guilt. It's an all-time favorite of mine.

—Mary Relyea, Canastota, New York

1-1/2 cups egg whites (about 10)
   1 cup cake flour
   2 cups sugar, *divided*
  1/2 cup baking cocoa
   1 teaspoon cream of tartar
   1 teaspoon vanilla extract
  1/4 teaspoon salt

GLAZE:
  1/2 cup semisweet chocolate chips
   3 tablespoons half-and-half cream

Place egg whites in a large mixing bowl; let stand at room temperature for 30 minutes. Sift together the flour, 1 cup sugar and cocoa twice; set aside.

Add the cream of tartar, vanilla and salt to the egg whites. Beat on medium speed until soft peaks form. Gradually beat in remaining sugar, about 2 tablespoons at a time, on high until stiff glossy peaks form and sugar is dissolved. Gradually fold in flour mixture, about 1/2 cup at a time.

Gently spoon into an ungreased 10-in. tube pan. Cut through batter with a knife to remove air pockets. Bake on the lowest oven rack at 350° for 40-50 minutes or until lightly browned and entire top appears dry. Immediately invert pan; cool completely, about 1 hour.

Run a knife around side and center tube of pan. Remove cake to a serving plate. For glaze, in a microwave-safe bowl, melt chocolate chips and cream. Stir until smooth. Drizzle over cake.

NUTRITION FACTS: 1 slice equals 235 calories, 3 g fat (2 g saturated fat), 2 mg cholesterol, 102 mg sodium, 49 g carbohydrate, 1 g fiber, 5 g protein.

Blackberry Cloud Parfaits

PREP: 30 Min. + Chilling   YIELD: 8 Servings

Here's a treat that saves calories and carbs by using sugar-free gelatin. The bright pink delight is made special with layers of fresh blackberries.   —Dorothy Reinhold, Malibu, California

- 1 package (.3 ounce) **sugar-free raspberry gelatin**
- 1 cup **boiling water**
- 1/2 cup **cold water**
- 1 carton (8 ounces) **frozen reduced-fat whipped topping,** thawed, *divided*
- 3 cups **blackberries,** *divided*
- 1 carton (6 ounces) **reduced-fat blackberry yogurt**

In a large bowl, dissolve gelatin in boiling water. Stir in cold water. Cover and refrigerate until syrupy, about 40 minutes.

Set aside 8 teaspoons whipped topping and eight blackberries for garnish. Fold yogurt and remaining whipped topping into gelatin.

Divide half of the gelatin mixture among eight parfait glasses or dessert dishes. Layer with remaining blackberries and gelatin mixture. Cover and refrigerate until set. Garnish with reserved whipped topping and berries.

NUTRITION FACTS: 1 parfait equals 122 calories, 4 g fat (3 g saturated fat), 1 mg cholesterol, 41 mg sodium, 18 g carbohydrate, 3 g fiber, 2 g protein. **DIABETIC EXCHANGES:** 1 starch, 1/2 fruit, 1/2 fat.

Peppermint Patty Cheesecake

PREP: 25 Min.   BAKE: 35 Min. + Chilling   YIELD: 16 Servings

Our Test Kitchen captures the coolness of winter in this dessert. Lower in fat and cholesterol, it's an indulgence you can afford.

- 1 cup **chocolate graham cracker crumbs** (about 5 whole crackers)
- 2 tablespoons **reduced-fat butter,** melted
- 2 packages (8 ounces *each*) **fat-free cream cheese**
- 1 package (8 ounces) **reduced-fat cream cheese**
- 1 can (14 ounces) **sweetened condensed milk**
- 3/4 teaspoon **peppermint extract**
- 2 **eggs,** lightly beaten
- 12 **chocolate-covered peppermint patties,** *divided*
- 1 teaspoon **all-purpose flour**

In a small bowl, combine cracker crumbs and butter. Press onto the bottom of a 9-in. springform pan coated with cooking spray. Place on a baking sheet. Bake at 325° for 8-10 minutes or until set. Cool on a wire rack.

In a large mixing bowl, beat cream cheese until smooth; beat in milk and extract. Add eggs; beat on low speed just until combined. Coarsely chop eight peppermint patties; toss with flour. Stir into batter. Pour over crust.

Bake at 325° for 32-40 minutes or until center is almost set. Cool on a wire rack for 10 minutes. Carefully run a knife around edge of pan to loosen; cool 1 hour longer. Refrigerate overnight.

Cut remaining peppermint patties into quarters; arrange on top of cheesecake. Remove sides of pan before cutting.

NUTRITION FACTS: 1 slice equals 228 calories, 8 g fat (5 g saturated fat), 50 mg cholesterol, 296 mg sodium, 30 g carbohydrate, trace fiber, 9 g protein. **DIABETIC EXCHANGES:** 2 starch, 1-1/2 fat.

Editor's Note: This recipe was tested with Land O'Lakes light stick butter.

Pina Colada Pudding Cups

(PICTURED ABOVE)

PREP: 15 Min. + Chilling   YIELD: 8 Servings

This dessert is so simple but it's chock-full of refreshing pineapple and coconut flavor. It's a nice treat after a big meal with make-ahead convenience for busy hostesses.

—Betty May, Topeka, Kansas

- 3 cups **fat-free milk**
- 2 envelopes **whipped topping mix**
- 2 packages (1 ounce *each*) **sugar-free instant vanilla pudding mix**
- 2 cans (8 ounces *each*) **unsweetened crushed pineapple,** undrained
- 1/2 teaspoon **coconut extract**
- 1/4 cup **flaked coconut,** toasted
- 8 **maraschino cherries**

In a large bowl, whisk the milk, whipped topping and pudding mixes for 2 minutes. Stir in the pineapple and extract.

Spoon into eight dessert dishes, 3/4 cup in each. Cover and refrigerate for 30 minutes or until chilled. Sprinkle each serving with 1-1/2 teaspoons coconut and top each with a cherry.

NUTRITION FACTS: 1 serving equals 171 calories, 3 g fat (3 g saturated fat), 2 mg cholesterol, 350 mg sodium, 31 g carbohydrate, 1 g fiber, 4 g protein. **DIABETIC EXCHANGES:** 1-1/2 starch, 1/2 fruit.

Raspberry Cream Cheese Coffee Cake

(PICTURED BELOW)

PREP: 25 Min.   **BAKE:** 25 Min. + Cooling   **YIELD:** 8 Servings

Because I need to watch my fat intake, I usually have to pass on desserts. But with reduced-fat cream cheese and egg substitute, I can enjoy this great berry cake.

—Christine Benner, Pottsville, Pennsylvania

      3 tablespoons butter, softened
    3/4 cup sugar, *divided*
    1/4 cup plus 2 tablespoons egg substitute, *divided*
      1 teaspoon grated lemon peel
      1 teaspoon vanilla extract
  1-1/4 cups all-purpose flour
  1-1/4 teaspoons baking powder
    1/4 teaspoon baking soda
    1/4 teaspoon salt
    1/2 cup buttermilk
      1 cup fresh raspberries
      2 ounces reduced-fat cream cheese
      1 teaspoon confectioners' sugar

In a large mixing bowl, beat butter and 1/2 cup sugar until crumbly, about 2 minutes. Beat in 1/4 cup egg substitute, lemon peel and vanilla. Combine the flour, baking powder, baking soda and salt; add to the butter mixture alternately with the buttermilk.

Pour into a 9-in. springform pan coated with cooking spray; sprinkle with berries. In a small mixing bowl, beat cream cheese and remaining sugar until fluffy. Beat in remaining egg substitute. Pour over berries.

Place pan on a baking sheet. Bake at 375° for 25-30 minutes or until a toothpick inserted near the center comes out clean. Cool on a wire rack for 10 minutes. Carefully run a knife around edge of pan to loosen; remove sides of pan. Sprinkle with confectioners' sugar. Serve warm. Refrigerate leftovers.

NUTRITION FACTS: 1 slice equals 221 calories, 6 g fat (4 g saturated fat), 17 mg cholesterol, 289 mg sodium, 37 g carbohydrate, 2 g fiber, 5 g protein. **DIABETIC EXCHANGES:** 2 starch, 1 fat.

Frosted Mocha Cake

(PICTURED ABOVE)

PREP: 20 Min.   **BAKE:** 30 Min. + Cooling   **YIELD:** 24 Servings

When creating this snack cake, our Test Kitchen used a combination of sugar and sugar substitute for the best taste and texture while still cutting calories and carbs.

    3/4 cup sugar blend for baking
    1/2 cup sugar
      2 eggs
    1/4 cup canola oil
      1 container (2-1/2 ounces) prune baby food
      3 teaspoons white vinegar
      1 teaspoon vanilla extract
      1 cup fat-free milk
      1 cup cold strong brewed coffee
      3 cups all-purpose flour
    1/3 cup baking cocoa
      2 teaspoons baking soda
      1 teaspoon salt
  FROSTING:
      1 teaspoon instant coffee granules
      1 teaspoon hot water
    1/2 teaspoon vanilla extract
      2 cups whipped topping

In a large mixing bowl, combine the first seven ingredients; beat until well blended. In a small bowl, combine milk and coffee. Combine the flour, cocoa, baking soda and salt; gradually beat into egg mixture alternately with milk mixture.

Pour into a 13-in. x 9-in. x 2-in. baking pan coated with cooking spray. Bake at 350° for 30-35 minutes or until a toothpick inserted near the center comes out clean. Cool on a wire rack.

In a small bowl, dissolve coffee granules in hot water. Stir in vanilla. Place whipped topping in a large bowl; gently fold in coffee mixture. Frost cake. Store in the refrigerator.

NUTRITION FACTS: 1 piece equals 151 calories, 4 g fat (1 g saturated fat), 18 mg cholesterol, 214 mg sodium, 25 g carbohydrate, 1 g fiber, 3 g protein. **DIABETIC EXCHANGES:** 1-1/2 starch, 1 fat.

Editor's Note: This recipe was tested with Splenda Sugar Blend for Baking.

Favorite Recipe Made Lighter

PERHAPS "Down-and-Dirty Dessert" would be a better name for Kristi Linton's Dirt Dessert, because you're going to want to put a spoon in each hand and go to town! But the tasty deliciousness in this creamy concoction means lots of fat and calories, and that's a problem for the Bay City, Michigan reader who asked for a makeover.

Luckily, our pros in the Test Kitchen discovered it to be a fairly straightforward task. Nearly every ingredient in the delectable dessert had a low-fat or fat-free equivalent, so the team started by using fat-free milk and reduced-fat cookies and whipped topping. They also replaced some of the cream cheese with the fat-free version. But to keep the original's richness, they opted to keep just enough of the regular cream cheese.

Next, they completely eliminated the margarine, which decreased the overall fat a great deal. The confectioners' sugar was lowered by a quarter, which reduced calories without cutting much of the sweetness. They also used sugar-free pudding mix. As a result, the calories were cut even further.

By focusing on smart ingredient choices, the makeover team was really able to put a dent in the amount of fat, calories and cholesterol found in the original. Calories were cut by a third, while fat and cholesterol were each slashed by over 60%.

The resulting Makeover Dirt Dessert is not only better for you, it's definitely an amazing after-dinner treat...perfect for kids of all ages. So break out the spoons and make sure you get a bite, because this is one dessert that won't be around for long!

Dirt Dessert

PREP: 30 Min. + Chilling   **YIELD:** 20 Servings

- 1 package (8 ounces) cream cheese, softened
- 1/4 cup margarine, softened
- 1 cup confectioners' sugar
- 3-1/2 cups cold milk
- 2 packages (3.4 ounces *each*) instant vanilla pudding mix
- 1 carton (12 ounces) frozen whipped topping, thawed
- 1 package (18 ounces) cream-filled chocolate sandwich cookies, crushed

In a large mixing bowl, beat the cream cheese, margarine and confectioners' sugar until smooth. In a large bowl, whisk milk and pudding mixes for 2 minutes; let stand for 2 minutes or until soft-set. Gradually stir into cream cheese mixture. Fold in whipped topping.

Spread 1-1/3 cups of crushed cookies into an ungreased 13-in. x 9-in. x 2-in. dish. Layer with half of the pudding mixture and half of the remaining cookies. Repeat layers. Refrigerate for at least 1 hour before serving.

NUTRITION FACTS: 1/2 cup equals 317 calories, 16 g fat (8 g saturated fat), 18 mg cholesterol, 387 mg sodium, 39 g carbohydrate, 1 g fiber, 4 g protein.

Makeover Dirt Dessert

(PICTURED ABOVE)

PREP: 30 Min. + Chilling   **YIELD:** 20 Servings

- 1 package (8 ounces) fat-free cream cheese
- 1 package (3 ounces) cream cheese, softened
- 3/4 cup confectioners' sugar
- 3-1/2 cups cold fat-free milk
- 2 packages (1 ounce *each*) sugar-free instant vanilla pudding mix
- 1 carton (12 ounces) frozen reduced-fat whipped topping, thawed
- 1 package (18 ounces) reduced-fat cream-filled chocolate sandwich cookies, crushed

In a large mixing bowl, beat cream cheese and confectioners' sugar until smooth. In a large bowl, whisk milk and pudding mixes for 2 minutes; let stand for 2 minutes or until soft-set. Gradually stir into cream cheese mixture. Fold in whipped topping.

Spread 1-1/3 cups of crushed cookies into an ungreased 13-in. x 9-in. x 2-in. dish. Layer with half of the pudding mixture and half of the remaining cookies. Repeat layers. Refrigerate for at least 1 hour before serving.

NUTRITION FACTS: 1/2 cup equals 208 calories, 6 g fat (4 g saturated fat), 6 mg cholesterol, 364 mg sodium, 33 g carbohydrate, 1 g fiber, 5 g protein. **DIABETIC EXCHANGES:** 2 starch, 1 fat.

Triple-Berry Cobbler
(PICTURED ABOVE)

PREP: 20 Min.   **BAKE:** 25 Min.   **YIELD:** 6 Servings

I combined several recipes to come up with this one. It's very versatile. Sometimes I use other fruits depending on what is available or on hand.   —Edna Woodard, Fredericksburg, Texas

   1/2 **cup sugar**
     3 **tablespoons cornstarch**
   1/4 **teaspoon ground cinnamon**
     1 **cup water**
     1 **cup fresh** *or* **frozen cranberries, thawed**
     1 **cup fresh blueberries**
     1 **cup fresh blackberries**
TOPPING:
   1/4 **cup sugar**
     2 **tablespoons butter, softened**
   1/3 **cup fat-free milk**
   1/4 **teaspoon vanilla extract**
   2/3 **cup all-purpose flour**
   3/4 **teaspoon baking powder**
   1/4 **teaspoon salt**

In a small heavy saucepan, combine the sugar, cornstarch, cinnamon and water until smooth. Bring to a boil; cook and stir for 2 minutes or until thickened. Remove from the heat; stir in the berries. Transfer the mixture to an 8-in. square baking dish coated with cooking spray.

For topping, in a small mixing bowl, beat sugar and butter until crumbly, about 2 minutes. Beat in milk and vanilla. Combine the flour, baking powder and salt; stir into butter mixture just until blended. Drop by tablespoonfuls over fruit mixture.

Bake at 375° for 25-30 minutes or until filling is bubbly and a toothpick inserted in topping comes out clean. Serve warm.

NUTRITION FACTS: 1 serving equals 235 calories, 4 g fat (2 g saturated fat), 10 mg cholesterol, 195 mg sodium, 49 g carbohydrate, 3 g fiber, 2 g protein.

No-Bake Pineapple Cheese Pie

PREP: 30 Min. + Chilling   **YIELD:** 8 Servings

My diabetic husband always liked the pineapple pie at a nearby restaurant, so I created something similar but healthier.
—Shirley Miller, North Judson, Indiana

Pastry for single-crust pie (9 inches)
     1 **package (.3 ounce) sugar-free lemon gelatin**
   1/2 **cup boiling water**
     1 **can (8 ounces) unsweetened crushed pineapple, undrained**
     1 **package (8 ounces) fat-free cream cheese**
     1 **package (3 ounces) cream cheese, softened**
     1 **carton (8 ounces) frozen reduced-fat whipped topping, thawed**

Line a 9-in. pie plate with pastry; trim and flute edges. Line pastry shell with a double thickness of heavy-duty foil. Bake at 450° for 8 minutes. Remove foil; bake 5 minutes longer. Cool on a wire rack.

In a small bowl, dissolve gelatin in boiling water. Cool for 10 minutes. Stir in pineapple. In a large mixing bowl, beat cream cheese until blended. Gradually beat in pineapple mixture. Fold in whipped topping. Spoon into pastry shell. Cover and refrigerate for 4 hours or until set.

NUTRITION FACTS: 1 piece equals 268 calories, 14 g fat (9 g saturated fat), 19 mg cholesterol, 311 mg sodium, 26 g carbohydrate, trace fiber, 7 g protein.

Chocolate Peanut Butter Cupcakes

PREP: 20 Min.   **BAKE:** 15 Min. + Cooling   **YIELD:** 2 Dozen

Though these fluffy cupcakes have only 7grams of fat, their rich flavor will keep anyone from guessing they're light.
—Donna Roberts, Shumway, Illinois

2-1/2 **cups all-purpose flour**
   2/3 **cup baking cocoa**

2 teaspoons baking soda

1/3 cup reduced-fat creamy peanut butter

1/4 cup canola oil

1 cup sugar

1/2 cup sugar blend for baking

2 cups fat-free milk

2 tablespoons white vinegar

1 teaspoon vanilla extract

FROSTING:

1/3 cup reduced-fat creamy peanut butter

1/4 cup reduced-fat butter

3 cups confectioners' sugar

3/4 cup baking cocoa

1/4 cup fat-free milk

2 teaspoons vanilla extract

1/4 teaspoon salt

1/2 cup orange jimmies *or* Halloween sprinkles

Sift the flour, cocoa and baking soda into a large bowl; set aside. In a small saucepan, cook peanut butter and oil over low heat for 2-3 minutes or until peanut butter is melted. Remove from the heat; stir in sugar and sugar blend until smooth. Stir in the milk, vinegar and vanilla. Pour into flour mixture; stir until blended.

Fill paper-lined muffin cups half full. Bake at 350° for 15-20 minutes or until a toothpick comes out clean. Cool for 10 minutes before removing from pans to wire racks to cool completely.

For frosting, in a large mixing bowl, beat peanut butter and butter until light and fluffy. Beat in the confectioners' sugar, cocoa, milk, vanilla and salt. Frost cupcakes. Sprinkle with jimmies.

NUTRITION FACTS: 1 cupcake equals 246 calories, 7 g fat (1 g saturated fat), 4 mg cholesterol, 197 mg sodium, 44 g carbohydrate, 2 g fiber, 5 g protein.

Editor's Note: This recipe was tested with Land O'Lakes light stick butter and Splenda Sugar Blend for Baking.

Apricot Angel Cake

PREP: 40 Min. **BAKE:** 50 Min. + Cooling **YIELD:** 12 Servings

Almond and apricot blend beautifully in this extra-low-fat angel food cake. With its tangy flavor, it could even serve as a fruit-flavored coffee cake. —Ellen Govertsen, Wheaton, Illinois

1-1/2 cups egg whites (about 10)

1-1/2 cups all-purpose flour

1-1/4 cups sugar, *divided*

2 teaspoons cream of tartar

1 teaspoon almond extract

1 teaspoon vanilla extract

1/4 teaspoon salt

1 cup apricot preserves

2 tablespoons water

Place egg whites in a large mixing bowl; let stand at room temperature for 30 minutes. Sift flour and 1/2 cup sugar together twice; set aside.

Add cream of tartar, extracts and salt to egg whites; beat on medium speed until soft peaks form. Gradually add remain-

ing sugar, about 2 tablespoons at a time, beating on high until stiff glossy peaks form and sugar is dissolved. Gradually fold in flour mixture, about 1/2 cup at a time.

In a small mixing bowl, beat apricot preserves and water until frothy. Gently fold in egg white mixture. Gently spoon into an ungreased 10-in. tube pan. Cut through batter with a knife to remove air pockets.

Bake on the lowest oven rack at 350° for 50-60 minutes or until lightly browned and entire top appears dry. Immediately invert pan; cool completely, about 1 hour.

Run a knife around sides and center tube of pan. Remove cake to a serving plate.

NUTRITION FACTS: 1 slice equals 221 calories, trace fat (trace saturated fat), 0 cholesterol, 110 mg sodium, 51 g carbohydrate, 1 g fiber, 5 g protein.

"Boo"rrific Kisses

(PICTURED BELOW)

PREP: 20 Min. **BAKE:** 40 Min. + Standing **YIELD:** 2-1/2 Dozen

It's easy to turn my recipe for meringue cookies into these whimsical kisses, perfect for Halloween. With just 15 calories, each little treat can be enjoyed guilt-free!
—Phyllis Eismann Schmalz, Kansas City, Kansas

2 egg whites

1/2 teaspoon vanilla extract

1/4 teaspoon almond extract

1/8 teaspoon cider vinegar

1/2 cup sugar

Orange food coloring, optional

1-1/2 teaspoons miniature semisweet chocolate chips

Place egg whites in a small mixing bowl; let stand at room temperature for 30 minutes. Add extracts and vinegar; beat on medium speed until soft peaks form. Gradually beat in sugar, 1 tablespoon at a time, on high until stiff glossy peaks form and sugar is dissolved, about 6 minutes. Beat in food coloring if desired.

Cut a small hole in the corner of a pastry or plastic bag; insert a #10 round pastry tip. Fill bag with egg white mixture. Pipe 1-1/2-in.-diameter ghosts onto parchment paper-lined baking sheets. Add two chips on each for eyes.

Bake at 250° for 40-45 minutes or until set and dry. Turn oven off; leave cookies in oven for 1 hour. Carefully remove from parchment paper. Store in an airtight container.

NUTRITION FACTS: 1 cookie equals 15 calories, trace fat (trace saturated fat), 0 cholesterol, 4 mg sodium, 3 g carbohydrate, trace fiber, trace protein. **DIABETIC EXCHANGE:** Free food.

Chocolate Orange Bites

FAT SALT CARB ▼ ▼ ▼

(PICTURED ABOVE)

PREP: 35 Min. + Chilling   **YIELD:** About 4 Dozen

Chocolate and orange blend beautifully in these special cookies that offer big taste. Better still, our home economists made sure the nibbles weighed in at only 35 calories each!

   1 package (9 ounces) chocolate wafers, crushed
Sugar substitute equivalent to 1/2 cup sugar
   1/4 cup reduced-fat butter, melted
   1/4 cup orange juice concentrate
   1 teaspoon grated orange peel
   1/2 cup confectioners' sugar
Baking cocoa *and/or* additional confectioners' sugar

In a small bowl, combine the first five ingredients. Shape into 3/4-in. balls; roll in confectioners' sugar. Cover and refrigerate for at least 2 hours.

Lightly sprinkle with cocoa and/or confectioners' sugar before serving. Store in an airtight container in the refrigerator.

NUTRITION FACTS: 1 piece equals 35 calories, 1 g fat (1 g saturated fat), 2 mg cholesterol, 37 mg sodium, 6 g carbohydrate, trace fiber, trace protein. **DIABETIC EXCHANGE:** 1/2 starch.

Editor's Note: This recipe was tested with Splenda No Calorie Sweetener and Land O'Lakes light stick butter.

Golden Thumbprints

SALT CARB ▼ ▼

(PICTURED ABOVE)

PREP: 30 Min.   **BAKE:** 15 Min./Batch   **YIELD:** 1-1/2 Dozen

I think these cookies taste as good as they look. I roll them in walnuts and bake them for friends and family at Christmas.
                              —Loraine Meyer, Bend, Oregon

   3 tablespoons butter, softened
   3 tablespoons brown sugar blend for baking

   2 tablespoons canola oil
   1 egg yolk
   1/2 teaspoon vanilla extract
   1 cup all-purpose flour
   1/4 teaspoon salt
   9 red *or* green candied cherries, halved

In a small mixing bowl, beat butter and brown sugar blend until well blended. Beat in the oil, egg yolk and vanilla. Combine flour and salt; gradually add to butter mixture and mix well.

Shape into scant 1-in. balls. Place 2 in. apart on ungreased baking sheets; flatten slightly. Bake at 375° for 5 minutes. Remove from the oven.

Using the end of a wooden spoon handle, carefully make an indentation in the center of each (cookie edges will crack). Fill each with a candied cherry half. Bake 6-8 minutes longer or until edges are lightly browned. Remove to wire racks.

NUTRITION FACTS: 1 cookie equals 75 calories, 4 g fat (1 g saturated fat), 17 mg cholesterol, 55 mg sodium, 9 g carbohydrate, trace fiber, 1 g protein. **DIABETIC EXCHANGES:** 1/2 starch, 1/2 fat.

Editor's Note: This recipe was tested with Splenda Brown Sugar Blend for Baking.

Chocolate Peanut Butter Crackles

SALT CARB ▼ ▼

(PICTURED BELOW RIGHT)

PREP: 40 Min. + Chilling   **BAKE:** 10 Min./Batch   **YIELD:** 4 Dozen

I make these every year and they always disappear fast. They have a lovely snowy look, making them perfect for the holidays, and the make-ahead dough is really a bonus.
                    —Giovanna Kranenberg, Cambridge, Minnesota

   1 cup sugar blend for baking
   1/2 cup canola oil
   2 eggs
   2 egg whites
   3 teaspoons vanilla extract
2-1/2 cups all-purpose flour
   2/3 cup baking cocoa
   2 teaspoons baking powder
Dash salt
Dash ground cinnamon
   24 miniature peanut butter cups, halved
   1/2 cup confectioners' sugar

In a large mixing bowl, beat the first five ingredients. Combine the flour, cocoa, baking powder, salt and cinnamon; gradually add to egg mixture and mix well. Cover and refrigerate for 4 hours or until easy to handle.

Roll dough into 1-in. balls. Flatten each ball and wrap around a peanut butter cup half; reshape into a ball. Roll in confectioners' sugar. Place 2 in. apart on ungreased baking sheets; flatten slightly.

Bake at 350° for 10-12 minutes or until set. Cool for 2 minutes before removing from pans to wire racks. Store in an airtight container.

NUTRITION FACTS: 1 cookie equals 91 calories, 4 g fat (1 g saturated fat), 9 mg cholesterol, 36 mg sodium, 13 g carbohydrate, 1 g fiber, 2 g protein. **DIABETIC EXCHANGES:** 1 starch, 1/2 fat.

Editor's Note: This recipe was tested with Splenda Sugar Blend for Baking.

Evergreen Cutouts

(PICTURED BELOW RIGHT)

FAT SALT CARB

PREP: 1-1/4 Hours + Chilling   **BAKE:** 10 Min./Batch
YIELD: About 3-1/2 Dozen

Our home economists created these eye-appealing cookies. The buttery bites will remind you of shortbread, but they have a wonderful, mild sweetness that sets them apart.

- 1/3 cup sugar blend for baking
- 1/4 cup butter, softened
- 1/4 cup almond paste
- 1/4 cup canola oil
- 1 egg
- 1 egg white
- 1/2 teaspoon vanilla extract
- 1/4 teaspoon almond extract
- 3 cups cake flour
- 1-1/2 teaspoons baking powder
- 1/4 teaspoon salt

TOPPING:
- 1 egg, *separated*
- 1/4 teaspoon water
- 6 to 8 drops green food coloring
- 2 tablespoons sugar blend for baking

In a large mixing bowl, beat sugar blend, butter and almond paste until well blended. Beat in the oil, egg, egg white and extracts. Combine the flour, baking powder and salt; gradually add to butter mixture and mix well. Divide into two portions; cover and refrigerate for 1-1/2 to 2 hours or until easy to handle.

On a lightly floured surface, roll each portion of dough to 1/8-in. thickness. Using a floured 2-1/2-in. round cookie cutter and a 1-1/2-in. tree-shaped cookie cutter, cut an equal number of circles and trees from dough.

Place circles 2 in. apart on ungreased baking sheets. Brush one side of trees with egg white; place egg white side down on circles. In a small bowl, combine the egg yolk, water and food coloring; brush over trees. Sprinkle with sugar blend.

Bake at 400° for 6-8 minutes or until edges are lightly browned. Remove to wire racks. Store in an airtight container.

NUTRITION FACTS: 1 cookie equals 70 calories, 3 g fat (1 g saturated fat), 12 mg cholesterol, 42 mg sodium, 9 g carbohydrate, trace fiber, 1 g protein. **DIABETIC EXCHANGES:** 1/2 starch, 1/2 fat.

Editor's Note: This recipe was tested with Splenda Sugar Blend for Baking.

Pistachio Pinwheels

(PICTURED BELOW RIGHT)

FAT SALT CARB

PREP: 40 Min. + Chilling   **BAKE:** 10 Min./Batch   **YIELD:** 5 Dozen

These whimsical surprises from our Test Kitchen look complex, but they're a cinch to assemble. You'll love the pistachio's nutty flavor combined with the dough's sweet taste.

- 1/3 cup butter, softened
- 1/3 cup sugar blend for baking
- 2 egg whites
- 3 tablespoons canola oil
- 1/2 teaspoon vanilla extract
- 2-3/4 cups cake flour

- 1 teaspoon baking powder
- 1/4 teaspoon salt
- Red paste food coloring
- 1/2 cup pistachios, finely chopped

In a large mixing bowl, beat butter and sugar blend until well blended. Beat in the egg whites, oil and vanilla. Combine the flour, baking powder and salt; gradually add to butter mixture and mix well.

Divide dough in half; add food coloring to one portion. Divide red and plain doughs into two portions. Between two sheets of waxed paper, roll out one portion of plain dough into an 8-in. x 6-in. rectangle. Repeat with one portion of red dough. Remove waxed paper; place red dough over plain.

Roll up tightly jelly-roll style, starting with a long side. Roll the log in pistachios; wrap in plastic wrap. Repeat with remaining doughs. Refrigerate for 2 hours or until firm.

Unwrap logs; cut into 1/4-in. slices. Place 2 in. apart on ungreased baking sheets. Bake at 375° for 7-9 minutes or until set. Remove to wire racks.

NUTRITION FACTS: 1 cookie equals 49 calories, 2 g fat (1 g saturated fat), 3 mg cholesterol, 33 mg sodium, 6 g carbohydrate, trace fiber, 1 g protein. **DIABETIC EXCHANGES:** 1/2 starch, 1/2 fat.

Editor's Note: This recipe was tested with Splenda Sugar Blend for Baking.

Spritz Wreaths

(PICTURED BELOW RIGHT)

FAT SALT CARB

PREP: 25 Min.   **BAKE:** 10 Min./Batch   **YIELD:** About 5 Dozen

At only 37 calories each, you can indulge your urge to eat more than one of these delightful cookies from our Test Kitchen. A tried-and-true holiday favorite, they are sure to jazz up any cookie tray.

- 1/3 cup sugar blend for baking
- 1/4 cup butter, softened
- 3 tablespoons canola oil
- 2 eggs
- 1/2 teaspoon vanilla extract
- 1-3/4 cups all-purpose flour
- 1/2 teaspoon baking powder
- 1/4 teaspoon salt
- 1/4 teaspoon ground allspice
- 1/8 teaspoon baking soda
- 6 drops green food coloring
- 1/4 cup holiday sprinkles

In a large mixing bowl, beat the sugar blend, butter and oil until well blended. Beat in eggs and extract.

Combine the flour, baking powder, salt, allspice and baking soda; gradually add to butter mixture and mix well. Beat in food coloring.

Using a cookie press fitted with a wreath-shaped disk, press dough 1 in. apart onto ungreased baking sheets. Decorate with holiday sprinkles.

Bake at 375° for 7-10 minutes or until set (do not brown). Remove to wire racks.

NUTRITION FACTS: 1 cookie equals 37 calories, 2 g fat (1 g saturated fat), 9 mg cholesterol, 25 mg sodium, 5 g carbohydrate, trace fiber, 1 g protein. **DIABETIC EXCHANGE:** 1/2 starch.

Editor's Note: This recipe was tested with Splenda Sugar Blend for Baking.

Favorite Recipe Made Lighter

IMPRESSIVE German Sweet Chocolate Cake is a real treat for Patricia Peebles and her sister. "We've adopted a healthy lifestyle," she writes from Springfield, Missouri, "and were hoping you could trim the cake down."

No problem, Patricia. See our makeover recipe at right! We cut half the fat and 40% of the calories!

German Sweet Chocolate Cake

PREP: 50 Min.   **BAKE:** 30 Min. + Cooling   **YIELD:** 16 Servings

    1 package (4 ounces) German sweet chocolate, chopped
1/2 cup water
    1 cup butter, softened
    2 cups sugar
    4 eggs, *separated*
    1 teaspoon vanilla extract
2-1/2 cups cake flour
    1 teaspoon baking soda
1/2 teaspoon salt
    1 cup buttermilk

FROSTING:

    1 cup sugar
1-1/3 cups evaporated milk, *divided*
    3 egg yolks, beaten
1/2 cup butter, cubed
1-1/3 cups flaked coconut
    1 cup chopped pecans
    1 teaspoon vanilla extract

Line three greased 9-in. round baking pans with waxed paper; grease the paper; set aside. In a saucepan, heat chocolate and water over low heat until chocolate is melted. Remove from the heat; cool.

In a mixing bowl, cream butter and sugar until fluffy. Add yolks, one at a time, beating after each addition. Beat in chocolate mixture and vanilla. Combine flour, baking soda and salt; add to creamed mixture alternately with buttermilk, beating after each addition.

In a small mixing bowl, beat egg whites until stiff peaks form; fold into batter. Transfer to prepared pans. Bake at 350° for 30 minutes or until a toothpick inserted near the center comes out clean. Cool for 10 minutes before removing from pans to wire racks to cool. Remove and discard waxed paper.

For frosting, in a Dutch oven, combine sugar and 1 cup milk. Bring to a rapid boil over medium heat. Boil for 6-8 minutes or until mixture is thickened and light caramel-colored, whisking constantly. Remove from the heat; gradually whisk in remaining milk. Let stand for 5 minutes to cool slightly, stirring occasionally.

Gradually whisk in yolks. Cook and stir over medium-low heat for 12-18 minutes or until frosting is slightly thickened and reaches 175°. (Frosting is done when a whisk pulled through it exposes the bottom of the pan for a few seconds.) Remove from the heat; stir in butter until melted. Stir in coconut, pecans and vanilla. Cool to room temperature. Place one cake layer on a serving plate; spread with a third of the frosting. Repeat layers twice. Refrigerate leftovers.

NUTRITION FACTS: 1 slice equals 553 calories, 31 g fat (16 g saturated fat), 145 mg cholesterol, 395 mg sodium, 66 g carbohydrate, 1 g fiber, 7 g protein.

Makeover German Sweet Chocolate Cake

PREP: 50 Min.   **BAKE:** 25 Min. + Cooling   **YIELD:** 16 Servings

    2 ounces German sweet chocolate, chopped
1/4 cup water
1/3 cup butter, softened
3/4 cup sugar
1/3 cup sugar blend for baking
    2 egg yolks
    1 package (5 ounces) prune baby food
    1 teaspoon vanilla extract
2-1/2 cups cake flour
1/4 cup baking cocoa
    1 teaspoon baking soda
1/2 teaspoon salt
    1 cup buttermilk
    4 egg whites

FROSTING:

2/3 cup sugar
3/4 cup plus 3 tablespoons reduced-fat evaporated milk, *divided*
    2 egg yolks, beaten
    5 tablespoons butter, cubed
3/4 cup flaked coconut, lightly toasted
3/4 teaspoon vanilla extract
1/4 cup finely chopped pecans, toasted

Coat three 9-in. round baking pans with cooking spray; line with waxed paper and coat the paper. In a saucepan, heat chocolate and water over low heat until chocolate is melted. Remove from the heat; cool.

In a mixing bowl, beat the next three ingredients until well blended. Add yolks, one at a time, beating well after each addition. Beat in the baby food, chocolate mixture and vanilla. Combine flour, cocoa, baking soda and salt; add to butter mixture alternately with buttermilk, beating after each addition.

In a small mixing bowl, beat egg whites until stiff peaks form; fold into batter. Transfer to prepared pans. Bake at 350° for 24-26 minutes or until a toothpick inserted near the center comes out clean. Cool for 10 minutes before removing from pans to wire racks to cool. Remove and discard waxed paper.

For frosting, in a Dutch oven, combine sugar and 3/4 cup milk. Bring to a rapid boil over medium heat. Boil for 5-6 minutes or until mixture is thickened and light caramel-colored, whisking constantly. Remove from the heat; gradually whisk in remaining milk. Let stand for 5 minutes to cool slightly, stirring occasionally.

Gradually whisk in yolks. Stir over medium-low heat for 8-12 minutes or until frosting is slightly thickened and reaches 175°. (Frosting is done when a whisk pulled through it exposes the bottom of the pan for a few seconds.) Remove from the heat; stir in butter until melted. Stir in coconut and vanilla. Cool to room temperature.

Spread a cake layer with a third of the frosting. Top with second cake layer, third of frosting and last cake layer. Stir nuts into remaining frosting; spread over top. Refrigerate leftovers.

NUTRITION FACTS: 1 slice equals 330 calories, 14 g fat (7 g saturated fat), 75 mg cholesterol, 284 mg sodium, 48 g carbohydrate, 1 g fiber, 6 g protein.

Editor's Note: This recipe was tested with Splenda Sugar Blend for Baking.

Chocolate-Dipped Strawberry Cheesecake

(PICTURED ABOVE)

PREP: 45 Min. + Chilling   **YIELD:** 12 Servings

Looking for a dessert for company? Try my light, creamy and airy treat. It always brings compliments and adds a touch of elegance to menus.   —Kathy Berger, Dry Ridge, Kentucky

- 1-3/4 cups chocolate graham cracker crumbs (about 9 whole crackers)
- 1/4 cup butter, melted
- 1 pound fresh *or* frozen strawberries, thawed
- 2 envelopes unflavored gelatin
- 1/2 cup cold water
- 2 packages (8 ounces *each*) fat-free cream cheese, cubed
- 1 cup (8 ounces) fat-free cottage cheese
- Sugar substitute equivalent to 3/4 cup sugar
- 1 carton (8 ounces) frozen reduced-fat whipped topping, thawed, *divided*
- 13 medium fresh strawberries
- 4 squares (1 ounce *each*) semisweet chocolate

In a small bowl, combine cracker crumbs and butter. Press onto the bottom and 1 in. up the sides of a 9-in. springform pan coated with cooking spray. Place on a baking sheet. Bake at 350° for 10 minutes or until set. Cool on a wire rack.

Hull strawberries if necessary; puree in a food processor. Remove and set aside. In a small saucepan, sprinkle gelatin over cold water; let stand for 1 minute. Heat over low heat, stirring until gelatin is completely dissolved. Transfer to the food processor; add cream cheese, cottage cheese and sugar substitute. Cover and process until smooth.

Add strawberry puree; cover and process until blended. Transfer to a large bowl; fold in 2 cups whipped topping. Pour into crust. Cover and refrigerate for 2-3 hours or until set.

For garnish, wash strawberries and gently pat with paper towels until completely dry. Cut tops off berries. In a microwave-safe bowl, melt chocolate at 50% power; stir until smooth. Dip each berry tip until half of the berry is coated, allowing excess to drip off. Place with tips pointing up on a waxed paper-lined baking sheet; refrigerate for at least 30 minutes.

Carefully run a knife around edge of springform pan to loosen; remove sides of pan. Arrange berries, chocolate tips up, around edge of cheesecake and place one in the center. Garnish with remaining whipped topping. Refrigerate leftovers.

NUTRITION FACTS: 1 slice equals 245 calories, 11 g fat (7 g saturated fat), 14 mg cholesterol, 377 mg sodium, 26 g carbohydrate, 2 g fiber, 10 g protein. **DIABETIC EXCHANGES:** 2 starch, 2 fat.

Editor's Note: This recipe was tested with Splenda No Calorie Sweetener.

Mango Fruit Crisp

(PICTURED BELOW)

PREP: 20 Min.   **BAKE:** 30 Min.   **YIELD:** 8 Servings

For many years, this was one of my most delicious summer desserts. I changed it to whole wheat flour to make it a bit more healthy.   —Judy Schatzberg, Livingston, New Jersey

- 4 medium peaches, peeled and sliced
- 3 medium mangoes, peeled and chopped
- 1/3 cup sugar
- 1/4 cup orange juice
- 2 tablespoons whole wheat flour
- 1 tablespoon lemon juice
- 1/2 teaspoon salt

TOPPING:

- 1/2 cup whole wheat flour
- 1/3 cup packed brown sugar
- 3 tablespoons cold butter
- 1/2 cup granola without raisins

In a large bowl, combine the first seven ingredients. Transfer to an 11-in. x 7-in. x 2-in. baking dish coated with cooking spray.

For topping, in a bowl, combine flour and brown sugar. Cut in butter until crumbly; stir in granola. Sprinkle over fruit.

Bake at 375° for 30-35 minutes or until topping is golden brown and fruit is tender. Serve warm.

NUTRITION FACTS: 1 serving equals 239 calories, 6 g fat (3 g saturated fat), 11 mg cholesterol, 199 mg sodium, 48 g carbohydrate, 5 g fiber, 3 g protein.

Shamrock Meringue Cups

(PICTURED BELOW)

PREP: 30 Min. + Chilling   **BAKE:** 45 Min. + Standing   **YIELD:** 12 Servings

This recipe is a low-fat take on a classic lime pie. The cute cups are always a hit at potlucks and church suppers.

—Jean Elimon, Thompsonville, Illinois

   4 egg whites
   1 teaspoon vanilla extract
1/4 teaspoon salt
1/4 teaspoon cream of tartar
   1 cup sugar
   1 can (14 ounces) fat-free sweetened condensed milk
1/2 cup lime juice
   2 cups reduced-fat whipped topping
   2 to 3 drops green food coloring, optional
 20 green candied cherries

Place egg whites in a small mixing bowl; let stand at room temperature for 30 minutes. Add vanilla, salt and cream of tartar; beat on medium speed until soft peaks form. Gradually beat in sugar, 1 tablespoon at a time, on high until stiff peaks form.

Drop meringue into 12 mounds on two parchment paper-lined baking sheets. With the back of a spoon, shape into 3-in. cups. Bake at 275° for 45-50 minutes or until set and dry. Turn off oven and do not open door; leave meringues in oven for 1 hour.

In a small mixing bowl, beat milk and lime juice until combined. Cover and refrigerate for 1 hour or until set.

Fold in whipped topping and food coloring if desired. Spoon 1/3 cup filling into each meringue cup. Cut 18 cherries in half and two into thin slivers; garnish each dessert with a shamrock shape.

NUTRITION FACTS: 1 serving equals 225 calories, 1 g fat (1 g saturated fat), 2 mg cholesterol, 110 mg sodium, 48 g carbohydrate, trace fiber, 4 g protein.

Easy Chiffon Pie

PREP: 25 Min. + Chilling   **YIELD:** 10 Servings

I received this pie recipe from my grandmother a couple of years ago. She's a cool grandmother, and so is this pie! You'll love the creamy tartness of the cranberry whipped filling. It's a delicious change-of-pace dessert come the holidays.

—April Easler, Norridgewock, Maine

1-1/2 cups reduced-calorie reduced-sugar cranberry juice
   1 package (.6 ounce) sugar-free raspberry gelatin
   1 can (16 ounces) jellied cranberry sauce
   1 carton (8 ounces) frozen reduced-fat whipped topping, thawed, *divided*
   1 extra-servings-size graham cracker crust (9 ounces)
 10 fresh raspberries

In a microwave-safe bowl, heat cranberry juice on high for 2-3 minutes or until boiling; add gelatin and stir until dissolved. Cover and refrigerate for 45-60 minutes or until mixture is slightly thickened.

In a large mixing bowl, beat cranberry sauce for 1-2 minutes or until smooth. Gradually beat in gelatin mixture. Cover and refrigerate for 45 minutes or until thickened.

Refrigerate 10 tablespoons whipped topping for garnish. Stir half of the remaining whipped topping into cranberry mixture; fold in remaining whipped topping. Spread filling evenly into crust. Cover and refrigerate for 8 hours or overnight.

Cut into slices; top each with 1 tablespoon whipped topping and a raspberry.

NUTRITION FACTS: 1 piece equals 256 calories, 9 g fat (4 g saturated fat), 0 cholesterol, 194 mg sodium, 40 g carbohydrate, 1 g fiber, 2 g protein. **DIABETIC EXCHANGES:** 2-1/2 starch, 1 fat.

Editor's Note: This recipe was tested in a 1,100-watt microwave.

Berry Oat Bars

PREP: 20 Min.   **BAKE:** 25 Min. + Cooling   **YIELD:** 9 Servings

I found this quick dessert in a cookbook for kids. I lightened it and increased the amount of oats for more fiber. My family couldn't even tell that I had changed the original recipe!

—Faye Mayberry, St. David, Arizona

1-1/2 cups quick-cooking oats
   1 cup all-purpose flour
1/2 cup packed brown sugar
1/4 teaspoon salt
1/2 cup butter, melted
1/2 cup seedless raspberry preserves, warmed
   2 cups fresh blueberries

In a small bowl, combine the oats, flour, brown sugar and salt. Stir in butter until blended.

Press 1-1/2 cups of oat mixture into an 8-in. square baking dish coated with cooking spray. Carefully spread preserves over crust; sprinkle with blueberries. Top berries with the remaining oat mixture.

Bake at 350° for 25-30 minutes or until lightly browned. Cool on a wire rack. Cut into bars. Refrigerate leftovers.

NUTRITION FACTS: 1 bar equals 300 calories, 11 g fat (6 g saturated fat), 27 mg cholesterol, 174 mg sodium, 47 g carbohydrate, 2 g fiber, 4 g protein.

Trimmed-Down Dishes for Two

If you're cooking for two…or just for you…you'll turn to this thorough chapter time and again. These lightened-up dishes yield smaller quantities so you can enjoy all the flavor without dealing with all the leftovers.

Herb-Rubbed Pork Chops, p. 242

Favorite Chicken Pasta
(PICTURED ABOVE)

PREP/TOTAL TIME: 30 Min.   **YIELD:** 2 Servings

This dish was a favorite of mine at a local restaurant, but when I saw the recipe, I knew it was too rich for my diet. I made some healthy changes, and now it's one of my favorites.
—Lynn Skilsky, Tucson, Arizona

1-1/4 cups uncooked bow tie pasta
  1/2 cup boiling water
  1/4 cup chopped sun-dried tomatoes (not packed in oil)
    1 teaspoon chopped shallot
    1 garlic clove, minced
    2 teaspoons olive oil
  1/4 cup white wine *or* reduced-sodium chicken broth
    2 tablespoons sliced ripe olives
    1 tablespoon prepared pesto
  1/8 teaspoon pepper
1-1/2 teaspoons all-purpose flour
  1/2 cup fat-free half-and-half
    1 package (6 ounces) ready-to-serve grilled chicken breast strips
    1 tablespoon shredded Parmesan cheese
    2 teaspoons pine nuts, toasted

Cook pasta according to package directions. Meanwhile, in a small bowl, combine water and sun-dried tomatoes; cover and let stand for 5 minutes.

In a large skillet over medium heat, cook and stir shallot and garlic in oil for 2 minutes. Stir in the wine or broth, olives, pesto and pepper; cook 1 minute longer.

Combine flour and half-and-half until smooth; stir into pan. Bring to a boil; cook and stir for 1-2 minutes or until thickened.

Drain pasta and tomatoes; add to shallot mixture. Stir in chicken; heat through. Sprinkle with Parmesan cheese and pine nuts.

NUTRITION FACTS: 1-3/4 cups equals 398 calories, 15 g fat (3 g saturated fat), 60 mg cholesterol, 1,150 mg sodium, 32 g carbohydrate, 2 g fiber, 29 g protein.

Spiced Acorn Squash

SALT MEAT-
LESS

PREP/TOTAL TIME: 25 Min.   **YIELD:** 2 Servings

This cinnamon-and-maple flavored squash dish is so quick and easy in the microwave. It's also a good source of vitamins A and C, potassium and fiber.   —George Mankin, Horsham, Pennsylvania

    1 medium acorn squash
    1 tablespoon butter, melted
    2 teaspoons maple syrup
  1/2 teaspoon cider vinegar
  1/8 teaspoon *each* ground ginger, cinnamon and mace

Pierce squash several times with a fork. Place on microwave-safe paper towels; microwave on high for 10 minutes. Let stand for 5-10 minutes.

In a small bowl, combine the butter, syrup and vinegar. Combine the ginger, cinnamon and mace. Cut squash in half; discard seeds. Brush cut sides with butter mixture; sprinkle with spice mixture.

Place on a large microwave-safe plate; cover with microwave-safe paper towels. Cook on high for 5-10 minutes or until squash is tender.

NUTRITION FACTS: 1/2 squash equals 155 calories, 6 g fat (4 g saturated fat), 15 mg cholesterol, 65 mg sodium, 27 g carbohydrate, 3 g fiber, 2 g protein. **DIABETIC EXCHANGES:** 1-1/2 starch, 1 vegetable.

Editor's Note: This recipe was tested in a 1,100-watt microwave.

Apple Orchard Chicken Salad

PREP/TOTAL TIME: 15 min.   **YIELD:** 2 servings

Here's a chunky and nutritious salad that's packed with crunchy apple and celery, dried cranberries, blue cheese and almonds. It's a wonderful blend of tastes and textures.

—Christine Vaught, Salem, Oregon

1-1/2 cups cubed cooked chicken breast
    1 celery rib, thinly sliced
    1/2 cup chopped red apple
    1/4 cup dried cranberries
    1/3 cup fat-free mayonnaise
    2 lettuce leaves
    1 bacon strip, cooked and crumbled
    2 tablespoons crumbled blue cheese
    2 tablespoons chopped almonds

In a small bowl, combine the chicken, celery, apple and cranberries. Stir in mayonnaise. Serve on lettuce; sprinkle with bacon, blue cheese and almonds.

NUTRITION FACTS: 1 serving equals 352 calories, 13 g fat (4 g saturated fat), 94 mg cholesterol, 572 mg sodium, 25 g carbohydrate, 4 g fiber, 35 g protein. **DIABETIC EXCHANGES:** 4 very lean meat, 2 fat, 1 starch, 1/2 fruit.

Stir-Fry for Two

PREP/TOTAL TIME: 30 Min.   **YIELD:** 2 Servings

When minutes matter, I stir up this tasty skillet supper. It's an easy stir-fry that's ideal on busy nights. For a change, you can add or substitute other vegetables.

—Evelyn Plyler, Apple Valley, California

    2 teaspoons cornstarch
    1/2 cup reduced-sodium chicken broth
    1/3 cup orange juice
    2 tablespoons reduced-sodium soy sauce
    2 teaspoons sugar
    2 teaspoons white wine vinegar
    1 teaspoon sesame oil
    1/2 pound boneless skinless chicken breasts, cut into strips
    2 teaspoons canola oil, *divided*
    1 small sweet red pepper, julienned
    1 cup fresh snow peas
    1 small onion, halved and sliced
    1 teaspoon grated orange peel
    1 garlic clove, minced
Hot cooked rice, optional

In a small bowl, combine cornstarch and broth until smooth. Stir in the orange juice, soy sauce, sugar, vinegar and sesame oil; set aside.

In a large nonstick skillet or wok, stir-fry chicken in 1 teaspoon canola oil over medium-high heat for 5-7 minutes or until juices run clear; remove and keep warm. Stir-fry the red pepper, peas, onion, orange peel and garlic in remaining oil for 3-5 minutes or until crisp-tender. Return chicken to the pan.

Stir orange juice mixture; pour over chicken mixture. Bring to a boil; cook and stir for 1 minute or until thickened. Serve with rice if desired.

NUTRITION FACTS: 1-1/2 cups (calculated without rice) equals 303 calories, 10 g fat (1 g saturated fat), 63 mg cholesterol, 820 mg sodium, 24 g carbohydrate, 4 g fiber, 28 g protein. **DIABETIC EXCHANGES:** 3 very lean meat, 2 vegetable, 1-1/2 fat, 1 starch.

Spicy Turkey Quesadillas
(PICTURED BELOW)

PREP/TOTAL TIME: 25 Min.   **YIELD:** 2 Servings

A bit of spice livens up cranberries and turkey while fat-free cream cheese rounds out the bold flavors in this appetizer for two from our Test Kitchen.

    3 ounces fat-free cream cheese
    1/4 cup chopped fresh *or* frozen cranberries, thawed
    1 tablespoon chopped green chilies
1-1/2 teaspoons honey
    1 teaspoon Louisiana-style hot sauce
    4 flour tortillas (6 inches)
    1 cup diced cooked turkey breast

In a small mixing bowl, beat cream cheese until smooth. Stir in the cranberries, chilies, honey and hot sauce until blended. Spread over one side of each tortilla. Place turkey on two tortillas; top with remaining tortillas.

Cook in a large nonstick skillet over medium heat for 2-3 minutes on each side or until lightly browned. Cut into wedges.

NUTRITION FACTS: 1 quesadilla equals 343 calories, 7 g fat (1 g saturated fat), 64 mg cholesterol, 751 mg sodium, 35 g carbohydrate, 1 g fiber, 33 g protein. **DIABETIC EXCHANGES:** 4 very lean meat, 2 starch, 1 fat.

Fresh Vegetable Omelet

(PICTURED AT FAR RIGHT)

CARB MEAT-LESS

PREP: 30 Min.   **BAKE:** 10 Min.   **YIELD:** 2 Servings

Healthy and simply delicious, this light and fluffy omelet is chock-full of fresh garden veggies, flavor and cheese. Try it with whatever veggies you have on hand.   —Edie DeSpain, Logan, Utah

    4 egg whites
1/4 cup water
1/4 teaspoon cream of tartar
    2 eggs
1/4 teaspoon salt
    1 teaspoon butter
    1 medium tomato, chopped
    1 small zucchini, chopped
    1 small onion, chopped
1/4 cup chopped green pepper
1/2 teaspoon Italian seasoning
1/3 cup shredded reduced-fat cheddar cheese

In a small mixing bowl, beat the egg whites, water and cream of tartar until stiff peaks form. In a large mixing bowl, beat eggs and salt until thick and lemon-colored, about 5 minutes. Fold in the whites.

Melt butter in a 10-in. nonstick ovenproof skillet coated with cooking spray. Add egg mixture. Cook over medium heat for 5 minutes or until puffed and lightly browned on the bottom. Bake, uncovered, at 350° for 10-12 minutes or until a knife inserted 2 in. from edge comes out clean.

Meanwhile, in a skillet, saute the tomato, zucchini, onion, green pepper and Italian seasoning until tender. Carefully run a knife around edge of omelet to loosen. With a sharp knife, score center of omelet. Place vegetables on one side and sprinkle with cheese; fold other side over filling. Slide onto a serving plate; cut in half.

NUTRITION FACTS: 1/2 omelet equals 222 calories, 11 g fat (5 g saturated fat), 231 mg cholesterol, 617 mg sodium, 12 g carbohydrate, 3 g fiber, 20 g protein. **DIABETIC EXCHANGES:** 3 lean meat, 2 vegetable, 1/2 fat.

Skillet Potatoes

(PICTURED AT FAR RIGHT)

MEAT-LESS

PREP: 25 Min.   **COOK:** 10 Min.   **YIELD:** 2 Servings

These savory, seasoned skillet potatoes with mushrooms make a hearty, versatile side dish with all kinds of meats. Served alongside a tossed salad, you could even serve them as a meatless meal for two.   —Mary Relyea, Canastota, New York

    1 large baking potato, cubed
1/3 cup chopped sweet red pepper
1/4 cup chopped celery
    1 garlic clove, minced
1-1/2 teaspoons olive oil
1/2 cup sliced baby portobello mushrooms
1/2 teaspoon paprika
1/4 teaspoon salt
1/8 teaspoon pepper

Place potato in a small saucepan and cover with water. Bring to a boil. Reduce heat; cover and simmer for 15-20 minutes or until tender. Drain and set aside.

In a nonstick skillet coated with cooking spray, cook the red pepper, celery and garlic in oil for 2 minutes. Stir in mushrooms; cook 3 minutes longer. Stir in the potato, paprika, salt and pepper; cook until lightly browned.

NUTRITION FACTS: 1 cup equals 194 calories, 4 g fat (1 g saturated fat), 0 cholesterol, 321 mg sodium, 37 g carbohydrate, 4 g fiber, 5 g protein. **DIABETIC EXCHANGES:** 2 starch, 1/2 fat.

Tomato Juice Cocktail

(PICTURED AT FAR RIGHT)

FAT

PREP: 15 Min.   **COOK:** 35 Min. + Chilling   **YIELD:** 2 Servings

This recipe came from my mother-in-law, and many say it's the best tomato juice they've ever tasted. It has a little eye-opening kick to it that's wonderful!   —Beverly Cottrell, Ipswich, Maine

3/4 pound tomatoes (about 4 small), sliced
1/3 cup chopped onion
1/4 cup coarsely chopped green pepper
1/4 cup water
    2 tablespoons sliced celery
1-1/2 teaspoons sugar
1/2 teaspoon salt
1/8 teaspoon pepper

In a small saucepan, combine all ingredients. Bring to a boil. Reduce heat; cover and simmer for 30-35 minutes or until vegetables are tender. Cool.

Transfer tomato mixture to a blender; cover and process until smooth. Refrigerate until chilled.

NUTRITION FACTS: 3/4 cup equals 69 calories, 1 g fat (trace saturated fat), 0 cholesterol, 614 mg sodium, 16 g carbohydrate, 3 g fiber, 2 g protein. **DIABETIC EXCHANGE:** 2 vegetable.

Dijon Chicken Caesar Salad

CARB

PREP/TOTAL TIME: 20 Min.   **YIELD:** 4 Servings

I dress up tender chicken with this zesty toss. Not only is it pretty to serve, but it's low in carbs and sodium, too.   —Peg Boehm, Sheboygan Falls, Wisconsin

    2 tablespoons lemon juice
    2 tablespoons olive oil
    1 tablespoon fat-free sour cream
    2 teaspoons water
    1 teaspoon Worcestershire sauce
    1 teaspoon Dijon mustard
    1 garlic clove, minced
1/4 teaspoon coarsely ground pepper
    2 tablespoons grated Parmesan cheese, *divided*
    7 cups torn romaine
    3 cups julienned cooked chicken breast, warmed

In a small bowl, whisk the lemon juice, oil, sour cream, water, Worcestershire sauce, mustard, garlic and pepper. Stir in 1 tablespoon Parmesan cheese.

Toss the romaine with 1/4 cup dressing; divide among four plates. Top with chicken; drizzle with remaining dressing. Sprinkle with remaining Parmesan cheese.

NUTRITION FACTS: 1 serving equals 254 calories, 11 g fat (2 g saturated fat), 83 mg cholesterol, 169 mg sodium, 5 g carbohydrate, 2 g fiber, 33 g protein. **DIABETIC EXCHANGES:** 4 very lean meat, 2 fat, 1 vegetable.

Orange Soy Milk Frappes

PREP/TOTAL TIME: 10 Min.   **YIELD:** 2 Servings

Light, frothy and filled with natural goodness, this creamy-topped orange smoothie from our home economists takes just a few ingredients...but makes a wholesome morning eye-opener.

    1/2 cup vanilla soy milk
    1/2 cup orange juice
      5 ice cubes
      2 teaspoons sugar
    1/4 teaspoon vanilla extract
Dash salt

In a blender, combine all ingredients; cover and process for 30-45 seconds or until smooth. Pour into chilled glasses; serve immediately.

NUTRITION FACTS: 1 cup equals 70 calories, 1 g fat (0 saturated fat), 0 cholesterol, 98 mg sodium, 13 g carbohydrate, 0 fiber, 2 g protein. **DIABETIC EXCHANGES:** 1/2 starch, 1/2 fruit.

Strawberry Tofu Smoothies

PREP/TOTAL TIME: 10 Min.   **YIELD:** 2 Servings

This is one sweet way to get more soy in my diet. It's light, tasty, and I can take it with me in an insulated mug with lid and straw. With only four ingredients, it comes together in a snap.
—Debbie Stepp, Ocala, Florida

        1 cup unsweetened apple juice
    1-1/2 cups frozen unsweetened strawberries
        4 ounces silken firm tofu, cubed
        1 teaspoon sugar

In a blender, combine all ingredients; cover and process for 45-60 seconds or until smooth. Pour into chilled glasses; serve immediately.

NUTRITION FACTS: 1 cup equals 136 calories, 2 g fat (trace saturated fat), 0 cholesterol, 25 mg sodium, 26 g carbohydrate, 3 g fiber, 5 g protein. **DIABETIC EXCHANGES:** 1-1/2 fruit, 1 lean meat.

Herb-Rubbed Pork Chops

CARB

(PICTURED ABOVE)

PREP/TOTAL TIME: 25 Min.   YIELD: 2 Servings

When time is short, I rely on this surefire recipe. It's healthy, economical and so easy to fix. Best of all, I'm not stuck with leftovers for days on end.   —Sharon Denton, Chester, Virginia

 1 teaspoon dried parsley flakes
 1 teaspoon dried marjoram
 1 teaspoon rubbed sage
 1/8 teaspoon garlic powder
 1/8 teaspoon salt
 1/8 teaspoon pepper
 2 bone-in pork loin chops (3/4 inch thick and 6 ounces each)
 1-1/2 teaspoons olive oil, *divided*
 1/4 cup reduced-sodium chicken broth
 2 tablespoons sherry *or* additional reduced-sodium chicken broth

In a small bowl, combine the parsley, marjoram, sage, garlic powder, salt and pepper. Brush both sides of pork chops with 1 teaspoon oil; rub with herb mixture.

In a large nonstick skillet coated with cooking spray, cook chops in remaining oil over medium heat for 3-4 minutes on each side or until lightly browned. Remove and keep warm. Add broth and sherry or additional broth to skillet, stirring to loosen browned bits. Bring to a boil.

Return chops to the pan. Reduce heat; cover and simmer for 4-5 minutes or until a meat thermometer reads 160°. Serve chops with pan juices.

NUTRITION FACTS: 1 pork chop with 3 tablespoons pan juices equals 221 calories, 11 g fat (3 g saturated fat), 74 mg cholesterol, 282 mg sodium, 1 g carbohydrate, trace fiber, 26 g protein. DIABETIC EXCHANGES: 3 lean meat, 1 fat.

Parmesan Vegetable Rice

MEAT-LESS

(PICTURED ABOVE)

PREP/TOTAL TIME: 20 Min.   YIELD: 2 Servings

With its red tomatoes and green pepper, this healthful rice dish is colorful enough to serve guests during the holidays, but I make it whenever I want a special rice dish any time of year at all!
    —Nola Nielsen, Darien, Illinois

 1/2 cup uncooked instant rice
 1/2 cup chopped green pepper
 1 garlic clove, minced
 2 teaspoons butter
 1 plum tomato, seeded and chopped
 1/4 teaspoon salt
 1/4 teaspoon celery salt
 1/4 teaspoon pepper
 2 tablespoons shredded Parmesan cheese, *divided*

Cook rice according to package directions. Meanwhile, in a small nonstick skillet coated with cooking spray, saute green pepper and garlic in butter for 2 minutes. Stir in the tomato, salt, celery salt and pepper; cook 2 minutes longer.

Add the rice and 1 tablespoon Parmesan cheese; heat through. Sprinkle with remaining Parmesan cheese.

NUTRITION FACTS: 1/2 cup equals 164 calories, 5 g fat (3 g saturated fat), 14 mg cholesterol, 609 mg sodium, 25 g carbohydrate, 1 g fiber, 4 g protein. DIABETIC EXCHANGES: 1 starch, 1 vegetable, 1 fat.

Turkey Chow Mein

PREP/TOTAL TIME: 30 Min.   YIELD: 2 Servings

Turkey dinner gets an Asian twist in this entree from our Test Kitchen. Fresh vegetables combine with tender turkey to create a nutritious and hearty chow mein that's sure to please.

    1 tablespoon cornstarch
    2 tablespoons plus 1/4 cup water, *divided*
    2 celery ribs, sliced
    1 medium onion, chopped
    2 teaspoons canola oil
    4 cups shredded Chinese *or* napa cabbage
    1/2 cup sliced fresh mushrooms
    3/4 cup reduced-sodium chicken broth
    1 tablespoon reduced-sodium soy sauce
    1/2 teaspoon sugar
    1/4 teaspoon garlic powder
    1 cup cubed cooked turkey
    1 cup hot cooked rice

In a small bowl, combine cornstarch and 2 tablespoons water until smooth; set aside. In a large nonstick skillet or wok, stir-fry celery and onion in oil for 3 minutes. Add cabbage and mushrooms; stir-fry 2 minutes longer. Add the broth, soy sauce, sugar, garlic powder and remaining water; cook and stir until vegetables are crisp-tender.

Stir cornstarch mixture and add to the pan. Bring to a boil; cook and stir for 2 minutes or until thickened. Add turkey; heat through. Serve with rice.

NUTRITION FACTS: 1-1/4 cups chow mein with 1/2 cup rice equals 353 calories, 9 g fat (2 g saturated fat), 53 mg cholesterol, 659 mg sodium, 38 g carbohydrate, 4 g fiber, 28 g protein. **DIABETIC EXCHANGES:** 3 very lean meat, 2 starch, 2 vegetable, 1 fat.

Dilled Stroganoff

PREP/TOTAL TIME: 25 Min.   YIELD: 2 Servings

I rely on baby portobello mushrooms and a hint of dill for my stroganoff. Served with whole wheat pasta, it makes a rich supper in moments that's just right for two.
— Katherine Preiss, Penfield, Pennsylvania

1-1/3 cups uncooked whole wheat spiral pasta
    1/3 pound lean ground turkey
    1 medium onion, chopped
2-3/4 cups sliced baby portobello mushrooms
    3/4 cup water
    1 tablespoon ketchup
1-1/2 teaspoons dill weed
    1 teaspoon reduced-sodium beef bouillon granules
    1/2 teaspoon Worcestershire sauce
    1/4 cup reduced-fat sour cream

Cook pasta according to package directions. Meanwhile, in a large nonstick skillet coated with cooking spray, cook turkey and onion over medium heat until meat is no longer pink; drain.

Add mushrooms; cook and stir for 1 minute. Stir in the water, ketchup, dill, bouillon and Worcestershire sauce. Bring to a boil. Reduce heat; simmer, uncovered, for 8-10 minutes.

Stir in sour cream; heat through (do not boil). Drain pasta; serve with turkey mixture.

NUTRITION FACTS: 2/3 cup meat mixture with 2/3 cup pasta equals 363 calories, 10 g fat (4 g saturated fat), 70 mg cholesterol, 355 mg sodium, 45 g carbohydrate, 5 g fiber, 24 g protein.

Cranberry Bread Pudding

FAT

PREP/TOTAL TIME: 30 Min.   YIELD: 2 Servings

I use leftover French bread and dried cranberries in this comforting treat.
— Irene Erickson, Lacona, New York

    1 cup cubed day-old French bread (1/2-inch cubes)
    2 tablespoons dried cranberries
    2/3 cup fat-free milk
    1/4 cup egg substitute
    2 tablespoons brown sugar
    1/2 teaspoon vanilla extract
    1/8 teaspoon ground cinnamon

Divide bread cubes and cranberries between two 10-oz. ramekins or custard cups coated with cooking spray. Place on a baking sheet.

In a small bowl, combine the remaining ingredients. Pour over bread mixture. Bake at 350° for 25-30 minutes or until a knife inserted near the center comes out clean. Serve warm.

NUTRITION FACTS: 1 serving equals 168 calories, 1 g fat (trace saturated fat), 2 mg cholesterol, 205 mg sodium, 33 g carbohydrate, 1 g fiber, 7 g protein. **DIABETIC EXCHANGES:** 1-1/2 starch, 1/2 fruit.

Lemon Sorbet

FAT SALT

(PICTURED BELOW)

PREP: 15 Min. + Freezing   YIELD: 2 Cups

Whether you serve it in chilled bowls or scooped into cut lemon halves, this creamy four-ingredient sorbet is both sweet and tart.
— Goldene Petersen, Brigham City, Utah

    1 cup sugar
    1 cup water
    3/4 cup lemon juice
    3 tablespoons grated lemon peel

In a small saucepan over medium heat, cook and stir sugar and water until mixture comes to a boil. Reduce heat; simmer, uncovered, for 2 minutes. Remove from the heat; cool to room temperature.

Stir in lemon juice and lemon peel. Freeze in an ice cream freezer according to manufacturer's directions. Transfer to a freezer container; freeze for at least 4 hours before serving.

NUTRITION FACTS: 1/3 cup equals 138 calories, trace fat (trace saturated fat), 0 cholesterol, 1 mg sodium, 36 g carbohydrate, trace fiber, trace protein.

Broiled Vegetable Sandwiches

(PICTURED BELOW)

PREP/TOTAL TIME: 30 Min.   **YIELD:** 2 Servings

Tender and crispy vegetables shine in this palate-pleasing recipe. Served on a warm toasted bun with fresh basil, mayonnaise and a dash of jalapeno pepper, a plate of veggies never tasted so good!
—Jane Jackson, Randolph, Iowa

- 6 slices peeled eggplant (1/4 inch thick)
- 1/2 cup sliced yellow summer squash (1/4 inch thick)
- 1/3 cup sliced zucchini (1/4 inch thick)
- 2 slices red onion (1/4 inch thick)
- 1 teaspoon Italian seasoning

Dash cayenne pepper

- 2 hard rolls, split
- 5 teaspoons reduced-fat mayonnaise
- 2 fresh basil leaves
- 2 fresh spinach leaves
- 1 cup julienned roasted sweet red peppers
- 2 slices tomato
- 2 teaspoons minced seeded jalapeno pepper
- 1/8 teaspoon pepper

Place the eggplant, yellow squash, zucchini and onion in a 15-in. x 10-in. x 1-in. baking pan coated with cooking spray. Coat vegetables with cooking spray; sprinkle with Italian seasoning and cayenne. Broil 4-6 in. from the heat for 5-7 minutes on each side or until tender and lightly browned.

Place rolls, cut side up, on an ungreased baking sheet. Broil for 2 minutes or until lightly browned. Spread roll bottoms with mayonnaise; layer with basil, spinach, red peppers, tomato and jalapeno. Sprinkle with pepper. Top with broiled vegetables; replace roll tops.

NUTRITION FACTS: 1 sandwich equals 290 calories, 7 g fat (1 g saturated fat), 4 mg cholesterol, 869 mg sodium, 44 g carbohydrate, 5 g fiber, 8 g protein. **DIABETIC EXCHANGES:** 2 starch, 2 vegetable, 1 fat.

Editor's Note: When cutting or seeding hot peppers, use rubber or plastic gloves to protect your hands. Avoid touching your face.

Mashed Potato Cakes

PREP/TOTAL TIME: 25 Min.   **YIELD:** 2 Servings

What a great way to use up any remaining mashed potatoes! These light cakes cook up golden brown and have a wonderful butter-and-onion flavor. Kids and adults alike will love our Test Kitchen's spin on the classic cakes!

- 1 egg white, lightly beaten
- 1 cup mashed potatoes (with added milk and butter)
- 1 tablespoon all-purpose flour
- 2-1/2 teaspoons finely chopped green onion
- 1/2 teaspoon minced fresh parsley
- 1/8 teaspoon salt
- 1/8 teaspoon pepper

Butter-flavored cooking spray

- 1 teaspoon reduced-fat butter

In a small bowl, combine the first seven ingredients. In a large nonstick skillet coated with butter-flavored cooking spray, melt butter over medium heat.

Drop potato mixture by 1/4 cupfuls into skillet; press lightly to flatten. Cook over medium heat for 4-5 minutes on each side or until golden brown. Serve warm.

NUTRITION FACTS: 2 potato cakes equals 147 calories, 6 g fat (4 g saturated fat), 16 mg cholesterol, 497 mg sodium, 21 g carbohydrate, 2 g fiber, 4 g protein. **DIABETIC EXCHANGES:** 1-1/2 starch, 1 fat.

Editor's Note: This recipe was tested with Land O'Lakes light stick butter.

Creamy Seafood Linguine

PREP: 20 Min.   **COOK:** 15 Min.   **YIELD:** 4 Servings

To dress up this creamy seafood dish, I serve it with steamed asparagus or a tossed salad and French bread. Try it with cubes of flounder, salmon or another full-flavored fish.
—Carole Floyd, Exmore, Virginia

- 6 ounces uncooked linguine
- 1 tablespoon cornstarch
- 1 cup fat-free evaporated milk
- 1 medium onion, finely chopped
- 2 garlic cloves, minced
- 2 teaspoons olive oil
- 1/2 pound uncooked large shrimp, peeled and deveined
- 1/2 pound bay scallops
- 3 tablespoons white wine *or* reduced-sodium chicken broth
- 1/2 cup grated Parmesan cheese, *divided*
- 2 tablespoons minced fresh parsley
- 1 tablespoon minced fresh basil *or* 1 teaspoon dried basil
- 1/2 teaspoon salt
- 1/8 teaspoon pepper

Cook linguine according to package directions. Meanwhile, in a small bowl, combine cornstarch and milk until smooth; set aside.

In a large nonstick skillet, saute onion and garlic in oil until tender. Stir in the shrimp, scallops and wine or broth. Cook, uncovered, for 3-5 minutes or until shrimp turn pink.

Stir milk mixture and add to skillet. Bring to a boil over medium heat; cook and stir for 1-2 minutes or until thickened. Stir in 1/4 cup Parmesan cheese, parsley, basil, salt and pepper. Drain linguine; top with seafood mixture. Sprinkle with remaining Parmesan cheese.

NUTRITION FACTS: 3/4 cup linguine with 1/2 cup seafood mixture and 1 tablespoon Parmesan cheese equals 394 calories, 7 g fat (3 g saturated fat), 113 mg cholesterol, 749 mg sodium, 46 g carbohydrate, 2 g fiber, 34 g protein. **DIABETIC EXCHANGES:** 3 very lean meat, 2-1/2 starch, 1 fat, 1/2 fat-free milk.

Grilled Lime-Teriyaki Shrimp

 CARB

(PICTURED ABOVE)

PREP: 10 Min. + Marinating   **GRILL:** 10 Min.   **YIELD:** 2 Servings

I make these seafood skewers often because we grill year-round. The side dishes may vary, but these shrimp are always a stellar main event. —Karen Tyson, Clawson, Michigan

- 3 tablespoons lime juice
- 2 tablespoons olive oil
- 2 tablespoons reduced-sodium teriyaki sauce
- 1 tablespoon balsamic vinegar
- 1 tablespoon Dijon mustard
- 1 teaspoon garlic powder
- 6 drops hot pepper sauce
- 6 uncooked jumbo shrimp, peeled and deveined

Combine the first seven ingredients in a large resealable plastic bag; add shrimp. Seal bag and turn to coat. Refrigerate for 1 hour, turning occasionally.

If grilling the shrimp, coat grill rack with cooking spray before starting the grill. Drain and discard marinade. Thread shrimp onto two metal or soaked wooden skewers. Grill, covered, over medium heat or broil 4 in. from the heat for 3-4 minutes on each side or until shrimp turn pink.

NUTRITION FACTS: 3 shrimp equals 119 calories, 4 g fat (1 g saturated fat), 168 mg cholesterol, 301 mg sodium, 2 g carbohydrate, trace fiber, 18 g protein. **DIABETIC EXCHANGES:** 3 very lean meat, 1/2 fat.

Crunchy Carrot Salad

FAT CARB MEAT-LESS

(PICTURED ABOVE)

PREP/TOTAL TIME: 15 Min.   **YIELD:** 2 Servings

These carrots make a beautiful presentation and are absolutely delicious. They're a hit with everyone who has tasted them, including my husband, who doesn't typically care for carrots. —Jennifer Cain, Bel Air, Maryland

- 1 tablespoon sugar
- 1 tablespoon white vinegar
- 1/4 teaspoon salt
- 2 medium carrots, julienned
- 2 tablespoons chopped sweet red pepper
- 1 tablespoon thinly sliced green onion (green part only)
- 1 tablespoon chopped almonds, toasted
- 1/8 teaspoon sesame seeds, toasted

In a small bowl, combine the sugar, vinegar and salt. Add carrots; toss to coat. Divide between two plates. Sprinkle with red pepper, onion, almonds and sesame seeds.

NUTRITION FACTS: 3/4 cup equals 78 calories, 2 g fat (trace saturated fat), 0 cholesterol, 318 mg sodium, 14 g carbohydrate, 3 g fiber, 2 g protein. **DIABETIC EXCHANGES:** 1 vegetable, 1/2 starch.

Turkey Lunch-Box Wraps
(PICTURED ABOVE)

PREP/TOTAL TIME: 15 Min.   **YIELD:** 2 Servings

You'll get a smart head start on your daily vegetable requirement with this wrap. The sandwiches taste wonderful cold or warmed in the microwave. They make a great brown-bag treat.
—Denise Marshall, Jacksonville, Florida

> 2 whole wheat tortillas (8 inches), room temperature
> 4 teaspoons honey mustard
> 6 ounces thinly sliced deli turkey
> 2 thin slices Muenster cheese
> 1 cup fresh baby spinach
> 1 medium carrot, shredded
> 1 bacon strip, cooked and crumbled
> 1/4 cup chopped seeded cucumber
> 1/4 cup chopped roasted sweet red pepper

Spread tortillas with mustard. Layer each with turkey, cheese, spinach, carrot, bacon, cucumber and red pepper; roll up tightly.

NUTRITION FACTS: 1 wrap equals 277 calories, 8 g fat (3 g saturated fat), 54 mg cholesterol, 1,408 mg sodium, 34 g carbohydrate, 4 g fiber, 26 g protein. **DIABETIC EXCHANGES:** 3 very lean meat, 1-1/2 starch, 1 vegetable, 1 fat.

Basil Tomato Soup   MEAT-LESS
(PICTURED ABOVE)

PREP: 20 Min.   **COOK:** 20 Min.   **YIELD:** 2 Servings

Fresh basil perks up the flavor in this creamy, from-scratch delight. My aunt shared the recipe years ago, and it's been one of my favorites ever since.   —Sarah Travis, Edina, Minnesota

> 1 medium onion, chopped
> 1 medium carrot, shredded
> 1-1/2 teaspoons butter
> 4 medium tomatoes, peeled and seeded
> 1/4 teaspoon sugar
> 1/4 teaspoon salt
> 1/8 teaspoon coarsely ground pepper
> 1/4 cup loosely packed fresh basil leaves
> 1 cup reduced-sodium chicken broth *or* vegetable broth

In a small saucepan, saute onion and carrot in butter until tender. Stir in the tomatoes, sugar, salt and pepper. Bring to a boil. Reduce heat; cover and simmer for 10 minutes. Cool slightly.

Transfer to a blender; add basil. Cover and process until smooth. Return to the pan; stir in broth and heat through.

NUTRITION FACTS: 1 cup equals 141 calories, 4 g fat (2 g saturated fat), 8 mg cholesterol, 673 mg sodium, 25 g carbohydrate, 6 g fiber, 5 g protein. **DIABETIC EXCHANGES:** 4 vegetable, 1/2 fat.

Family-Style Suppers

It's so satisfying to create mealtime memories with your family, but it's even more rewarding when the food you serve is nutritious. Here, six cooks share the dinner menus most-requested at their homes. We're sure these heart-warming suppers will spark smiles at your table as well.

Veal with Mushroom-Wine Sauce, p. 257
Roasted Rosemary Potatoes, p. 257

flavorful meal's
sure to delight

A Colorado cook makes a healthy menu exciting and teaches lessons to last a lifetime.

Teaching kids about healthy eating comes naturally to Becky Oliver of Fairplay, Colorado. As a high school English teacher, Becky sees all sorts of eating habits, and they're not always very impressive. "I really see what poor eating can do to kids," she explains.

Becky's tried to make better choices for her family. "I was raised with healthy eating habits," she notes, "but after some researching, I planned even more nutritious meals for my family. The changes helped my husband, Rod, lower his blood pressure and cholesterol levels significantly."

By keeping good-for-you food accessible and fun, Becky taught her two toddlers, Lanaya and Race, to make smart choices early on. "My children are the only kids I know who actually get excited about shrimp and salmon and avoid cake," Becky says with a smile.

To keep meals interesting, Becky involves her son and daughter in just about every aspect of food preparation—from deciding what to cook to preparing dinner. "I take my kids grocery shopping," she says. "Lanaya picks out foods that are different. She recently found asparagus. I let her push the buttons to cook it in the microwave, and she ate it all."

DELICIOUS CHICKEN DINNER

The menu Becky shares here is full-flavored, nutritious and always well-received by her family. For a quick and colorful appetizer, she serves Texas Caviar. "I adapted this recipe from a cookbook I received a long time ago, and now I can't imagine a get-together at my house without it," she relates.

Seasoned Chicken Strips make an appealing entree on any menu. The tender strips are treated to a crispy coating before they're baked to perfection. "They're designed for kids, but tasty enough for company," Becky says.

A super-easy side dish, Cauliflower Puree with Onions, rounds out suppers with some fun. The creamy cauliflower is topped with sweet caramelized onions. "We call it 'silly cauliflower,'" Becky notes. "My kids think the caramelized onion topping tastes just like candy."

Seasoned Chicken Strips

(PICTURED AT LEFT)

PREP/TOTAL TIME: 25 Min.   YIELD: 4 Servings

   1/3 cup egg substitute
     1 tablespoon prepared mustard
     1 garlic clove, minced
   3/4 cup dry bread crumbs
     2 teaspoons dried basil
     1 teaspoon paprika
   1/2 teaspoon salt
   1/4 teaspoon pepper
     1 pound chicken tenderloins

In a shallow bowl, combine the egg substitute, mustard and garlic. In another shallow bowl, combine the bread crumbs, basil, paprika, salt and pepper. Dip chicken in egg mixture, then roll in crumbs.

Place on a baking sheet coated with cooking spray. Bake at 400° for 10-15 minutes or until golden brown and chicken juices run clear.

NUTRITION FACTS: 3 ounces cooked chicken equals 188 calories, 2 g fat (trace saturated fat), 67 mg cholesterol, 525 mg sodium, 14 g carbohydrate, 1 g fiber, 30 g protein. **DIABETIC EXCHANGES:** 3 very lean meat, 1 starch.

Cauliflower Puree with Onions

CARB MEAT-LESS

(PICTURED AT FAR LEFT)

PREP/TOTAL TIME: 25 Min.   YIELD: 4 Servings

     1 package (16 ounces) frozen cauliflower
     2 tablespoons water
4-1/2 teaspoons olive oil, *divided*
   1/4 teaspoon salt
   1/4 teaspoon pepper
     1 large sweet onion, thinly sliced
     2 tablespoons sugar

Place cauliflower and water in a microwave-safe bowl. Cover and cook on high for 6 minutes; stir. Cook 1-2 minutes longer or until tender. Cool slightly. Drain, reserving 2 tablespoons cooking liquid.

Place the cauliflower, reserved liquid, 1-1/2 teaspoons oil, salt and pepper in a food processor or blender; cover and process until blended. Keep warm.

In a small nonstick skillet coated with cooking spray, cook onion over medium-high heat in remaining oil for 6 minutes. Stir in the sugar; cook 7-10 minutes longer or until the onion is tender and lightly browned. Serve with the cauliflower puree.

NUTRITION FACTS: 1/2 cup cauliflower with 2 tablespoons onions equals 111 calories, 5 g fat (1 g saturated fat), 0 cholesterol, 176 mg sodium, 15 g carbohydrate, 3 g fiber, 3 g protein. **DIABETIC EXCHANGES:** 1 vegetable, 1 fat, 1/2 starch.

Editor's Note: This recipe was tested in a 1,100-watt microwave.

Texas Caviar

FAT MEAT-LESS

PREP: 20 Min. + Chilling   YIELD: 5 Cups

     2 cans (15-1/2 ounces *each*) black-eyed peas, rinsed and drained
     1 can (10 ounces) diced tomatoes and green chilies, drained
     1 medium green pepper, finely chopped
     1 small red onion, finely chopped
   1/2 cup fat-free Italian salad dressing
     2 tablespoons lime juice
   1/4 teaspoon salt
   1/4 teaspoon pepper
     1 medium ripe avocado, peeled and cubed
Baked tortilla chips *or* scoops

In a large bowl, combine the peas, tomatoes, green pepper and onion. In a small bowl, whisk the dressing, lime juice, salt and pepper. Pour over black-eyed pea mixture and stir to coat. Cover and refrigerate for at least 1 hour.

Stir in avocado just before serving. Serve with chips.

NUTRITION FACTS: 1/2 cup (calculated without chips) equals 113 calories, 3 g fat (1 g saturated fat), trace cholesterol, 522 mg sodium, 17 g carbohydrate, 4 g fiber, 5 g protein. **DIABETIC EXCHANGES:** 1 starch, 1/2 fat.

TASTY TIP
Becky Oliver says allowing her children to help cook expands the foods they'll eat. When making Texas Caviar, let little ones rinse the peas and do the stirring.

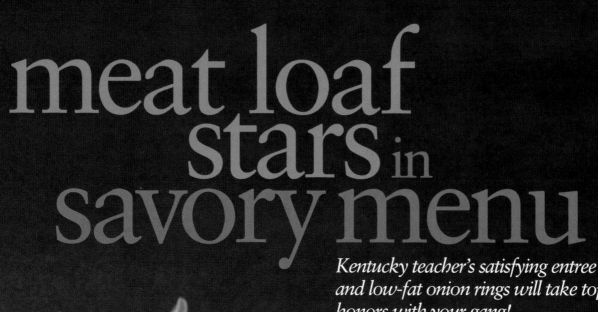

meat loaf
stars in
savory menu

Kentucky teacher's satisfying entree and low-fat onion rings will take top honors with your gang!

When it comes to cooking up healthy family meals, Tonya Vowels of Vine Grove, Kentucky has it down to a science! As a high school physics and chemistry teacher, she says labs are always a favorite part of classes—both for her and her students. "I think that correlates with my love of cooking, since I do a lot of experimenting in the kitchen," Tonya laughs.

Husband Eric, director of alternative programs for a local school system, encourages her to try new things and supports her efforts to make menus healthier.

"I had some weight to lose after the births of our children, Caroline and Charlie," Tonya recalls, "and not much energy or time for exercise. I knew we had to make some changes.

"I started by preparing more meals at home so I could better control the amount of fat. I looked for ways to limit or lighten up our snacks and tried to serve more baked and grilled lean meats instead of fried. I even found a new way to make 'oven-fried' chicken using cornflakes that tastes crunchy but cuts a lot of calories...and now it's one of my staples."

In her spare time, Tonya enjoys scrapbooking. "I recently compiled a book of my great-grandmother's recipes, with pictures of the kids and me making each one. I want to do this with my grandmother's recipes as well. It's a fun way to try new dishes and makes a heartwarming keepsake."

LIGHT, LUSCIOUS FAMILY FARE

It's easy to get your family eating healthier with menus as delicious as the one Tonya shares here. Crispy Baked Sweet Onion Rings are a perfect match for just about any entree. "These are a real family favorite—especially when Vidalias are in season," she says. Boost the flavor even more with seasoned bread crumbs or a shake or two of different spices.

No one would suspect that the main course, mini Bacon-Cheddar Meat Loaves, is light. Moist, tender and topped with bacon and melted cheese, they're savory sensations that you'll be asked to prepare time and again.

Zesty BLT Bread Salad finishes Tonya's healthy supper and always draws raves. "It tastes just like a BLT, has a light vinaigrette dressing and goes well with so many main dishes," she says. Since a meal this filling doesn't leave much room for dessert, a scoop of fat-free ice cream or frozen yogurt will do the job nicely!

Baked Sweet Onion Rings

(PICTURED AT LEFT)

PREP/TOTAL TIME: 30 Min.   YIELD: 4 Servings

    1/2 cup egg substitute
    2/3 cup dry bread crumbs
    1/2 teaspoon salt
    1/4 teaspoon pepper
      1 sweet onion, sliced and separated into rings

Place egg substitute in a shallow dish. In another shallow dish, combine the bread crumbs, salt and pepper. Dip onion rings into egg, then roll in crumb mixture.

Place onion rings on a baking sheet coated with cooking spray. Bake at 425° for 15-18 minutes or until golden brown, turning once.

NUTRITION FACTS: 1 serving equals 66 calories, 1 g fat (trace saturated fat), 0 cholesterol, 312 mg sodium, 12 g carbohydrate, 1 g fiber, 3 g protein. DIABETIC EXCHANGE: 1 starch.

Bacon-Cheddar Meat Loaves

(PICTURED AT FAR LEFT)

PREP: 20 Min.   BAKE: 40 Min.   YIELD: 4 Servings

      4 egg whites
    1/2 cup crushed reduced-fat butter-flavored crackers (about 13 crackers)
    1/3 cup plus 8 teaspoons shredded reduced-fat cheddar cheese, divided
    1/4 cup chopped onion
    1/2 teaspoon salt
    1/4 teaspoon pepper
      1 pound lean ground beef
      2 turkey bacon strips, cut in half

In a large bowl, combine the egg whites, crackers, 1/3 cup cheese, onion, salt and pepper. Crumble beef over mixture and mix well. Shape into four small loaves; place in an ungreased 11-in. x 7-in. x 2-in. baking dish. Top each with a half strip of bacon.

Bake at 350° for 35-40 minutes or until a meat thermometer reads 160°. Sprinkle with remaining cheese; bake 2-3 minutes longer or until cheese is melted.

NUTRITION FACTS: 1 meat loaf equals 296 calories, 15 g fat (6 g saturated fat), 86 mg cholesterol, 672 mg sodium, 9 g carbohydrate, trace fiber, 30 g protein. DIABETIC EXCHANGES: 4 lean meat, 1/2 starch, 1/2 fat.

BLT Bread Salad

(PICTURED AT FAR LEFT)

PREP/TOTAL TIME: 20 Min.   YIELD: 4 Servings

      3 cups cubed French bread
      1 tablespoon water
      1 tablespoon white wine vinegar
      1 tablespoon reduced-fat mayonnaise
    1-1/4 teaspoons sugar
      1 teaspoon olive oil
    1-1/2 cups torn leaf lettuce
      1 large tomato, chopped
      2 tablespoons crumbled cooked bacon
      1 tablespoon chopped green onion

Place bread cubes on an ungreased baking sheet; coat lightly with cooking spray. Bake at 400° for 8-10 minutes or until they are golden brown.

For dressing, in a small bowl, whisk the water, vinegar, mayonnaise, sugar and oil until smooth. In a large salad bowl, combine the lettuce, tomato and bread cubes. Sprinkle with bacon and onion. Drizzle salad with dressing and toss to coat.

NUTRITION FACTS: 1-1/4 cups equals 118 calories, 4 g fat (1 g saturated fat), 4 mg cholesterol, 288 mg sodium, 17 g carbohydrate, 2 g fiber, 4 g protein. DIABETIC EXCHANGES: 1 starch, 1 vegetable, 1/2 fat.

TAKE A TIP FROM THE COOK

"Buy lean meats and keep easy-to-prepare ingredients on hand so that you aren't tempted to stop by a fast-food drive-thru at the end of the day," Tonya advises.

simple perfection

This Minnesota reader turns her
summer meal into a special event.

For Sarah Newman, eating right has been key to maintaining a healthy lifestyle for quite a while. "For a number of years, I've tried to cook low-fat recipes," Sarah explains from Brooklyn Center, Minnesota, "but I was just cooking for myself. When my husband, Paul, and I were married in 2003, I had to expand my repertoire."

In order to balance Paul's love of flavorful, hearty foods with her wish to keep meals light, Sarah began looking for new ways to serve satisfying menus they'd both enjoy. "Now I also consider sodium, fiber and whole grains and other nutrients in addition to fat grams when I prepare a meal," Sarah says.

After the birth of the couple's daughter in 2005, Sarah became even more diligent about nutritious eating. "Grace doesn't eat many of the same foods we do, but we know that whatever we eat will influence her habits. That gives me additional incentive to continue my healthy cooking habits," Sarah relates.

Because Paul is a full-time student in addition to his job, Sarah is primarily in charge of taking care of the couple's growing family. "I've been very fortunate to be a full-time, stay-at-home mom, and I absolutely love it!" she says. "It's certainly a challenge at times, but I can't imagine doing anything else."

LIGHT MENU SATISFIES

Getting meals ready on time can be a struggle for this busy mom. The meal shared here, however, is ideal when it comes to time management, taste and nutrition.

Much of hearty Shrimp and Penne Supper may be made ahead. Sarah writes, "I saute the garlic and onion in the morning and add the tomatoes. I also stir together the milk, flour and half-and-half and put both mixtures in the refrigerator. When it's close to dinnertime, I just cook the pasta and shrimp and put the few remaining ingredients together."

Marinated Vegetable Salad makes a refreshing side dish that couldn't be much simpler to whip up. "This recipe is so easy," Sarah notes. "Marinating the vegetables overnight gives them a great flavor and texture."

Sarah tops off this delicious dinner with Chocolate Chip Snack Cake. After some makeovers to the original recipe, which came from her mom, Sarah says, "It's just as good, with a lot less guilt!"

Marinated Vegetable Salad
(PICTURED AT LEFT)

FAT CARB MEAT-LESS

PREP: 20 Min. + Chilling   YIELD: 6 Servings

        2 cups fresh broccoli florets
        2 cups fresh cauliflowerets
        1 medium cucumber, halved and thinly sliced
        1 cup sliced fresh mushrooms
        1 cup cherry tomatoes, halved
      1/3 cup finely chopped red onion
      1/2 cup fat-free Italian salad dressing

In a large bowl, combine broccoli, cauliflower, cucumber, mushrooms, tomatoes and onion. Add dressing; toss to coat. Cover; refrigerate for 8 hours or overnight.

NUTRITION FACTS: 1-1/3 cups equals 48 calories, trace fat (trace saturated fat), 1 mg cholesterol, 306 mg sodium, 9 g carbohydrate, 3 g fiber, 3 g protein. DIABETIC EXCHANGE: 2 vegetable.

Shrimp and Penne Supper
(PICTURED AT LEFT)

PREP: 35 Min.   COOK: 20 Min.   YIELD: 6 Servings

        2 cups uncooked whole wheat penne pasta
        1 medium onion, chopped
        3 garlic cloves, minced
        2 teaspoons olive oil, *divided*
        1 can (14-1/2 ounces) diced tomatoes with basil, oregano and garlic
        2 teaspoons Italian seasoning
      1/2 teaspoon salt
      1/2 teaspoon crushed red pepper flakes
      1/4 cup all-purpose flour
        1 cup fat-free half-and-half
      3/4 cup fat-free milk
        1 package (10 ounces) fresh spinach, torn
      1/2 cup shredded Parmesan cheese *divided*
        1 pound uncooked medium shrimp, peeled and deveined

Cook pasta according to package directions. Meanwhile, in a large nonstick skillet coated with cooking spray, cook onion

and garlic in 1 teaspoon oil over medium heat for 3 minutes. Stir in the tomatoes, Italian seasoning, salt and pepper flakes.

Combine the flour, half-and-half and milk until smooth; gradually stir into skillet. Bring to a boil, stirring constantly. Add spinach; cook and stir for 2 minutes or until spinach is wilted and sauce is thickened. Stir in 1/4 cup Parmesan cheese. Drain pasta and place in a serving bowl. Add sauce and toss to coat; keep warm.

In the same skillet, cook the shrimp in remaining oil over medium heat for 3-4 minutes or until shrimp turn pink. Place over pasta mixture; sprinkle with remaining Parmesan cheese.

NUTRITION FACTS: 1-1/3 cups equals 342 calories, 6 g fat (2 g saturated fat), 117 mg cholesterol, 852 mg sodium, 47 g carbohydrate, 5 g fiber, 25 g protein. DIABETIC EXCHANGES: 2-1/2 starch, 2 very lean meat, 1 vegetable, 1 fat.

Chocolate Chip Snack Cake
(PICTURED AT FAR LEFT)

PREP: 25 Min.   BAKE: 20 Min. + Cooling   YIELD: 15 Servings

      1/4 cup butter, softened
        1 cup sugar
        1 egg
        2 egg whites
        1 cup (8 ounces) reduced-fat sour cream
      2/3 cup unsweetened applesauce
        1 teaspoon vanilla extract
        1 cup all-purpose flour
        1 cup whole wheat flour
    1-1/2 teaspoons baking powder
      1/2 teaspoon salt
      1/4 teaspoon baking soda
TOPPING:
      1/3 cup sugar
        1 teaspoon ground cinnamon
      1/2 cup miniature semisweet chocolate chips

In a large mixing bowl, beat butter and sugar until crumbly, about 2 minutes. Add egg, then egg whites, beating well after each addition. Beat in the sour cream, applesauce and vanilla (mixture will appear curdled). Combine the flours, baking powder, salt and baking soda; stir into butter mixture just until blended.

Pour half of the batter into a 13-in. x 9-in. x 2-in. baking pan coated with cooking spray. Combine sugar and cinnamon; sprinkle half over batter. Top with half of the chocolate chips.

Gently top with remaining batter; spread evenly. Sprinkle with remaining cinnamon-sugar and chips. Bake at 350° for 20-25 minutes or until a toothpick inserted near the center comes out clean. Cool on a wire rack.

NUTRITION FACTS: 1 piece equals 215 calories, 7 g fat (4 g saturated fat), 28 mg cholesterol, 194 mg sodium, 36 g carbohydrate, 2 g fiber, 4 g protein. DIABETIC EXCHANGES: 2 starch, 1 fat.

TAKE A TIP FROM THE COOK

"The original snack cake recipe called for regular chocolate chips, but I reduced the amount and used mini chips to limit fat while covering more area," Sarah points out.

southwestern fare goes light

This North Carolina mom lowers the fat, but not the flavor, in these traditional family recipes.

Like many expectant moms, Anna Yeatts of Kernersville, North Carolina embraced the phrase "eating for two" when pregnant with her daughter, Ayla. "I took that adage literally and gained 35 pounds, despite already being at my heaviest," she laughs. "I got so tired of being out of shape, I knew I had to do something."

After she and husband Fabian welcomed their new baby, Anna began to make some changes. "I wanted to set a good example for my daughter," she explains. "So I joined a local gym and weight-loss center, and drastically overhauled how I ate." She soon learned about portion control, fat and calories. "I was amazed by how much better I felt when eating healthy yet tasty dishes," Anna says. In the process, Anna

also became a personal trainer. She now teaches several classes—including kickboxing, yoga and Pilates—part-time.

Along the way, Anna realized her family's eating habits needed a major overhaul, too. "I made my first change when I met my husband, who transformed me from a picky eater into a lover of delicious Mexican food," she says. "I made the next change when I realized all those great Mexican recipes were loaded with fat and calories."

To bring reduced-fat dinners to the table, Anna searched for flavor in seasonings and spices rather than in rich ingredients. "My husband loves that I experiment with the foods he grew up with, as well as other cuisines. He never knows what he may come home to!" she says.

Anna's wish to slim down her husband's family recipes produced the flavorful menu she shares here.

For the main course, she serves a lighter Southwestern classic. "Everyone loves this recipe for Fabulous Taco Salad," says Anna. "It's like eating decadent Mexican food while keeping the calories under control."

Taco salad only gets better when topped with Anna's colorful Fresh Salsa. With ripe tomatoes, crisp onion and a touch of minced serrano pepper, it also makes a great side dish or appetizer with crunchy baked tortilla chips.

Finish the fiesta with a piece of moist and refreshing Tres Leches Cake. "I always try to replace full-fat dairy products with light versions when baking," explains Anna. Though it's been trimmed-down, the charm of this Mexican dessert isn't lost. It's the perfect end to a mouth-watering meal.

Fabulous Taco Salad

CARB

(PICTURED AT LEFT)

PREP/TOTAL TIME: 30 Min.   YIELD: 4 Servings

     1 pound extra-lean ground turkey
     1 medium onion, finely chopped
     3 garlic cloves, minced
     1 teaspoon olive oil
     4 plum tomatoes, chopped
 1/4 teaspoon salt
 1/4 teaspoon pepper
 1/4 cup minced fresh cilantro
     6 cups torn romaine
 1/2 cup shredded reduced-fat Mexican cheese blend
 1/2 cup salsa

In a large nonstick skillet over medium heat, cook the turkey, onion and garlic in oil until meat is no longer pink. Stir in the tomatoes, salt and pepper; cook for 3-4 minutes or until tomatoes are tender. Remove from the heat; stir in cilantro.

Divide romaine among four plates; top each with 3/4 cup turkey mixture, 2 tablespoons cheese and 2 tablespoons salsa.

NUTRITION FACTS: 1 serving equals 224 calories, 6 g fat (2 g saturated fat), 55 mg cholesterol, 467 mg sodium, 11 g carbohydrate, 3 g fiber, 35 g protein. DIABETIC EXCHANGES: 4 very lean meat, 2 vegetable, 1 fat.

Fresh Salsa

 FAT SALT CARB MEAT-LESS

(PICTURED AT LEFT)

PREP/TOTAL TIME: 15 Min.   YIELD: 2 Cups

     4 plum tomatoes, chopped
     1 small onion, finely chopped
 1/4 cup minced fresh cilantro
     1 serrano pepper, seeded and minced
     1 garlic clove, minced
     1 teaspoon lime juice
 1/4 teaspoon salt
 1/4 teaspoon pepper
Baked tortilla chip scoops

In a small bowl, combine the first eight ingredients. Cover and refrigerate until serving. Serve with chips.

NUTRITION FACTS: 1/4 cup (calculated without chips) equals 11 calories, trace fat (trace saturated fat), 0 cholesterol, 77 mg sodium, 2 g carbohydrate, 1 g fiber, trace protein. DIABETIC EXCHANGE: Free food.

Editor's Note: When cutting or seeding hot peppers, use rubber or plastic gloves to protect your hands. Avoid touching your face.

Tres Leches Cake

 FAT SALT

(PICTURED AT FAR LEFT)

PREP: 35 Min.   BAKE: 20 Min. + Chilling   YIELD: 15 Servings

     5 eggs, *separated*
     1 cup sugar, *divided*
     1 tablespoon butter, softened
 1/3 cup fat-free milk
     1 teaspoon vanilla extract
     1 cup all-purpose flour
     1 teaspoon baking powder
MILK SYRUP:
     1 can (14 ounces) fat-free sweetened condensed milk
     1 can (12 ounces) fat-free evaporated milk
     1 cup fat-free half-and-half
     3 teaspoons vanilla extract
    15 tablespoons frozen reduced-fat whipped topping
    15 fresh strawberries

Let egg whites stand at room temperature for 30 minutes. Coat a 13-in. x 9-in. x 2-in. baking dish with cooking spray and dust with flour; set aside.

In a large mixing bowl, beat egg yolks on high speed for 5 minutes or until thick and lemon-colored. Gradually beat in 3/4 cup sugar and butter. Stir in milk and vanilla. Sift flour and baking powder; gradually add to yolk mixture and mix well (batter will be thick).

In a small mixing bowl with clean beaters, beat egg whites on medium speed until soft peaks form. Gradually beat in the remaining sugar, 1 tablespoon at a time, on high until stiff peaks form. Gradually fold into the batter.

Spread evenly into prepared dish. Bake at 350° for 18-22 minutes or until cake springs back when lightly touched. Place on a wire rack.

In a large saucepan, combine the condensed milk, evaporated milk and half-and-half. Bring to a boil over medium heat, stirring constantly; cook and stir for 2 minutes. Remove from the heat; stir in vanilla. Cool slightly.

Cut cake into 15 pieces, leaving cake in the baking dish. Poke holes in cake with a skewer. Slowly pour a third of the milk syrup over cake, allowing syrup to be absorbed into the cake. Repeat twice. Let stand for 30 minutes.

Cover and refrigerate for 2 hours before serving. Top each piece with whipped topping and a strawberry.

NUTRITION FACTS: 1 piece equals 233 calories, 3 g fat (2 g saturated fat), 76 mg cholesterol, 126 mg sodium, 42 g carbohydrate, 1 g fiber, 8 g protein.

> ### HEALTHY OUTLOOK
> Anna trimmed down her Fabulous Taco Salad by swapping out the olive oil for vegetable oil and substituting ground turkey for ground beef.

standout dinner

A Maryland family's journey to a heart-smart lifestyle.

For many women, losing baby weight is a major motivator for adopting a healthy lifestyle. But for Julie Kocur of Abingdon, Maryland, the choice to lighten menus came well before the baby-weight worries.

Five years ago, Julie, her husband, Dave, and their daughter, Meghan, awaited the birth of new baby Emily. Tragically, Emily was stillborn, and doctors speculated that Julie had developed gestational diabetes after her 24-week glucose-tolerance test.

After several years of healing, Julie and Dave prepared to welcome their daughter Kristin. Though gestational diabetes was never confirmed for Julie, she followed a diabetic diet for most of the pregnancy. "I actually had a glucose test come back borderline for diabetes, and after what happened to Emily, I wasn't going to take any chances with Kristin," she explains.

Kristin was born completely healthy at 37 weeks, and soon after, Julie joined a weight-loss program and shed 35 pounds. "If I learned anything from losing Emily, it's that life is too short to make choices knowingly that will end it sooner," says Julie. "My kids mean the world to me, and I want to be around to enjoy them for as long as I can!

"I still splurge occasionally...peanut butter cups are my downfall...but I balance things out with regular exercise and healthy choices," she adds.

SPECIAL SUPPER HAS A LIGHT TOUCH

Creating an impressive meal that fits into a nutritious diet can be challenging, but Julie's found a delectable menu that's as perfect for company as it is for special family dinners.

A tender and luscious main course, Veal with Mushroom-Wine Sauce brings a touch of elegance to the dinner table. "This delicious entree came from a cookbook filled with low-fat recipes. We altered it a bit to better suit our tastes," Julie says.

Roasted Rosemary Potatoes are a perfect accompaniment to the veal and lend a homey appeal. A hint of rosemary makes this dish an attention-getter, and it takes only five ingredients to prepare! "To make the assembly even easier, I toss all the ingredients into a plastic bag and shake it up," writes Julie.

Cheesecake with Berries offers a grand finale that will bring rave reviews. It's so rich and tasty, you'll have a hard time believing it's light. "This creamy cheesecake is ideal for any special occasion," Julie says. We're sure you'll agree!

Veal with Mushroom-Wine Sauce
(PICTURED AT LEFT)

CARB

PREP/TOTAL TIME: 30 Min.   YIELD: 4 Servings

    4 veal cutlets (4 ounces *each*)
1/2 teaspoon canola oil
    1 pound sliced fresh mushrooms
    1 small onion, chopped
    1 garlic clove, minced
1/2 cup white wine *or* reduced-sodium chicken broth
    4 teaspoons all-purpose flour
1/4 cup water
    2 tablespoons minced fresh parsley
1/4 teaspoon salt
1/8 teaspoon pepper

In a large nonstick skillet coated with cooking spray, cook the veal in oil over medium heat for 2-3 minutes on each side or until no longer pink. Remove and keep warm.

Add mushrooms, onion and garlic to the skillet; cook over medium-high heat for 5-8 minutes or until tender. Add wine, stirring to loosen browned bits from pan.

Combine flour and water until smooth; stir into mushroom mixture. Bring to a boil; cook and stir for 2 minutes or until thickened. Stir in the parsley, salt and pepper. Serve over veal.

NUTRITION FACTS: 1 cutlet with 1/2 cup mushroom sauce equals 231 calories, 12 g fat (4 g saturated fat), 74 mg cholesterol, 281 mg sodium, 9 g carbohydrate, 2 g fiber, 23 g protein. DIABETIC EXCHANGES: 3 lean meat, 1 vegetable, 1/2 fat.

Roasted Rosemary Potatoes
(PICTURED AT LEFT)

MEAT-LESS

PREP: 10 Min.   BAKE: 30 Min.   YIELD: 4 Servings

    4 medium potatoes, peeled and cubed
4-1/2 teaspoons olive oil
3/4 teaspoon dried rosemary, crushed
1/2 teaspoon salt
1/4 teaspoon pepper

Place potatoes in a 15-in. x 10-in. x 1-in. baking pan coated with cooking spray. Drizzle with oil and sprinkle with seasonings; toss to coat.

Bake at 425° for 30-35 minutes or until golden brown, stirring once.

NUTRITION FACTS: 3/4 cup equals 147 calories, 5 g fat (1 g saturated fat), 0 cholesterol, 300 mg sodium, 24 g carbohydrate, 2 g fiber, 2 g protein. DIABETIC EXCHANGES: 1-1/2 starch, 1 fat.

Cheesecake with Berries
(PICTURED AT RIGHT)

PREP: 25 Min.   BAKE: 40 Min. + Chilling   YIELD: 12 Servings

1-2/3 cups crushed reduced-fat vanilla wafers
    (about 50 wafers)
Sugar substitute equivalent to 1/4 cup sugar
1/4 cup reduced-fat butter, melted
    2 packages (8 ounces *each*) reduced-fat cheese
    1 cup (8 ounces *each*) reduced-fat cheese cup
    (8 ounces) reduced-fat sour cream

1/3 cup sugar
    1 tablespoon cornstarch
    2 eggs, lightly beaten
    2 egg whites, lightly beaten
    1 teaspoon vanilla extract
    3 cups sliced fresh strawberries

In a small bowl, combine wafer crumbs and sugar substitute; stir in butter. Press onto the bottom and 1/2 in. up the sides of a 10-in. springform pan coated with cooking spray. Place on a baking sheet. Bake at 350° for 6-8 minutes or until lightly browned. Cool on a wire rack.

In a large mixing bowl, beat the cream cheese, sour cream, sugar and cornstarch until smooth. Beat in the eggs, whites and vanilla on low speed just until combined. Pour into crust.

Place pan on a double thickness of heavy-duty foil (about 18 in. square). Securely wrap foil around pan. Place in a large baking pan; add 1 in. of hot water to larger pan.

Bake at 300° for 40-45 minutes or just until center is set. Remove pan from water bath. Cool on a wire rack for 10 minutes. Carefully run a knife around edge of pan to loosen; cool 1 hour longer. Refrigerate overnight.

Remove sides of pan. Cut into slices; top with strawberries. Refrigerate leftovers.

NUTRITION FACTS: 1 slice with 1/4 cup strawberries equals 256 calories, 14 g fat (8 g saturated fat), 75 mg cholesterol, 272 mg sodium, 26 g carbohydrate, 1 g fiber, 8 g protein.

Editor's Note: This recipe was tested with Splenda No Calorie Sweetener and Land O'Lakes light stick butter.

TAKE A TIP FROM THE COOK
"The veal recipe is quite easy to cut in half for two," Julie says.

taking things
light &easy

This Ohio mom offers a healthy supper
that's perfect for get-togethers.

Like many of us, Jenny Witcraft has been watching her weight for years. But after she was diagnosed with breast cancer in 2004, health took center stage for her entire family. "I've been more aggressive about our diet since then," she says.

The bookkeeper from Cleveland, Ohio decided to make some changes immediately, like cutting salt usage and not drinking soda. Others were more gradual. "Most have been small ones, here and there—such as switching to skim milk and using light or fat-free ingredients," she says.

"My husband, Gary, fought the changes at first. I learned quickly that if he didn't know I'd substituted light ingredients, he couldn't tell the difference in most cases. My 13-year-old son, Mark, has grown up with light and fat-free items, so for him, it's been no big deal.

"These days, I try to buy more organic foods without breaking the bank to pay for them. And I read nutrition labels. Shopping sure takes a lot longer than it did when I first got married!"

Jenny's family tries to stay active, although sometimes it's a struggle. "We've participated in the Race for the Cure every year since my diagnosis. Gary also helps coach Mark's baseball team, and I critique from the bleachers. I'm still trying to find 'fitness activities' I don't lose interest in after a week," she laughs.

By subtly making adjustments to their diets, Jenny and her family moved to a healthier way of life. "The changes worked for us," Jenny says, "because I lightened up a little at a time. If you ask me, it's a waste to try to 'go light' all at once. I mean, if nobody will touch the food you've made, you're not taking big steps toward a healthier lifestyle."

FAMILY-FRIENDLY MEAL

If you're looking to feed a crowd, Jenny's got the answers. And the best part is that her menu is delicious, nutritious and appeals to a wide variety of tastes. In addition, it fits with nearly any time of year…a spring lunch at Easter or a New Year's Eve buffet.

For the main course, she serves a moist and lean Breaded Pork Roast. "The five-ingredient entree has become a tradition on our New Year's Day menu," she says. "I'm really flattered that my mom asked me how to make it."

Simple to prepare yet sophisticated to the palate, Basil-Garlic Green Beans are a perfect match with the pork roast. "These are a result of trying to get my son to eat green beans. He loves them extra garlicky," says Jenny, "and I'm happy to oblige."

To go with the meal, try Dilled Wheat Bread. It's great with this dinner, but Jenny likes it with hearty soups and stews, too. It may take an extra bit of prep work, but the homemade results are unbeatable. Best of all, you can take comfort in knowing that you're feeding your family and friends healthy fare they'll remember for ages to come.

TASTY TIP

To save time, roll the pork roast in the bread crumb mixture and place the roast in the pan the day before your event. Cover and store in the refrigerator. The day of your party, all you'll have to do is cook it.

Breaded Pork Roast

(PICTURED AT FAR LEFT)

PREP: 15 Min.   **BAKE:** 1-1/4 Hours + Standing   **YIELD:** 12 Servings

- 9 garlic cloves, minced
- 1 boneless whole pork loin roast (3 pounds)
- 2/3 cup seasoned bread crumbs
- 2 tablespoons grated Parmesan cheese
- 2 teaspoons rubbed sage

Press garlic onto the roast. In a shallow pan, combine the bread crumbs, Parmesan cheese and sage. Gently roll roast in crumb mixture until coated. Place fat side up on a rack in a shallow roasting pan. Bake, uncovered, at 350° for 1-1/4 to 1-1/2 hours or until a meat thermometer reads 160°. Let stand for 10-15 minutes before slicing.

NUTRITION FACTS: 3 ounces cooked pork equals 152 calories, 5 g fat (2 g saturated fat), 57 mg cholesterol, 61 mg sodium, 2 g carbohydrate, trace fiber, 22 g protein. **DIABETIC EXCHANGE:** 3 lean meat.

Basil-Garlic Green Beans

(PICTURED AT FAR LEFT)

PREP/TOTAL TIME: 25 Min.   **YIELD:** 12 Servings

- 3 pounds fresh green beans, trimmed
- 5 tablespoons reduced-fat butter, cubed
- 6 garlic cloves, minced
- 1 tablespoon dried basil

Place beans in a large kettle and cover with water. Bring to a boil; cover and cook for 8-10 minutes or until crisp-tender. Drain and keep warm. In the same pan, melt butter. Add garlic; cook and stir until golden. Add basil and beans; toss to coat.

NUTRITION FACTS: 3/4 cup equals 56 calories, 3 g fat (2 g saturated fat), 9 mg cholesterol, 37 mg sodium, 8 g carbohydrate, 4 g fiber, 2 g protein. **DIABETIC EXCHANGES:** 1 vegetable, 1/2 fat.

Editor's Note: This recipe was tested with Land O'Lakes light stick butter.

Dilled Wheat Bread

(PICTURED AT FAR LEFT)

PREP: 10 Min.   **BAKE:** 3 Hours   **YIELD:** 1 Loaf (1-3/4 Pounds, 12 Slices)

- 1-1/4 cups water (70° to 80°)
- 1 tablespoon butter, softened
- 2 tablespoons sugar
- 2 teaspoons dill weed
- 1-1/2 teaspoons salt
- 2 cups whole wheat flour
- 1-1/4 cups all-purpose flour
- 1-1/2 teaspoons active dry yeast

In bread machine pan, place all ingredients in order suggested by manufacturer. Select basic bread setting. Choose crust color and loaf size if available. Bake according to bread machine directions (check dough after 5 minutes of mixing; add 1 to 2 tablespoons of water or flour if needed).

NUTRITION FACTS: 1 slice equals 134 calories, 1 g fat (1 g saturated fat), 3 mg cholesterol, 307 mg sodium, 27 g carbohydrate, 3 g fiber, 4 g protein. **DIABETIC EXCHANGE:** 1-1/2 starch.

Let's Celebrate!

Cheers! It's time to celebrate with loved ones, good friends and, of course, phenomenal food. Ideal for entertaining, the following menus are guaranteed to impress guests without expanding their waistlines.

WELCOME spring with a meal fit for a king...or a queen. This elegant menu features fork-tender leg of lamb. Seasoned with an herbal rub and a hint of lemon, it's a delightfully refreshing main course.

The lamb is paired with a colorful side dish of fresh vegetables and couscous, in addition to oven-fresh hot cross buns. Together, the combination makes for a classic meal that your guests won't soon forget.

Lemon-Herb Leg of Lamb

CARB

(PICTURED AT LEFT)

PREP: 10 Min. + Marinating   **BAKE:** 1-3/4 Hours + Standing
YIELD: 12 Servings

Lemon and a variety of herbs give this lamb recipe great flavor. I created the recipe from a combination of several others. It's the only way my daughter would eat lamb when she was young.
—Patricia Crandall, Inchelium, Washington

- 2 teaspoons lemon juice
- 1-1/2 teaspoons grated lemon peel
- 1 teaspoon garlic salt
- 1 teaspoon dried oregano
- 1 teaspoon dried thyme
- 1 teaspoon dried rosemary, crushed
- 1 teaspoon ground mustard
- 1 boneless leg of lamb (4 pounds), rolled and tied

In a small bowl, combine the first seven ingredients. Rub over leg of lamb. Cover and refrigerate overnight.

Place lamb on a rack in a shallow roasting pan. Bake, uncovered, at 325° for 1-3/4 to 2-1/4 hours or until meat reaches desired doneness (for medium-rare, a meat thermometer should read 145°; medium, 160°; well-done, 170°). Let stand for 15 minutes before slicing.

NUTRITION FACTS: 4 ounces cooked lamb equals 198 calories, 8 g fat (3 g saturated fat), 92 mg cholesterol, 225 mg sodium, trace carbohydrate, trace fiber, 28 g protein. **DIABETIC EXCHANGE:** 4 lean meat.

Vegetable Medley with Couscous

MEAT-LESS

(PICTURED AT LEFT)

PREP: 30 Min.   **COOK:** 10 Min.   **YIELD:** 10 Servings

I tried this recipe from a cookbook because I'd never had couscous before. Now I love it! It was divine with the vegetables and a good alternative to rice.   —Ruth Cowley, Pipe Creek, Texas

- 3 cups reduced-sodium chicken broth **or** vegetable broth
- 3 tablespoons butter
- 3 tablespoons minced fresh parsley
- 1/4 teaspoon pepper
- 2-1/4 cups uncooked couscous
- 3 medium sweet red peppers, cut into 3/4-inch pieces
- 2 tablespoons canola oil
- 3 medium zucchini, halved and sliced
- 3 yellow summer squash, halved and sliced
- 1 tablespoon minced fresh basil **or** 1 teaspoon dried basil
- 1-1/2 teaspoons salt
- 1/3 cup grated Parmesan cheese

In a large saucepan, bring the broth, butter, parsley and pepper to a boil. Stir in couscous. Cover and remove from the heat; let stand for 5 minutes.

Meanwhile, in a Dutch oven, saute the red peppers in oil for 4 minutes. Stir in the zucchini, yellow squash, basil and salt; cook 6-10 minutes longer or until tender.

Fluff couscous with a fork; serve with vegetables and sprinkle with Parmesan cheese.

NUTRITION FACTS: 3/4 cup vegetables with 2/3 cup couscous equals 249 calories, 8 g fat (3 g saturated fat), 11 mg cholesterol, 628 mg sodium, 38 g carbohydrate, 4 g fiber, 9 g protein. **DIABETIC EXCHANGES:** 2 starch, 1-1/2 fat, 1 vegetable.

Spiced Fruited Hot Cross Buns

FAT SALT

(PICTURED AT FAR LEFT)

PREP: 40 Min. + Rising   **BAKE:** 20 Min.   **YIELD:** 2 Dozen

With fat-free milk, ground flaxseed, whole wheat flour and dried fruit, these tantalizing, healthy treats can be prepared easily in the bread machine without a bit of guilt.
—Alina Niemi, Honolulu, Hawaii

- 1-1/2 cups fat-free milk (70° to 80°)
- 1/4 cup water (70° to 80°)
- 1/4 cup butter, melted
- 1 teaspoon salt
- 2/3 cup sugar
- 2 tablespoons ground flaxseed
- 1 tablespoon grated orange peel
- 2 teaspoons grated lemon peel
- 1/4 teaspoon *each* ground cardamom, cinnamon and nutmeg
- 2-1/4 cups whole wheat flour
- 2 cups all-purpose flour
- 1 package (1/4 ounce) active dry yeast
- 1/2 cup golden raisins
- 1/4 cup dried cranberries
- 1/4 cup finely chopped candied ginger

ICING:
- 3/4 cup confectioners' sugar
- 3/4 teaspoon grated orange peel
- 2 to 3 teaspoons lemon juice

In bread machine pan, place the first 14 ingredients in order suggested by manufacturer. Select dough setting (check dough after 5 minutes of mixing; add 1 to 2 tablespoons of water or flour if needed). Just before the final kneading (your machine may audibly signal this), add the raisins, cranberries and candied ginger.

When cycle is completed, turn dough onto a lightly floured surface. Divide into 24 portions; shape each into a ball. Place 2 in. apart on baking sheets coated with cooking spray. Cover and let rise in a warm place until doubled, about 40 minutes.

Bake at 350° for 20-25 minutes or until golden brown. Remove from pans to cool on wire racks. Combine the icing ingredients; pipe an X on each bun.

NUTRITION FACTS: 1 bun equals 160 calories, 3 g fat (1 g saturated fat), 5 mg cholesterol, 129 mg sodium, 32 g carbohydrate, 2 g fiber, 4 g protein. **DIABETIC EXCHANGE:** 2 starch.

special supper
with a
steakhouse
flair

YOU DON'T have to go to a fancy restaurant to enjoy a wonderful steak dinner. These rich and satisfying dishes come together quickly for a healthy supper any time at all. The meal is ideal whenever you plan to entertain friends, but you could also cut the ingredients in half and serve a special meal for two.

Steaks with Mushroom Sauce

(PICTURED AT LEFT)

PREP: 15 Min. **COOK:** 20 Min. **YIELD:** 4 Servings

These scrumptious steaks are smothered in a succulent mushroom-wine sauce. The savory entree dresses up any plate.
—Stephanie Allee, Chambersburg, Maryland

> 1 cup boiling water
> 1/2 cup sun-dried tomatoes (not packed in oil), julienned
> 2 cups whole fresh mushrooms, quartered
> 2 garlic cloves, minced
> 1 shallot, chopped
> 2 teaspoons butter
> 1/2 teaspoon pepper
> 1/4 teaspoon salt
> 4 boneless beef sirloin steaks (6 ounces *each*)
> 1 tablespoon olive oil
> 1/2 cup dry red wine *or* reduced-sodium beef broth
> 1/4 teaspoon dried thyme
> 1 to 2 tablespoons all-purpose flour
> 1-1/4 cups reduced-sodium beef broth

In a small bowl, pour boiling water over sun-dried tomatoes. Cover and let stand for 5 minutes. Drain and set aside.

In a large nonstick skillet coated with cooking spray, saute the mushrooms, garlic and shallot in butter for 3-4 minutes or until mushrooms are tender. Remove and keep warm.

Combine pepper and salt; rub over steaks. In the same skillet, cook steaks in oil for 5-6 minutes on each side or until meat reaches desired doneness (for medium-rare, a meat thermometer should read 145°; medium, 160°; well-done, 170°). Remove and keep warm.

Add wine or broth to the skillet, stirring to loosen any browned bits. Stir in thyme. Bring to a boil. Reduce heat; simmer, uncovered, for 5-7 minutes or until mixture is reduced by half.

In a small bowl, combine flour and broth until smooth. Gradually stir into skillet. Bring to a boil; cook and stir for 2 minutes or until thickened and bubbly. Stir in sun-dried tomatoes and mushroom mixture; heat through. Serve with steaks.

NUTRITION FACTS: 1 steak with 1/2 cup sauce equals 333 calories, 14 g fat (5 g saturated fat), 101 mg cholesterol, 521 mg sodium, 10 g carbohydrate, 2 g fiber, 36 g protein.

Creamy Blue Cheese Dressing

(PICTURED AT LEFT)

PREP/TOTAL TIME: 15 Min. **YIELD:** 1-1/2 Cups

I have been making this incredible salad dressing for about 40 years, and I always get raves. The thick, creamy dressing is surprisingly light and makes it easy to jazz up simple greens.
—Joan Smith, Claremore, Oklahoma

> 1 cup reduced-fat salad dressing
> 1/2 cup fat-free sour cream
> 1/4 cup minced fresh parsley
> 3 tablespoons fat-free milk
> 2 tablespoons chopped onion
> 1 tablespoon cider vinegar
> 1 tablespoon lemon juice
> 1 garlic clove, minced
> 1/4 teaspoon salt
> 1/4 teaspoon pepper
> Dash cayenne pepper
> 1/4 cup crumbled blue cheese

In a small bowl, whisk the first 11 ingredients until blended. Stir in blue cheese. Cover and refrigerate until serving.

NUTRITION FACTS: 2 tablespoons equals 74 calories, 5 g fat (1 g saturated fat), 9 mg cholesterol, 275 mg sodium, 6 g carbohydrate, trace fiber, 2 g protein. **DIABETIC EXCHANGES:** 1 fat, 1/2 starch.

Editor's Note: This recipe was tested with Miracle Whip Light salad dressing.

Whole Wheat Sage Rolls

(PICTURED AT FAR LEFT)

PREP: 40 Min. + Rising **BAKE:** 15 Min. **YIELD:** 20 Rolls

On Friday nights, my daughters and I like to try new dishes. This heartwarming recipe for sage rolls is one we especially enjoy.
—Harriet Stichter, Milford, Indiana

> 2 to 2-1/2 cups all-purpose flour
> 1/4 cup packed brown sugar
> 2 packages (1/4 ounce *each*) active dry yeast
> 1 to 2 tablespoons minced fresh sage
> 1 teaspoon salt
> 1-3/4 cups fat-free milk
> 1/4 cup butter, cubed
> 2 cups whole wheat flour
> 1/2 cup plus 2 tablespoons cornmeal, *divided*

In a large mixing bowl, combine 1 cup flour, brown sugar, yeast, sage and salt. In a small saucepan, heat milk and butter to 120°-130°. Add to dry ingredients; beat just until moistened. Add whole wheat flour and 1/2 cup cornmeal; beat until smooth. Stir in enough remaining all-purpose flour to form a firm dough.

Turn onto a lightly floured surface; knead until smooth and elastic, about 6-8 minutes. Place in a bowl coated with cooking spray, turning once to coat top. Cover and let rise in a warm place until doubled, about 30 minutes.

Coat two baking sheets with cooking spray and sprinkle with remaining cornmeal; set aside. Punch dough down. Turn onto a lightly floured surface; divide into 20 pieces. Shape each piece into a roll.

Place 2 in. apart on prepared baking sheets. Cover and let rise until doubled, about 30 minutes.

Bake at 375° for 14-16 minutes or until golden brown. Remove to wire racks.

NUTRITION FACTS: 1 roll equals 142 calories, 3 g fat (2 g saturated fat), 7 mg cholesterol, 155 mg sodium, 26 g carbohydrate, 2 g fiber, 4 g protein. **DIABETIC EXCHANGES:** 1-1/2 starch, 1/2 fat.

it's a
shore
thing!

WONDERING what to serve when family and friends of all ages—and special dietary needs—get together? Cater to the crowd with a wholesome, low-fat meal that just about anyone can enjoy. Moist corn muffins, a tasty shrimp boil and refreshing iced tea make this a menu you'll turn to time and again. Best of all, each of the mouth-watering recipes in this warm-weather spread comes together in minutes!

Jalapeno Corn Muffins

FAT MEAT-LESS

(PICTURED AT LEFT)

PREP/TOTAL TIME: 30 Min.   YIELD: 16 Muffins

These cheerful muffins will dress up any gathering. With corn and red pepper, the sweet baked goods are sure to be a great accompaniment to summer buffets.   —Judie White, Florien, Louisiana

  1-1/2 cups yellow cornmeal
  1-1/4 cups all-purpose flour
      2 tablespoons sugar
      1 tablespoon baking powder
      1 teaspoon salt
      1 teaspoon ground cumin
      2 eggs
      1 cup fat-free milk
      3 tablespoons butter, melted
      2 tablespoons minced fresh cilantro
      1 can (8-3/4 ounces) whole kernel corn, drained
    1/2 cup chopped sweet red pepper
    1/2 cup chopped seeded jalapeno peppers

In a large bowl, combine the first six ingredients. In another bowl, combine the eggs, milk, butter and cilantro; stir into dry ingredients just until moistened. Stir in the corn, red pepper and jalapenos.

  Coat muffin cups with cooking spray; fill two-thirds full. Bake at 425° for 12-16 minutes or until a toothpick comes out clean. Cool for 5 minutes before removing from pans to wire racks. Serve warm.

NUTRITION FACTS: 1 muffin equals 136 calories, 3 g fat (2 g saturated fat), 33 mg cholesterol, 303 mg sodium, 22 g carbohydrate, 2 g fiber, 4 g protein. DIABETIC EXCHANGES: 1-1/2 starch, 1/2 fat.

Editor's Note: When cutting or seeding hot peppers, use rubber or plastic gloves to protect your hands. Avoid touching your face.

Spiced Shrimp Boil

FAT

(PICTURED AT LEFT)

PREP: 20 Min.   COOK: 1 Hour   YIELD: 6 Servings

I created this recipe by accident one night when I didn't have the usual spices on hand. Now friends often furnish the shrimp just to have me cook it this way!
—Norma Reynolds, Overland Park, Kansas

      1 medium lemon, halved
  2-1/2 pounds medium red potatoes (about 10), quartered
      1 teaspoon ground coriander
      1 teaspoon cayenne pepper
    1/8 teaspoon ground allspice

    1/8 teaspoon ground cloves
    15 whole peppercorns
     4 garlic cloves, peeled and halved
     4 bay leaves
     2 teaspoons mustard seed
    1/2 teaspoon dill seed
     4 celery ribs, halved
     1 bunch parsley
     2 medium onions, cut into wedges
     5 quarts cold water
     3 medium ears sweet corn, husked and cut into 2-inch pieces
  1-1/2 pounds uncooked shell-on jumbo shrimp (about 18)
     1 teaspoon salt

Squeeze juice from lemon halves into a large bowl; add lemon and potatoes to bowl. Sprinkle with coriander, cayenne, allspice and cloves; toss to coat. Set aside.

  Place peppercorns, garlic, bay leaves, mustard seed and dill seed on a double thickness of cheesecloth; bring up corners of cloth and tie with string to form a bag. Place the spice bag, celery, parsley and onions in a soup kettle; add water. Bring to a boil; cover and boil for 15 minutes.

  Strain, reserving liquid and spice bag. Discard parsley and vegetables. Return cooking liquid with spice bag to the heat; carefully add potato mixture. Bring to a boil. Reduce heat; simmer, uncovered, for 15 minutes. Add corn; simmer 15-20 minutes longer or until potatoes and corn are tender.

  Stir in shrimp; cook for 3 minutes or until shrimp turn pink. Drain; discard spice bag and lemon. Transfer shrimp mixture to a large serving bowl. Sprinkle with salt; toss to coat.

NUTRITION FACTS: about 2-2/3 cups equals 263 calories, 2 g fat (trace saturated fat), 168 mg cholesterol, 605 mg sodium, 39 g carbohydrate, 5 g fiber, 23 g protein. DIABETIC EXCHANGES: 3 very lean meat, 2-1/2 starch.

Iced Cranberry-Mint Tea

FAT SALT CARB

PREP: 20 Min. + Standing   YIELD: 8 Servings (2 Quarts)

Raise a toast to friends, family, sunshine and warm weather with this bright cranberry cooler from our Test Kitchen. The lovely drink has a hint of mint and a refreshing splash of lemon. After one sip, it's sure to become a family favorite.

     4 cups water
   2/3 cup loosely packed fresh mint leaves
     2 tablespoons sugar
     8 lemon herbal tea bags
  3-1/2 cups reduced-calorie reduced-sugar cranberry juice
     1 tablespoon lemon juice
Ice cubes
Lemon slices, optional

In a large saucepan, bring the water, mint and sugar to a boil. Remove from the heat; add the tea bags. Cover and steep for 15 minutes.

  Discard tea bags. Cover and let stand 45 minutes longer. Strain and discard mint leaves. Stir the cranberry and lemon juices into tea. Serve over ice with lemon slices if desired.

NUTRITION FACTS: 1 cup equals 34 calories, trace fat (trace saturated fat), 0 cholesterol, 4 mg sodium, 8 g carbohydrate, trace fiber, trace protein. DIABETIC EXCHANGE: 1/2 starch.

rustic
elegance

COMFORTING, hearty and full of down-home appeal, this satisfying trio of tastes is a wonderful way to welcome guests to your table.

Loaded with potatoes, savory ground turkey, mushrooms and more, our golden frittata makes a substantial main course any time of the year. Serve hefty wedges alongside homemade Wild Rice Bread and our change-of-pace pear and blue cheese salad for an incredible meal that's guaranteed to receive compliments.

Hearty Potato Frittata
(PICTURED AT LEFT)

PREP: 20 Min.　**COOK:** 20 Min.　**YIELD:** 6 Servings

Great flavor and subtle spices surround each bite of my home-style frittata. Ground turkey and fresh vegetables make it an eye-opening dish.　　　　　—Mary Relyea, Canastota, New York

　3/4 pound lean ground turkey
　1/2 cup chopped green pepper
　1/2 teaspoon rubbed sage
　1/2 teaspoon crushed red pepper flakes
　1/8 teaspoon ground nutmeg
　1/2 cup sliced fresh mushrooms
　　2 green onions, chopped
　　4 small red potatoes, thinly sliced
　　4 teaspoons butter
　　8 egg whites
　　4 eggs
　　3 tablespoons fat-free milk
　　1 teaspoon salt
　1/4 teaspoon pepper

In a 12-in. ovenproof skillet coated with cooking spray, cook the turkey, green pepper, sage, pepper flakes and nutmeg over medium heat for 3 minutes. Add the mushrooms and onions; cook 4-5 minutes longer or until the meat is no longer pink and the vegetables are tender. Drain and set aside.

In the same skillet, cook potatoes in butter until lightly browned and almost tender. Return turkey mixture to the pan. In a large bowl, whisk the egg whites, eggs, milk, salt and pepper. Pour over turkey mixture. Cover and cook over low heat for 8-12 minutes or until almost set.

Uncover skillet. Broil 3-4 in. from the heat for 3-5 minutes or until the eggs are completely set. Let stand for 5 minutes before cutting.

NUTRITION FACTS: 1 serving equals 263 calories, 11 g fat (4 g saturated fat), 193 mg cholesterol, 596 mg sodium, 20 g carbohydrate, 2 g fiber, 21 g protein. **DIABETIC EXCHANGES:** 3 lean meat, 1 starch, 1/2 fat.

Blue Cheese Pear Salad
MEAT-LESS
(PICTURED AT LEFT)

PREP: 20 Min.　**BAKE:** 15 Min. + Cooling　**YIELD:** 6 Servings

Sweet pears and rich blue cheese turn a bed of greens into this elegant side salad.　　　—Cindy Dyrnes, Deptford, New Jersey

　　3 medium Bartlett pears, cored and halved
　　6 teaspoons lemon juice, *divided*
　1/3 cup water

　　2 tablespoons plus 1 teaspoon olive oil
2-1/4 teaspoons balsamic vinegar
　1/4 teaspoon salt
　1/8 teaspoon pepper
　1/2 cup crumbled blue cheese
　　2 tablespoons chopped walnuts, toasted
　　3 tablespoons chopped green onions
　　6 cups torn leaf lettuce

Place pears cut side down in an 11-in. x 7-in. x 2-in. baking dish. Brush with 2 teaspoons lemon juice. Add water and remaining lemon juice to pan.

Bake, uncovered, at 350° for 15-20 minutes or just until pears are tender. Drain and cool to room temperature.

In a small bowl, whisk the oil, vinegar, salt and pepper. In another bowl, combine the blue cheese, walnuts and onions.

Just before serving, divide lettuce among six plates; drizzle with dressing. Top each with a pear half and 2 tablespoons blue cheese mixture.

NUTRITION FACTS: 1 serving equals 161 calories, 10 g fat (3 g saturated fat), 8 mg cholesterol, 261 mg sodium, 16 g carbohydrate, 3 g fiber, 4 g protein. **DIABETIC EXCHANGES:** 2 fat, 1 vegetable, 1 fruit.

Wild Rice Bread
FAT ↓　MEAT-LESS
(PICTURED AT FAR LEFT)

PREP: 20 Min. + Rising　**BAKE:** 40 Min. + Cooling
YIELD: 2 Loaves (16 Slices Each)

I add texture and a subtle, nutty flavor to homemade bread by mixing in nutritious wild rice. Moist and heartwarming, this recipe makes for a terrific snack or side.
　　　　　　—Bonnie Groh, Manistique, Michigan

　　3 cups whole wheat flour
　　3 cups all-purpose flour
　　2 packages (1/4 ounce *each*) active dry yeast
2-1/2 teaspoons salt
　　1 cup water
　　1 cup fat-free milk
　1/4 cup butter, cubed
　1/4 cup honey
　　2 cups cooked wild rice

In a large mixing bowl, combine the whole wheat flour, 1 cup all-purpose flour, yeast and salt. In a small saucepan, heat the water, milk, butter and honey to 120°-130°. Add to dry ingredients; beat until smooth. Stir in the wild rice and enough remaining all-purpose flour to form a stiff dough.

Turn onto a lightly floured surface; knead until smooth and elastic, about 6-8 minutes. Place in a bowl coated with cooking spray, turning once to coat top. Cover and let rise in a warm place until doubled, about 40 minutes.

Punch dough down. Turn onto a lightly floured surface; divide in half. Shape into loaves. Place in two 9-in. x 5-in. x 3-in. loaf pans coated with cooking spray. Cover and let rise until doubled, about 30 minutes.

Bake at 375° for 40-45 minutes or until golden brown. Remove from pans to wire racks to cool completely.

NUTRITION FACTS: 1 slice equals 116 calories, 2 g fat (1 g saturated fat), 4 mg cholesterol, 203 mg sodium, 22 g carbohydrate, 2 g fiber, 4 g protein. **DIABETIC EXCHANGE:** 1-1/2 starch.

spotlight
on fall fruit

SUMMER doesn't always have to steal the show; the season for fruit is fall. Why not create a cozy meal featuring these models of nutrition? Perfect for entrees, side dishes, salads and, of course, desserts, fall fruit is a natural fit with healthy eating.

This menu includes apples, grapes, cranberries and more. With all of these incredible flavors, your guests will happily discover how delicious eating right can be.

Pork with Savory Quince Compote
(PICTURED AT FAR RIGHT)

PREP: 30 Min.   **COOK:** 40 Min.   **YIELD:** 6 Servings (1-1/2 Cups Compote)

The L&T staff relied on white wine to boost the flavors of quince and rosemary in this sweet, savory compote for pork tenderloin.

> 3/4 teaspoon salt
> 1/2 teaspoon dried thyme
> 1/4 teaspoon ground ginger
> 1/4 teaspoon pepper
> 2 pork tenderloins (1 pound *each*)
> **COMPOTE:**
> 1 small onion, chopped
> 1 tablespoon butter
> 2 medium quinces, peeled and cut into 1/2-inch pieces
> 1 cup reduced-sodium chicken broth
> 1/2 cup white wine *or* additional reduced-sodium chicken broth
> 1/4 cup honey
> 2 teaspoons minced fresh rosemary *or* 1/2 teaspoon dried rosemary, crushed
> 1 bay leaf
> 1/2 teaspoon salt
> 1/4 teaspoon pepper

Combine the salt, thyme, ginger and pepper; sprinkle over pork. Place on a rack in a shallow roasting pan lined with heavy-duty foil.

Bake, uncovered, at 425° for 30-35 minutes or until a meat thermometer reads 160°.

Meanwhile, in a large nonstick skillet over medium heat, saute onion in butter until tender. Stir in the remaining ingredients; bring to a boil. Reduce heat; cover and simmer for 8 minutes. Uncover; simmer 25-30 minutes longer or until quinces are tender and liquid is thickened. Discard bay leaf.

Let the pork stand for 5 minutes before slicing. Serve with the compote.

NUTRITION FACTS: 4 ounces cooked pork with 1/4 cup compote equals 274 calories, 7 g fat (3 g saturated fat), 89 mg cholesterol, 677 mg sodium, 18 g carbohydrate, 1 g fiber, 31 g protein. **DIABETIC EXCHANGES:** 4 lean meat, 1 starch.

Apple and Goat Cheese Salad
(PICTURED AT RIGHT)

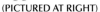
SALT MEAT-
LESS

PREP/TOTAL TIME: 20 Min.   **YIELD:** 8 Servings

This makes a light and lovely salad for almost any meal.
—Radelle Knappenberger, Oviedo, Florida

> 6 cups torn mixed salad greens
> 2 medium apples, chopped
> 1/2 cup raisins
> 1/2 cup green grapes, halved
> 2 tablespoons olive oil
> 4-1/2 teaspoons balsamic vinegar
> 1 tablespoon honey
> 1-1/2 teaspoons lemon juice
> 1 garlic clove, minced
> 3 tablespoons chopped walnuts, toasted
> 2 tablespoons crumbled goat cheese

In a bowl, combine the greens, apples, raisins and grapes. In a jar with a tight-fitting lid, combine the oil, vinegar, honey, lemon juice and garlic; shake well. Pour over salad; toss to coat. Sprinkle with nuts and goat cheese. Serve immediately.

NUTRITION FACTS: 3/4 cup equals 133 calories, 6 g fat (1 g saturated fat), 3 mg cholesterol, 31 mg sodium, 19 g carbohydrate, 2 g fiber, 3 g protein. **DIABETIC EXCHANGES:** 1 vegetable, 1 fruit, 1 fat.

Cran-Orange Ice Cream Cake
(PICTURED AT RIGHT)

PREP: 30 Min. + Freezing   **COOK:** 15 Min. + Chilling   **YIELD:** 12 Servings

Layers of ice cream and cranberries will delight family and friends who try this festive ice cream cake from our Test Kitchen.

> 3/4 cup crushed gingersnap cookies (about 30 cookies)
> 1/4 cup sugar
> 1/4 cup reduced-fat butter, melted
> 1-1/2 cups fresh *or* frozen cranberries
> 1/3 cup packed brown sugar
> 1/4 cup orange juice
> 1/8 teaspoon ground cloves
> 6 cups reduced-fat vanilla ice cream, softened
> 1 tablespoon grated orange peel

In a small bowl, combine the cookie crumbs, sugar and butter; press onto the bottom of a 9-in. springform pan coated with cooking spray. Freeze for 1 hour or until firm.

In a small saucepan, combine the cranberries, brown sugar, orange juice and cloves. Cook over medium heat for 10-15 minutes or until berries pop, stirring occasionally. Cool slightly. Transfer to a food processor; cover and process until blended. Refrigerate for 30 minutes or until chilled, stirring occasionally.

In a large bowl, combine ice cream and orange peel. Spread half over the crust; gently spread cranberry mixture over ice cream. Freeze for 30 minutes or until firm; freeze remaining ice cream mixture.

Soften remaining ice cream mixture; spread over cranberry layer. Cover and freeze for 6 hours or until firm. Remove from the freezer 15 minutes before serving.

NUTRITION FACTS: 1 slice equals 234 calories, 7 g fat (4 g saturated fat), 16 mg cholesterol, 204 mg sodium, 42 g carbohydrate, 1 g fiber, 4 g protein.

Editor's Note: This recipe was tested with Land O'Lakes light stick butter.

Favorite Recipe Made Lighter

PARTY TIME means great finger foods, dips and spreads...but it doesn't have to mean lots of calories, sodium and fat. For example, when our Test Kitchen home economists tasted Kathi Mulchin's elegant Crab Appetizer Mold, they loved the flavor, but not its fat and calories.

The cook from Salt Lake City, Utah knew her recipe was indulgent and turned to us for help. "This easy dish is ideal for parties, but it's far from being light," she writes. "I'd love for you to make it healthier."

In this case, a great makeover was just a few steps away. First, our pros determined that although the combination of cream of mushroom soup, mayonnaise and cream cheese gives the recipe a wonderful taste, it also brings too much fat and calories. The team opted for reduced-fat or fat-free varieties of the ingredients instead. An easy swap like this works perfectly with no-bake recipes, since fat-free products can break down and lose their smooth consistency when heated. The team also chose to decrease the onions slightly to showcase the crab flavor even more.

Makeover Crab Appetizer Mold is everything our makeover team hoped it would be! The flavors of the delicate crab and savory green onions come through in each bite. Though it's been slimmed down, this appetizer is just as luscious as the original.

Crab Appetizer Mold

PREP: 30 Min. + Chilling   **YIELD:** 4-1/2 Cups

> 1 envelope unflavored gelatin
> 3 tablespoons cold water
> 1 can (10-3/4 ounces) condensed cream of mushroom soup, undiluted
> 1 package (8 ounces) cream cheese, cubed
> 1 cup mayonnaise
> 2 cans (6 ounces *each*) crabmeat, drained, flaked and cartilage removed
> 2 celery ribs, finely chopped
> 4 green onions, finely chopped

Assorted crackers

In a small microwave-safe bowl, sprinkle gelatin over cold water; let stand for 1 minute. Microwave, uncovered, on high for 20 seconds. Stir; let stand for 1 minute or until gelatin is completely dissolved.

In a large saucepan, combine the soup, cream cheese, mayonnaise and gelatin. Cook and stir over medium heat for 5-7 minutes or until smooth. Remove from the heat; stir in the crab, celery and onions.

Transfer to a 5-cup ring mold coated with cooking spray. Cover and refrigerate for 4 hours or until set. Unmold onto a serving platter; serve with crackers.

NUTRITION FACTS: 1/4 cup (calculated without crackers) equals 151 calories, 14 g fat (4 g saturated fat), 32 mg cholesterol, 262 mg sodium, 2 g carbohydrate, trace fiber, 5 g protein.

Makeover Crab Appetizer Mold

(PICTURED ABOVE)

PREP: 30 Min. + Chilling   **YIELD:** 4-1/2 Cups

> 1 envelope unflavored gelatin
> 3 tablespoons cold water
> 1 can (10-3/4 ounces) reduced-fat reduced-sodium condensed cream of mushroom soup, undiluted
> 1 package (8 ounces) reduced-fat cream cheese, cubed
> 1 cup fat-free mayonnaise
> 2 cans (6 ounces *each*) crabmeat, drained, flaked and cartilage removed
> 2 celery ribs, finely chopped
> 3 green onions, finely chopped

Assorted crackers

In a small microwave-safe bowl, sprinkle gelatin over cold water; let stand for 1 minute. Microwave, uncovered, on high for 20 seconds. Stir; let stand for 1 minute or until gelatin is completely dissolved.

In a large saucepan, combine the soup, cream cheese, mayonnaise and gelatin. Cook and stir over medium heat for 5-7 minutes or until smooth. Remove from the heat; stir in the crab, celery and onions.

Transfer to a 5-cup ring mold coated with nonstick cooking spray. Cover and refrigerate for 4 hours or until set. Unmold onto a serving platter; serve with crackers.

NUTRITION FACTS: 1/4 cup (calculated without crackers) equals 72 calories, 4 g fat (2 g saturated fat), 28 mg cholesterol, 294 mg sodium, 4 g carbohydrate, trace fiber, 6 g protein. **DIABETIC EXCHANGES:** 1 very lean meat, 1/2 fat.

celebrate the season!

WHY NOT HOST a rise-and-shine holiday brunch for family, friends or out-of-town guests this year? It couldn't be easier with this light and lovely spread of convenient, make-ahead reader favorites. Best of all, starting the day with a healthy breakfast can help boost energy for the busy days ahead, while cutting down on snacking and helping to beat overeating.

Peach-Stuffed French Toast

MEAT-LESS

(PICTURED BELOW)

PREP: 25 Min. + Chilling   **BAKE:** 25 Min.   **YIELD:** 10 Servings

With its make-ahead convenience and scrumptious flavor, this recipe is ideal for holiday brunches. It's a standout main dish.
          —Julie Robinson, Little Chute, Wisconsin

- 1 loaf (1 pound) French bread, cut into 20 slices
- 1 can (15 ounces) sliced peaches in light syrup, drained and chopped
- 1/4 cup chopped pecans

- 4 eggs
- 4 egg whites
- 1-1/2 cups fat-free milk
- 3 tablespoons sugar
- 1-1/4 teaspoons ground cinnamon, divided
- 1 teaspoon vanilla extract
- 1/4 cup all-purpose flour
- 2 tablespoons brown sugar
- 2 tablespoons cold butter

Reduced-calorie pancake syrup, optional

Arrange half of the bread in a 13-in. x 9-in. x 2-in. baking dish coated with cooking spray. Top with peaches, pecans and remaining bread.

In a small bowl, whisk the eggs, egg whites, milk, sugar, 1 teaspoon cinnamon and vanilla; pour over bread. Cover and refrigerate for 8 hours or overnight.

Remove from the refrigerator 30 minutes before baking. Bake, uncovered, at 400° for 20 minutes.

In a small bowl, combine the flour, brown sugar and remaining cinnamon; cut in butter until crumbly. Sprinkle over French toast. Bake 5-10 minutes longer or until a knife inserted near the center comes out clean. Serve with syrup if desired.

NUTRITION FACTS: 1 piece (calculated without syrup) equals 267 calories, 8 g fat (3 g saturated fat), 92 mg cholesterol, 368 mg sodium, 39 g carbohydrate, 2 g fiber, 10 g protein. **DIABETIC EXCHANGES:** 2-1/2 starch, 1-1/2 fat.

Turkey Breakfast Sausage Patties

CARB

(PICTURED AT LEFT)

PREP: 15 Min. + Chilling   **COOK:** 10 Min.   **YIELD:** 8 Servings

I experimented with so many spices to finally attain what I think is the next best thing to pork sausage. These are especially good drizzled with maple syrup.   —Marla Swoffer, Novato, California

- 1 pound lean ground turkey
- 1 teaspoon rubbed sage
- 1/2 teaspoon salt
- 1/2 teaspoon fennel seed
- 1/2 teaspoon dried thyme
- 1/8 teaspoon garlic powder
- 1/8 teaspoon pepper

Dash *each* white pepper, cayenne pepper, ground allspice, ground cloves and ground nutmeg

In a large bowl, combine all ingredients. Shape into eight 2-1/2-in. patties. Cover and refrigerate for at least 1 hour.

In a large skillet coated with cooking spray, cook patties over medium heat for 4-6 minutes on each side or until no longer pink.

NUTRITION FACTS: 1 patty equals 86 calories, 5 g fat (1 g saturated fat), 45 mg cholesterol, 201 mg sodium, trace carbohydrate, trace fiber, 10 g protein. **DIABETIC EXCHANGE:** 1 lean meat.

> **TASTY TIP**
> Round out the brunch with a fast fruit medley, orange juice and cups of hot coffee.

General Recipe Index

This handy index lists every recipe by food category, major ingredient and/or cooking method, so you can easily locate recipes to suit your needs.

● Table-ready in 30 minutes or less.

Alphabetical Index

*This handy index lists every recipe in alphabetical order
so you can easily find your favorite dish.*

● Table-ready in 30 minutes or less.

Reference Index

Use this index to locate the many healthy cooking hints (by chapter) located throughout this book.